SOCIAL ENTREPRENEURSHIP

SOCIAL ENTREPRENEURSHIP

New Models of Sustainable Social Change

Edited by
Alex Nicholls

OXFORD
UNIVERSITY PRESS

OXFORD

UNIVERSITY PRESS

Great Clarendon Street, Oxford OX2 6DP

Oxford University Press is a department of the University of Oxford.
It furthers the University's objective of excellence in research, scholarship,
and education by publishing worldwide in

Oxford New York

Auckland Cape Town Dar es Salaam Hong Kong Karachi
Kuala Lumpur Madrid Melbourne Mexico City Nairobi
New Delhi Shanghai Taipei Toronto

With offices in

Argentina Austria Brazil Chile Czech Republic France Greece
Guatemala Hungary Italy Japan Poland Portugal
Singapore South Korea Switzerland Thailand Turkey Ukraine Vietnam

Oxford is a registered trade mark of Oxford University Press
in the UK and in certain other countries

Published in the United States
by Oxford University Press Inc., New York

A catalogue record for this title is available from the British Library

Library of Congress Cataloging in Publication Data
Data available

Typeset by SPI Publisher Services, Pondicherry, India
Printed in Great Britain
on acid-free paper by
Ashford Colour Press Ltd, Gosport, Hampshire

ISBN 978–0–19–928387–3 (Hbk.)   978–0–19–928388–0 (Pbk.)

10 9 8 7 6 5 4 3 2

Preface

Jeff Skoll

The rapid industrial and technological advancements of the last century have led to many breakthroughs, but they have also left us to confront an uncertain future. With real threats of environmental and economic collapse, terrible diseases, over-population, war, terrorism and menacing new forms of weaponry, we have much to overcome. Efforts by our governments and institutions have proven insufficient to reverse these destructive trends. Our best hope for the future of humanity lies in the power and effectiveness of socially motivated, highly empowered, individuals to fight for changes in the way we live, think, and behave.

Those four sentences perfectly capture the case for social entrepreneurship. But they are not unique to our time: the same could have been said 100 years ago, 200 years ago, 300 years ago at the beginning of the Industrial Revolution. One of the great ironies of history is that the solutions to current challenges frequently create new challenges even more menacing. Industries that have improved the quality of our lives have also created new problems that threaten our very existence. Technological innovations that were developed to increase the efficiency of life have frequently been used to increase the efficiency of taking life. We can split the atom, walk on the moon, communicate with another person anywhere in the world in the blink of an eye, and yet poverty, violence, and illness in much of the world are as pervasive as they have ever been.

But the nature and the wonder of humanity is that while there are always tumultuous events and seemingly overwhelming challenges to face, people, exceptional individuals, and ideas and movements emerge to face and find solutions to these challenges.

Social entrepreneurs are those people—the practical dreamers who have the talent and the skill and the vision to solve the problems, to change the world for the better. Social entrepreneurs have a unique approach that is both evolutionary and revolutionary, operating in a free market where success is measured not just in financial profit but also in the improvement of the quality of people's lives. Social entrepreneurs take workable value creation models and adapt them for the benefit of all our communities. They do not buy into the notion that only governments and powerful individuals and corporations are in a position to determine where and how resources are allocated. They believe that any individual has the potential to make positive changes not just in our communities, but also in society as a whole. And they put that belief into action, in creative ways that are described throughout this book.

At the world's great foundations, universities and charitable institutions, social entrepreneurship has rapidly become the most influential idea of our time. For these institutions, theories of social entrepreneurship offers a powerful tool to identify, train and support individuals with the potential to create major social change. For the entrepreneurs themselves, it presents a roadmap to realize their dreams.

Yet, for all of this, social entrepreneurship remains as much an idea as a movement. There is a great need for ongoing scholarship and publications that serve as a call to arms to current social entrepreneurs, as an inspiration to budding social entrepreneurs, and to document the field for institutions, academics, and legislators.

The Skoll Foundation has supported the Skoll Centre for Social Entrepreneurship to contribute to meeting this need, and to promote the advancement of social entrepreneurship worldwide. This volume, synthesizing research and lessons from practice by leading social entrepreneurs and scholars in the field who gathered for the first Skoll World Forum on Social Entrepreneurship in March 2004, exemplifies the Centre's aim to produce work that both engages with theory and is also valuable to practitioners in the field.

Social entrepreneurs have a vision of the future and will stop at nothing to see that future come true. It is up to us to help them succeed in order to ensure that the failures of the past do not become the failures of the future, and to build a world where all people, regardless of geography, background, or economic status, enjoy and employ the full range of their talents and abilities.

Preface to the Paperback Edition

Alex Nicholls
Rowena Young

The Publication of this book in 2006 attempted to capture the landscape of thinking and research in social entrepreneurship as it looked at the time of the first Skoll World Forum in Social Entrepreneurship in 2004. From this perspective, social entrepreneurship represented an exciting and emergent set of new models offering hope for systemic, positive, social and environmental change. However, it was something of a well-kept—and often contested—secret. Whilst it was clearly a hot topic for some policy makers and civil society groups, social entrepreneurship was poorly defined, widely misunderstood, and even controversial. Did it simply represent business capturing the social agenda or government privatising welfare by another means? Was it just a fad dressing up well-established civil society action in new trendy clothes? Could it be a threat to important, established, organizations already generating social welfare in innovative ways? Indeed, during the first Skoll World Forum in Social Entrepreneurship, some unidentified 'activists' even put up a series of posters in the Said Business School's lavatories warning delegates: 'Beware social entrepreneurship: a wolf in sheep's clothing'!

Much has changed since then in terms of both scholarship and practice and this new preface will sketch out the most significant of these developments. Three important themes can be identified: new start-ups and existing organisations going to scale; mainstreaming; changing research agendas.

New Start-Ups and Existing Organisations Going to Scale

Despite patchy empirical data, it seems clear that over the last four years there has been steady growth in the number of socially entrepreneurial organizations globally and that their interventions in institutional voids or suboptimal markets are making a significant difference (e.g. Bornstein, 2004; Economist, 2005c; Drayton, 2006; Harding and Cowling, 2006; Cabinet Office, 2006). For example, Ashoka has continued to grow its network of social entrepreneurs, identifying new fellows in developed countries in the North for the first time. This represents an important broadening of their focus and recognises the power of social entrepreneurship to address social and environmental issues across all countries, not only those that are primarily in need of economic development. However, it is not the absolute number of socially entrepreneurial organisations that is most important, but rather that their impact is rising and, in this respect, evidence from a range of new start-ups and the scaling of successful existing models suggests exciting progress is being made across the world.

India, one of the most fertile arenas for social entrepreneurship globally, has seen an explosion of new activity including: Western models being adapted to local circumstances (UnLtd India, Social Impact); local models transferring to the global North (ChildLine, Just Change); new alliances between government and civil society; and exciting new models from social entrepreneurs in education (Toybank in Mumbai), health (SERP in Andhra Pradesh), renewable energy generation (SELCO, an Ashden Award winner in 2005 and 2007), waste recovery (BIOTECH in Kerala, also an Ashden Award winner in 2007) and economic development (India Fair Trade Forum).

In Africa, mobile telephony is revolutionalising banking for the poor by opening up access to financial services for those without a bank account, hugely improving the process of transferring remittances from the North to the South (e.g. Vodafone's M-PESA initiative). Internet technology is also facilitating the provision of market intelligence and commercial trading platforms across developing countries such as Tradebiz (www.home.tradebiz. com.pk). In Latin America, youth focussed organizations such as Ecoclubes are engaging and empowering young people across the continent with environmental activism and community development, whilst expanding microfinance vehicles such as FIS Microcredito continue to build new financial services for the poor in the same region.

Whilst social entrepreneurs are adept at these sorts of social innovation start-ups, they have also been busy developing, scaling, and – in some cases - rejuvenating existing organizations to grow social impact and better achieve mission objectives. BRAC and others have codified their experience of diversifying and replicating their services in one setting (Bangladesh), and are attempting to establish blue-printed programmes in Africa and elsewhere, experimenting with US and UK fundraising offices along the way. Their prior track record is proving attractive to commercial financiers too.

Fundacion Paraguaya de Cooperacion y Desarrollo provides one of the most successful examples of spinning out the core insight at the heart of their success to date: Teach a Man to Fish now has a network of 400 independent initiatives spanning 65 countries, and growing. All its members are experimenting with the best ways to grow self-sustaining agricultural colleges. CAMFED has achieved escape velocity, breaking through in its fundraising profile with opportunities such as the Financial Times' Christmas charity campaign (which was subsequently syndicated by a major donor). The strength of its network has grown apace with an expansion of its programmes delivering educational opportunities to girls and young women in Sub-Saharan Africa.

People Tree, the international company pioneering Fair Trade and ecological fashion, has achieved a different kind of first by furthering its mission to persuade Northern consumers that Fair Trade can move into the mainstream. Its designer collaborations are giving it legitimacy to lobby an industry whose human rights abuses have dominated newspaper headlines this year to clean up its act. Patient Opinion, a UK social enterprise, has been so successful in demonstrating the value and role of service user evaluation of health services in real time that the Department of Health has specified and commissioned a replica to scale. While there remain real barriers to spreading innovations, these very different strategies signal a new depth of purpose, and growing confidence that the social entrepreneurs' highest ambitions can be realised.

Mainstreaming

A second striking change is that social entrepreneurship is now better defined, more widely understood, and has been increasingly mainstreamed in global debates around everything from climate change to the Millennium Development Goals. A very public acknowledgement of this transition is that in the past three years the Nobel Prize for Peace has been awarded to social entrepreneurs: Wangari Maathai of the Greenbelt movement in 2005; Muhammad Yunus founder of Grameen Bank in 2006 (the 'father' of microfinance and a contributor to this book); and former Vice-President Al Gore in 2007 (an environmental campaigner and a speaker at the Skoll World Forum in Social Entrepreneurship 2006). Media coverage of social entrepreneurship has also grown and become more serious. For example, the Financial Times has commented on the subject (e.g. Guthrie, 2006; Jack, 2007) and the Economist now regularly covers on social entrepreneurship around the world, (e.g. Economist, 2005a, 2005b, 2005c, 2006a, 2006b, 2006c, 2006d, 2007a, 2007b). Overseas, Japan's leading national broadsheet, Asahi Shimbun, has also carried pieces which explore the relevance of social entrepreneurship to local problems.

Social entrepreneurship has increasingly become a feature of public policy discourse across governments too. The UK's Labour government has been at the forefront of this development. In 2006, it built on its commitment to social entrepreneurship first shown with the establishment of a Social Enterprise Unit within the Department of Trade and Industry (DTI, 2002) by creating an Office for the Third Sector (OTS) within the Cabinet Office (Cabinet Office, 2006). There is now a Minister dedicated to the Third Sector who has a specific brief to develop social enterprise policy, action, investment, and debate across the UK. Some departments have made social enterprise their own, arguing its case as a tool for, variously, increasing patient choice (Department of Health) and developing rural communities (DEFRA). Public procurement officers are now routinely required to consider the contributions of charities and social enterprises when tenders are issued (DTI, 2003). The debate about further enablers, such as the inclusion of social clauses within public procurement or the encouragement of a social stock exchange, is also heating up. The opposition Conservative Party has also signalled its commitment to social entrepreneurship going forward, including a proposal for social enterprise zones in the most deprived neighbourhoods to mimic the tax-advantaged enterprise zones of the 1980s (Social Enterprise Zones Task Force, 2007). This cross-party consensus suggests that social entrepreneurship will be a feature of the UK policy landscape for the foreseeable future. The risk of social entrepreneurship being seen as a policy fad in the UK now seems minimal.

However, it is not only in the UK that social entrepreneurship has become mainstreamed within policy. In China, for example, the government has opened up opportunities for innovative NGOs and social entrepreneurs as part of a move towards a more 'harmonious society'. While there remains considerable unease about government intentions in China, and it is clear that restrictions could still be put on NGO activity from the centre, social innovation is alive and well in the municipalities and successes are rapidly rolled out. Furthermore, this new space for social entrepreneurship has encouraged commercial players to enter as well. Teams at the McKinsey Shanghai office were the first to introduce a venture philanthropy fund, Non-Profit Partners, in 2005 (China Economic Review, 2007). In the process this created a more enabling environment for others such as the Non-Profit Incubator, NPI, which aims to couple the dissemination of social entrepreneurship with new venture philanthropy models.

Elsewhere, action is accelerating at a state level. In South Australia, for example, universities such as Carnegie Mellon and Adelaide are promoting social entrepreneurship, buoyed by the personal support of the Premier and his Thinker in Residence programme (www.thinkers.sa.gov.au/home.html). The results of this programme are being implemented in numerous state departments with social innovation initiatives emerging in areas ranging from sustainable planning to aboriginal affairs. In other cases, it is enthusiastic individuals who propagate support and champion social entrepreneurs' efforts at a policy level. For example, the Brazilian Minister for Development, Industry, and Foreign Trade, Luiz Fernando Furlan, has supported businesses with social goals as an intrinsic part of the landscape for increasing national competitiveness, in no small part due to his earlier involvement as a mentor for Ashoka.

Social entrepreneurship is also gaining traction with mainstream businesses. Major financial institutions such as Morgan Stanley and Citigroup are now brininging capital into microfinance by bundling securitized loans from in-country intermediaries with front-line oversight for the mainstream debt market. Tellingly, Morgan Stanley see this as the first step towards a diversified 'sustainable business' unit. In consumer markets, Fair Trade sales have grown at double digit rates for ten years across the North, with Nestle, Starbucks, Marks and Spencer, and Dunkin' Donuts amongst others all now engaging (Nicholls and Opal, 2005; Raynolds et al, 2007). In the UK about 5% of businesses with employees are now thought to be a social enterprise and, at £27bn per annum, their contribution to GDP equals that of the agriculture sector (Cabinet Office, 2006). Lex Mundi, the international legal services firm, has launched a foundation dedicated to providing pro bono support to social entrepreneurs around the globe. Furthermore, Environmental Resources Management (ERM), the world's largest environmental consultancy, has also made social entrepreneurship a focus of its foundation activity, and is now adding an investment fund aimed at social enterprises within the low carbon businesses sector.

In universities, scholarly engagement with social entrepreneurship has also been transformed in the past few years. 2006 marked a watershed in social entrepreneurship scholarship with the publication of four new academic books, in addition to this one, on the topic (Mair et al; Austin et al: Nyssens; Mosher-Williams; Perrini). In the same year, the Journal of World Business issued the first special edition of a scholarly journal on social entrepreneurship (volume 41). The second - in Entrepreneurship Theory and Practice - has been recently announced. Aimed at more popular audiences, Innovations also launched, and the China Economic Review (2007) published a special edition on social enterprise. In 2007, the Social Enterprise Research Conference celebrated its fifth year in London, the Skoll World Forum in Social Entrepreneurship hosted its fourth event in Oxford, and the International Social Entrepreneurship Research Conference held its third annual meeting in Copenhagen. In addition, in 2007, the Social Entrepreneurship Colloquium was held for the first time at the Saïd Business School over five research-intensive days. Co-hosted by the Skoll Centre for Social Entrepreneurship and the Center for Advancement of Social Entrepreneurship at Duke University, this meeting brought together scholars from five continents and a dozen disciplines to explore the topic of social entrepreneurship, critique current work, and set out new research agendas. Many of the attendees were engaging with the subject for the first time and the meeting aimed to both broaden and deepen scholarly engagement with social entrepreneurship.

Another field-building project was launched in 2006, with the establishment of the University Network for Social Entrepreneurship (www.universitynetwork. org). This is a joint project between Ashoka, the Skoll Centre for Social Entrepreneurship, the Social Enterprise Knowledge Network (www.sekn.org), and EMES (www.emes.net) and its objectives are twofold. In the first instance, it aims to build on the valuable regional co-ordination of scholarly community building and dialogue among these prior research networks, and connect different traditions internationally, and second, to provide practitioners and students with a gateway to the growing knowledge base and its instigators. The site provides information about current research, teaching, and events in social entrepreneurship globally and is steadily building its database of resources. In future, the site will offer interactive spaces for academic discussions and working papers to help generate new research projects and partnerships and support the building of social entrepreneurship as a serious field of scholarly work.

The number of taught courses in social entrepreneurship has also increased substantially across the world, perhaps by as much as a factor of ten in four years (e.g. Brock, 2006; Aspen, 2006). A survey carried out by the Global Academy within Ashoka identified more than 250 scholars worldwide currently teaching social entrepreneurship in some form (Kim and Davis, 2007). In addition to the new scholarly books noted above, many more international case studies are now available in the subject, including exciting initiatives in Latin America (eg SEKN), Africa (e.g. the new Case Study Centre at the African Institute of Management, Dakar) and North America (e.g. Wei-Skillern et al, 2007). As scholarly engagement in social entrepreneurship as a unit of analysis has been transformed over the past few years, so the research agendas around the subject have also moved on. This represents the third important development in the field.

Evolving Research Agendas

In 2004/5 the question of how to define social entrepreneurship dominated research in the field (e.g. Dees, 1994, 1996, 1998). In this book, we suggest that the search for a single definition was a sterile activity and proposed instead a set of boundaries for social entrepreneurship arguing that a key part of what makes social entrepreneurship so successful is that it resists isomorphic pressures to conform to set types of action preferring instead to remain fluid and adaptable to fill institutional voids in environmental or social provision. Such action defies easy classification at an individual or organizational level. We set the boundaries around social entrepreneurship as the product of any individual, organizational, or network activity that demonstrates some element of sociality, innovation, and market orientation, irrespective of its legal form (charity, business), resource strategy (for-profit, not-for-profit, voluntary sector) or sectoral home (public, private, or civil society) (Nicholls and Cho, 2006). Whilst the boundaries of social entrepreneurship may still be contested at times, such an 'umbrella' approach appears now to have been broadly accepted in more recent scholarly work in the field that has largely moved on from sometimes monological attempts simply to parse 'social' and 'entrepreneurship' from a management perspective (see Cho, 2006, for a critique) to look instead at more substantive questions that have social entrepreneurship as the unit of analysis for multi-disciplinary lines of enquiry (e.g. Alvord et al,

2004; Light, 2006; Nicholls, 2006, 2008a, 2008b; Peredo and Chrisman, 2006; Peredo and McLean, 2006; Baron, 2007; Chell, 2007; Dorado, 2006; Haugh, 2007; Ridley-Duff, 2007; Shaw and Carter, 2007; Sullivan, 2007; Tracey and Jarvis, 2007; Weerawardena and Sullivan Mort, 2007; Mair and Seelos, forthcoming). Three specific lines of ongoing research enquiry are emerging as important: the process of social entrepreneurship; the political context of social entrepreneurship; the resource strategies available to social entrepreneurship.

In 2004, the inchoate field of practice and research in social entrepreneurship was largely dominated by a focus on 'hero entrepreneurs'. This was mainly a product of a rise in philanthropic/grant giving interest being directed at such individuals within a Northern cultural milieu (witness the Fellowship/awards programmes of key early players such as Ashoka, Echoing Green, the Schwab Foundation, the Skoll Foundation, UnLtd etc). However, this has been increasingly understood as only offering part of the picture: effectively the tip of a socially entrepreneurial iceberg. Most social entrepreneurship is, in reality, not the product of single charismatic individuals but of ideas generated, propagated, and operationalised by groups, networks, and formal or informal organizations. Whilst it is clearly useful shorthand for grant-givers and policy makers to recast this collective action in terms of extraordinary individual stories, a careful survey of extant research in the field challenges the accuracy of such representations as culturally contingent rather than absolute (e.g. Alvord et al, 2004).

One of the academic objectives of the Skoll Centre for Social Entrepreneurship has been to bring together the very diverse research traditions in social entrepreneurship that had already developed during the last ten years. What became apparent early on was that there was a particularly strong contrast between the North American view that typically prioritised business solutions to social problems and, consequently, focussed largely on the social enterprise part of the social entrepreneurship spectrum (e.g. Brinckerhoff, 2000; Dees et al, 2001, 2002: Boschee and McClurg, 2003; Austin et al, 2006) and the European tradition of studying innovation in the broader social economy, with a strong interest in co-operatives (Borzaga and Defourny, 2001; Spear and Bidet, 2005; Nyssens, 2007). The former typically built their account of social entrepreneurship around familiar narratives from the world of commercial entrepreneurship (itself something of a myth). These presented social entrepreneurship as innovative start-ups that were the product of extraordinary individuals and their personal traits and qualities (creativity, risk-taking, transformatory leadership etc). However, the latter saw social entrepreneurship more as collective action, rooted in communities, and often innovating within existing organizations or institutional settings. This debate between different traditions has served to critique the 'hero' entrepreneur model and offer a richer and more substantive account of how social entrepreneurship works and why it matters.

New scholarship that explores social innovation (e.g. Mulgan, 2005) and uses systems thinking to explore social change has also highlighted how inaccurate 'hero'/start-up models are as holistic accounts of the process of delivering significant social and environmental impact. Whilst management based research clearly has value in exploring organisational level strategy and operations, the key questions for social entrepreneurship in practice—largely concerning replication and impact—often demand a more socio-political academic turn. This has been understood in Third Sector scholarship more generally for years (e.g. Powell, 1987; Salamon and Anheier, 1997).

As a consequence, the second important development in social entrepreneurship research concerns its political context. As scholarship in the field has matured and engaged more disciplinary perspectives across the social sciences—sociology, anthropology, human geography, political science, ethics—the discourse around social entrepreneurship has moved away from business school centred accounts that simply applied established neo-liberal economic models and strategic approaches from the commercial world to social problems. In its place is emerging a more nuanced understanding of the politics of social and environmental entrepreneurship. At an institutional level this is evidenced by the increased engagement with the subject by scholars in schools of public policy (for example in the Kennedy School at Harvard and the Wagner School at New York University). From this perspective, social entrepreneurship is not simply a new mechanism by which to fix malfunctions in existing economic systems by somehow tweaking markets better to optimise their social value creation, but rather represent a challenge to their continued existence as static institutions (see Offer, 2006, for the general context, if not the specifics). Until recently this macro dimension has been underplayed in favour of more micro-level attention to organizational structures and, particularly, resource strategies (hence the fascination with social enterprise).

Social entrepreneurship focuses on change in social and cultural arrangements via participative structures and democratic processes. It is typically highly embedded in community and frequently uses advocacy to support action. It is this challenge to extant institutional structures that makes all social entrepreneurship inherently political. Social entrepreneurs instinctively grasp this in two ways.

First, they never ignore governmental action and often work with the public sector. Today, evidence suggests that the majority of social entrepreneurial work across the globe is funded by public money, whether via direct government contracts (more than 50% of the UK charity sector income in 2006, for example, NCVO, 2007), grants, international aid, or other support from transnational bodies such as the United Nations (Meehan et al, 2004). Even unincorporated social movements that shun government support have been shown to co-develop their campaigning repertoire with the governments and their representatives with whom they dynamically interact (Tilly, 2004).

Furthermore, social entrepreneurs within and without formal government are bringing about reforms in the public sector that are every bit as innovative and impactful as any private action. For example, the Commission on Unclaimed Assets in the UK is looking to establish a new Social Investment Bank that will leverage considerable resources to pump prime social innovation and social enterprise (Commission on Unclaimed Assets, 2006). In a very different example, the incrementalism of state-owned enterprise reform by Chinese civic entrepreneurs, contrary to perceptions of gross inefficiency among the Western commentariat, has created the stability so essential for one of the most successful waves of social innovation in our lifetimes (Guthrie, 2007).

New boundary spanning hybrid organizations are also emerging across government, the private sector, and civil society that are driving social innovation and changing institutional arrangements. For example, at the Skoll Centre for Social Entrepreneurship, we have pioneered a programme for social entrepreneurs within the public heath system who will act as pathfinders in reforming the most significant source of welfare in the UK. Similarly, new 'state-sponsored' social enterprises are emerging to increase the responsiveness of public services by bringing them closer to their beneficiaries whilst also building new models that are more efficient and creative in the way they use public resources.

Second, social entrepreneurs develop micro-level political structures to challenge established institutional patterns that are blocking social change (Alvord et al, 2004). Whether through direct action, advocacy, or new models of cooperation and solidarity, social entrepreneurs work to realign power structures within and without markets better to address inequalities in the distribution of public and environmental goods. At its heart, social entrepreneurship is about disruptive social justice: a project that combines moral and political aims with practical implementation (see e.g. Nicholls and Opal, 2005).

The third area of new ideas in social entrepreneurship is resource strategy. There has been a move away from the assumption that philanthropy is the only source of finance for social change towards an engagement with a broader range of innovative mechanisms based around existing capital market structures. There are a number of drivers behind this shift. First, the amount of capital available in mainstream markets dwarfs philanthropic capital. Second, accessing philanthropic capital is often difficult and inefficient, by some estimates costing 25% of the sums raised (up to five times more costly than raising conventional finance, see Meehan et al, 2004). Third, mainstream investors and institutions are recognising new opportunities in social enterprise markets (Nicholls, 2007). That is not to say—as noted above—that social entrepreneurs are not challenging market conventions, but rather that they are reconfiguring them to recognise new forms of value, return, and the nature of investment. A good example is Generation Investment Management that is pioneering new enhanced social and environmental analytics to identify long-term, high growth, investment opportunities that conventional approaches typically undervalue (http://www.generationim.com).

The Skoll Centre for Social Entrepreneurship has commissioned a suite of short papers on different aspects of social finance and investment that explore this emerging landscape and represent the most comprehensive account of its rapid development currently available. The research includes two framing, overview, pieces (Nicholls and Pharoah, 2007; Emerson and Spitzer, 2007) as well as accounts of specific financial models such as Venture Philanthropy (John, 2006, 2007), social risk capital (Emerson et al, 2007), environmental investing (Harold et al, 2007), real estate investing (Spitzer et al, 2007) and public offerings within an 'ethical' stock market (Hartzell, 2007).

Conclusions

In summary the last four years have seen major changes in the social entrepreneurship landscape both academic and in praxis. In many ways social entrepreneurship is moving out of its start-up phase and into early maturity both as a field of action and research. However, there remain some major challenges. For the continued development of the academic field there are three main priorities: more and better empirical data: deeper and more rigorous theory building and testing across disciplines; and establishing academic credibility by publishing in the top journals.

Some progress is being made across all three areas, but a tipping point has yet to be reached in terms of academic participation. As noted elsewhere in this collection (Dees and Battle Anderson, 2006), the university setting for research in social entrepreneurship still remains a challenge and it is incumbent on all those already engaged with the subject to strive to bring in new colleagues and work relentlessly to broaden and deepen the research base. This is a demanding objective, but one that looks more achievable than ever today.

For praxis, the four areas highlighted in the Endnote to the first edition of this book remain critical: finding new resource streams; improving governance structures and practices; reviewing organizational impact and performance holistically; and building out the socially entrepreneurial landscape from lone organisations to bigger ecosystems.

As has already been suggested, the last four years has seen significant new work towards building a 'social' finance marketplace, but the truth is that the extant institutional arrangements remain fragmented and ill equipped to provide the quantum leap in the resource base needed to drive the next wave of social entrepreneurship forward (Emerson and Spitzer, 2007; Nicholls and Pharoah, 2007). One possible solution will be to encourage charities and foundations to use their investments better to further their social mission. Such mission related investments (MRIs) can significantly add capital to the social finance marketplace. For example, if 10% of UK charity investments went into social entrepreneurship rather than commercial firms, an additional £8 billion of capital would be available to grow social value (NCVO, 2007). In the absence of such a market, the move towards self-sustainable business models—as structured in the social enterprise model—has become increasingly attractive. This could represent a dangerous polarisation of the movement and must be balanced by more vigorous government and civil society action to ensure the integrity of social entrepreneurship is preserved and the full range of its impacts and interventions exploited.

An important strand in the ongoing development of the resource base is the growth of ethical markets. Changes in consumption patterns and a reconfiguring of organizational value chains—both partly driven by social entrepreneurs—are offering new market opportunities to add social and environmental value as well as to derive economic sustainability (Nicholls, 2007). Thus, the rise of Fair Trade is both the consequence of, and an opportunity for, social entrepreneurs. Equally, innovative social enterprises, such as the Furniture Resource Centre, use all their value chain activities to address their social mission in terms of inputs, process, and outputs. This represents a positive deconstruction of the social innovation opportunity landscape perfectly in line with social entrepreneurs' key characteristics of sociality, innovation, and market orientation.

In terms of governance and accountability, there has also been progress. Two new initiatives that have been developed recently are particularly interesting. The first, has been pioneered by two NGOs with a long history of addressing issues around governance: Keystone and Accountability. Working within the coalition of organisations known as BOND (British Overseas NGOs for Development) this has taken the form of a series of quality performance standards for action driven by beneficiary voice (BOND, 2006). Building on work by ActionAid and others that devolved performance measurement and strategic decision making to the field level actors, BOND has developed a framework for performance accountability that radically challenges conventional models and represents a major social innovation in the development landscape. This important work reflects a number of the observations made by Jacobs in this volume (Jacobs, 2006). The second initiative concerns a series of pieces of research around organizational legitimacy that recasts socially entrepreneurial performance as partly a function of accountability to key stakeholders (Nicholls, 2008a). This work is developing an Organisational Legitimacy Toolkit that will allow social entrepreneurs—and, indeed, other organisations—better to understand how their right to operate is configured and, thus, deliver more responsive and effective goods, services, and transformatory interventions whilst also improving their chances of establishing the sustainability of their social impacts (Nicholls, 2008b).

There has also been new work recently addressing impact measurement and performance innovation in social entrepreneurship. Following on from work done by the Roberts Enterprise Development Fund (REDF) in the 1990s on

Social Return on Investment (e.g. Emerson, 1999), Nef (the New Economics Foundation) has built up a programme of work looking at performance measurement and impact in social entrepreneurship (e.g. Walker et al, 2006; Sanfillipo and Lawlor, 2007). This important work has been consolidated into a web-based toolkit that offers social entrepreneurs a range of metrics to account for their impact and develop and test mission driven strategies. (www.proveandimprove.org/new). Recent empirical work has also explored the strategic context of impact measurement regimes within social entrepreneurship with particular reference to how such data is used in organizational accountability and innovation (Nicholls and Nicholls, 2007). What this work demonstrates is that social entrepreneurs tend to use measurement as part of a resource strategy to satisfy or attract funders rather than as a mechanism strategically to improve their own accountability and mission impact. This suggests a major missed opportunity to use available data to make practical recommendations for performance enhancement in social entrepreneurship going forward. Furthermore, the impact metrics landscape is currently fragmented and contested. If social entrepreneurs were to agree to standardised performance measurements there would be a strong incentive to both implement them across the sector and use them more proactively.

However, for all the forward momentum in these three important areas, the final set of issues remains an anomaly for the social entrepreneurship movement. Perhaps because its leading advocates have been at pains to try to delineate what is distinctive about social entrepreneurship, they have not yet built strong alliances with the broader social development field. Of course, many social entrepreneurs understand the overlaps in their work, and are fully cognisant of the operating alliances that are essential to the outcomes they seek. But the level of relationships with more established charitable foundations, policy makers, and development and aid agencies remains limited, and, at times, even hostile. It seems increasingly clear the social entrepreneurship movement will need to participate in a wider intra-sectoral debate if its members wish to see it grow and mature.

An important fault-line has also emerged within the movement itself. A passionate group of advocates has argued that it is particular organisational forms, namely the 'hybrid' businesses which combine a social imperative with a commercial economic model that really set social entrepreneurship apart from earlier generations of social development. For reasons we have already set out, this does not appear to threaten the scope of the movement at a conceptual level. But it is indicative of the contests all significant social movements need to go through if they are to unearth deeper insights as well as heart-felt commitments and institutional innovations from subscribers (Tilley, 2004). From a sociological perspective, it can be said that the purpose of exchanges within the movement to date has been to confirm belonging and claims to authenticity through expressions of a considerable degree of conformity. By contrast, the movement will need to develop greater resilience to contention and specialisation within it ranks, while maintaining sufficient overall coherence to act as a major force for societal change.

The number of key actors stewarding the social entrepreneurship movement, and particularly those engaged in shaping and sustaining an international platform, is as yet very small. For them to be successful during this early phase, they have necessarily worked with a strong regard for self-interest. Their ability to raise the game or at least attract attention for the movement has been synonymous with gaining recognition for themselves and has not tended to spread the credit for key developments. But both driver and symptom of an expansion in social entrepreneurship will be greater diversity and its corollary, more competition. At present, it is difficult to see where that will come from: mechanisms for collectivising voice from social entrepreneurs themselves are weak, and new resources would be needed to amplify their demands.

A reflection on the academic work within the field of social movements tells us that permanent, systemic, social change ultimately comes from a realignment of wider societal cognitive frames of reference, rather than isolated private ventures. This is achieved not only by framing contested issues in a new way—something that is central to the existing social entrepreneurship landscape—but by then constructing networks and alliances and using these new institutions to develop collective action processes to embed change (e.g. Hargrave and Van de Ven, 2006; Thekaekara and Thekaekara, 2007). This is a political and collaborative process. The social entrepreneurship movement needs to build such collective action processes from the ground upwards. As a consequence, the self-appointed stewards of social entrepreneurship will need to loosen their control of the development of the field going forward—typically based upon their own internal agendas—and increasingly accept diversity, contradiction, and independence as the life blood of social entrepreneurship as it moves further into collective maturity.

References

Alvord, S., Brown, L, Letts, C. (2004), 'Social entrepreneurship and societal transformation: an exploratory study', *Journal of Applied Behavioral Science*, 40.3, pp. 260–83.

Aspen (2006), *A Closer Look At Business Education: Social Entrepreneurship/Social Enterprise*, Aspen Institute.

Austin, J., Gutierrez, R., Ogliastri, E, Reficco, R. (eds) (2006), *Effective Management of Social Enterprises*, Harvard: David Rockefeller Center Series on Latin American Studies.

Baron, D. (2007), 'Corporate Social Responsibility and Social Entrepreneurship', *Journal of Economics & Management Strategy*, 16.3, pp. 683–717.

BOND (2006), A BOND Approach to Quality in Non-Governmental Organisations: Putting Beneficiaries First, available at: http://www.bond.org.uk/futures/standards/index.htm

Bornstein, D. (2004), *How To Change The World: Social Entrepreneurs and the Power of New Ideas*, Oxford: Oxford University Press.

Borzaga, C. and Defourny, J. (2001), *The Emergence of Social Enterprise*. New York: Routledge.

Boschee, J., and McClurg, D. (2003), *Toward a Better Understanding of Social Entrepreneurship: Some Important Distinctions*. Minnesota: Institute for Social Entrepreneurs.

Brinckerhoff, P. (2000), *Social Entrepreneurship: The Art of Mission-Based Venture Development*. New York: John Wiley & Sons.

Brock, D. (2006), *Social Entrepreneurship Teaching Resources Handbook*, Berea College.

Cabinet Office (2006), *Social Enterprise Action Plan: Scaling New Heights*, London: Office of The Third Sector, available at: http://www.cabinetoffice.gov.uk/third_sector/social_enterprise/action_plan.aspx

Chell, E. (2007), 'Social Enterprise and Entrepreneurship', *International Small Business Journal*, 25.1, pp. 5–26.

China Economic Review (2007), 'Giving Back, Corporate Style', August.

Cho, A. (2006), 'Politics, Values, and Social Entrepreneurship: A Critical Appraisal', in Mair, J., Robinson, J., and Hockerts, K., *Social Enrepreneurship*, Palgrave MacMillan, pp. 34–56.

Commission on Unclaimed Assets (2006), *Social Investment Bank: A Consultation Paper*, available at: *http://www.unclaimedassets.org.uk/CUA_report_16pp.pdf*

Dees, J. G. (1994), *Social Enterprise: Private Initiatives for Common Good*. Harvard: Harvard Business School Press.

—— (1996), *The Social Enterprise Spectrum: from Philanthropy to Commerce*. Harvard: Harvard Business School Press.

—— (1998), *The Meaning of Social Entrepreneurship* at *http://faculty.fuqua.duke.edu/centers/case/files/dees-SE.pdf*

—— Emerson, J., and Economy, P. (2001), *Enterprising Non-profits: A Toolkit for Social Entrepreneurs*. New York: Wiley Non-Profit Series.

—— —— —— (2002), *Strategic Tools for Social Entrepreneurs: Enhancing the Performance of Your Enterprising Non-profit*. New York: Wiley Non-Profit Series.

—— and Battle Anderson, B. (2006), 'Rhetoric, Reality, and Research: Building a Solid Foundation for the Practice of Social Entrepreneurship', in Nicholls, A. (ed), *Social Entrepreneurship: New Models of Sustainable Social Change*, Oxford University Press, pp. 144–68.

Department for Trade and Industry (DTI), Social Enterprise Unit (2002), *Social Enterprise: A Strategy for Success*, London.

—— (2003), *Public Procurement: A Toolkit For Social Enterprises*, London: DTI.

Dorado, S. (2006), 'Social Entrepreneurial Ventures: Different Values So Different Process of Creation, No?', *Journal of Developmental Entrepreneurship*, 11.4, pp. 319–44.

Drayton, W. (2006), 'The Citizens' Sector Transformed', in Nicholls, A. (ed), *Social Entrepreneurship: New Models of Sustainable Social Change*, Oxford University Press, pp. 45–55.

Economist (2005a), 'Hale and Healthy', April 14th.

—— (2005b), 'Calling an End to Poverty', July 7th.

—— (2005c), 'Good for Me, Good for My Party', November 24th.

—— (2006a), 'The Rise of the Social Entrepreneur', February 23rd.

—— (2006b), 'Special Topic: The Business of Giving', February 23rd.

—— (2006c), 'The New Powers in Giving', June 29th.

—— (2006d), 'The Fight over a Big Idea', July 20th.

—— (2007a), 'Fish versus AIDS', August 30th.

—— (2007b), 'The Clinton Factor', September 25th.

Emerson, J. (1999), 'Social Return on Investment: Exploring Aspects of Value Creation', *REDF box set*, vol. 2, chapter 8, San Francisco: Roberts Enterprise Development Foundation.

—— Freundlich, T., and Fruchterman, J. (2007), *Nothing Ventured*, Skoll Centre for Social Entrepreneurship, available at: http://www.sbs.ox.ac.uk/skoll/research/Short+papers/Short+papers.htm

—— and Spitzer, J. (2007), *From Fragmentation to Functionality*, Skoll Centre for Social Entrepreneurship, available at: http://www.sbs.ox.ac.uk/skoll/research/Short+papers/Short+papers.htm

Guthrie, J. (2006), 'Let this social enterprise malarkey bloom', *Financial Times Comment*, May 25th.

Guthrie, D. (2007), 'Social Entrepreneurship and Innovation in China', paper presented at the International Forum on Social Entrepreneurship, Hangzhou, May 27th.

Harding, R., and Cowling, M. (2006), *Social Entrepreneurship Monitor: United Kingdom 2006*, London: Global Entrepreneurship Monitor.

Hargrave, T., and Van de Ven, A. (2005), 'A Collective Action Model of Institutional Innovation', *Academy of Management Review*, 31.4, pp. 864–88.

Harold, J., Spitzer, J., and Emerson J. (2007), *Blended Value Investing: Integrating Environmental Risks and Opportunities into Securities Valuation'*, Skoll Centre for Social Entrepreneurship, available at: http://www.sbs.ox.ac.uk/skoll/research/Short+papers/Short+papers.htm

Hartzell, J. (2007), *Creating An Ethical Stock Exchange*, Skoll Centre for Social Entrepreneurship, available at: http://www.sbs.ox.ac.uk/skoll/research/Short+papers/Short+papers.htm

Haugh, H. (2007), 'New Strategies for a Sustainable Society: The Growing Contribution of Social Entrepreneurship', *Business Ethics Quarterly*, 17.4, pp.743–9.

Jack, A. (2007), 'Beyond charity? A new generation enters the business of doing good', *Financial Times*, April 5th.

Jacobs, A. (2006), 'Helping People is Difficult: Growth and Performance in Social Enterprises Working for International Relief and Development', in Nicholls, A. (ed), *Social Entrepreneurship: New Models of Sustainable Social Change*, Oxford University Press, pp. 247–69.

John, R. (2006), *Venture Philanthropy: The Evolution of High Engagement Philanthropy in Europe*, Skoll Centre for Social Entrepreneurship, available at: http://www.sbs.ox.ac.uk/skoll/research/Short+papers/Short+papers.htm

—— (2007), *Beyond The Cheque: How Venture Philanthropists Add Value*, Skoll Centre for Social Entrepreneurship, available at: http://www.sbs.ox.ac.uk/skoll/research/Short+papers/Short+papers.htm

Kim, M., and Davis, S. (2007), *Social Entrepreneurship Faculty Directory*, Ashoka Global Academy.

Light, P. (2006), 'Reshaping Social Entrepreneurship', *Stanford Social Innovation Review*, Fall, pp. 47–52.

Mair, J., Robinson, J., and Hockerts, K. (2006), *Social Entrepreneurship*, Palgrave MacMillan.

—— Seelos, C. (forthcoming), 'Profitable Business Models and Market Creation in the Context of Deep Poverty: A Strategic View', *Academy of Management Perspectives*.

Meehan III, W., Kilmer, D., and O'Flanagan, M. (2004), 'Investing in Society', *Stanford Social Innovation Review*, Spring, pp. 35–41.

Mosher-Williams, R. (2007), *Research on Social Entrepreneurship: Understanding and Contributing to an Emerging Field*, ARNOVA.

Mulgan, G. (2007), *Social Innovation*, Skoll Centre for Social Entrepreneurship, available at: http://www.sbs.ox.ac.uk/skoll/research/Short+papers/Short+papers.htm

National Council for Voluntary Organisations (NCVO) (2007), *UK Voluntary Sector Almanac 2007*.

Nicholls (2008a), A., and Opal, C. (2005), *Fair Trade: Market-Driven Ethical Consumption*, London: Sage.

—— (2006), 'Playing the Field: A New Approach to the Meaning of Social Entrepreneurship', *Social Enterprise Journal*, 2.1, pp. 1–5.

—— Cho, A. (2006), 'Social Entrepreneurship: The Structuration of a Field', in Nicholls, A. (ed), *Social Entrepreneurship: New Models of Sustainable Social Change*, Oxford University Press, pp. 99–118.

—— (2007), *What is the Future of Social Enterprise in Ethical Markets?*, London, Office of The Third Sector, available at: http://www.cabinetoffice.gov.uk/third_sector/Research_and_statistics/social_enterprise_research/think_pieces.aspx

—— Nicholls, J. (2007), 'Social Impact Measurement and Planning for Innovation', paper presented at the 3rd International Social Entrepreneurship Conference, Copenhagen, June 18th.

—— Pharoah, C. (2007), *The Landscape of Social Finance*, Skoll Centre for Social Entrepreneurship, available at: http://www.sbs.ox.ac.uk/skoll/research/Short+papers/Short+papers.htm

—— (2008), 'Capturing the Performance of the Socially Entrepreneurial Organisation (SEO): An Organisational Legitimacy Approach', in Robinson, J., Mair, J., and Hockerts, K. (eds), *International Perspectives on Social Entrepreneurship Research*, Palgrave MacMillan (forthcoming).

—— (2008b), 'What Gives Fair Trade Its Right To Operate? Organisational Legitimacy and the Strategic Management of Social Entrepreneurship', in MacDonald, K., and Marshall, S. (eds), Fair Trade, Corporate Accountability and Beyond: Experiments in Global Justice Governance Mechanisms, Ashgate (forthcoming).

Nyssens, M. (ed) (2007), *Social Enterprise*, Routledge.

Offer, A. (2006), *The Challenge of Affluence*, Oxford University Press.

Peredo, A., Chrisman, J. (2006), 'Towards a Theory of Community-Based Enterprise', *Academy of Management Review*, 31.2, pp. 309–38.

—— McLean, M. (2006), 'Social entrepreneurship: A critical review of the concept', *Journal of World Business*, 41, pp. 56–65.

Perrini, F. (ed) (2007), *The New Social Entrepreneurship*, Edward Elgar.

Powell, W. (1987), *The Nonprofit Sector: A Research Handbook*, Yale: Yale University Press.

Raynolds, L., Murray, D., and Wilkinson, J. (eds) (2007), *Fair Trade. The Challenges of Transforming Globalization*, Routledge.

Ridley-Duff, R. (2007), 'Communitarian Perspectives on Social Enterprise', *Corporate Governance*, 15.2, pp. 382–93.

Robinson, J., Mair, J., and Hockerts, K. (eds), *International Perspectives on Social Entrepreneurship Research*, Palgrave MacMillan.

Salamon, L., and Anheier, H. (1997), *Defining the Nonprofit Sector: A Cross-National Analysis*, Manchester University Press.

Sanfillipo, L., and Lawlor (2007), 'Measuring Real Value: A DIY Guide to Social Return on Investment', New Economics Foundation, available at: http://www.neweconomics.org/gen/z_sys_PublicationDetail.aspx?pid=241.

Shaw, E., and Carter, S. (2007), 'Social entrepreneurship; Theoretical antecedents and empirical analysis of entrepreneurial processes and outcomes', *Journal of Small Business and Enterprise Development*, 14.3, pp. 418–29.

Social Enterprise Zones Task Force (2007), *Social Enterprise Zones*, Conservative Party, available at: http://www.conservatives.com/pdf/socialenterprise.pdf

Spear, R., and Bidet, E. (2005) 'Social Enterprises for Work Integration in 12 European Countries: A Descriptive Analysis', *Annals of Public and Cooperative Economics*, 76.2, pp. 195–231.

Spitzer, J., Emerson J., and Harold, J. (2007), *Blended Value Investing: Innovations in Real Estate*, Skoll Centre for Social Entrepreneurship, available at: http://www.sbs.ox.ac.uk/skoll/research/Short+papers/Short+papers.htm

Sullivan, D. (2007), 'Stimulating Social Entrepreneurship: Can Support From Cities Make a Difference?', *The Academy of Management Perspectives*, 21.1, pp. 77–8.

Thekaekara, S., and Thekaekara, M. (2007), *Social Justice and Social Entrepreneurship*, Skoll Centre for Social Entrepreneurship, available at: http://www.sbs.ox.ac.uk/skoll/research/Short+papers/Short+papers.htm

Tilly, C. (2004), *Social Movements, 1768–2004*, Paradigm.

Tracey, P., and Jarvis, O. (2007), 'Toward a Theory of Social Venture Franchising', *Entrepreneurship Theory and Practice*, 31.5, pp. 667–85.

Walker, P., Lewis, J., Lingayah, S., and Sommer, F. (2006), *Prove it! Measuring the Effect of Neighbourhood Renewal on Local People*, available at: http://www.neweconomics.org/gen/newways_socialaudit.aspx

Weerawardena, J., and Sullivan Mort, G. (2006), 'Investigating social entrepreneurship: A multidimensional model', *Journal of World Business*, 41, pp. 21–35.

Wei-Skillern, J., Austin, J., Leonard, H., and Stevenson, H. (eds) (2007), *Entrepreneurship in the Social Sector*, Sage.

Contents

Contents

Contents

Acknowledgements

First, I should like to thank all the outstanding contributors to this collection who so generously gave their time, thinking, and research. Their patience with me throughout the—sometimes tortuous—process of editing this historic volume has been exemplary and is much appreciated.

Second, I owe a considerable debt of gratitude to my academic 'patrons'— Jeff Skoll and Prof. Anthony Hopwood—without whose material support this book could never have been written.

Third, I want to single out for thanks my mother Catherine Nicholls, who has been tireless and fearless in her support of my work over the years. She is truly an extraordinary woman. Sam and Harriet have also been vital to me as this book has come together and are always in my thoughts.

I want to praise the Skoll Centre for Social Entrepreneurship support team— Kathryn Smyth and Mona Turnbull—for their good humour and skill whilst making considerable contributions to the Skoll World Forum in Social Entrepreneurship and the running of the Centre in general. Finally, I also need to express my most affectionate thanks to my extraordinary colleague at the Skoll Centre, Rowena Young, who helped me frame my arguments and structure the book throughout its production.

This book is dedicated to Isabel, my guiding star.

'Social Entrepreneurs need always to be ten years ahead of their time and to be prepared to be ridiculed. This is the only way to bring about real change.'

Bunker Roy, Barefoot College (Campinas, Brazil, 2004)

List of Figures

List of Tables

Abbreviations

List of Abbreviations

AIMS	Aid Information Mapping Services
ALMO	Arm's-Length Management Organization
ALNAP	Active Learning Network for Accountability and Practice
ALPS	Accountability, Learning, and Planning System
AMA	American Medical Association
ANCA	Associacao Nacional de Cooperacao Agricola
BRAC	Bangladesh Rural Advancement Committee
CAF	Charities Aid Foundation
CEP	Center for Effective Philanthropy
CFO	Chief Finance Officer
CIC	Community Interest Company
CNFA	Citizens Network for Foreign Affairs
COO	Chief Operating Office
CSE	Corporate Social Entrepreneurship
CSI	Center for Social Innovation (Stanford)
CSR	Corporate social responsibility
DdG	Diálogo de Gestiones
DfID	Department for International Development
DTI	Department for Trade and Industry
EU	European Union
FUSION	Future Social Innovators Network (Stanford)
GSB	Graduate School of Business (Stanford)
GDP	Gross Domestic Product
GEM	Global Entrepreneurship Monitor
GEXSI	Global Exchange for Social Investment
GMA	Global Micro-Entrepreneurship Awards
GTZ	German Development Agency
HBS	Harvard Business School

Abbreviations

ICG	International Crisis Group
IEA	Institute for Economic Affairs
INGO	International Non-Governmental Organization
IOWH	Institute for One World Health
IPP	Institute of Public Policy
ISERC	International Social Entrepreneurship Conference
KSG	Kennedy School of Government (Harvard)
LLCs	Limited Liability Corporations
LPs	Limited Partnerships
MIS	Management Information Systems
MIT	Massachusetts Institute of Technology
MNC	Multinational Corporation
MS&E	Management Science and Engineering (Stanford)
NEPAD	New Partnership for Africa's Development
NESsT	Non-Profit Enterprise and Self-Sustainability Team
NFF	Nonprofit Finance Fund
NGOs	Non-Governmental Organizations
NHS	National Health Service
NPOs	Not-For-Profit Organizations
NPV	Net Present Value
ODI	Overseas Development Institute
OED	Oxford English Dictionary
PMP	Public Management Program (Stanford)
RISE	Research Initiative in Social Entrepreneurship
ROI	Return on Investment
SAMOPN	Southern African Marula Oil Producers Network
SE Lab	Social Entrepreneurship Collaboratory (Stanford, Harvard)
SEKN	Social Enterprise Knowledge Network
SEP	Social Entrepreneurship Programme
SIIS	Stanford Institute for International Studies
Social E-Challenge	Social Entrepreneurs Challenge (Stanford)
SROI	Social Return on Investment
UK	United Kingdom
UPAs	Urban Priority Areas
USA	United States of America
VESC	Virginia Eastern Shore Corporation
WEF	World Economic Forum

Currency	Conversion rate
Euro1	$1.18
Euro1	£0.69
$1	£0.58
£1	$1.72

A Note on Currency Conversions

This book includes figures in US dollars ($) and UK pounds (£). The exchange rates calculations used are correct at the time of going to press (December 2005) and are as follows:

A Note on the Meaning of 'Not-for-Profit'

There appears to be a degree of substitution of the terms 'nonprofit' and 'not-for-profit' across international scholarship. Both are used to describe social purpose ventures that often—but not always—have special tax advantages. However, there is some confusion over whether these terms describe the strategic function of the organization (i.e. that its mission is not to make a profit) or the process of what it actually does (i.e. its activities are not profitable). There is a further complexity in that both terms can be extended at times to the sense of 'profitable, but not profit distributing' (i.e. without external shareholders). Indeed, in the USA, legally a nonprofit organization is one that does not declare a profit and instead utilizes all revenue available after normal operating expenses in service to the public interest. This sense may be applied particularly to successful social enterprises, but also allows large corporations such as the John Lewis Partnership (which is owned by its workforce) to be technically classed as 'nonprofits', even though such a large and profitable organization would not be typically thought of by many as a not-for-profit.

Nonprofit is typically used in the USA to describe social purpose organizations that serve the public interest and are registered as 501(c)(3) tax-exempt organizations. These would often be recognized as charities in the UK. Not-for-profit is used more commonly in the UK for a range of social purpose organizations including charities, co-operatives, and voluntary organizations.

It is also possible to include under this heading a distinct category of social enterprises that uses equity, or equity-like, finance and which may distribute some profits, but is mission driven and not set up for private gain. In such cases equity will have been offered as a strategy for accessing new finance and will be made available under terms that cannot jeopardize the 'social' or community ownership of the venture. In 2005, the UK government acknowledged this innovative type of social enterprise by introducing a new legal form for such organizations—the Community Interest Company (CIC). The CIC features an 'asset lock' and limits the amount of dividend distribution to encourage a wider range of finance into social ventures without risking mission drift.

To achieve clarity for the reader of this book, the term not-for-profit is used exclusively throughout. As used here, the term describes any venture that has, as its prime strategic aim, a social purpose and is either not profit distributing or offers only limited dividends in accord with its social mission, whether it is tax paying or not and irrespective of its income mix.

About the Authors

Alex Nicholls

Dr Nicholls is the first lecturer in social entrepreneurship appointed in the UK. His research and teaching experience fall across a range of subjects centred on social and ethical issues. Nicholls has a background in retail marketing and, before that, medieval lexicography, but in recent years has developed particular interests in Fair Trade, business ethics, and the interface between marketing and society. He has been working in the specific area of social entrepreneurship for some time and acted as the external consultant for the establishment of the Skoll Centre for Social Entrepreneurship at the Saïd Business School.

Nicholls has published in a range of refereed journals, including the *European Journal of Marketing* and *Service Industries Journal*, and has presented papers at many international conferences. He has also co-authored a major research book *Fair Trade: Market Driven Ethical Consumption* for Sage Publishers (2005). Nicholls has held lectureships at a wide variety of academic institutions including: the University of Toronto, Canada; Leeds Metropolitan University; University of Surrey; Aston Business School.

Nicholls is a fellow of the Academy of Marketing Science and member of the Institute of Learning and Teaching. He also sits on the regional social enterprise expert group for the South East of England Development Agency.

Jeff Skoll

Jeff Skoll served as eBay's first full-time employee and first president, creating the business plan that the company still follows. In 1998 he inspired the company to take an active role in philanthropy, pioneering creation of the eBay Foundation through the allocation of pre-IPO shares. This innovation sparked similar initiatives by other young companies in high-technology hubs across the USA. In 1999 Skoll created the Skoll Foundation, which takes an entrepreneurial approach to philanthropy, seeking out and empowering the world's most promising social entrepreneurs in order to effect lasting, positive social change worldwide. Today, he serves as chairman of the Skoll Foundation and continues to build the foundation, which has tripled in size over the past year.

In addition to his role as Skoll Foundation chairman, Skoll directs his investment group, Capricorn Management, and leads a venture in Hollywood to produce feature films highlighting social entrepreneurs who overcome the injustice of social inequity. He also serves as a board director for the eBay

Foundation and Community Foundation Silicon Valley and is a member of the advisory board of the Stanford Graduate School of Business, among others. He holds a BSc in electrical engineering from the University of Toronto and an MBA from the Stanford Graduate School of Business.

His recent honours and awards include Canada's 1999 Leafy Award for his contributions to high technology; a 2001 Visionary Award from the Software Development Forum; the 2002 Outstanding Philanthropist Award from the Silicon Valley chapter of the Association of Fundraising Professionals; the 2003 Outstanding Philanthropist Award from the International Association of Fundraising Professionals; and, in 2003, an honorary Doctor of Law degree from his alma mater, the University of Toronto. In 2002, Skoll was identified by *Business Week* as one of the most innovative philanthropists of the past decade.

Muhammad Yunus

Professor Yunus is the founder and managing director of Grameen Bank which currently operates 1,537 branches providing credit to 4.7 million poor people residing in 54,022 villages in Bangladesh. He originated the concept of Grameen Bank, i.e. banking without collateral for the poorest of the poor. Yunus studied economics at Vanderbilt University, USA and received his Ph.D. in economics in 1970. He taught economics at Middle Tennessee University from 1969 to 1972. Returning to Bangladesh in 1972, he joined the University of Chittagong as Head of the Economics Department. He started the Grameen Bank Project in 1976. It was transformed into a formal bank in 1983. The Grameen Bank offers small loans for self-employment to the rural poor, especially poor women.

In addition to Grameen Bank, Yunus has created a number of companies in Bangladesh to address diverse issues of poverty and development. Among them are: Grameen Phone (a mobile telephone company); Grameen Cybernet (Internet Service Provider); Grameen Communications (Rural Internet Service Provider); Grameen Software company; Grameen Information Technology Park; Grameen Fund (Social Venture Capital Company); Grameen Capital Management Company; Grameen Textile Company; Grameen Knitwear Company; Grameen Renewable Energy Company; Grameen Health Company; Grameen Education Company; Grameen Agriculture Company; Grameen Fisheries and Livestock Company; and Grameen Business Promotion Company.

Yunus has been widely honoured. Amongst his awards are: Ramon Magsaysay Award (1984) from the Philippines; Aga Khan Award for Architecture (1989) from Switzerland; Mohamed Shabdeen Award for Science, Socio-Economic (1993) from Sri Lanka; World Food Prize (1994) from USA; Simon Bolivar Prize (1996) from Venezuela; Man for Peace Award (1997) from Italy; Prince of Austurias Award for Concord (1998) from Spain; Ozaki (Gakudo) Award (1998) from Japan; Indira Gandhi Award (1998) from India; Sydney Peace Prize (1998) from Australia; Rotary Award for World Understanding (1999) from USA; Golden Pegasus Award (1999) from Italy; Roma Award for Peace and Humanitarian Action (1999) from Italy; King Hussein Humanitarian Leadership Award (2000) from Jordan, International Cooperation Prize Caja de Granada (2001) from Spain; 'NAVARRA' International Aid Award (2001) from Spain; Grand Prize of the Fukuoka Asian Culture Prize (2001) from Japan; Mahatma Gandhi Award (2002) from USA; Volvo Environment Prize (2003) from Sweden; Citta di Orvieto Award (2004) from Italy; Nikkei Asia Prize (2004) from Japan; The Economist Award for Social and Economic Innovation (2004) from USA. Within Bangladesh, he received the President's Award (1978); Central Bank Award (1985); and Independence Day Award (1987), the highest national award. He was the first chair of the Policy Advisory Group of CGAP (Consultative Group to Assist the Poorest). He has been appointed as an International Goodwill Ambassador for UNAIDS by the United Nations. Yunus has also been inducted as a member of the Legion d'Honneur by President Chirac of France.

Bill Drayton

Bill Drayton has been a social entrepreneur since he was a New York City elementary school student. He was born to a mother who emigrated from Australia as a young cellist and an American father who, also unafraid to step into the unknown, became an explorer at an equally young age. Public service and strong values run through the stories of both parents' families—including several of the earliest anti-slavery abolitionist and women's leaders in the USA. These family influences, the rich diversity and openness of life in Manhattan—as well as America's deep cultural concern with equity, which flourished during the Civil Rights years—all interacted with one another and with Drayton's temperament to plant Ashoka's earliest roots. In elementary school, Drayton loved geography and history and was equally unmotivated in Latin and maths. His real passion in those years went to sailing, and starting and running a series of newspapers in his school and beyond. In high school he created and built the Asia Society into the largest student organization. By high school he was also a NAACP member and actively engaged in and deeply moved by civil rights work. At Harvard he founded the Ashoka Table; and, at Yale Law School, he launched Yale Legislative Services which, by the time he graduated, engaged one-third of the student body in helping key legislators throughout the northeast design and draft legislation.

Drayton's deepening commitments to Asia, especially South Asia, and to civil rights were closely linked. Martin Luther King, Jr. followed Mahatma Gandhi's way, and anyone concerned with inequity within the USA could only be more disturbed by the greater inequalities between the world's North and South. Once focused on such a chasm, any entrepreneur would have to ask: 'What can I do?'. At Harvard and Oxford, Drayton did ask. Fully appreciating how central to significant change ('development') entrepreneurs are, his answer was the Ashoka idea. Drayton is also a manager and management consultant—choices that also grow from his fascination with how human institutions work. Although he loves and thinks first in historical terms, he is trained in economics, law, and management, the three key-interventionist disciplines. He was a McKinsey & Company consultant for almost ten years, gaining wide experience serving both public and private clients.

For four years, he was assistant administrator at the US Environmental Protection Agency, where he had lead responsibility for policy, budget, management, audit, and representing the environment in Administration-wide policy development, notably including budget, energy, and economic policy. He successfully 'intrapreneured' a series of major innovations and reforms in the field, ranging from the introduction of emissions trading to the use of economics-defined incentives to remove the advantage of delaying compliance. Later he founded and led Save EPA (an association of professional environmental managers that helped the Congress, press, Administration, citizen groups, and public understand and then block much of the radically destructive policies proposed by the Administrator Ann Gorsuch and others). Drayton also founded and led Environmental Safety (which helps develop and spread better ways of implementing environmental laws). He also served briefly in the White House, and taught both law and management at Stanford Law School and Harvard's Kennedy School of Government. He is currently significantly involved as board chair of Get America Working! and Youth Venture, both major strategic innovations for the public good.

Drayton has received many awards for his achievements. He was elected one of the early MacArthur fellows for his work, including the founding of Ashoka. Yale School of Management gave him its annual Award for Entrepreneurial Excellence. The American Society of Public Administration and the National Academy of Public Administration jointly awarded him their National Public Service Award, and the Common Cause gave him its Public Service Achievement Award. He has also been named a Preiskel-Silverman Fellow for Yale Law School and is a member of the American Academy of Arts and Sciences.

Rowena Young

Rowena Young has been involved in the formation of the social entrepreneurship movement in the UK since its inception in the late 1990s. She is Director of the Skoll Centre for Social Entrepreneurship at the Saïd Business School. The Centre was launched in November 2003 at the Saïd Business School, Oxford University, to promote the advancement of social entrepreneurship worldwide.

Before joining Saïd, Young was Chief Executive of the School for Social Entrepreneurs. The School was launched by Michael Young, acknowledged to be the world's most prolific serial social entrepreneur, and founder of the Open University and the Consumers' Association.

Previously Young was development director at Kaleidoscope, a leading drug treatment service in London where she launched Simplyworks, a web-enabling business creating training and employment for long-term drug users. In 2002 she published *From War to Work: drug treatment, social inclusion and enterprise* with the Foreign Policy Centre.

She has overseen operations at Children's Express, a national news agency run by children and young people – where successes included helping children to shape government policy – and at the think tank Demos, which played an influential role in shaping the policy agenda for a newly elected Labour government in 1997.

Geoff Mulgan

Dr Geoff Mulgan is Director of the Young Foundation, which in previous incarnations was run by Michael Young (described as 'probably the most successful entrepreneur of social enterprises in the world' by Harvard's Professor Daniel Bell). Previously he was head of policy in Prime Minister Tony Blair's office; director of the UK government's Strategy Unit; and founder and director of the think tank Demos. His last book was *Connexity*, published by Harvard Business Press. He is a visiting professor at London School of Economics and University College London.

Albert Cho

Albert Cho is a management consultant and independent researcher. He holds an AB in social studies, *summa cum laude* and Phi Beta Kappa, from Harvard College, as well as an MSc in development economics and an MBA with distinction from Oxford University, where he was a Rhodes Scholar. Cho has worked at the World Resources Institute and the United Nations Millennium Project and serves as a trustee of the Telluride Association, a not-for-profit educational institution. He has previously published on social entrepreneurship, international trade and environmental policy, and identity politics. He lives in Brooklyn, NY.

Paola Grenier

Paola Grenier is a Dahrendorf Scholar at the Centre for Civil Society, London School of Economics and Political Sciences, where she is pursuing a doctorate in social policy. She has researched and published on social entrepreneurship in the UK and internationally, as well as on social movements and social capital. Before entering academia she worked for ten years in the not-for-profit sectors in the UK and in Hungary, specializing in social housing, homelessness, medical self-help, and mental health.

J. Gregory Dees

J. Gregory Dees is professor of the Practise of Social Entrepreneurship and the founding faculty director of the Center for the Advancement of Social Entrepreneurship at Duke University's Fuqua School of Business. Dees is widely recognized as an academic pioneer in the area of social entrepreneurship and has written extensively on the topic. With Jed Emerson and Peter Economy, he published two books: *Enterprising Nonprofits* (2001, Wiley) and *Strategic Tools for Social Entrepreneurs* (2002, Wiley).

Prior to coming to Duke, Dees served as the Miriam and Peter Haas Centennial Professor in Public Service at Stanford University's Graduate School of Business, where he was also founding co-director of the Center for Social Innovation. Much of Dees' academic career was spent at Harvard Business School where he helped launch the Initiative on Social Enterprise. In 1995, he created a new course on 'Entrepreneurship in the Social Sector' for which he received Harvard Business School's Apgar Award for Innovation in Teaching.

From 1996 until 1998, Dees interrupted his academic career to work with the Mountain Association for Community Economic Development in Berea, KY, on strategies for promoting entrepreneurship in central Appalachia. He started his academic career on the faculty of the Yale School of Management and previously worked as a management consultant and engagement manager with McKinsey & Company. He serves on the board of directors of the Bridgespan Group. His is also a board member and treasurer of SJF Advisory Services, a not-for-profit affiliate of the Sustainable Jobs Fund. He is on advisory boards for the *Fast Company*'s Social Capitalist Awards, REDF, Communities by Choice, and Management Leadership for Tomorrow. Over the years, he has had other formal advisory or board roles with numerous organizations and projects, including the Kauffman Foundation, the Denali Initiative, New Schools Venture Fund, and Partners for Youth with Disabilities. Dees has a Ph.D. in philosophy from the Johns Hopkins University, a masters in Public and Private Management from Yale, and a BA with high honours in philosophy from the University of Cincinnati.

Beth Battle Anderson
Beth Anderson now Vice President, National Foundation Relations at Teach for America, formerly lecturer and managing director at the Center for the Advancement of Social Entrepreneurship (CASE) at Duke University's Fuqua School of Business. Previously, she served as a research associate and acting administrative director at Stanford Business School's Center for Social Innovation and as a summer associate at McKinsey & Company. She has presented on topics related to social entrepreneurship at numerous events and conferences in the USA and abroad. With Professor Greg Dees, she has co-authored papers and chapters on blurring sector boundaries, for-profit social enterprise, scaling social innovations, developing earned income strategies, and the process of social entrepreneurship. She has also supervised, researched, written, and edited several cases on social entrepreneurship and philanthropy. Additionally, at Stanford she helped develop and served as a teaching assistant for a Public Policy course 'Business Skills for the Social Sector'. She received her MBA from Stanford after working for five years in the not-for-profit sector and graduating *magna cum laude* with a BA in Classics from Williams College.

James E. Austin

Dr Austin holds the Snider Professorship of Business Administration, Emeritus at the Harvard Business School. He has been a member of the Harvard University faculty since 1972. His Doctor of Business Administration and MBA degrees are from Harvard University.

Austin was the co-founder of the School's Social Enterprise Initiative. He has authored sixteen books, dozens of articles, and over a hundred case studies on business organizations. His most recent award-winning book is *The Collaboration Challenge: How Nonprofits and Business Succeed Through Strategic Alliances*. Austin has given seminars and served as an advisor to managers and government officials around the world, including being a special advisor to the White House. He has served on many not-for-profit and corporate boards.

Herman Leonard

Herman B. ('Dutch') Leonard is professor of Business Administration at the Harvard Business School and the George F. Baker, Jr. professor of Public Sector Management at Harvard University's John F. Kennedy School of Government. In addition he serves as co-chair of the HBS Social Enterprise Initiative. He teaches extensively in executive programmes at the Business School and the Kennedy School and around the world in the areas of general organizational strategy, governance, performance management, crisis management and leadership, and corporate social responsibility.

His work on leadership focuses on innovation, creativity, effective decision-making, and advocacy and persuasion. His current work in leadership and management is focused on the relationship between governance, accountability, and performance, and emphasizes the use of performance management as a tool for enhancing accountability. He has also worked and taught extensively in the area of crisis management and on issues related to corporate social responsibility.

He is the author of *Checks Unbalanced: The Quiet Side of Public Spending* (1984), of *By Choice or By Chance: Tracking the Values in Massachusetts Public Spending* (1992), and (annually from 1994 to 1999) of *The Federal Budget and the States* (an annual report on the geographic distribution of federal spending and taxation).

Professor Leonard is a member of the board of directors of Harvard Pilgrim Health Care, an 800,000-member Massachusetts HMO, of the Hitachi Foundation for the USA, and of CIVIC Investments. He was for a decade a member of the board of directors of the Massachusetts Health and Educational Facilities Authority and was a member of the Massachusetts Commission on Performance Enhancement. He has been a financial advisor to the Connecticut Governor's Office of Policy and Management, to the Massachusetts Turnpike Authority, and to the Central Artery-Third Harbor Tunnel Project. Professor Leonard was a member of the Governor's Council on Economic Policy for the State of Alaska, of the Governor's Advisory Council on Infrastructure in Massachusetts, and of the US Senate Budget Committee's Private Sector Advisory Committee on Infrastructure. He served as chairman of the Massachusetts Governor's Task Force on Tuition Prepayment Plans, on the National Academy of Sciences Committees on National Urban Policy and on the Superconducting Supercollider, and on the New York City Comptroller's Debt Management Advisory Committee. In addition to his academic studies and teaching, he has been chief financial officer and chief executive officer of a human services agency and has served as a director of public, not-for-profit, and private sector organizations.

Ezequiel Reficco
Ezequiel Reficco is a senior researcher at the Social Enterprise Initiative within Harvard Business School.

Jane Wei-Skillern
Jane Wei-Skillern is an assistant professor of Business Administration in the General Management Unit and Social Enterprise Group at the Harvard Business School. She teaches the second-year MBA elective, Entrepreneurship in the Social Sector. Professor Wei-Skillern earned her BSc in Business from the Haas School of Business at the University of California at Berkeley, an MA in Business Research and a Ph.D. in Organizational Behaviour, both from the Graduate School of Business at Stanford University. Prior to joining the faculty at Harvard, she was an assistant professor of Organizational Behaviour at London Business School.

Doug Foster
Dr Foster's extensive professional experience includes work in the health service, self-employment, and voluntary sector. His previous academic post was as a lecturer at the University of Portsmouth, where he also studied for a PhD focused on Social Entrepreneurship. He currently teaches and researches in Organizational Behaviour, Entrepreneurship and Business Ethics at the University of Surrey. His specific research interests include: spirituality and work, comparative socio-economic complexes and ethics, and critical management theory. He has recently contributed a module on Social Enterprise and Social Entrepreneurship to a new MSc Entrepreneurship programme for launch in September 2006.

Sutia Kim Alter
Kim Alter is founder and principal of Virtue Ventures LLC, a management consulting firm specialized in social entrepreneurship and Visiting Fellow of the Skoll Centre for Social Entrepreneurship at the Saïd Business School, University of Oxford. Alter has over a dozen years of experience in the social enterprise field, first as a social entrepreneur directing the start-up of a 100 per cent self-financed international volunteer organization, Visions in Action, then as a consultant supporting not-for-profit ventures and social enterprises

in more than thirty countries worldwide. Prior to starting her own company, she worked as a technical specialist in microfinance and small/medium enterprise development for major international organizations, Save the Children and Catholic Relief Services. Under Virtue Ventures, her projects and clients have won several awards for global innovation including: Schwab Foundation Social Entrepreneur of the Year (2002); World Bank's Development Marketplace (2003), and Yale School of Management and Goldman Sachs Foundation National Business Plan competition (2003).

Alter is author of *Managing the Double Bottom Line: A Business Planning Guide for Social Enterprises*, and its workbook accompaniment (2001, Pact Publications), and contributing author to *Sustaining Nonprofits through Income Generation* (2004, Jossey-Bass), as well as author of several articles on not-for-profit sustainability strategies and social entrepreneurship. Alter holds a bachelor's degree in international relations and an MBA.

Charles Leadbeater

Charles Leadbeater is an independent writer, speaker, and advisor to leading companies on innovation, entrepreneurship, and the knowledge economy.

After graduating from Balliol College, Oxford with a first class degree in politics, philosophy, and economics, Leadbeater worked for the breakfast television station TV-am, and then joined the *Weekend World*, the current affairs programme, before moving to the *Financial Times*, where he worked as labour editor, industrial editor, Tokyo Bureau Chief, and finally features editor. In 1994 he became assistant editor at *The Independent* where, with Helen Fielding, he devised Bridget Jones's Diary column. In 1999 he won the David Wall prize for journalism.

Leadbeater's work on social entrepreneurship began in 1997 with his report on *The Rise of the Social Entrepreneur,* published by the independent think tank Demos. He is a senior research associate with Demos and has been an advisor to the Downing Street Policy Unit and the British government's Department of Trade and Industry on the rise of the Internet and the knowledge-driven economy. He also drew up the initial plan for the Department of Culture's £10 million project Culture Online, which is promoting digital access to publicly funded museums, galleries, and arts.

Leadbeater is currently a visiting fellow at the Skoll Centre for Social Entrepreneurship.

Alex Jacobs

Alex Jacobs is the CEO of Mango, a not-for-profit organization based in Oxford that provides consultancy services to NGOs in financial management, the management of humanitarian and development projects, and governance.

In 2002, Mango won a special award for contribution to Management Accounting from the Chartered Institute of Management Accountants and in 2001 was shortlisted for Best New Charity at the UK Charity Awards.

Jacobs has carried out major evaluations of humanitarian practice. He currently sits on the board of BOND, the umbrella body for UK NGOs, as well as Oxfam's audit committee. He has extensive experience of NGO operations, ranging from field experience in sub-Saharan Africa to management, board, consultancy, and funding agency appointments. He has worked with rural communities and NGOs in the Democratic Republic of Congo, Kenya, Rwanda, Zimbabwe, and many other countries.

As a Visiting Skoll Fellow at the Skoll Centre for Social Entrepreneurship Jacobs is undertaking research into the governance of international NGOs.

He has published a number of papers drawing on his experience of financial management in NGOs, including *Financial Management Evaluation of the Performance of British Aid Agencies in their Response to the Gujarat Earthquake of 2001* (published by the Disaster Emergencies Committee, 2002), *Financial Management Evaluation of the DEC Agencies' Response to the Southern Africa Food Crisis 2003* (published by the Disaster Emergencies Committee, 2004), and *Mango's Health Check, Standard Finance System for NGOs and Accounting Packs* (published by Mango, 2000 and 2003). He has co-written a new CD, *Finance for the Non-Financial Manager*, and carried out original research into NGO Management while a visiting fellow at Duke University, North Carolina.

Jacobs has a degree in social anthropology from Cambridge University and qualified as a Chartered Management Accountant while working as a private-sector management consultant.

Gordon Bloom

Professor Gordon M. Bloom is director and founder of Harvard's Social Entrepreneurship Collaboratory (SE Lab), a principal of the Hauser Center for Nonprofit Organizations and an affiliate of the Center for Public Leadership at Harvard's John F. Kennedy School of Government.

Prior to Harvard he taught a course series on social entrepreneurship at Stanford University, where he was a lecturer on the Public Policy Program faculty in the School of Humanities & Sciences, and a faculty affiliate of Stanford's Center for Social Innovation at the Graduate School of Business. At Stanford Bloom created the Social Entrepreneurship Collaboratory (SE Lab) an innovative, Silicon Valley influenced incubator where student teams create and develop pilot programmes for US and international social sector initiatives. His teaching and research interests are primarily in the area of strategy and vision for US and international not-for-profits, and social entrepreneurship. Bloom's interest in entrepreneurship is also informed by work in the private sector in the USA, Europe, and Asia as CEO of a medical technology company and in international strategy consulting.

He graduated magna cum laude with an AB in History and Science from Harvard and later received his MBA from Stanford and an MFA from Columbia after working in the nonprofit and private sectors in New York and London.

Sally Osberg

Sally Osberg joined the Skoll Foundation as its first president and CEO in 2001. Inspired and empowered by the foundation's visionary founder, Jeff Skoll, she leads the organization's entrepreneurial team in advancing systemic change to benefit communities around the world by investing in, connecting, and celebrating social entrepreneurs. She brings to the foundation more than twenty years of social sector leadership, with special expertise in organizational development, strategic positioning, and innovative public programming.

Prior to the Skoll Foundation, she was executive director of the Children's Discovery Museum of San Jose, which she guided from its inception to national recognition as a leader in the museum field and the broader arena of informal learning. The museum received the National Award for Museum Service from the White House in 2001. Osberg served as a member of the board and as president of the Association of Youth Museums, on the board of the American Association of Museums and on both the Silicon Valley chapter and national boards of the American Leadership Forum, among others. Currently, she sits on the boards of the Oracle Help Us Help Foundation and Women & Philanthropy, and on the advisory board of the John Gardner Center for Youth and Their Communities. She earned her MA in literature from the Claremont Graduate School and her BA in English from Scripps College, where she was elected to Phi Beta Kappa. In 1998 she received the John Gardner Leadership Award from the American Leadership Forum, and in 1999 the *San Jose Mercury News* named her as one of the 'Millennium 100', which recognized individuals who have shaped and led Silicon Valley.

Pamela Hartigan

Dr Hartigan is the managing director of the Schwab Foundation for Social Entrepreneurship. The Foundation's work is dedicated to advancing the field of social entrepreneurship globally, building and supporting its practitioners whose efforts have achieved transformational social change. She holds masters' degrees in economics and public health and a PhD in cognitive psychology. Her career includes positions with academic and community-based organizations as well with the World Bank and the World Health Organization (WHO). Before joining the Schwab Foundation, Hartigan was executive director of the Department of Health Promotion at WHO. In November 2000, Klaus Schwab, founder and president of the World Economic Forum, invited her to spearhead the Schwab Foundation for Social Entrepreneurship. Hartigan also teaches on a course in social entrepreneurship at the University of Geneva's graduate school of business and is the author of numerous articles on the subject.

Jerr Boschee

Jerr Boschee has spent the past 25 years as an advisor to social entrepreneurs in the USA and elsewhere. To date he has delivered seminars or conducted master classes in forty-one US states and thirteen countries and has long been recognized as one of the founders of the social enterprise movement worldwide. Boschee is executive director of the Institute for Social Entrepreneurs, which he created in 1999, and is Chairman and CEO of Peace Corps Encore!, a not-for-profit he co-founded in 2003 to send former Peace Corps Volunteers back into service on short-term assignments. He is the former president and CEO of The National Center for Social Entrepreneurs, is one of the six co-founders of the Social Enterprise Alliance, and was recently named by the *Nonprofit Times* in its not-for-profit sector 'Power & Influence Top 50' list. He served from 2001 to 2004 as an advisor to England's Department of Trade and Industry Social Enterprise Unit and is the author of *The Social Enterprise Sourcebook* (2001). Boschee is also a former general manager for a Fortune 100 company, managing editor for a chain of forty-four newspapers, and a Peace Corps Volunteer.

Jed Emerson
Jed Emerson is senior fellow with the Generation Foundation, of Generation Investment Management of London, England. He has served as a lecturer in Business at Stanford Business School and was the Bloomberg Senior Research Fellow in Philanthropy at Harvard Business School. He was founding director of the Roberts Enterprise Development Fund, and founding director of the Larkin Street Youth Center, both of San Francisco, CA. He is widely recognized as a thought leader on issues of social entrepreneurship, strategic philanthropy, social investing, and related areas. His main focus of work is the Blended Value Proposition that explores the intersect of value creation through the leveraging of both market rate and below market rate capital. Emerson has spoken widely on these topics in both the USA and internationally. Emerson is currently a Visiting Fellow at the Skoll Centre for Social Entrepreneurship.

Foreword

While the extraordinary industrial and technological innovations of recent decades have led to many breakthroughs, they have also left us to confront an uncertain future. With real threats of environmental and economic collapse, terrible diseases, over-population, war, terrorism and menacing new forms of weaponry, we have much to overcome. Efforts by our governments and institutions have proven insufficient to reverse these and other destructive trends. Our best hope for the future of humanity lies in the power and effectiveness of socially motivated, highly empowered individuals who fight for changes in the way we live, think and behave.

Those four sentences perfectly capture the case for social entrepreneurship. But they are not unique to our time: the same could have been said 100 years ago, 200 years ago, even 300 years ago at the beginning of the Industrial Revolution. One of the great ironies of history is that the solutions to current challenges frequently create new challenges even more menacing. Industries that have improved the quality of our lives have also created new problems that threaten our very existence. Technological innovations that were developed to increase the efficiency of life have frequently been used to increase the efficiency of taking life. We can split the atom, walk on the moon, communicate with another person anywhere in the world in the blink of an eye, and yet poverty, violence and illness in much of the world are as pervasive as they have ever been.

But the nature and the wonder of humanity is that while there are always tumultuous events and seemingly overwhelming challenges to face, people, exceptional individuals and ideas and movements emerge to face and find solutions to these challenges. Social entrepreneurs are those people– the practical dreamers who have the talent, the skill, and the vision to solve the problems, to change the world for the better. Social entrepreneurs have a unique approach that is both evolutionary and revolutionary, operating in an enlightened market environment where success is measured not by financial returns alone, but by tangible improvements to the quality of people's lives. Social entrepreneurs take workable models and adapt them for the benefit of people, communities, nations and the planet. They don't accept the notion that only governments and powerful individuals and corporations are positioned to determine where and how resources should be allocated.

They believe that any individual has the potential to make positive changes not just in our communities, but in society as a whole. And they put that belief into action, in creative ways that are described throughout this book.

At the world's great foundations, universities and charitable institutions, social entrepreneurship has become one of the most influential ideas of our time. For these institutions, social entrepreneurs are the catalysts for significant social change. For the entrepreneurs themselves, the growing credibility and scale of the field world-wide represents unprecedented momentum to tip communities, nations and the world toward new possibilities and a better future.

Yet, for all of this, social entrepereneurship remains as much an idea as a movement, a field that's a work in progress. There remains great need for bridging the worlds of theory and practice, for supporting the development of both the scholarship and the practical knowledge needed to inform policy-makers, investors, the media and others who could do more—far more—to get behind those dedicated men and women on the front lines of social change. It should go without saying that social entrepreneurs are core to the field's evolution; the problems they address, the innovations they develop, and the contexts in which they work are crucial to building the knowledge base from which the most important questions can be raised. Ideally, the evolution of the field along these lines will benefit social entrepreneurs in untold ways, providing them with practical means of advancing their own effectiveness and—perhaps most significantly—a precious opportunity to reflect upon and learn from the experience of others.

The Skoll Foundation has supported the Skoll Centre for Social Entrepreneurship to contribute to meeting these needs and to promote the advancement of social entrepreneurship worldwide. This volume, synthesizing research and lessons from practice by leading social entrepreneurs and scholars in the field who gathered for the first Skoll World Forum on Social Entrepreneurship in March 2003, exemplifies the Centre's aim to produce work that engages with theory but is also applicable and useful to practitioners in the field.

Social entrepreneurs have a vision of the future and will stop at nothing to see that future come true. Social entrepreneurs are our truth-tellers: they see the world as it is and as it can be. Yes, they confront realities—negative trends spiking into territory from which we may never recover– but then they see something the rest of us miss: a new path, an innovative solution, potential for change. Microloans, carbon credit trading, nonprofit pharmaceuticals, and new education, conflict resolution, and trading systems are just a few of the examples of what social entrepreneurs can do and powerful proof that their innovations can create lasting, large scale change. Now it is up to us. We must do everything in our power to help those courageous men and women tackling our toughest challenges. We must make sure that the potential they see, the visions to which they dedicate their lives, becomes future reality.

Introduction

Alex Nicholls

In 2003, according to the World Bank (World Bank 2004) the population of the globe stood at around 6.3 billion people. Of these roughly half lived on less than $2 (£1.16) per day. Over 1 billion suffered from malnutrition, a similar amount lacked potable water, and 2.4 billion did not have access to proper sanitation. As a result the Bank estimated that more than 10 million children die of preventable diseases every year. Furthermore, the HIV/AIDS pandemic continues to sweep across Africa and many other developing countries and is predicted to affect over 100 million people globally by 2010. At the same time the level of economic inequality between the richest and the poorest continues to grow, with the poorest 50 per cent of the world's population accounting for just 5 per cent of global income (Bornstein 2004: 6–10).

In the face of such mounting crises, governments and multilateral agencies have increasingly struggled to provide timely and effective interventions. Indeed, in many countries (both developed and developing) there has been a systematic retreat of government from the provision of public goods (as defined by Samuelson 1954) in the face of new political ideologies that stress citizen self-sufficiency and that give primacy to market-driven models of welfare (Martin 2002). As a result, in many territories, the 'supply side' of resources available for public goods has remained static or diminished. The increase in humanitarian and environmental crises—of which the South East Asian Tsunami of 2005 is the most recent terrible example—combined with the failure of conventional institutions to address them has also led to a rapid growth in the 'demand side' for new models that create social and environmental value.

However, the global picture is more complex—and hopeful—than these bare facts might suggest. For example, post the collapse of the Soviet Union and communist Eastern Europe there are more democratically elected governments in place across the world than at any previous time in history (see, e.g. *The Economist* 1999 and 2005*a*). During the twentieth century, whilst global inequality has grown by most measures, so has per capita wealth, particularly

1

in developing countries (*The Economist* 2004*a*). As a result, the productive lifetime of many citizens has dramatically increased and this has encouraged more social mobility. Similarly, life expectancies have improved in most countries as have education levels, although the AIDS crisis is threatening to reverse this trend in parts of Africa (Bornstein 2004). Finally, the gradual dissemination of new technologies and the advent of powerful global communications networks have better connected the disparate communities across the world. Thus, a number of the circumstances that can support a growth in the supply side of new social goods that encompass a range of public, private, and hybrid approaches to creating social impact are also in place (see Table I.1).

At the same time as these extraordinary changes have come about across the world's citizenry, multinational corporations have grown to dominate the international landscape, many with turnovers in excess of the Gross Domestic Product (GDP) of sovereign nations. For example, Wal-Mart—the world's largest company by market capitalization in 2003—had a turnover in 2002 greater than the GDP of Turkey, Denmark, South Africa, and many other countries (Young and Welford 2002). Indeed, the largest three hundred multinationals now own more than a quarter of the world's assets (Bornstein 2004). The outstanding success of this business model has demonstrated—amongst other matters—how to scale operations internationally and to maximize value creation through innovation and technology.

In recent years, social entrepreneurship has emerged as a global phenomenon in the context of these social and environmental demand- and supply-side developments (see Nicholls, A. 2004, 2006; Mair, Robinson, and Hockerts 2006). Driven by a new breed of pragmatic, innovative, and visionary social activists and their networks, social entrepreneurship borrows from an eclectic mix of business, charity, and social movement models to reconfigure solutions to community problems and deliver sustainable new social value. Throughout history, of course, there have been extraordinary social change-makers (Florence Nightingale, Susan B. Anthony, Gandhi, etc.), but what is different today is the scale and reach of the new social impact being generated (often at a

Table I.1 Drivers behind the growth of social entrepreneurship

Supply side	Demand side
Increase in global per capita wealth/ improved social mobility	Rising crises in environment and health
Extended productive lifetime	Rising economic inequality
Increase in number of democratic governments	Government inefficiencies in public service delivery
Increased power of multinational corporations	Retreat of government in face of free market ideology
Better education levels	More developed role for NGOs
Improved communications	Resource competition

systemic level), as well as the extraordinary variety of approaches being employed.

There has been an unprecedented wave of growth in social entrepreneurship globally over the last ten years (see Bornstein 2004: 3–6). For example, as part of the 2004 Global Entrepreneurship Monitor (GEM) report a survey was conducted of social entrepreneurship activity in the UK: these data suggested that new 'social' start-ups are emerging at a faster rate than more conventional, commercial ventures (Harding and Cowling 2004: 5). Other research has also shown that employment rates in social sector ventures are significantly out-stripping those in conventional businesses across a number of developed countries (Salamon and Anheier 1999). Salamon (2003) has also calculated that the not-for-profit sector generated $1.3 trillion (£754 billion) of aggregate expenditures in 1999, accounting for 5.1 per cent of the combined GDPs of the countries in which they operated. This made the sector the seventh largest global 'economy', ahead of Italy, with nearly 40 million full-time equivalent workers and close to 200 million volunteers. In Europe more than 3.5 million jobs are provided by social enterprises (Social Enterprise London—SEL 2000), and it has been estimated that 1.5 million people are regularly engaged in community economic activities (NEF 1999). Whilst all of these not-for-profit ventures will not, necessarily, be socially entrepreneurial, such data still under-pins the proposition that social entrepreneurship has become a powerful global phenomenon (Drayton 2002; Harding 2004).

More significantly still, the impact that social entrepreneurs and their new models of social value creation are actually achieving today is also far more ambitious than ever before. For example, in the USA, a quarter of the popu-lation belongs to a credit union (Smallbone et al. 2001) and the Grameen Bank in Bangladesh now serves more than 2.4 million micro-credit customers across Bangladesh and Afghanistan, transforming the economic development of thousands of very poor villages. Equally striking, the Bangladesh Rural Advancement Committee (BRAC) is the largest single employer in the region after the government, employing four times more staff than the largest private firm. Socially entrepreneurship is proving not only to be highly effective at delivering social impact but also highly efficient. For example, a survey of job creation in England and Wales found that social entrepreneurs delivered new jobs at a third of the cost of the public sector (Smallbone et al. 2001: 19).

Social entrepreneurs are also bringing about systemic change by influencing social behaviour for the good on a global scale. For example, the Fair Trade movement has seen its sales internationally grow at double-digit rates for more than a decade towards an estimated $1.8 billion (£1 billion) by 2007 (Demetriou 2003). In the process, it has helped catalyse a revolution in the way many consumers view their relationship with producers and has underpinned a policy-level reassessment of global Trade Justice culminating in the Make Poverty History campaign in 2005 (see also Nicholls and Opal 2005: 55–76).

3

The role of international non-governmental organizations (INGOs) has also changed dramatically, becoming both more influential and entrepreneurial in recent years (as discussed in Chapter 12). Increasingly, development INGOs have moved from being small-scale pressure groups to functioning as the operational division of multi-lateral aid programmes. For example, in 2003 almost 20 per cent of the World Bank's and US Agency for International Development's funding was dispensed by INGOs (Quelch and Laidler-Kylander 2005: 4). Similarly, BRAC has collaborated actively with the Bangladeshi government in its educational and health programmes. In the process, established INGOs have also developed powerful global brands. In Europe, for example, Amnesty International, the World Wildlife Fund, Greenpeace, and Oxfam all scored above major corporate brands such as Microsoft, Bayer, the Ford Motor Company, and Coca-Cola in terms of consumer trust (Quelch and Laidler-Kylander 2005: 11). Such high levels of trust are (often almost accidentally) built upon longevity of action, clarity of mission, and consistent media accounts of fieldwork. The increasingly dynamic combination of advocacy and operations demonstrated by some forward-looking INGOs reflects the approach of many social entrepreneurs more generally.

As has already been suggested, social entrepreneurship is an international phenomenon (see Figure 1.1). In Europe it has been increasingly supported by government and European Union policy, particularly in the UK with such initiatives as the establishment of the Social Enterprise Unit within the Small Business Service of the Department of Trade and Industry (Department for Trade and Industry—DTI 2002). In the USA the 'venture' philanthropy and emerging foundation agenda have driven much new activity forward (*The Economist* 2004b). Beyond Northern, developed, countries social entrepreneurship takes other forms again. For example, in Latin American co-operative models of social ventures that centre on civil society rather than on government or the private sector are particularly popular (Davis et al. 2003). However, such models are often rejected in the former communist countries of Eastern Europe as a consequence of a political and cultural legacy of corrupt centralized control. Here, social entrepreneurship ventures often look to hybrid commercial models that blend economic and social value creation, often known as social enterprises (Alter 2002). In many emerging economies in Asia, the role of the market is still largely unrealized by social ventures and the interface between civil society and state is more fertile location for socially entrepreneurial activity.

Finally, several countries ground social entrepreneurship in other significant cultural factors. For example, a key part of the enormous success of the Grameen Bank micro-credit network in rural Bangladesh came from the recognition of the vital role that could be played by women in managing loans. Alternatively, in many Catholic countries, social entrepreneurs emerge from the religious community. Thus, the Mondragon co-operative (the largest

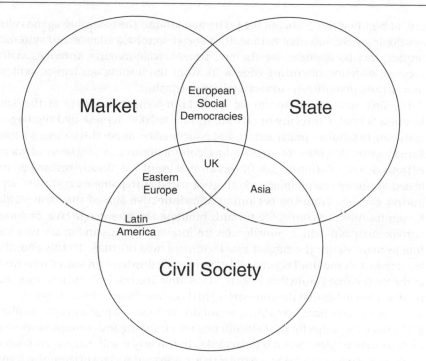

Figure I.1 Positioning of social entrepreneurship internationally

single employer in the Basque region of northern Spain) largely survived the fascist Franco-led regime due to its links to organized religion in the towns and villages where it operated. Historically such activity was the product of a range of drivers, many of which can still be discerned in today's social entrepreneurs. These included: individual ethical or religious motives, personal altruism, community or political contexts, professional interests, cultural mutuality, and the development of solidarity.

Social entrepreneurship, therefore, represents an umbrella term for a considerable range of innovative and dynamic international praxis and discourse in the social and environmental sectors. To some the socially entrepreneurial paradigm offers a panacea for addressing social market failures (Drayton 2002), to others it is a manifestation of the usurping supremacy of 'business' models across all aspects of modern life (Dart 2004). Nevertheless, however contextualized, social entrepreneurship is clearly no longer a marginal activity pigeon-holed under the headings of 'not-for-profit management' or 'charity governance', but rather a driver of significant social change that is developing rapidly into an autonomous field of research and practice. This book recognizes this shift in both the perceived and actual impact of social entrepreneurship across the globe and aims to contribute to the ongoing task of building this inchoate field. Themed around the emerging agendas for developing new, sustainable models of social sector excellence and systemic impact, this book offers, for the first time, a wide-ranging, internationally focused, selection of cutting-edge work from the leading academics, policy-makers, and practitioners in social entrepreneurship.

The first Skoll World Forum in Social Entrepreneurship, held at the Saïd Business School, University of Oxford, in March 2004, represented the largest gathering of scholars, practitioners, and policymakers under this banner to date. Subsequently described by one leading commentator as the 'Davos of social entrepreneurship' (Hutton 2005), this annual event has already become established as one of the premier gatherings of social entrepreneurs and their supporters globally. From the beginning, the distinctive aim of the Skoll World Forum has been to contribute towards building the knowledge base of social entrepreneurship both to provide relevant input into praxis and to advance the intellectual case for the subject as a legitimate field of study. To this end, the leading writers and thinkers in social entrepreneurship have presented new work at the Skoll World Forum that is both provocative and original and it is from this pool of scholarship that the contents of this book are drawn. The ambition is that *Social Entrepreneurship: New Models of Sustainable Social Change* will take its place as the research primer for the field, offering new thinking and conceptual models of value to practitioners and scholars alike. In this way it will make a serious and useful contribution to the emerging discourse around social entrepreneurship.

This introduction serves to set the scene for the rest of the book. First, it surveys the existing academic landscape with respect to the field. Then it goes on to consider how social entrepreneurship may be defined as a distinct and influential paradigm of new praxis within social sector activity. Finally, the structure and logic of the book as a whole is explained.

Research Context of Social Entrepreneurship

Whilst there is a growing body of commercial, mass media, and academic articles written on the subject of social entrepreneurship (see Bibliography), there has yet to be published an international collection of the current thinking in the field spanning policy, praxis, and academic research though see Mair et al, 2006, for a recent research conference volume on the subject. The range of books on social entrepreneurship to date has been limited to think tank or policy documents (Leadbeater 1997; Leadbeater and Goss 1998; Social Enterprise Coalition 2003), practitioner guides (Brinckerhoff 2000; Boschee 2001; Dees, Emerson, and Economy, 2001, 2002), descriptive accounts of social entrepreneurs and their actions (Alter 2002; Bornstein 2004), or academic books addressing specific issues within the sector (Austin 2000; Borzaga and Defourny 2001; Bernholz 2004; Dacanay 2004).

This body of writing can be conceptualized as falling at the intersection of the established fields of not-for-profit management and commercial entrepreneurship within a conventional business and economics context. The former field already has an extensive literature largely exploring how to start and sustain successful charitable ventures (e.g. James and Rose-Ackerman 1986; Powell 1987; James 1989; Oster 1995; Hammack 1998; Oster, Massarsky, and Beinhacker 2004). The latter has today established entrepreneurship as a meaningful locus of academic teaching and research (e.g. Burch 1986; Casson 1990; Hirsch and Peters 1998; *The Harvard Business Review* 1999). However, this is not to suggest that social entrepreneurship as a field of study sits at a fixed point between these two, better established, literatures, rather it takes inspiration from both—and other scholarship too—to drive its own agenda forward. Other disciplines that are already proving valuable in social entrepreneurship research include: marketing (Quelch and Laidler-Kylander 2005), business ethics (Moore 2004), cultural studies (Holt 2004), political economics (Putnam 2001, 2004), and sociology (DiMaggio and Anheier 1990; Dart 2004).

Banks (1972: 53) first coined the term 'social entrepreneur' in the context of an analysis of different approaches to management and their values orientation with reference to Robert Owen. Banks noted that managerial skills could be deployed to address social problems, as well as business challenges.

Soon after this, research into social entrepreneurship focused on the management of non-profit organizations. Etzioni (1973) suggested that neither the state nor the market alone could catalyse the necessary innovations and reforms of society but rather that the source would be 'a third alternative' that could combine the efficiency of the entrepreneurial market place with the welfare orientation of the state. Chamberlain (1977) also used the term 'social entrepreneur', although it was in the context of the perceived arrival of a new breed of more socially motivated business executives who might commit themselves and their corporations to constructive approaches to social problems by changing the rules under which they themselves operate.

Subsequent academic research into social entrepreneurship has largely been focused on defining what it is and what it does and does not have in common with commercial entrepreneurial activity (Dees 1994, 1996, 1998*a*, 1998*b*; Boschee 1995, 2001; Leadbeater 1997; Brinckerhoff 2000; Thompson, Alvy, and Lees 2000; Dees, Emerson, and Economy 2001, 2002; Drayton 2002; Thompson 2002; Austin, Stevenson, and Wei-Skillern 2003; Boschee and McClurg 2003; Sullivan Mort, Weerawardena, and Carnegie 2003). However, despite some promising work thus far, a consensus over the boundaries of social entrepreneurship remains elusive. Johnson acknowledged this in a review of the available published research on social entrepreneurship (2000: 5), she commented,

Defining what social entrepreneurship is, and what its conceptual boundaries are, is not an easy task ... in part because the concept is inherently complex, and in part because the literature in the area is so new that little consensus has emerged on the topic.

This chapter will return to the question of the meaning of social entrepreneurship later.

Despite the current challenges of establishing such a young field of study, academic interest has been considerable. Over the last ten years, a number of dedicated teaching and research centres in social entrepreneurship have been set up at universities in North America and Europe, starting with the Initiative on Social Enterprise at Harvard Business School in 1993 (see Table I.2). In addition, there has also been a significant growth in the number of courses offered in social entrepreneurship and social enterprise across a variety of other international universities. These courses typically reside within either a business school or public policy environment and many are allied to established not-for-profit programmes and centres. The majority are postgraduate options (see Table I.3).

In terms of new scholarship, two useful academic research networks already exist. The first is the Social Enterprise Knowledge Network (SEKN) that connects eleven universities across Latin America and Spain and has been driven forward by Harvard Business School (see www.sekn.org). The second is the European focused EMES group (see www.emes.net/en/index.html) that brings together nine university research centres that work on the 'social economy', including the Open University (UK), the University of Liège (Belgium), and University of Trento (Italy). However, there is still a real need—and an opportunity—better to coordinate the growing research activity in social entrepreneurship across nations. A global academic network would offer a coherent picture of research activity and materials to the field, encourage new cross-national collaborative research and ensure that scarce resources were not being misspent in duplicated projects. The establishment of such a network is one of the strategic objectives of the UK-based Skoll Centre for Social Entrepreneurship.

Table I.2 University centres for social entrepreneurship

Institution	Research centre
University of Alberta, Canada	Canadian Centre for Social Entrepreneurship www.bus.ualberta.ca/ccse/
Columbia Graduate School of Business, USA	Research Initiative on Social Enterprise www-1.gsb.columbia.edu/ socialenterprise/academics/research/
Fuqua Business School, Duke University, USA	Center for Advancement of Social Entrepreneurship www.fuqua.duke.edu/centers/case/
Harvard Business School, USA	The Initiative on Social Enterprise www.hbs.edu/dept/socialenterprise/
Herriot-Watt University, UK	Social Enterprise Institute www.sml.hw.ac.uk/socialenterprise/
Saïd Business School, University of Oxford, UK	Skoll Centre for Social Entrepreneurship www.sbs.ox.ac.uk/html/faculty_skoll_main.asp
Seattle University, USA	Center for Non-Profit and Social Enterprise Management www.seattleu.edu/asbe/ec/
Stanford Graduate School of Business, USA	Center for Social Innovation www.gsb.stanford.edu/csi
Stern School of Business, New York University, USA	Stewart Satter Program in Social Entrepreneurship w4.stern.nyu.edu/berkley/ social.cfm?doc_id=1868

Table I.3 Universities (without a dedicated social entrepreneurship centre) offering research and/or teaching in social entrepreneurship

University of the Andes
University of San Andrés, Argentina
Berea College, USA
Haas Business School, University of Berkeley, USA
University of Bologna, Italy
Brigham Young University, USA
Anderson Business School, University of California and Los Angeles, USA
Judge Institute, University of Cambridge, UK
Catholic University of Chile, Chile
University College Cork, Ireland
Tuck Business School, Dartmouth University, USA
University of East London, UK
ESADE, Spain
IESA, Venezuela
IESE Business School, University of Navarra, Spain
INSEAD, France
Kellogg Business School, North Western University, USA
University of Liège, Belgium
London Business School, UK
London School of Economics, UK
Catholic University of Louvain-la-Neuve, Belgium
Open University, UK
University of the Pacific, Peru
University of Sao Paulo, Brazil
Roberts Wesleyan College, USA
Sloan Business School, MIT, USA
University of Texas at Austin, USA
University of St Gallen, Switzerland
University of Trento, Italy
University of Ulster, UK
University of Westminster, UK
Yale School of Management, USA

Furthermore, there are also several important network and support organizations that have grown up around social entrepreneurship (see Table I.4), many of them investing in practitioner-driven research. These include: specialized grant-giving institutions (the Skoll Foundation; NESsT; UnLtd), bespoke consultancy groups (Bridgespan; New Sector Alliance), venture philanthropy organizations (New Philanthropy Capital; Acumen Fund; New Profit Inc; EVPA), representative 'trade' bodies (Social Enterprise Coalition; Social Enterprise Alliance), and elected membership communities (Schwab Foundation for Social Entrepreneurship). Perhaps the most influential and well established of these non-governmental network organizations is Ashoka (see www.ashoka.org). Founded by an ex-McKinsey and Co. consultant, Bill Drayton, over twenty years ago, Ashoka identifies, invests in, and connects leading social entrepreneurs through all phases of their career. These individuals are elected as Ashoka 'Fellows' for life. To date over 1,500 Fellows have been elected globally.

Table I.4 Network support organizations for social entrepreneurs

Organization	Founded
Ashoka (International) www.ashoka.org	1982
Bridgespan (USA) www.bridgespangroup.org	2000
Community Action Network (UK) www.can-online.org.uk	1998
The Institute for Social Entrepreneurs (USA) www.socialent.org	1999
NESsT (South America/Eastern Europe) www.nesst.org	1997
Net Impact (International) www.netimpact.org	1993
New Philanthropy Capital (UK) www.philanthropycapital.org	2001
New Sector Alliance (International) www.newsector.org	2000
Roberts Enterprise Development Fund (USA) www.redf.org	1997
School for Social Entrepreneurs	1998
The Schwab Foundation for Social Entrepreneurship (International) www.schwabfound.org	1998
Skoll Foundation (International) www.skollfoundation.org	1999
Social Enterprise Alliance (USA) www.se-alliance.org	1998
Social Enterprise Coalition (UK) www.socialenterprise.org.uk	2000
Social Venture Network (USA) www.svn.org	1987
Social Ventures Australia (Australia) www.socialventures.com.au	2002
UnLtd (UK) www.unltd.org.uk	2002

The research outputs of this diverse group of organizations have included: social investment 'sector reports' (New Philanthropy Capital), case studies (NESsT), global action networks and customized individual-level engagements (Ashoka's Global Academy), toolkit guides (Social Enterprise Coalition), and longitudinal data-sets (GEM).

Having outlined the research context for social entrepreneurship to date, this introduction will now move on to address the thorny issue of the meaning(s) of social entrepreneurship.

Beyond Definitions: The Meanings of Social Entrepreneurship

As has already been noted the definition of social entrepreneurship is often seen as contested and unclear. Interestingly, the main cause of this apparent lack of clarity over the meaning of social entrepreneurship is, in fact, also the basis of its extraordinary impact—namely its dynamic flexibility.

Social entrepreneurs and their networks demonstrate an unrelenting focus on systemic social change that disregards institutional and organizational norms and boundaries. These disruptive change-agents are often sectoral iconoclasts operating in a more diverse and dynamic strategic landscape than conventional businesses or social ventures. Whilst aiming never to compromise social mission, social entrepreneurs will look for alliances and sources of resources wherever they may be found most easily. Thus, many engage simultaneously with government, philanthropic institutions, the voluntary sector, and banks, as well as the commercial market to secure funding and other support where necessary. Similarly, social entrepreneurs will often exploit a range of organizational forms—often-unique hybrids—from charity to not-for-profit to commercial venture to maximize social value creation. Social entrepreneurs also move easily across sectors, often diversifying from their core mission to expand overall social impact and increase resource flows. For example, the Furniture Resource Centre in Liverpool (see www.frcgroup. co.uk) began as a furniture recycling, removal, and employment training social venture engaged with social landlords, but diversified into community waste collection and recycling (Bulky Bob's), retailing (among other things, partnering with Ben and Jerry's ice cream), and finally—as its profile grew—into social sector consultancy (Cat's Pyjamas). Another case is Cafédirect—the Fair Trade coffee company—that transitioned from being a charity-funded start-up to a PLC offering share equity to the consumer market (see www.cafedirect.org).

For social entrepreneurs, the extraordinary breadth of their operational contexts and organizational forms makes classification highly problematic. They defy the traditional isomorphic forces that often constrain and categorize organizational innovation (see DiMaggio and Powell 1983; DiMaggio and Anheier 1990), preferring instead constantly to challenge the status quo by reconfiguring accepted value creation boundaries (public/private, for-profit/not-for-profit, and economic/social). As is discussed below in Chapters 5 and 6, social entrepreneurship often defies structuration as an organizational field-making classifications problematic. Indeed, in recognition of this, the UK government has recently introduced a new legal form of incorporation, the Community Interest Company, which represents a hybrid organizational type part not-for-profit, part equity offering limited company (DTI 2004).

The question of how to fund these new social ventures is at the heart of their diversity. Despite the increase in supply-side issues noted previously, a similar advance in available resources has not matched the pace of growth of new social ventures. The result has been heightened competition for what funding is available (Emerson 1999a). One of the products of this mismatch between resource supply and demand has been for social entrepreneurs to consider strategic moves into new markets to subsidize their social activities either through exploiting profitable opportunities in the core activities of their not-for-profit venture or via for-profit subsidiary ventures and cross-sector partnerships with commercial corporations. This new organizational model has attracted considerable public policy attention in developed countries. It is widely known as 'social enterprise' (see Alter 2003; Boschee and McClurg 2003).

Whilst social enterprise and social entrepreneurship are sometimes used as synonyms (particularly in the USA), the former is, in fact, a subset of the latter fitting within a broader social entrepreneurship 'spectrum' (see Figure I.2; Dees 1996). Many social ventures can be highly entrepreneurial without generating independent profit streams: this could include innovation in the public sector, for example, or pure welfare ventures like Childline International (see Bornstein

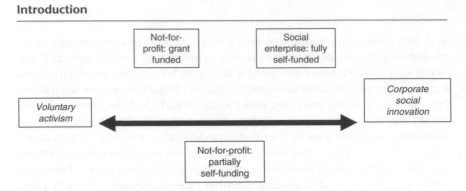

Figure I.2 Funding dimensions of social entrepreneurship
Source: Adapted from Dees 1998*b*; Alter 2002.

2004). Therefore, the primary distinction here lies in which funding model is adopted with respect to achieving a social objective, namely social enterprises look to move away from grant dependency towards self-sufficiency via the creation of income streams. Ultimately, the aim is to be more sustainable, though how far reliance on the market can actually support sustainability is contested. This debate is at the heart of much of the emergent strategic thinking on social entrepreneurship and is well illustrated by a comparison of Chapters 7 and 16 below.

Therefore, social entrepreneurship is best understood as a multi-dimensional and dynamic construct moving across various intersection points between the public, private, and social sectors. The organizational mechanisms employed are largely irrelevant: social entrepreneurs work in the public, private, and social sectors alike, employing for-profit, not-for-profit, and hybrid organizational forms (or a mix of all three) to deliver social value and bring about change. Such ventures can variously be incorporated as: charities, co-operatives, companies limited by shares or guarantee, community businesses, development trusts, as well as more conventional private limited companies. Leadbeater (1997) acknowledged the presence of social entrepreneurship across all three sectors of society by discerning three organizational milieus of social entrepreneurs:

- Public sector adoption of business skills
- Socially affirmative businesses or businesses focusing on social ends
- The voluntary and not-for-profit sector adopting more entrepreneurial approaches

Emerson (2003) broadly concurred in his definition of the types of social entrepreneur:

- Civic innovator
- Founder of a revenue generating social enterprise
- Launcher of a related revenue generating activity to create a surplus to support social vision

As a consequence, the organizational landscape of social entrepreneurship can be conceptualized as a dynamic continuum ordered by the range of available funding structures (see Figure I.2). The boundaries of this continuum are set, at one extreme, by voluntary activism (fully reliant on donated assets and volunteers) and, at the other, by corporate social innovation (dedicated social ventures within the context of a private sector organization; see Kanter 1999). Lying along the continuum are alternative social organizational types ordered according to the proportion of their operations that are self-funded. These range from fully grant funded via those that are partially self-sufficient, having developed some internal sources of income, to social ventures that are fully self-sufficient.

However, this two dimensional spectrum requires additional dimensions to capture the full richness of social entrepreneurship. First, a public sector dimension needs to be added that recognizes institutional innovation such as participatory budgets or carbon exchanges. Second, network models that combine organizations and individuals dynamically need to be mapped to recognize the extraordinary variety in different loci of control across socially entrepreneurial ventures.

For all the organizational and institutional complexity of the social entrepreneurship model noted earlier, it is still possible to set boundaries around it. Simply put, social entrepreneurship is defined by its two constituent elements: a prime strategic focus on social impact and an innovative approach to achieving its mission. Thus, the combination of an overarching social mission and entrepreneurial creativity marks out social entrepreneurship as distinct from other public, private, or civil sector activity. In practice, to differentiate social entrepreneurship from other ventures requires attention to two organizational elements: the social mission focus (the context and outcomes of action that establishes the social component) and the operational processes (the approach to action that establishes the 'entrepreneurial' component). Each of these will now be considered in turn (see further Nicholls, A. 2004, 2006).

Social Mission Focus

For social entrepreneurs the social mission is explicit and central. This obviously affects how social entrepreneurs perceive and assess opportunities. Mission-related impact becomes the central criterion, not wealth creation. (Dees 1998a: 2)

As has already been noted, the primacy of the social mission over all other organizational objectives is the first key determinant of a potentially socially entrepreneurial venture. Social mission focus equates to an identification of an unmet social need or a new social value creation opportunity (although see Chapters 5 and 6 for a discussion of the problematic issues around normalized concepts of the social). The social mission is most clearly defined in two ways: the operational context of the venture and its outcomes and impact. A third, operational processes, can also be significant in defining both the social and entrepreneurial (see Table 1.5).

13

Table I.5 Defining the 'social' in social entrepreneurship

Defining characteristic	Examples	Contested issues
Context of social venture	Public welfare; environmentalism; development and aid	Acts as a privatization of public goods; does not address underlying political issues; narrow focus can create dependency
Process of social venture	Close engagement with key stakeholders; employ and train disenfranchised; act as trade intermediary	Stakeholder selection criteria/exclusion from process; empowerment of stakeholders
Outcomes and impacts	Improved public welfare; individual empowerment; crisis alleviation	Social impact often unmeasured; short-termism

Many examples of social entrepreneurship share the same objectives noted by Smallbone et al. (2001: 18) specifically for social enterprises,

- To provide goods and services which the market or public sector is either unwilling or unable to provide
- To develop skills
- To create employment
- To foster pathways to integrate socially excluded people

However, the full spectrum of socially entrepreneurial activity goes further than this. Historically, the main operational areas in which social entrepreneurs create change have been (Bornstein 2004):

- Poverty alleviation through empowerment, for example the microfinance movement
- Health care, ranging from small-scale support for the mentally ill 'in the community' to larger-scale ventures tackling the HIV/AIDS pandemic
- Education and training, such as widening participation and the democratization of knowledge transfer
- Environmental preservation and sustainable development, such as 'green' energy projects
- Community regeneration, such as housing associations
- Welfare projects, such as employment for the unemployed or homeless and drug and alcohol abuse projects
- Advocacy and campaigning, such as Fair Trade and human rights promotion

Of course, these are not distinct categories in reality and work in one often overlaps with another (e.g. a project like the Kaleidoscope initiative in London working with drug users, can span the health, community, employment, and welfare fields simultaneously). Indeed, some of the most successful and innovative social entrepreneurs consciously develop cross-category activity to maximize social impact (and resource availability) across their whole value chain.

In accordance with this focus on community the EMES research group defined the social element of social enterprises by five operational features (Spear and Bidet 2003: 8):

- An activity launched by a group of citizens
- Decision-making power not based on capital ownership
- A participatory nature involving those affected by the venture
- Limited profit distribution
- An explicit aim to benefit the community

Social entrepreneurs typically address areas of unmet social need or new social opportunity creation that the public or private sectors have failed to address. In many cases, these can be considered as failures in the social market of public goods. Such a market may be inherently dysfunctional due to a range of reasons including a lack of credible performance information, high transaction costs, and a lack of innovation (see Emerson 2003). Hence the historic need for public sector interventions. The range of social market failures addressed by social entrepreneurs can be grouped as follows: grassroots, institutional, political, spiritual, and philanthropic. Further, a variety of entrepreneurial approaches appropriate to each—innovative 'means' to social capital generating 'ends'— can also be discerned (see Table I.5).

Social market failures at a grassroots level are typically the product of a lack of institutional support at either a macro or micro level that generates the need for new community action. Many such ventures are allied to advocacy and have roots in powerful social movements. As such these actions may be categorized as critical social entrepreneurship, since they often challenge existing institutional structures and aim to build alternatives. The co-operative organizational model pioneered in Rochdale, UK, in the nineteenth century is, perhaps, the most powerful example of community driven social entrepreneurship (see www.archive.co-op.ac.uk/pioneers.htm). Today, co-operatives are the most widely spread organizational format in the world and have transformed economic and political power relationships from Nicaragua to Dhaka. For example, by grouping small-scale producers into co-operatives the Fair Trade model has countered the problem of price monopsony often exploited by middlemen and returned more of the commodity value-chain back to farmers (Table I.6) (Nicholls and Opal 2005: 32–54).

Another powerful example can be seen in community housing. The Coin Street Housing Association grew out of a community's reaction to the lack of affordable public or private accommodation in a part of inner city south London (see www.designforhomes.org/projects/planned/coinst/coin.html). The project developed a new model of community housing that addressed this social market failure by leveraging local social capital and building a new institutional structure within existing legal boundaries. Such an approach also generated a replicable social franchise model for other communities.

Table I.6 Social market failures addressed by social entrepreneurs

Origins	Social market failure	Means	Ends	Example
Grassroots	Lack of institutional support	Critical social entrepreneurship	Co-ordinated creation of social capital through local/community action	Co-operatives
Institutional	Changing social landscape	Normative social entrepreneurship	Social entrepreneurship champions new social institution	Open University
Political	Retreat of centralized government control from society	Market socialism	Introduction of enterprise /private sector market philosophy into public sphere	Social enterprise
Spiritual	Decline of church influence in society	Commercialization of congregation and church-based activities	Revitalize role of faith in public affairs	CAFOD/Fair Trade Foundation
Philanthropic	Lack of finance for development of social capital	Foundations coordinating charity giving as social entrepreneurial start-up funding	Link business and social innovation	Skoll Foundation and community education

Addressing institutional social market failures tends to be more resource hungry, but aims for larger-scale impacts and has a broader social focus. This form of social entrepreneurship responds to changes in the macro-social landscape that require large-scale solutions. Such action often operates within established institutional norms, whilst still aiming to introduce innovation and change. As such it may be considered as normative social entrepreneurship —using existing conventions in innovative ways. In the UK, Lord Michael Young was an extraordinary example of a normative social entrepreneur. The Open University, the Consumers' Association, the Institute of Community Studies (now renamed the Young Foundation), and the School for Social Entrepreneurs are all examples of his new configurations of conventional institutional forms that target particular social impacts.

Similarly, the Tateni (a Nguni term of affection) project started by Veronica Khosa in South Africa (Bornstein 2004: 183–99) provides a further good example. In this case, the social entrepreneur reacted to the inadequacy of institutional support for victims of the catastrophe of AIDS/HIV by creating a home-care service that would both complement the existing welfare system and offer a new model of community-based training and action in health care. Between 1995 and 1999, the project's staff made over 200,000 home visits and trained over 1,000 new home carers.

Social market failures in the political context represent the failure of the state to provide sufficient or appropriate public goods. In some cases—particularly in developing countries—this may be the result of acute shortages of resource. In others, it comes from deliberate policy—best understood as the trend towards the retreat of government from public sector provision across many developed states in the 1980s and 1990s (see Le Grand and Bartlett 1993; Giddens 1998, 2000). The impact of this shift in a specific context (the Church of England) is considered in Chapter 9. The socially entrepreneurial response to these failures has been expressed both within and without government. On the one hand there has been a move towards 'reinventing' government in a number of countries (Osbourne and Gaebler 1992). This entails bringing more entrepreneurial or business thinking into public sector departments and operations in order to enhance their efficiency and impact. On the other, as governments in northern countries have increasingly retreated from their traditional role as providers of public goods, new models of provision have emerged. These have often taken the form of hybrid organizations that mix public and private agendas (the Public–Private Finance Initiatives in the UK are typical examples). In the USA and the UK, this movement has been characterized as the 'Third Way' or 'market' socialism (Giddens 1998, 2000). Finally, in developing countries in the south, other manifestations of the political agenda of social entrepreneurship can be seen. For example, in Brazil, the rationale behind the planning and execution of the extraordinary civic entrepreneurship embodied in the Curatiba community was entirely political (this is discussed in detail in Chapter 11: also see, e.g. Leadbeater and Goss 1998; Spengler and Ford 2002).

There is a long tradition of social action across a range of cultures from the Quaker philanthropists of the UK (including the Cadbury, John Lewis, and Sainsbury families: see Kennedy 2001) to the educational role of Buddhist monks in Asia. However, the decline of organized religion in some cultures has provided another set of social market failures. In this space, social entrepreneurship flourishing within religious institutions aims at both reviving faith communities and mobilizing faith-based resources towards wider social problems (see Chapter 9).

The former represents the commercialization (or 'Japanization') of some congregations where exploiting the money raising possibilities of a parish to support and sustain it has become a strategic norm. The latter reflects the long tradition of faith-based solutions to social problems within civil society and is an emergent component of public sector policy in some countries, particularly the USA. Pastor Rick Warren and his development of the Saddleback Church in the USA is a good example (*The Economist* 2005*b*). Saddleback—the 'Purpose Driven Church' (see www.purposedrivenlife.com/rickwarren.aspx)—has been an outstanding example of how innovation has reinvented faith communities not only multiplying worshippers exponentially but also mobilizing substantial resources for good works within and without the community itself. Similarly, in the UK, the association between the Fair Trade movement and church groups has long been important in generating social and financial capital. Indeed, the bulk of sales for Traidcraft—one of the leading Fair Trade enterprises in the UK—still come from retail activity rooted in Christian congregations across the country.

Finally, the imbalance between supply and demand of philanthropic resources to the social sector represents another area of market failure. This has led to the evolution of new paradigms of social 'investment' through more engaged models of venture philanthropy (Letts, Ryans, and Grossman 1997; Meehan, Kilmer, and O'Flanagan 2004). These are social venture funds characterized by high levels of engagement with the social entrepreneur, long-investment horizons, higher levels of risk-taking, and a rigorous focus on auditing social impacts, where possible. Thus, venture philanthropy is, in essence, the philanthropic application of venture capital principles and practice. Moreover, in addition to funding, venture philanthropists typically provide networking, management advice, and an array of other supports to organizations within their portfolio. The emergence of a number of significant venture philanthropy organizations in recent years—such as the Acumen Fund, New Philanthropy Capital, the European Venture Philanthropy Association, and New Profit Inc.—demonstrates the growing interest in this model of social investment. However, it is important to note that the volume of funds currently under management by venture philanthropy groups still remains very small, typically less than 1 per cent of total giving. As a result, the most significant contribution being made by the venture philanthropy model currently lies in its demonstration of a more 'engaged' approach to social investment rather than in the funds that it is directly contributing.

In summary, the strategic mission focus of a socially entrepreneurial venture will be defined by its operational context and is likely to be quite distinct from conventional business and, indeed, many less risk-taking social actions. However, equally important in establishing the social within social entrepreneurship are the outcomes and impacts driven by the mission. There are a number of distinctive issues here too.

First, social entrepreneurs often work towards a combined value proposition that blurs the traditional view that the creation of economic value is quite separate from its social equivalent. Thus, value creation could include not only superior service delivery, but also more nebulous effects such as empowerment and systems innovation. This is conceptualized in the notion of Blended Value that combines fully monetized social impacts with more conventional financial data to judge the outcomes of a social venture (Emerson 2003; Nicholls, J. 2004). Such an approach is a prerequisite of appropriate performance measurement, since a purely financial account will almost certainly undervalue operational success. Given that social entrepreneurs often operate in the spaces that conventional markets ignore, it is unrealistic to assume that they will always generate a market rate return on investment. However, to consign their performance to a nebulous definition of 'good works' is also insufficient. Social impact can be measured and should be combined with any other value creation achieved to give a proper picture of a social entrepreneur's success or failure. This 'double' or 'triple bottom line' approach is central to interpreting social venture outcomes (see Alter 2000; Elkington 2001).

Second, social entrepreneurs look to create social impact both as a result of an operational process and, often, as part of the process (see Table I.5). Thus, they seek out opportunities to add social impact throughout their entire value chain, often employing and training disenfranchised groups as a part of delivering their social mission or revitalizing depleted community resources such as housing stock. The process of social entrepreneurship, therefore, may typically be characterized by a range of social missions that are addressed at different points in the 'social' value chain. For example, Youth Industries Inc. in the USA built a series of social enterprises that not only produced goods and services high in social capital (via a community restaurant and a recycled clothes shop: see also Putnam 2001), but also employed and trained homeless young people as the staff. Furthermore, the profits from the commercial enterprises were reinvested in mentoring programmes and accommodation for the employees as part of their transition back into normal society. Such an approach would be commercially unviable for most non-social ventures. The significance of mission driven 'values' within the value creation process is crucial here. In many ways ethos matters as much as strategy.

Finally, measuring social impact and social value creation demands different metrics from conventional business. A number of qualitative performance measures have been developed for social ventures over the last ten years including: Triple Bottom Line accounting (Elkington 2001), the Balanced Scorecard for not-for-profits (Kaplan 2002), the Family of Measures (Sawhill and Williamson 2001), and social reporting (Zadek 1998). Whilst these metrics have a strategic value in establishing mission alignment and stakeholder engagement they are of limited use in attracting investment or establishing benchmarks. For this a more quantitative approach is needed. The Social Return on Investment (SROI) model provides such an approach. Pioneered by Jed Emerson at the Roberts Enterprise Development Fund (REDF) in California (Emerson 1999*b*), SROI has subsequently been refined by the New Economics Foundation in the UK (Acron-Thomas et al. 2003; Nicholls, J. 2004). However, these metrics have yet to become fully accepted across the social sector, let alone widely used (indeed, REDF themselves have recently abandoned recommending the use of SROI). Consequently, there are few comparable social impact benchmarks available to social entrepreneurs and their stakeholders. Indeed, social value creation will always be at least partly contingent on subjective and negotiated judgements across stakeholders (see further Chapter 3).

It has also been argued that a third dimension to the social element in social entrepreneurship may also be discerned in an analysis of the personality traits of the socially entrepreneurial individual. The individual level of analysis of social entrepreneurship has often been defined in terms of established models of the commercial, private-sector entrepreneur ('who the entrepreneur is': McClelland 1961; Brockhaus 1980) and has typically presented the entrepreneur as a uniquely skilled leader and innovator or 'business hero' with outstanding personal qualities (Gartner 1988; Venkataraman 1997). In this way, Casson (1982: 23) characterized the entrepreneur as 'someone who specialises in taking judgemental decisions about the co-ordination of scarce resources' and who has 'imagination and foresight and skill in organising and delegating work'. This tradition of the 'heroic leader' set apart from the conventional landscape is also clearly evident in some of the more descriptive accounts of social entrepreneurs and their actions (Leadbeater 1997; Boschee 2001; Alter 2002; Bornstein 2004). Furthermore, Drayton (2002) noted the special creativity found in many social entrepreneurs at the level of personal traits and others have highlighted their unique leadership skills (Henton, Melville, and Walesh, 1997; Thompson, Alvy, and Lees 2000). The growth of support organizations celebrating and connecting social entrepreneurs as 'Fellows' or award winners noted earlier also lionizes the individual social change-maker.

However, whilst many social entrepreneurs do, indeed, demonstrate qualities usually associated with their commercial counterparts—particularly leadership, vision, drive, and opportunism—there is also a crucial difference. For social entrepreneurs there is always a 'socio-moral motivation' or social-mission focus to their entrepreneurial activity and ambition (Casson 1994: 3; Dees 1998a). It is in this spirit that Ashoka includes the presence of 'ethical fibre' as one of the key determinants in electing to its Fellowship. Bornstein (1998) also highlighted the social entrepreneur's unique ethical make-up and drive towards a social mission as being centrally important (see also Boschee 1995). Finally, Catford (1998) identified a strong commitment to social justice as being a defining characteristic. The personality traits associated with the social entrepreneur are also of significance in the second distinctive element of social entrepreneurship: operational processes.

Operational Processes

An analysis of a venture's strategic mission and outcomes identifies its social dimension, as does the character and personality of the social entrepreneur. However, to establish whether or not such an organization is socially *entrepreneurial* requires closer attention to its operational processes.

The established literature on commercial entrepreneurship acknowledges the process level of operations as highly significant in determining entrepreneurial activity at an individual or group level (i.e. 'what the entrepreneur does': Kent, Sexton, and Vesper 1982; Gartner 1988). This approach sometimes combines with the personality traits level of analysis noted earlier in a unified entrepreneurial paradigm based on unexpected opportunity recognition and its innovative exploitation (e.g. Shane and Venkataraman 2000: 18; also see Drucker 1985). In organizational terms this level of analysis identifies the entrepreneur as being both a situational (Hersey and Blanchard 1982) and transformational leader (Stogdill 1974) that applies innovation and risk-taking creativity effectively in highly contingent ways.

Building on the established entrepreneurship literature, a number of distinguishing process features of social entrepreneurship have already been identified. These can be summarized in two dimensions: innovation and market orientation (see further Chapter 5). However, both elements are operationalized with features distinct to a social context. First, several authors have highlighted a distinctive approach towards innovation, opportunity creation, and recognition in social entrepreneurship (Dees and Battle Anderson 2002; Thompson 2002; Austin, Stevenson, and Wei-Skillern 2003; Sullivan Mort, Weerawardena, and Carnegie 2003; Dees, Battle Anderson, and Wei-Skillern 2004). This research has presented socially entrepreneurial processes as models that bring together multiple contextual elements to provide frameworks for strategic growth planning in a social setting. Thus, Austin, Stevenson, and Wei-Skillern (2003) focused on an analysis of the key differences between commercial and social entrepreneurship across four components behind successful growth: people, context, deals, and opportunities. Alternatively, Guclu, Dees, and Battle Anderson (2002) developed a two-stage model of opportunity creation for social ventures that combined personal factors (defined as individual 'social assets') with operational issues (namely, developing a viable operating model, a convincing social impact theory, and an effective resource strategy).

Second, it has been suggested that social entrepreneurs demonstrate creative network building as an important strategic tool in a far broader range of contexts than conventional entrepreneurs (Dennis 2000; Blundel and Smith 2001; BarNir and Smith 2002). Thus, social entrepreneurs engage with network activity not only to leverage resources and strengthen their own venture but also to deliver impact and create new social value. Central to this strategic approach is a stakeholder worldview that prioritizes maximizing positive impact across the web of external and internal actors connected to a social venture ahead of traditional economic objectives such as organizational growth and maintaining competitive advantage. Similarly, a deeper understanding of network models often informs social venture development, since effective mechanisms for social impact creation are rarely linear and purely transactional processes. A good example is Fair Trade, where building social connections across a reconfigured value chain has delivered both a new trading model and a new consumption and marketing paradigm to deliver innovative social value (see Nicholls and Opal 2005: 151–78; Nicholls and Alexander 2006).

Third, social entrepreneurs typically view growth in a strategically different light from commercial entrepreneurs (see Leat 2003 for example). Since the former are focused primarily on social impact, rather than profit maximization, the drive to scale may not always be relevant. Indeed, maximum impact may best be achieved by staying small and local, deepening rather than broadening activities. The deeply embedded community origins of much of social entrepreneurship also militate against hierarchical models of growth. More typical are 'broad and flat' organizational structures (e.g. co-operatives). Looser 'social franchise' or network models may be used to spread social impact creation most effectively (e.g. the Ecoclubes youth environmental project in Latin America: see www. ecoclubes.org).

Thus, according to Alvord, Brown, and Letts (2004), social entrepreneurship is characterized by three types of innovation:

- *Transformational*: By building local capacity this approach alters local norms, roles, and expectations to transform the cultural context for the better (e.g. BRAC and local village-based training initiatives)

- *Economic*: By developing bespoke 'packages' to solve problems this approach provides tools and resources to enhance productivity and transform economic circumstances (e.g. Grameen Bank and microfinance)

- *Political*: By building local movements to challenge power this approach increases the voice of marginalized communities to increase their political influence (e.g. the Self-Employed Women's Association in India)

Finally, social entrepreneurs often aim for a Schumpeterian 'creative destruction' that aims to change the landscape of social provision systemically for the better. Social entrepreneurship often works at the level of social movements and social entrepreneurs are often highly politicized (though not necessarily aligned party politically). They are effective activists, advocates, and catalysts of wider change. The drive towards systemic change within their own operating sectors, not for their own benefit, but rather for the benefit of their stakeholders, also marks out social entrepreneurs as quite unlike their commercial counterparts. Paradoxically, the ultimate (though usually unattainable) aim of many social ventures is to be so successful in addressing a given social need that they effectively remove their need to exist. For example, if, in a perfect world, the Fair Trade movement could ever end global trade injustice for good it would put itself out of business.

Much of the, admittedly to date limited, literature interpreting the socially entrepreneurial paradigm has used this process-oriented approach (Dees 1998a; Dees and Elias 1998; Alter 2000; Thompson, Alvy, and Lees 2000; Boschee 2001; Dees, Emerson, and Economy 2001, 2002; Dees and Battle Anderson 2002; Dees, Battle Anderson, and Wei-Skillern 2004). Most notably, Dees's seminal analysis (1998a) of the meaning of social entrepreneurship drew specifically upon established economic conventions of entrepreneurial activity to frame his research in process terms. For example, drawing on Say's suggestion (2001) that a commercial entrepreneur creates new value by shifting economic resources out of an area of lower yield and into an area of higher productivity and greater yield, Dees argued that social entrepreneurs also create new (social) value by pulling together resources in more effective ways to address issues. Similarly, Schumpeter (1980) proposed that innovation was at the heart of the entrepreneurial approach by declaring that the function of entrepreneurs was, above all, to reform or revolutionize the patterns of production. In this context, Dees noted that social entrepreneurs relentlessly search for new and better means of delivering social value. Finally, where Drucker (1985) suggested that an entrepreneur plays a key role as a catalyst for change by searching for new paradigms and exploiting them as fresh opportunities, Dees stressed that social entrepreneurs also often aim for systemic social change in order to ensure the sustainability of their innovative interventions.

Dees (1998a: 4) summarized his thinking by combining both the individual traits and the process levels of analysis of entrepreneurship when he defined social entrepreneurs as acting as change agents by:

- Adopting a mission to create and sustain social value (not just private value)
- Recognizing and relentlessly pursuing new opportunities to serve that mission
- Engaging in a process of continuous innovation, adaptation, and learning
- Acting boldly without being limited by resources currently in hand
- Exhibiting a heightened sense of accountability to the constituencies served and for the outcomes created

Bearing in mind the discussion above, social entrepreneurship, in this collection, will be defined as follows:

Innovative and effective activities that focus strategically on resolving social market failures and creating new opportunities to add social value systemically by using a range of resources and organizational formats to maximize social impact and bring about change.

Structure of the Book

Social Entrepreneurship: New Models of Sustainable Social Change consists of seventeen chapters organized into four parts: New Perspectives, New Theories, New Models, and New Directions. The tone of the book is deliberately highly varied with contributions from field actors as well as academics and policy-makers. Included here are descriptive accounts of social entrepreneurship in action as well as more theorized reflections on practice. Whilst some may find the variety of narrative textures and authorial voices unusual, it perfectly reflects the current state of this emergent field of study and such diversity is unashamedly celebrated here. However, the structure of the book is designed to group the contributions stylistically and, thus, to give its contents greater conceptual clarity and ease the reader's way through the material.

After this introduction, Part I—New Perspectives—features four chapters from eminent practitioners with outstanding track records in social entrepreneurship. This section provides an introduction to the book as a whole, exploring different aspects of the praxis and policy that underpin the emergent academic field. Part II—New Theories—takes the discussion into a more theoretical dimension and presents five new academic perspectives on social entrepreneurship from leading researchers in the field. Part III—New Models—sets out four paradigms of how social entrepreneurship can reconfigure social issues and add new value. The book concludes with Part IV—New Directions—that addresses four important challenges for the future of social entrepreneurship: foundation support, creating a social finance marketplace, developing strategic competencies around sustainability, and pursuing a blended value approach to measure success. The collection ends with some concluding remarks that highlight a number of directions for future research.

Part I opens with Muhammad Yunus, the 'father' of microfinance, founder of the Grameen Bank, and one of the world's most famous social entrepreneurs, issuing a call to arms for a reconfiguration of capitalism as a model for social change. He argues for a new conceptualization of what capitalism is and what it can achieve in tandem with effective social actors who can run ventures beyond the point of full cost recovery. This new hybrid is termed a 'social business entrepreneur'. Yunus then sets out a number of key themes to support this new type of entrepreneur that will be echoed and developed elsewhere in the collection. These include: the research opportunity for new theoretical models to support practice, the need for a new social capital market to provide more finance for social projects, the value of foundation support and awards, and the need for new metrics and transparent performance information. Interestingly, these observations are in tune with the recent observations by the managing partner of McKinsey and Co. (Davis 2005) that the continued separation of the social and the economic is strategically unsustainable for big business.

Next Bill Drayton, the founder of Ashoka, sets the context for the rise of social entrepreneurship when he considers how the 'citizens' sector' (also known as civil society) has changed dramatically in recent years. Drayton notes how the 'business/society productivity gap', in place since the Industrial Revolution, is now rapidly closing with huge numbers of new social sector groups appearing across the globe and generating jobs, new flows of services and finance, and great social impact. He then goes on to set out four critical design challenges for the field going forward: global operational integration, social/business reintegration, disciplined entrepreneurial judgement, and social investing innovation.

In Chapter 3, Rowena Young, the Director of the Skoll Centre for Social Entrepreneurship at the University of Oxford, discusses the nature of value creation in social ventures and how this relates to key issues for social entrepreneurship. Of particularly interest is the juxtaposition of value creation and value systems. The author identifies five important elements within social-added value: its subjectivity, contestability, contingency, heterogeneity, and values base. Young then discusses the role of social metrics in establishing the real value of social impact and the chapter concludes by dissecting notions of social value creation under several headings: social-added value, empowerment and social change, social innovation, and systemic change.

Geoff Mulgan—the Director of the Young Foundation—concludes Part I by presenting a policy analysis of the key issues facing social entrepreneurship today. Mulgan highlights the 'other invisible hand'—the government sponsored legal and fiscal frameworks that support civic activities—to develop a discussion around the role of government policy in catalysing new social ventures. He considers the nature of the public value created by the social entrepreneurship paradigm and then goes on to set out what government can do to maximize this value creation. Mulgan surveys some of the UK government initiatives in this area in which he had particular involvement and then proposes a new policy agenda to maintain the momentum. Finally, he challenges researchers to consider nine key topics and generate robust data that can contribute to the ongoing debate and policy development around social entrepreneurship both in the UK and abroad.

Part II of the book moves from practitioner perspectives to a more theoretical set of discussions that aim to broaden the academic field of social entrepreneurship by engaging with a range of social science disciplines and established literatures. This part opens with Chapter 5 that takes a particular sociological perspective on social entrepreneurship. Alex Nicholls, university lecturer in social entrepreneurship at the Skoll Centre for Social Entrepreneurship, University of Oxford, and Albert Cho, a researcher at the United Nations, test several foundational concepts that underpin an understanding of social entrepreneurship. The authors identify three key definitional features of social entrepreneurship – sociality, innovation, and market orientation – and then proceed to explore the contested issues around each. Finally, the chapter engages with structuration theory to argue that by defying easy categorization (as reflected in its resistance to organizational isomorphism) the social entrepreneurial paradigm actually maximizes its operational effectiveness and, in this way, also enhances its legitimacy across different stakeholder groups. Paola Grenier, a doctoral researcher at the London School of Economics and Political Science, contributes Chapter 6. Grenier contextualizes social entrepreneurship within a broader set of debates around globalization and issues of control and agency. Drawing on the work of Giddens and Beck particularly, she develops the notion of 'individuation'—the individual level freedom to act outside of hierarchies and established structures—in terms of 'global' civil society and its new organizational manifestations encompassing social entrepreneurship. Moving on, Grenier then explores the motives and 'moral individualism' associated with social entrepreneurs as social actors that have 'a powerful sense of their own agency and values'. Next she places such actors within a globalized context of loci of social market failures or 'endemic dissatisfaction'. A survey of the support networks for social entrepreneurs follows and leads to a discussion of such organizations in the larger global landscape—what is notable is that all the key players are located in the North and West, despite the fact that much of social entrepreneurial activity is actually located in the South and East. As a result, Grenier suggests that the concept of social entrepreneurship, as currently conceived, is a 'Western notion' with a focus on the 'hero' individual entrepreneur imbued with the language and conventions of neo-liberal business. She argues that this is a poor representation of the complex realities 'on the ground' and may restrict the impact of support mechanisms.

In Chapter 7, Beth Battle Anderson and Greg Dees from the Fuqua Business School at Duke University highlight the need for more rigorous research to test some of the current thinking around social entrepreneurship. They particularly focus on the role of earned income in the social enterprise subset of activities within social entrepreneurship by setting out five key areas for future research. These include: the question of self-sufficiency versus dependency, what constitutes sustainability, how earned income can contribute to financial freedom, how scalability can be approached strategically, and what is the relationship between funding and social impact. In the second part of their chapter, Battle Anderson and Dees argue that effectively to address these issues, academics need to move away from the established traditions of 'non-profit' research towards a more holistic view of how social impact can be achieved most effectively across a range of organizational forms. They argue that there is much to learn from existing research traditions in business and management that has long been resisted by not-for-profit scholars. To this end, the chapter concludes by considering five current obstacles that lie in the way of greater engagement between business school scholars and social sector research and proposes a range of practical strategies to overcome these hurdles.

A team from Harvard Business School, led by Jim Austin, contributes Chapter 8. In this discussion the case is made for 'Corporate Social Entrepreneurship' (CSE), described as more 'robust forms of strategic corporate citizenship'. The chapter lays out both the push and pull factors that are driving businesses to consider this new level of social engagement and then goes on to describe four key areas for operationalizing CSE: leadership, strategy, structures, and systems. Finally, the research identifies seven types of CSE change agents that together can move a company towards this more engaged social agenda.

Part II concludes with Doug Foster—of the University of Surrey—presenting an analysis of an extensive empirical study exploring the role of social entrepreneurship in a spiritual or sacred context, namely in the actions and attitudes of a sample of Church of England vicars. Foster builds a theorization of social entrepreneurship in the context of a broader discussion of public and private professionalism and then goes on to use a range of examples from his qualitative survey to test the boundaries of socially entrepreneurial behaviour in a specific diocese. He identifies a range of such activity amongst the sampled clergy and suggests some future directions for 'sacred' innovation. Foster's wide ranging use of literature embraces not only sociological theory (Beck, Giddens, etc.), political commentary (Hobbs, Burrows, etc.), and the philosophy of ethics (MacIntyre) but also more mainstream business and entrepreneurship scholarship (Kirzner, Leadbeater, etc.).

The third section of this collection considers new models of social entrepreneurship from around the world in an applied context. First, Sutia Kim Alter, Founder of Virtue Ventures and a Visiting Fellow at the Skoll Centre for Social Entrepreneurship, sets out an extensive typology of social enterprise organizational forms. Alter reminds us that the social enterprise model combines both social impact and financial value creation by adopting various business elements within the context of achieving a social mission. The objective is to diversify funding in order to support sustainability and longer-term impact. However, she also acknowledges that this model will not be appropriate for every social entrepreneur. Drawing on her extensive experience of consulting with social sector groups across Latin America, Eastern Europe, Central Asia, and elsewhere, Alter distinguishes three forms of social enterprise: mission-centric, mission-related, and unrelated to mission. Building on this analysis, the chapter then goes on to identify three operational types of social enterprise: embedded, integrated, and external. Alter explores seven specific prototypes of organizational forms across these three types. Each prototype is set out with a detailed case study example. The next section of the chapter considers combined models that bring together two or more of the seven prototypes as either 'complex', 'mixed', or 'enhancing' organizational forms. Alter concludes by reminding us of the limitations of the social enterprise approach and warns against assuming it is the 'holy grail' of social entrepreneurship.

Chapter 11 is a contribution from Charles Leadbeater. Leadbeater is an established thinker and writer on social and community issues and was one of the first opinion leaders to use the phrase social entrepreneur in the UK (Leadbeater 1997) He is a Visiting Fellow at the Skoll Centre for Social Entrepreneurship. In the chapter, he discusses the case of the city of Curitiba in Brazil as an example of 'network' social entrepreneurship at a civic level. In this context, Leadbeater explores the notion of 'structured self-organization' to create social goods (here both more effective social housing and more efficient waste recycling) and sets out five key elements behind this approach: leadership, shared platforms, a pragmatic philosophy, distributed resources, and collaborative civic engagement. Next, he goes on to develop a model of networked social entrepreneurship in contrast to the more conventional organizational model. The chapter concludes by critiquing some of the key features of social entrepreneurship as currently perceived in the light of this new thinking, notably: the social entrepreneur's motivations and impacts, the nature of social venture leadership, the blurring of contexts for socially entrepreneurial activities, and the outcomes of such activities. Leadbeater ends by returning to the example of Curitiba to suggest that increasing social impact may not only be driven by organizational growth but also by the scaling up and connection of key networks.

The next chapter addresses the important issue of performance measurement and accountability in social ventures, focusing particularly on aid and development NGOs. Alex Jacobs, the CEO of Mango and a Visiting Fellow at the Skoll Centre for Social Entrepreneurship, argues that the bureaucratic and organizational arrangements across the social sector actually serve to undermine attempts to improve performance and strengthen accountability. Jacobs suggests that current NGO institutional arrangements have grown up in an unplanned way that has given rise to a number of systemic factors that slow the pace and reduce the chance of change and improved operational effectiveness. These are grouped into four sets of issues: conceptual confusion, funding pressures, internal organizational factors, and external factors. Each, in turn, is then explored in detail. The chapter concludes that raising the quality of NGO performance to more consistent heights depends on developing more appropriate conceptual units and organizational arrangements that specifically aim to support and release the energies of field staff.

Part III of the collection concludes with Professor Gordon Bloom from the Kennedy School of Government at Harvard discussing his own innovative approach to new social venture creation, the social entrepreneurship 'collaboratory' or student-driven project incubator. Bloom begins by noting that the pedagogic opportunities for students interested in social entrepreneurship have been limited and, with particular reference to his own experiences at Stanford and Harvard, he goes on to explain in detail the rationale behind, and genesis of, the collaboratory approach as a solution to this educational gap that mixes both praxis and theory. Of particular value here is the analysis of an emerging social entrepreneurship curriculum for universities. By means of a number of brief case study examples, Bloom demonstrates the impact of this model both for teaching and for empowering the social entrepreneurs of the future within the student body.

Sally Osberg, the CEO of the Skoll Foundation based in Palo Alto, California, opens Part IV, New Directions. Osberg considers how modern philanthropy is reinventing itself in the context of significant new players entering the landscape, particularly a new breed of wealthy entrepreneurs. These new donors are driving new models of giving and engagement forward and are often described as 'venture philanthropists', typically characterized by closer relationships between grant giver and recipient. Osberg sets out a diagram bringing together three key elements of the new philanthropy: the value proposition, the terms of engagement, and the results. The chapter then goes on to consider each in turn with a range of examples. The discussion ends with some observations concerning the implications of this new philanthropic agenda for social entrepreneurs.

In the next chapter Pamela Hartigan, the Managing Director of the Schwab Foundation for Social Entrepreneurship, addresses the key issue of the lack of finance currently available to social entrepreneurs by presenting a detailed, historical case study of the development of the Global Exchange for Social Investment (GEXSI). The chapter falls into two sections. First, a discussion focuses mainly on the process of establishing effective performance criteria with which to identify and promote promising social investment opportunities to potential investors. Following an overview of the background to the initiative Hartigan goes on to explore the criteria set out for the GEXSI with reference to specific ventures. Second, the chapter acknowledges and analyses the operational difficulties encountered by the GEXSI as it initially struggled to deliver its mission of brokering significant new resources into socially entrepreneurial projects. The case is brought up to date with a concluding discussion of the promising new partnership with ACCESS (a separate, 'social' ratings agency recently renamed 'Keystone') to overcome some of the GEXSI's initial operational hurdles.

Chapter 16 offers a wide-ranging discussion concerning how to develop sustainable strategies for social enterprises in the USA. Contributed by Jerr Boschee, the Founder and Executive Director of the Institute for Social Entrepreneurs, this discussion sets out a very practical analysis of the key issues behind building successful social enterprises that can last. Boschee draws upon a large number of individual cases to illustrate his points and includes a significant amount of input drawn from a range of semi-structured interviews. In contrast with Greg Dees and others elsewhere in the book, Boschee is adamant that any truly entrepreneurial social venture must move towards a market-based self-sufficiency strategy that aims to generate independent earned income. The chapter begins by setting the historical context for a move towards the social enterprise model in the USA and then defines its key terms of reference including: innovation, entrepreneurship, social entrepreneurship, earned income, social purpose business, and the differences between innovators, entrepreneurs, and professional managers. Next, Boschee considers the obstacles that lie in the way of innovation and 'entrepreneurship' in social ventures. Finally, he lists fourteen critical success factors for sustainable social enterprises drawn from his extensive field experience.

Part IV of this collection ends with a rousing call to arms for the future of social entrepreneurship by Jed Emerson, a Senior Visiting Research Fellow at the Skoll Centre for Social Entrepreneurship. Emerson develops his extensive work on Blended Value to analyse five key topics within the emerging field of social entrepreneurship: the nature of the firm, capital investment, performance tracking, the dissemination and development of intellectual capital, and how the field may be organized in future. The chapter contributes both operational and conceptual insights and concludes that there is a pressing need for an expanded vision of social entrepreneurship that encompasses the full range of Blended Value social impact creation opportunities. Furthermore, new value networks must be built to facilitate this expanded vision and to generate more systemic approaches to social change.

The book concludes with an endnote from the editor and also includes a comprehensive bibliography that brings together for the first time in print, the full range of academic work related to social entrepreneurship across a number of academic disciplines.

Conclusion

The impact of the new social entrepreneurship model has been felt across the range of socially focused activities. On the one hand, the model has contributed to a reconfiguring of existing social ventures such as charities, not-for-profits, and NGOs. On the other, social entrepreneurs have helped catalyse the public sector to become more effective, accountable, and flexible in its approaches to social provision. Furthermore, social entrepreneurship also demonstrates how commercial enterprise and established business models can be integrated with social value creation. This reveals opportunities and challenges for the corporate world.

For social entrepreneurs traditional measures of performance have been re-engineered to increase social impact and accountability. Outputs have been recast as outcomes framed in terms of social value creation and impact rather than simple numbers. For example, a charity would cease to be judged on its ability to raise money and remain solvent but rather on the effectiveness with which it addressed its social mission. Similarly, asset structures need to take increasing account of social, as well as financial and physical capital. Thus, measures of successful relationship building, trust, networks, and cooperation become more important in strategic planning and assessment. This fits well with social ventures' typical ownership structures highlighting key stakeholders. Of course, all of this revolutionary thinking is contested and problematic, not least in terms of metrics. But what is patently clear is that social entrepreneurship is generating entirely new paradigms of social value creation and systemic change that are creating their own definitional terms and taxonomies as they emerge.

The subsequent chapters of this book will explore the multiple dimensions of social entrepreneurship across the world from a variety of perspectives in the hope of providing practitioners and academics alike with both new thinking and new models of action.

References

Aeron-Thomas, D., Nicholls, J., Forster, S., and Westall, A. (2003). *Social Return on Investment: Miracle or Manacle*? London: New Economics Foundation.

Alter, K. (2000). *Managing the Double Bottom Line: A Business Planning Reference Guide for Social Enterprises*. Washington, DC: PACT Publications.

—— (2002). *Case Studies in Social Entrepreneurship*. Washington, DC: Counterpart International.

—— (2003). *Social Enterprise: A Typology of the Field Contextualized in Latin America*. Washington, DC: IDB.

Alvord, S., Brown, L., and Letts, C. (2004). 'Social Entrepreneurship and Societal Transformation: An Exploratory Study', *Journal of Applied Behavioral Science*, 40(3): 260–83.

Austin, J. (2000). *The Collaboration Challenge: How Non-Profits and Businesses Succeed Through Strategic Alliances*. San Francisco, CA: Jossey-Bass.

—— Stevenson, H., and Wei-Skillen, J. (2003). *Social Entrepreneurship and Commercial Entrepreneurship: Same, Different, or Both?*, Harvard Business School, Working Paper.

Banks, J. (1972). *The Sociology of Social Movements*. London: Macmillan.

BarNir, A. and Smith, K. (2002) 'Interfirm Alliances in the Small Business: The Role of Social Networks', *Journal of Small Business Management*, 40(3): 219–32.

Bernholz, L. (2004). *Creating Philanthropic Capital Markets*. Hoboken, NJ: John Wiley & Sons.

Blundel, R. K. and Smith, D. (2001). *Business Networking: SMEs and Inter-Firm Collaboration, a Review of the Research Literature with Implications for Policy*. Report to Small Business Service PP03/01, Department of Trade and Industry, Small Business Service, Sheffield.

Bornstein, D. (1998). 'Changing the World on a Shoestring', *Atlantic Monthly*, 281(1): 34–9.

—— (2004). *How to Change the World: Social Entrepreneurs and the Power of New Ideas*. Oxford: Oxford University Press.

Borzaga, C. and Defourny, J. (2001). *The Emergence of Social Enterprise*. New York: Routledge.

Boschee, J. (1995). 'Social Entrepreneurship', *Across the Board*, 32(3): 20–5.

—— (2001). *The Social Enterprise Sourcebook*. Minneapolis, MN: Northland Institute.

—— and McClurg, D. (2003). *Toward a Better Understanding of Social Entrepreneurship: Some Important Distinctions*. Minnesota, MN: Institute for Social Entrepreneurs.

Brinckerhoff, P. (2000). *Social Entrepreneurship: The Art of Mission-Based Venture Development*. New York: John Wiley & Sons.

Brockhaus, R. (1980). 'Risk Taking Propensity of Entrepreneurs', *Academy of Management Journal*, 23(3): 509–20.

Burch, J. (1986). *Entrepreneurship*. New York: John Wiley & Sons.

Casson, M. (1982). *Entrepreneur: An Economic Theory*. London: Edward Elgar.

—— (ed.) (1990). *Entrepreneurship*. Aldershot, UK: Edward Elgar.

—— (1994). *The Economics of Business Culture*. Oxford: Clarendon Press.

Catford, J. (1998). 'Social Entrepreneurs Are Vital for Health Promotion—But They Need Supportive Environments Too', *Health Promotion International*, 13(2): 95–7.

Chamberlain, N. (1977). *Remaking American Values*. New York: Basic Books.

Dacanay, M. (2004). 'Creating Space in the Market. Social Enterprise Stories in Asia', *Asian Institute of Management*.

Dart, R. (2004). 'The Legitimacy of Social Enterprise', *Nonprofit Management and Leadership*, 14(4): 411–24.

Davis, I. (2005). 'The Biggest Contract', *The Economist*, 26 May.

Davis, L., Etchart, N., Jara, M., and Milder, B. (2003). *Risky Business: The Impacts of Merging Mission and Market*. NESsT, Santiago, Chile.

Dees, J. G. (1994). *Social Enterprise: Private Initiatives for Common Good*. Harvard, MA: Harvard Business School Press.

—— (1996). *The Social Enterprise Spectrum: From Philanthropy to Commerce*. Harvard, MA: Harvard Business School Press.

—— (1998a). *The Meaning of Social Entrepreneurship*, Available at: http://faculty.fuqua.duke.edu/centers/case/files/dees-SE.pdf

—— (January–February, 1998b). 'Enterprising Nonprofits', *Harvard Business Review*, 76(1): 54–67.

—— and Battle Anderson, B. (2002). 'Blurring Sector Boundaries: Serving Social Purposes Through For-Profit Structures', *CASE Working Paper Series*, 2. Duke Fuqua School.

—— and Elias, J. (1998). 'The Challenges of Combining Social and Commercial Enterprise', An Essay on Norman Bowie's University-Business Partnerships: An Assessment, *Business Ethics Quarterly*, 8(1): 1–17.

—— Emerson, J., and Economy, P. (2001). *Enterprising Non-profits: A Toolkit for Social Entrepreneurs*. New York: Wiley Non-Profit Series.

—— —— —— (2002). *Strategic Tools for Social Entrepreneurs: Enhancing the Performance of Your Enterprising Non-profit*. New York: Wiley Non-Profit Series.

—— Battle Anderson, B., and Wei-Skillern, J. (Spring, 2004). 'Scaling Social Impact', *Stanford Social Innovation Review*: 24–32.

Demetriou, D. (2003). 'Consumers Embrace Ethical Sales, Costing Firms £2.6bn a Year', *The Independent*, 9 December, p. 7.

Dennis, C. (2000). 'Networking for Marketing Advantage', *Management Decision*, 38(4): 287–292.

DiMaggio, P. and Anheier, H. (1990). 'The Sociology of Nonprofit Organizations and Sectors', *Annual Review of Sociology*, 16: 137–59.

—— and Powell, W. (1983). 'The Iron Cage Revisited: Institutional Isomorphism and Collective Rationality in Organizational Fields', *American Sociological Review*, 48: 147–60.

Drayton, W. (2002). 'The Citizen Sector: Becoming as Entrepreneurial and Competitive as Business', *California Management Review*, 44(3): 120–32.

Drucker, P. (1985). *Innovation and Entrepreneurship*. London: Harper-Business.

DTI—Department for Trade and Industry, Social Enterprise Unit (2002). *Social Enterprise: A Strategy for Success*. London: DTI.

DTI—Department for Trade and Industry (2004). *Community Interest Companies. An Introduction to Community Interest Companies*. London: DTI.

Elkington, J. (2001). 'The Triple Bottom Line for 21st Century Business', in R. Strakely and R. Welford (eds.), *Business and Sustainable Development*. London: Earthscan, pp. 20–43.

Emerson, J. (1999*a*). 'The US Non-Profit Capital Market', in *REDF Box Set*, vol. 2, chapter 10. San Francisco, CA: Roberts Enterprise Development Fund.

—— (1999*b*). 'Social Return on Investment: Exploring Aspects of Value Creation', in *REDF Box Set*, vol. 2, chapter 8. San Francisco, CA: Roberts Enterprise Development Fund.

—— (2003). 'The Blended Value Proposition: Integrating Social and Financial Returns', *California Management Review*, 45(4): 35–51.

Etzioni, A. (1973). 'The Third Sector and Domestic Missions', *Public Administration Review*, 33: 314–23.

Gartner, W. (1988). 'Who Is the Entrepreneur? Is the Wrong Question', *American Journal of Small Business*, 12: 11–32.

Giddens, A. (1998). *The Third Way*. Cambridge: Polity Press.

—— (2000). *The Third Way and Its Critics*. Cambridge: Polity Press.

Guclu, A., Dees, J., and Battle Anderson, B. (2002), 'The Process of Social Entrepreneurship: Creating Opportunities Worthy of Serious Pursuit', *CASE Working Paper Series*, 3. Duke Fuqua School.

Hammack, D. (ed.) (1998). *Making the Nonprofit Sector in the United States*. Bloomington, IN: Indiana University Press.

Harvard Business Review (1999). *Harvard Business School on Entrepreneurship*. Boston, MA: HBS.

Harding, R. (2004). 'Social Enterprise: The New Economic Engine?', *Business Strategy Review*, 15(4): 39–43.

Harding, R. and Cowling, M. (2004). *Social Entrepreneurship Monitor: United Kingdom 2004*. London: Global Entrepreneurship Monitor.

Henton, D., Melville, J., and Walesh, K. (1997). 'The Age of the Civic Entrepreneur: Restoring Civil Society and Building Economic Community', *National Civic Review*, 86(2): 149–56.

Hersey, P. and Blanchard, K. (1982). *Management of Organizational Behaviour*. New Jersey, NJ: Prentice-Hall.

Hirsch, R. and Peters, M. (1998). *Entrepreneurship*. Boston, MA: Irwin/McGraw-Hill.

Holt, D. (2004). *How Brands Become Cultural Icons*. Harvard, MA: HBSP.

Hutton, W. (2005). 'How Would Confucius Vote?', *The Observer*, 27 March, p. 26.

James, E. (1989). *The Nonprofit Sector in International Perspective*. Yale, CT: Yale Studies on Nonprofit Organizations.

—— and Rose-Ackerman, S. (1986). *The Non-Profit Enterprise in Market Economics*. London: Routledge.

Johnson, S. (2000). 'Literature Review on Social Entrepreneurship', *Canadian Centre for Social Entrepreneurship Discussion Paper*, Available at: http://www.bus.ualberta.ca/ccse/WhatIs/Lit.%20Review%20SE%20November%202000.rtf.

Kanter, R. (May–June, 1999). 'From Spare Change to Real Change. The Social Sector as Beta Site for Business Innovation', *Harvard Business Review*: 122–32.

Kaplan, R. (2002). 'The Balanced Scorecard and Nonprofit Organizations', *Balanced Scorecard Report*: 2–6.

Kennedy, C. (2001). *Business Pioneers: Sainsbury, John Lewis, Cadbury*. London: Random House.

Kent, C., Sexton, D., and Vesper, K. (1982). *Encyclopaedia of Entrepreneurship*. New Jersey, NJ: Prentice-Hall.

Leadbeater, C. (1997). *The Rise of the Social Entrepreneur*. London: Demos.

—— and Goss, S. (1998). *Civic Entrepreneurs*. London: Demos.

Leat, D. (2003). *Replicating Successful Voluntary Sector Projects*. London: Association of Charitable Foundations.

Letts, C., Ryan, W., and Grossman, A. (March–April, 1997). 'Virtuous Capital: What Foundations Can Learn From Venture Capital', *Harvard Business Review*: 36–44.

Mair, J., Robinson, J., and Huckerts, K. (2006). *Social Entrepreneurship*. Basingstoke, UK: Palgrave Macmillan.

Martin, M. (2002). 'Between Entrepreneurship and Surveillance: An Interpretive Political Economy Perspective on the Globalizing Organization', *Entwicklungsethnologie*, 11(1): 83–110.

McClelland, D. (1961). *The Achieving Society*. Princeton, NJ: Van Nostrand.

Meehan, W., Kilmer, D., and O'Flanagan, M. (Spring, 2004). 'Investing in Society', *Stanford Social Innovation Review*: 34–43.

Moore, G. (2004). 'The Fair Trade Movement: Parameters, Issues and Future Research', *Journal of Business Ethics*, 53: 73–86.

NEF—New Economics Foundation (1999). *Regional Community Investment Partnerships*. London: NEF.

Nicholls, A. (2004). 'Social Entrepreneurship: The Emerging Landscape', in S. Crainer and D. Dearlove (eds.), *Financial Times Handbook of Management*, 3rd edn. Harlow, UK: FT Prentice-Hall, pp. 636–43.

—— (2006). 'Social Entrepreneurship', in D. Jones-Evans and S. Carter (eds.), *Enterprise and Small Business: Principles, Practice and Policy*, 2nd edn. Harlow, UK: FT Prentice-Hall.

—— and Alexander, A. (2006). 'Rediscovering Consumer-Producer Involvement: A Network Perspective on Fair Trade Marketing in the UK', *European Journal of Marketing*, 40 (forthcoming).

—— and Opal, C. (2005). *Fair Trade: Market-Driven Ethical Consumption*. London: Sage.

Nicholls, J. (2004). *Social Return on Investment: Valuing What Matters*. London: New Economics Foundation.

Osbourne, D. and Gaebler, T. (1992). *Reinventing Government*. Reading, MA: Addison-Wesley.

Oster, S. (1995). *Strategic Management for Nonprofit Organisations: Theory and Cases*. Oxford: Oxford University Press.

—— Massarsky, C., and Beinhacker, S. (2004). *Generating and Sustaining Nonprofit Earned Income*. San Francisco, CA: Jossey-Bass.

Powell, W. (1987). *The Nonprofit Sector: A Research Handbook*. Yale, CT: Yale University Press.

Putnam, R. (2001). *Bowling Alone*. New York: Simon & Schuster.

—— (ed.) (2004). *Democracies in Flux: The Evolution of Social Capital in Contemporary Society*. New York: Oxford University Press.

Quelch, J. and Laidler-Kylander, N. (2005). *The New Global Brands*. Mason, OH: Thomson.

Salamon, L. (2003). *The Resilient Sector: The State of Nonprofit America*. Washington, DC: Brookings Institution Press.

—— and Anheier, H. (1999). *The Emerging Sector Revisited*. Baltimore, MD: Johns Hopkins University.

Samuelson, P. (1954). 'The Pure Theory of Public Expenditure', *Review of Economics and Statistics*, 36(4): 387–9.

Sawhill, J. and Williamson, D. (2001). 'Measuring What Matters in Nonprofits', *McKinsey Quarterly*, 2: 98–107.

Say, J.-B. (2001). M. Quddus and S. Rashid (eds.), *A Treatise on Political Economy*. London: Transaction Publishing.

Schumpeter, A. (1980). *Theory of Economic Development*. London: Transaction Publishing.

Shane, S. and Venkataraman, S. (2000). 'The Promise of Entrepreneurship as a Field of Research', *Academy of Management Review*, 25(1): 217–26.

Smallbone, D., Evans, M., Ekanem, I., and Butters, S. (2001). *Researching Social Enterprise*. Middlesex University.

Social Enterprise Coalition (2003). *There's More to Business Than You Think. A Guide to Social Enterprise*. London: SEC.

Social Enterprise London—SEL (2000). *Enterprise for Communities—Creating Sustainable Social Enterprises*. London: SEL.

Spear, R. and Bidet, E. (2003). *The Role of Social Enterprise in European Labour Markets*, EMES Working Papers Series 3/10.

Spengler, J. and Ford, T. (2002). *From the Environmentally Challenged City to the Ecological City*, Available at: http://www.earthscape.org/p3/ger01/ger02.pdf.

Stogdill, R. (1974). *Handbook of Leadership*. New York: Free Press.

Sullivan Mort, G., Weerawardena, J., and Carnegie, K. (2003). 'Social Entrepreneurship: Towards Conceptualisation', *International Journal of Nonprofit and Voluntary Sector Marketing*, 8(1): 76–88.

The Economist (1999). 'Is There a Crisis?', 15 July.

—— (2004a). 'More or Less Equal?', 11 March.

—— (2004b). 'Doing Well and Doing Good', 29 July.

—— (2005a). 'Something Stirs', 3 March.

—— (2005b). 'The Glue of Society', 14 July.

Thompson, J. (2002). 'The World of the Social Entrepreneur', *International Journal of Public Sector Management*, 15(5): 412–31.

—— Alvy, G., and Lees, A. (2000). 'Social Entrepreneurship—A New Look at the People and the Potential', *Management Decision*, 38(5): 328–38.

Venkataraman, S. (1997). 'The Distinctive Domain of Entrepreneurship Research. An Editor's Perspective', in J. Katz and R. Brockhaus (eds.), *Advances in Entrepreneurship, Firm Emergence, and Growth*, vol. 3. Greenwich, CT: JAI Press, pp. 119–38.

World Bank (2004). *World Development Report 2004: Making Services Work for Poor People*, Available at: http://econ.worldbank.org/WBSITE/EXTERNAL/EXTDEC/EXTRE SEARCH/EXTWDRS/0,,contentMDK:20227703~pagePK:478093~piPK:477627~theSi-tePK:477624,00.html.

Young, W. and Welford, R. (2002). *Ethical Shopping*. London: Fusion Press.

Zadek, S. (1998). 'Balancing Performance, Ethics, and Accountability', *Journal of Business Ethics*, 17(13): 1421–41.

Part I

New Perspectives

1

Social Business Entrepreneurs Are the Solution

Muhammad Yunus

Capitalism Is Interpreted too Narrowly

Many of the problems in the world remain unresolved because we continue to interpret capitalism too narrowly. In this narrow interpretation we create a one-dimensional human being to play the role of entrepreneur. We insulate him from other dimensions of life such as religious, emotional, and political dimensions. He is dedicated to one mission in his business life—to maximize profit. He is supported by masses of one-dimensional human beings who back him up with their investment money to achieve the same mission. The game of free market works out beautifully with one-dimensional investors and entrepreneurs. We have remained so mesmerized by the success of the free market that we never dared to express any doubt about it. We worked extra hard to transform ourselves, as closely as possible, into the one-dimensional human beings as conceptualized in theory to allow the smooth functioning of free market mechanisms.

Economic theory postulates that you are contributing to the society and the world in the best possible manner if you just concentrate on squeezing out the maximum for yourself. When you get your maximum, everybody else will get his or her maximum. As we devotedly follow this policy sometimes doubts appear in our mind whether we are doing the right thing. Things do not look too good around us. We quickly brush off our doubts by saying all these bad things happen because of 'market failures'; a well-functioning market cannot produce unpleasant results.

I think things are going wrong not because of 'market failure'. It is much deeper than that. Let us be brave and admit that it is because of 'conceptualization failure'. More specifically, it is the failure to capture the essence of a human being in our theory. Everyday human beings are not one-dimensional entities; they are excitingly multi-dimensional and indeed very colourful.

Their emotions, beliefs, priorities, and behaviour patterns can be more aptly described by drawing an analogy with the basic colours and millions of colours and shades they produce.

Social Business Entrepreneurs Can Play an Important Role in the Market

Let us suppose that we postulate a world with two kinds of people, both one-dimensional, but having different objectives. One type is the existing type, i.e. the profit maximizing type. The second is a new type of person, who is not interested in profit maximization. He is totally committed to make a difference to the world. He is social-objective driven. He wants to give a better chance in life to other people. He wants to achieve his objective through creating and supporting sustainable business enterprises. Such businesses may or may not earn profit, but like any other business they must not incur losses. They create a new class of business that we may describe as 'non-loss' business.

Can we find this second type of person in the real world? Yes, we can. Are we not familiar with 'do-gooders'? Do-gooders are the same people who are sometimes referred to as 'social entrepreneurs' in formal parlance. Social entrepreneurship is an integral part of human history. Most people take pleasure in helping others. All religions encourage this quality in human beings. Governments reward them by giving tax breaks. Special legal facilities are created for them so that they can create legal entities to pursue their objectives.

Some social entrepreneurs use money to achieve their objectives; some just give away their time, labour, talent, skill, or such other contributions that are useful to others. Those who use money may or may not try to recover part or all of the money they put into their work by charging a fee or a price.

We may classify the social entrepreneur, who uses money, into four types:

1. No cost recovery
2. Some cost recovery
3. Full cost recovery
4. More than full cost recovery

Once a social entrepreneur operates at 100 per cent or beyond the cost recovery point he has entered the business world with limitless possibilities. This is a moment worth celebrating. He has overcome the gravitational force of financial dependence and now is ready for space flight! This is the critical moment of significant institutional transformation. He has moved from the world of philanthropy to the world of business. To distinguish him from the first two types of social entrepreneurs listed earlier, we will call him 'social business entrepreneur'.

With the introduction of social business entrepreneurs, the marketplace becomes more interesting and competitive. Interesting because two different kinds of objectives are now at play, creating two different sets of frameworks for price determination: competitive because there are more players now than before. These new players can be equally aggressive and enterprising in achieving their goals as traditional entrepreneurs.

Social business entrepreneurs can become very powerful players in the national and international economy. Today if we added up the assets of all the social business entrepreneurs in the world, it would not add up to even a tiny fraction of the global economy. It is not because they lack growth potential, but because conceptually we have neither recognized their existence nor have we made any room for them in the market as yet. They are considered freaks, and kept outside the mainstream economy. We do not pay any attention to them, because our eyes are blinded by the theories taught in our schools.

If social business entrepreneurs exist in the real world—as it seems they surely do—it makes no sense that we do not make room for them in our current conceptual frameworks. Once we have recognized them, supportive institutions, policies, regulations, norms, and rules will come into being to help them enter the mainstream.

The neoliberal free market is often considered to be ill-equipped to address social problems. Indeed, the market is often identified as significantly contributing to creating social problems (such as environmental hazards, inequality, health problems, unemployment, ghettoes, crimes, etc.). Since the market is perceived as having no capacity to solve social problems, this responsibility is typically handed over to the public sector. This arrangement was widely considered as the only solution until command economies—such as the former Soviet Union—were created where the state took over everything, abolishing the free market.

But this did not last long. With command economies gone we are back to the artificial division of work between the market and the state. In this arrangement, the market is turned into the exclusive playground of the personal gain seekers, overwhelmingly ignoring the common interest of communities and the world as a whole.

With the global economy continuing to expand year-on-year, personal wealth in many developed countries reaching unimaginable heights, technological innovations supporting the continuation of economic growth, globalization threatening to wipe out the weak economies and the poor from the economic map, it is time to consider the case for social business entrepreneurs more seriously than we ever did before. Not only is it not necessary to leave the market solely to the personal-gain seekers, it is extremely harmful to mankind as a whole to do that. It is time to move away from a narrow interpretation of capitalism and broaden the concept of the market by giving full recognition to social business entrepreneurs. Once this is done, social business entrepreneurs can flood the market and make it work for social goals as efficiently as it does for personal goals.

Social Stock Market

So, how do we encourage creation of social business entrepreneurs? What are the steps that we need to take to facilitate social business entrepreneurs to play a bigger and bigger role in the marketplace?

First, we must recognize the social business entrepreneur in our theory. Students must learn that businesses are of two kinds:

1. Businesses to make money
2. Businesses to do good for others

Young people must learn that they have a choice to make about which kind of entrepreneur they would like to be. If we broaden the interpretation of capitalism even more, they will have a wider choice of mixing these two basic types in proportions just right for their own personal objectives.

Second, we must make the social business entrepreneurs and social business investors visible in the marketplace. As long as social business entrepreneurs operate within the cultural environment of present stock markets they will remain restricted by the existing norms and conditions of trading. Social business entrepreneurs must develop their own norms, standards, measurements, evaluation criteria, and terminology. This can be achieved only if we create a separate stock market for social business enterprises and investors. We can call it the 'social capital market'. Investors will come here to invest their money for the cause they believe in, and in the company they think is doing the best in achieving a particular mission. There may be some companies listed in this social capital market who are excellent in achieving their mission whilst at the same time making very attractive profits. Obviously, these companies will attract both kinds of investors, social goal oriented as well as personal gain oriented.

Making profit will not disqualify an enterprise from being a social business enterprise. The basic deciding factor for this will be whether the social goal remains the enterprise's overarching goal, and it is clearly reflected in its decision-making. There will be well-defined, stringent, entry and exit criteria for a company to qualify to be listed in the social capital market and to lose that status, where necessary. Soon companies will emerge which will succeed in mixing both social goals and personal goals. Investors must remain convinced that companies listed in the social capital market are truly social business enterprises.

Along with the creation of the social capital market, we will need to create rating agencies, appropriate impact assessment tools, indices to understand which social business enterprise is doing more of and/or better than others. In this way, social investors can be correctly guided. This new industry will need its own *Social Wall Street Journal* and *Social Financial Times* to bring out all the exciting, as well as the terrible, news stories and analyses to keep social entrepreneurs and investors properly informed.

Within business schools we can start producing social MBAs to meet the demand of the social business entrepreneurs, as well as preparing young people to become social business entrepreneurs themselves. I think young people will respond very enthusiastically to the challenge of making serious contributions to the world by becoming this new form of entrepreneur.

We will need to arrange financing for social business entrepreneurs. New bank branches specializing in financing social business ventures will have to appear. New investment 'angels' will have to come forth. Social venture capitalists will have to join hands with the social business entrepreneurs.

How to Make a Start

One good way to get started with creating social business enterprises would be to launch a design competition for social business enterprises. There could be a local, a regional, and a global competition. Prizes for successful designs could come in the shape of financing for the enterprises or as partnerships for implementing the projects. All submitted social business proposals could be published so that these can become the 'open source' starting points for the social entrepreneurs in the next cycle.

A social business entrepreneur could start the social capital market itself as a social business enterprise. One business school, or several business schools, could join hands to launch this as a project and then start serious business transactions.

Let us not expect that a social business enterprise will come up, from its very birth, with all the answers to a social problem. Most likely, it will proceed in steps. Each step may lead to the next level of achievement. Grameen Bank is a good example in this regard. In creating Grameen Bank I never had a blueprint to follow. I moved one step at a time; always thinking this step will be my last step. But it was not. That one step led me to another step, a step, which looked so interesting that it was difficult to walk away from it. I faced this situation at every turn.

I started my work by giving a small amount of money to a few poor people without any collateral. Then I realized how good the people felt about it. I needed more money to expand the programme. To access bank money, I offered myself as a guarantor. To get support from another bank, I converted my project into the bank's project. Later, I turned it into a central bank project. Over time I saw that the best strategy would be to create an independent bank to do the work that we did. So we did. We converted the project into a formal bank, borrowing money from the central bank to lend money to the borrowers. Since donors became interested in our work, and wanted to support us, we borrowed and received grants from international donors. At one stage we decided to be self-reliant. This led us to focus on generating money internally by collecting deposits. Now Grameen Bank has more money in deposits than it lends out to borrowers. It lends out half a billion dollars a year, in loans averaging under $200 (£116), to 4.5 million borrowers, without collateral, and maintains a 99 per cent repayment record.

We introduced many programmes into the bank—housing loans, student loans, pension funds, loans to purchase mobile phones to become the village telephone ladies, loans to beggars to become door-to-door salesmen. One came after another.

If we create the right environment, social business entrepreneurs can use market mechanisms to significant effect and make the market an exciting place for fighting social battles in ever more innovative and effective ways. Let us get serious now about social business entrepreneurs. They can brighten up this gloomy world for us all.

2

The Citizen Sector Transformed

Bill Drayton

Over the last two and a half decades, the operating half of the world that deals with social issues has gone through an historical transformation of unprecedented speed and scale. It has gone from pre-modern to entrepreneurial and competitive—in precisely the same sense as those words are used in business.

This is a profound change in architecture. It is a change with huge relevance for almost everyone. For millions it is a career change waiting to happen. For those running businesses, governments, universities, and—certainly—citizen groups, it is bringing profound changes to the strategic environments facing these institutions. Five years ago, for example, business strategists could afford to pay little attention to the sector. If they do so five years hence, they will probably be committing malpractice. The same is true for scholars or journalists whose job it is to understand and explain the forces at work in society.

It is the world's leading social entrepreneurs who have been driving this transformation of the citizen sector. Florence Nightingale transformed public health, nursing, housing codes, even the use of statistics in public discourse. She was at least as powerful an entrepreneur as Andrew Carnegie. Today's Nightingales include Mohammed Yunus, who marketed microcredit globally, and Jeroo Billimoria, whose Childline free telephone hotline for and staffed by street children has swept India and is now spreading globally.

The defining quality of leading social entrepreneurs is that they cannot come to rest until they have changed the pattern in their field *all* across society. Their life vision is this new pattern. Scholars and artists take delight in seeing and expressing an insight; professionals in serving a client; managers an institution. It is only the entrepreneurs who cannot stop until they have changed the whole society. Once one understands this, one understands why they are equally focused on the 'how to's'—How am I going to get from here to there? How do I solve this problem? How can I make these pieces fit together?—as on the vision. And why they will stick with it for many years, even decades.

As the number of such top tier social entrepreneurs multiplies, the rate and scope of social innovation multiplies—just as it did earlier once business entrepreneurs were set free and encouraged.

The wise economist, William J. Baumol, reports that from the time of ancient Rome to 1700 there was *zero* growth in per capita income in the West. And then, over the next three centuries, it grew 20, 200, and 740 per cent (Baumol 2002, 2004).

What caused this dramatic take-off? Business became entrepreneurial and competitive. This profound change in the architecture of this half of society set in motion a compounding of innovation and its spread. The newspapers over these three centuries continued to focus on wars and earthquakes, but the underlying historical force that drove everything before it was this change in human architecture.

From 1700 until roughly 1980, the social other half of society remained stuck. Despite individual exceptions like Nightingale and Maria Montessori, it did not become structurally competitive and, therefore, experienced little innovation and productivity growth.

Why did it fall so dramatically behind? First, there was no pressure because it was so easy to tax the *new* wealth being created by business to pay for the canals, roads, schools, and welfare systems. Second, the money flowed through monopoly institutions—and no monopoly, regardless of sector, welcomes competition because it cannot long survive it. With no pressure to change and the paymaster opposed, the sector fell into a state of acute relative squalor: poor performance, low repute and self-esteem, miserable salaries, little élan. That is where the sector languished until just a few decades ago.

Around 1980 the dam broke. The business/social productivity gap (and the consequent imbalances of the 'consumer society') became too extreme. Too many serious social problems festered unsolved. Democracy, education, and self-confidence were growing. The first generation of post-colonial adults was coming of professional age; and, unlike the prior generation whose dream it was to wrest control of government from the British or the Dutch, it was not focused only on government. Moreover, between 1980 and 1989, the generals retreated in Latin America and the Berlin Wall fell.

Except where fearful governments blocked it (e.g. Myanmar), the citizen sector became structurally entrepreneurial and competitive across the continents with a speed and energy that is probably historically unparalleled.

Whereas the business/social gap within the most societies has been less recognized than the world's north/south gap, it is often as wide. On the other hand, it is easier for a brother in the citizen sector to learn from a sister in business than it has been for Thais to learn from Germans. As a result, the citizen sector has been rapidly closing the productivity gap over the last twenty-five years. Ashoka estimates that the citizen sector is halving the gap every ten to twelve years in the countries and regions where it is large and competitive.

One measure of the sector's growing productivity is its rapid progress from isolated local efforts (the 'They're just a drop in the ocean' phase) to national force (e.g. the impeachment of President Collor in Brazil) and, now, to global connectedness and power.

The only reason we now have the International Criminal Court is that 2,000 citizen groups got together and blasted it out of the attic where the nation states had kept it locked up for over fifty years.

And that is only the beginning. Ideas now move from Bangladesh to the USA to Brazil—in fact, all across the world—quickly. This new wiring is one example of how the sector's productivity is growing dramatically.

With every such acceleration in its productivity catch-up, the citizen sector attracts a larger share of society's resources. Hence the sector's explosive growth over the last several decades:

- In the UK, the sector's contribution to GDP grew 260 per cent from 1991 to 2001 (NCVO 2004)

- In Germany from 1960 to 2000 full-time equivalent employment shrank 2 per cent in business, roughly doubled from 1960 to 1990 then stalled in government, but almost quadrupled in the citizen sector (see Figure 2.1)

- In the USA, the number of citizen sector organizations almost tripled from 1982 to 2002 (with the rate of increase accelerating over the last decade) while religious congregations barely grew 10 per cent and all other organizations grew somewhat more than 60 per cent (Weitzman 2002)

- In Indonesia, the number of known environmental organizations grew from 1 in 1983 to over 2,000 in 1997 (Bornstein 2004: 4)

- In Brazil, the number of citizen groups grew from at most 36,000 but probably less than 5,000 to 400,000 registered and an estimated total of 1,000,000 in the twenty years since the military withdrew (Bornstein 2004: 4) (Bornstein and Ashoka analysis – WD)

- In forty-eight countries, the average annual growth rate in the number of citizen organization members and volunteers accelerated over the 1990s. For example, the annual membership growth rate expanded from 3 to 5 per cent in community action; from 2 to 3 per cent in human rights; from 4 to 6 per cent in the environment, and from 1 to 2.5 per cent in peace (Salamon et al. 2003)

These figures and many more document a primary historical wave.

Even so, they do not capture the sector's growing sophistication and effectiveness. When a region has hundreds of thousands or millions of citizen groups, the productivity-sharpening effect of competition is unavoidable.

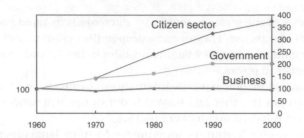

German employment indexed to 1960

Figure 2.1 The same historical forces are at work even in the German heart of Europe
Source: McKinsey analysis of data from Johns Hopkins nonprofit sector series.

Moreover, as the field matures, large, sophisticated second and third generation citizen groups emerge. In Bangladesh, for example, in terms of full-time equivalent paid employment, the largest citizen group, BRAC, is four times bigger than the biggest business. And the second largest, Grameen, is tied for third place with the second largest business.

Moreover, the field is, as we discussed, moving forcefully onto the global playing field. The number of registered international citizen groups increased 450 per cent from 1990 to 2000 (Drayton 2005).

How do a small number of pattern-change leading social entrepreneurs trigger such an extraordinary primary historical force? The process is very similar to that reported in the familiar literature describing the diffusion of primary scientific ideas—how each moves down and across society, sector by sector, over time.

When a social entrepreneur successfully introduces a fundamental pattern change, something very similar occurs. Consider the entrepreneur's impact on a local community. The entrepreneur's new idea challenges existing patterns, be it how the schools organize sports or how poor people obtain housing—and the assumption that things cannot be changed. These impacts are a bit like ploughing the earth before seeding.

At the same time, the entrepreneur is planting a seed—his/her idea. That seed has been carefully designed to be as simple and user-friendly as possible. Why? Because the entrepreneur cannot succeed unless local people in thousands of communities take up his/her idea and make it fly.

As primary social entrepreneurs plough and seed, the number of local change makers multiplies. Someone in the local community says 'ah, I see an opportunity'. And then that person plants the seed and grows it. And thereby becomes a local role model just as much as the originating entrepreneur.

As the number of primary social entrepreneurs in a country increases, the rate of ploughing and seeding in any local community accelerates. As the citizen sector wires itself together globally, as ideas suddenly move easily from Bangladesh to Poland and the USA, every community experiences more and more ploughing and seeding, more and more local change makers. As the number of local change makers increases, barriers are replaced by support institutions and respect, which encourages yet more family, friends, and neighbours to step up and take on other challenges.

As this base across society builds, each new generation of leading social entrepreneurs will find its task easier. And its numbers will increase as at least a few local change makers learn and grow in confidence.

This dynamic lies close to the heart of the change I have been describing. The idea that one can become a change maker, not just an object, is highly contagious. And the energy that anyone so empowered brings to bear is extraordinary.

Increasingly, Ashoka has come to understand that, indeed, its ultimate objective is to make 'everyone a change maker'—a world where everyone, as he/she courses through society will take delight in and be capable of solving any problem encountered. This is a world very different from that of the preceding 15,000 years.

The agricultural revolution produced only enough surplus to enable a few per cent to move into the small towns, develop culture, and rule everyone else. A few per cent have, by and large, ruled ever since.

As Jeff Skoll, co-founder of eBay, commented, 'With social entrepreneurship, we're talking about nothing less than the democratization of power' (Skoll 2004).

And it is the only way society can plausibly overcome the complexity and scale of the problems we now face. When everyone is a change maker, the problems can no longer outrun the solutions.

There is only one thing more powerful than a big idea in the hands of a leading entrepreneur (business or social), and that is when they work together. And, indeed, increasingly social entrepreneurs and the larger citizen sector behind them (many millions of organizations) are becoming a field.

Just how intelligently these entrepreneurs and citizen organizations across the planet learn to work together (and with the other dimensions of society) is now by far the field's most important challenge. Now that the field has huge momentum, its long-term patterns and institutions are developing and crystallizing very quickly—simply because all these practitioners need pattern and predictability. However, without wise leadership, there is no guarantee that this crystallization will see logic overcome inertia.

The stakes are enormous. That is so because once the field has crystallized, significant change becomes all but impossible. Why? Because, by then, the field will have become an organism in which each part connects to and reinforces many other parts. Thousands of valued cross-cutting synergies will have taken hold. A reformer who tries to pull on any one piece will quickly find that he/she faces resistance from the many other elements that will be affected. This difficulty, a bit like trying to pull one stick from a beaver dam by hand, is why management consultants have long since learned that, for any one change to stick, they must change all dimensions of an organization. Otherwise, the larger organism will kill the change much as the body rejects (kills) foreign organs introduced into it.

Let me outline four critical design choices now facing the field, choices that will be made, for good or ill, before too many more years pass. In each case, the outcome hangs uncertainly in the balance.

Global Operational Integration

This is the first field, especially its cutting edge of leading social entrepreneurs, which needs to be operationally integrated globally. Very few social problems now are not, at least in significant part, global. Further, even when solutions can be implemented at a lower level, there are enormous economies that come from thinking and problem solving together across the globe.

Moreover, if the world is to grow together and not disintegrate, weaving its leading creators of the future together in a trusting community may well make a critical difference.

This is especially important once one grasps that binding the world together is not likely to come from the leadership of one person or group who will do for all humanity what Jean Monnet and his colleagues did a half century ago for Europe. Instead, it is the dynamic of a competitive citizen sector increasingly operating at the global level that, more than any other force, will do the job.

Once one pioneer social entrepreneur and his/her group operating at this level succeed, competitors will seek out the next step. Otherwise they risk falling behind. For example, now that there is an International Criminal Court, however limited, human rights and other groups will try to get the court's jurisdiction expanded to cover their issues, to persuade new countries to adhere to the court, and otherwise to compete by finding new ways to strengthen global jurisprudence.

This is the promise.

However, one citizen group after another has failed to build an operationally integrated global institution. One after another, they have been reduced to little more than shared brand names—wrecked on the reefs of jealously divisive national laws. Much practised use of national, religious, ideological, and other fault lines for power purposes. And a still weak grasp of just how important integration is.

Social/Business Reintegration

For three centuries the social and business halves of society drifted apart. So far apart that they developed different languages, styles, legal structures, and mutually negative stereotypes of one another.

This compounding division was an historical accident, a giant navigational error. Nonetheless, the inertia of division remains strong.

Every major need that a person has—be it housing or health care—is now served by separate business and social systems that have not talked for centuries. It is hard to imagine a more incompetent way of doing things: or a bigger opportunity—a huge societywide productivity gain.

Building on the experience of over 400 of the 1,700 Fellows whose work is focused on ensuring full economic citizenship for everyone, Ashoka is now well into a programme that is demonstrating just how enormously profitable for all parties—businesses, citizen organizations, and the ultimate consumers—seizing this productivity gain opportunity is. Major corporations in building products and irrigation equipment on several continents have entered into contractual agreements with leading citizen organizations, with Ashoka helping both parties. Negotiations are in progress in the forest and health areas. The goal is to create new production, financing, and distribution chains that draw on the relative strengths of each side to produce much enhanced value for everyone.

For example, in Mexico, a partnership between Amanco, which produces drip irrigation equipment, and rural citizen groups that grew rapidly over the last decade and now serve many, many thousands of small farmers, is enabling these smallholders to gain access to this technology for the first time. The citizen groups know the farmers and have very low operating costs. Amanco has the advantage in manufacturing. Combining these strengths gives the farmers larger and more stable incomes, water conservation, and environmental benefits. The citizen groups gain competitive leverage by bringing these advantages to their clients plus a very major and growing new source of revenue that will free them from dependence on governments and foundations. Amanco is the first company in its industry to open this major new and highly profitable market. It is also learning how to work with the newly competitive citizen sector, a skill that will later help it open other new markets ahead of its competitors.

Once Ashoka has successful demonstrations in four industries, it and its partners will market this new paradigm to business schools and publications, to the citizen sector, and to management consulting firms. Because building these new production and distribution systems will create decades of business for, and many new partners in, the consulting firms, Ashoka hopes within a few years to hand off its catalytic role to the consultancy firms.

This business/social production and distribution system work is one of a large portfolio of high leverage investments Ashoka is making in building bridges between the two sectors. The levers that give this example its power work in many of the other cases as well. Now that both sectors are highly competitive, competition will drive other businesses and other citizen groups to enter once the advantages of doing so are clear. Moreover, once buttoned-up business managers and down dressing citizen group leaders decide that working together is *really* profitable, they will begin tearing down the stylistic and other barriers built up over centuries.

The field needs to develop new relationships with other sectors, including governments and universities. However, no relationship needs more work or is more important than that with business. Nor is any more promising given that both now are entrepreneurial and competitive and given that the productivity gap is eroding fast.

Disciplined Judgement

There is one area where the citizen sector should *not* be like business. It must not be driven to overreliance on numeric analysis in decision-making at the expense of judgement: least of all when the most important application of judgement—to value-based vision and its close cousin, ethical fibre—is called for.

Selecting pattern-change social entrepreneurs (or other types of leaders) at the start of their careers requires this sort of disciplined judgement. This is what Ashoka's five-step selection process does (Ashoka 2005a). It achieves consistent results on every continent every year over five years of evaluations. Five years after selection, 88 per cent have had their innovation copied by independent institutions and between 50 and 60 per cent have changed national policy.

There is significant risk here. Too many scholars, foundation officers, government grant managers, and business executives—all reinforcing one another rather like an echo chamber—are pressing the sector in this direction.

There is nothing wrong with numbers or with analysing them.

However, if the discussion focuses disproportionately here, and if numeric tools are better developed, more accessible, and more valued than judgement, the field will suffer. Business seems to have suffered from just such an imbalance. This is the prime theory advanced to explain why privately held companies have been doing better (even in financial terms) than their publicly held peers.

By contrast, the legal system has been built to make judgements. Its core challenge is to *judge* who is telling the truth, a task not readily delegated to statistical analysis. Hence its reliance on juries on the one hand and on judges controlling the presentation of arguments and evidence so as to maximize the probability of a just result on the other.

The citizen sector cannot afford to fear judgement. It must decide where it must make judgements and develop disciplined, generalizable ways of doing so (Ashoka 2005*b*). This is not an easy challenge, but it is practicable and well worth the effort. Not investing heavily here now risks the field settling into patterns that could well prove intellectually crippling in the long term.

Social Investing Innovation

The rapid transformation and explosive growth of the citizen sector's operations over the last twenty-five years is beginning to stimulate a wave of innovation in social financing. Socially responsible investing and microfinance are, for example, now both well established.

However, very little has changed in the provision of institutional finance to operating citizen organizations. With quantitatively minute exceptions, the only options are government agencies, foundations, and (very limited) corporate foundations. As the sector is growing many times faster than foundation assets, the current situation is pushing the citizen sector back into growing dependence on government—precisely the situation that led to its three century productivity lag.

Moreover, despite the efforts of the many dedicated people working in these institutions, their structure makes it very difficult for them to serve social entrepreneurs well. The entrepreneur needs an institution that will back his or her new idea, but government agencies serve legislated goals and foundations follow their own internally created 'strategies'. The social entrepreneur needs investors who are comfortable cutting across categories, since the most interesting new solutions typically are cross-cutting—but this makes a programme officer's job far more difficult because it requires consultation and power sharing with other offices. The entrepreneur needs to build an institution, but that is 'overhead'. The social entrepreneur needs even longer term financing than business peers given the stickiness of public decision-making, but these investors are short term.

This is not a job for the social entrepreneur; it is a life calling. Every day, year in, year out, without which significant pattern change is impossible. Sustained *personal* loyalty to the social entrepreneur is critical for both the venture and its creator—but this is impossible for such institutions.

The current structures are also stultifying for many who wish to engage in social investing. Assistant secretaries and division chiefs, foundation presidents and officers are channelled and hedged about by their legislation, strategies, and organizational stovepipes as firmly as are their investees. What structures, for example, are ready to accommodate a social investor who would most enjoy making a big, multi-year commitment to a great idea–entrepreneur combination once every few years and then spend 85 per cent of his or her time working with two or three such partners?

When a service industry's clients have changed radically and it has not, and when clients and even many members of the industry feel crimped, the time is ripe for social entrepreneurs to go to work.

Where are the richest opportunities? While it is always highly dangerous to predict what a wave of entrepreneurship will produce, let me outline one of the most important options.

The for-profit finance industry constitutes roughly 10 per cent of the world economy. It is a highly competitive, flexible industry. Its job is to seek out opportunities to connect investors and investees and to do so in the most mutually beneficial ways.

What if this industry began to experience immense new opportunities, on both supply and demand sides, as a result of the emergence worldwide of a highly competitive, competent citizen sector that is now both huge and growing several times faster than the rest of the economy? The opportunities increasingly are there. The citizen sector now has many large, trustworthy institutions. The reintegration with business both makes the sector more understandable and is multiplying investment opportunities that will yield positive economic as well as social and engagement returns. Consider the Amanco–Ashoka–citizen sector collaboration that provides small farmers access to irrigation described earlier. The citizen groups need start-up funding until they reach break even, and the small farmers need loans to purchase the equipment. The latter (adequately secured) loans, moreover, would benefit from a securitized secondary market.

Once a few pioneer financial firms succeed in breaking open a profitable social investing market, their competitors will have to follow. At that point, these institutions' product development departments and bankers will launch an enduring competition to find and serve new investor/investee opportunities. These institutions could well eventually dominate the social investing market. In any case, they certainly will inject a much needed competitive, client-oriented spirit to the sector. Their engagement will also subtly, steadily encourage business–social bridging.

The new socially entrepreneurial/competitive citizen sector has matured to the point that it is the most hopeful force driving history. It is now crystallizing patterns that will define its effectiveness for the long term. Ensuring that these patterns are as intelligent as possible could not be more important.

References

Ashoka (2005*a*). *Selecting Leading Social Entrepreneurs*, Available at: www.ashoka.org

—— (2005*b*). *Alternative Financial Services*, Available at: www.ashoka.org

Baumol, W. (2002). *The Free-Market Innovation Machine*. Princeton, NJ: Princeton University Press.

—— (2004). Personal Conversations with the Author.

Bornstein, D. (2004). *How to Change the World*. Oxford: Oxford University Press.

Drayton, W. (2005). 'Where the Real Power Lies', *Alliance*, 10(1): 29–30.

National Council for Voluntary Organizations (2004). 'Exploring the Role of the Third Sector in Public Service Delivery and Reform'.

Salamon, L., Anheier, H., List, R., Toepler, S., and Sokolowski, W. (eds.) (2003). *Global Civil Society: Dimensions of the Non-Profit Sector*. Baltimore, MD: Johns Hopkins University.

Skoll, J. (March 2004). 'Social Entrepreneurship: The 21st Century Revolution', delivered at Saïd Business School, Oxford University, UK.

Weitzman, M. (2002). *The New Nonprofit Almanac & Desk Reference: The Essential Facts and Figures for Managers, Researchers, and Volunteers*. San Francisco, CA: Jossey-Bass.

3

For What It Is Worth: Social Value and the Future of Social Entrepreneurship

Rowena Young

Introduction: Social Value and Its Discontents

All entrepreneurs try to create value. Whatever their business, value is their stock in trade. For entrepreneurs in the commercial sector, there are well-established methods for determining how much value they make. It is also clear who does the valuing. At least in the economies driven by international capital markets, the owners of capital and their agents determine business worth. None of their methods is perfect. All of them rely on the considerable exercise of judgement. But at least commercial entrepreneurs can expect to participate in shared assumptions and shared processes of valuation (e.g. looking at price/earnings ratios). Whatever other sorts of value businesses create as they go about their work, the financial profit, the traditional bottom line, is accepted as the most important measure of value.

By contrast, social entrepreneurs are said to create value which is social. Whatever it is, it benefits people whose urgent and reasonable needs are not being met by other means. This output appears to strike the majority as so obvious that it has evaded much comment. The people developing new metrics (see, e.g. http://www.neweconomics.org/gen/newways_socialreturn.aspx for an overview of one of the new approaches, 'social return on investment') have been preoccupied with capturing the value emanating from the social sector, but their work has not required them to reflect further on what it is or how it is comprised, or where they have, these considerations have not been a priority. Perhaps the ways we think about business have become so embedded and persuasive—and of increasing influence in the social sector—that we have simply transposed the idea of one sort of value creation for another.

The world is currently replete with methods for analysing value. They range from contingent valuation methods and hedonic pricing in economics to whole life cost methodologies and ecological footprints; from balanced scorecards, triple bottom lines, and social audits in business to benchmarking, cost benefit analysis, and customer satisfaction surveys in public sector, not excluding a wide variety of human development and quality of life indices.

Most of these themselves combine diverse elements. They generally include quantitative and qualitative elements; varied timescales; public and private benefits; a wide range of types of valuation in terms of reliability and certainty (e.g. varying from the value of a building to the much less predictable value of cutting crime); and often try to make sense of widely varying interests.

The field is changing fast, but from the perspective of social entrepreneurship five particularly crucial features of value should be emphasized:

- First, value is subjective; it is a matter of real life experiences. The processes of consumption, participation in, and co-construction of social value are intimately related to their effects. So, for example, the social value of a programme for disadvantaged young people cannot simply rely on traditional economic measures of income gained and employability: it also needs to reflect their own experience, and whether they felt empowered or disempowered. Similarly, the value of care for the disabled depends greatly on how it is delivered as well as on objective outcomes.

- Second, social value is negotiated between stakeholders. So, to pursue the example given earlier, in Britain, the government's employment service (known as Job Centre Plus) counts the number of entrants to work who remain in their jobs thirteen weeks later. At the same time, with the same individuals, a youth homelessness charity may monitor a set of factors in their clients' circumstances, all of which have a bearing on their prospects of sustaining employment. These might include their housing security, the quality of their friendships, their drug use and mental well-being, and their continuing socialization into work and skills development. Both have come to a recognition that the concept of social exclusion more readily encapsulates the condition these young people experience, and its correlate—social inclusion—provides a more reliable guide to their economic status than joblessness per se. But they are beholden to different stakeholders, with somewhat different motivations and demands. The government needs to demonstrate efficiency with taxpayers' money. The charity needs to demonstrate to its donors that it is doing everything it can to enable young people to overcome their difficulties. Both are acting responsibly, but differently and together.

- Third, social value is contingent and open to reappraisal. So too is commercial value. However, the price mechanism supplies a means by which economic value is defined at the point of sale at a certain point in time. At the point of sale, supplier and consumer agree on the economic value of the exchange. The relationship is one of equivalence (at least outside of monopolistic settings). Demand may ebb and flow, but businesses enjoy a reliable means of determining their current value and making predictions based on this information in ways that investors and other stakeholders accept. The social sector enjoys no such certainty. What seems valuable to one generation becomes a legacy of guilt and destruction to the next, as in the cases of colonialism, communism, or disposable consumption. Similarly, but more fortuitously, people may multiply an investment in their skills over and over during their lifetimes. The relationship between resources expended and perceived social return can often seem asymmetrical.

• Fourth, social value brings together incommensurable elements which cannot easily be aggregated within a single metric; for example, the relative value of equality and asset values; sustainability for future generations and income streams.

• Finally, there is no escaping the fact that values are inseparable when it comes to social activity. Ideas of justice, self-determination, and respect are all inherent to social value generation since the processes of exchange that enable value to be realized affect all participants and often reflect their relative standings and power. Attempts to define or measure social value must, therefore, start with some explicit discussion of values and which are relevant and why.

In real life environments the sort of comparability that is so important in traditional financial markets becomes much less feasible for units of social value. If, for example, your concern as a philanthropist is to fund viable businesses in post-tsunami Aceh, it matters less whether businesses elsewhere offer a higher social return, since your intention is to understand what will work in local conditions, with local people. Even within a mature field with good comparative data, such as illicit drug treatment, it may not be relevant how agencies elsewhere perform, if your specific goal is to help Merseysiders or Manhattanites. In terms of social value, perhaps the goal of 'harmonization' across approaches, of cultivating a better informed craft based on shared knowledge and new evaluative practices, is a more realistic goal than an attempt to create a more 'scientific' metrical regime which privileges the outcomes of one tool or another. This is not to say that social value is irredeemably subjective and hopelessly open-ended. We can discern distinct categories of social value, and can draw meaningful conclusions. The remainder of this chapter reflects this and falls into three parts:

• The next section considers the relationship between process and outcomes foci for social ventures. It also identifies some of the factors which have influenced the way social entrepreneurs have defined problems and codified responses of different kinds. The importance of clear value systems is reinforced.

- Following this discussion, the chapter moves on to address the nature of social value and its measurement. Concrete examples illustrate the core properties of social value creation noted earlier: its subjectivity, contestability, contingency, heterogeneity, and values base. The debate around social metrics and their use is also set out.

- The final part of the chapter sets out a framework for mapping social value and impact across four dimensions: social added value, empowerment and social change, social innovation, and systemic change. It concludes with some observations about new areas for discussion in light of recognition of the importance of social added value.

The Social Entrepreneur's Dilemma

It is easy to focus on organizational forms. But what is new and most distinctive about social entrepreneurship is not the particular organizational forms that are used but the entrepreneur's continual pursuit of greater social or environmental impact. However, few have had much to say about what precisely characterizes that impact, or what all the different examples of it might share in common (although, see Introduction and Chapter 5 for some observations). Most accounts quickly retreat from the difficult and messy business of defining or understanding what makes a social difference, preferring instead to concentrate on process and inputs; for example, the traits of socially entrepreneurial behaviour and the ways entrepreneurs work or the methods they use. On the whole, most commentators concentrate on the 'entrepreneurial' in social entrepreneurship and what constitutes good managerial practices of a certain kind, and, perhaps surprisingly, tend to neglect the social, that might make better social goals than others.

This emphasis has had some benefits. Many in the social sector need new skills to deliver their vision and many of those skills parallel the skills needed in business. There are also advantages in providing social entrepreneurs with a shared language and a common lexicon of ways of getting things done. These can help to legitimize work which is otherwise marginalized; it can teach people in the private sector about the links between the social and the economic; and it can help in the business of moving social entrepreneurship from the margins to the mainstream through the replication of proven models such as Fair Trade businesses or cooperative wind farms.

However, this focus also carries some risks. No method, entrepreneurial or otherwise, has a pre-eminent moral claim to social benefit, and none can claim to be inherently valuable and virtuous, as history constantly reminds us. In the late nineteenth and early twentieth centuries, for example, businesses such as the Rowntree and Cadbury confectionary companies in Britain were at the cutting edge of socially committed service provision, improving their employees' housing, health, and education out of enlightened self-interest. But seen through a modern lens these models now look extremely paternalistic and even disempowering to their employees.

Similarly, charities, which now have high levels of public trust (91 per cent in Britain respect what they do: NCVO 1997) at a time when confidence in other institutions is being eroded, have in the past periodically lost trust, and come to be seen as much as a problem as a solution. For example, in the post-1945 period they were generally seen as inefficient, undemocratic vestiges of an aristocratic society, or—earlier—the Charity Organising Society was seen as one of the worse expressions of upper class power over the poor (Harris 1972). At the very least, opinion on what constitutes social value can change, and today there are some warning signs of a similar swing, whether in the form of new legislation on the objects of charity (e.g. the UK Charities Bill), critiques of poor accountability (Edwards 2000) or claims that many of the forms of giving and aid are counterproductive (Hoffman 2005).

The second major problem with too narrow a concentration on entrepreneurial process is that it can distort the value proposition from 'using entrepreneurial approaches to optimize social (or environmental) impact' to 'deriving private benefits/profits from social markets'. A recent Canadian example of social entrepreneurship, described by Dart (2005), is indicative of the confusion. Dart's study centred on an urban counselling centre which offered sustained help to individuals and families experiencing emotional ill health and mental distress, often homeless people with complex problems. A zealous new director, the social entrepreneur, looked at the finances, the long waiting list, and protracted cases, and set out on an entrepreneurial path of reform. The agency adopted brief intervention counselling as its primary service, waiting lists were cut and the organization enjoyed sound financial health once more. Clients with complex needs which are unresponsive to this one-size-fits-all approach lost a valued service and no steps were taken to ensure a suitable alternative. In other words the social need was sacrificed to the needs of enterprise.

Ethos and values matter. A good illustration is the current shifts underway in the UK in the organization of public services which have opened up new opportunities for social enterprise. In health, and specifically the provision of general practice services, the conditions for greater institutional pluralism have been created recently as the relevant contracts have been wrested from doctors' control. Though the public perception of general practice is that these partnerships are public bodies, in the past they have generally been privately owned, with doctors extracting surpluses in high salaries for themselves. Now it has, in theory, become viable for social enterprises to enter this field. The social entrepreneurs, nurses, and other alternative health providers who could seize this opportunity may identify more closely with patients than many general practitioners and are likely to be more open to experimenting with bold new ways of working. However, the only way to grasp the key differences between the alternative players is through understanding their values and motivations—rather than market structures or organizational forms.

The third problem with favouring process over results is that it may be preventing the social entrepreneurship field from winning over important potential allies. As the social entrepreneurship movement has rapidly established itself on the global stage it has sometimes alienated others. For example, institutions which act as guardians to the social justice and community development fields, and the expert practitioners within these respective groups have too often felt their work has been discounted for want of relevance or overlooked for want of quality. They feel at worst aggrieved, at best sceptical. In philanthropic circles, some feel social entrepreneurship just re-badges what they have always looked for anyway—dynamic people with good and viable ideas—or, more parochially, that it represents (yet another) US imposition (a rather odd viewpoint given the very strong histories of social entrepreneurship over the last 150 years in Europe and around the world, but nevertheless quite a common one). One of the problems which has exacerbated this reaction has been a confusion in places between social entrepreneurship and social enterprise, the first being an approach which can be used in a wide range of settings, the latter a category of market-based businesses trading for a social purpose. Some appear to have taken the social enterprise sector as the sum of the social entrepreneurship field when, in fact, it represents but one set of organizational arrangements which lend themselves to resolving some of the objectives social entrepreneurs hold (see Introduction). It is also plausible, and even likely, that this reaction represents a defence mechanism. Social entrepreneurs have, after all, introduced more demanding expectations of social change agents at the same time being more willing to work with powerful institutions that many parts of the social development field more typically see as the enemy (business, government). Closer attention to ends, to the social impact in social entrepreneurship, offers the prospect of a more engaging way to move forward.

There is also another factor to be taken into account. Social entrepreneurs themselves want to achieve social outcomes; this is what generally motivates them more than anything. A skill- and tool-based approach to social entrepreneurship education, support, and research, therefore, only partially aligns itself with a socially entrepreneurial mindset or heuristic. Spinosa, Flores, and Dreyfus (1997) drew analogies between citizen activists and entrepreneurs and shamans, describing them as vividly imagining new worlds and new social realities, and conjuring them into being by enabling others to believe in what does not yet exist. We need to ensure that our concepts and analysis do not lose sight of this bigger—more visionary—picture.

What Is Social Value?

Social value offers a way of conceiving the role social entrepreneurs play in societies and the contributions they make. Jed Emerson, the most notable thinker and writer on value in the social entrepreneurship movement (see www.blendedvalue.org), has argued that value cannot so easily be disaggregated into its economic, social, and cultural components and that to think in such narrow terms is 'to leave value on the table'. Instead, he would have us reconstitute value in 'blends', managing all kinds, not just some. This approach is helpful for guiding investors and businesses to achieve greater social and environmental impact. Although such a 'blended value' approach certainly can help social agencies to marshal their financial assets more effectively, it does not have much to say about the 'right' objectives and social—or for that matter public—purpose of a venture. The social may be found in everything, but the idea of value that people in social purpose organizations have in mind bears closer resemblance to my opening definition of benefiting 'people whose urgent and reasonable needs are not being met by other means'.

In business it is often assumed that value is something objective, derived from the laws of supply and demand, and then managed through enterprises. But closer inspection shows value to be more complex than this. In the first place all value comes from consumers: their willingness to spend money on goods and services which itself is constantly changing under the influence of fashion and taste. Second, within organizations, value turns out to be anything but objective. Rather the allocation of costs turns out to be fraught and complex, which is why generations of accountants have had to innovate new ways of handling value (e.g. Johnson and Kaplan 1991). Anyone in any doubt about the fluid nature of value in business needs only look at the history of the Internet boom, a heady and reckless exercise in valuation, or the changing approaches to valuation of intangibles such as brands, or even the accounting scandals at Enron.

All of the methods used to make sense of value share the feature that they are tools for supporting conversations: in the case of business these are conversations between managers and divisions, and between managers and shareholders. Sometimes they are conversations between managers and regulators. In the public sector too the emerging field of public value recognizes that such value can only be understood in the context of the key conversations that shape public sectors: between politicians, managers, and other stakeholders. The language of public value is a way of relating the things that are achieved—like better services, lower crime—in a more coherent way.

For social entrepreneurs, as well, the broader goals of social improvement translate into a series of rather different kinds of conversation about value: with foundations and philanthropic funders often concerned with impact;

with investors possibly wanting a mix of commercial and social returns; with public agencies offering contracts and demanding some measurable results. But what counts as social value then has to be at root about activities and services which are valued by the groups not being adequately served by the market or political systems—the marginalized and dispossessed.

Many NGOs are now attempting to measure the value they create. But often the methods they use raise more questions than they answer. For example one UK agency, which has a keen interest in improving the quality of information in the social sector, recently used the following example as an illustration of: (1) how effective charities can be and (2) how sometimes judging worth is really simple (*The Economist* 2005). In the example, a local elder care charity employed staff to help their customers apply for welfare payments from the government in a minimum income guarantee scheme. It is known that millions fail to gain the awards they are entitled to, despite extreme need. It takes staff around 20 minutes to help an individual complete the necessary form. For every £1 ($1.72) expended, £26 ($44.72) of benefit are received, resulting, so it was claimed, in a 2,500 per cent return on investment (ROI).

Unfortunately, this example probably does not illustrate (1) or (2). Technically, the ROI calculation is correct. But it is a financial calculation and does not correspond with social value. First, no value is added in the transaction. Strictly speaking all that is happening is that money is being transferred from one group (taxpayers) to another (poor pensioners). This may be a desirable outcome but it is very different from creating new value. Second, this example forces attention onto the question of why elder care charities do not spend a modest and one-off amount on a really effective campaign and if necessary, training scheme, to get the government to do its job properly or, if their networks and culture make them ideally placed to do the work on behalf of government, why they do not hold government accountable for the administration costs.

Examples of this kind illuminate the tricky question of what to measure and how to measure it. This has been the subject of greater attention most recently in both the social entrepreneurship field (e.g. the Charities Evaluation Service, the Social Audit Network, REDF—formerly the Roberts Enterprise Development Fund, the New Economics Foundation); the related activities of triple bottom line accounting (e.g. SustAinability); the development of a public value ethos (e.g. Moore 1995; Kelly, Mulgan, and Muers 2002); the practices of accountability (e.g. Keystone); and the emergence of analytic sector reporting (e.g. New Philanthropy Capital, the World Bank's GEMs, or Gender Enterprise Markets). The originators of these tools are sophisticated but none believes measurement is a magic bullet. None asserts the ubiquity of their particular methodology, or even that any is definitive. Most are highly conversant with the fluid nature of value. However, in the absence of a broader framework for thinking about value such as the one set out here, and less time to reflect, many who form the audience for these tools have jumped in downstream, believing that metrics can guide them to the right objectives and provide certainty where the reality is rather more open to dispute.

The risk with any metric is that people will come to see it as a description of a reality, rather than as a tool for a conversation about that reality. Moreover, it can be all too easy to mistake what is measured as a proxy for value as being the value itself (the crass cliché that only what can be measured can be managed must share some of the blame).

Metrics can be helpful: in conversation with donors or investors and for internal management, with the people affected by an organization's work, and with peers or the general public. But all these conversations are different and call for different kinds of evidence. In some instances, such as where models are mature, or where public funders are involved and large data sets have been compiled, there may exist common indicators which can provide reliable clues to the worth of different interventions. Benchmarking can give a reasonable indication of relative efficiency and effectiveness in turning resources into results.

In experimental models, by contrast, evaluation may be far more speculative. There are unlikely to be reliable data, clear boundaries around the activity or direct comparators. Trying too hard to squeeze a new activity into these boxes may be harmful and may constrain innovation. Even in an age of evidence-based policymaking, bureaucrats use evidence only to inform their understanding. They too have to patch together incomplete information, information which has often been gathered from models no longer in use, information which is historic. The sensible ones do not pretend it can direct their decisions or guarantee future innovations. It is worrying then that some metrics, such as social return on investment (SROI), appear to promise a finer grained accuracy, though they are, in fact, built on much looser assumptions. They appear to seek a far higher degree of certainty than public officials would ever ask of their data sets. They appear to offer the answer, when they should function as the invitation to begin a conversation.

In practice, few investors—even those from venture finance backgrounds that are used to the equivalent metrics in commercial contexts—like to be so insulated from the real issues (see Cunningham and Ricks 2004; Kramer 2005). Conversely, at the other end of the spectrum, some practitioners, particularly those identifying with the social justice movement, have shunned any kind of measurement, believing it to be too hard or inappropriate to their goal of empowering particular marginalized groups. But metrics have uses for them too. The 'returns' on effective advocacy can be mind-blowing and metrics such as SROI, used judiciously, can be used to better make the case for the longer-term investment approach so necessary to this sort of work (Scott and Carson 2003; Paton 2004).

What clearly remains the case in any sort of social change is that one metric or another can only function well when it is in service to a higher vision, when managers know why they are measuring and for whom. As Bill Drayton of Ashoka has argued, there is no instance in which we can absolve ourselves from making judgements about the things we are trying to do. Social entrepreneurs have to and do take personal responsibility for the inferences they make and the decisions they act on.

A second related question is whether to use integrative approaches to value, or to celebrate the diversity of different kinds of value. There are more or less transformative approaches to social entrepreneurship and different ways of thinking about value. Which ways predominate depends on which frame is being used. The philosopher Joseph Raz in his book *The Practice of Value* (2005) has written of evaluative frames, and the way human beings tend to think in genres first, and only later come to judge the quality of one instance or another. He draws on cultural genres in the arts to make his point, but argues that our tendency to think in these ways is broader, extending to the emergence, use and negotiation of any cultural category (indeed, if one thinks of the way toddlers overapply words such as 'apple' to broader classes of objects such as 'fruit' when they are acquiring language, it is hard to imagine this propensity is anything other than hard-wired). Any model of value essentially functions this way; as a frame that makes sense in particular contexts and conversations.

The beauty of Raz's approach (2005) to value is that it favours plurality. It allows you to apply different lenses as needs must. So if you are the supply chain manager at Marks and Spencer, in the example described below, you may sit with producers and apply a social value perspective to persuade them that they should invest their trust, time, and skills in working with you, while persuading yourself and your investors at the Shell Foundation that your social impact strategy is robust. With your managers and corporate affairs team, you may adopt a blended value perspective which balances social and commercial performance. Your senior directors may explain your success to the board in financial terms only.

It is not a sign of backwardness that social entrepreneurs need and use multiple ways to adequately describe what they are trying to do. Rather it is a strength and one that is shared with a wide spectrum of the most valuable human activities including culture, religion, politics, and family life, to name just a few. Each of them affords the entrepreneur the opportunity to tell their story in the most compelling way possible. As Charles Tilley has shown (Tilley 2006), whenever we use a story to explain something we are also often trying to change the person we are talking to. So it is with social entrepreneurship. Our conversations about value constitute the relationships with key stakeholders—but they are also often used to try to change the perceptions of investors, governments, regulators. And very often, by orchestrating these different sorts of stories, social entrepreneurs are changed themselves, triangulating insight derived from different perspectives to enrich their work. This chapter now concludes by setting out the key dimensions of social value.

A Framework of Social Value

Social Added Value

Seen through the eyes of the social entrepreneur themselves there is a common thread across all their activities. Usually this can best be described as a focus on the creation of social added value. Namely, they aim to return more value to their intended beneficiaries for comparable resources expended than other ventures. So, for example, Kids' Company in South London is different from many other groups working with street children and highly troubled young adults because crucially, it asks its staff to bring love and attachment into their work over and above their professional skills as therapists, educators, and youth workers. Only this way, they argue, can they hope to garner the trust of people who have learned constantly to repel others, cultivate a real sense of belonging and a personal investment in processes of participating, healing, learning, and ultimately constructing new ways of organizing their lives. Similarly Childline International, which supports advice services in numerous countries around the world, has recognized the legitimacy gap felt by young consumers in other offerings and has overcome their distrust by staffing its helplines with young people themselves. People Tree, a fashion company trading in Japan and the UK, employs all the usual features of the Fair Trade model—such as paying guaranteed prices at above-market levels and capacity-building among, in this case, over 200 groups of poor producers—but, critically, and unlike many other companies selling artisan-made clothes and crafts, it also makes a high quality design input. In this way it contributes to greater market access by ensuring local expertise and traditions are presented to Northern consumers in the most appealing ways. The prospects of sustained and growing trade, and generations of economic and social benefits in poor communities, are thereby increased.

The models creating added social value are very varied, combining personal, family, and community resources, and market and government levers in novel combinations. Thus, the Care Collective, a model currently being incubated by Launchpad,[1] aims to provide a twofold improvement on alternative childcare models by being genuinely community-based and combining volunteer parental inputs with a backbone of paid professional supervision. This way, children enjoy sustained carer relationships and a wider activity mix, and the cost to entry is reduced to a point where childcare becomes affordable to all. In the USA, the Heron Foundation, which supports social and economic development among poor communities, is surprisingly unusual among its peers for exacting more impact by investing around a quarter of its assets in debt and equities which further its mission, as well as providing grants and subordinated loans directly to beneficiary groups. A number of Latin American countries including Mexico and Brazil have recently introduced the 'bolsa familia' which aims to achieve a range of public health and education goals by, for the first time, coupling mandatory participation in for example, immunization and literacy programmes, with the receipt of family welfare payments. The employee ownership movement represents a different sort of example again, encouraging the value in modest family businesses to be sustained when the owner seeks an exit. Admittedly, these represent very different sorts of added value, but perhaps what they share in common is that they all represent additional inputs which improve the quality of beneficiaries' experience, or the ability of an organization to enable its beneficiaries to participate in wider processes.

Empowerment and Social Change

Many social entrepreneurs do not stop at creating added social value. Their work also brings about a sustained shift in the social or economic relations of disadvantaged groups. So, for example, there is a set of models which harness economic forces to create employment for economically impoverished groups, but which also provide jobs for groups who are seen by other parts of society to be taboo, dysfunctional, or undeserving in some way. For example, the international 'social firms' movement has achieved much in shifting employer and public attitudes to adults with learning disabilities and mental health problems, by enabling people to encounter them in familiar social roles as employees in packing companies, or hotels and office maintenance companies. The Green Hotel in Mysore, southern India, provides a model of environmental and social tourism, employing abused women and *dalits*, the 'untouchables'. The power of these models is in part derived from the fact that unlike, say, rights-based approaches, which seek to change political, legislative, and judicial regimes which lie in others' control, the desired change lies within their gift. If social change lies in the alignment of shifting practices, structures, and beliefs (Thekaekara 2005), then these approaches are promising because they can simultaneously tackle all three. There is nothing as effective in revealing and unsettling deep-rooted cultural prejudices as encountering an experience which quite clearly refutes the basis on which they have been held.

Another set of examples lies in the ethical retail models, more commonly found in the Global North. Both household chains such as The Body Shop, and product lines which qualify for one or other of the recognized ethical kitemarks—such as the Rugmark, FSC sustainable forestry mark for timber products, or the certified organic cotton award—are particularly effective because they present the ethical consumption proposition to a wide cross section of the public, and where they succeed, create a context whereby taking care over the particular social affects of your purchasing choices is perceived as according the consumer with good social standing. Where these strategies achieve critical mass, they affect social change because they create a new benchmark for the way a sector or industry must behave. They make child slavery, the erosion of ecological resilience, and other social abuses non-competitive. They also help inculcate new social norms which in turn make new kinds of debates possible, with correspondingly higher degrees of sophistication. It was inconceivable only a few years ago, for example, that concepts such as carbon-trading or the environmental or local economic impact of 'food miles' would be the subject of the mainstream newspaper coverage and public debate there is today.

Empowerment often allows otherwise marginalized groups to exercise their rights. In a low-level way, community broadcasters, for example, enable special populations (the blind, prisoners, Muslim youth, etc.) to access the public information they need to enact aspects of their roles as citizens. Examples like CAMFED ostensibly provide access to educational opportunities for upwards of 150,000 girls and young women in sub-Saharan Africa, but perhaps their most enduring legacy will prove to be a new idea of 'girlhood' to which elders, parents, and public officials all subscribe and from which multiple outcomes accrue. Human rights movements such as International Bridges to Justice in China or Witness are, in different ways, enabling people to exercise the rights which, though ascribed to them in theory, often prove elusive in reality. They recognize that where the rule of law or social norms supporting a human rights settlement is weak, alternative social infrastructure is vital.

The National Slum Dwellers Initiative in Mumbai, India, is another example which now enjoys widespread replication internationally. This model is smart for not only politicizing and skilling groups of poor, landless, and disenfranchised people to campaign successfully for the resources to create safe, durable housing, clean water, and other public services such as education, but also for insisting that its members undertake the work themselves, making them creditworthy to other lenders and employers in the process. Illustrative of the newer models of governance needed for a globalizing world, are transnational examples such as the International Crisis Group (ICG). This NGO identifies the precursors to significant conflict and mobilizes international agencies to be proactive, thereby preventing death, hunger, disease, and the mass displacement of peoples, with all the consequences such large-scale disruptions can exert. These models are interesting, not least because while it may be possible to conceive of direct beneficiaries 'in far flung places' in conventional ways, the so-called international community is equally enabled in its role as good global citizen, and constituent members of it can, if they choose to count the benefits thus, consider a modest preventive investment in an organization like ICG now as a massive saving on the bill of war later. Corporations, too, are beginning better to understand the ways they can integrate inclusive practices in blends which are good for the excluded and dispossessed while at the same time furthering the corporate business case (see Godeke, Nielsen, and Simmons 2004, as well as Chapter 8) in innovations which go far beyond the superficiality of earlier generations of corporate social responsibility (CSR). In an interesting example of business-to-business philan-thropy, a model which itself deserves closer attention, the Shell Foundation for one has demonstrated its conviction in the role of business in development by giving the British retailer Marks and Spencer a grant to provide market access for poor Southern producers. Shell understood that a large demand-side inter-vention was much needed to complement the work small trade justice organ-izations are undertaking to improve supply chains. For its part, Marks and Spencer felt compelled to manage its supply chain differently due to customer demand for better ethical standards. Finally, Celtel International, the fastest growing mobile telecommunications company in Africa, is distinctive for reaching very poor consumers, enabling them to access the information to skip a generation of (expensive, less accessible, hard to maintain) computer technology and access the information they need to change their lives.

Social Innovation

Some of social ventures are extremely innovative; others are not. Innovation creates social value if it allows people to achieve more for less, or to solve problems that are otherwise insoluble. Examples of genuine social innovations include: the work of eBay, which has connected thousands of small traders and isolated home hobbyists; the idea of the *Big Issue*, a magazine to be sold by homeless people; the Korean *OhMyNews*, a cheap, online citizen news service where readers are the writers and which exerted a decisive influence in the last general election. So, too, are the social technologies of participatory budget planning: a mechanism which augments representative democracy in a grow-ing number of locations around the world. The concept of 'carbon trading' is another example.

Innovations often come from combining existing elements in new ways, but only over time does it become clear whether they really are creating new value. In part that is a matter of their scale. But it also reflects what they do, as well as the implications of what they do. Take the hands-on work and immediate effects of KickStart, the Intermediate Technology Group, or International Development Enterprises, India, for example, all of which show how cheap, simple, durable, technology such as water pumps or irrigation design can transform the income poor farmers can generate from their land. In fifty years' time it is possible that their ultimate value will be perceived to be that they prove the statement that 'poor people are not poor for inherent reasons and can trade their way to wealth and well-being' over the competing idea that 'poor people should be pitied, need and will always need our help and handouts' (and, by the way, that poor people are other people too—they are sisters, musicians, comics, and villains). Much follows from a shift like this.

As these examples demonstrate some social innovation derives from new things, some from new applications and combinations of old things. This can be seen in the cases of two technologies which have found renewed social purpose: cross country skis and the humble bicycle. Finland found the answer to rapidly increasing obesity and ever higher levels of heart disease when its government aggressively promoted the benefits of daily skiing. Similarly in London in the summer of 2005, 50 per cent more people rediscovered the joys of cycling when terrorists hit the London Underground transport network. In the process of retreating from fear, they also learned that cycling is very often the fastest, most reliable form of transport in the city. As urbanization puts many more cities around the world in gridlock, a return to mass cycling—as still happens in parts of Asia—may prove an important part of the solution, ensuring we enjoy comparable well-being to the Finns at the same time. In the world of social value creation, context is king.

Systemic Change

In the final analysis, however, the greatest social value comes neither from double dividends or innovation but rather from systemic change which transforms the architecture of how things work. Small groups of committed people can find points of powerful leverage—and achieve a tipping point. So, for example, the work of Fazle Abed and colleagues at BRAC and Mohammad Yunus and company at the Grameen group, have achieved a transformation in the prospects of many Bangladeshi people, particularly women, because of their scale. Their principal activity is the delivery of services, but they have grown so large that these no longer represent a safety net or critique of the system: they are the system and have become almost a parallel state, with all the problems and tensions that the system brings.

Martin Burt and colleagues at Fundación Paraguaya have shown how market forces can be hitched to systemic social value creation by using philanthropy to bankroll the poor and create the market for the country's leading retail bank to serve. As a result, the Fundación has today been able to redirect its efforts to enterprise development among the same target group in order that they can make the most of this new access to finance. Wendy Abt and colleagues are interesting too, in this regard. They are passionate about providing money, development opportunities, optimism, and independence to the world's poorest people. To do so, they are exploiting the tools of capitalism to raise venture funds, buy up the leading retail banks across sub-Saharan Africa and mass market microfinance products. Critics could argue this is the new, invidious face of imperialism and will prove just as deadly as the abuses of old. Others will say that until the poor can fight fire with fire, they will always be on the sharp end of inequalities in a global capitalist system and approaches like Wendy's represent the cutting edge of social entrepreneurship. To my mind, the more important point is to have that debate framed by considerations of value—including the views of the bank's prospective customers—than around ideology, since ideology tells us more about the competing perspectives (inputs) of, usually, Northern arbiters, whereas value can give us access to outcomes and the experiences of the critical stakeholders.

Newer, and as yet unproven, but no less illustrative of this search and the range of people now bringing entrepreneurial approaches to social change, are experiments such as Generation and Just Change. The brainchild of Al Gore, formerly vice president of the United States, and David Blood, formerly chief executive of Goldman Sachs Asset Management, Generation is an investment fund. Its thesis is that it is foolhardy, as well as morally reprehensible, to treat demographic shifts, population movements, conflict, crisis, disease pandemics, and environmental risks as 'externalities'—unrelated to business actions—whose impact can be disregarded. They aim to show that longer-term investment horizons which take these factors into account will prove good for investors and good for society. They will succeed if their financial performance is more competitive than alternatives. Their impact will be to reconnect the economic and the social where they should never have been shorn apart. We should care because if they are right, they will help shepherd the capitalist system towards a more benign path, affecting millions of people, and the health of the ecologies they inhabit in the process. Another example is Just Change, where a bottom-up approach is attempting to institutionalize a new balance of power between investors of capital, labour, and consumption and, in so doing, could inject a step change in the degree of justice with which corporations of different kinds interact with market forces and the people affected by them.[2] Stan and Mari Thekaekara, the activists driving the thinking and implementation of these models, have drawn inspiration from the economic relations of the fisherfolk community in Tamil Nadu. In contrast to agrarian societies and their economic offspring, the asset-owners in the fishing communities of southern India do not enjoy automatic privileges. Instead, risks are shared with labourers, whose expertise is invested along with capital assets such as boats and equipment. If these relations could be replicated globally, their repercussions would be significant.

For What It Is Worth

If we take seriously the social value created by social entrepreneurs new areas for discussion emerge. First, it opens up a major direction of research to map more precisely the great diversity of outputs and outcomes associated with social entrepreneurship: the results of this work are likely to be complex, overlapping with the growing evidence base on efficacy in fields like health and welfare, and with the ever more sophisticated understandings of the relationships between spending and results.

Second, it should help to maintain the concern for needs, and in particular needs which are not being adequately met by the market, governments, or the traditional voluntary sector. The most important argument for social entrepreneurship is that it recognizes these needs better and acts on them more effectively. Yet sometimes these claims are asserted rather than proved.

Third, it should encourage a more systemic view of change and methods of education, like the 'action learning' approaches advocated by the School for Social Entrepreneurs, which deepen social entrepreneurs' impulses to scan widely to understand their operating environment and to be highly reflective about the significance of their interventions. Gerard Lemos (2005), one of the designers of the programme's methodology, once remarked that most students thought they needed to be harder-headed, when, in his view, they would achieve more by becoming higher-minded. His is a useful corrective.

Fourth, it points to the need to find, socialize (and be socialized by), and embrace a far wider range of people in the social entrepreneurship movement, since organizations in all sectors can act in socially focused ways.

Finally, it should remind us that, at its best, social entrepreneurship is about living a more compelling life that is more directly engaged and that integrates vision and impact. This is why any discussion of value in this field should never stray too far from a clear sense of values, or borrow too uncritically from a business world that often works most effectively when it is ethically neutral in its calculus; and why educational, capacity-building, research, or infrastructure debates should continue to grapple with the things that make social entrepreneurship different.

Notes

1. Launchpad is run jointly by the Skoll Centre for Social Entrepreneurship and the Young Foundation. For details see www.youngfoundation.org.uk
2. Stan and Mari Thekaekara are preparing a forthcoming paper on this work as Fellows at the Skoll Centre.

References

Cunningham, K. and Ricks, M. (Summer 2004). 'Why Measure: Nonprofits Use Metrics to Show That They Are Efficient. But What If Donors Don't Care?' *Stanford Social Innovation Review*: 44–51.

Dart, R. (2005). *Unintended Consequences of Social Entrepreneurship: The Complex Structure and Effects of Radical Service Delivery Improvement in a Canadian Human Services Organization*, presented at the International Social Entrepreneurship Conference (ISERC), Barcelona, April.

Edwards, M. (2000). *NGO Rights and Responsibilities*. London: NCVO.

Godeke, S., Nielsen, D., and Simmons, A. (2004). *Private Investment for Social Goals: Building the Blended Value Capital Market*, Report from a workshop sponsored by the World Economic Forum, the International Finance Corporation, and the Rockefeller Foundation in Geneva.

Harris, J. (1972). *Unemployment and Politics: A Study in English Social Policy, 1886–1914*. Oxford: Clarendon Press.

Hoffman, K. (2005). *Enterprise Solutions to Poverty*. London: Shell Foundation.

Johnson, H. and Kaplan, R. (1991). *Relevance Lost: The Rise and Fall of Management Accounting*. Cambridge, MA: Harvard Business School Press.

Kelly, G., Mulgan, G., and Muers, S. (2002). *Creating Public Value: An Analytical Framework for Public Service Reform*. London: Prime Minister's Strategy Unit.

Kramer, M. (2005). *Measuring Innovation: Evaluation in the Field of Social Entrepreneurship*. Skoll Foundation and Foundation Strategy Group.

Lemos (2005). Personal Conversation with the Author.

Moore, M. (1995). *On Creating Public Value: Strategic Management in Government*. Cambridge, MA: Harvard University Press.

NCVO (1997). *Blurred Vision: Public Trust in Charities*. On-going research programme, Available at: www.ncvo-vol.org.uk

Paton, R. (2004). *Managing and Measuring Social Enterprise*. London: Sage.

Raz, J. (2005). *The Practice of Value*. Oxford: Oxford University Press.

Scott, J. and Carson, N. (2003). 'Who's Afraid of Real Returns?' *Alliance*, 8(3): 12.

Spinosa, C., Flores, F., and Dreyfus, H. (1997). *Disclosing New Worlds: Entrepreneurship, Democratic Action, and the Cultivation of Solidarity*. Cambridge, MA: MIT Press.

The Economist (2005). 'Virtue's eBay', 19–25 November, p. 33.

Thekaekara, S. (2005). A *Social Change Manifesto for the Poor*, Skoll Centre for Social Entrepreneurship lecture series on social change, Saïd Business School, Oxford University, June.

Tilley, C. (2006). *Why?*

Web Resources

Charities Evaluation Service—www.ces vol.org.uk
Gender Enterprise Markets, World Bank Group—www.ifc.org/gem
Keystone—www.keystonereporting.org
New Economics Foundation—www.neweconomics.org
New Philanthropy Capital–www.philanthropycapital.org
REDF (formerly the Roberts Enterprise Development Fund)—www.redf.org
Social Audit Network—www.socialauditnetwork.org.uk
www.socialenterprise.org.uk—choose 'search resources', then search by subject for 'quality building and impact measurement'.
Sustainability—www.sustainability.com

4

Cultivating the Other Invisible Hand of Social Entrepreneurship: Comparative Advantage, Public Policy, and Future Research Priorities

Geoff Mulgan

This collection is one of many signs that social entrepreneurship is increasingly becoming part of the mainstream. As a phenomenon it is becoming now common, from drug treatment projects in India to sexual health in Vietnam, environmental protection in China to job creation in US inner cities. So it comes as a surprise to discover just how new the idea of entrepreneurship, let alone social entrepreneurship, is in our language. The first edition of the *Oxford English Dictionary* (OED 1897) still defined an entrepreneur as 'the director of a public musical institution'. Only in a later edition was the word used in its more modern sense, as the editors acknowledged that the control and direction of capital and labour in a modern economy might be so difficult and different from past experience that a new class of person was needed and with it a new word, adopted from the French. The idea that this role has a social equivalent—and that the handling of social and economic assets in advanced societies might be so difficult that a new class of person is needed—is only a few decades old, and has only in the last decade become visible in discussions of public policy.

In this chapter I examine the relationship between government and social entrepreneurship. I show that the latter is highly dependent both on the underlying conditions that governments create—the rule of law, property rights, freedoms to organize and criticize—and on the degree to which governments provide more active support, as contractors and funders. I look in particular at the experiences of government in the UK that have probably given a higher priority to the cultivation of enterprise and entrepreneurship in civil society, as well as in public services, than any other country. The UK has both pioneered new approaches and run up against some of the problems and tensions that are inherent to the relationship between a national state and entrepreneurship in all its forms. The chapter also looks at some of the broader issues raised by this relationship: the nature of the comparative advantage which social entrepreneurship offers; the nature of the value to which it contributes; the current state of knowledge; and what remains to be discovered.

The Invisible Hand

Social entrepreneurship sits within a broader context of social change. People living in modern market economies are reasonably familiar with the idea of the invisible hand that was first described by Bernard Mandeville and Adam Smith in the eighteenth century. In Smith's classic account the combination of markets, legal frameworks, and property rights translates the self-interest and greed of millions of individuals into a force that promotes the prosperity of all. The brilliance of the market mechanism is that it is automatic: by harnessing motives and energies that are already there it avoids the need for a king or a commander to 'run' the economy. Instead the economy runs itself and rewards both performance and innovation (see further Baumol 2003).

In the eighteenth century Adam Smith was equally famous for a very different set of writings that looked at the 'moral sentiments' of sympathy and compassion that hold societies together. Although he didn't put it in these terms, the two strands of his work can be brought together in the idea that all modern societies depend not only on the invisible hand of the market but also on another invisible hand: the legal and fiscal arrangements that serve to channel the moral sentiments, the motivations of care, civic energy, and social commitment into practical form and, thus, into the service of the common good (Mulgan and Landry 1996).

Amitai Etzioni provided another useful framework for thinking about these sentiments. In his classic works on organizational structure in the 1960s he showed that all organizations fit into three broad types: there are the coercive organizations usually associated with the state that achieve their objectives through command and violence; there are instrumental organizations that achieve their objectives through payment, exchange, and self-interest; and there are normative organizations that achieve their objectives through shared values (e.g. Etzioni 1961). In practice, most organizations combine more than one of these characteristics. Seen in this light, the drive towards social entrepreneurship can only be understood as part of a much broader movement to expand the sway of this third group of organizations that are based on values, consent, and mutual commitment. They are, in this sense, an overt challenge both to business (and, in particular, to the evangelists of business who would like to turn every social relationship into a market transaction) and to governments (and, in particular, to anyone who believes that for every problem there is a governmental solution).

In many societies the arrangements to support normative organizations of any kind are weak or non-existent. Indeed in much of the world the main barriers to social entrepreneurship remain quite basic. These include: a lack of adequate legal forms for independent not-for-profit organizations (NPOs); fair, let alone favourable, tax rules for donations or for trading; laws and a political environment that make it possible to argue, criticize, and campaign; and protections from violence or the arbitrary caprice of bureaucrats. This is why so many social entrepreneurs in much of the world live embattled lives, constantly struggling to survive, appeasing powerful interest groups and suspicious states.

However, in some countries these basic conditions are well established. Citizens' rights to demonstrate and advocate and to organize trade unions and political parties sit alongside legal frameworks that make it easy to create new organizations, to employ staff, to trade, to fund-raise, and to innovate. These are the results of several centuries of struggle, and they have enabled societies to adapt more rapidly to changing needs and wants. Just as markets draw on the energies and creativity of entrepreneurs willing to risk money and prestige, so does social change draw on the often invisible fecundity of tens of thousands of individuals and small groups who spot needs and innovate solutions. At any one time there may be many thousands who believe that they can meet needs that are unmet by the state or the market, and then struggle to find the resources—the people, money, buildings, customers—to put their insight into effect. Many are motivated by personal factors: problems, mistreatments and bad luck. Behind the facades of any great modern city like Oxford or London, Chicago or Mumbai, Berlin or São Paulo, there lie thousands of small conspiracies to reshape the world, some in embryonic NGOs, some in units of the public sector like schools and hospitals, some finding a home in commercial companies. These are much easier to see in retrospect: the histories of such ventures as Oxfam and Barnardos, the National Health Services (NHS) and the hospice movement, show that in their early days they looked fairly unpromising. Most remained well below the radar of the rich and powerful and of course many failed. But others took root and became permanent institutions.

The biography of Michael Young, Britain's, and perhaps the world's, greatest serial social entrepreneur, illuminates the point. Throughout his career he repeatedly identified unmet needs and then put together people, legal vehicles, money, and, patronage in a relentless struggle to make the idea a reality. Some became very large-scale enterprises—like the Open University and the Consumers' Association; others remained small, like the National Funerals College or the Baby Naming Society; some paved the way for public sector innovations, like phone-based diagnostic services, or the out-of-school clubs pioneered by Education Extra; some ended up as for-profit companies, like Language Line which provided translation services; and many failed, like the new university on Robben Island in South Africa, or the self-service garage. One of his last creations was the School for Social Entrepreneurs, with branches around the UK, which was designed to nurture many more people like him.

The general point is that social entrepreneurship, in its wider sense, is a discovery mechanism: through the hard graft of trying to put an idea into practice in a world where there is intensive competition for resources, loyalty, and time, social entrepreneurs learn whether there really is a need and whether there is a coherent business model for meeting it. However brilliant the policy-makers or the analysts in consultancies may be, they will not be reliable judges of what will and will not work: indeed the higher up the hierarchy they have climbed the less they may be able to imagine something radically new. In this wide sense social entrepreneurship is one of the ways our societies adapt and learn, drawing not on the concentrated brainpower of the university, bureau-cracies, and global companies, but the distributed intelligence of thousands of people who take it on themselves to be self-appointed leaders (this concept emerged in the literature on the patterns of social change, e.g. LaPiere 1965).

What are their characteristics? The simplest definitions of social enterprise and entrepreneurship stick closely to the words: they are about institutions and activities which are social (and therefore not private), that is to say con-cerned with a social mission and benefit; and they are concerned with enter-prise, that is to say risk-taking, trading, and exchange, and therefore distinct from the many other kinds of institution which modern societies depend on, from churches to private limited companies, schools to state bureaucracies.

Yet many soon find themselves drawn away from nouns and binary defin-itions to qualitative descriptions. George Gilder's definition of the essential entrepreneurial virtues works well for this group (see Spinosa, Flores, and Dreyfus 1997). He mentions three characteristics of entrepreneurs. The first, he says, is giving. As an example of giving he describes Henry Ford offering low prices to create the market for his cars; a temporary sacrifice for future reward. The second, he says, is humility by which he means entrepreneurs being willing to spend a lot of time in 'the grit and grease and garbage of their business'. He also means the ability to listen. Entrepreneurs, he writes, must be 'meek enough and shrewd enough to endure the humbling of self that comes in the process of profound learning from others'. The third is commitment by which he means people who 'give themselves, their time, their wealth, their sleep', people who 'leverage their lives to their belief in a redemptive idea'.

Gilder was writing about entrepreneurs in business. But his comments apply equally to social entrepreneurs—they are frequently anything but the angels that some of the more hagiographic literature portrays. Many social entrepre-neurs are stubborn, bloody-minded, and difficult to work with. But at their heart there is a moral commitment that is about giving a community what it needs, not what it expects or even knows that it wants.

The Current Climate of Social Entrepreneurship

Social entrepreneurs have emerged in large numbers during past periods of rapid social transformation. Nineteenth century Britain, for example, gave birth to dozens of new social ventures that grew rapidly, including large building societies that became lynchpins of the twentieth century financial services industry (see, e.g. Prochaska 1988; Harris 1994). Many of the UK's most important innovations occurred during this period beyond the scope of both the state and the market—for example, in childcare (Barnardos), housing (Peabody), community development (the Edwardian settlements), and social care (Rowntree). Europe created a broad-based social economy of mutual societies, cooperatives, and associations during the same period, some inspired by the radical philosophies of Bukharin and Proudhon and Kropotkin, others offshoots of the trade unions and the new social democratic parties. The aftermath of the Second World War was a similar accelerator and in Germany, for example, gave birth to a plethora of large social organizations, many under the aegis of the Church and funded by a special tax.

Three interlocking trends have driven the more recent growth of social entrepreneurship. The first is a change in thinking about government, a long shift away from the traditional idea of a commanding state monopolizing authority that was accelerated by the collapse of communism in 1989. Many countries have sought to reform public services to allow their individual units more autonomy, for example, to define their own employment policies, to use assets in more creative ways, and to reshape their relationship with those they serve. Many governments have sought new forms of the state that are more personal (with bureaucrats turned into 'advisers'); organizational structures that turn government into a commissioner, purchaser, or regulator of more diverse, innovative, providers, and less like a monolithic bureaucracy. These policy shifts have created new markets for social entrepreneurs to provide services in fields such as residential care and waste and recycling (see further Salamon 2000). The parallel shift to methods of policy and decision-making that are more transparent, porous, and inclusive has provided space for social entrepreneurs to act as advocates, alongside roles as service providers and as an alternative to the traditional state. As I will show there are no guarantees that social entrepreneurs will be more competent, accountable, or more responsive than state or for-profit entities; the point is that these changes have given them more scope to prove their worth.

The second set of trends has come from within business. There is fairly clear evidence that over time both consumers and employees have become more demanding about the ethical standards of business. CSR has been a response both to pulls from stakeholders and to pushes from people working in business who want life to mean more than a fatter profit line. As a result more businesses have set themselves overt social goals (examples like the Body Shop and

Ben and Jerry's being particularly prominent); more investors have sought to bridge the gap between classic business in the pursuit of shareholder value and not-for-profit ventures achieving a mix of different kinds of value; more businesses have started to use richer metrics of value; and many have become attracted to a vision of capitalism that is more founded on lasting relationships than on fleeting transactions. These trends can easily be exaggerated: in the UK, for example, corporate giving remains low and possibly falling, as well as being dramatically lower than the public believes it to be. The involvement of business also raises new problems, for example, around who captures the value from cause-related marketing, or the often-manipulative agendas of CSR. But these trends have opened up a great deal of space for creativity in ways that bear little relationship to the traditional charitable donation from the chairman of the board.

The third set of trends has come from within the charitable sector. These are best understood as part of the long-term rethinking of traditions of paternalistic charity that was often criticized for creating unequal relationships of dependence. On the one hand, social movements have campaigned for more democratic and modern forms of charity in which beneficiaries' voices and needs were taken into account, while on the other many charities have started to bump up against legal prohibitions on trading activities.

Together these trends have given rise to a new wave of social entrepreneurship to match that of the nineteenth century. In the UK some enterprises like CaféDirect and the Big Issue are household names. Others like Coin Street Community Builders, the Day Chocolate Company, the Bromley by Bow project, Kaleidoscope, the Wise Group, Greenwich Leisure, or the Furniture Resource Centre are now firmly established. A similar pattern can be found in many countries, from Canada, the USA and Mexico to India, Brazil, and Korea.

The Relative Position of Social Entrepreneurship

Social entrepreneurship can be found in any kind of organization—from state schools to a retail business. Social enterprise—namely social ventures that have independent revenue streams—has a narrower meaning and has to be judged in its context. Most social enterprises compete either directly or indirectly with private firms and state agencies. However, in some analyses of the comparative performance of NPOs, public ones and private ones in fields where they coexist, NPOs turned out to be less innovative and less responsive to customers. Remarkably little serious research has been done on the relative merits of different kinds of organizational form, and it is still common to hear advocates praising the inherent virtues of public organization, private business, or social enterprises without a shred of evidence to support their claims (although see Leat 1993). Most experience suggests that organizational form counts for much less in determining the qualities and behaviours of organizations than the nature of their relationships, the competition they face, and the patterns of power within which they operate.

So where is social entrepreneurship likely to have a comparative advantage over private enterprise or public enterprise? There are three areas where it may have an edge:

The first is an ability to mobilize more inputs—notably the contribution of voluntary labour or the willingness to work for less than a for-profit. A good example might be remote rural bus services which are strictly uneconomic in a traditional for-profit or public sector model but which can become viable with volunteer drivers. Similarly, social entrepreneurship may be able to achieve a cheaper cost of capital through investors' willingness to take lower returns.

The second source of advantage may be an ability to design and run more effective processes—ways of working, motivating teams, distinct methods (like small schools), or business models (like the Big Issue) which are not transferable to for-profit or state organizations. This may be particularly the case where they bring together diverse activities in ways that are synergistic: a simple example is the way that an organization running many different kinds of activity may be better placed to ensure that buildings are used from early in the morning to late at night.

The third may be that their outputs contain an added value embedded in the product or service itself either through the ethos of the organization (as in the case of Fair Trade products) or through the ways in which the service is shaped—for example a neighbourhood wardens scheme may feel different if it is rooted in the community, as will a childcare project provided on your street and run by your neighbours.

These three sets of potential advantages enable social entrepreneurs to create more value (social and economic) relative to inputs than other organizations. The three are likely to count for far more in sectors that are relatively labour intensive, more face-to-face and less commoditized than others. Defence contracting, large-scale IT, or shipbuilding are not likely to prove propitious for social entrepreneurship. However, scale is not an inherent barrier: one of the UK's largest retailers (the Co-operatives UK), and some of its biggest financial service companies (the mutual building societies) are social enterprises.

The only way to discover where social entrepreneurship has advantages is through the discovery process of market competition: ensuring a reasonably level playing field either through competition policy in the private sector, or through the terms of contracts in public markets. In advance it is rarely possible to guess which organizations will do best. Many projects that look impressive will fail when subjected to rigorous analysis or the tests of the market. Because many are fairly experimental in nature, early results can also be misleading: 'Hawthorn effects' (the added motivation that is associated with pilots) can exaggerate performance, while early positioning on learning curves can have the opposite effect, understating the potential impact of new models. In the design of public markets one important conclusion is that a clear distinction needs to be made between the encouragement of social entrepreneurship to do new things and innovate—which requires flexible contracts that allow time for learning curves to take effect—and contracts for mature markets in which there can be a level playing field between providers from different sectors.

The Roles of Government

For governments the key contribution of social entrepreneurship is that it can create social value more effectively than the state can on its own: the value associated with producing outputs and outcomes, but also a more intangible value of rebuilding social capital.

There is a widely held view that states and societies exist in a zero sum game and that a more powerful state necessarily means a weaker society. This view has been expounded by many great minds, including Peter Drucker (1990), one of the first users of the term social enterprise. It became something of a conventional wisdom on the right of American politics in the 1980s.

Many social entrepreneurs see government as the enemy. Bureaucracies tend to prefer process to outcomes; they are suspicious of rule breaking; keen to impose common standards, and prescribe common methods. Their requirements for accountability—both accountability for spending and results, and accountability through the democratic process—are often at odds with the buccaneering and individualist style of social entrepreneurs.

Yet the view that government is the enemy of social entrepreneurship is at odds with the historical evidence, and at odds with contemporary experience. The true story is subtler, and more interesting. States that commandeer all powers and resources do indeed squeeze out the space for social entrepreneurship. But lean, mean retreating states can be just as bad for social entrepreneurship—usually it is organized crime that fills the space, which was the experience of parts of the USA in the 1980s and, in a very different way, of Russia in the 1990s. The available evidence—some of which is covered in Skocpol's excellent recent book (2003) on the history of American civic life—shows that the best states for social entrepreneurship are ones that engage with civil society, that are open, accessible, active, and supportive. In the USA in the early twentieth century, and again in the 1960s and 1970s, she writes, 'civic voluntarism was thoroughly intertwined with government activities'. The same message comes over in a recent piece of research on local government and civil society in Britain. In some cities the local councils are open, engaged, and supportive of a thriving civic scene; narrow cliques control others, and civil society suffers. Where states come to see social enterprises as competitors, life can quickly become difficult—as has arguably happened in Bangladesh in the 2000s.

The economic facts also dispel the simplistic clichés about government. In most developed societies a substantial proportion of voluntary sector income is derived from the state (the 37 per cent level in the UK is roughly comparable to every other developed country, including the USA). As Salamon, Sokolowski, and List (2003) have pointed out there is a widespread pattern of 'third party government' in which governments at all levels enlist third parties—lower levels of government, private banks, insurance companies, businesses, and not-for-profit organizations—to carry out their programmes and respond to public needs.

This pattern has certainly been visible in the UK. In his very first major speech as Prime Minister in June 1997 Tony Blair spoke of the importance of social enterprise to his new administration. He saw it as an essential part of the drive towards a more flexible, adaptable state, more in touch with real communities, and better able to make the most of limited resources.

Like other governments, the UK recognized that social entrepreneurship had the potential to generate types of value that were not easily created by business or public agencies. However, we were very aware that we could not move faster than the available capacity. As Blair's chief adviser on social policy I was one of those who concluded very early on in favour of not grand plan but a more evolutionary approach, designed to push forward the drivers of social entrepreneurship and remove some of the barriers so as to allow for organic growth. The worst thing that we could have done would have been to pump too much money into social entrepreneurship, raise expectations too high, and then see inexperienced leaders and organizations crash into disappointment.

The key, instead, was to remove as many of the barriers to social entrepreneurship as possible, and to provide some of the enablers where they were absent: finance, networks, support, and development so that the other invisible hand could do its work. Consequently, in a series of Budgets we tried to make it as easy as possible for citizens to commit money through a steady improvement in the tax treatment of donations to charities, which now matches any regime elsewhere in the world. We encouraged the development of larger, and more flexible sources of independent finance through the Community Investment Tax Credit (which has led to a wave of new Community Finance Institutions). A new Charity Bank was licensed as a source of cheap capital while the mainstream banks were encouraged to be less conservative in meeting the needs of excluded communities. Small, often very small, funding packages were provided for individual social entrepreneurs via the lottery-funded Charity Board, the Millennium Commission, and then UnLtd (which was funded with a £100 million ($172 million) endowment left over from the Millennium Commission), so that thousands of people with the germ of an idea could have the chance to try putting it into practice.

We tried to make it simpler for people to give time through volunteering initiatives from Millennium Volunteers to Timebank, a huge expansion of funding for mentoring, and a reform of benefit rules to make it easier to volunteer without jeopardizing entitlements. We tried to make it as easy as possible to create vehicles for action through simplifying and deregulating the process of creating voluntary organizations and charities, and in 2004 passed into legislation a new legal vehicle for social enterprises—the Community Interest Company (CIC). The definition of CICs has not been straightforward: it has raised important issues about how to constrain the transfer of assets into other activities; whether there should be upper limits on equity and dividends to demarcate CICs from for-profit organizations; and how to manage the relationship between CICs and parent organizations. But it marks a major step towards creating a more flexible legal environment for social enterprise.

We invested in capacity through a series of funding streams, of which the most recent is well over £100 million ($172 million) in Futurebuilders, focused on infrastructure and working capital for voluntary organizations. We expanded the sources of advice and support through mainstream routes like Business Links (since many of the types of advice needed are very similar to those sought by small firms), through specialist networks like the Community Action Network, and through learning projects like the School for Social Entrepreneurs. We sought to make it easier for smaller social enterprises to get engaged in decision-making, through funding voluntary sector participation in Local Strategic Partnerships (the umbrella bodies for strategy, planning, and regeneration in local areas), and the radical decentralization of the New Deal for Communities that has put small communities in charge of multi-million pound regeneration budgets.

Most radically, we opened up new space for social enterprises in public services by promoting greater contestability and a more level playing field between public, private, and not-for-profit sectors. Some very large new ventures like the Surestart programme for under-3s have been almost entirely voluntary sector led. Other policies have greatly expanded the scope of the sector, notably in childcare, housing, welfare, social care, and drug treatment.

Some of these national moves have been mirrored locally. For example Sheffield City Council has developed a commitment that 10 per cent of procurement should come through social enterprises. Fifty-five thousand homes have been transferred into the management of an arm's-length management organization (ALMO) called 'Sheffield Homes', 10 per cent of whose £1 billion ($1.72 billion) budget will be delivered through social enterprises.

One of the major factors which has made it easier to support social entrepreneurship is that, increasingly, governments have tried to tie funding to outcomes—no longer giving the public sector a guaranteed monopoly. So, for example, the new National Offender Management Service which is designed to provide a much more holistic approach to correctional services will evolve over the next few years into a purchaser of a diverse range of services, some from prisons and probation groups, some from private firms, and some from social enterprises: the key consideration will be whether better outcomes can be achieved—for example, with less recidivism—rather than just paying to keep people in prison for the period of their sentence. Much of the broader public sector reform agenda in the UK—including the promotion of Foundation Hospitals, more independent schools within the state framework (such as City Academies—which are an important new avenue of philanthropy each with millions of pounds donated alongside the majority of funding from government), areas such as Employment Zones, which allow for the maximum flexibility in getting people into work, or the growth of Community Support Officers in policing—are all pointing towards a radically different vision of the public sector with far greater diversity and much more provision rooted in communities.

There has also been a strong emphasis on innovation—the use of zones, pilots, public venture funds like the multi-hundred million pound 'Invest to Save' budget—and the encouragement of constructive rule breaking like the clause in the Education Act which allows head teachers to ignore national rules if they think they can do better—in direct emulation of the Empress Maria Theresa's famous medal for officers who turned the tide in battle by disobeying orders (a reminder too of Katherine Hepburn's comment that 'if you obey all the rules you miss all the fun').

So far this strategy has worked reasonably well. There has been a continued growth in the quantity and range of social entrepreneurship, new jobs (around 85,000), new volunteers (a million or so according to the most recent evidence), and all the signs of an emerging industry—with niches, funds, and umbrella bodies. Social entrepreneurship has played a part in the creation of new activities and in innovation in old ones.

Yet public policy towards social entrepreneurship is never unproblematic. Nor is it finished business. No government has yet found the ideal way to support capacity building in the sector. Much of the public sector—in particular local government—continues to resist competition and contestability (ideology and vested interests come together). Some of the most important general funding streams are coming to an end without clarity about what will replace them: the smallest community-based social enterprises are often most vulnerable because they are the least likely to have multiple sources of income. Such small community organizations also find it hard to take part in decision-making. Government is itself rather incoherent with multiple and sometimes conflicting agendas coming from different departments, despite repeated attempts to streamline and simplify overlapping programmes. There have also been important, and continuing, arguments around funding and procurement (including the use of full-cost recovery so that public contracts adequately cover overheads), and the timescales of contracts that have substantial practical importance for social entrepreneurs.

The Nature of Value

The comparative advantages of social entrepreneurship derive from a better ability to manage and create social value. This takes us straight into the difficult territory of thinking about value. All of the other concepts of economics are essentially derivative from ideas about value. Money, for example, is simply a tool for handling value: storing it, transacting it, and so on. Similarly, capital is meaningful only as an asset which creates value, or which has the potential to create value. This may be a stock of money that can be invested in a trading project; or it may refer to a factory, or a design, or a retail centre.

Recent years have brought a proliferation of new definitions of value and capital. Human capital is a straightforward application: qualifications and skills enable individuals to earn more, and, indeed, UK evidence shows very high returns to certain kinds of education. Over time, the value of the capital depreciates, and in periods of rapid change this pace of depreciation may accelerate. 'Social' capital is more problematic (see Putnam 2001, 2004). The phrase has become extremely popular in recent years, although this popularity has not led to a stable definition or accepted means of measurement. Some, for example, suggest that it is best understood in very similar terms to human capital as an attribute of the individual: their ability to make connections, use networks, deal with people from varying backgrounds. Others situate it in social relationships. So far social capital has not made the transition into practical use as a policy tool, although large-scale surveys are now being used to map it and to compare levels of capital in different geographical areas and age cohorts (Home Office 2004).

Social entrepreneurs have been keen to develop more rigorous metrics that can bridge the worlds of business and social policy. It is often assumed that value in business is a relatively unproblematic concept that is easily defined, measured, and managed. However, this is not the case. There has been a long history of innovation in accounting techniques to capture shifting patterns of value in different industries—from railways and the telegraph, to large-scale aerospace production and, more recently, the Internet—and of major failures that have resulted from the mis-measurement of costs, assets, and potential returns. In each of these cases value turned out to be much harder to pin down than one might expect: how for example to allocate the costs of design, development, testing, and vast factories in the manufacture of aeroplanes (see Johnson 1991)? Capital values in infrastructures have generally been very volatile (a high proportion of early railways went bankrupt; the huge overinvestment in third generation mobile phone licences is a more recent example). There remains little consensus on how to judge the capital value of brands or intellectual property or the culture and ethos of an organization, although no one doubts that these have many of the qualities of other forms of capital (and, in theory, these are all captured in market capitalizations).

These problems are mirrored within the state. Governments also try to manage value, either explicitly or implicitly, and the public value they are concerned with often overlaps with the value being created by social entrepreneurs. A lot of work is underway to give more substance to this concept—involving, amongst others, the BBC (who made the concept central to their charter renewal bid), the government's Strategy Unit, the Work Foundation, the Kennedy School of Government (KSG) at Harvard University, and others (Mulgan 2003). It is generally agreed that whereas private value is determined in markets, public value is determined by citizens' preferences, expressed through a variety of means and refracted through the decisions of elected politicians. For something to be of value it is not enough for citizens to say that it is desirable in a survey or consultation. It is only of value if citizens—either individually or collectively—are willing to give something up in return for it. Sacrifices are not only made in monetary terms through paying taxes and charges. They can also involve granting coercive powers to the state (e.g. in return for security), disclosing private information (e.g. in return for more personalized services), or giving time (e.g. serving as a part-time special police officer). The idea of opportunity cost is therefore central to public value: if it is claimed that citizens would like government to create something, but they are not willing to give anything up in return, then it is doubtful that the asset or activity in question will genuinely create value.

Traditional market failure analysis provides one set of explanations for public action: where there are public goods that are not excludable (such as defence), information failures (as in health, e.g.) and externalities (such as climate change). But public preferences go beyond these classic examples: people often want a public expression of identity and community (e.g. through major public buildings) and they often place a strong value on issues such as distributional equity (who gets fair treatment?) and due process. Citizens themselves are often involved in the production of services provided by social entrepreneurs and public agencies in a way that is not the case in relation to private services (e.g. in the areas of public health, education, and community safety citizens typically provide as much of the critical input that contributes to outcomes as paid professionals).

There are no neat dividing lines between different kinds of value: economic and social, public and private. Moreover, most social entrepreneurs work across a range of different kinds of value: indeed this is arguably one of the things that distinguish them. In some of their work they may be producing returns in ways not dissimilar to a private company doing the same things: offering goods and services and making a profit. They may be producing a value which only government can pay for—like reducing the likelihood of teenagers committing crimes, or improving the quality of public spaces. Or they may create value that others are willing to pay for, such as foundations or private donors. Ultimately however social entrepreneurship, like any other kind of enterprise, rests on its ability to create value and the extent to which people or individuals with the means to pay recognize that value.

There have been many attempts in recent years to synthesize new measures of value: cost–benefit analyses, QUALYs (which assess health impacts in terms of years of healthy life), the balanced scorecards proposed by Kaplan (2002), the blended value methods proposed by Emerson (2003), and the SROI models currently being used by the New Economics Foundation amongst others (Nicholls 2004). These work well with some social enterprises but not with others. For example, scorecards can be useful tools for individual organizations, but cannot easily capture the different perspectives that there may be around a community project. SROI analyses can be useful for understanding the indirect effects of projects working to regenerate communities or cut crime, although the numbers involved are always open to challenge. But methods that seek to aggregate diverse numbers into a single figure (like cost–benefit analyses and SROIs) can seek to impose an inappropriate consistency onto what is inevitably a complex picture made up of data of very uneven reliability. Moreover, the theoretical underpinnings of most of these methods remain very weak—with rather unconvincing accounts of the nature of value and the role of quantification.

An alternative to attempts to synthesize single metrics is to use 'Value Maps'—visual diagrams which set out in graphic form the relationships between different types of value and the flows of value they achieve, combining quantitative and qualitative aspects of value (Mulgan 2005). These aim to combine harder data on those values which can be easily measured—such as market returns and capital values, alongside the less easily measured contributions to social outcomes—crime, health, education. Some of these can be given rough monetary equivalents—what it would cost to achieve equivalent goals through other means. Such maps can also describe other dimensions of value ranging from community perceptions, trust, and employee development and so on without trying to quantify them in the same way as market prices. Ideally any assessments of value then need to be adjusted with an appropriate discount rate, based on differential depreciation to reflect the levels of risk and asset lives in order to give measures of net present values (NPVs). Such maps also have to be explicit about the degrees of certainty around different numbers (e.g. through a star rating), since indirect effects are likely to be much less certain than value that is directly paid for by consumers or contractors.

The main purpose of such maps, like all descriptions of value, is not to claim objectivity but rather to support better decision-making and in this case to provide some common frames for the different stakeholders in a social enterprise to consider options and opportunity costs. Ultimately all considerations of value involve conversation between different groups with different perspectives: there is no single objective value. So the most important questions for any metric of value are whether it can support the right kind of conversation, and whether the pictures it portrays prove to be robust against experience.

Social Entrepreneurship and Poverty

If social entrepreneurship works best when it creates new kinds of social value, this is more likely in areas that have been deserted by the traditional economy. Prosperous areas tend to be quite good at mobilizing their resources: physical assets and time are both highly valued and used. Social entrepreneurship has tended to spring up fastest in areas with underused assets, in particular high unemployment, and derelict or redundant buildings and land. Social entrepreneurs are often better able to discern the potential value of new activities, and can usually provide services and activities at much lower cost than public agencies that depend on professionals who live outside the area, and have to pay for overheads in more expensive city centres.

However, although the potential of social entrepreneurship may be greatest in poor areas, its practice can be harder. The research on social capital in Britain has revealed a very stark pattern. Whereas in the USA there is clear evidence of decline, and in many North European countries there is clear evidence that social capital has strengthened in recent decades, in the UK the picture is more ambiguous. Overall levels of social capital have remained constant or even risen. But what has changed is the class distribution—a strengthening in middle class areas that are now even denser webs of clubs, associations, and activities than before, and a marked decline in working class areas that has coincided with falling levels of political participation, labour market participation, and exclusion in all its forms (Halpern 2005).

In many estates in Glasgow, or Hackney, or for that matter Luton or Blackbird Leys in Oxford this soon becomes apparent. The decay of public buildings and spaces, and the loss of jobs in the 1980s, coincided with a decay of community in all its senses. A generation ago the community was held together by the rhythm of work, the rhythm of family life fitted to work, the rhythm of community life, and by powerful civic organizations. Most of these have weakened alongside the loss of the social bonding that comes from many people doing things together (Putnam 1994).

As governments sought to regenerate poor areas, their strengths and weaknesses were thrown into sharp relief, as was the uneven capacity of communities to organize themselves. There are many things that only states can do: raising large sums of money to rebuild buildings, create jobs, or revive schools. There are other things that only the market could do—preparing people for employability, managing large-scale developments. But neither states nor markets are competent at creating a sense of common purpose. Hence, alongside the investment of money in regeneration, a substantial amount of effort has gone into rebuilding the capacity of community organizations and social enterprises to run things themselves. It is where need has been married to capacity—in places like Easterhouse and Castlemilk in Glasgow, Manor Park in Sheffield, Balsall Heath in Birmingham, the 'projets' around the big French cities, or the Bronx and Detroit—that social entrepreneurship and enterprise have achieved the most, often weaving together diverse activities and acting as a bridge between the world of big organizations, big business and big government, and the localized small-scale communities in which people live their lives.

Next Phases of Public Policy

Over the next few years public policy will undoubtedly evolve in the light of assessments of what has and has not worked. More sophisticated contracting and funding methods seem certain to evolve along with more sophisticated metrics for assessing value. In the UK I would predict that as government seek to accelerate provision in new growth areas they will encourage social entrepreneurs to play a central role, providing more strategic funding, for example, to help with working capital, skills development, or IT infrastructure. Examples of sectors in which this kind of strategic approach is likely include: domestic households (i.e. measures to increase energy efficiency, reduce waste), childcare, eldercare in all its forms, and care for chronic diseases.

The development of new thinking about public value will also have an impact on social entrepreneurship: involving the public in the design of contracts (e.g. specifying the measures that will be used to determine payments to a contractor in housing), weighting payments to public satisfaction (e.g. payments to bus services reflecting satisfaction rather than simply rewarding punctuality), developing underused bases for social organization (e.g. empowering neighbourhoods and streets to appoint block leaders to motivate and mobilize their neighbours in such things as crime reduction and recycling), and the use of participatory budgeting to involve the community in setting priorities. Each of these examples will increase the scope for social entrepreneurs while also making them more accountable.

A more radical agenda might go further: for example, should social enterprises be guaranteed a proportion of public purchasing (rather as small and medium-sized enterprises currently benefit from guaranteed shares of government funding and research); should more be done to overcome the barriers to transferring assets to communities so that they can raise income for themselves? Are new vehicles needed for long-term contracting?

The other area of likely advance is in methods for dealing with systemic change. The last few years have seen great advances in understanding the nature of complex systems and their dynamics. Policymakers have moved away from the classic silo models of analysis and policy design, and from one-discipline methods of analysis. In areas as diverse as poverty, crime, and climate change, transformational change has to cope with a series of inter-connected systems—economic, social, attitudinal—and with the complex feedback loops that link them together. In some fields—notably health and crime—the professions have become much more attuned to the use of systems methods (see Chapman 2002).

Within central government the UK Strategy Unit has pioneered the use of systems methods in public policy, including much more holistic mapping of interconnections that explain how systems work. So, for example, the work on education has sought to model the connections between family cultures, school performance, and the pull of economic opportunities. In crime and correctional services, it has shown the complex links between sentencing policies, media coverage of crime, political discourse, and the cost drivers of the prisons system. These systemic analyses often bring out counterintuitive results: for example, showing how success in seizing illegal drugs can increase the sales of the drugs market (because of the dynamic impact of the price rises that result); or how building new roads increases rather than reduces conges-tion. Systemic analyses also often point to the need for structural change to reshape incentives and feedback mechanisms—and can be very challenging for existing vested interests.

Some social entrepreneurs intuitively understand these connections and think holistically. This is one reason why many combine advocacy and action. Some can imagine possible step changes. But usually they lack the analytical tools for working out which types of intervention will achieve the greatest leverage, and very few are proficient at quantitative analysis. Potentially there should be a great scope for collaboration between more holistic policymakers and institutional designers and social entrepreneurs.

A Research Programme—What Remains Unknown

In policy terms this is a relatively new field. It is short of concepts, empirical evidence and road-tested argument. There is no common body of knowledge on social innovation, enterprise, or entrepreneurship (though the Young Foundation has recently brought together theories, examples, and evidence on social innovation, see Mulgan 2006). There are many case studies of social innovations—though these fail to aggregate learning—and of the work of individual social entrepreneurs. There is abundant research on innovation within different fields, such as health, education, or criminal policy, which, though suggestive, does not seek to investigate common patterns. There is also an emerging body of research into the voluntary sector's capacity to innovate in the delivery of public services—but this tests one aspect of a sector's putative innovative capacity not social innovation as such (see Osborne 1998; Alcock, Brannelly, and Ross 2004). The subject of social enterprise (understood as trading in the market to achieve social aims) is becoming better understood but there are still no widely accepted concepts or empirical time series data to draw on (see Bristol City Council 1999; Birmingham Social Economy Consortium 2001; Amin, Cameron, and Hudson 2002; Westall 2002). There is some limited emerging work on the replication of successful voluntary sector initiatives but even this remains in its infancy (see Leat 2003). Meanwhile within the sector many of the umbrella organizations remain more in the advocacy and celebration mode, at home in a culture of anecdotes about heroic individuals with carefully burnished stories of success against the odds. They have proved slow to evolve towards more rigorous analysis, quantitative evaluation, and more nuanced judgements about the contribution social enterprise can make.

However the time is now right for the sector to move on, and the following are likely to be some of the areas where reasonably rapid progress could usefully be made.

The first is a better understanding of social entrepreneurs themselves. What is it that leads people to take risks, to switch from being an ordinary citizen to becoming a leader of change? Are there common personality types and personal histories? Are social entrepreneurs more likely to have failed at school, for example, or to have hit some other kind of barrier? Do they plan to become entrepreneurs or stumble into it?

The second is a better understanding of teams. A common flaw in much of the writing about social entrepreneurship is that it exaggerates the role of heroic individuals. As in business and science, although individual heroes often dominate the histories, on closer inspection creative social entrepreneurship is more often the product of the chemistry between people rather than stemming from a single source (this is one reason why often, when the front person is taken away from their context, they find it hard to create the same magic—successful serial social entrepreneurs are very rare). Teams are also crucial to understanding change in big organizations and systems—in government, for example, decisive change comes most often when a small number of key individuals—a leading minister, an official, an adviser—all share a common mission to achieve change.

The third is a better understanding of growth. There appear to be common life cycles and patterns for social ventures, just like businesses. Most start out rather chaotically: isolated, trying to do too much, and lacking credibility. The successful ones at some point have to grapple with difficult questions around growth: how to strike the right balance between organic growth, mergers and takeovers, or the various varieties of franchising (which tend to be very different from franchising in business, partly because the services to be delivered are less easily specified and partly because of the importance of values and relationships in most social enterprises). However, there is little agreement on the terms to use (those taken from business fit imperfectly in social fields) and on whether there are any general patterns influencing what works best. A very common issue is the problem of succession from a charismatic founder; the characteristics that are most successful in growing a new enterprise are rarely suitable for consolidation and growth. Another issue is the 'valley of death' faced when ventures try to grow and have to decide at precisely which point to introduce more formalized structures, metrics, and reporting arrangements (the difficulty of doing this in values-driven organizations explains why so many have flunked expansion). In all fields, growth in scale leads to changes in form, but this is particularly difficult for social ventures. The spark and passion is hard to routinize and scale up. This should be an important area of research: we need to understand the lessons of organic growth, franchising, and takeovers; what can be transplanted and what cannot; and why so many of the great social enterprises founded a century or so ago became bureaucratized (like Britain's building societies or the various mutual credit organizations set up in Europe).

The fourth set of issues concern governance. There is an inherent tension between entrepreneurship and risk-taking on the one hand, and the traditional roles of trustees acting as guardians of values who are, therefore, almost constitutionally risk averse. Boards have to juggle the competing interests of donors, contractors, beneficiaries, and potential future beneficiaries, often without much guidance. Larger organizations generally need to reform governance to reflect a changed mix of stakeholders, but this usually means less discretion for the founders and in some cases may undermine the organization's values. A great deal of innovation is underway in governance around the involvement of beneficiaries, stakeholders, and communities, but much of it is messy, weak on principles, and lacking in evidence.

The fifth is better understanding of networks. Social entrepreneurs often achieve their impact by mobilizing networks more effectively than public and for-profit organizations. Social network analysis has the potential to provide great insights into how they work. For example, recent work has mapped the networks of support that operate in towns and cities. They have looked at the partnerships involved in tackling domestic violence in Northampton or burglary in Nottingham and, by mapping who helps whom, and who values whom, revealed that often the key links are not between organizations but between people. Often quite junior people can turn out to be the crucial hubs that weave the system together. Similarly, the best social entrepreneurs often work to weave together disparate organizations, making things work in ways that bear little relationship to formal 'organograms'.

The sixth area in which new research is needed is better understanding of systems. The curse of social entrepreneurship is that brilliant projects can often leave bigger systems untouched. Genuine systemic transformation usually means working in many more dimensions, engaging with politics, public opinion, and funding flows. At the rhetorical level, many involved in social entrepreneurship have become engaged with systems thinking, but we lack good tools for making sense of how social entrepreneurship can best reinforce policy change, advocacy, or a changing role for businesses.

The seventh area is better understanding of innovation. Great progress has been made in recent years in understanding innovation in business. This work has demonstrated the importance of competition and the types of market structures that are most likely to accelerate innovation. Work in some industries has suggested that the optimum market structure is oligopolistic rather than highly competitive between small units. This work has profound implications for public services. Most public services generally combine the two features that are least likely to promote innovation: monopoly on the one hand and very small units, such as schools, hospitals, and prisons, on the other. But it also has implications for social entrepreneurship, where hard knowledge about the extent and nature of innovation is almost completely absent.

The eighth area for future research is a better understanding of the core skills involved in social entrepreneurship. It is arguably misleading to see social entrepreneurship as a profession. Professions are based on stable bodies of knowledge; policed boundaries; recognized social roles, and status. Parts of business certainly are professions. But other business specialisms—such as entrepreneurship and innovation—are not, and are unlikely to be helped by attempts at professionalization. Clarifying this matters: we want social entrepreneurs to support each other but not to fall into the trap of erecting barriers around themselves and taking on the trappings of pomp and self-importance that they grew up attacking.

Finally, we need better cross-national comparisons: what policies have worked well in accelerating the growth of social entrepreneurship. In most policy fields at the moment the best ideas are coming from the margins. The best performing nations by most measures are the smaller countries: within Europe the northern countries like the Netherlands and Denmark rather than Germany or France, Estonia rather than Russia; in North America, Canada rather than the USA; in Asia Korea, Taiwan, and Singapore rather than Japan. Being on the edge appears to be an advantage: two of the most innovative societies in recent years have been Finland and New Zealand. But so far we know relatively little about which countries have produced the best policy environments, and which are travelling fastest in terms of achievements.

In most countries the share of gross domestic product (GDP) contributed by social entrepreneurship in any strict definition remains very small—well under 1 per cent in the UK, for example (even though the more broadly

93

defined civil sectors are a lot bigger). Yet there is a realistic prospect that social entrepreneurship in all its forms will continue to grow in size, complexity, capacity, and confidence. There is no reason why it could not double as a share of GDP each decade.

As Baumol (2003) has written in his classic book on innovation, capitalism is a machine well-designed for perpetual, relentless innovation. In the commercial marketplace the 'invisible hand' of competition and profit translates individual self-interest into the common interest of growing wealth. In the social field there are good reasons for wanting to cultivate the other invisible hand with just as much determination.

Seen in the long view social entrepreneurship is part of the much broader story of democratization: of how people have begun to take control over their own lives, over the economy, and over society. It is, in some respects, a cousin of business entrepreneurship, in other respects inseparable from the rise of social movements, and the growth of a non-religious voluntary sector. It thrives only in societies where power is reasonably widely distributed, and where the poor as well as the rich have property rights. And it is to a large extent a phenomenon found only where there are democracy, rights, and freedoms. It thrives in these environments because it is best understood as one of the ways in which sovereignty is institutionalized, born of the insight that where there is a need or an aspiration, anyone can create the solution, and that solution can then take institutional form, and thus live longer, reach more people, and achieve more. It is, in other words, an expression of the very modern idea that institutions are not given or limited by traditions, but are rather malleable, adaptable, and plastic.

References

Alcock, P., Brannelly, T., and Ross, L. (2004). *Formality or Flexibility? Voluntary Sector Contracting*. London: NCVO.

Amin, A., Cameron, A., and Hudson, R. (2002). *Placing the Social Economy*. London: Routledge.

Baumol, W. (2003). *The Free-Market Innovation Machine: Analyzing the Growth of Miracle Capitalism*. Princeton, NJ: Princeton University Press.

Birmingham Social Economy Consortium (2001). *Social Enterprise: What Implications for the Voluntary Sector?*

Bristol City Council (1999). *Bristol Social Economy Audit*.

Chapman, J. (2002). *System Failure*. London: Demos.

Drucker, P. (1990). *Managing the Non-Profit Organization*. New York: HarperCollins.

Emerson, J. (2003). 'The Blended Value Proposition: Integrating Social and Financial Returns', *California Management Review*, 45(4): 35–51.

Etzioni, A. (1961). *A Comparative Analysis of Complex Organizations*. New York: Free Press.

Halpern, D. (2005). *Social Capital*. London: Polity Press.

Harris, J. (1994). *Private Lives, Public Spirit: Britain 1870–1915*. London: Penguin.

Home Office (2004). *Citizenship Survey: People, Families and Communities*. London: Home Office.

Johnson, T. (1991). *Relevance Lost: The Rise and Fall of Management Accounting*. Harvard, MA: Harvard University Press.

Kaplan, R. (2002). 'The Balanced Scorecard and Non-Profit Organizations', *Balanced Scorecard Report*, pp. 2–6.

LaPiere, R. (1965). *Social Change*. London: McGraw-Hill.

Leat, D. (1993). *Managing Across Sectors: Similarities and Differences Between For-Profit and Voluntary Non-Profit Organizations*. London: Centre for Voluntary Sector and Not-for-Profit Management, City University.

——(2003). *Replicating Successful Voluntary Sector Projects*. London: Association of Charitable Foundations.

Mulgan, G. (2003). *Creating Public Value*. London: The Government Strategy Unit, Available at: www.strategy.gov.uk

——(2005). *Value Maps*. London: Commission on Architecture and the Built Environment.

——(2006). *Social Silicon Valleys: A Manifesto for Social Innovation*. London: The Young Foundation.

——and Landry, C. (1996). *The Other Invisible Hand*. London: Demos.

Nicholls, J. (2004). *Social Return on Investment: Valuing What Matters*. London: New Economics Foundation.

Osborne, S. (1998). *Voluntary Organizations and Innovation in Public Services*. London: Routledge.

Prochaska, F. (1988). *The Voluntary Impulse*. London: Chatto.

Putnam, R. (1994). *Making Democracy Work: Civic Traditions in Modern Italy*. Princeton, NJ: Princeton University Press.

——(2001). *Bowling Alone*. New York: Simon & Schuster.

——(ed.) (2004). *Democracies in Flux: The Evolution of Social Capital in Contemporary Society*. New York: Oxford University Press.

Salamon, L. (2000). *The Tools of Government*. Oxford: Oxford University Press.

——Sokolowski, M., and List, R. (2003). *Global Civil Society: An Overview*. Baltimore, MD: Kumarian Press.

Skocpol, T. (2003). *Diminished Democracy: From Membership to Management in American Civic Life*. Oklahoma, OK: University of Oklahoma Press.

Spinosa, C., Flores, F., and Dreyfus, H. (1997). *Disclosing New Worlds: Entrepreneurship, Democratic Action, and the Cultivation of Solidarity*. Cambridge, MA: MIT Press.

Westall, A. (2002). *Value Led, Market Driven*. London: IPPR.

Part II
New Theories

5

Social Entrepreneurship: The Structuration of a Field

Alex Nicholls and Albert Hyunbae Cho

As noted in the introduction, social entrepreneurship is a dynamically evolving phenomenon that engages a broad range of stakeholders and is articulated across different organizational approaches. Yet despite the growing importance of social entrepreneurship as a means of addressing critical social issues globally (Nicholls 2004, 2006), to date our understanding of the field remains largely limited to anecdotal case studies and instrumental analyses of efficiency and operational best practices (see, e.g. Leadbeater 1997; Bornstein 2004). Indeed, the chief theoretical location of social entrepreneurship has been within business studies with a methodological preference towards strategic reflection on specific examples of innovative praxis often under-pinned by profiles of 'hero' social entrepreneurs (Dees 1998; Dees, Emerson, and Economy 2001). Whilst such an approach has helped raise the profile of the field of research, it has yet to offer much in the way of serious theoretical discourse. Of particular note has been the lack of any sociological inter-pretations of the phenomenon to date. As a young, still-evolving, and largely undertheorized area of practice and research, social entrepreneurship is still in the process of self-definition. As a consequence, it is now timely to explore and develop a range of foundational concepts of social entrepreneurship drawn from the existing sociology of organizations (though see Mair and Marti 2004; Cho 2006, for some initial discussions of possible theoretical approaches).

This chapter attempts to develop some useful analytical frameworks for the study of social entrepreneurship. It explores a set of issues that logically underpin a theoretically grounded understanding of this locus of action, proceeding in two parts. Initially, it defines social entrepreneurship as a distinct field of organizational activity mapped across three key dimensions, which we call sociality, market orientation, and innovation. This analysis is important not only because it situates social entrepreneurship within the broader context of social purpose organizations and private enterprises, but also because in doing so, it illuminates a number of useful theoretical frameworks for understanding the social, political, and operational features of entrepreneurial social ventures. Indeed, a key argument of this chapter is that these components of social entrepreneurship—sociality, market orientation, and innovation—are themselves sociologically important categories and that, as a result, sociological theory can help identify important conceptual issues for social entrepreneurs.

The second part of this chapter begins with the premise that these conceptual dimensions of social entrepreneurship are susceptible to sociological analysis, and applies insights from various fields to suggest potential directions for future research. As an exemplar, it analyses the political dimension of 'sociality', drawing upon insights from critical theory. It then applies Giddens' analysis (1984) of structuration to explore the relationship between social entrepreneurs and the contexts in which they operate and to consider two issues in organizational activity: the use of legitimating assets and resistance to field-level isomorphic pressures. These examples are far from exhaustive and our treatment of them here can only be exploratory, but they suggest that a sociological approach to social entrepreneurship can open up new and fruitful frontiers for future research in the field.

Unpacking 'Social Entrepreneurship': Foundational Concepts

This section explores the basic characteristics of social entrepreneurship with a view to identifying the key organizing principles of the field. Any serious attempt to understand the meanings of social entrepreneurship must logically begin with a rigorous examination of its foundational concepts: 'social' and 'entrepreneurship', both individually and in relation to each other. Initially, social entrepreneurship is meaningful only insofar as it can be distinguished significantly from entrepreneurship that is not social. Hence it is essential to understand what social means in this context, and how the objectives of social entrepreneurship differ from the objectives of (by extension) non-social entrepreneurship. On the other hand, so-called social ventures themselves are not new. If social entrepreneurship is substantively distinct from traditional socially oriented organizational forms such as not-for-profits or philanthropic foundations, its entrepreneurial dimension must separate it from other non-entrepreneurial social ventures. Consequently, it is also important to flesh out the critical differentiating elements of entrepreneurship. As was noted in the introduction, both the social and entrepreneurship elements can usefully be framed from a variety of perspectives drawing on their operational processes, outputs, or contexts. However, in this chapter, we will set out a more sociologically inflected definitional approach in an attempt to drive down towards a deeper understanding of this emergent field of action and study.

Social entrepreneurship ventures are often social by a process of normative self-construction that does not admit to easy interpretation. Social organizations are ostensibly social because they advance specific social objectives, but this merely begs the questions of what social objectives include, what the nature and boundaries of society are, and how the answers to these questions are determined. The use of the phrase social as a modifier for entrepreneurship raises two questions, one conceptual and one empirical: first, which objectives can legitimately be considered social, and second, to what extent does a given organization actually advance these objectives? Our ability to call an organization an example of social entrepreneurship implicitly presupposes the ability to assess whether a given organization has legitimate objectives and whether it can make an operational contribution towards these goals (the question of legitimacy is addressed further later). Furthermore, while these goals are distinguished from private objectives, it is not always clear what they include. Hence, *sociality*—the extent to which an organization intentionally and effectively pursues the advancement of social objectives (however defined) is a critical, but problematic dimension for distinguishing socially entrepreneurial ventures from other organizations (see further Cho 2006). Some of the contested issues around the social are discussed later.

Entrepreneurship is the second conceptual building block of social entrepreneurship, and it, too, evokes a complicated set of questions. Drawing distinctions between traditional social purpose organizations and socially entrepreneurial ventures implicitly involves assessing the extent to which a given organization is entrepreneurial, which in turn involves defining entrepreneurship. As was suggested in the introduction, there are a number of competing definitions of entrepreneurship, each emphasizing different elements of entrepreneurial behaviour and each with a number of different meanings, often including profit-making, risk-taking, and innovation. For the purposes of this analysis, these various meanings will be clustered around two primary characteristics of entrepreneurship that correspond to what Casson (2005) calls the 'Schumpeterian' and the 'Austrian' approaches to entrepreneurship.

The Schumpeterian narrative of entrepreneurship emphasizes the role of the entrepreneur as innovator. Entrepreneurs draw upon the 'dream and the will to found a private kingdom', developing 'new combinations' of goods, services, and organizational forms in the service of a relentless drive to create (Schumpeter 1934: 93). Casson (2005: 17) calls innovation 'high-level entrepreneurship': the kind of drive that 'historically, has led to the creation of railroads, the birth of the chemical industry, the commercial exploitation of colonies, and the emergence of the multidivisional multinational firm'. Put in the context of social objectives, social entrepreneurs are essentially social innovators, a definition embraced by several social entrepreneurship funding and support agencies. The Skoll Foundation (2005) noted that 'unlike business entrepreneurs who are motivated by profits, social entrepreneurs are motivated to improve society'; they are 'change agents for society, seizing opportunities others miss and improving systems, inventing new approaches and creating sustainable solutions to change society for the better'. In other words, creativity, innovation, and resourcefulness are the elements of entrepreneurship most relevant to social entrepreneurs. Hence the Skoll Foundation includes among its exemplary social entrepreneurs Maria Montessori and Jane Addams, both of whom revolutionized social service provision in various sectors without necessarily adopting a market-oriented strategy. From this perspective, what sets social entrepreneurship apart from traditional social service providers is precisely that they are non-traditional; they are disruptive in their approach, pioneering, and entrepreneurial. Hence *innovation* appears to be one of the principally important dimensions defining social entrepreneurship often aiming at systemic change.

Casson contrasts the Schumpeterian, high-level mode of entrepreneurialism with the low-level entrepreneurship he associates with the Austrian School approach to entrepreneurship. The Austrian entrepreneur, in the context of the market economy, exploits arbitrage opportunities to buy cheap and sell dear. He or she is motivated by profit and seeks to generate efficiencies that will produce more arbitrage opportunities. In the context of social entrepreneurship, the relevant principle is not necessarily arbitrage, but *market orientation*, which similarly involves the rationalized search for financial returns. Within the spectrum of social entrepreneurship, this approach is particularly relevant in the subset of ventures commonly called social enterprises that combine social impact with an independent commercial income stream. For example, the Institute for Social Entrepreneurs (2005) defines social entrepreneurship as 'the art of simultaneously pursuing both a financial and a social return on investment' (the 'double bottom line'), clearly enumerating the market oriented dimension of social entrepreneurship. Likewise, Alter (2000: 1) defines social enterprise as a 'generic term for a nonprofit enterprise, *social-purpose business or revenue-generating venture* founded to support or create economic opportunities for poor and disadvantaged populations *while simultaneously operating with reference to the financial bottom line*' (emphasis added).

However, the application of market orientation to social purpose ventures is a more complex construct than simply a path to generating financial, as well as social, returns. Today, successful social entrepreneurs not only have to work within a market context when seeking earned income, but also the grant funding landscape has become an increasingly competitive and demanding marketplace. Indeed, the development of a new set of accountability mechanisms and performance ratings agencies around social ventures—such as Guidestar or Keystone—demonstrates the competitive pressures that affect social purpose organizations irrespective of their income streams. This greater degree of accountability is welcome since it encourages organizations to maximize social impact subject to resource constraints, but it introduces a new set of issues for decision-makers to consider. In both of these senses, the broad principle of market orientation appears, therefore, to be another key dimension of entrepreneurship relevant to the study of social entrepreneurship. Finally, social entrepreneurs also address 'social' market failures where institutions are failing to address the need for new public goods. This 'social' disequilibrium often demands systemic interventions.

These three elements: sociality, market orientation, and innovation, map out a set of conceptual dimensions for the field of social entrepreneurship. We analyse them not to attempt an exclusive or constrained definition of social entrepreneurship, but rather to provide structure to the field so that its salient features can be isolated, understood, and evaluated. Indeed, any particular social purpose organization will be situated at a different set of coordinates in this three-dimensional space (see Figure 5.1). Some organizations are socially oriented and innovative but lack a particularly strong market orientation, such as the initial innovation of hospice and palliative care. Others might be socially oriented and market oriented, but at the same time be reproductions of existing concepts and therefore not innovative, such as the replication of microfinance

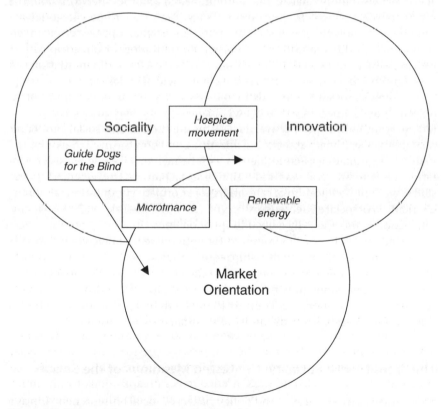

Figure 5.1 Dimensions of social entrepreneurship

facilities. Others still might be market oriented and innovative, but have a less clearly defined or more contested sociality, such as environmental projects focusing on renewable energy or projects targeted at improving access to reproductive health interventions. Furthermore, many social ventures move dynamically between these dimensions, shifting as they aim to maximize social impact and bring about change with often limited resources. For example, witness the move towards greater market orientation by the long-established UK charity Guide Dogs for the Blind driven by the arrival of a new director, Geraldine Peacock. It should be stressed that this framework is intended to open, not close, discussion about the theoretical boundaries of social entrepreneurship.

Indeed, by focusing attention on the loci of difference—the set of features that differentiate social entrepreneurship ventures from other organizations—this framework also opens up a broader set of questions about the nature of these ventures and their relationship to the contexts in which they operate. It is a key contention of this chapter that each of these elements—sociality, market orientation, and innovation—raises interesting questions about the interaction between individual agents (entrepreneurs) and their networks and the social contexts in which they operate, suggesting that these categories are themselves sociologically appropriate phenomena that can be better understood through the application of appropriate frameworks from sociology, as well as political and social theory. Examining these axes of differentiation can therefore enrich our basic understanding of the field of social entrepreneurship.

For example, sociality implicitly invokes a set of questions about how 'social' objectives are defined, negotiated, and pursued—a line of inquiry taken in Cho (2006). From another perspective, it raises the question of how social enterprises manage their legitimacy as social organizations, and how the need to acquire and maintain legitimating assets influences their behaviour. Likewise, market orientation raises questions about the division of social burdens between markets and states; the commodification of care; and, more normatively, questions about the distribution of social entrepreneurship's benefits (see, e.g. Brickell 2000). Finally, innovation is also a socially embedded phenomenon, in that it both influences and is influenced by the environment for entrepreneurial behaviour. Properly apprehending social entrepreneurship requires that we go further than simply to identify the key differentiating features of the field; we must also analyse these underlying dimensions and understand them sociologically, within the broader context of social phenomena. The next section of the chapter takes up a subset of these issues to demonstrate the utility of this analytical approach.

The Trouble with Sociality: Contested Meanings of the Social

The construction by scholars and policymakers of social entrepreneurship as a distinct category over the last few years implicitly opposes the concepts of social and conventional/commercial entrepreneurship. This immediately raises the question of exactly what the social dimension of social entrepreneurship entails. Existing definitions are of limited use in answering this question, as they tend merely to define social entrepreneurship along the established behavioural and operational lines preset in business research on commercial entrepreneurship, but typically with an ill-defined social focus (Cho 2006). Such approaches neither ask key questions surrounding the issue of how entrepreneurship actually plays out in social contexts nor challenge the—often tautological—application of such a term to social ends, providing little guidance as to what those ends might be. Yet social entrepreneurship can only be considered a discrete focus of inquiry on the basis of the unique features of its social dimension. Research that neglects this substantive dimension leaves the most important aspect of the field unexplored. Social entrepreneurship links the instrumental means of entrepreneurship (and its attendant characteristics, market orientation and innovation, *inter alia*) to putatively social objectives. Absent a critical examination of those ends and the study of social entrepreneurship become an analysis of means oriented towards ends that remain wholly unclear.

This gap in the research is particularly surprising because the social is a deeply complex and contested category. The first problem with neglecting the social is that this omission leaves the field without a stable substantive core. Failure to engage with theories of the social leads to an interesting lacuna similar to the one Neidorf (2005: 15) encountered in a conversation with an 8-year-old about the good objectives of public service:

NEIDORF: Now here's a 'philosophy' question for you. What makes a person good?
CHILD: Oh, that's an easy one! A good person is somebody who helps other people.
N: Really? So what does a good person help others to do?
C: Whatever they are trying to do.
N: Does a good person help others to do anything they might be trying to do, no matter what it is?
C: Well . . . no, I guess not.
N: Okay, then, out of all the things people try to do, which ones does a good person help them to do?
C: Oh, that's easy! He helps them do things that are good.

Social entrepreneurship, like the concept of service learning that Neidorf critiques, begs an important question: what is the nature of the social objectives that entrepreneurs are trying to pursue? Public service is only as valuable as the ends that are being served; likewise, social entrepreneurship is only as interesting as the social objectives it advances. Without a more sophisticated inquiry into this set of foundational issues, the definition of social entrepreneurship remains tautological, even jejune.

The second problem, as argued by Cho (2006), is that speaking of social entrepreneurship without acknowledging the deeply contested nature of social objectives presupposes an unrealistic homogeneity of social interests. Visions of the social are inextricably linked to varying sets of potentially incompatible values and normative commitments. In the inescapable context of social heterogeneity, talking about social entrepreneurship without acknowledging the possibility of fundamentally divergent social objectives makes little sense. It may, in fact, be an act of discursive marginalization, reflecting the social interests of the dominant public while neglecting the needs and objectives of what Nancy Fraser (1992: 123) calls 'subaltern counter-publics'. Heterogeneity of interests means that social is not simply a descriptive category; rather, it inevitably raises political and normative questions about whose interests are being furthered, and at whose expense. Social heterogeneity suggests that the narrative linking social entrepreneurship to social objectives is not simple or unambiguous, and demands critical analysis to uncover potential conflicts between ostensibly social ends.

A third complicating factor is that social visions can be articulated in monological or dialogical ways, and that the choice of approaches has normative implications (Cho 2006). Implicit in the narrative of the innovative, romantic hero social entrepreneur is the desire to remake the world in the creator's image, or at least in the image of the utopian vision articulated by the social entrepreneur. This monological, subject-centred image is hard-wired in many definitions of social entrepreneurship. Dees, Emerson, and Economy (2001: 4), for example, described social entrepreneurs as: 'reformers and revolutionaries', whose 'visions are bold', who 'break new ground, develop new models, and pioneer new approaches'. This monological approach contrasts sharply with a consensus-based, participatory, dialogical approach to the identification of social problems and solutions, and indeed raises questions about the means appropriate for social action (Cho 2006).

Social entrepreneurship is productive precisely because it is disruptive, innovative, and progressive, but the untrammelled pursuit of a messianic social vision can be destructive as well as redemptive. How should social entrepreneurs negotiate the need to be single-minded and disruptive with the need to pursue inclusive and sustainable processes? Are social entrepreneurs' versions of what Hegel (1988: 32) called 'world-historical individuals', heroic men and women 'with insight into what was needed and what was timely', whose 'deeds and . . . words are the best of their time'? A world-historical individual 'commits himself unreservedly to one purpose alone . . . so it happens that such individuals treat other interests, even sacred ones, in a casual way—a mode of conduct certainly open to moral censure.' Must 'so great a figure . . . necessarily trample on many an innocent flower, crushing much that gets in his way'? Or does the omnipresent multiplicity of legitimate social visions militate in favour of a more democratic, less hubristic approach to social change? Perhaps disruptive strategies are needed in early stages of social entrepreneurship to force issues to the fore, whereupon more inclusive procedures for resolving them can be pursued (e.g. social movement theory, see Davis et al. 2005). Or perhaps social change should be seen as a competitive marketplace—or battleground—of unique social visions. Or perhaps the complexity and potential disharmony of social objectives suggests the need for greater humility and receptivity to competing worldviews. Should strategies for social change be evaluated teleologically and *ex post,* or are there procedural issues that bear legitimate claims for consideration *ex ante*? Whatever the case, the intrinsic diversity of social objectives calls for greater scholarly attention to be paid to the political and normative implications of strategies for social change.

Market Orientation

Market orientation is a second feature that differentiates social entrepreneurship ventures from other social organizations. By market orientation, we mean the dimension of entrepreneurship that entails rationalizing strategic operations in response to exogenous variables traditionally conceived as competitive market pressures. Many social purpose organizations are located in dysfunctional or non-existent markets, but social entrepreneurs nevertheless recognize the value of a market orientation that gives primacy to the most effective deployment of resources towards achieving a social goal. Market orientation is present in descriptions of social entrepreneurship that describe a 'double or triple bottom line', cost or full-cost recovery, or the development of independent profit-making ventures, such as social enterprises. With its implicit focus on efficiency and effective use of resources, market orientation distinguishes many social entrepreneurship ventures from traditional models of not-for-profit social service delivery or advocacy, as well as much of the public sector.

Market orientation can resolve many of the complaints associated with traditional social service delivery operations, by encouraging accountability, economy, and innovation (Bartlett and LeGrand 1993). However, market orientation may also participate in a broader shift towards monological social agenda setting. This is particularly true for social enterprises with a mixed social and economic strategic agenda: focusing on generating economic, as well as social, value in such initiatives can precipitate conflicts with other terminal social objectives (see further Dart 2004; Weisbrod 2004; Foster and Bradach 2005). Lottery marketing and investments in ecotourism ventures are just two examples of cases where the market orientation of social ventures may create outcomes incompatible with social objectives the social entrepreneur may not have included in her decision-making calculus. In the first case, social programmes end up being subsidized by those least able to afford the expense, and in the second, the rights of displaced communities frequently come into conflict with the desire to extract economic value from environmental conservation (Cho 2006). Indeed, in the context of social heterogeneity, the market-oriented dimension of social entrepreneurship can be a double-edged sword, creating both progress and regress relative to social outcomes desired by different groups.

A market-oriented approach may also raise legitimate normative and ethical issues, particularly in the context of social service delivery. On the one hand, in the context of the retreat of the welfare state and the privatization of social services, lines between social entrepreneurship, public–private partnership, and outright privatization become increasingly blurry. The application of quasi-market principles to the public sector has been a key feature of government policy in a number of developed economies in the last twenty years (see LeGrand and Bartlett 1993; LeGrand 2003). This model typically applied socially entrepreneurial approaches to public welfare delivery as part of an agenda to 'reinvent government' along more efficient and impactful lines (Osbourne and Gaebler 1992). The application of such policies has often been highly controversial (see Eikenberry and Kluver 2004) and the empirical evidence for their success remains mixed (see, e.g. Docteur and Oxley 2003), but there is an increasing consensus developing around the value of bringing a market orientation to the delivery of public goods funded by the state that parallels some of the market-driven approaches typified in other successful social entrepreneurship ventures (see also Giddens 1998). This gradual hybridization of functions is neither intrinsically good nor bad, but it does call for closer critical analysis. Similarly, innovative models that increase the market orientation of social services raise legitimate ethical questions about shifting expectations about full cost recovery. Particularly in tendering scenarios where not-for-profits compete directly with for-profit companies.

Hospice care, for example, is a social innovation directed towards the provision of palliative care for terminally ill patients at the end of life. In the USA, ownership patterns in the hospice sector differ in terms of market orientation; some are not-for-profits, frequently run by religious charities; others are for-profit corporations. The American government provides fixed Medicare payments to support hospice care on a per diem basis, while costs vary. This feature of hospice economics provides financial incentives for hospice managers to control costs, and for-profit and not-for-profit hospices respond to these incentives in very different ways (Weisbrod and Lindrooth 2004). Because patient costs tend to follow a U-shaped pattern (with marginal costs high at the beginning of care as patient care plans are developed, lower during an intermediate period, then higher again in the patient's final days), hospices have a financial incentive to attract patients with a longer length of stay, thereby maximizing the length of the profitable intermediary period. Preliminary empirical research suggests that for-profit hospices maximize lengths of stay by admitting patients significantly earlier into hospice programmes than their not-for-profit counterparts, and by selectively admitting patients whose diagnoses are associated with longer expected lengths of stay (Weisbrod and Lindrooth 2004: 24). By contrast, not-for-profits also pursue patients with high expected lengths of stay, but use these profits to subsidize patients with illnesses associated with low profitability in the service of their mission. Weisbrod finds that not-for-profits are no less efficient at service provision than for-profit hospices; market orientation merely shifts the patient recruitment strategy and produces de facto discrimination based on the profitability associated with the patient diagnosis.

Market orientation, then, may have mission-related implications for socially innovative organizations. Hence, it is important to underscore that market orientation is a continuous rather than a discrete variable. Not-for-profit ventures that seek to control input costs and achieve operational efficiency exhibit a certain kind of market orientation; profit-seeking ventures exhibit another. While neither is intrinsically superior to the other, the degree to which an organization responds to market incentives is a substantively important question that deserves further consideration and research.

Structuration and Innovation in Social Entrepreneurship

Innovation is the third major distinguishing feature of social entrepreneurship. Thinking about entrepreneurship as innovation suggests that the disruptive creation of new models and techniques is—as Schumpeter suggested—a critical driver of social change. It also implicitly raises the question of how social innovators behave, and of what constrains and influences their action. Social entrepreneurs stand in a dynamic relation to the social contexts that produce them, and which they seek to influence through new behaviours. This inter-activity lends itself to a discussion of the relationship between structure and agency, for which we turn to the theory of structuration, as developed by Giddens (1984).

Structuration

The theory of structuration attempts to resolve a basic debate in sociology about the relationship between structure and agency. Loosely put, structuralist arguments emphasize the contextual social forces that structure and deter-mine individual choices. Strict structuralists tend to downplay the scope for truly independent behaviour by social actors, arguing that social organization always influences the choices available to them. On the other hand, agency theorists argue that individual agents have much greater scope to choose courses of behaviour. They emphasize the creative and disruptive abilities of individual actors, suggesting that social structures are fluid and malleable in the hands of agents (Cohen 1989).

Giddens (1984) argued that the pure opposition between structure and agency is misguided and needlessly dualist. He suggested that agents are

109

neither powerless nor omnipotent relative to the social contexts in which they operate; rather, structure and agency exist in a complicated, endogenously determined, continuously evolving relationship with each other. In the theory of structuration, competent agents actively and reflexively reproduce the conditions that determine their behaviour, but they do so in a way that enables changes to occur. Structuration theory suggests that agents are not always free to pursue an unlimited array of choices, nor are they powerless in the face of a hegemonically deterministic social structure. Rather than leading us into a choice between duelling caricatures of social existence, Giddens suggested that agents operate in an evolving and dynamic relationship with their social environments, an interesting and far less deterministic account of social behaviour. As he noted, 'According to the notion of the duality of structure, the structural properties of social systems are both medium and outcome of the practices they recursively organise' (Giddens 1984: 25).

Giddens' work on structuration has also been applied outside of the narrow sociological domain in business and management scholarship, most notably strategy (see Pozzebon 2004 for a useful survey). In the spirit of this wider application of Giddens' solution to the structure and agency dichotomy, structuration can also inform many of social entrepreneurship's basic concepts. Social entrepreneurship operates at the horizon between agency and structure as the concept that bridges individual or networked entrepreneurship and the social concerns that lie above and outside the individual. We can also view social entrepreneurship as a particular genus of social behaviour pursued by independent agents and their networks. If normatively meaningful engagement with society is a defining characteristic of social entrepreneurship, then understanding the relationship between agents and the social environment in which they operate is a critical element of understanding this field.

Structuration theory suggests a number of tools and approaches for analysing key questions concerning the drivers and constraints in social entrepreneurship. Are social entrepreneurs, indeed, world-historical individuals, innovators whose creative agency permits them to shape social outcomes according to their subjective and exogenous desires? To what extent are their behaviours, objectives, and strategies constrained and ultimately determined by structural features of the environments in which they originate? What analytical tools can help us better understand the disruptive dimension of socially entrepreneurial behaviour?

For example, structuration theory may help us think about how the emerging field of social entrepreneurship can avoid the stasis that affects more traditional social ventures. Giddens (1984: 54) suggested that 'all human action is carried on by knowledgeable agents who both construct the social world through their action, but yet whose action is also conditioned and constrained by the very world of their creation.' Yet even within the structurationist dynamic, different balances between structure and agency are possible. In contrast with more established organizational fields, social entrepreneurs may produce an imbalance in this dynamic: a greater propensity towards Fuchs' concept (2003) of 'self-organizing' (see also Chapter 11). Namely, the social entrepreneurial individual or network often consciously challenges the societal status quo by disrupting dysfunctional structures to innovate, change, and deliver greater social or environmental impact. Thus, the influence of extant social structures on social entrepreneurs may be far less than in other areas of 'self-organizing' action and—conversely—their impact on society far greater. However, the important role of market orientation, noted earlier, does provide a corrective to extending this line of thinking too far.

Furthermore, it is evident that the dynamic and cross-sectoral activities typical of social entrepreneurship often defy being constrained within established organizational frames of reference or societal norms. Indeed, this boundary-blurring flexibility is often their key strategic advantage. Such conceptualizations are best theorized within an important subset of structuration theory: institutional isomorphism.

Institutional Isomorphism

One of the reasons social entrepreneurship has received so much attention in popular and academic discussions recently is that it is perceived to be a source of new and innovative solutions to persistent social problems. As has been noted earlier, to some extent, the field has crystallized thus far around the image of the social entrepreneur as romantic hero: the creative, risk-taking actor who tackles social problems using new approaches, untapped resources, and his or her bare hands (Dees 1998; Bornstein 2004). Indeed, social entrepreneurs do typically develop and promulgate approaches that differ significantly from existing (and presumably inferior) methods of service delivery. Originality, diversity, and the ability to disrupt stable systems are some of the most important tools of the social entrepreneur.

However, if innovation, originality, and difference are such critical elements of social entrepreneurship, then it is worthwhile to ask how this new breed of entrepreneurship might escape the fate of more traditional organizations such as firms and some not-for-profits, which exhibit a 'startling homogeneity of organizational forms and practices' (DiMaggio and Powell 1983). DiMaggio and Powell cited research in a wide range of sectors, including hospitals, public schools, the radio industry, and the textbook industry, that demonstrates an inexorable Weberian tendency for organizations to fall into an 'iron cage' of conformity and 'institutional isomorphism'.

Furthermore, they suggested that organizational homogeneity is a direct consequence of the 'structuration of organizational fields', which constructs sectors into environments subject to powerful isomorphic pressures. Isomorphic forces include coercive, mimetic, and normative pressures (DiMaggio and Powell

1983: 150) that interact with features of the competitive and institutional environment to encourage the adoption of similar organizational structures and behaviours. Coercive pressures are the consequence of political or social imperatives, such as regulation or social taboos. By establishing a clear set of rules and expectations, they encourage organizations to adopt similar practices. Mimetic pressures are the consequence of organizational responses to situations of environmental uncertainty and risk. Organizations tend to model themselves on other examples that are perceived to be successful in their field, a process typified by the widespread diffusion of 'best practices'. Finally, normative pressures are generated by increasingly rationalized professional structures within an organizational sector. For example, recruitment processes may establish employment profiles consonant with organizational culture, then carefully filter all subsequent job applicants to match existing criteria. McKinsey & Co.'s early decision to hire recent MBA graduates as management consultants, for example, derived from its organizational culture, and this norm gradually diffused throughout the sector. Across any sector, the development of standardized and comparable roles—such as assistant, associate, and full professors in US universities—facilitates normative isomorphism.

The more strongly the organizations within a sector become identified as members of a single 'field', the more strongly these isomorphic pressures will operate. The structuration of a field is a dynamic and interactive process; coercive, mimetic, and normative pressures help construct the field at the same time as they stimulate new isomorphic pressures. Hence the iron cage to which DiMaggio and Powell (1983) referred.

The tendency towards institutional isomorphism partially explains why social entrepreneurship has been such a welcome disruptive force, and raises important questions about how social entrepreneurs navigate isomorphic pressures that created stable but insufficient structures in the first place. Does the construction of the field of social entrepreneurship contain the seeds of its own destruction, in that such structuration could generate isomorphic pressures contrary to the ideals of disruptive, Schumpeterian, social entrepreneurship? Are the concepts of 'scaling up' or 'mainstreaming' social entrepreneurship intrinsically paradoxical? Or can social entrepreneurs adopt modes of rationalization and professionalization consistent with the need to escape these pressures?

In order better to understand how social entrepreneurship often escapes organizational isomorphism at a field level, this chapter will conclude with a final theoretical model drawn from within structuration—legitimation.

Legitimation

The strategic drive towards organizational legitimacy has been defined as part of the process of isomorphism. In the context of an institutional theory analysis of social enterprises, Dart (2004: 415) noted,

From an institutional perspective, legitimacy is...the means by which organizations obtain and maintain resources...and is the goal behind an organization's widely observed conformance or isomorphism with the expectations of key stakeholders in the environment.

Further, Suchman (1995: 574) defined organizational legitimacy as 'a generalized perception or assumption that the actions of an entity are socially desirable, proper, or appropriate within some socially constructed system of norms, values, beliefs and definitions'. He also identified two approaches to establishing legitimacy: the organizational and strategic (that deploys established symbolic patterns of action and selective internal information to garner societal support); and the institutional (that encompasses sectorwide issues beyond individual organizational control). In the former category lie social auditing mechanisms and accountability regimes. In the latter lie broader notions of what a social venture should look like (i.e. a charity, for example) and are often bounded by legal and cultural traditions.

Drawing on Suchman (1995), Dart (2004) noted the significance of three levels of legitimacy for social enterprises: pragmatic, moral, and cognitive (these categories have been extended by amongst others: Lister 2003; Jepson 2005; Nicholls, Jepson and Jacobs 2006). With reference to the discussion earlier, each of these maps against an institutionally isomorphic pressure: pragmatic against coercive; moral against mimetic; cognitive against normative. An analysis of the socially entrepreneurial approach to each of these three forms of legitimacy reveals how the field has avoided the isomorphic pressures that would have both reduced its operational impact and facilitated its categorization and definition (see Table 5.1).

Building pragmatic legitimacy is typically based on simple exchange calculations where the external actor asks the question, what do I get from this organization and does it conform to my expectations? Establishing pragmatic legitimacy with key stakeholders is clearly a strategic objective of all social ventures. However, there are a number of problematic issues here. First, whilst establishing social accountability and impact measurement is particularly important in establishing pragmatic legitimacy, it is also particularly difficult. Convincing and established social metrics are few and there are, as yet, no reliable benchmarking data against which to judge social performance, even when it is adequately captured. Second, even where sophisticated social metrics

Table 5.1 Relationship between organizational isomorphism and legitimacy

Isomorphic pressure	Example	Organizational legitimacy	Example
Coercive	Programme related investment	Pragmatic	Social impact metrics
Mimetic	Social enterprise model	Moral	Community focus
Normative	Social activist engagement	Cognitive	'Public Good' test for charities

mechanisms have been put in place, there remains the issue of identifying who actually benefits from a social venture and, thus, where to focus an analysis of the development of pragmatic legitimacy is also problematic. As a consequence, social entrepreneurs can avoid many of the coercive isomorphic pressures typically experienced by other organizations from outside forces. For example, the effectiveness of foundation grant-giving to not-for-profits remains largely unmeasured, in stark contrast to shareholder accountability in normal businesses.

In contrast, moral legitimacy is based upon normative estimations of whether an organization fits accepted societal frameworks of behaviour or not. The central question here is not 'have I received what I expect from this organization?', but rather, 'does this organization behave as it should?'. Dart (2004: 420) argued that, at this level, the changing institutional context around social ventures in many countries has been the main driving force behind a social enterprise model that emphasizes self-sufficiency and internal revenue streams. From this perspective, the macroinstitutional priority given to neoliberal market economics in recent years has been the main catalyst for the rise of social enterprise. Whilst there may indeed be some truth in these observations with respect to the social enterprise—profit making—model, when the wider spectrum of social entrepreneurship is considered (as conceptualized by Dees 1998) the situation is rather different.

Moral legitimacy maps against mimetic isomorphism in its reflection of an organization's need to correspond to accepted patterns of action and behaviour at the field level. However, here too, social entrepreneurs represent a special case. The focus on—perhaps contested—social objectives carries with it moral legitimacy that may supersede operational effectiveness. Many donors are content to accept the not-for-profit organizational form (or its successful marketing communications) as a cipher for organizational impact. Furthermore, the community or stakeholder foundations of many social ventures bring with them a level of moral legitimacy both internally and externally that belies the need for mimetic behaviour even in the context of high uncertainty, as is typically the case for social entrepreneurs who often lack resources, capacity, or mimetic models. Finally, the bespoke diversity of much successful social action plays against mimetic forces and embodies a focus on social objectives rather than organizational form.

Finally, cognitive legitimacy is seen as less evaluative and is typically based upon a 'deep' conceptualization of an organization that suggests that it would literally be ontologically unthinkable for the organization to be other than it is. At this level, the enduring presence of social ventures is only possible because a society has fully accepted the three estates of the private, public, and social/civil sectors as defining the organizational landscape of modern life. The relationship between social ventures and existing social movements is important here. Cognitive legitimacy can be generated not via the adoption of structural processes such as audit trails or the reporting of performance measurements, but in the engagement of public constituencies in informed discussion of social values, issues, and strategy. This is because all social ventures are—to a lesser or greater degree—rooted in a normative assumption of the value of community integration and the history of social movements. Although, interestingly, the disruptive nature of much socially entrepreneurial activity has challenged this status quo and, as such, is often questioned in terms of its right to operate (both by internal, social, actors and by those outside the sector): witness, for example, the divisive arguments concerning the 'mainstreaming' of Fair Trade.

Cognitive legitimacy is played out in normative isomorphic pressures that demand a fixed organizational position within the broader socio-structural architecture as a precursor to a venture having a basic right to exist for the wider population. However, as noted earlier, social entrepreneurs disrupt these structures and work most effectively outside of established organizational patterns. As such—and in common with many innovative organizations— social entrepreneurship typically lacks cognitive legitimacy, but rather than this be a barrier to effective operations it, in fact, becomes a means towards greater impact. It is also, ultimately, why social entrepreneurship is widely misunderstood and often seen as ill-defined outside of the sector itself.

The management of what may be conceived as the 'legitimating assets'—or the particular actions, behaviours, documents etc that support legitimacy judgements—of a social venture can increasingly be seen as central to maintaining its right to operate in the judgement of key stakeholders (see Nicholls, Jepson and Jacobs 2006). Using a legitimacy framework to explore the dynamic effectiveness of social entrepreneurship reveals not only their resistance to institutionally isomorphic pressures but also suggests the need to research deeper into the foundations of such legitimacy and its creation and maintenance.

Conclusions

Social entrepreneurship research is still in search of compelling theoretical foundations. This chapter suggests that any discussion of social entrepreneurship must begin by grappling with the sociological boundaries of the phenomenon, and has presented an approach to understanding what social entrepreneurship includes and how to analyse its key dimensions. We suggest that social entrepreneurship differs from other organizational forms primarily with respect to its social mission, its emphasis on innovation, and its general market orientation. Particular social entrepreneurship ventures will include these elements to differing degrees, but they are useful markers for mapping out the structure of the field.

These markers are also useful for highlighting a new set of directions for social entrepreneurship research grounded in the nature of the phenomenon itself. Sociality, market orientation, and innovation are all concepts susceptible to analysis, both in themselves and in interaction with each other. Insights from organizational sociology can shed light on these essential components of social entrepreneurship and help researchers and practitioners to develop a more rigorous understanding of the phenomenon.

For example, complications in the social dimension of social entrepreneurship mean that social entrepreneurs need to grapple explicitly with the nature of their missions and do so in a manner that demonstrates openness to competing visions for social change. It also means that the pursuit of social outcomes needs to be conducted in a way that secures legitimating assets for the organization. Likewise, market orientation can generate operational efficiencies and encourage social innovation. However, it can also generate unexpected and perverse consequences, including ethically complicated incentive systems. Market orientation operates along a continuum, and organizations will need to identify the degree to which market orientation is consistent with, supports, or conflicts with their mission(s). Finally, innovation is a hallmark of social entrepreneurship, and understanding its relationship to field-level isomorphic pressures is an important part of helping to realize its potential for social change.

Yet these are only a limited set of the potentially fruitful directions for foundational research and theory building in social entrepreneurship. If the monological definition of social objectives is a problematic concept, then the role of social and organizational networks deserves further consideration. Likewise, if coercion is an important isomorphic pressure, then cultural and geographic issues are likely to be important too. Or if market orientated solutions do not address the fundamental drivers of social pathologies, then more innovative approaches targeted at social change might be appropriate. At this early stage in the evolution of social entrepreneurship as an area of research, the questions are more satisfying than the answers, but further inquiry will help us better apprehend the dynamics of the field.

In many ways social entrepreneurship presents an interesting example of the Hegelian–Marxian dialectic (see Zeitz 1980). The conjunction of new organizational models to deliver social goods with traditional social structures is creating a dynamic thesis of alternatives that are struggling to find synthesis across institutional boundaries. There are clear tensions in the disruptive patterns of much social entrepreneurship that offer complex and sometimes confrontational solutions to social problems. Similarly, the pursuit of a blended value (Emerson 2003) approach to outputs and outcomes that refutes the distinction between the economic and the social confronts accepted metrical norms that bound traditional conceptions of exchange value. However, there is an ongoing process of antithesis that is a function of how social entrepreneurs challenge existing, dysfunctional, social welfare delivery structures. Indeed, *contra* Marx and Hegel, there seems to be no evidence that the move to a final synthesis is either desirable or likely. The more social entrepreneurs continue to avoid institutional isomorphism and sectoral assimilation by defying the logic of Hegelian–Marxian synthesis, the more legitimating assets they will accrue and the more systemic and sustainable social impact they are likely to achieve.

References

Alter, K. (2000). *Managing the Double Bottom Line: A Business Planning Reference Guide for Social Enterprises*. Washington, DC: PACT Publications.

Bartlett, W. and LeGrand, J. (1993). 'The Theory of Quasi-Markets', in J. LeGrand and W. Bartlett (eds.), *Quasi-Markets and Social Policy*. Basingstoke, UK: Palgrave Macmillan, pp. 13–34.

Bornstein, D. (2004). *How To Change The World: Social Entrepreneurs and the Power of New Ideas*. Oxford: Oxford University Press.

Brickell, P. (2000). *People Before Structures*. London: Demos.

Casson, M. (2005). 'Entrepreneurship', in D. Henderson (ed.), *The Concise Encyclopedia of Economics*. Liberty Fund: Library of Economics and Liberty. Available at: http://www.econlib.org/library/Enc/Entrepreneurship.html

Cho, A. (2006). 'Politics, Values and Social Entrepreneurship: A Critical Appraisal', in J. Mair, J. Robinson, and K. Hockerts (eds.), *Social Entrepreneurship*. Basingstoke, UK: Palgrave Macmillan, pp. 34–56.

Cohen, I. (1989). *Structuration Theory: Anthony Giddens and the Constitution of Social Life*. New York: St Martin's Press.

Dart, R. (2004). 'The Legitimacy of Social Enterprise', *Nonprofit Management and Leadership*, 14(4): 411–24.

Davis, G., McAdam, D., Scott, R., and Zald, M. (2005). *Social Movements and Organizational Theory*. Cambridge, UK: Cambridge University Press.

Dees, J. G. (1998). *The Meaning of Social Entrepreneurship*. Available at: http://faculty.fuqua.duke.edu/centers/case/files/dees-SE.pdf

——Emerson, J., and Economy, P. (2001). *Enterprising Non-Profits: A Toolkit for Social Entrepreneurs*. New York: Wiley Non-Profit Series.

DiMaggio, P. and Powell, W. (1983). 'The Iron Cage Revisited: Institutional Isomorphism and Collective Rationality in Organizational Fields', *American Sociological Review*, 48: 147–60.

Docteur, E. and Oxley, H. (2003). *Health-Care Systems: Lessons from the Reform Experience*, OECD Health Working Papers.

Eikenberry, A. and Kluver, J. (2004). 'The Marketization of the Nonprofit Sector: Civil Society at Risk?' *Public Administration Review*, 64(2): 132–40.

Emerson, J. (2003). 'The Blended Value Proposition: Integrating Social and Financial Returns', *California Management Review*, 45(4): 35–51.

Foster, W. and Bradach, J. (2005). 'Should Nonprofits Seek Profits?', *Harvard Business Review*, February, 92–100.

Fraser, N. (1992). 'Rethinking the Public Sphere: A Contribution to the Critique of Actually Existing Democracy', in C. Calhoun (ed.), *Habermas and the Public Sphere*. Cambridge, MA: MIT Press, pp. 109–42.

Fuchs, C. (2003). 'Structuration and Self-Organisation', *Systemic Practice and Action Research*, 16(2): 133–67.

Giddens, A. (1984). *The Constitution of Society*. Berkeley, CA: University of California Press.

—— (1998). *The Third Way*. Cambridge: Polity Press.

Hegel, G. (1988). *Introduction to the Philosophy of History*. Indianapolis, IN: Hackett.

Institute for Social Entrepreneurs (2005). *Social Entrepreneurship: A Glossary of Useful Terms*. Available at: http://www.socialent.org/pdfs/GLOSSARY.pdf

Jepson, P. (2005). 'Governance and Accountability of Environmental NGOs', *Environmental Science and Policy*, 8: 515–24.

Leadbeater, C. (1997). *The Rise of the Social Entrepreneur*. London: Demos.

LeGrand, J. (2003). *Motivation, Agency, and Public Policy: Of Knights and Knaves, Pawns and Queens*, Oxford: Oxford University Press.

—— and Bartlett, W. (eds.) (1993). *Quasi-Markets and Social Policy*. Basingstoke, UK: Palgrave Macmillan.

Lister, S. (2003). 'NGO Legitimacy—Technical Issue or Social Construct?', *Critique of Anthropology*, 23: 175–92.

Mair, J. and Marti, I. (2004). *Social Entrepreneurship Research: A Source of Explanation, Prediction, and Delight*, IESE Working Paper 546, March.

Neidorf, D. (2005). 'What's Not Served in Service Learning', *The Common Review*, 2: 13–9.

Nicholls, A. (2004). 'Social Entrepreneurship: The Emerging Landscape', in *Financial Times Handbook of Management*, 3rd edn. London: Financial Times/Prentice-Hall pp. 636–43.

—— (2006). 'Social Entrepreneurship', in S. Carter and D. Evans-Jones (eds.), *Enterprise and Small Business: Principles, Practice and Policy*, 2nd edn., (forthcoming). London: Financial Times/Prentice-Hall.

——, Jepson, P., and Jacobs, A. (2006). *Improving the Performance of Social Organizations: Legitimacy as a Tool for Analysis and Strategic Management, Skoll Centre for Social Entrepreneurship Working Paper*.

Osbourne, D. and Gaebler, T. (1992). *Reinventing Government*, Reading, MA: Addison-Wesley.

Pozzebon, M. (2004). 'The Influence of a Structurationist View on Strategic Management Research', *Journal of Management Studies*, 41(2): 247–72.

Schumpeter, J. (1934). *The Theory of Economic Development: An Inquiry into Profits, Capital, Interest, and the Business Cycle*. Cambridge, MA: Harvard University Press.

Skoll Foundation for Social Entrepreneurship (2005). *About Social Entrepreneurship*. Available at: http://www.skollfoundation.org/aboutsocialentrepreneurship/index.asp

Suchman, M. (1995). 'Managing Legitimacy: Strategic and Institutional Approaches', *Academy of Management Review*, 20(3): 571–610.

Weisbrod, B. (Winter 2004). 'The Pitfalls of Profit', *Stanford Social Innovation Review*, 40–7.

—— and Lindrooth, R. (2004). 'Do Nonprofit and For-profit Organizations Respond Differently to Incentives? Behavior in the Mixed Hospice Industry', *Working Paper* 05–13, Institute for Policy Research, Northwestern University.

Zeitz, G. (1980). 'Interorganizational Dialetics', *Administrative Science Quarterly*, 25(1): 72–88.

6

Social Entrepreneurship: Agency in a Globalizing World

Paola Grenier

This chapter focuses on the emergence of social entrepreneurship as a distinct concept and organizational field within the context of globalization. Where social entrepreneurship highlights the role of agency[1] and leadership in bringing about positive social change and furthering social justice, globalization appears as an inexorable force, unstoppable and unchangeable, dominated by economics, and altering societies around the world for better or for worse. What difference can social entrepreneurs make within such a world, where globalization leaves almost no space for human agency? And is social entrepreneurship a helpful way of conceptualizing the role of individuals in effecting change for the good?

The main purpose of this chapter is to explore how human action, the agency so clearly apparent in social entrepreneurship, can influence what at first seem to be the agent-less processes of globalization. Another purpose is to explore how social justice and social change are pursued globally, when economics and finance seem to rule. The argument presented here is that social entrepreneurship cannot be fully understood as a significant societal phenomenon without locating it within the increasingly dominant global processes of economic and social integration (Bornstein 2004; Martin 2004).[2] Similarly the impact and potential of social entrepreneurship depend on its ability to engage with the often unpredictable and erratic unfolding of globalization as it is felt differentially across the world. Social entrepreneurship, it will be suggested, is not simply about changing national practices and systems, or even of spreading beneficial social innovations internationally. Rather, it is about the abilities and opportunities of those pursuing social justice within the loosely defined field of social entrepreneurship to create global platforms and networks through which they can interact with and influence globalization, and start to fashion better worlds across the globe.

There are several reasons for conceptualizing social entrepreneurship specifically as a global issue. One is to try and account for the particular contemporary emergence and relevance of social entrepreneurship, and in particular to paint a broader picture than ones currently portrayed where social entrepreneurship is linked with the retreat of the welfare state (Edwards 2002), the dominance of the market (Dees 1998a, 1998b; Dart 2004) and the growing size and influence of NPOs and civil society (e.g. Defourny 2001; Drayton 2002; Bornstein 2004). Perspectives on globalization would suggest that all of these trends reflect deeper changes running through societies. Second, is to demonstrate that globalizing processes are neither as homogenous nor as absolute as sometimes presented (e.g. Hay 2001; Hutton and Giddens 2001), but that they are influenced and caused by the ideas and actions of people as well as the effects of structural and institutional powers. By definition, social entrepreneurs are examples of people who have 'made a difference', often within communities which are impoverished and disenfranchised from the benefits of globalization. Social entrepreneurs, therefore, provide important examples of the kind of impact that people can have within a globalizing world, and how such impact may be achieved.

There are a variety of definitions and approaches to social entrepreneurship, some of which are similar to each other, and some of which are markedly different (Taylor et al. 2000), and because social entrepreneurship is a relatively new, and at times somewhat muddled field, it is important to clarify some of the terms adopted here. Broadly speaking, social entrepreneurship can be understood in two main ways. One is in terms of individual change makers and innovators—social entrepreneurs—people who are pursuing a social mission, often as leaders and founders of not-for-profit or non-governmental initiatives. Such social entrepreneurs are engaged with a wide variety of largely not-for-profit activities, and are innovating and breaking new ground in their chosen field—this might be HIV/AIDS, working with homeless people, disability, mental health, preservation of endangered habitats, conflict resolution, and so on. Historically, these are the people who found organizations that are now part of the established landscape, such as Oxfam in the UK, the International Committee of the Red Cross, the Sierra Club in North America, Médecins sans Frontières in France. This understanding of social entrepreneurship is closely associated with the work of the Ashoka Foundation and the Schwab Foundation for Social Entrepreneurs. The former provides the following comment:

The job of a social entrepreneur is to recognize when a part of society is stuck and to provide new ways to get it unstuck. He or she finds what is not working and solves the problem by changing the system, spreading the solution and persuading entire societies to take new leaps. (www.ashoka.org)

The second broad definition is as the development of commercial, income-generating activities within not-for-profit or 'pro-social' organizations. Such activities tend to complement a social mission, either simply by providing a supporting income stream, or by combining economic and social goals to create more holistic approaches to social change. These approaches are associated with the cooperative and mutual movements found in parts of Europe and much of Latin America, and also with the international development work of organizations such as NESsT and Virtue Ventures. Such organizations are usually known as social enterprises, as the NESsT website notes: 'Social enterprises—mission-driven businesses that increase the financial sustainability and social change impact of civil society organizations.'

This chapter adopts the first definition—that of social entrepreneurs as individual change makers and innovative leaders. Furthermore, the field of social entrepreneurship is understood here not only as consisting of those individual social entrepreneurs, but also of the organizations and initiatives which support and promote social entrepreneurship, and which are seeking to define the field and mobilize interest and resources. This means that the actions, roles, and discourses of the networks of social entrepreneurs, such as Ashoka and the Schwab Foundation, as well as of the individuals who are within those networks, are considered significant in constructing social entrepreneurship as a field.

Having introduced some parameters for this chapter, what follows is divided into four parts. First, some perspectives on globalization are reviewed, and its characteristics and effects are outlined. Second, the nature of agency within globalizing processes is considered. Third, social entrepreneurship is conceived in relation to globalization, in terms of space and the relationships between the local and global, and in terms of the emergence of networks as a characteristic form of organizing within globalization. Finally, the conclusion draws together some implications and issues faced by social entrepreneurship as a field.

Globalization

Globalization is a much discussed and much referenced term in academia, in public policy and politics, in economics and development, and increasingly in the media and with the general public. For Giddens, a leading sociologist and one of the most influential writers on the topic, globalization is 'the most significant debate going on in the social sciences and in politics' (Giddens 1999).

Broadly speaking, globalization is the growing interdependence and integration between economies and societies around the world. Four main spheres can be identified where the processes and effects of globalization are apparent: economic, social, cultural, and political. It is the economic sphere that generally receives the greatest attention and is the main focus for global policy initiatives. The World Bank refers to 'the common or core sense of' globalization as 'the expansion of cross-border economic ties' (PREM 2000). While the idea of globalization as an economic phenomenon is the most prevalent, many authors and commentators also recognize it as having social, cultural, and political implications, and some would even assert that these are the more important drivers and effects of globalization.[3] Globalization is apparent socially in the migration of people across borders, and the growing ethnic and religious diversity found in many cities and countries. Similarly globalization is experienced culturally on a day-to-day basis around the world, in the form of Hollywood films, CNN, Big Brother, Manchester United, McDonald's, and Eminem (Toynbee 2001). And in political terms, globalizing processes are manifested through the development of supranational governance mechanisms, such as the World Trade Organization (WTO), as well as regionally based multilateral institutions and initiatives, such as the European Union and NEPAD (the New Partnership for Africa's Development).[4]

Perhaps in part because of the dominance of certain social and economic forces and the sense of powerlessness felt by many, globalization is often presented in terms of inevitable and immutable structural changes (Rose 2000; Hay 2001). Such changes are taking place with or without the involvement or consent of peoples and societies. The language used to describe and talk about globalization assumes it represents change that is not under the control of human agency: Hay (2001: 1) refers to globalization as 'a process without a subject'; and Giddens (1999) talks about a 'juggernaut' and a 'runaway world'. There is a sense of needing to join in and respond or be left behind, and much less sense that nations and peoples can actually create and shape the globalizing world on their own terms. Hutton has also echoed these sentiments:

Globalisation is so powerful an idea because of the sense of there being no escape. It's coming down the tracks straight at you (Hutton, in Hutton and Giddens 2001: 4)

To add to this, the benefits and reach of globalization are unevenly and unequally felt, and have contributed to profound differences in wealth both between and within countries (Cummings 2003). Certainly the USA is a dominant force in the international arena in terms of its economic, military, and cultural power, and some would argue that it is driving the globalization train or the juggernaut (Giddens 1999). Yet Giddens also argues that globalization is neither so homogenous nor is it controlled in any kind of effective manner by the USA or some coalition of Western powers. The experience of many developing countries, nevertheless, is of the dominance of Western ideas, Western money, Western companies, and Western ways of life. Often this is through the interventions of multilateral institutions such as the World Bank, the WTO, and the IMF and it needs to be acknowledged that the agendas of these institutions are entangled with the interests of global capitalism and neoliberalism (e.g. Hutton in Giddens and Hutton 2001). Power differences between countries and inequalities within countries, resulting in the lack of voice and influence that many people and parts of the world experience, are significant characteristics of globalization, and are key issues when considering social entrepreneurship.

Globalization has simultaneously created new opportunities and resources for actors, at the same time as contributing to a range of social, environmental, and economic problems and risks. Opportunities include the rapid technological development and diffusion that has been central to globalization. The use of computers and mobile phones and access to television and digital media are affecting the nature of relationships, access to knowledge, and flows of information. For Giddens (1990), this has led to the disembedding of space and time, where face-to-face experiences are replaced or complemented by interactions that can take place across time and across space. Globalization is closely associated with the emergence of the 'network society' and 'knowledge economy', where information, expertise, and connections between people and between organizations are central. The Internet is perhaps the archetypal example of a decentralized network, where information is held in nodes rather than a central store, and can be accessed through a variety of hubs, from anywhere in the world.[5] It can be seen, therefore, that global knowledge and global action are not centralized and homogenous, but rather an interactive set of relationships and content which is often locally generated, and indicative of the local–global relations that characterize globalization. Such networks are not ephemeral but are sustained—involving regular interaction between the actors involved—and are evolving. Social networks between people and organizations can be developed and brought to life with far fewer resources than in the past by drawing on technology, and to far greater and more rapid potential global effect.

Global processes are not benign, let alone unerringly positive, and while some argue that the growth in free global trade has, overall, been beneficial for both rich and poor countries and people (e.g. PREM 2000), there are many serious social and environmental problems that also constitute globalization. Issues such as global warming, HIV/AIDS, and the growth of genetically modified foods transgress national borders and necessitate global responses.[6] Equally, local and regional issues, such as conflict in the Middle East, Africa, and Asia, are understood not only as having international impact, but as part of a global reality where other actors, be they nation states, individuals, or corporations, influence how such issues play out. Even economic globalization, which undoubtedly receives the most policy attention and could be assumed, therefore, to be under some level of control, can be turbulent and damaging, for example, contributing to the economic collapses experienced in Argentina and Asia in the 1990s (Soros 2001). Concerns about these sorts of issues and the impact of neoliberalism has prompted 'anti-globalization' protests, which might be seen as attempts to mitigate these damaging effects and to reassert local controls. As earlier, this emphasizes the concurrent decentralizing tendencies of globalization alongside the dominance of certain powers and nations, and indicates the importance of linking local issues with a global stage.

Globalization is a complex phenomenon, mixing cultural, social, economic, technological, and political trends, to create a world that is qualitatively different from the one experienced during much of the modern period (Giddens 1999; Beck 2004). Such changes are entangled with existing institutions, and rooted in the enlightenment and modernity. As such, globalization does not represent a clear or coherent new world or theoretical framework (Beck 2004). For the purposes of this chapter, theories and thinking on globalization offer a number of concepts and trends that can inform an analysis of social entrepreneurship. In particular they point to the creation of new needs and new opportunities for social actors, especially in reframing and taking issues to a global level. They highlight the significance of networks and networking as forms of action and mobilization, and emphasizes the importance of connecting local and global. At the same time it is unclear what the role and potential of individual agency is, and, because, this is central to understanding social entrepreneurship the notion of agency within globalization is considered in more detail in the next section.

Agency, Globalization, and Civil Society

Globalization incorporates some paradoxical notions of agency. On the one hand, globalization is associated with individuation and the growing capacity of individuals to author their own lives, free from the constraints of traditional roles and expectations: Beck comments that 'individual agency now assumes a central place' (Beck 2004: 65). On the other hand, globalization is, as detailed earlier, a 'process without a subject', where the majority of people and countries in the world seem to have little power or say in how they are affected by global processes. This section reviews the patterns and contradictions of individuation, and goes on to look at some of the key ways in which people are motivated and able to impact on the world around them, finding expression as part of a value-driven global civil society.

Increasing individualism is a widely acknowledged and well-recognized facet of modern societies. It is also a much-decried trend, as notions of solidarity, community, collective action, and mutual responsibility are replaced by the self-interested and egotistical *homo oeconomicus* of capitalism. Both Beck and Giddens, however, argue that there is an important distinction between this—what could be called selfish individualism—and what is sometimes referred to as individuation. Individuation is the freeing up of people from their traditional roles and deference to hierarchical authority, and their growing capacity to draw on wider pools of information and expertise and actively chose what sort of life they lead. Individuation is not, as Beck points out, about being able to chose between 'ten kinds of yoghurt' (2004: 92), but is more about the politicization of day-to-day life;[7] the hard choices people face are not over what shampoo to buy, but in crafting personal identities and choosing how to relate to issues such as race, gender, the environment, local culture, and diversity. The opening up of roles has been especially apparent for women, alongside the growth of universal human rights, and these trends well illustrate some of the profound and essentially practical effects of individuation.

Individuation has a range of social implications, many of which seem paradoxical. Whilst many people have more choice and control over their lives, the fear of freedom has led to powerful normative conventions. One example of this is the emphasis on work, reinforced by deeply felt criticisms of 'scrounging', as the only form of legitimate and productive life. It has also inspired national and religious fundamentalism and a reawakening of authoritarian right-wing politics, certainly throughout Europe (Beck 2004). Even though one of the key changes in a globalizing world is the emphasis on relationships and networks, there is nevertheless a decline in social solidarity. Where people's roles are no longer tightly defined by social structures, there is a need to build new social institutions and find new ways of engaging with others on the basis of more fluid identities. In addition there are some deep contradictions and paradoxes coming to light between existing institutions, for example as men and women struggle to define a balance between their work and private lives, and people seek to bridge and combine a range of cultural and social backgrounds both personally and in their relationships (Beck 2004). The capacity for people to author their own lives, and to adopt multiple and changing personal identities, is seriously constrained, even within the most modern societies. This does not, however, diminish the significance of the changing nature of many social institutions, and the need for people to ascertain more personal ways of expressing and interpreting these institutions—be it in family, religion, or work—within their lives. As Beck commented:

No matter what their ideology, they are almost forced into becoming an alternative kind of entrepreneur, a social entrepreneur, because they can only construct their chosen lives by entering into a continuous process of harmonizing their projects with those of others. (Beck 2004: 75)

Such attempts to define and understand the self and to construct a life that is in harmony with others create the need and potential for the social entrepreneur (Cerny 2000: 451). This is partly in response to the inadequacy of existing identities and life styles, or as Cerny points out 'the endemic dissatisfaction with existing institutions and processes of governance' (2000: 451). This notion of a social entrepreneur as crafting the self, alongside the process of 'harmonizing' with others, contains within it notions of a more ethical and morally oriented individual than the self-interested individualism of capitalism would imply. In fact, Moore argues that this is giving rise to a 'moral individualism', an altruistically oriented motive, looking to support social justice and to create a better world (Moore 2002). Such moral individualism is born from personal reflection in relation to self-identity, the development of personal philosophies and spiritualities, and the aspiration for a 'self-actualizing' life (Beck 2004). This acts as the basis for the moral and political dimensions to agency that are apparent as part of globalization. Giddens comments:

It becomes more and more apparent that lifestyle choices, within the settings of local–global interrelations, raise moral issues which cannot simply be pushed to one side. Such issues call for forms of political engagement which the new social movements both presage and serve to help initiate. (Giddens 1990: 5)

The emergence of a 'global civil society', markedly different from national and even international forms of civil society, has been heralded (Cerny 2000; Global Civil Society Yearbook 2001, 2002, 2003, 2004/5; Kaldor 2003; Keane 2003). Global civil society is said to be the space between the market, state, and household where individuals, groups, organizations, and social movements express ideas, values, and interests. It is concerned with 'the meaning and practice of human equality'; the pursuit of social justice; finding and giving voice, status, and power to people otherwise marginalized; and providing a platform and legitimacy for such people. It is intentionally plural and often discordant, as an arena for competing values and for working through moral dilemmas. And it is within the space of global civil society that individual agents can express their interests and act out their moral agendas in relation to globalization.

Global civil society has taken a number of forms, which, as with all aspects of globalization, are intermingled with existing forms of civil society. Civil society is most commonly associated with NGOs, NPOs, the voluntary sector, charities, philanthropic organizations, the 'third sector'—different terms are used in different countries. Essentially these refer to formally constituted organizations and a bounded sector. In fact, civil society means something much broader, and it also includes those hard to identify and pin down loose networks, social movements, cooperative relationships, and community action, which are easily missed out in empirical investigations and statistical measurement. Perhaps one of the most distinct developments of a networked or more loosely structured global civil space has been the development of the World Social Forum, originally held in Porto Alegre in Brazil, and aiming to create a public forum through which it can be realized that 'another world is possible' (see World Social Forum (2005) website). The idea has now expanded and morphed into a range of different issue-specific, local, national, and regional social forums, held at (ir)regular intervals throughout the world. There are other manifestations of global social action, such as: the rise of Internet activism and what John Clark has termed 'dot causes' so evident in the Coalition to Ban Landmines (Clark and Themudo 2003); the development of transnational activist networks (Kekk and Sikkink 1998); the new social movements based on single issues and the 'personal as political'; the 'new' new social movements, such as the trade justice and the debt relief campaigns; and the 'rooted cosmopolitans' of Tarrow (2004), people who bridge local and global needs and structures. Of course, leadership and entrepreneurship play a part in many of these new forms and new initiatives within civil society, though the structural opportunities created by globalization and the networked and collective nature of the responses tend also to be emphasized in the literature (e.g. Tarrow 2001; Clark 2003).

Yet, in practice, global civil society is as uneven as many other facets of globalization.[8] Taking internationally focused NGOs as a part of the infrastructure of global civil society, their headquarters are predominantly located in the USA and western Europe (Kaldor et al. 2003), though the same authors also note that the reach of global civil society is becoming more evenly spread, as more parts of the world engage with it more actively. Equally, issues which become defined and perceived as 'global' issues are more likely to have been identified as such in the North and West than in the developing countries of the South (Chandhoke 2003). It is then for those in the South to take advantage of opportunities that have been created elsewhere, and to seek to shape agendas which are so often predetermined for them.[9]

Despite the seemingly inexorable spread of globalization and the dominance of certain powers, there are ways in which people are challenging and changing the system. The growth, not only in the not-for-profit and non-governmental sectors (Salamon and Anheier 1999), but more specifically in the emergence of global civil society, is part of the space that people are forcing open as a means through which they can act and express their values and interests. The emergence of social entrepreneurship as a category for certain forms of social action can also be seen as part of this process, and one which places particular emphasis on the power and potential of individual agency.

Social Entrepreneurship

What then of social entrepreneurs, and their role as 'moral' agents within globalization and as part of global civil society? This section first briefly describes the field of social entrepreneurship, the key organizations, and the way in which it has developed. It identifies the key actors within social entrepreneurship as the individuals who are recognized as social entrepreneurs and the organizations that recognize and support them as such. Social entrepreneurship is, therefore, understood not only as the actions and motives of the social entrepreneurs themselves, but also in terms of the organizations which act as the gatekeepers to the field, which determine who is and who is not a social entrepreneur, and are therefore important in shaping definitions and understandings of social entrepreneurship. The intention is to offer a more sociologically oriented analysis than has been present in much of the literature to date, which tends to focus on individual attributes (e.g. Dees 1998*a*), stories and case studies (Henton et al. 1997; Bornstein 2004), and organizational issues experienced by social entrepreneurs relating to growth, replication, and effectiveness (Guclu, Dees, and Battle Andersen 2002).

Social entrepreneurship is a term that started to be used by a handful of people and organizations during the 1980s and 1990s within the broad arenas of civil society and international development. Since then it has become an increasingly popular term in these specialist areas and also in the media more generally (Taylor et al. 2000). Social entrepreneurship is identified with the actions of individual social entrepreneurs, people who are seen as incisive, energetic, and innovative leaders who provide 'new ideas to solve intractable social problems' and who can transform societies (Echoing Green website). It is about an approach rather than specific social issues, where an entrepreneurial process is portrayed as relevant to all areas of social change and as equally effective within all contexts. The Schwab Foundation provides the following definition:

Social entrepreneurs create social value through innovation and leveraging financial resources. They transform groups, organizations, or institutions. Social entrepreneurs take risks, they act courageously, they pursue new ways, and they are engaged and committed to create social value, to serve society, particularly the poor and marginalized. (Schwab 2000)

Social entrepreneurship is consciously defined and promoted by a growing number of organizations which find it a useful and relevant concept in seeking to offer support to innovative social leaders—social entrepreneurs. In all cases these organizations have a range of criteria that they apply to identify social entrepreneurs, and often a rigorous process through which social entrepreneurs are then selected to join the network, membership, or fellowship. Specialist support designed specifically for social entrepreneurs is then available to those who are recognized or accredited in this way. This support may be financial, access to expertise and information, training and education programmes, organizational and personal development, networking opportunities. These organizations also act as mutual support networks, and at times this can be one of their most powerful functions. Some of the main ones are listed below:[10]

Ashoka, which was set up in the USA in 1980 provides support and networking opportunities for 'leading' social entrepreneurs internationally. It has 1,472 fellows in 48 different countries.

Echoing Green, which was set up in the USA in 1987–8 supports 'emergent' social entrepreneurs internationally, though the majority are in the USA. It has 371 fellows in 30 countries.

LEAD, which was set up in the UK in 1991 and supports leadership and networks between leaders working towards sustainable environmental development. It has 1,402 fellows in more than 70 countries.

Avina, which was set up in Switzerland in 1994 supports partnership development between social entrepreneurs and business leaders throughout Ibero-America. It has 324 partners in 20 countries.

School for Social Entrepreneurs, which was set up in the UK in 1998 provides a year-long training and personal development programme for potential UK-based social entrepreneurs. By 2004, there were about 200 existing and former students from the UK.

Schwab Foundation for Social Entrepreneurship, which was set up in Switzerland in 2000 works with 'outstanding' social entrepreneurs internationally. It has 78 members in 30 countries.

UnLtd, which is an endowed grant-making foundation, was set up in the UK in 2001 to provide funding and support to UK-based social entrepreneurs at the grassroots level.

People who are identified and recognized as social entrepreneurs tend not to have defined themselves as such. Rather they acquire the label and status as a result of the recognition, and what could be thought of as a kind of accreditation, from those support organizations. Social entrepreneurship as a concept and phenomenon can therefore be seen and understood through the actions and identities of the individual social entrepreneurs who have been recognized in this way, and also through the criteria and the ambitions of the support organizations which are largely responsible for articulating the boundaries and the priorities for social entrepreneurship as a field.

The next part of this section looks in more detail at the motives and actions of individual social entrepreneurs themselves, and attempt to assess to what extent these are predicated on the changing role of individuals and individual identities within globalization and the notion of 'moral individualism'. Following this, the kind of support offered by the organizations promoting and identifying social entrepreneurs is reviewed in relation to the growing significance of networking, the development of global civil society, and the uneven and often Western dominated nature of globalization processes and effects.

Social Entrepreneurs

The list of social entrepreneurship support organizations above gives an idea of the numbers of social entrepreneurs who have thus far been recognized and supported. This part looks at the stories and lives of some of those individuals who are part of the Ashoka fellowship and the Schwab network of social entrepreneurs, as both these organizations identify social entrepreneurs working in any field and almost any geographical area, and are therefore more global in their reach than many of the others. In addition, Ashoka is the longest-standing organization supporting social entrepreneurs and is a widely acknowledged leader in the field. This provides a broad initial base from which to start to explore some of the motives and actions of social entrepreneurs. The analysis offered here is based on a selection of about thirty Ashoka and Schwab social entrepreneurs, chosen to cover a wide range of issues, approaches, and locations. In some cases this involved reading about them, and in others interviewing and talking with them. In all cases, social entrepreneurs proved to be interesting and responsive people to read about, work with, and research.

Two specific areas are explored later, and come directly out of the review of globalization and agency in the previous sections. The first relates to the motives and values of social entrepreneurs, and investigates to what extent they embody the 'moral individualism' that Moore (2002) proposes. The second looks at the contradictory institutional frameworks that social entrepreneurs are attempting to 'harmonize', and how social entrepreneurs are instrumental in finding ways of addressing the 'endemic dissatisfaction' with existing institutions that Cerny (2000) talks about.

MOTIVES AND 'MORAL INDIVIDUALISM'

Why people do what they do is a source of constant fascination for others, and no more so that in the case of social entrepreneurs who seem to embrace a life of ongoing struggle, often for very few material rewards. When the author and journalist David Bornstein asked a leading Ashoka fellow why he did what he did, Fabio Rosso, who has developed an extraordinary system for delivering electricity to people in rural Brazil, was quoted as saying: 'I am trying to build a little part of the world in which I would like to live' (Bornstein 2004: 239). On the one hand this is a very simple statement, on the other it is indicative of someone who has thought about and questioned the kind of world in which he currently lives and what sort of world he wants to live in. Rosso is not focused on creating a better world for himself through advancing his personal career and status, but rather by making change happen in the world around him. Helmy Abouleish, a Schwab social entrepreneur, heads up an Egyptian business company with a strong and explicit spirituality running through its work. He believes that for a truly spiritual path to develop in an organization, or even a country, it requires input from all people; and it is only by building bridges between religions and peoples that this can be achieved.

This kind of deeply felt and thought through personal philosophy seems typical of social entrepreneurs, and originates in a variety of ways. Several are responding to very personal experiences, such as Erzsebert Szekeres who has a physically disabled child and has gone on to pioneer new ways for disabled children to interact with each other and to participate in Hungarian society

(Bornstein 2004). Or Muhammud Yunus, who founded the Grameen Bank which went on to inspire the microcredit movement around the world, is said to have been profoundly affected by his experiences of the famine in Bangladesh in 1974 (Bornstein 2004). Yet other social entrepreneurs were born into families where values and ethics were central, and where they saw and were part of the commitments of parents and grandparents, as was the case with Abouleish and many others. And for some, their philosophy has been expressed through a kind of vocational ethic, and many of the social entrepreneurs have a professional background and training as teachers, doctors, nurses, lawyers (this tendency for a professional background has been noted by the Schwab foundation; see also Bornstein 2004; Grenier 2004).

This is consistent with globalization theorists, such as Beck and Giddens, who emphasize the motives of people in a globalizing world to self-actualize and develop personalized philosophies and spiritualities. Whilst Beck and Giddens present idealized versions of people as free to self-actualize, social entrepreneurs really do seem to have a powerful sense of their own agency and their own values. Social entrepreneurs act as if they have the choice and capacity to develop and adopt a personal approach to life, often based on values and ethics that are not so commonly expressed through capitalism and the economic forces of globalization. And such values do seem to reflect the notion of moral individualism. Social entrepreneurs often embark on their own personal journeys, where they are unlikely simply to adopt a set of values that have been articulated in their family or within a religion or profession, but rather take these as points of inspiration from which to develop their own personal motive and value systems. In some cases, personal suffering or deprivation may have sparked a desire to take action, and in other cases, contact with others who are suffering may provoke action. What is notable in both cases is that values are expressed in very personal terms.

INSTITUTIONAL PARADOXES AND 'ENDEMIC DISSATISFACTION'

Social entrepreneurs work in an incredible variety of fields and issues, and are said to focus on the most acute and intractable social problems. They often operate where there are paradoxes and tensions, where existing institutional systems do not work or where people are no longer prepared to put up with such levels of disadvantage, and hence they are associated with poverty reduction, citizen action, education, health, the environment, and so on. This could be by enabling homeless and excluded people to live and work together, as the Barka Foundation is doing in Poland—an initiative which has been recognized by both Ashoka and Schwab. Or it could be about researching and developing medical treatments which address the needs of people in developing countries rather than prioritizing the development of new treatments for those in the richer West; as is being pursued by Victoria Hale, a Schwab social entrepreneur. Many of these issues are those which globalization has brought to the fore, as outlined in the earlier sections, and are some of the paradoxes that people experience which can only be resolved by systemic changes to existing institutions. Of course this is a broader historical process, and much of the work of the social entrepreneurs is building on the achievements of those who have gone before them. It would not be possible for Paul Rice, a Schwab social entrepreneur, to be developing fair trade in the USA, without a strong movement that had already developed in other parts of the world.

Social entrepreneurs can therefore be seen as operating at the edges of institutional paradox and failure, where there is 'endemic dissatisfaction' with how things are done, and from where they are attempting to change or create new institutions and practices. But this is consistent with much social change activism that has taken place historically, and what makes social entrepreneurship a phenomenon that is particularly relevant to globalization is the way in which it connects and mediates between the global and local. Social entrepreneurs tend to be experts in the fields and institutional contexts within which they are working. They are also often very committed to the particular geographical location where they are based. They are certainly not people who change jobs at regular intervals, switching between countries and issues, looking for something more interesting or more challenging. But together with this focused commitment to a place and issue, many social entrepreneurs do operate at the international level, raising resources and furthering their cause. They can be considered to be 'rooted cosmopolitans', people who are deeply committed to a locale, but who are able to connect with and operate as part of an emerging cosmopolitan class (Grenier 2004; Tarrow 2004). Few social entrepreneurs aim to operate at a global level, and they are unlikely to be convinced by a one-size-fits-all approach to social change. They are more likely to seek to inspire others to take up their ideas and localize their work, as has been the case with Muhammud Yunus and the Grameen Bank.

It is the way in which social entrepreneurs understand and frame issues as globally significant, and the ways in which they connect the local and global, that are distinctive about their work. They are not building the not-for-profit equivalents of multinational corporations such as McDonald's, but are rather seeking new ways through which ideas and practices can spread. Even where people are operating globally, it is through networks of organizations and hubs of activity and information, such as the international support network of Childlines that Jeroo Billimoria is developing. This is typical of globalizing processes, where networks and hubs of activity are more powerful in diffusing an idea than a centralized and standardized mechanism that would roll out a single form across the globe.

Theories of globalization provide some insight into the nature of the social needs and that institutional tensions that social entrepreneurs address. Social entrepreneurs can be viewed as mediators between the local and global: for example, by developing a new practice which has potential application and benefits internationally; by taking an idea developed in one location, and rooting it into another; or by reframing local needs in terms of their global implications. Globalization theories also suggest ways in which motives and values become personalized as people seek to develop their own forms of spiritual expression. The work of social entrepreneurs does seem to represent an ethical thread within globalizing social processes. This would also suggest that 'social entrepreneur' is an emerging and evolving personal identity, where those accredited as social entrepreneurs come to see themselves as such. Such an identity would sit alongside the development of the multiple and fluid personal identities seen within globalization, as people seek to determine their own place in society, combining roles as parent, manager, entrepreneur, environmentalist, feminist, doctor, and so on. Potentially such insights could complement the research and theory development that is more often found in studies of social entrepreneurship, whereby personal identity and institutional analysis could add to existing research into personality traits, behaviours, and organizational processes.

Supporting Social Entrepreneurs

Ashoka pioneered the term social entrepreneurship during the 1980s; it was not until the mid- to late 1990s that several other organizations adopted a similar terminology and, perhaps more significantly, a similar rationale for interventions which would catalyse positive social change. In fact, many of the organizations, set up to support social entrepreneurs, are also explicit about wanting to develop social entrepreneurship as a distinct and recognizable organizational field (Scott 2001; Hoffman 1999). Their intention seems to be to define a certain type of civil society leader and certain forms of innovative social change as social entrepreneurship, requiring a specific mix of funding and support which is not readily available from within the mainstream. Providing grants, training and support to organizations, projects and programmes has been the most widespread form of support for effecting social change within civil society. In contrast, those interested in social entrepreneurship have tended to direct their support to specific individual social entrepreneurs, emphasizing the idea and capability of the individual rather than of the organization, project, or programme. Hence the need for new organizations which not only provide these new types of support opportunities, but at the same time also seek to define and refine the nature of social entrepreneurship such that the phenomenon is better understood and achieves broader recognition.

From the list of organizations presented earlier, it can be seen that social entrepreneurship operates across a range of social issues and at multiple levels.

It has emerged at the national level within the UK; at the regional level in the Ibero-American world; and at the international level through organizations such as Ashoka and Schwab. This simultaneous, though still very much embryonic, emergence of social entrepreneurship at multiple levels points to social entrepreneurship as a global phenomenon rather than as isolated or coincidental developments. This part follows directly from the previous part, focusing on the work of Ashoka and the Schwab Foundation, as they both operate internationally and have been developing forms of support for individuals that have not been commonplace in international development. What follows reviews these support organizations on the basis of concepts taken from the account of globalization set out earlier: the nature and significance of networks; the location of the support organizations within global civil society; and the extent to which they offer an alternative approach within international development and civil society, or conform with existing dominant discourses represented by neoliberalism and global capitalism.

NETWORKS OF SUPPORT

Being selected as either a Schwab or an Ashoka social entrepreneur is a long and challenging process, involving nomination by people from within a country, and several stages of interviews, as well as written information. It also requires the social entrepreneurs to demonstrate and talk through their own ideas, their approach, and the potential of their work, often developing it further than have done so to date. So becoming an Ashoka or a Schwab social entrepreneur is a process of challenge and discovery, one which is clearly different from the traditional forms of grant application and assessment. From the beginning, social entrepreneurship is about establishing and developing relationships. Neither Ashoka nor Schwab wanted to be like a funding body, where relationships with grant recipients are often characterized in terms of the power differentials between those that have money and those that need it.

Whilst Ashoka provides a local salary for three years to its fellows, its more important role is in providing international recognition, moral support, and access to networks of mutual support across issues, sectors, and countries. A striking example of the way in which Ashoka operates as a global platform and facilitates relationships is the development by Indonesian fellows of a joint response to the tsunami and earthquake in Aceh, which took place in December 2004. Similarly, in South Africa and in Poland, social entrepreneurs have got together and started to support emerging social entrepreneurs, something that would not have happened without the relationships formed within Ashoka and Schwab.

Many of the fellows I interviewed said that the credibility, confidence, contacts and ideas they gained through Ashoka were more valuable than the money. (Bornstein 2004: 237)

The Schwab Foundation invites its social entrepreneurs to attend the World Economic Forum (WEF) in Davos, and by doing this provides access to some of the most powerful people in the world—people who are otherwise inaccessible to most social change agents. Membership of Schwab provides a certain legitimacy, but attending the WEF with a national president can make a profound difference to how a social entrepreneur is viewed in his or her home country, and in particular where a regime is authoritarian and oppression of civil initiatives is common. The WEF also provides opportunities to influence the thinking and priorities of political and economics leaders. Social entrepreneurs make presentations alongside such world leaders, providing a very different perspective on the urgent needs of societies and what can be done. This attempt to bring together leading social entrepreneurs with leading business and political leaders is still very much in its early stages. Though much of the potential is as yet unrealized, there are indications that the social entrepreneurs are increasingly able to make use of the opportunity, and that they are increasingly well received and taken seriously. However, they are a tiny proportion of the people present and represented at the WEF, and unless there is some attempt to provide an even more equal footing and status for social entrepreneurs alongside the economic and political, the social, health, and environmental needs of the world may always remain a small and underrepresented voice.

The Foundation plays a critical role in disseminating the examples of Schwab entrepreneurs to the ever-growing number of corporations, high net worth individuals and foundations eager to identify and support highly effective social purpose organizations. Thus, the Foundation acts as a broker between social entrepreneurs in its community and social investors worldwide seeking to maximize their social contributions. (From Schwab Foundation 2003)

As global networks, Ashoka and Schwab enable the development of sustainable and evolving relationships between the social entrepreneurs themselves, and access into other networks, often of business leaders. It can also help social entrepreneurs to reach for and stand on a global platform, presenting social and environmental issues as of global significance. More generally the centrality of networking as a way in which social entrepreneurs can develop the means to support and further their work is a defining characteristic of globalization.

LOCATING SOCIAL ENTREPRENEURSHIP WITHIN GLOBAL CIVIL SOCIETY

The organizations supporting social entrepreneurs and spreading the concept globally are all located in the West, be it the USA or western Europe. The fact that social entrepreneurship is a concept and form of support which originated in the West, and continues to be located and sourced in the West, gives credence to beliefs that it is a Western notion which is being transmitted, however usefully and effectively, across the globe. In some ways this makes social entrepreneurship typical of global civil society, which is itself predominantly headquartered in the USA and western Europe, but not part of the most progressive and inclusive parts of global civil society which are increasingly found in the South and developing parts of the world.

Similarly, even though both Ashoka and Schwab are international, there are significant geographical gaps in their memberships. Most notably the Middle East and Central Asia are all but absent from the maps of social entrepreneurship; and Russia and the former Soviet States are also clearly very difficult areas in which to identify social entrepreneurs, though it is a large and globally significant region (see Grenier 2004 where Table 6.1 details the geography of social entrepreneur support organizations). At the time of writing this chapter, the Ukraine and Georgia have seen some of the most dramatic and effective processes of social change, as protests and democracy movements have reshaped politics in both countries. It seems unlikely that there were no social entrepreneurs within these movements. These may simply be a part of the world that are currently beyond the reach and contacts of the support organizations. Or it may have something to do with their particular conceptualizations of social entrepreneurship, and that social entrepreneurs are recognized and selected on the basis of ideas which have developed in such different (Western) contexts that they are unrecognizable in such countries.

The Western conceptualization of social entrepreneurship is especially apparent in the highly individualistic notion of the social entrepreneur that is the dominant field rationality. Interestingly, even in the business world, entrepreneurship is increasingly understood in terms of the dynamics between people, culture, and context, as a process rather than the preserve of a single person. In fact research in entrepreneurship has consistently failed to identify personality traits, as have leadership studies, and theory development is moving towards more contingent and constructionist approaches (e.g. Gartner 1988; Bruyat and Julien 2000; Chell 2000; Hjorth, Johannisson, and Steyaert 2003; Hjorth and Steyart 2004). Thinking on social entrepreneurship, however, is currently based more on impressions and stories than on rigorous research and analysis, and the dominant understanding of social entrepreneurs are as, for example: 'people with new ideas to address major problems who are relentless in their pursuit of their visions' (Bornstein 2004: 1). But the relentless pathbreaker characterized by Bornstein, and who appears in the work of Ashoka and Schwab, can easily smack of the World Bank come to town. It can also offer similar narratives to those of such multilateral institutions, of developing countries as needing to import and learn Western ideas and practices in order to progress. This could be contrasted with locally constructed and driven processes of change and development which are inclusive and responsive, and in many ways are more what social entrepreneurship is intended to be about, and is certainly what you are more likely to find when looking at the process and impact of social entrepreneurship. Yet it is the presentation of this kind of larger-than-life visionary figure which can be so alienating for some, particularly in societies which are not as individualized and look more to collective action and collective identities.

Global civil society has tended to see ideas cascaded and taken up in different ways depending on the context. Where the World Social Forum devolved, albeit somewhat chaotically, into local social forums, social entrepreneurship remains more tightly controlled, and has not seen a devolution of power to define and shape the concept and practice into the countries where it is being enacted. This may be necessary if organizations such as Ashoka and Schwab are to retain their standards and quality control over who is admitted into their networks. However, it does limit ownership of the notion as a global phenomenon, and may potentially limit its global reach and influence. In some ways the organizational models practised by the support organizations are not in tune with globalization as a process that thrives on decentralization, on hubs and nodes and relationships, rather than on centralized standards and controls.

GLOBALIZATION, NEOLIBERALISM, OR AN ALTERNATIVE?

Social entrepreneurs are consistently referred to as like business entrepreneurs, with an emphasis on the similarities in style and approach that both adopt: 'Social and business entrepreneurs have much in common. They combine innovation, resourcefulness and opportunity to discover new ways of doing things. In addition, social entrepreneurs are committed to using business principles, including transparency, efficiency, market research and impact evaluation, to solving social issues' (Hartigan 2002). The language of social entrepreneurship certainly seems to frame it as reflecting the dominance of the market and business in society, the de-politicization of social action, and the privileging of a business-like rationale. This is also reflected in that many, if not all, the newly developing university centres and departments focusing on social entrepreneurship are located in business schools.[11]

When reviewing the work of social entrepreneurs, and experiencing the energy and nature of the networking events that are held, there is less evidence that these are people who are especially business oriented. In fact, it is the creativity, coupled with warmth and enthusiasm, that is so engaging when meeting social entrepreneurs. It is not a corporate experience, even though the social entrepreneurs may well be professional and knowledgeable about their field and work in the way that good business executives are. The need to continuously represent social entrepreneurs as business-like seem not to be based on empirical evidence relating to the work of the social entrepreneurs. Rather, it appears that social entrepreneurship is seeking its learning and legitimacy from business, as well as seeking to make connections into the business world where civil society organizations have generally struggled and often failed. As such, the rationale presented within the field of social entrepreneurship position it as close to the corporate world, as oriented towards business, and as using similar language and concepts. This helps to enable effective communication and build relationships, and establishing a rapport with the corporate world is clearly a priority within this emerging field.

In an analysis of the sociological origins of social entrepreneurship, Dart (2004: 420) employed notions of legitimacy from new institutional theory to show that the development of social enterprise and social entrepreneurship has taken place, not because it offers a more effective way of meeting social needs, but rather because it is a more morally legitimate form where being 'business-like' is societies' preferred method of problem solving and organizing. He concludes that social entrepreneurship is likely to drift away from broad ideas of entrepreneurship, which encompass the kind of social change leadership that has been discussed in this chapter, and towards 'a narrower frame of market-focused revenue-generating', as this is the predominant societal discourse and therefore the more effective way of gaining legitimacy. Within these perspective, social entrepreneurship looks more like the expansion of global capitalism and neoliberalism, than of the cultural and social changes that broader notions of globalization are premised on. In fact there is some evidence of this happening, especially as the organizations promoting social change leaders (rather than income generating) place so much emphasis on being business-like and making use of market mechanisms (e.g. Schwab 2000). Equally, there is an increasing emphasis on financial sustainability and developing independent sources of income (Hartigan 2002). Whilst this may be valuable for many organizations, it may also exclude some powerful and effective examples of social change that place a greater emphasis on mobilizing people and engaging a wide range of support than developing independent commercially based income streams. This may be the direction that social entrepreneurship goes in, but it should be acknowledged that this would exclude many social movements and organizations that have affected some of the more profound social changes throughout history, such as the anti-slavery movement and the women's movement. For example, the founding of the International Criminal Court, which Drayton, founder and head of Ashoka, cited as an example of social entrepreneurship at the 2004 Skoll World Summit, was a complex political process with little concern for business-like mechanisms, and no special interest in developing an income stream to support itself independently (Glasius 2003). Some care therefore needs to be taken as to what extent social entrepreneurship offers an alternative to existing forms of social change, or to what extent it is simply the extension and intrusion of 'business' into the 'social' and political arenas.

In looking at the nature and work of the organizations supporting social entrepreneurship, there are some critiques and problematic issues that become apparent. Such organizations do offer unique networking opportunities and provide a global platform for leading social change agents. At the same time, they are based in the West, rooted in Western notions and thinking, and strongly influenced by the dominant societal paradigm of global capitalism. Social entrepreneurship is an example of the entanglement between neoliberalism and globalization, and between existing institutional mechanisms, which are hierarchical and centralized, and emergent systems which are localized and networked. Current trends indicate that the field of social entrepreneurship is becoming more economically focused, and less sensitive to the cultural and social processes of globalization.

Conclusion

This chapter was written with the idea of showing some ways in which agency is not only apparent but also powerful and effective in influencing and shaping processes of globalization. In order to explore this, social entrepreneurship was taken as a compelling example of agency, both in terms of the actions of social entrepreneurs and in terms of the emergence of a global field which supports such forms of transformative social action. It does appear that social entrepreneurs are an emerging group of people, identified and singled out by accrediting organizations such as Ashoka and Schwab. Their engagement with one another and their ability to make use of the resources and opportunities presented to them, especially in taking issues to a global stage, is encouraging in terms of a movement of social change agents who provide an ethical and value-driven vision of what is possible in society. It may be a small and emerging field, but there is clearly a power and energy within it, within the relationships that are being formed between the social entrepreneurs and the connections that are developing into other sectors and arenas. There are signs of emerging webs of influence which may impact positively on the social and cultural trajectory of our globalizing world, giving space and voice to those who seem powerless against the 'juggernaut' of globalization. But, as with many phenomenon that appear global, Western thinking and ideas are immanent in social entrepreneurship. Equally, the insistence, by many of those who are supporting and developing social entrepreneurship, of modelling and comparing such work with business and likening it to market processes seems naive when looking at the reality of what people are doing and the kinds of motives that they have. This not only limits the notion of social entrepreneurship, but limits it within ways of thinking and idea, which are largely Western and not rooted in other cultures and societies, and therefore may have little natural resonance other than as another facet of the unevenness of globalization. In fact, it seems more likely that social entrepreneurship will be increasingly associated with what could be termed ethical economic activity, where social and economic goals are pursued simultaneously. While there is a value in this and greater development is needed to understand better the complex relationships between economic and social well-being, it is different from those who are trying to change social and cultural practices in society, and are not necessarily invoking the economic. The call that is being made by those who are marginalized from the benefits of globalization is for something different rather than more of the same.

Notes

1. The term agency is used here to refer to the actions and effects of human actors. Agency is conceptualized as a legitimate authority that has arisen historically through Western civilization, as the authority of external forces and institutions such as the deity, the church, the state have declined and relocated to the self and the individual. Meyer (2000) refers to this understanding of agency as the dominant, legitimate, and assumed way in much of contemporary social sciences. Meyer (2000: 101) takes the position 'that the modern 'actor' is a historical and ongoing cultural construction', and looks at the way in which agency has been relocated over time from the exogenous forces of the 'gods' to the church, to the state, and to individual souls and citizens. He goes on to suggest that the modern social actor (i.e. the person) is an 'authorized agent', not only for the self but also on behalf of 'others' (p. 102). He comments that 'In the Western picture, humans have the capacity and responsibility to modify society and to intervene in lawful nature, in order to reduce discrepancies between mundane realities and transcendental chartered goals' (p. 102). It is in this 'Western' sense that agency is employed in this chapter, and it is in this sense that it is argued that agency is constructed within the discourse of social entrepreneurship.
2. Several other authors similarly see social enterprise and the social economy as directly relating to processes of globalization, see in particular Favreau (2000) who comments that the social economy can contribute 'towards a new definition of the relationships among populations, the intermediate structures of civil society, the market and the State' at a time 'when many issues remained unsettled' (p. 236).
3. This seems to depend largely on the perspective being adopted, so it should not be surprising that an institution such as the World Bank emphasizes the economic, and sociologists such as Giddens and Beck emphasize social and cultural elements.
4. Whilst these structures are governed by representative from participating nations, and therefore provide a key role to the nation state, the laws and regulations they embody and enact are at a level above those of the nation state.
5. The Internet is, of course, not in practice accessible from anywhere in the world, as many countries are still poorly developed and do not have adequate electricity or phone supplies. The 'digital divide' is one of the main ways in which globalization is 'uneven'.
6. Beck's seminal work on 'risk society' provides a detailed analysis of the changing nature of risk, its unpredictable and radical nature, and its global and at times catastrophic implications.
7. Beck notes that the neoliberal thinking of the new political right supports the de-politicization of life, and seems to believe that commodification and consumerism can address all needs without the state or a political arena. Beck cautions against this, as he notes that capitalism has only been possible through the development of certain

political forms and practices, and that in fact it is politics which defines the world more than the economic market. Without political engagement, he warns, democracy and freedom will be undermined, and any benefits of capitalism will erode (see Beck 2004).

8. For a more detailed analysis of global civil society see Keane (2003) and the Global Civil Society Yearbooks published annually since 2001.

9. An example of this is the way in which 'Third World' debt relief became an issue in the North, and then through the campaigns of the Jubilee 2000 movements became a global issue. For a more detailed analysis of this see Grenier (2003).

10. The figures quoted below for Ashoka, Echoing Green, Avina, and Schwab are taken from Grenier (2004: 152–3).

11. This tendency to locate social entrepreneurship as a business function contrasts, for example, with the Centre for Civil Society at the London School of Economics (where I am based) which is located in the Department of Social Policy.

References

Ashoka website. *What is a Social Entrepreneur?* Available at: http://www.ashoka.org/fellows/social_entrepreneur.cfm

Beck, U. (2004). In U. Beck and J. Willms, *Conversations with Ulrich Beck*. Cambridge: Polity Press.

Bornstein, D. (2004). *How to Change the World. Social Entrepreneurs and the Power of New Ideas*. New York: Oxford University Press.

Bruyat, C. and Julien, P.-A. (2000). 'Defining the field of research in entrepreneurship', *Journal of Business Venturing*, 16: 165–80.

Cerny, P. (2000). 'Political Agency in a Globalizing World: Toward a Structurational Approach'. *European Journal of International Relations*, 6(4): 435–63.

Chandhoke, N. (2003). 'The Limits of Global Civil Society', in M. Glasius, M. Kaldor, and H. Anheier (eds.), *Global Civil Society Yearbook 2003*. Oxford: Oxford University Press, pp. 35–53.

Chell, E. (2000). 'Towards Researching the 'Opportunistic Entrepreneur': A Social Constructionist Approach and Research Agenda', *European Journal of Work and Organizational Psychology*, 9(1): 63–80.

Clark, J. (ed.) (2003). *Globalising Civic Engagement*. London: Earthscan.

—— and Themudo, N. (2003). 'The Age of Protest: Internet-Based 'Dot Causes' and the 'Anti-Globalization' Movement' in J. Clark (ed.), *Globalising Civic Engagement*. London: Earthscan, pp. 109–26.

Cummings, D. (2003). 'Globalisation Puts Corporate Profits Before People', *An Intelligence Debate at the Royal Geographical Society*, Available at: http://www.culturewars.org.uk/2003-02/globalisation.htm

Dart, R. (2004). 'The Legitimacy of Social Enterprise', *Nonprofit Management and Leadership*, 14(4): 411–24.

Dees, J. G. (1998*a*). *The Meaning of Social Entrepreneurship*, Available at: http://www.the-ef.org/resources-Dees103198.html

—— (January–February, 1998*b*). 'Enterprising Nonprofits', *Harvard Business Review*, 76(1): 54–67.

—— (2003). 'Social Entrepreneurship Is About Innovation and Impact, Not Income'. Available at: http://skoll.socialedge.org/?293@21.D0y7ae6ubQ9.53535@.1ad86d9e

—— and Anderson, B. (2004). 'Scaling Social Impact. Strategies for Spreading Social Innovations', *Stanford Social Innovation Review*: 24–32.

Defourny, J. (2001). 'Introduction: From Third Sector to Social Enterprise', in C. Borzaga and J. Defourny (eds.), *The Emergence of Social Enterprise*. London: Routledge, pp. 2–27.

Drayton, W. (2000). *The Entrepreneur's Revolution and You*, Available at: www.ashoka.org

—— (2002). 'The Citizen Sector: Becoming As Entrepreneurial and Competitive As Business', *California Management Review*, 44(3): 120–32.

Echoing Green website. Available at http://www.echoinggreen.org/

Edwards, S. (2002). 'Social Enterprise: Changing the Landscape of Welfare Provision in the United Kingdom and Ontaria, Canada?' Paper presented at ISTR Conference, Cape Town, South Africa.

Favreau, L. (2000). 'The Social Economy and Globalisation: An Overview', in J. Defourny, P. Develtere, and B. Foneneau (eds.), *Social Economy North and South Belgium*. Katholieke Universiteit Leuven and Universite de Liege, pp. 227–41.

Gartner, W. (Spring, 1988). ' 'Who is the Entrepreneur?' is the Wrong Question', *American Journal of Small Business*: 11–32.

Giddens, A. (1990). *The Consequences of Modernity*. Cambridge, UK: Polity Press.

—— (1999). 'Runaway World: The Reith Lecture Revisited', *The Director's Lectures, Lecture 1*, 10 November.

Glasius, M. (2003). 'Expertise in the Cause of Justice: Global Civil Society Influence on the Statute for an International Criminal Court', in M. Glasius, M. Kaldor, and H. Anheier (eds.), *Global Civil Society Yearbook 2003*. Oxford: Oxford University Press, pp. 35–53.

Global Civil Society Yearbook (2001). Oxford: Oxford University Press.

—— (2002). Oxford: Oxford University Press.

—— (2003). Oxford: Oxford University Press.

—— (2004/5). London: Sage.

Grenier, P. (2003). 'Jubilee 2000: Laying the Foundations for a Social Movement', in J. Clark (ed.), *Globalising Civic Engagement*. London: Earthscan, pp. 86–108.

—— (2004). 'The New Pioneers: The People Behind Global Civil Society', in M. Kaldor, M. Glasius, and H. Anheier (eds.), *Global Civil Society Yearbook 2004/5*. London: Sage.

Guclu, A., Dees, J.G., and Andersen, B. (2002). *The Process of Social Entrepreneurship: Creating Opportunities Worthy of Serious Pursuit*, Center for the Advancement of Social Entrepreneurship, Duke University, the Fuqua School of Business, November.

Hartigan, P. (2002). *Social Entrepreneurship: What Is It?* Available at: http://www.schwabfound.org/news.htm?articleid=30&sid=10

Hay, C. (2001). 'What Place for Ideas in the Structure-Agency Debate? Globalisation As a 'Process Without a Subject' ', in *First Press: Writing in the Critical Social Sciences*. Available at: http://www.raggedclaws.com/criticalrealism/archive/cshay_wpisad.html

Henton, D., Melville, J., and Walesh, K. (1997). 'The Age of the Civic Entrepreneur: Restoring Civil Society and Building Economic Community', *National Civic Review*, 86(2): 149–56.

Hjorth, D. and Steyart, C. (2004). *Narrative and Discursive Approaches in Entrepreneurship: A Second Movement in Entrepreneurship Book*. Cheltenham, UK: Edward Elgar.

—— Johannisson, B., and Steyaert, C. (2003). 'Entrepreneurship As Discourse and Life Style', in B. Czarniawska and G. Sevón (eds.), *The Northern Lights*. Copenhagen Business School Press, pp. 91–110.

Hoffman, A. (1999). 'Institutional Evolution and Change: Environmentalism and the U.S. Chemical Industry', *Academy of Management Journal*, 32(4): 351–71.

Hutton, W. and Giddens, A. (eds.) (2001). *On the Edge. Living with Global Capitalism*. London: Vintage.

Kaldor, M. (2003). *Global Civil Society: An Answer to War*. London: Polity Press.

—— Anheier, H., and Glasius, M. (2003). 'Global Civil Society in an Era of Regressive Globalization', in M. Kaldor, H. Anheier, and M. Glasius (eds.), *Global Civil Society Yearbook 2003*. Oxford: Oxford University Press, pp. 3–33.

Keane, J. (2003). *Global Civil Society?* Cambridge: Cambridge University Press.

Kekk, M. and Sikkink, K. (1998). *Activists Beyond Borders: Advocacy Networks in International Politics*. Ithaca and London: Cornell University Press.

Martin, M. (2004). 'Surveying Social Entrepreneurship: Toward an Empirical Analysis of the Performance Revolution in the Social Sector', *Arbeitspapiere Band 2*. University of St Gallen.

Meyer, J. (2000). 'The 'Actors' of Modern Society: The Cultural Construction of Social Agency', *Sociological Theory* 18(1): 110–20.

—— and Scott, R. (1992). *Organizational Environments: Ritual and Rationality*. Newbury Park, CA: Sage.

Moore, H. (2002). 'Social Entrepreneurs and the Responsible Economy', Available at *Fathom*, http://www.fathom.com/feature/35522/

NESsT website. Available at http://www.nesst.org/

PREM (2000). Economic Policy Group and Development Economics Group. 'What is Globalization?' Paper 1: *World Bank Briefing Papers, Assessing Globalization*.

Salamon, L. and Anheier, H. (1999). 'Civil Society in Comparative Perspective', in L. Salamon, H. Anheier, R. List, S. Toepler, W. Sokolowski, and Associates (eds.), *Global Civil Society: Dimensions of the Nonprofit Sector*. Baltimore, MD: The Johns Hopkins Centre for Civil Society Studies.

Schwab Foundation (2003). *Some of the Benefits of Belonging to the Schwab Foundation's Network of Outstanding Social Entrepreneurs*. Available at http://www.schwabfound.org/benefits.htm

Schwab, K. (2000). *Social Entrepreneurship*. Address delivered by Klaus Schwab, Founder and President of the World Economic Forum and the Schwab Foundation for Social Entrepreneurship, at the American International Club, Geneva.

Scott, W. (2001). *Institutions and Organizations*, 2nd edn. London: Sage.

Soros, G. (2001). 'The New Global Financial Architecture', in W. Hutton and A. Giddens (eds.), *On the Edge. Living with Global Capitalism*. London: Vintage, pp. 86–92.

Tarrow, S. (2001). 'Transnational Politics: Contention and Institutions in International Politics', *Annual Review of Political Science*, 4: 1–20.

—— (2004). 'Rooted Cosmopolitans and Transnational Activists', unpublished working paper, October.

Taylor, N., Hobbs, R., Nilsonn, F., O'Halloran, K., and Preisser, C. (2000). 'The Rise of the Term Social Entrepreneur in Print Publications', *Frontiers of Entrepreneurship Research*, Babson College. Available at: http://www.babson.edu/entrep/fer/XXXVI/XXXVIB/XXXVIB.htm

Toynbee, P. (2001). 'Who's Afraid of Global Culture?' in W. Hutton and A. Giddens (eds.), *On the Edge. Living with Global Capitalism*. London: Vintage, pp. 191–212.

World Social Forum (2005) website. Available at: http://www.forumsocialmundial.org.br

7

Rhetoric, Reality, and Research: Building a Solid Foundation for the Practice of Social Entrepreneurship

Beth Battle Anderson and J. Gregory Dees

The practice of social entrepreneurship may be quite old, but as a distinct field of academic inquiry, it is still in its infancy. It appears that the first dedicated course in this arena was launched at Harvard Business School (HBS) in Spring 1995 as part of the new Initiative on Social Enterprise. Since then, numerous other schools have launched similar courses, initiatives, and centres. This dramatic increase in activity at academic institutions represents tremendous progress in a relatively short time frame. However, a review of the top programmes reveals a potentially damaging weakness. Many of the new courses are staffed by practitioners who bring an invaluable depth of experience to this work, but who have limited research experience and are not on the regular tenure track at their institution where rigorous research is required. As a result, relative to other academic fields, social entrepreneurship is not yet blessed with a wealth of serious researchers.

Educational programmes, particularly those situated in leading universities, cannot stand without a firm foundation of knowledge behind them. The 'wisdom' of experience can be extremely helpful, but it must be tested, refined, tempered, and deepened by rigorous research. It is natural for those with experience to generalize from a very limited data-set, in some cases from one organization in one operating context. This tendency is particularly problematic in the social sector with its inherent diversity of purposes, covering everything from pollution to poverty and education to health care. Furthermore, the settings for this work vary widely. Differences in culture, wealth, infrastructure, government, history, and legal system can matter a great deal. Lessons learned fighting AIDS in Africa might not translate to launching a microenterprise programme in London or protecting the rain forest in Brazil. Only through systematic research can we reliably and responsibly identify cross-cutting patterns, formulate principles, and structure frameworks that

144

can help guide social entrepreneurs operating in a variety of settings with different purposes.

The need for research is even more acute in a young field that is fraught with rhetoric. Rhetoric often dominates early discussions of any new idea, particularly one with passionate adherents. Passionate promoters tend to generalize from a small number of highly visible successes while paying less attention to failures and disappointing efforts. This situation often leads to unfounded, exaggerated, or simplified assertions that are widely promoted through convincing rhetoric. Moreover, in their enthusiasm, proponents frequently adopt value-laden language that casts the new idea in a favourable light, while denigrating old approaches. In a world full of contending beliefs, information overload, and inherent scepticism, this kind of rhetoric may be essential to get attention and overcome resistance to change. Unfortunately, at the same time, this use of rhetoric makes it difficult to sort the good ideas from the bad. And rhetoric without research has the potential to harm practitioners who take actions based on unproven claims. Furthermore, for a nascent field like social entrepreneurship, one that is trying to establish itself as a legitimate arena of inquiry, rhetoric without research yields a fragile knowledge base that is vulnerable to attack by sceptics.

Thus, it is critical that we build a stronger foundation of knowledge around social entrepreneurship. In order to establish social entrepreneurship as a field, not a fad, universities around the globe must mount serious efforts to engage in rigorous research that will deepen our informal knowledge base. To illustrate this point, we explore below what we do not know about earned income, a major topic in social entrepreneurship. Systematic research into earned income and many of the other emerging themes of social entrepreneurship will help educators, students, and practitioners sort the rhetoric from the reality, enhancing the impact of social entrepreneurs and of the field as a whole.

What We Do Not Know About Earned Income

For readers who are not familiar with the term, 'earned income' primarily refers to income derived from selling products or services.[1] It is typically contrasted with philanthropic donations and government subsidies, and it is one of the most widely discussed concepts in social entrepreneurship. In recent years, with significant foundation support, major universities have launched business plan competitions focused on earned income ventures.[2] Many books and articles have been written on the topic, and numerous organizations have been created to advance practice and support the increasing number of social entrepreneurs seeking to develop and implement earned income strategies.[3] In fact, according to one consulting firm, the art of developing earned income has become a growing new 'field of practice'

145

(Community Wealth Ventures 2003). Some proponents even argue that social entrepreneurship should be defined in terms of the pursuit of earned income alone (Boschee and McClurg 2003).

While we do not embrace this definition of social entrepreneurship, we do see earned income as a potentially powerful tool for social entrepreneurs. We have written on the topic ourselves (Dees 1998, 2004; Battle Anderson, Dees, and Emerson 2001; Dees and Battle Anderson 2003) and have also been involved with several of the organizations promoting the exploration of earned income. Yet we are painfully aware of the lack of systematic knowledge about earned income strategies in the social sector. So here we identify five important research topics that arise out of the rhetoric surrounding earned income and illustrate the limits of our current understanding. Our goal is not to be critical of earned income promoters. We aim simply to point out where initial claims regarding the benefits of earned income need to be strengthened, refined, revised, or, perhaps, even rejected based on solid conceptual and empirical research. The pioneers have made great progress in establishing this new field of practice. We are deeply indebted to them, but it is time to move beyond a value-laden rhetoric supported primarily by anecdotal arguments and success stories.

Research Topic 1: 'Self-Sufficiency'

KEY QUESTIONS

What does it mean for an organization to be 'self-sufficient'? Is it fair to describe organizations that depend on earned income as self-sufficient and those that rely on other sources as 'dependent'? What are the value judgements that underlie the promotion of earned income?

Many proponents talk about earned income as a form of self-sufficiency and other sources of revenue as a form of 'dependency'. Perhaps the clearest example of this framing comes from earned income advocates Boschee and McClurg (2003), who describe self-sufficiency as something that 'can be

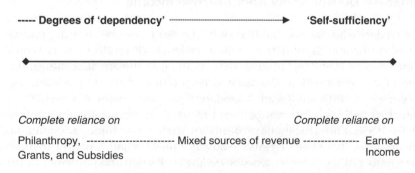

Figure 7.1 A perspective on financial strategies: Dependency vs. self-sufficiency

achieved only by relying *completely* on earned income, and is the *ultimate goal* of the *most ambitious* social entrepreneurs' (emphasis added). They refer to reliance on 'philanthropy, voluntarism, and government subsidy' as the 'dependency model'. In using this language, they are urging social entrepreneurs to move to one extreme of the full continuum of available financial options.[4]

Starkly contrasting different sources of funding in terms of dependency and self-sufficiency is seriously misleading. A financially self-sufficient organization, like a perpetual motion machine, is a myth. No matter where they are on this continuum, every organization is dependent on outsiders for resources and support.[5] Earned income comes from customers who often have a choice of many other organizations with which to do business. Earned income ventures are also dependent on suppliers for key inputs, on labour markets for talent, and often on bankers or investors for capital. If these dependencies do not seem real, consider the tens of thousands of companies that file for bankruptcy each year. The closest thing to a financially self-sufficient organization is one that is fully and generously supported by endowment, and even these organizations depend on well-functioning capital markets through which to invest their endowment.

Why do some people regard it as natural and appropriate to refer to earned income as a form of self-sufficiency and philanthropy as a form of dependency? No one would complain that businesses are too 'customer dependent'. This language appears to reflect a value judgement. Dependency is generally regarded as bad—a sign of weakness and vulnerability. Self-sufficiency is regarded as unequivocally good—a sign of strength. What are the values implicit in the use of these terms? Are they grounded in a market-oriented ideology? It is possible that being dependent on customers is, on average, better than being dependent on foundations, major donors, or the government. Yet until we have the research to support this kind of claim, it seems unfair to use language of self-sufficiency to encourage dependence on one source of funds rather than another. Understanding the values behind the language may yield useful insights into the growing popularity of earned income strategies.

Of course, the term earned income itself is value-laden, seemingly implying that the donations, grants, and government support that social sector leaders work so hard to attract and use for important social purposes are not 'earned'. Attracting these resources requires talent, effort, and an appealing value proposition, just like attracting paying customers. In fact, some writers have suggested that we should think of donors as 'customers' (see, e.g. Jones 1994), others see donors as 'investors' (Sprinkel 1997). Referring to earned income as 'revenue from sales' would be a more neutral description, but potential research questions about the language and values implicit in the rhetoric surrounding earned income go much deeper. Perhaps the answers lie in some of the other benefits that have been claimed for earned income, namely greater sustainability, financial freedom, and scalability.

Research Topic 2: Sustainability

SAMPLE QUESTIONS

Is earned income inherently more 'sustainable' than other forms of income for social entrepreneurs? Under what conditions is it most likely to be sustainable? Is 'sustainability' the right measure for assessing financial strategies?

Promoters of self-sufficiency often also tout the role of earned income in achieving sustainability. Indeed, sustainability has become the rallying cry for many proponents of earned income strategies. A groundbreaking 2003 report documenting the rise of earned income ventures in the USA is titled *Powering Social Change: Lessons on Community Wealth Generation for Nonprofit Sustainability* (Community Wealth Ventures 2003). That same year, Boschee and McClurg claimed 'as long as nonprofits continue to be dependent on contributions from individuals, grants from foundations, subsidies from government and other forms of largesse, they will *never* become sustainable or self-sufficient' (Boschee and McClurg 2003: 3).

Unfortunately, we are not aware of any systematic evidence that earned income is inherently more sustainable than other forms of revenue for social purpose organizations. It is true that earned income can be a very important part of the financial mix for social entrepreneurs, and it is widely recognized that a diversified funding strategy, often including some earned income, can contribute to financial stability. But it is not clear that earned income is intrinsically more reliable than all other sources. In fact, given the notoriously high failure rate for new businesses, we wonder why the failure rate would not also be high for earned income ventures started by social entrepreneurs. We may find a higher failure rate among social purpose organizations relying heavily on earned income than those relying more on philanthropy and government funding, but no systematic study has been done. We know that many of these ventures do fail or yield disappointing results, though we have no idea of the overall failure rate or the organizational impact of unsuccessful strategies.

Admittedly, a few failures have been documented. For example, in the 1990s, the media followed with interest the high profile dissolution of the earned income licensing agreement between the American Medical Association (AMA) and Sunbeam Corporation, a debacle that cost the AMA upwards of $13 million (£7.5 million) according to one estimate (Wolinsky 1999). Subsequently, HBS completed a series of teaching cases on this fiasco (Nanda and Haddad 2001). In another instance, two major philanthropic organizations funded an extensive analysis of the failure of The Nature Conservancy's establishment of the Virginia Eastern Shore Corporation (VESC), an earned income venture that was founded with three goals: profitability, job creation, and environmental protection (see Dabson, Plastrik, and Turner 2001). After four years, having run through millions of dollars in investments while generating significant losses, VESC was dissolved. The report examining this effort is a valuable step forward in generating some hypotheses about not-for-profits operating business ventures for social purposes, especially in the environmental arena, but these hypotheses need further testing and refinement through analysis of past and future successes and failures. In the short term, reports such as this one, and cautionary examples such as AMA–Sunbeam, need greater attention and more widespread dissemination to temper the rhetoric of earned income and its inherent sustainability.

A thoughtful research agenda would also explore the notion of sustainability in some depth. What does it mean? Why is it so attractive? Is it the right measure for assessing financial strategies? We suspect that despite the prevalence of the term, sustainability does not fully capture what attracts most proponents to earned income strategies. If we want to promote sustainability, we would be urging the creation of endowments, not active forms of earned income. For a not-for-profit, no income source is more sustainable than a prudently and conservatively invested endowment fund. Institutions such as Harvard University, with over $22 billion (£12.8 billion) in its endowment, and Ford Foundation, with an endowment close to $10 billion (£5.8 billion), are among the most sustainable organizations in the world as a result of their endowments. Yet proponents of sustainability rarely mention endowments. Endowments usually come from donors, and they buffer the organization from market discipline. Proponents of earned income tend to eschew 'donor dependency' and favour 'market discipline', suggesting that sustainability does not adequately capture what they find attractive about earned income.

Regardless of what is driving the attraction to sustainability, research could help us understand whether sustainability is really a problem in the social sector. In promoting the shift to earned income, Boschee claims, 'The very survival of many social service, arts, and other organizations is at stake' (Boschee 1998). He may be right, but we know of no systematic evidence showing that large numbers of effective social purpose organizations are going out of business, or that social sector organizations have inappropriately short lives. It is quite possible that the contrary is true. Perhaps too many ineffective organizations stay alive too long. While we do not have data on the average lifespan of social sector organizations, business organizations do appear to have relatively short lives. According to Arie de Geus, even large multinational corporations can only expect to live forty or fifty years on average (de Geus 1997). The life expectancy for smaller businesses is much lower, with one survey estimating 12.5 years for all firms. De Geus bemoans this state of affairs, but it may not be a bad thing for society. In fact, it results from what economist Joseph Schumpeter called 'creative destruction', whereby more innovative, efficient, and effective players drive weaker competitors out of business (Schumpeter 1950). This process imposes discipline on performance through competition in customer and capital markets, ensuring that only those organizations creating value efficiently survive.

Ironically, many proponents of earned income and the quest for sustainability seem to be drawn to the idea of 'market-based' solutions, yet in a well-functioning market, many organizations will not be sustainable for long periods. Nor should they be. Indeed, to get the benefits of market dynamics in the social sector, we may need to accept more of a process of creative destruction, which requires emphasizing social performance rather than organizational sustainability. If we fail to do so, earned income proponents may risk increasing the ranks of what some organizational scholars call 'permanently failing organizations' (Meyer and Zucker 1989). We could end up with ventures that succeed financially but fail socially (see Backman and Smith 2000).

Research Topic 3: Financial Freedom

SAMPLE QUESTIONS

Does earned income give social entrepreneurs more flexibility in how they spend their money? Is complete reliance on earned income optimal for social entrepreneurs? How difficult is it to generate profits from earned income ventures in the social sector?

Another alleged feature of earned income ventures that makes them attractive is the promise of financial freedom and flexibility. The Institute for Social Entrepreneurs' website quotes a not-for-profit CEO, 'The beauty of making a profit is that you can do a *lot* with the money, you can do what *you* want to do. You can do it *how* you want to do it for as *long* as you want to do it and you don't have to make anybody happy except your own Board and staff. You don't have to meet *anybody* else's expectations.'

As appealing as it might be to social entrepreneurs, it is far from clear whether it is a good thing to free them from meeting 'anyone else's expectations'. External accountability, when it is at least roughly aligned with an organization's mission, can play a valuable role. Research could explore the advantages and disadvantages of being accountable to donors to test the value of financial freedom.

Furthermore, while fundraising can undoubtedly be burdensome, we fear that the freedom ascribed to earned income ventures is often overstated. Ironically, one of the potential merits of earned income is that it imposes market discipline, requiring an organization to meet or exceed the expectations of its customers, usually in a competitive marketplace. If those expectations are not completely aligned with the organization's mission, just like foundation grants, government contracts, and individual philanthropists, customer demands may impose restrictions, expectations, and risks of 'mission-drift' on an organization. And for any venture, while customers may not dictate exactly how an organization spends the money it collects from them, they generally do demand that the organization deliver value to them over time at a competitive price. To call this form of revenue 'unrestricted' is to ignore the requirements of delivering value competitively (see Dees 2004: 11–12).

In reality, only if there are funds left over after covering all costs associated with delivering customer value does an organization have money that it can spend freely on whatever management chooses. Even then, most business ventures require a significant portion of the profits to be reinvested or to pay-off debts. Only the cash that remains after satisfying these demands will be available for the organization to use freely. In a business with a 10 per cent total return on sales that also requires half of those profits to be reinvested in the business (both generous estimates), it will take $1 million (£580,000) in sales to generate $50,000 (£29,000) in free cash flow. Especially if the venture is not completely aligned with the organization's mission, social entrepreneurs must ask if this earned income strategy is the most effective way for them to generate $50,000 (£29,000) in unrestricted cash.

Are earned income ventures in the social sector typically profitable? Do they often generate free cash flow for the organization to use as it pleases? It is not at all clear that they are or do. A paper reporting the results of a 2000 survey of enterprise in the US, not-for-profit sector claims, 'Nonprofit organizations operating ventures see a bottom line benefit.' Notably, support for this finding was that 'on average, survey respondents currently operating ventures say that their enterprises generate 12 per cent of annual net revenue' (Massarsky and Beinhacker 2002). It is unclear exactly what was meant by 'net revenue' in this context, which was probably an issue for the respondents as well. In business, net revenue refers to total sales less discounts, returns, and allowances. It does not take into account total expenses, and thus is closer to the 'top line' than to the 'bottom line' of an income statement. Earned income's contribution to revenues does not necessarily translate into a 'bottom line benefit'. Moreover, in addition to having a 'survivor bias' that fails to capture the costs of failed ventures, this kind of survey is a poor method for verifying profitability. Respondents may not know if their organization's ventures were profitable. Few not-for-profit organizations have accounting systems that fully and appropriately allocate costs to different ventures and programmes. A very different story can emerge when costs are fully taken into account, as suggested in recent work undertaken by the Bridgespan Group (Foster and Bradach 2005). Without rigorous in-depth research, we have no idea about the level of financial 'bottom line impact' business ventures are having on not-for-profit organizations.

Finally, if total reliance on earned income truly were optimal for social entrepreneurs, providing them with the ultimate freedom to pursue their mission, then one might expect to see far more social entrepreneurs adopting a for-profit form. Notably, of the relatively few who do, many have felt the need to have not-for-profit affiliates or partners that use philanthropy and government subsidies to support essential activities that cannot be sustained by the for-profit (see Dees and Battle Anderson 2003). The 'financial freedom' afforded these for-profit social ventures by their earned income activities does not seem sufficient to allow them to pursue their missions effectively. Even they appear to need some form of philanthropic support. Why should it be any different for not-for-profits?

Research Topic 4: Scalability

SAMPLE QUESTIONS

Does greater reliance on earned income make it easier to scale a successful social venture? How and under what conditions does earned income contribute to scalability?

Recently, proponents of earned income have started to emphasize another potential benefit—its scalability. The issue of scale has been a central one in the social sector where the spread of effective innovations appears to be very slow, especially when compared to business. In fact, Grameen Bank and Ashoka recently hosted an event for social entrepreneurs that specifically focused on the role of 'business-social ventures' in scaling the size and impact of social entrepreneurship efforts (Herbst 2004). Muhammad Yunus, founder of Grameen Bank, spoke of the power of earned income when seeking to scale, stating, 'The more we can move in the direction of business, the better off we are—in the sense that then we are free; we have unlimited opportunities to expand and do more, and replication becomes so much easier' (Herbst 2004).

Does reliance on earned income improve the scalability of social purpose organizations? Again, we have little systematic evidence one way or the other. It is true that businesses seem to scale much faster than not-for-profits, even when operating in the same industries (Hansmann 1996b).[6] This finding might lend some credibility to the idea that scale is easier with earned income. Yet we have seen powerful conflicting evidence. A quick glance at the youngest organizations on the *2003 Nonprofit Times 100* list of largest US-based not-for-profits reveals that these high-growth not-for-profits are highly dependent on philanthropic or government support. We looked at organizations that made it from their founding to the top 100 list in thirty years or less. Even if we exclude the fundraising organizations, such as the Fidelity Gift Fund, and the post-September 11 charities, such as the Twin Towers Fund, we still see a powerful bias for public and government support, with most of the organizations over 90 per cent dependent on these sources. Programme service fees were more than 20 per cent in only one case, Habitat for Humanity, where they are still well below donated funds, and that analysis of Habitat probably does not include the enormous dollar value of donated volunteer time.[7] If earned income were a better source of funding for scale, would we not expect to see that reflected in these rapid growth organizations? Yes, this sample has a US bias, but the levels of earned income in these organizations are abnormally low even for US-based not-for-profits.[8]

In fact, we face a glaring absence of compelling examples of social purpose organizations with very high levels of earned income scaling quickly. Proponents of earned income often cite Grameen Bank as an earned income venture that has successfully achieved scale, serving millions of families in Bangladesh while inspiring and providing guidance to many others around the world. Grameen certainly merits credit and attention for its success. Muhammad Yunus reports with well-deserved pride that the bank stopped taking philanthropic support and concessionary funding in the mid-1990s. He has wondered aloud why the bank did not make this move earlier.

The answer seems relatively straightforward. Grameen benefited from many millions of dollars of outside funding throughout its first and most crucial fifteen years of operation. As a result, during this period, it grew from a small experimental programme into a bank with over 1,000 branches. In nearly a decade since it stopped taking concessionary funding, it has added just over 100 branches to this network. Grameen stopped taking subsidized funding *after* most of the bank's infrastructure was built, its reputation was established worldwide, and it had a large base of savings deposits from its customers. If Grameen had always relied only on its retained earnings, savings, and market-rate capital, its growth rate would have been slowed considerably in the crucial early years.

Furthermore, before generalizing from this one powerful success story, we must remember that as a bank, Grameen is authorized to accept savings deposits. Savings have created a unique, low-cost, and appropriate base of capital to expand Grameen's lending programmes. Unfortunately, few social entrepreneurs are in a position to take savings deposits from the people they serve. They are fighting AIDS in Africa or serving street children in India. Even many other microcredit programmes are not classified as banks and are prevented by law from taking deposits. Thus, they have not been able to follow Grameen's lead, either in giving up outside support or in achieving significant scale. Grameen is a powerful model, but we cannot conclude from this one case that earned income is the best route. Much more thorough research is needed to explore the hypothesis that high levels of earned income make it easier to scale.

Research Topic 5: Social Impact

KEY QUESTIONS

How and under what circumstances can earned income strategies be used to improve social impact? Does the 'double bottom line' metaphor make sense? How should social entrepreneurs make decisions about the best funding strategy for maximizing their social impact?

In the end, self-sufficiency, sustainability, financial freedom, and scalability are only important if they lead to greater positive social impact by social entrepreneurs. We fear that social impact can get lost in the focus on financial impacts. Indeed, one of the catchphrases of the earned income movement is the double bottom line, which focuses on both financial and social or mission impact. Yet, with notable exceptions such as the work done by Roberts Enterprise Development Fund, there is little concrete evidence of the demonstrated social impact of social sector earned income ventures. For example, 87 per cent of respondents to a 2000 survey of not-for-profits that were operating businesses said 'the goals of the venture relate to the mission of the organization to a great or significant extent', but only 8 per cent reported actually calculating the social return their venture generates (Massarsky and Beinhacker 2002). This reality raises the question of whether there truly is an operable double bottom line for these ventures. In another research project on double bottom line private equity investors, only half of the funds responded that they evaluate the social impact of their investments in any way (Clark and Galliard 2003). And even for organizations that do attempt to measure both financial and social impact, we would argue that there is only one 'ultimate bottom line' for a social entrepreneur, which is mission impact (see Dees 2004). Thus, given the lack of strong data supporting either the financial or social impact of earned income ventures, we find the assertion of double bottom line benefits premature at best.

In pursuing the ultimate social bottom line, all social entrepreneurs must develop a financial strategy that will allow them to carry out their social mission effectively. In doing so, they have a choice of financial strategies, and they can, and often do, mix government, philanthropic, and earned income sources. They must position themselves on the continuum described in Figure 7.1, taking into consideration, among other things, the organization's mission, resource environment, and stage of development. For this reason, earned income strategies should be presented, considered, and pursued within the context of an overall financial strategy for social impact. Therefore, in order to promote this practice, and move beyond the simplified rhetoric of the double bottom line, solid research is needed that sheds light upon the link between financial strategy and social impact, between organizational sustainability and mission-related performance. We recognize that social impact is often hard to measure, but that should not allow it to get lost in the rhetoric regarding the other benefits of earned income.

Open Window of Opportunity for Research

The five preceding topics point to a serious need for more research around earned income strategies. Nonetheless, we believe that earned income has many attractive characteristics, particularly when it can be aligned with a social mission. Social entrepreneurs should consider it seriously and creatively. However, it is time to promote, support, and engage in rigorous research to deepen our understanding of this tool and other important social entrepreneurship concepts. In doing so, we will be capitalizing on the current surge in interest in social entrepreneurship amongst universities, foundations, the media, and even some governments. We should also take advantage of the recent growth of an increasingly vibrant community of researchers focused on the issues associated with the not-for-profit 'sector'.[9] These scholars have produced a rich base of knowledge on which we can build. However, this perspective is not appropriate for seizing the window of opportunity that has been created by the increasing attention on social entrepreneurship. Not-for-profit researchers tend to start with a particular legal form of organization in mind; many appear to see business methods and ideas as risky, potentially corrupting of their sector; and most take a social science approach, focusing on public policy implications rather than management issues. These biases must be overcome by moving beyond the field of not-for-profit research to establish a strong cohort of social entrepreneurship researchers.

The Need to Move Beyond Not-for-Profit Research

Some not-for-profit research is excellent and thought provoking, but even the best work in this area can hide subtle, perhaps even unconscious, biases against for-profit organizations, markets, and business-inspired approaches. In a thoughtful and inspiring observation about the future of the not-for-profit sector, Salamon (1997) comments:

[W]e should respond to the challenges the nonprofit sector is facing not with a vain attempt to return to a mythical golden age of supposed nonprofit purity, nor a policy of continued drift toward commercialization, but by using this as an occasion, and an opportunity, for renewal. This would entail rethinking the nonprofit sector's role and operations, re-examining the prevailing mythology in light of contemporary realities, and seeking a new consensus, a new settlement, regarding the functions of nonprofit organizations, the relationships they have with citizens, with government, and with business, and the way they will operate in the years ahead.

We agree with the spirit of this eloquent call for renewal, but we see in Salamon's language and framing of the issue some of the limits and biases that social entrepreneurship research must avoid. Three specific aspects can be outlined.

Shifting Away from a Narrow Focus on One Organizational Form

Not-for-profit researchers tend to see the world in terms of distinct legal forms of organizations. It is true that they have observed the blurring of sector boundaries and have documented trends such as the expansion of for-profit providers into many traditionally not-for-profit or public sector fields (see, e.g.

Salamon 2003). However, these trends seem to have reinforced the commitment of this group of researchers to the not-for-profit form of organization. Yet social entrepreneurship is not limited to this form alone. Social entrepreneurship researchers should not be constrained by this limitation either.

While many social entrepreneurs do adopt a not-for-profit form of organization, they, and those researching them, should view the choice of legal form as a strategic decision, not a state of being. Legal forms of organization are artefacts; tools people have designed to serve various purposes. The world is full of different organizational forms with different strengths and weaknesses (Hansmann 1996a). Social entrepreneurship research must encompass the full range of organizations that can serve a social purpose, regardless of legal structure. By focusing on purpose rather than form, the field will also be open to new organizational forms, such as the CIC that has recently been proposed in Great Britain.[10] Unfortunately, organizations such as these would currently fall outside the domain of traditional not-for-profit research.

Some of the language employed by not-for-profit researchers illustrates the challenge many of them have divorcing purpose from organizational form. Not-for-profit economist Burton Weisbrod uses the phrase 'for-profit in disguise' to identify organizations that are legally not-for-profits but appear to be maximizing profit or revenue instead of quality social outcomes (Weisbrod 1998: 11–12).[11] Extending this idea further, in an e-mail correspondence with one of us, a leading not-for-profit researcher referred to the for-profit community development bank Shorebank Corporation as a 'nonprofit in disguise', meaning a for-profit organization that serves a social purpose. But Shorebank and other social purpose businesses are clear about their objectives and are not 'in disguise'. They have merely strategically chosen to pursue their social objectives through a for-profit structure. Like social entrepreneurs themselves, social entrepreneurship researchers should focus first on purpose, then on organizational form.

Reducing Resistance to Business Concepts and Ideas

The intrinsic value not-for-profit researchers place on the not-for-profit form is often accompanied by a deep-seated scepticism of ideas and concepts from business. Indeed, in a rejection of the idea that not-for-profits should be more 'business-like', Paul Light of the Brookings Institution urges them to be more 'nonprofit-like'. Light (2002: 24) expresses a concern about how far in the direction of business not-for-profits can go 'without altering their character'. This comment echoes what Salamon (2003: 80–3) has called the 'distinctiveness imperative' for the not-for-profit sector. However, for social entrepreneurs, the point is not to be more business-like or more nonprofit-like. It is to be more *effective* at changing the world, using whatever organizational forms or management methods are most conducive to that. The distinctive character of the not-for-profit sector, if it has one, should be preserved only as long as its preservation is linked to better social performance. Otherwise, further evolution of the sector may be preferable to preservation of its current character. Distinctive is not always better.

Ironically, Light's own survey suggests that business-inspired reforms have been among the most valuable in enhancing performance in the not-for-profit sector (Light 2002: 112). He surveyed 250 executives of high performing not-for-profits and asked them how much various reforms had improved performance in the sector. If we combine the top two response categories ('Great deal' and 'Fair amount'), the most helpful reforms out of the thirteen listed were: 'Encouragement to do more strategic planning' (84 per cent), 'Increased openness to using standard business tools' (82 per cent), and 'Increased emphasis on outcomes measurement' (79 per cent). A case can be made that all three of these were at least partly business inspired. Certainly, the reference to 'standard business tools' speaks clearly to the value of cross-sector learning.[12] Spreading of practices, knowledge, and norms across sector boundaries has apparently been beneficial.

Despite this finding, throughout not-for-profit research, we have found a tendency to use terms with negative connotations to refer to business-inspired practices. Even Salamon, after rejecting the myth of 'nonprofit purity', describes increased earned income activities as a 'drift towards commercialization'. Commercialization seems like an innocent term. We have even used it ourselves in early work. However, it has negative connotations. Can you think of any occasion when someone expressed enthusiasm for the increasing 'commercialization' of anything? We frequently bemoan the commercialization of holidays, national parks, or historic sites. Compare Salamon's phrase drift towards commercialization with an alternative reading, such as 'strategic shift towards earned income'. Drift towards commercialization implies an aimless movement in the direction of base, market-oriented, money-centred values. A strategic shift towards earned income implies a deliberate change in financial strategy towards a source of funds that sounds attractive. As long as we describe earned income activity as commercialization, it will sound inherently objectionable. Some not-for-profit researchers even use the stronger term 'commercialism' (James 2003); that suggests a value system or ideology that places commercial interests above other more important values. We cannot afford to have research on social entrepreneurship led primarily by researchers whose language is fundamentally anti-business. Business-inspired methods certainly pose risks that need to be understood and explored, but they clearly offer potential benefits as well.

Emphasizing Management Rather than Social Science and Public Policy

The field of social entrepreneurship needs researchers with a practical, managerial orientation. Consider the difference between a course in 'art appreciation' and a course in painting or sculpting. One aims to enhance students' understanding of the field from an observer's point of view; the other aims to develop students' skills from a practitioner's point of view. They can inform each other, but they have different objectives.

Traditional research on the not-for-profit sector has been more on the level of art appreciation. It involves social scientists observing the sector and describing its operations. When practical conclusions are drawn, they are usually public policy conclusions. Largely because the researchers tend to reside in social science departments or public policy schools, not-for-profit researchers have been far less interested in managerial issues than their business school counterparts. For instance, one might expect a book with the title *To Profit or Not to Profit* to provide guidance to entrepreneurs and managers about which form of organization they might want to adopt (Weisbrod 1998). Any social entrepreneur who picks up this book with that hope will soon be disappointed. It presents some fascinating research on trends and patterns that could inform managerial conclusions, but it is clear from the start that doing so is not the goal of the seventeen authors who contributed. Their goals were to advance the economic and sociological theory of different organizational forms and to inform public policy. These are important goals, but only indirectly useful to social entrepreneurs. Someone needs to translate this kind of work into a form that is more useful for practitioners. Fortunately, some not-for-profit researchers are beginning to move in this direction and also engage business school researchers in their work (Young 2004). This trend is promising, but we need to accelerate the development of organizational and managerial social entrepreneurship research.

Engaging Business School Researchers

Ultimately, the field of social entrepreneurship research must include a community of researchers from varying disciplines and perspectives. The mix should reflect the diversity of social issues, the range of strategies for social change, the various organizational structures that could be used, and the multiple stakeholders involved. However, for at least three reasons, we feel that the most critical audiences to engage at this stage are business school faculty and doctoral students. First of all, business and management faculty are more likely to have a practical orientation that, coupled with their familiarity with markets and business tools, has great potential to advance knowledge and influence practice. Second, there appears to be a thirst from the field for more knowledge around business-inspired methods and approaches, creating both a need and an opportunity for rigorous research informed by a business perspective. Admittedly, business school faculty may have a bias towards market-based approaches and business-inspired methods, but this perspective could help counterbalance the existing biases against business. Finally, many of the academic initiatives focused on social entrepreneurship are being established at business schools, providing a wonderful opportunity for engaging faculty. Unfortunately, student or donor, rather than faculty, demand is driving many business school initiatives. They will not endure or reach their potential without significant support and leadership from influential tenured faculty members who are actively contributing to the development of the field through research as well as teaching.

We have already seen some promising developments on the business school research front. These efforts are still relatively new, and much of the initial research is more descriptive than grounded in theory. In many ways, this type of research represents a critical first step in establishing social entrepreneurship as a field of academic inquiry. As a case in point, Columbia University's Business School Research Initiative in Social Entrepreneurship (RISE) conducted the first survey of US-based equity investors in early stage for-profit ventures considered to have positive social or environmental impacts. *The RISE Capital Market Report: The Double Bottom Line Private Equity Landscape in 2002/2003* presents the results of this survey (Clark and Galliard 2003). It represents a significant step forward in helping to define and document an emerging area of social entrepreneurship, offering useful insights while also raising significant questions and identifying areas for further research. It is powerful in part because it is practical, is helping to provide structure to a previously undefined area of inquiry, and has support, participation, and audiences across sector boundaries.[13] We hope to see an increasing number of similar efforts at business schools around the world. Nonetheless, this work is purely descriptive and is not driven by theory. To take the research deeper, we need to push further to engage tenure-track and tenured business school faculty who have been trained in research methods to apply their expertise and build theory specifically for the field social entrepreneurship. While this task will not be easy, it is paramount.

Common Obstacles to Faculty Involvement

On the basis of our experiences at Harvard, Stanford, and Duke, we have identified a number of common obstacles to engaging business school faculty. Our efforts have met with limited success, but we have learned a few lessons along the way.[14] We hope they will be useful to others in the field that are interested in deepening the research base supporting social entrepreneurship.

Limited Understanding of Social Entrepreneurship

Most business school faculty members have only a vague sense, at best, of the field of social entrepreneurship. This reality is not surprising. The field is new and the boundaries are unsettled. Some see it as a branch of Corporate Social Responsibility (CSR), others as a branch of not-for-profit management. Without a clear understanding of the field and its issues, it is hard for them to see the relevance of their expertise.

Limited Availability of Reliable Data Sources

Many business researchers have come to rely on the wide array of existing databases with significant amounts of relevant business data. However, for most social entrepreneurship research questions, the required databases will have to be built. And while some researchers might not mind collecting field data, they are more comfortable doing so in familiar fields where they are more confident what kind of data to collect.

Few Obvious Outlets for Publishing

Very few of the leading academic journals in the business disciplines have published anything on social entrepreneurship, perhaps because they have received few submissions in this area. Whether they would welcome a submission related to social entrepreneurship is uncertain, further increasing the risk, especially for junior, tenure-track faculty who must publish in the right journals. The field of not-for-profit research has a couple of journals that would probably be receptive to social entrepreneurship research, but these are generally not known or held in high regard by business school faculty.

Limited Time Available for New Research Agendas

One of the biggest constraints on any faculty research is time. In our conversations with faculty, the issues surrounding social entrepreneurship intrigue many of them, but with heavy teaching loads, existing research and writing projects, and oftentimes leadership or administrative responsibilities within the school or their departments, they just do not have time to commit to exploring a new arena in any depth.

Limited Demand for Social Sector Researchers

While the need for social entrepreneurship research is great, the market demand for social entrepreneurship researchers is still weak. This lack of demand is a major deterrent for junior faculty and Ph.D. candidates. Most initiatives in this area are staffed by adjuncts (primarily academically inclined practitioners) and faculty who have already received tenure on the basis of other research. Few tenure-track possibilities exist. A leading academic in the area of social marketing once told us that he felt obligated to advise doctoral students and junior professors not to pursue research in this area until they were established as it could be 'career suicide'.

Potential Methods for Overcoming the Obstacles

These obstacles are not surprising in a new field that is still perceived as marginal in many universities. Fortunately, they are not totally insurmountable, and addressing them is critical to building a solid foundation of social entrepreneurship research. Success will require the concerted effort of many individuals and initiatives at multiple schools. The following methods should help.

Build Interest and Understanding

The first step in attracting new faculty to this field is to build their interest in, and understanding of, the field in order to help them see specifically how and where their existing knowledge and expertise might apply. We have found a combination of the following three tactics to be effective.

FIND NATURAL LINKS TO INDIVIDUAL INTELLECTUAL INTERESTS

It is critical to understand the motivations of each individual faculty member. What type of research questions intrigues them? What work have they already done that might have interesting implications for social entrepreneurs? Are there social sector contexts that might offer attractive opportunities for them to test or refine their theories? For example, we are currently in discussions with a faculty member interested in online communities, distributed teams, and organization design. We have connected her and one of her Ph.D. students with a social entrepreneur seeking to enhance her organization's efforts to transfer knowledge and facilitate learning across its diverse network of members. We are hopeful that a research project will emerge that will have significant impact on the organization, inform the general field of practice, serve as an example to other faculty members, and perhaps lead to additional social entrepreneurship research by this one.

ENGAGE THEM IN GET-ACQUAINTED ACTIVITIES

We have found it useful to engage faculty in other activities that will help them learn more about the field and get them thinking about ways that their research might apply. While it can be difficult to attract faculty to events, having them hear a speech by, or have dinner with, distinguished leaders in the field can provide them with greater insight into the nature of social entrepreneurship and inspire them to get more involved. Another low-cost way to involve tenured faculty is to ask them to serve as advisors, to your overall initiative, to a student team working on a problem in their area of expertise, or to other social entrepreneurship faculty on a paper or research project related to their area of expertise. Finally, you may be able to stimulate their interest by asking them to teach a session in their area of expertise to an executive programme for social sector leaders.

ENCOURAGE INTERDISCIPLINARY RESEARCH

Promoting collaboration between business faculty and researchers with expertise in a field more clearly related to the social sector can help extend management research into new arenas. For example, one of our leading marketing professors teamed up with a faculty member from the Department of Theatre Studies to explore the relationships between entrepreneurial orientation and stakeholder support in not-for-profit theatres. In instances such as these, the non-business researcher can provide the contextual understanding while the business researcher has the opportunity to test her theories and hypotheses in a different environment without having to invest significant time in learning a whole new field. If an appropriate academic colleague is not available, working with a thoughtful practitioner might be an option. At the very least, we should be prepared to connect interested faculty with leaders and experts in the field for interviews, recommended resources, and general information that will help inform the research and increase the faculty member's understanding of the particular context and issues in an efficient manner.

CAST A BROAD NET

It can be helpful to be flexible about the kind of research you will encourage or support. We embrace a definition of social entrepreneurship that does not encompass CSR or not-for-profit management, but we are open to supporting research in these areas. We will consider working with any faculty member whose research in some way incorporates themes related to social impact and addresses a managerial question. We do negotiate with the faculty member to bring the topic as close to our core interests of social entrepreneurship as possible, without being rigid. This approach allows us to build our base of institutional support, while involving faculty members who might later do work more directly related to social entrepreneurship.

Address Resource Constraints

As one of our faculty members once pointed out to us, there are four key resources that if too scarce or of poor quality will undermine any faculty research project: money, data, time, and research questions.

PROVIDE SOME FUNDING

Though money may be the least important issue, we do recognize that it is critical and thus recommend that new initiatives establish a pool of funds to support social sector research.[15] The funding provides clear advantages, and the process of announcing and awarding funding also offers the chance to promote social entrepreneurship research amongst a wide range of faculty members.

ASSIST IN DATA ACQUISITION

Funding can ease the data burdens by paying for the development or acquisition of data. It is also helpful to point faculty in the direction of good primary and secondary data sources. While we do not limit social entrepreneurship to the not-for-profit sectors, many social entrepreneurs choose this form of organization. Thus, high quality not-for-profit sector data can be a starting point for interested faculty. Through organizations such as the National Center for Charitable Statistics, initiatives such as Guidestar,[16] and groundbreaking research such as Lester Salamon's global Comparative Nonprofit Sector Project,[17] the quantity, quality, and availability of not-for-profit data is undoubtedly increasing (see ABS 2002a, 2002b).

HELP FREE UP FACULTY TIME

As previously mentioned, time is possibly the scarcest faculty resource. Money can help, but money alone is not enough. A supporting Dean's Office can be crucial. One approach is to get approval from the administration to lighten or shift interested faculty members' responsibilities, such as 'buying out' their time from teaching an existing course, to do research related to social entrepreneurship. Another strategy is to provide funds to support research done in conjunction with a doctoral student. It is cheaper to pay for doctoral students' time, and they are often looking for interesting projects and sources of funding. Ph.D. candidates can make significant progress on research under the supervision of a strong faculty member. Moreover, if the initial research is promising, the doctoral student may adopt the theme, or something related, as a dissertation topic, advancing the social entrepreneurship research base and cultivating future faculty leaders. The faculty supervisor may also get more interested.

HELPING FACULTY DEVELOP RESEARCH QUESTIONS

To some extent, cultivating researchers has to be done on an individual faculty member basis. However, it is possible to develop a research agenda using ideas from this book, conversations with social entrepreneurs, and a review of relevant articles, reports, and case studies. A broad research agenda will help identify faculty with applicable expertise and provide a starting point for conversations with appropriate faculty members (see Dees and Battle Anderson 2006).

163

Be Sensitive to Demand Issues

The lack of demand is perhaps the most challenging obstacle to overcome. There are no simple solutions for making social entrepreneurship research a viable path to academic recognition and success. In the short term, it probably makes sense to focus attention on tenured faculty members who do not face the same publishing pressures as those early in their careers. Some tenured faculty will welcome the challenge of bringing their expertise to a new area. When involving junior faculty, our advice is to attempt to reduce the risks while realistically managing expectations. We recommend seeking the advice of the department head before recruiting junior faculty to work in this area. We also recommend thinking through the publication strategy in advance to increase the chances of a strong journal placement. There are at least two strategies for addressing the need for faculty members to publish in mainstream journals.

FRAME THE RESEARCH IN A CONTEXT-NEUTRAL WAY

A 'context-neutral' approach involves designing the research to explore questions whose answers are not dependent on a particular organizational context. For example, a topic high on our research agenda is related to scaling social innovations—the mechanisms and conditions that facilitate the effective and efficient spread of promising social innovations. Though a number of issues related to scale are specific to the social sector, social entrepreneurs could improve their scaling strategies simply with a better understanding of the general factors that enhance the effective transfer and adoption of innovations. Thus, we are supporting a couple of experimental research projects related to the role of learning and adapting to changing information and understanding during the scaling process. These experiments will be conducted in a neutral context, thus maintaining relevance to mainstream audiences and publications. Depending on the results, we may also work closely with the researchers to develop a paper that attempts to place some of the findings in the context of social entrepreneurship.

MAXIMIZE THE BENEFITS OF A CONTEXT-SPECIFIC APPROACH

The social sector can be a rich context for generating new knowledge. This strategy borrows from the approach to entrepreneurship adopted by HBS in the early 1980s. According to Howard Stevenson, HBS faculty members decided that 'entrepreneurship should *not* be what scholars study but rather the entrepreneurial firm should be *where* people study.' This approach 'emphasize[s] the 'how' of entrepreneurship rather than the 'who' or 'what''' (Stevenson 2000). Similarly, a better understanding of how things happen in social purpose organizations could surface intriguing research questions that are relevant to existing domains of business research. This context might make a good laboratory for questions that emerge in slightly different ways in business. For example, lessons about measuring social impact may yield insights for measuring intangibles in a business setting.

We recognize that promoting both 'context-neutral' and 'context-specific' research will not solve the demand problem or eliminate the risks of engaging in social entrepreneurship research, particularly for junior business school faculty. However, we have some reason for optimism. We have heard at least one well-respected faculty member, who has also been an associate editor or editorial board member of several leading academic journals, claim that research papers that have both social and managerial implications actually stand out during the review process. Perhaps we will soon see an increase in articles related to social entrepreneurship appearing in journals that are attractive outlets for business school faculty.

Conclusion

The time is ripe for making significant progress in social entrepreneurship research that will build a solid foundation for practice, education, policy, and further research. Attention to the field is increasing. Business schools are responding. Social entrepreneurs are seeking knowledge, and some public officials are even looking for guidance on shaping policy that will promote social entrepreneurship. We must seize this opportunity to begin establishing a community of researchers that includes business school faculty and can build on the experience, knowledge, and efforts of leading social entrepreneurs, social sector observers, and not-for-profit researchers to help us sort the rhetoric from the reality and establish a vibrant field of social entrepreneurship within our universities.

Notes

1. This definition is a simplified one. Technically, passive income from investments or real estate is classified as earned income, but the proponents of earned income strategies for social entrepreneurs are advocating the more active forms of earned income. Earned income promoters also use a variety of phrases to describe their various earned income activities, including nonprofit or social purpose ventures, social enterprises, community wealth generation, or simply earned income strategies.
2. For example, the Yale School of Management-Goldman Sachs Foundation Partnership on Nonprofit Business Ventures and the Global Social Venture Competition run by London Business School, Columbia Business School, and the Haas School of Business at Berkeley.

3. For example, Community Wealth Ventures, Institute for Social Entrepreneurs, National Center for Social Entrepreneurs, National Center on Nonprofit Enterprise, Nonprofit Enterprise and Self-sustainability Team, Roberts Enterprise Development Fund, Social Enterprise Alliance, and Virtue Ventures.

4. For an alternative description of the continuum of financial strategies, see Dees (1998).

5. One major stream in organizational theory is the 'resource dependence' perspective. For a description see, Pfeffer and Salanick (1978).

6. Interestingly, they also seem to shrink more quickly as markets decline.

7. The organizations we examined also included Conservation International, America's Second Harvest, Mercy Corps International, the Local Initiatives Support Corporation, and Focus on the Family.

8. In 1998, USA reporting public charities, excluding hospitals and higher education, received 50 per cent of their revenues from fees for goods and services while 36.3 per cent came from public support (private contributions and government grants). See Weitzman (2002).

9. Some dispute the inclination to call this a sector because of the enormous diversity within it. See Warren (2003).

10. See http://www.dti.gov.uk/cics/

11. Weisbrod generally rejects the idea that nonprofits he has studied behave like 'for-profits in disguise'.

12. Note that 'Increased openness to using standard business tools' was the number two response behind strategic planning even if we only look at the top category 'Great deal'. No other reforms drew more than 40 per cent in the 'Great deal' category or over 80 per cent in the combined response.

13. For example, in addition to Columbia Business School, sponsors of the project included mutual fund management firm Calvert Group, Ltd.; venture capital funds Commons Capital, LP, Expansion Capital Partners, LLC, SJF Ventures, and Underdog Ventures, LLC; and The Rockefeller and Surdna Foundations. Of the fifty-nine funds included in the survey, ten were philanthropic funds or charitable organizations and forty-nine were structured as limited liability corporations (LLCs), limited partnerships (LPs) or C-Corporations. Notably, several of the 'for-profit' funds combined the LCC and nonprofit structures.

14. The authors would like to thank and acknowledge Fuqua School of Business Professors Will Mitchell, Christine Moorman, and Manju Puri whose comments on a faculty panel on this topic in October 2003 were invaluable in informing our practice and this section of the chapter.

15. See Center for Advancement of Social Entrepreneurship website, http://www.fuqua.duke.edu/centers/case/faculty/research.html

16. Guidestar is focused on facilitating access to information about the operations and finances of US-based nonprofit organizations. www.Guidestar.org

17. See http://www.jhu.edu/~cnp/

References

ABS (American Behavioral Scientist) (June, 2002*a*). 'Resources for Scholarship in the Nonprofit Sector: Studies in the Political Economy of Information, Part 1: Data on Nonprofit Industries', *The American Behavioral Scientist*, 45(10).

——(June, 2002*b*). 'Resources for Scholarship in the Nonprofit Sector: Studies in the Political Economy of Information, Part 2: Resources for Comparative Institutional Research', *The American Behavioral Scientist*, 45(11).

Battle Anderson, B., Dees, J. G., and Emerson, J. (2001). 'Developing Viable Earned Income Strategies', in J. G. Dees, J. Emerson, and P. Economy (eds.), *Strategic Tools for Social Entrepreneurs*. New York: John Wiley & Sons, pp. 191–234.

Backman, E. and Smith, S. (2000). 'Healthy Organizations, Unhealthy Communities', *Nonprofit Management & Leadership*, 10(4): 355–73.

Boschee, J. (1998). *Merging Mission and Money: A Board Member's Guide to Social Entrepreneurship*. Washington, DC: The National Center for Nonprofit Boards.

——and McClurg, J. (2003). *Toward a Better Understanding of Social Entrepreneurship: Some Important Distinctions*. Minnesota, MN: Institute for Social Entrepreneurs.

Clark, C. and Gaillard, J. (2003). *RISE Capital Market Report: The Double Bottom Line Private Equity Landscape in 2002/2003*. Columbia Business School: Rise Capital Market Report.

Community Wealth Ventures (2003). *Powering Social Change, Lessons on Community Wealth Generation for Nonprofit Sustainability*. Washington, DC: Community Wealth Ventures.

Dabson, B., Plastrik, P., and Turner, R. (2001). *Lessons from the Life and Death of the Virginia Eastern Shore Corporation*. Washington, DC: Corporation for Enterprise Development.

Dees, J. G. (January–February, 1998). 'Enterprising Nonprofits', *Harvard Business Review*, 76(1): 54–67.

——(2004), 'Putting Nonprofit Business Ventures in Perspective', in S. Oster, C. Massarsky, and S. Beinhacker (eds.), *Generating and Sustaining Nonprofit Earned Income: A Guide to Successful Enterprise Strategies*. San Francisco, CA: Jossey-Bass, pp. 3–18.

——and Battle Anderson, B. (2003). 'For-Profit Social Ventures', in M. Kourilsky and W. Walstad (eds.), *Social Entrepreneurship, special issue, International Journal of Entrepreneurship Education*, Vol. 2. Senate Hall Academic Publishing, pp. 1–26.

—— —— (2006). 'Framing a Theory of Social Entrepreneurship: Building on Two Schools of Practice and Thought', in R. Mosher-Williams (ed.), *Research on Social Entrepreneurship: Understanding and Contributing to an Emerging Field*. Association for Research on Nonprofit Organizations and Voluntary Action (ARNOVA).

de Geus, A. (1997). *The Living Company*. Boston, MA: Harvard Business School Press.

Foster, W. and Bradach, J. (February, 2005). 'Should Nonprofits Seek Profits?', *Harvard Business Review*, 92–100.

Hansmann, H. (1996*a*). 'The Changing Roles of Public, Private, and Nonprofit Enterprise in Education, Health Care, and Other Human Services', in V. Fuchs (ed.), *Individual and Social Responsibility: Child Care, Education, Medical Care, and Long-Term Care in America*. Chicago, IL: University of Chicago Press, pp. 245–71.

——(1996*b*). *The Ownership of Enterprise*. Boston, MA: Harvard University Press.

Herbst, K. (2004). 'Business-Social Ventures: Reaching for Major Impact', *Ashoka Changemakers.net*

James, E. (2003). 'Commercialism and the Mission of Nonprofits', *Social Science and Modern Society*, 40(4): 29–35.

Jones, T. (May, 1994). 'A Customer by Any Other Name: Rethinking the Donor Relationship', *Advancing Philanthropy*: 12–8.

Light, P. (2002). *Pathways to Nonprofit Excellence*. Brookings Institute.

Massarsky, C. and Beinhacker, S. (May 2002). *Enterprising Nonprofits: Revenue Generation in the Nonprofit Sector*. Yale School of Management – The Goldman Sachs Foundation Partnership on Nonprofit Ventures.

Meyer, M. and Zucker, L. (1989). *Permanently Failing Organizations*. Newbury Park, UK: Sage.

Nanda, A. and Haddad, K. (2001). *The American Medical Association—Sunbeam Deal (A): Serpent on the Staff Meets Chainsaw Al*. Harvard Business School Case N1-801-326.

Pfeffer, J. and Salanick, G. (1978). *The External Control of Organizations: A Resource Dependence Perspective*. New York: Harper & Row.

Salamon, L. (1997). *Holding the Center: America's Nonprofit Sector at the Crossroads*. Cummings Foundation.

—— (2003). *The Resilient Sector: The State of Nonprofit America*. Brookings Institution Press.

Schumpeter, J. (1950). *Capitalism, Socialism, and Democracy*, 3rd edn. New York: Harper & Row.

Sprinkel, G. (1997). *Beyond Fund Raising: New Strategies for Nonprofit Innovation and Investment*. New York: John Wiley & Sons.

Stevenson, H. (2000). 'Why Entrepreneurship Has Won!', *Coleman Foundation White Paper*.

Warren, M. (2003). 'The Political Role of Nonprofits in a Democracy', *Social Science and Modern Society*, 40(4): 46–51.

Weisbrod, B. (1998). *To Profit or Not To Profit: The Commercial Transformation of the Nonprofit Sector*. Cambridge: Cambridge University Press.

Weitzman, M. (2002). *The New Nonprofit Almanac & Desk Reference: The Essential Facts and Figures for Managers, Researchers, and Volunteers*. San Francisco, CA: Jossey-Bass.

Wolinsky, H. (1999). 'AMA Board Under Fire; Resolution Would Hold It Liable for Sunbeam Deal', *Chicago Sun-Times*, 9 April, p. 52.

Young, D. (ed.) (2004). *Effective Economic Decision-Making by Nonprofit Organizations*. The Foundation Center.

8

Social Entrepreneurship: It Is for Corporations, Too

James E. Austin, Herman B. Leonard, Ezequiel Reficco,
and Jane Wei-Skillern

Corporations and Social Entrepreneurship

Social entrepreneurship is not just for the social sector. Corporations can also be social entrepreneurs. In fact, leading companies seeking to create more robust forms of strategic corporate citizenship are engaging in what we refer to as 'Corporate Social Entrepreneurship' (Austin et al. 2005). This chapter addresses four questions:

1. What is corporate social entrepreneurship?
2. Why invest in it?
3. How is it done?
4. Who are corporate social entrepreneurs?

What Is Corporate Social Entrepreneurship?

Historically, entrepreneurship has been the basic engine that gives rise to new ventures—the driving force behind the dramatic growth and development of the business sector. Entrepreneurs identify business opportunities and mobilize resources to create new enterprises. Recognizing that traditional management approaches did not often produce the dynamic innovation that characterized new venture entrepreneurship, corporate leaders have in recent decades attempted to bring entrepreneurial processes into their organizations. This 'corporate entrepreneurship' is aimed at spotting and redefining market opportunities through innovative strategies, processes, and organizations that would generate new competitive advantage. Parallel to this trend, the social sector saw the emergence of the practice of 'social entrepreneurship', which aimed at achieving greater social impact through innovation and adaptation of the discipline and tools from the business world in support of a social mission.

The concept of corporate social entrepreneurship (CSE) draws on these other three conceptions of entrepreneurship, and is defined here as 'the process of extending the firm's domain of competence and corresponding opportunity set through innovative leveraging of resources, both within and outside its direct control, aimed at the simultaneous creation of economic and social value.' Like all entrepreneurship, CSE involves opportunity and innovation. However, unlike either corporate or social entrepreneurship, it is as much about mobilizing internal as external resources in order to generate both economic and social value.

The CSE process takes companies beyond traditional patterns of charitable giving to more robust forms of corporate citizenship. Businesses have historically been significant sources of philanthropic capital for the social sector. In 2003, corporate giving in the USA amounted to $13.46 billion (£7.81 billion), an increase of 4.6 per cent over the previous year (AAFRC 2003). Virtually all major corporations are engaged in various forms of charitable work that benefit the larger community. Many have set up foundations to handle these activities. So CSE is not about convincing companies to be socially responsible, but rather explores the question of why companies would be willing to make larger and deeper engagements in the social enterprise sphere.

Why Invest in CSE?

Companies worldwide are facing a combination of push and pull factors that propel them towards more robust forms of CSR. While the social dimension has been present in the world of private business, these tectonic movements are reshaping the landscape and raising the bar of what is expected of businesses in the social realm. Companies need to find a process to respond to this challenge, and move their social initiatives to a higher level; CSE is that process.

Push Factors

These factors have a forcing effect on corporate behaviour even in the face of reticence to move in this direction of their own volition. Responses to these factors tend to be reactive, aimed at avoiding adverse consequences; they are often just a form of risk mitigation. Even so, they can represent powerful impulses. A major force in this regard is changing expectations by the public at large and key stakeholder groups such as consumers, employees, and communities. These groups express sentiments that point towards a much more active role for companies in resolving social problems beyond their traditional role of producing goods and services.

The global survey data shown in Figure 8.1 reveal how sampled members of the public feel about the extent of companies' responsibility for helping solve major social problems like crime, poverty, and lack of education. About 40 per cent of the respondents in North America and Western Europe deemed the companies to be very or completely responsible, and in emerging markets it was even higher, at about 45 per cent.

When the responsibility is more sharply focused on improving education and skills in the communities where the companies operate, the expectations of those considering private business very or completely responsible rise to well over 50 per cent in all regions, as indicated in Figure 8.2.

The public's expectations about corporate responsibility extend to companies' value chains. There is an overwhelming expectation that companies are responsible for whether the inputs along their supply chains have been produced in a socially and environmentally responsible manner, as revealed in Figure 8.3.

Unmet expectations can produce adverse consequences. The public is neither passive nor without power to affect corporate results—and, therefore, corporate behaviour. Figure 8.4 reveals that around half of the respondents have considered punishing companies they considered as socially irresponsible.

The forms of punishment are multiple and serious, as revealed in Figure 8.5. As consumers they can boycott companies and urge others to do the same. As investors they can withhold their capital. As workers they can choose other employers or be less loyal. Irresponsible firms run the risk of losing markets, capital, and talent. Bad business can be bad for business.

The push factors tend to generate largely defensive reactions—responses that are focused on protecting rather than creating economic value. The aspirations of CSE are to go beyond reactive, protective response—to entrepreneurial, value-creating action. It is to this—the pull factors—that we now turn.

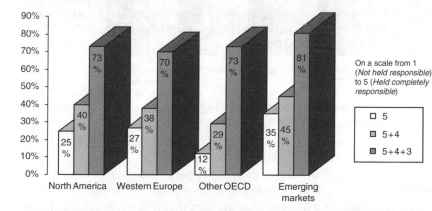

Figure 8.1 Changing expectations: Should large companies be held responsible for helping solve social problems like crime, poverty, and lack of education?

Source: Derived from 2003 Corporate Social Responsibility Monitor, GlobeScan.

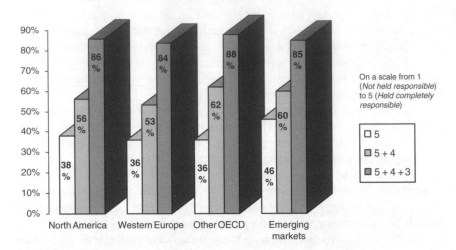

Figure 8.2 Changing expectations: Should large companies be held responsible for improving education and skills in communities where they operate?

Source: Derived from 2003 Corporate Social Responsibility Monitor, GlobeScan.

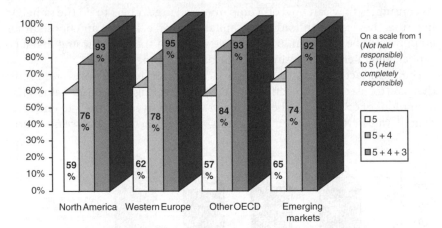

Figure 8.3 Changing expectations: Should large companies be held responsible for ensuring that its supplies have been produced in a socially and environmentally responsible manner?

Source: Derived from 2003 Corporate Social Responsibility Monitor, GlobeScan.

Pull Factors

These factors comprise positive incentives in that they present opportunities for greater value creation. The CSE is rooted in the pursuit of social and economic value-generating opportunities, so these pull factors are particularly

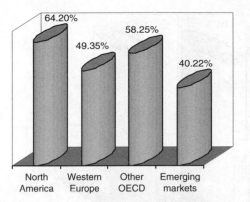

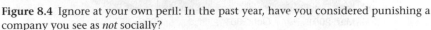

Figure 8.4 Ignore at your own peril: In the past year, have you considered punishing a company you see as *not* socially?

Source: Derived from 2003 Corporate Social Responsibility Monitor, GlobeScan.

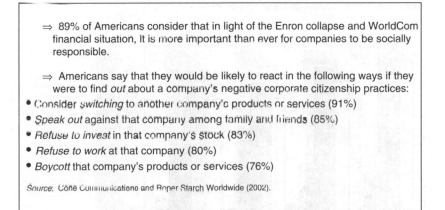

Figure 8.5 Ignore at your own peril

relevant forces. Just as consumers can punish, so, too, can they reward. As Figure 8.6 shows, faced with products equal in price and quality, most consumers in the USA will give preference to the company they deem to be more socially responsible.

Being able to differentiate on this basis can be a powerful advantage in the marketplace. A basic CSE proposition is that creating social value creates business value. There are even indications that consumers might pay a premium for products produced in environmentally and socially responsible ways, as suggested in Figure 8.7.

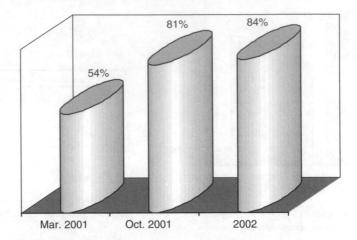

Figure 8.6 Buying preferences: I would be likely to switch brands to one associated with a good cause, if price and quality are similar

Source: Cone Communications and Roper Starch Worldwide (2002).

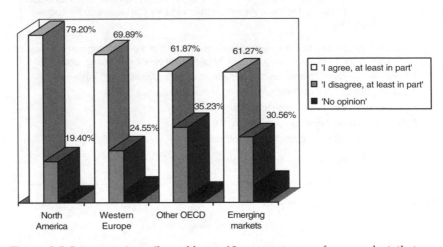

Figure 8.7 Price premium: 'I would pay 10 per cent more for a product that was produced in a socially and environmentally responsible way...'

Source: Derived from 2003 Corporate Social Responsibility Monitor, GlobeScan.

A company's social commitment is also important in the decision-making of communities, prospective employees, and potential investors. Just as these stakeholders can withhold their support from social laggards, they are motivated to provide their resources to companies that have generated a positive social track record. As Figure 8.8 illustrates, a company's social performance

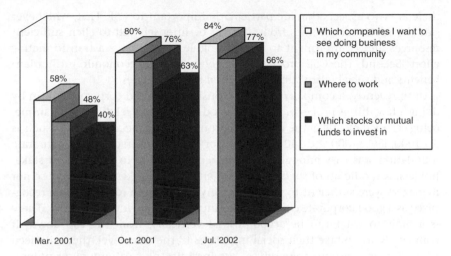

Figure 8.8 Competitive advantage: 'A company's commitment to social issues is important when I decide . . . '

Source: Cone Communications and Roper Starch Worldwide (2002).

has become an increasingly salient factor, over time, among stakeholders when deciding whether to support a company.

From the foregoing, it is evident that there are multiple sets of forces that motivate companies to invest in social actions. Research indicates that the motivations are varied in practice with some being more altruistic in nature and others being more utilitarian (Austin et al. 2004). As Figure 8.9 depicts,

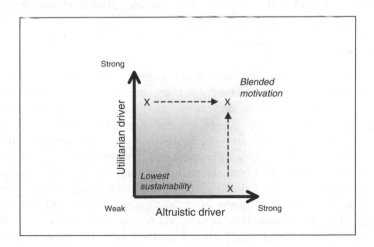

Figure 8.9 Motivational spectrum

there are two aspects that are particularly important to CSE. First, whichever side the motivation comes from, it must be intensely felt to elicit sufficient resources and commitment to be sustainable and to have a transformative effect. Second, the CSE process must generate both economic (utilitarian) benefits and social (altruistic) benefits and their synergies.

Until recently, a company could be considered a good corporate citizen by doing a few things properly. Having a good community relations programme, being certified by one of the various environmental or social standards (such as AA 1000, ISO 14000 and 14001, SA8000, or TBL),[1] or even creating a corporate foundation was easy enough to do and good enough to satisfy most stakeholders. A modicum of social awareness and a few strokes of a pen by senior managers were sufficient to put a company on the path towards being recognized as a good corporate citizen. This is increasingly no longer the case. There is a limit to what can be accomplished vertically, from the top down. If companies are to take their social initiatives to the next level, they will need to rethink and reshape themselves, tapping into the creativity of every individual. Taking on this challenge will require bolder and more creative steps. CSE combines the willingness and desire to create joint economic and social value with the entrepreneurial redesign, systems development, and action necessary to carry it out.

How to Do It

Assuming that the motivations of the company are sufficiently strong to engage in the CSE process, the challenge then is carrying out the task. We offer suggestions in four areas: leadership, strategy, structures, and systems.

Leadership

Major entrepreneurial transformations within companies do not occur without strong leadership. There are three important dimensions. First is vision. The leader needs to be able to envision a company in which the social dimension is a central and integral part of the corporation's very being. Second is legitimization. The leader needs to create an internal environment that signals the appropriateness and desirability of the CSE process. One needs to stimulate organizational receptivity to the transformational change intrinsic to CSE. Third is empowerment. The leader needs to enable other leaders and change agents in the company to build and execute that process. This entails allocating human and financial resources to establish a cadre of corporate social entrepreneurs who will have the capacity to realize important change.

Strategy

There are three key strategy elements for CSE. The first is alignment. The social dimensions and the business dimensions of the company's strategy must be aligned with each other. The closer the alignment, the greater the potential for joint value creation. While one alignment will rarely be complete, the more connections there are, the greater the opportunity to undertake innovative actions that generate social value and business benefit.

A second strategy element is leveraging core competencies. CSE is about going beyond the traditional strategy of charitable giving. Its focus is on discovering creative ways to mobilize and deploy the company's key assets, those components of the business that are key to its business success, such as technology, talent, image, infrastructure, procurement and distribution systems, and communications. Writing cheques for socially oriented activities can also be helpful, but it often leaves a great deal of potential value untapped. The CSE is the process for unlocking that value. When the resources mobilized are the key business assets, then the connections between social and business value multiply to create far greater economic and social value.

The third strategy element is partnering. While there are many CSE actions that are unilateral and internal, creating alliances with other entities is a particularly powerful form of entrepreneurship. Such collaborations enable the company to gain access to new and different resources and competencies beyond its own. Creating an alliance is very much an entrepreneurial undertaking, akin to, but different from, creating a new enterprise. The opportunity set for value generation is richer because of the possibility of creating new resource configurations that can produce innovative approaches to old problems. These collaborations can be transactional in nature: sharply targeted around specific activities or projects such as cause-related marketing, event sponsorships, or employee volunteer service programmes. Others have moved further along the 'collaboration continuum' to discover opportunities for integration that mesh their strategies, mission, values, activities, and organizations (Austin 2000).

Structures

Structure needs to follow strategy, so the corporate social entrepreneur needs to create innovative organizational forms within the corporation to advance the new social dimensions. A dual organizational approach seems advisable, 'T-shaped', with a 'vertical' component that deepens the company's social commitment, and a 'horizontal' one, entrusted with the mission of spreading it across silos. On the one hand, there needs to be an entity with the primary responsibility to deepen the company's engagement in social entrepreneurship. This should not, however, be mistaken for the traditional approach of creating a separate entity to which one can relegate the social activities such as a foundation. Too often such departments or offices were kept quite separate from company operations, with two adverse effects. First, they were marginalized from the central power structures of the company. Second, they robbed the rest of the organization of the opportunity to deploy their key resources to the social agenda and, thereby, also inhibited the reciprocal generation of business benefits. The function of the CSE entity is to promote the integration of social action with the rest of the business. Because CSE seeks to initiate a significant organizational transformation, a well-staffed organizational focal point to foster the change process is essential. At the same time, cross-functional engagement is critical because social value generation transcends functional business boundaries. Finding new forms of interdepartmental collaboration is part of the CSE process. The CSE goal of integration also implies inserting the social entrepreneurship dimension into the daily operations of the operating units as part of their ongoing responsibilities.

Systems

Systems need to follow structures, so CSE also calls for a set of systems that, first, enhance learning about the process and, second, enable the effective execution of it. Three seem particularly relevant. The first requisite is a decision-making process that integrates the consideration of economic and social value creation. The social dimension needs to be woven into the company's regular business decisions so that one is routinely asking about the social effects and social value opportunities, just as one would be asking about other dimensions such as financial or market position. The second requisite process is a combined learning- and performance-oriented measurement and management system. CSE needs to have goals and managers need to be held accountable and rewarded for achieving them—but they also need learning-oriented tools to help them work out how to produce better performances those goals demand. Businesses know how to do this very well with economic goals. Measuring social value and return, however, is more complicated. This is perhaps the least developed area of CSE, yet its pursuit is essential. We are deploying resources and should assess our return—economic and social—on those investments. Our goal is to attain higher returns. The third crucial system is an effective economic and social value communications process. CSE needs to ensure that the company's social actions and impact are adequately reported to internal and external stakeholders. While some companies are hesitant to seek publicity for their good works, thinking that such an approach might cast their altruistic motivations in a negative light, it is important to let others know of significant CSE. Internal communications help make employees proud of their company and fuels deeper involvement.

External communications encourage similar engagement by other companies as well as enhancing the company's image with external stakeholders. Many companies have found that undercommunicating their actions has inhibited them from harvesting more fully many of the benefits from their actions, thus undercutting or failing to mobilize internal support for continuing or enhancing the programmes. While social performance should be integrated into regular corporate reports (annual, etc.), there is also merit in having separate social reports to spotlight this dimension and to set forth goals for which the corporation will be accountable.

Who Are the Corporate Social Entrepreneurs?

Corporate social entrepreneurship is not the product of a single leader but rather a cadre of entrepreneurs. They are all change agents that play a multitude of roles critical to the transformation process. Seven such roles stand out.

- *Champions* are the advocates for the cause. They continually stand up and push for the generation and integration of social and business value as a central tenet for the company.

- *Communicators* are particularly articulate about the rationale and importance of the transformation. They are skilled and active listeners to various stakeholders and are able to speak to these groups in ways that reveal how the social action is relevant to their needs and interests.

- *Creators* are the inventors of new possibilities. Entrepreneurship is all about innovation. Corporate social entrepreneurs invent new resource configurations, actions, and relationships. They are not managers of the status quo but creators of the new.

- *Catalysts* inspire and create synergies in the work of others. Being an innovator does not mean doing it all yourself. Rather these entrepreneurs catalyze a process that unleashes the transformative process and energy of people across the corporation.

- *Coordinators* reach across internal and external boundaries, inspiring, mobilizing, and harmonizing action. Social entrepreneurship often involves mobilizing and configuring resources and actions in new ways that transcend traditional boundaries. This requires a coordinating function to ensure strategic coherence across the organization.

- *Contributors* support the work and success of others. Rather than being perceived as building a new power centre, corporate social entrepreneurs need to enable and enhance the success of other groups.

- *Calculators* project and monitor results. They need to be skilled calculators in two senses. First, as organizational change engineers, they need to be able to assess how fast and far they can move the transformational process within the realities of the organization. Second, they need to be able to calculate carefully and creatively the costs and benefits of the social entrepreneurship process.

Looking Ahead

Social entrepreneurship will be a growing force in this century. Harnessing its energy and potential will be increasingly central to enabling corporations to move to higher levels for generating economic and social value. The push and pull forces noted above create the incentives for such engagement and CSE provides the process through which corporations can become even more powerful economic and social value-generating engines in society.

Note

1. For a comprehensive list, see Emerson and Bonini (2004: 89–90).

References

AAFRC (2003). *Giving USA 2003*. Bloomington, IN: AAFRC Trust for Philanthropy.

Austin, J. (2000). *The Collaboration Challenge: How Nonprofits and Businesses Succeed Through Strategic Alliances*. San Francisco, CA: Jossey-Bass.

Austin, J., Leonard, H., Reficco, E., and Wei-Skillern, J. (2005). 'Corporate Social Entrepreneurship: The New Frontier', in M. Epstein and K. Hanson (eds.), *The Accountable Corporation*. Westport, CT: Praeger.

Austin, J., Reficco, E., Berger, G., Fischer, R., Gutierrez, R., Koljatic, M., Lozano, G., and Ogliastri, E. (2004). *Social Partnering in Latin America: Lessons Drawn from Collaborations of Businesses and Civil Society Organizations*. Cambridge, MA: Harvard University Press.

Cone Communications and Roper Starch Worldwide (2002). *The 2002 Cone Corporate Citizenship Study: The Role of Cause Branding*. Boston, MA: Cone Communications and Roper Starch Worldwide.

Emerson, J. and Bonini, S. (2004). *The Blended Value Map: Tracking the Intersects and Opportunities of Economic, Social and Environmental Value Creation*, Available at: http://www.blendedvalue.org/Papers/97.aspx [cited 15 October 2004].

GlobeScan (2002). *The 2003 Corporate Social Responsibility Monitor*. Toronto: GlobeScan.

9

Social Entrepreneurship: Exploring a Cultural Mode Amidst Others in the Church of England

Doug Foster

Introduction

This chapter explores social entrepreneurship via a particular conceptualization of cultural modes, through competition and/or conflict with alternatives so configured (MacIntyre 1985: 163), and in the context of a particular shared socio-economic space. The approach here is to suggest social entrepreneurship is distinctly 'social' and 'entrepreneurial', and *not* 'profit' or 'professionalism' orientated. This might otherwise seem unremarkable if it were not for the contrast with those that suggest, a potential profession of social entrepreneurship (e.g. Drayton 2002). The discussion begins, therefore, with the rationale for, and subsequent theorization of, four different cultural modes, and then selects a socio-economic space where understandings of cultural modes can be explored; that socio-economic space is a sampled element of a particular diocese of the Church of England which is charged, according to one account (Ecclestone 1988), with the 'cure or care of souls' of all within its community. The chapter concludes with an overview of how convincing this conceptual differentiation is and a view on the potential of the Church of England in the socially entrepreneurial arena.

A Theorization: Towards Four Cultural Modes or Characters

This theorization begins with the idea, not just that 'the professional' is challenged by 'the entrepreneurial', but that this claim can be further segmented. Let us also start with the period claimed as initiating the 'entrepreneurial revival' because it is a key point where debate can be historically drawn back or pulled forward in order to substantiate analytical argument. In the pre-Thatcherite UK of the 1970s the label entrepreneur was used as a form of mild abuse (Hobbs 1988, 1991; Burrows 1991). The underlying belief system related to this view does not seem to have been in any way confined to a particular political grouping such as the Left. Indeed, as the Thatcher era began, the label seemed to be retaining its association with the unsavoury with at least part of that unsavouriness being related to its seeming focus on financial gain—and this by the very people who might be thought most in favour of it. For example, within six months of the first Thatcher government coming to power in 1979, the Institute for Economic Affairs (IEA), an essentially right-wing, 'free market', think tank, hosted a colloquium where there was a discussion centred on a paper by MacRae (1980) asking if the entrepreneur had shifted 'From Villain to Hero?'. During this debate, Hannah (1980: 128) stated that, on approaching businessmen for entries in a Dictionary of Business Biography, while they happily stated that they were on hospital management committees, but when they were prompted by the interviewers to say that they made money, became very upset.

All this seems a world away from the contemporary English mainstream cross-party enthusiasm for all things business and entrepreneurial today, though a greater sophistication and distinctiveness has arguably been brought both between and within these conceptual areas during the interval of time. The so-called Left, social democratic, 'Third Way' claimed enthusiastic endorsement of social entrepreneurship (Giddens 1998), but this in the end is as much part of the post-Thatcher 'market consensus', as the 'Middle Way' (Macmillan 1938) was part of the post-Attlee one on welfare. Further, the Labour party connection with the 'Thatcherite project' can be historically drawn back further; the economic part of our theorization starts with the end of the welfare-state consensus marked by the 'Brighton revolution', when the British prime minister, the late Jim Callaghan, addressed the governing Labour party conference of 1976 (Grant and Nath 1984; Grant 1993). Of relevance here too are important related responses to the long-term decline of the British economy (Elbaum and Lazonik 1986) and a broader critique of modernity that suggests a contemporary inability to resolve moral debate (MacIntyre 1985). Nevertheless, it is within the post-1979 Thatcher era that attempts to dismantle the 'bureaucratic ethos' (Niskanen 1973) really came into their own, as did the project of reviving the entrepreneurial (Sheldon 1980*a*).

Following Perkin (1989, 1992), however, this theorization supports the claim that the 'entrepreneurial revival' is empirically overdrawn, and that a broader, business-focused, private professionalism absorbs this challenge, with a stronger general business and commercial orientation picking up some entrepreneurial qualities on the way. Innovation and entrepreneurship still play a part in the 'revolt against professionalism' (Perkin 1989) from the 1960s through to the 1980s, which in turn can be understood as having resulted in the more specific challenging of 'welfare-state consensus' public professionalism, the pre-1979 dominant mode of the professional. The latter is usurped, first, socially, by political moderates (Titmuss 1960) highlighting a 'self-interest' orientation of public professionals rather than one towards those of their client group, and then radicals follow, advocating and/or undertaking *social innovations* (Laing 1967; Illich 1974). The language of entrepreneurship is absent in these social spaces at this time; however, a point of little surprise given the broad pre-1980's distaste for the entrepreneurial label, yet is there not justification for an analytic using some form of entrepreneurial terms to grasp a better understanding of these radicals? Does Illich identify opportunistic moments in the failures of educational and medical professionalism and Laing the opportunity, within marginality, of change in attitudes towards, and care of, the mentally ill? Second, as we have already noted, public professionalism is economically critiqued by profit/private gain-orientated anti-bureaucratic and pro-entrepreneurship analysis (Niskanen 1973; Kirzner 1980).

Both of these revolts against public professionalism make a common accusation that any claim to professional service is being undermined by self-interest, but they part company on recommended alternatives; the social critique suggests a more genuinely engaged, responsive, and innovative ethic and practice, the economic, that self-interest has to be an accepted part of human nature, and the best way to manage this is through market mechanisms. However, private/for-profit entrepreneurship is not distinguished simply by self-interest, and this may be just one instance of rhetoric covering a broader business perspective. Another example is brought out by Parsons (1988) critique of the Conservatives bringing entrepreneurial culture into the UK public sector. Parsons focuses on the Austrian School of Economics, inclusive of Kirzner, but also others (Hayek 1967, 1986; Shackle 1972, 1979), who, he suggested, have the most coherent approach to entrepreneurship, emphasizing subjectivist and *ex ante* perspectives:

...although individuals may perceive lost opportunities after the event, it is acting according to the anticipated exploitation of profit opportunities which defines entrepreneurial activity. (Parsons 1988: 37)

The demands of the 'new' public sector on the other hand, Parsons claimed, are *ex post* focused, with objective costs and outcomes based on past or current time events, and with individuals allocated to be 'entrepreneurs' (Parsons 1988: 38). The split between *ex ante* and *ex post* here matches closely Shackle's between *enterprise* and *policy*, respectively (Shackle 1979: 140–1). Yet if Parsons is interpreted as offering an argument against the invasion of private sector values into the public sector realm per se, then an obvious retort to this is the prevalence of just such *ex post* focus in private sector organizations as well. Parsons' argument is made with regard to particular ideological challenge, but in any respect, the very claim to a broad, *ex post*, private sector focus highlights

183

the limitations of private entrepreneurship in even the private sector of the economy (Foster 2001: 128).

For Thatcher's claim to enterprise culture to have been as ideologically strong and plausible as it was however, it had to have sufficient enough a base in reality to manufacture such a convincing element of façade. This can be understood by its actual, if sometimes tangential, link to the Austrian School of Economics; a flirtation with Kirzner for sure, but an actual courting of Hayek who, unlike those who became ever closer to subjectivism and epistemological relativism (and with distinctiveness that Parson's analysis overlooks), converted to Popper's realism and 'piecemeal social engineering' (Popper 1962, 1984). Further, not only did the Conservative government have latterly to resort to 'engineering enterprise culture' (Morris 1991), but Margaret Thatcher is known to have read Magee's book (1979) on Popper four times and very much praised it (somewhat to the bemusement of the author). A more limited entrepreneurial development, then, was absorbed into a private professional ethos. However, while the claim has been that the switch to entrepreneurial culture has been more in rhetoric rather than reality, this is far from saying there has been no effect, one of which, in more recent times, has been where, in terms of social orientation, Illich's reference to social innovation has inadvertently been built on, and any ideological concern with reference to 'the entrepreneurial' seemingly overcome. There have subsequently been claims to a more distinct role for, and/or the rise of, the social entrepreneur (Beardshaw and Towell 1990; Atkinson 1994; Handy 1997; Leadbeater 1997; Giddens 1998). Yet can entrepreneurial theory really accommodate 'social objects'? Let us return to some earlier analysts.

Sheldon (1980b: xii) initially imported Kirzner (1980) to suggest interest rather than just self-interest as capturing the potential scope of the entrepreneurial motive, for whilst Kirzner clearly seems to emphasize profit as the primary exemplar of pure gain, he also mentions status, power, and helping others. However, Sheldon's claim towards this is undermined, not merely by him seeming to re-assert self-interest as of particular importance in assessing the genealogy of the entrepreneurial, but by attempting to switch focus away from intent altogether and towards potential good consequences (Sheldon 1980c: 127). Further, Kirzner, while not reverting to a consequentialist approach, cast an overall suspicion on claims to a broader entrepreneurial agenda:

It is doubtful in the extreme if ideals such as benevolence or patriotism can be relied upon in general, to enable a potential discoverer to identify his own personal interest with that of the discovery of an opportunity for a desirable re-allocation of resources for society. (Kirzner 1980: 20–1)

Rather than accepting Kirzner's doubt over other non-self-interest entrepreneurial possibilities, we might alternatively suppose there is all the more justification for distinguishing between the two; for, however much Kirzner may wish to doubt it, there are those whose action seems best understood as *social* entrepreneurship. Thus, while what may differentiate private entrepreneurship from social entrepreneurship may be the former's primary engagement with profitable gain and the latter's with helping others or 'social objects', we should also remind ourselves that, of whatever orientation, entrepreneurship is something rather more distinct than just everyday business, moneymaking, or not-for-profit organizing. It is the seeking, being alert to, and 'discovering' of opportunities (Kirzner 1980; Osbourne and Gaebler 1992; Drucker 1994); intuiting, 'knowing', and/or venturing towards them in a way not reducible to rational calculation (Knight 1921; Graves 1952; Foster 2001); and then innovatively recombining resources to produce new processes, products, or services (Schumpeter 1934).

While an interesting contentiousness exists in respect of a potential private/social entrepreneurial split, Perkins claimed public/private professionalism split has also been contested (Hanlon 1998). All this is suggestive of a contest between cultural modes for socio-economic and moral space, and the need for further conceptual work to develop understanding. One approach is to develop a typology based around MacIntyre's concept of character:

A character is an object of regard by the members of the culture generally or some significant segment of them. He [the character] furnishes them with a cultural and moral ideal. Hence the demand is that, in this kind of case, role and personality are fused. Social type and psychological type are required to coincide. The character morally legitimilses a mode of social existence. (MacIntyre 1985: 29)

Foster (2001) suggested a different set of characters that are less the modernist 'straw-men' MacIntyre offers, them having greater substance in the values they hold and demonstrate as 'objects of regard', and relating to the modes of culture discussed earlier: the public professional (state-based or state-like, service oriented, non-judgemental or with disinterested judgement, public institutionalized, focused on policy and planning), the private professional (corporate-/market-/profit-oriented with an emphasis on accounting and finance, marketing and/or rational managerial frameworks focused around commercial/commercial-like activity), the private entrepreneur (economically spontaneous, alert to opportunity discovery, intuitive, innovative around objects of private interest/profit), the social entrepreneur (socially spontaneous, alert to opportunity discovery; intuitive; innovative around social objects). What fruitful research arena might be appropriate to explore these contesting modes of character?

The Church of England is a particularly pertinent research field to explore potential varieties of character. As a counter-revolt against the 'entrepreneurial revival', clergy who saw the rolling back of the welfare state as wanting to put the Church back in a 'poor relief' role might be expected to be amongst those wishing to retain a more distinctly religious role and support previous public professionalism. Yet Conservative politicians tended to be the ones calling for clergy to stick to their 'religious' roles, for accusations of Marxism became associated with Church proposals for urban, and later rural, regeneration. *Faith in the City* (ACURA 1985) and *Faith in the Countryside* (ACORA 1990) came out as reports to present criticism and to provoke action. Further, combined with the rise of radical interest in the symbolic, identity, and the 'post-material' if largely via new social movements (Beck 1992; Kriesi 1995), a more missionary approach to 'being Church' developed a primary opportunity through a spiritual agenda being added to a more socially orientated and community building change of emphasis (Warren 1995). Yet added to the contrast between a pastoral/public professional mode and a missionary/social entrepreneurial mode is the intrigue of private entrepreneurship and private professionalism, with the Church's financial crisis of the early 1990s presenting a potential acute orientation towards the financial survival of the Church and its own paid members. Foster (2001) undertook research to explore this area, and in particular then, the research focused on the possible struggle of vicars between the private professional and social entrepreneurial—but also more distinctly sacred—modes. Whilst focusing on a single diocese—given the pseudonym *Seagull diocese* here—the research's value orientation towards interest in social entrepreneurship engaged with the work of an official on the diocese's Board of Social Responsibility to locate the vicars within a socio-economic profile. Quite what meaning this 'locating' had with regard to the vicar's claims to practice was part of the research's empirical concern.

The Case Study

Introduction

As mentioned briefly earlier, a potentially distracting element to the engagement of the Church of England with social entrepreneurship hit it in the early 1990s, and was substantively to challenge its resource base. Poor investment decisions by the 1990s Church Commissioners incurred substantive losses and nearly brought the Church's operations to its knees. These events formed the background of the Turnbull Report (ACOCE 1995) and led to subsequent changes in Church structure. Thus, while the Church had historically been able to rely on its inherited wealth to sustain a contemporary presence, it now needed to bring in finance from the parishes to keep its clergy in post and as a presence in the community. By one reading of the situation, it might have been expected that the Church would be too engrossed in keeping itself financially afloat to engage with the broader concept of social entrepreneurship. Alternatively, the crisis did present an opportunity to link religiosity, sociability, and enterprise together—what better time to engage the Church into social mission mode than the millennial 'decade of evangelism' (Warren 1995, 1996)? Seagull diocese had authorized its Council for Social Responsibility to produce its own 'social profile', in the wake of the ten-yearly national population census, as a basis for assessment of need and quota to the diocese. The great diversity of this diocese was conceptualized in terms that located individual vicars within their parishes, in a way comparable to other vicars in the diocese, and compatible with research concerns. Seagull diocese itself is one of the forty-four Church of England dioceses. It includes a population in excess of 700,000, covering an area of more than 400 square miles. Within its boundaries are approximately 140 parishes, divided into 8 deaneries and 2 archdeaconries. It seems appropriate at this point to consider how its data helps to establish a needs contextualization of research.

A summary of the social profile analysis of 'Seagull diocese' by one of its authors concluded:

The range of difference, both within and between parishes, has increased; the gainers still outnumber the losers, but such wide differences encourage tension, bitterness, and social discord, as the increasing crime and urban riots of the decade have demonstrated. (4/10/93)

The basis of these comments was that, according to the analysis, between the years of 1981 and 1991 the diocese had developed three urban priority areas (UPAs). This new, lower order, of category was created because of these areas' acute problems centred on rising unemployment and reliance on social housing that may be unsuitable for children. Table 9.1 illustrates some of the differences that the report suggests, by presenting data on particular indicators from the respective profiles of 1981 and 1991, with examples from three categories of profile—UPA, category 1, and category 5. The social profile was based on the most comprehensive data on the diocese population at the time of the field research; fluctuations and changes of need post-1991 are likely, but

Table 9.1 Examples of parish profile variation within 'Seagull diocese'

Parish profile indicator	Urban priority area* (%)		Category 1 (%)		Category 5 (%)	
	1981	1991	1981	1991	1981	1991
Social rented housing	79	80	83	52.1	15	9.2
Owner occupier housing	16	15.9	16	46	81	88
No car	69	68.9	47	43.4	28	21.8
2+ cars	3	4.7	9	13.3	18	29.2
Professional manager	5	4.5	8	7.7	19	15.7
Unemployed						
male	14	23.7	15	16.7	6	6.8
female	8	6.9	8	5.6	5	2.7

* Previously category 1 under 1981 classification.

a substantive UK government policy influence such as that affecting house ownership change between 1981 and 1991 is not apparent in respect of data relevance for 1996–7. Even in respect of the areas affected by change in the housing situation from 1981 to 1991, there is some evidence of a different form of housing problem rather than a categorical elevation of the area. Thus, there appears an arguable continuity in the general amount of deprivation or affluence in an area, based on consistent indicators, over the past fifteen to twenty years.

Qualitative semi-structured interviews were used as the core method of this research and documentary sources were used for contextualizing the interviews with vicars. These mainly constituted parish magazines, but also diocesan newsletters, parish SWOT analyses and plans, and sermon notes. The thirty vicars interviewed in this 1996–7 research are distinguished for purposes of this chapter by letter allocation from A to ZD and fall into social profile banding in the following ways (inclusively); 'vicars in deprivation' (UPAs and category 1), vicars A–C; 'vicars on the edge of deprivation/middle England' (category 2), vicars D–K; 'vicars in middle England' (category 3), vicars L–U; and 'vicars in affluence' (categories 4 and 5), vicars V-ZD. Only select samples of them are mentioned here. It should also be noted that 'vicars' constitute those designated either 'vicar' or 'rector' of their benefice (area of responsibility that may include one or more parishes). The purpose of this research approach was to see how their thoughts and reflections on practice could be located in terms of their parish category and the various cultural modes or *characters* as adopted here from MacIntyre (1985).

But the question could be posed: why select a diocese as the unit for research rather than a deanery, a town, or a rural or inner city area? And why select Seagull diocese particularly? Marcourt, Thompson, and Webberburn (1996) have noted the concentration of investigations into the parish system either focused on the inner city (ACURA 1985) or rural areas (ACORA 1990), as distinct from the towns that they chose to research. A diocesan wide project could cover all three of these if the right diocese was selected. The focus on this particular diocese brings all three together: an inner city area with high population; rural areas where some inhabitants are claimed by research interviewees never to have been to the nearest town let alone the city area; and the town life in between.

Test of Character: Resources, Opportunities, and Innovations

OPPORTUNITIES: FROM THE DOORSTEP AND BEYOND, ACROSS THE CATEGORIES

Vicar G and vicar N, one on the edge of, and one firmly within middle-England respectively, can both be understood in their different ways to be asserting a claim to act as an 'old-fashioned, valued priest' (in vicar N's words) with a distinct priestly character. For vicar N, in particular, both social and financial matters are claimed as impeding the sort of priestly character he wished to pursue; regarding 'the social' aspects of his work, for example, he says:

...I suppose, in a sense, if you look through my diary...in a week I suppose...five or six, if I'm *absolutely* honest, five or six people will come to have a heart-to-heart each week...that's a very hidden thing...but again that's the essence of being a priest... who else are they going to go to? CAB [Citizen's Advice Bureau]? Their doctor? Who?...[...]...and people come to talk about a multitude of things, not necessarily couched in God terms...I mean...um...I had a chap here...um...earlier this week I expect it was...yes it was....who's unemployed,...[...]...well...you know ...um...he wants to talk about it...and perhaps I can give some sort of reflection upon it which is different to what the job-centre might say...

This 'hidden' social work of vicar N is suggestive of its persistence, despite his apparent reluctance to acknowledge it as such: work deemed more appropriate for social workers or other public professionals rather than a social opportunity for an innovative response by a vicar.

Vicar ZC, working in an affluent parish more comfortably accommodates such a view. He looks as his work from a more inclusive and holistic perspective:

I will talk to somebody about the problems they are having with their children, which is about relationships and married life...I will talk about problems they are having with their neighbour...which may need a call to a solicitor or the CAB, if fences are being pulled down...I'll talk to them about their finances, if they're in debt, if there are concerns there...if they want to talk about their prayer life, their understanding of theology...um...[...]...they may not express it...they may not choose it through the formal worship of the church...[...]...and it's not the vicar trying to bring the conversation round to spiritual things...I think the spiritual things are there... um...and I think people know they're there...and often want to explore them...so I'm a social worker, I'm a solicitor...I'm a welfare officer, I'm a probation officer, I'm a pastor...I'm a spiritual friend...I'm a confessor...

Vicar B, based in a UPA has similar aspirations towards a more distinct religious role (though vicar B preaches and practises from an evangelical theology), and has a comment of relevance for the multi-role claims of vicar ZC, mentioned later. For vicar B, needs other than those 'distinctly spiritual ones' are not necessary prerequisites for meeting spiritual need:

...spiritual care is concerned with their relationship with God...their relationship with God is not dependent upon their social well-being

and this *should* define the priority of such interventions for him in his terms. Yet if vicar N had difficulty in dispensing with the social aspects of his work, this is nigh on impossible for vicar B, whose context might challenge even the laid-back vicar ZC noted below:

People come straight off the street, knock on the front door... asking for money, or food or whatever... if you look in our porch, you'll find there are stains where drinks have been thrown around... [...] ... and sitting in a very intimidating way in the porch with dogs and all the rest of it, demanding this, that, and the other, while they roll new cigarettes from old... er... and my wife has come to the point where, because of the sort of negative things, she will now not give food and drink... which is difficult for me to live with... but on the other hand, they will not go to any other house down the street, even if it's a house with Christians in it, a Christian wouldn't treat them in the same way a minister is expected to...

Vicar B does not mention any figure to suggest the scale of these visits to his vicarage, but this might be suggested by the experience of vicar A, whose benefice is a scale up, in category 1; he also takes a rather different theological approach:

...of the many drunk and homeless people we have on the doorstep... [...] ... obviously I wouldn't sit and talk to them about prayer unless they particularly wanted to talk about it... but... um... I do have many callers at the door for food... its as many as forty some weeks... it's a lot... and their needs are very much physical needs... but we try to meet them as people... sit and talk to them and... and again with social issues... God's justice, we do have the poorest church area in (X) and we are trying to get the church engaged with the poor in that area.

We should note vicar A's claim to his benefice's inclusion of the poorest church area, something not specifically picked by the overall social profile analysis. What, however, might be made of the reflections highlighted here so far?

Vicar A's approach has an affinity towards a Maslowian approach (Maslow 1973) to need in contrast to the congregational and evangelical approach of vicar B. This said, practising an evangelical theology does not necessitate a narrow spiritual focus. A key background work to the Church of England's *Faith in the City* was Bishop David Sheppard's *Bias to the Poor* (Sheppard 1983). Sheppard was an evangelical who also chaired the sponsoring group of the CCBI (1997) report. Vicar A would seem more comfortable with being open to meeting a variety of need, and similarly being engaged with the broader community, but, in importing Maslow's hierarchy of need into such practical engagement, he seems to be distracted from the possibility of addressing needs simultaneously. Vicar B, in virtually turning Maslow on his head (and virtual it is, since humanistic psychology does not feature in his approach) wishes to distance himself from other needs for purposes of clear demarcation, and those coming to his door who only wish to exploit a traditional hospitality without any inclination to pursue a spiritual journey in congregation. To be clear, vicar B does 'inevitably' engage with meeting other social needs, though most often this is with a directed focus on his congregation, such as the debt counselling service, but he does not see this as what he is particularly called to do. He has given some hint as to why ministers (and, again, the use of the concept of 'minister' rather than that of 'priest' is reflective of his theological approach) in particular may get doorstep callers. Vicar C, in a category 1 area, puts them in a comparative context, but also attempts clearly to embed his congregation in community:

...and very much...[...]...being part of the community....and living *in* the community...um...we're very much involved with the...other sort of...what I suppose you'd call professional carers...y'know, like social workers...and meet together on a regular basis...um...to help this community in which *I live*...in which they *don't live*...they tend to live outside the community...we're required to live over the shop as it were...and that's a great task in an area like this, because there's a great deal of deprivation,...[...]...but...um...when they wanted to have a drop-in centre for the aged, which Age Concern run, we were very much involved in the planning...and members of the congregation are involved in the manning of the facility...um.... and members of the congregation are involved in the community centre...and the various things that meet there...toy libraries, youth clubs...but being in the community...um...I think realising that...there are no financial resources in a parish like this...

This living in the same community as those of whom they are charged with 'curing souls', marks out points of distinction for vicars across the diocese from their professional peers, sometimes bringing stress and conflict, but also presenting significant opportunity. The re-appropriation of the doorstep opportunities for new forms of social entrepreneurship, the ability to 'move on' towards a more substantive fulfilment of need for those who call on vicars in these various circumstances, would surely be of benefit not only to the callers, but the vicars themselves, although another consideration is that the stress of coping with these sort of conditions for a vicar may take their toll. Vicar A's theological orientation and vicar C's working class background make them comfortable with their circumstances for the time being; although they both have some way to go to catch up with vicar B's eight years in his. In the meantime, some of the evident initiatives of vicar C and his congregation highlights the importance, in financially challenged areas, of embedding congregational 'human resources' within the community.

The gap between a UPA and a category 3 middle-class benefice is exposed in the different experiences of vicar B and vicar L (interestingly a former IBM employee) in terms of access to congregational human resources and 'business' input and a private professional ethos more generally. Vicar B cannot find anybody to take on the role of treasurer; this poses no such problem for vicar L, but finding someone willing to 'lower' themselves to mow the church lawn does. However, even vicar Y, in an affluent benefice, finds difficulty in filling a treasurer's post on one of the Parochial Church Councils he covers. In the Church of England post the Church Commissioners' crisis, there is much greater pressure on parishes to raise finance, even in some of the poorer categories. Vicar C, in his category 1 benefice, captures this well:

Sadly it drains a lot . . . it drains a lot of our energy . . . fund raising . . . [. . .] . . . but a lot of people round here are quite poor . . . [. . .] . . . but they have to find £8,000 ($13,760) towards . . . y' know . . . towards the quota . . . to . . . um . . . to send to the diocese . . . but of course the Church Commissioners and the diocese heavily subsidize this parish because . . . they pay my stipend y' know . . . and my colleagues . . . so . . . um . . . but it's a big problem yeah . . . um . . . [. . .] . . . when I was in chaplaincy, we only took it to give to charity . . . we took collections but it was all shelled out again . . . but it's a drain on us really . . . absorbs too much time and too much energy . . . unfortunately, that's it . . .

Here then is not only a claim about the pressures of raising finance and the time and energy it absorbs, but an additional one about it diverting money away from charitable and social causes. Yet vicar C does manage to sustain much social engagement in his area, despite the considerably greater burden carried in meeting their diocesan quota. Vicar B, despite his own scepticism about professionalism in the Church of England itself, finds the lack of professionals and professionalism in his benefice a definite inhibition to progress. This may, in part, be related to his own professional middle class background, in contrast to the working class background of vicar C. Thus, vicar B frames the problem as not being resourced for a post with expertise in applying for grants: a particular form of public professionalism. This is a perfectly understandable way of framing the problem: but are there other possibilities? Let us consider certain other claims made of an affluent part of the Seagull diocese.

Vicar X, who seemed anxious to be moved to a deprived parish, has a link between his parish and one in a deprived London borough. As part of developing such links, an issue of vicar X's parish magazine thanks one of its parishioners for his significant human resource contribution to work in the London borough. Having played a major role in renovating the local church hall, this particular parishioner is claimed to have spent hundreds of hours assisting with the refurbishment and development of a church hall centre, which houses a nursery, a child centre, a counselling room, and a range of support groups and social activities. A key element of that work has been the securing of two major grants: £100,000 ($172,000) from City Challenge and £50,000 ($86,000) from the National Lottery (Foster 2001: 397).

Given the apparent affluence of vicar X's parishes and the total contrast with that of vicar B, it is no surprise that vicar X's parishioners have the appropriate skills to secure and develop this project, but also that the project is not for the parish itself but for a much more deprived area. Hundreds of hours are not being spent raising money for the quota to the diocese, despite the fact of that quota being significantly higher. Whether it is the lack of specific funding or the lack of expertise within his congregation, vicar B, conversely, cannot get further funding for projects—but is this just a default in technical expertise? The seeking out of opportunity, and imagining and innovating around the problem might have been brought about by another sort of initiative: a diocesan initiative or an initiative on behalf of either particular benefice could have put vicars B's and X's parishes in contact with each other. However, no such initiative occurred suggesting a different 'entrepreneurial landscape' across the two parishes.

FROM 'WORKER', THROUGH 'OLD-FASHIONED VALUED', TO 'MANAGERIAL' PRIEST

Vicar Q suggests the most radical agenda for the future of the clergy—to abandon full-time stipendiary ministry altogether, and shift completely over to non-stipendiary 'worker priests'. Such an agenda might give freedom from raising Church resources, but his recommendation is made from the security of his own 'middle England' benefice and in close proximity to his own retirement. Another alternative is to go the other way and adopt a more 'businessing' approach, something like that of vicar L. Would this have positive impact (e.g. secure financial resource base) or negative (competing cultural modes) on socially entrepreneurial possibilities? It, perhaps, seems surprising to be discussing vicar N in this context; in the statement later he appears to be admitting a problematic role for such business and management matters but also an awkward distancing from it:

In terms of finance...I don't have anything to do with finance at all...I mean we're a middle-class parish...I've got lots of very good managers in their own right...[...]... I want to be known as a priest who cares for souls...and wants converts...*that's* what I'm on about...and money actually—and of course the church—and not a lot of people realise this because so often the clergy are talking about money—actually the church says the building is nothing to do with the priest...it's the churchwardens' legal responsibility, not mine at all...and...um...we've just done something a wee bit naughty (laughter)...um...er...and the churchwardens realised it's their responsibility, not mine...so I want to have a clear divide...

This reinforcement of his 'old-fashioned valued priest' statement seemed tainted with a sense of anxiety, so the claims regarding matters of legal responsibility were further investigated.

Quite contrary to vicar N's assertion, the Church building is not just the churchwardens' responsibility (Macmorran and Briden 1996: 64–8), and, thus, the 'naughtiness' not theirs alone. Further, in a parish magazine five months earlier vicar N exhibits a rather different character to that of the strongly demarcated priest; he recounts a meeting organized by the deanery:

The speaker was a Roman Catholic Deacon who at that time worked part-time for IBM, and he spoke to us about the whole area of aims, objectives, and mission statements and ownership, most of which was even then old hat to industry and business, but which was very new to most of us.

Enthused by the experience, vicar N goes back to his Parish Church Council and they produce a collectively owned mission statement:

As we now have it, the Statement is the measure for all our decisions and action. All our committee work has been reorganised, each has its own aims and objectives according to the Statement; so everyone can see what we are aiming to do and to be under the five main headings of:

1. Worship
2. Ministry, education, and fellowship
3. Children and Youth
4. Buildings, finance, and resources
5. The wider Church

At last we feel there is both a harmony in the work we are doing, and a common basis for the work we do.

We have already noted the legal position over the church building, but here too the mission statement claims a collective ownership of mission in regard to buildings, just as suggested by the part-time IBM deacon. However, five months on, this venture into the private professional ethos has not produced the 'harmony in work' of the mission statement, but quite the opposite: an apparent financial scandal, an unstable resource base to do other work, and a defensive and demarcating approach. While the adoption of the private professional character itself would have created distinction from the socially entrepreneurial, the demarcating reaction against also does so; 'social work' is not what a priest should be engaged with, and so the opportunity such possibilities present are not taken up.

Another venture into this sort of approach is exemplified by vicar P's development of a team ministry within the diocese, a structure that would seem to particularly align with a 'businessing' ethos. Here, interestingly, particular distinction between rector and vicar is revived, with 'team rector' being the leader of 'team vicars'. For (team) vicar P, temporal job status was part of the way of contemporary society, and the idea of incumbency an extravagance. Unlike vicar Q, vicar P believes in and is actually living with job temporality. There were no financial scandals on his patch, but what seemed an even stronger theme in vicar P's mode of church was a greater sense of social disengagement, his valuing of more proximate association with other 'long-term decision-makers' (senior managers), and his increasing distance from the 'front-line' of practice:

Some people get very het up about the administration part of the job taking them away from pastoral care...um...I think my view is...that by making sure everything happens properly, I'm allowing other people to be free to do pastoral care...and do it more effectively....I could spend a lot of time, beavering around visiting people...but then the broader picture of what's happening would get lost...it's the longer term I'm interested in...but that's how the job has evolved...it's just good practice to support the people who are 'hands-on'...

This does give an opportunity for others to report back on their experiences and for innovative projects to be developed in response to these, the priest allowing and supporting the 'prophecy' of others a la Gill (1992), perhaps. Vicar P and his team would seem to have the lot; a mission statement; strategy; long term, medium, and short-term planning; however:

We tend to be very reactive, to what's been happening during the week... it's much more difficult to sit down and plan really effectively what we're doing... but what we haven't done at all, as I was saying, is to move on from the planning to the appraisal... y' know (laughter)... [...]... planning is wonderful, but was it really worth it?...

The dislocation between the day-to-day and the whole variety of plans seems not only to put the question of whether all the planning itself (to which vicar P is greatly devoted) is worth it, but the question as to what constitutes 'worth'.

There seems a curious vacuum at the core of this evident pursuit of the private professional character, echoing MacIntyre's claims (1985) about the moral poverty of the bureaucratic manager pursuing efficiency. Contra MacIntyre however, it is claimed here that bureaucracy is not necessarily about efficiency. It appears that the private professional ethos is at least roughly distinct in terms of its broader commercial managerial focus and that the sense of emptiness within the practice may be as much to do with a lack of institutional fit for such a mode of professional undertaking that either becomes cut off from fulfilling its *telos* (with worth hidden, giving the sense of emptiness) or exposes a corrupting influence on its institutional arena. There is also a distinct lack of reference to entrepreneurial concepts such as opportunity or innovation amongst all this—yet vicar P, and those he supports, are not the only ones seemingly trapped into being 'reactive'.

BEYOND BEING REACTIVE AND BACK TO OPPORTUNITY

Vicar D works in a category 2 benefice, and reflecting this 'on the edge' category, experiences a rather less intense version of the doorstep callers than those in UPA and category 1 areas. He takes on a contemporary version of the established 'learned member of the community' role for a clergyman:

I think a lot of our work as educated people if you like... and who know the system is actually getting people into that system... [...]... the social services and people like that are excellent if they are asked... but of course they don't go looking for work, they're not pro-active... and I think that's the same with us, we're not proactive, we're reactive, but helping people to find out... we're helping them along... we're a bit of a CAB [Citizen Advice Bureau] as well... people come along ... 'I can't fill out this form, can you help me'... there's a lot of illiteracy and innumeracy, and I discovered that being a school governor for two schools as well...

Though vicar D does not use the language of 'social inclusion', something like that is eluded to here. He compares priestly 'reactiveness' to that of social services, though this does not explain why, nevertheless, he is more accessible than social services. As vicar C put it, 'living over the shop' is at least part of that, but for the 'doorstep' to be approachable in the first place, must represent an opportunity, a 'moment' part created by the ministry itself. A possible impediment may have been particular understandings about where opportunity, pro-activity, and innovation should take place—'out there', beyond the buildings and vicarage. Yet whilst, indeed, opportunity comes to the doorstep, being out 'scanning the environment' would seem to increase 'being in the right place at the right time' in a variant number of circumstances, though what use is made of those opportunities is another matter. A number of responses from vicars in Seagull diocese capture this opportunity seeking. Vicar E, in a benefice on the edge of deprivation/middle England, states:

...it's a being thing...and that's why you should be reasonably public...that's why for me wearing a clerical collar...so people know you're there...without making a song and dance about it, but you are there...so often I think some of the best work you do, is taking my children to school, at the school gates, you are just there...some people might stop you...'could I have a chat'...'could I have a word with you'.

Such could not be further from the approach of vicar P. In her affluent benefice, vicar ZA also makes herself available to parishioners:

I've possibly put a human face...and people...well, they've said things, I don't know whether I should tell you, 'you're the most unholy, holy person that we know'...being in the village, the shopping, the being part of the community, not driving...I don't pass through...I'm around, I'm one of—y' know there's a lot of breaking down the barriers, of images...

In an era that, despite global warming and the possible causes of it, remains obsessed with car transport, the possibilities of social engagement through not driving are sometimes overlooked. Yet 'getting around' in a country parish is something rather different from doing the same in a deprived urban area. The killing of vicar Christopher Grey by a psychiatrically disturbed man in his deprived inner-city parish being a case in point. However, neither his numerous doorstep callers nor the burdens of administration stop vicar A being 'out and about' in his deprived benefice:

...by becoming over efficient and organized we can squeeze out the gospel...and there isn't the space to be with the person in sadness and in sorrow...and just being around...I try to walk round the parish when I can...just to be seen, to be there...[...]...but it is also being available to people...many pastoral contacts happen unexpectedly...

All such opportunity seeking and its response may seem trivial compared with the 'grand' innovations of some of the social entrepreneurs discussed earlier; but such substantive moments and their exploitation are just large scale versions of smaller scale opportunities and innovations, which apart from their worth in themselves, may also feature as part of, or as additions to, such grand projects. An example of such a moment comes from Erin Pizzey's early days of setting up the Women's Refuge at Belmont Terrace:

I was in the local park at 1 o'clock with my goddaughter Rachel. I saw a small, plump woman sitting by herself on a bench and I walked over and introduced myself to her. She had been a nurse and had a varied career so I asked her what she did all day now. She said 'Nothing much.' So that solved that and she came down to Belmont Terrace for a look at the place and is now worked to death and invaluable to everybody. (Pizzey 1974: 20)

It would seem arguable that Pizzey's opportunistic recruitment approach is strongly intuitively based as one would expect; this would seem to be in line with what Kirby (2003: 293) suggests features in many entrepreneurial approaches: a proneness to mistakes (although, elsewhere, he claims more measured, rational approaches also seem unreliable: Kirby 2003: 251). A particularly worrying example of this approach in Seagull diocese is the claim of 'opportunistic exploiting' by vicar ZC of those who feel 'called' to work with children to undertake such work— though it should be remembered that Pizzey's 'bench sitting nurse' could as easily been contra-indicated to work with children, and Pizzey's refuge included many children who had also been abused. Additional checking of these entrepreneurial intuitions should at least be advised in the case of children. This is, however, entrepreneurship in the raw, warts and all, without all the professional and managerial surroundings that sometimes become confused and associated with it.

This section has focused a great deal on opportunities and moments and much less on innovations. Part of the explanation of the greater focus on opportunities and moments rather than their appropriation is simply that while there have been plenty of opportunities the innovative responses to them have been rather more limited. To reiterate, this is not to say there have not been responses, and initiatives are claimed to have been undertaken. As individual responses vicars have, at least at times, echoed the sort of welfare entrepreneurship conceptualized by Taylor-Gooby (1999), through developing that precisely where opportunity seeking is undertaken. For example, vicar C's congregation demonstrates various social engagements with Age Concern, a Community Centre, youth clubs, and a playschool. Rather differently, vicar X, in his affluent benefice, has co-ordinated one of his parishioners to make a significant impact on an adopted London borough parish. Others, such as vicar I, in his category 2 'on the edge' benefice and following his particular mode of 'charismatic' church, combine innovation in church services while also bringing initiatives to pursuing a social agenda. He states, 'A drop-in facility is available for people on the streets, with a shower, a clothes store and the regular attendance of a community nurse.' These are all seen by Vicar I as responding to social needs. Indeed, the appropriation of such social opportunities is further enhanced by being accepted by 'guys sitting on a bench having a can' in a way that other members of the church are not.

It is an approach that seems very much 'in the spirit' of Warren's 'missionary' recommendations (1995, 1996), though Warren is not specifically promoting the Charismatic mode of church. Another, also promoting a Charismatic mode of church in the same band of deprivation, is vicar J. When describing the scope of work undertaken in his benefice, he states:

I mean here for example... we put a lot of resources into young families in all kinds of ways... because there are a lot of young families around here... so we have a playschool that meets everyday, which we staff... properly... we have a coffee shop, where you can get a good lunch or snack here deliberately to... and I think those are as valuable as any other things we do... we have an active youth group, Sunday school... we have a mothers' and toddlers' type thing... but I mean I don't think I want to break them all down... I think... I feel that what we're meant to be doing is that every opportunity... bringing, what I see as, the riches of the Gospel into peoples lives...

While these may not be groundbreaking innovations, they still represent interventions that are meaningful and appropriate to the opportunities that arise, and open the pathway to opportunities and innovative possibilities. Elsewhere, indeed in an affluent benefice, some of the parishioners themselves are the focus of particular interventions. Vicar W outlines the plight of farmers, for example:

... where once they were the centre of the community, they are now very much on the periphery of it... and they might not see another human being all day... so... their role in society has changed massively—I said seventy years, but it's changed massively even in the last twenty years.... um... suicide is the second most common cause of death among farmers... and that's an horrendous statistic... um... we try to address it a little bit by setting up a helpline... or liaising with the Samaritans and encouraging farmers to avail themselves of the opportunity at any rate... but we've had a farming suicide in the area...

Vicar W has not only challenged assumptions about 'affluent' parishes, but also highlighted particular problems and developed a project to address them.

Conclusion and Overview

In the analysis earlier, the potential for a socially entrepreneurial character is contested by combinations of alignment to public professionalism and an 'old-fashioned valued priest' and apparent flirtations with a private professional character. While attempts to be more concrete in matters cultural is always likely to meet frustration, evidence for particular cultural affiliation may sometimes be deceptively simple and only overlooked through over-interpretation. Take the case of vicars L and N, with direct, if different, business influences through IBM. In both cases they draw on these IBM experiences to produce 'mission statements' in their parishes. Whilst Gill and Burke (1996) quite rightly point out that, preceding the current vogue in business thinking, mission statements were actually associated with religious communities, this is of no relevance in interpreting the experiences of vicar L and N here; in both cases mission statements are treated as a business idea. It is, perhaps, debatable whether it is the character of the private professional that is problematic here or, rather, the crude interpretation and/or misunderstanding by the vicars themselves of such a character that is the core of the issue. For example, vicar P's claim to be concentrating on the development of close association with elite professional peers may suggest a distinct lack of 'market' focus.

What does seem clear, however, is that if the Church of England is to make a significant contribution towards the development of social entrepreneurship, then it must continue to seek out opportunities and innovations. As has already been noted, a number of the vicars discussed earlier are doing just that (e.g. vicars A, E, and ZA), while other vicars in the study, however, clearly wished to distance themselves from social objects (vicars B and N) and others still actually distanced themselves by becoming integrated into the social circles of a perceived managerial elite (vicar P). There are indications here of social entrepreneurial possibility in the claims to practice of these vicars, but so often, what vicars so orientated are good at are recognizing, and even going out in their environment and scanning for, opportunities. What these opportunity recognizers and seekers seem less good at doing is innovating in response to the opportunities presented or discovered. This is not to say that significant projects have not got off the ground and such were noted with vicars I, J, W, and X; yet there remains a sense of 'opportunity lost' in many respects, even where opportunities literally come knocking at the door.

So the emulation of a private professional character is either problematic in itself for vicars or they misunderstand it. This might very well be for the good encouraging more assistance in taking on the character of the social entrepreneur. But, here to, innovation does not seem to match up with opportunistic possibility. Yet why should any of this be a surprise? Indeed, it is not for those supporting the 'old-fashioned (though actually pre-1979?) valued priest' and public professionalism, where welfare professionals attended the plight of the poor and needy, and vicars just got on with their rituals of 'hatches, matches, and dispatches' (baptisms, marriages, and funerals). This latter argument is not entirely convincing on two accounts. First, although the public professional and the welfare state will always have a key social and economic role in contemporary British society, even when that intervention was at its most substantive, such professionalism proved somewhat problematic with problems remaining at the margins of social and professional interest, or were not recognized at all. Thus, R. D. Laing and other anti-psychiatrists created new responses to those diagnosed with severe mental illness, Erin Pizzey 'discovered' domestic violence and created Women's Refugees, and the Reverend Eric Blakebourgh innovated harm reduction responses in the marginal social and health arena of drug misuse. As the case material presented in this chapter should have suggested, Blakebourgh is not alone in having been in places of 'social opportunity'—where he is different from some is what he has done once given it.

Second then, to return to the arguments for old-fashioned valued priest, with a reliance on the continued flow of 'business-as-usual' issues, must be seen as a retrograde step; particularly since part of Archbishop Runcie's rationale for *Faith in the City* was to continue to demonstrate the 'significance' of the Church. For many of course the Church of England has long been of no significance and its fate does not matter. Yet despite the need to raise human and financial resources to keep the Church itself going, it still so often has human and financial capacity over to offer for social objectives—it is only that it might do better with opportunities that it proactively encounters and otherwise seeks out.

References

Archbishop's Commission on the Organisation of the Church of England (ACOCE) (1995). *Working As One Body*. London: Church House Publishing.

Archbishop's Commission on Rural Areas (ACORA) (1990). *Faith in the Countryside*. London: Church House Publishing.

Archbishop's Commission on Urban Priority Areas (ACURA) (1985). *Faith in the City*. London: Church House Publishing.

Atkinson, D. (1994). *The Common Sense of Community*. London: Demos.

Beardshaw, V. and Towell, D. (1990). *Assessment and Case Management*. London: Kings Fund Institute, Briefing Paper 10.

Beck, U. (1992). *The Risk Society*. London: Sage.

Burrows, R. (ed.) (1991). *Deciphering the Enterprise Culture: Entrepreneurship, Petty Capitalism, and the Restructuring of Britain*. London and New York: Routledge.

Council of Churches for Britain and Ireland (CCBI) (1997). *Unemployment and the Future of Work*. London: CCBI.

Drayton, W. (2002). 'The Citizen Sector: Becoming as Competitive and Entrepreneurial as Business', *California Management Review*, 44(3): 120–32.

Drucker, P. (1994). *Innovation and Entrepreneurship*. Oxford: Butterworth-Heinemann.

Ecclestone, G. (ed.) (1988). *The Parish Church?* London and Oxford: Mowbray.

Elbaum, B. and Lazonick, W. (1986). *The Decline of the British Economy*. Oxford: Clarendon Press.

Foster, D. (2001). *Social Entrepreneurship, Private Professionalism or Something more Sacred*. Unpublished Ph.D. thesis, University of Portsmouth.

Giddens, A. (1998). *The Third Way*. Cambridge: Polity Press.

Gill, R. (1992). *Moral Communities*. Exeter, UK: University of Exeter Press.

——and Burke, D. (1996). *Strategic Church Leadership*. London: SPCK.

Grant, W. (1993). *The Politics of Economic Policy*. London: Harvester Wheatsheaf.

—— and Nath, S. (1984). *The Politics of Economic Policy Making*. Oxford: Blackwell.

Graves, R. (1952). *The White Goddess*. London: Faber & Faber.

Handy, C. (1997). *The Hungry Spirit*. London: Hutchinson.

Hanlon, G. (1998). 'Professionalism as Enterprise', *Sociology*, 32(1): 43–63.

Hannah, L. (1980). 'Questions and Discussion', in A. Sheldon (ed.), *The Prime Mover of Progress*. London: IEA, pp. 127–8.

Hayek, F. (1967). *Studies in Philosophy, Politics and Economics*. London and New York: Routledge.

—— (1986). *The Road to Serfdom*. London: Ark (1st pub. 1942).

Hobbs, D. (1988). *Doing the Business*. Oxford: Oxford University Press.

—— (1991). 'Business as a Master Metaphor: Working Class Entrepreneurship and Business-like Policing', in R. Burrows (ed.), *Deciphering the Enterprise Culture: Entrepreneurship, Petty Capitalism and the Restructuring of Britain*. London and New York: Routledge, pp. 107–25.

Illich, I. (1974). *Celebration of Awareness*. London: Penguin Books.

Kirby, D. (2003). *Entrepreneurship*. London: McGraw-Hill Education.

Kirzner, I. (1980). 'The Primacy of Entrepreneurial Discovery', in A. Sheldon (ed.), *The Prime Mover of Progress*. London: IEA, pp. 3–31.

Knight, F. (1921). *Risk, Uncertainty and Profit*. Chicago, IL: University of Chicago Press.

Kriesi, H. (1995). *New Social Movements in Western Europe: A Comparative Analysis*. London: University College Press.

Laing, R. (1967). *The Politics of Experience and the Bird of Paradise*. Harmondsworth, UK: Penguin.

Leadbeater, C. (1997). *The Rise of the Social Entrepreneur*. London: Demos.

MacIntyre, A. (1985). *After Virtue*, 2nd edn. London: Duckworth.

Macmillan, H. (1938). *The Middle Way*. London: Macmillan.

Macmorran, K. and Briden, T. (1996). *A Handbook for Churchwardens and Parochial Church Councillors*. London: Mowbray.

Macourt, M., Thompson, C., and Webberburn, A. (1996). *Parish: Church or Community?* Conference paper to BSA Sociology of Religion Group, Religion, Culture and Ideology conference, April.

MacRae, D. (1980). 'From Villan to Hero?' in A. Sheldon (ed.), *The Prime Mover of Progress*. London: IEA, pp. 117–27.

Magee, B. (1979). *Popper*. London: Fontana.

Maslow, A. (1973). *The Farther Reaches of Human Nature*. Harmondsworth, UK: Penguin.

Morris, P. (1991). 'Freeing the Spirit of Enterprise: The Genesis and Development of the Concept of Enterprise Culture', in R. Keat and N. Abercrombie, *Enterprise Culture*. London and New York: Routledge, pp. 21–37.

Niskanen, W. (1973). *Bureaucracy: Servant or Master?* London: IEA.

Osbourne, D. and Gaebler, T. (1992). *Reinventing Government*. Reading, MA: Addison-Wesley.

Parsons, S. (1988). 'Economic Principles in the Public and Private Sectors', *Policy and Politics*, 16(1): 29–39.

Perkin, H. (1989). *The Rise of Professional Society: England Since 1880*. London and New York: Routledge.

—— (1992). 'The Enterprise Culture in Historical Perspective: Birth, Life, Death and Resurrection?' in P. Heelas, and P. Morris (eds.), *The Values of Enterprise Culture: A Moral Debate*. London and New York: Routledge, pp. 36–60.

Pizzey, E. (1974). *Scream Quietly Or The Neighbours Will Hear.* London and Harmondsworth: Penguin.

Popper, K. (1962). *The Open Societies and its Enemies,* vol. II. London: Routledge.

—— (1984). *Objective Knowledge: An Evolutionary Approach.* Oxford: Clarendon Press.

Schumpeter, J. (1934). *The Theory of Economic Development.* Cambridge, MA: Harvard University Press.

Shackle, G. (1972). *Epistemics and Economics: A Critique of Economic Doctrines.* Cambridge: Cambridge University Press.

—— (1979). *Imagination and the Nature of Choice.* Edinburgh, UK: Edinburgh University Press.

Sheldon, A. (ed.) (1980*a*). *The Prime Mover of Progress.* London: IEA.

—— (1980*b*). 'Preface', in A. Sheldon (ed.), *The Prime Mover of Progress.* London: IEA, pp. xi–xiv.

—— (1980*c*). 'Questions and Discussion', in A. Sheldon (ed.), *The Prime Mover of Progress.* London: IEA, pp. 127–8.

Sheppard, D. (1983). *Bias to the Poor.* London: Hodder & Stoughton.

Taylor-Gooby, P. (1999). 'Markets and Motives: Trust and Egoism in Welfare Markets', *Journal of Social Policy,* 28(1): 97–114.

Titmuss, R. (1960). *The Irresponsible Society.* London: Fabian Society.

Warren, R. (1995). *Building Missionary Congregations.* London: Church House Publishing.

—— (1996). *Signs of Life.* London: Church House Publishing.

Part III

New Models

10

Social Enterprise Models and Their Mission and Money Relationships[1]

Sutia Kim Alter

Introduction

The hallmark of social entrepreneurship is its ability to combine social interests with business practices to effect social change. Its hybrid world—part business–part social—has spawned a new breed of practitioner, the social entrepreneur, as well as a new brand of organization, the revenue earning social enterprise. Traditionally people think of not-for-profits as being responsible for creating social value and for-profits for creating economic value; social entrepreneurship brings these dichotomies together, marrying social interest and market mechanisms to create both social and economic value with a new type of institution.

The social enterprise is driven by two strong forces. First, the nature of the desired social change often benefits from an innovative, entrepreneurial, or enterprise-based solution. Second, the sustainability of the organization and its services requires diversification of its funding stream, often including the creation of earned income opportunities (see Reis 1999). Social enterprise introduces a new not-for-profit paradigm for creating sustainable value for people and the planet.

The early years of social entrepreneurship have been characterized by tremendous innovation; this, in turn, has produced a diverse landscape of social enterprises. Nonetheless, distinct patterns are emerging. The occupation of classifying and organizing social enterprise models provides a common conceptual framework in this nascent field. Social enterprise models impart prototypes for replication, inspire creative approaches for value generation, inform design by establishing operational blueprints, and motivate new methodologies for not-for-profit mission accomplishment.

The emergence of the social enterprise is often attributed to shifting stakeholder expectations of not-for-profit organizations to achieve larger-scale social impact while also diversifying their funding (Reis 1999). In recent times, not-for-profits have come under heavy scrutiny. Pressure is on for these organizations to professionalize their services, increase social impact, and be accountable for results. Furthermore, support from traditional, philanthropic, and government sources is declining, and competition for available funds is increasing. Concurrently, with more not-for-profits to choose from and scarce resources, funders are becoming savvier about treating grants as social investments for which they expect a quantifiable return. Thus, not-for-profit market forces are galvanizing practitioners to explore alternative financing approaches, and more effective programming methods. Not-for-profit leaders understand that to be competitive they must render high quality services to clients as well as realize significant social returns. They also recognize that their organizations' survival rests on the ability to augment or replace grants by other means. Attaining these ends has required not-for-profit practitioners to shift from traditional approaches to new paradigms. In a word, necessity spurred the invention of the social enterprise.

The result has been stronger, more innovative, and entrepreneurial not-for-profit organizations. The integration of business tools and practices within not-for-profits builds organizational capacity that can improve performance and increase their ability to effect lasting change. The social enterprise paradigm also provides not-for-profits with a mechanism to deepen their social impact. Organizations can strengthen, expand, or enhance their missions by creating more meaningful social impact, by reaching new client markets, or by diversifying their social services. In addition, social enterprise provides not-for-profit leaders with an institutional framework for establishing an independent means of financing. Income earned and financial leveraging through business-oriented resource management enables practitioners to make new programme-related investments and ensure that their organizations will be ongoing concerns.

Mission and Money Relationships

The crux of the individual social enterprise lies in the specifics of its dual objectives—depth and breadth of social impact to be realized, and amount of money to be earned. Mission drives social value creation, which is generated through not-for-profit programmes. Financial need and market opportunities drive economic value creation, which is delivered through business models. As a result, money and mission are intertwined like DNA in the social enterprise, yet they are not always equal partners. Although all social enterprises create both types of value, the decision to pursue a social enterprise is generally motivated by either the monetary gain or the programme benefit it renders the not-for-profit parent organization. The purpose of a social enterprise is defined by the emphasis and priority given to its financial and social object-ives. Purpose also determines whether a practitioner engages in social enter-prise as a programme strategy or a financial strategy.

From a programme perspective, social enterprise addresses one of the most pressing issues not-for-profit organizations face—how to achieve sustainable impact. In organizations where high compatibility between business and social mission exists, social enterprise is a natural programme fit. For example, programme activities of economic development organizations revolve around work and wealth creation, an obvious business–social interrelationship. The missions and objectives of social welfare organizations focused on employ-ment development or welfare-to-work transitioning also mesh neatly with a social enterprise programme methodology. Agricultural organizations offer ample opportunities to marry sustainable crop cultivation programmes with social enterprises that process food and sell Fair Trade coffee and cocoa. In these cases, the social enterprises are central to the organization's mission and function as a self-funding programme strategy, accomplishing mission goals while simultaneously increasing financial self-sufficiency.

Opportunities to utilize a social enterprise approach for programme execu-tion are less evident in some organizations. Here, social enterprise is a com-plimentary activity that augments the organization's mission and programmes while generating income, but does not operate integrally as a social programme. For example, an arts and culture not for-profit may com-mercialize its products (i.e. sell art) to the benefit of its organization and artist clients, yet its mission and corresponding programmes are aimed at the cultural preservation of traditional crafts An environmental organization concerned with reforestation may launch an eco-tourism enterprise to earn supplemental income while also educating the public about conservation and employing community members in alternative, low environmental-impact jobs. Therefore, clear mission-related benefits realized by this enterprise also enlarge the organization's mission, and subsequently its activities beyond reforestation. Where the social enterprise is not a seamless match with an organization's mission, the impetus to begin a social enterprise might be financially motivated, nevertheless the social enterprise can serve to enhance or expand the organization's social programmes and strengthen its mission. In these cases, social enterprise's activities are related to the mission, but are employed as a funding strategy, which at once earns income to finance social programmes and augments the mission.

The third group is organizations where no logical programmatic opportun-ity exists for employing a social enterprise. In this category, organizations incorporate social enterprises as an auxiliary activity without concern for social benefit. In these instances, social enterprises are often unrelated to the mission and are employed solely as a funding strategy.

Although many not-for-profits pursue social enterprise as an instrument to achieve self-sufficiency through earned income, social enterprises' financial purposes differ among organizations. The financial objective of a social enterprise is *not* by default profit—generating net revenue to provide funding to the parent organization—or even viability—breakeven to cover social programme costs. Social enterprises do not need to be profitable to be worthwhile. They can improve the efficiency and effectiveness of an organization by (Dees 1998):

1. Reducing the need for donated funds
2. Providing a more reliable, diversified funding base, or
3. Enhancing the quality of programmes by increasing market discipline.

For many not-for-profits, social enterprise is a strategy to diversify their funding base, decrease reliance on donors, and recover programme costs or subsidize social programmes. The social enterprise is a means to reduce programme deficits and employ resources more efficiently. Organizations seeking to diversify income may set modest financial objectives by for-profit standards. For example, a programme previously 100 per cent grant-funded that covers 40 per cent of its costs with earned income could be considered a success for many not-for-profit organizations. Organizations using social enterprise to diversify income are more apt to practise mission-centred models.

Financial self-sufficiency is achieved by generating adequate income to cover an organization's operating and social programmes costs without continued reliance on donor funding. This is no easy task, as it requires that organizations run lucrative businesses, often in addition to their not-for-profit programmes. Organizations seeking to achieve full financial self-sufficiency will opt for non-mission-oriented social enterprises that offer the greatest profit-making potential over less productive enterprises geared towards achieving social benefit.

Other organizations engage in social enterprise as a means to make best use of their resources and to reduce costs. Financial objectives are tied to programme objectives. Sharing back office functions, streamlining systems, and increasing operational efficiencies to improve performance achieve cost savings. Leveraging not-for-profit assets to generate income optimizes resources. Tangible assets—facilities, equipment—or intangible assets—methodology, relationships, goodwill, and expertise—provide the basis of the social enterprise. Unrestricted income enables the organization to reimburse programme costs and make internal investments in hard-to-fund projects such as pilot programmes or overheads.

Despite the social enterprise's purpose, social mission remains the cornerstone of the not-for-profit parent organization and central to its ethos and activities. As value creation properties are intertwined in the social enterprise, purpose and mission are inextricably linked. The interrelationship between business activities and social programmes is dictated by the social enterprise's

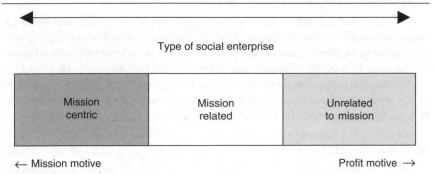

Figure 10.1 Social enterprise type by mission orientation

purpose and relevance to the parent organization's mission. Therefore, a system of classification based around 'mission orientation' provides one determinant of social enterprise type (Figure 10.1).

In the mission-centric social enterprise business activities are central to the parent organization's social mission. These social enterprises are created for the express purpose of advancing the mission using a self-financing model (Box 10.1).

BOX 10.1 MISSION CENTRIC SOCIAL ENTERPRISE EXAMPLE

The mission of Association Paysan (this organization's name has been changed to preserve anonymity) in rural Haiti is 'to establish at the community level cooperative enterprises that allow the peasants to advance economically'. Association Paysan's mission is the foundation of its social programmes, guiding decisions ranging from which industries to enter to how to design its business models. Association Paysan uses social enterprise as strategy to create economic opportunities for its clients—Haitian peasants—by creating jobs, opening markets, and supporting self-employment. Clients benefit from Association Paysan's social enterprises in four ways, as employees, business owners, customers, and community members. The enterprises also achieve impact by mitigating another critical social problem clients face: food insecurity.

In central Haiti, where food supplies are unreliable, little sustainable farming knowledge exists and peasants lack access to agricultural inputs; so people often go hungry. To address this problem and accomplish its mission, Association Paysan began three mission-centric cooperative enterprises: a bakery that makes and sells traditional Haitian flat bread; a store that sells agricultural and farm inputs; and a farm. The bakery provides twenty-four jobs for Association Paysan's clients and a reliable supply of food to the community. The store promotes sustainable cultivation and food production and, hence, fosters self-employment (farming) as well as creating jobs. The third business, a 50-acre farm, grows produce and animal feed, and raises livestock, also providing food to the local population and over 100 jobs. In sum, Association Paysan's three businesses create nearly 200 jobs for local peasants and supply essential goods and services to the community. Financially, the social enterprises are self-sufficient, not only covering their own costs but also earning a surplus that Association Paysan uses to subsidize its literacy, advocacy, micro-loans, and agricultural education programmes.

209

In the mission-related social enterprise business activities are related to the organization's mission or social services. Mission-related social enterprises have synergistic properties, creating social value for programmes and generating income to subsidize programme costs or operating expenses (Box 10.2).

Commercialization of social services is a common form of mission-related social enterprise. One example is a family services organization that provides free meals to the children of low-income families enrolled in the organization's day care programmes. By utilizing its industrial kitchen, staff dietitian, and cooks, the organization starts a catering business serving the 'social institutional' market segment—schools, day care centres, hospitals, senior service organizations—that are willing and able to pay for this service.

Mission expansion is another type of mission-related social enterprise. An example is a women's economic development organization that supports self-employed single mothers through small business consulting services. The organization expands its mission by opening a sliding-scale fee-based childcare social enterprise to enable clients more time to focus on their business

---

BOX 10.2 MISSION RELATED SOCIAL ENTERPRISE EXAMPLE

IONA Senior Services is an example of a not-for-profit organization that launched a mission-related social enterprise, Essential Eldercare. IONA is 'dedicated to enabling older people to live with dignity and independence. Through its professional staff, corps of volunteers, and close collaboration with other organizations, IONA provides services and access to programmes designed to meet the needs of seniors and their families'. IONA accomplishes its mission by providing free and subsidized eldercare services to low income elderly residents of Washington, DC, which includes adult day care, fitness, computer classes, recreational activities, counselling, meals, etc.

IONA commercialized its social services to start Essential Eldercare, a premier eldercare social enterprise, as a means to generate income to support the organization's programme activities. Essential Eldercare sells premium eldercare services to middle- and high-income seniors in the greater Washington Metro area. Although there are marginal differences between the types of eldercare services rendered by IONA and Essential Eldercare, the main difference is the markets they serve, thus Essential Eldercare social enterprise's activities are related to IONA's mission. It is important to note that IONA's mission does not dictate the economic status of the seniors it serves. Therefore, by expanding eldercare services into an affluent market, IONA is able to reach a greater number of seniors and increase its social impact.

Essential Eldercare is structured as a profit centre within its not-for-profit parent organization, IONA. Assets and synergies are leveraged across the not-for-profit and social enterprise. For example, it charges social workers and eldercare specialists either to social services (IONA) or Essential Eldercare based on the client and it also shares back office functions, such as reception, intake, and accounting and their related expenses. Essential Eldercare benefits from IONA's location, superb facility, name recognition, and stellar reputation to sell its products. The programme and financial inter-relationship between IONA and Essential Eldercare is evidenced in the latter's mission 'to provide families premium quality eldercare services with compassion and integrity. By meeting the needs of an affluent target market, Essential Eldercare will generate excess revenue and capacity to serve more economically and socially disadvantaged frail seniors'.

BOX 10.3 SOCIAL ENTERPRISE UNRELATED TO MISSION EXAMPLE

Save the Children is a not-for-profit dedicated to 'creating real and lasting change for children in need'. In addition to traditional not-for-profit fundraising activities and child sponsorship, Save the Children has established a corporate licensing social enterprise. Licensing relationships are sought with companies in consumer products industries, based on the mutually beneficial goal of increased profit for companies and a significant and steady income stream for Save the Children's work worldwide. Licensees use Save the Children's name and logo. Enclosed with each licensed item is a tag that describes the organization's mission and work. Corporate partners benefit from Save the Children's reputation to boost their image and to attract socially conscious consumers. The first licensing agreement in 1992 was for an exclusive line of neckties featuring original artwork created by children. Since, Save the Children has developed licensing agreements with some thirty companies representing a wide range of products distributed through major retailers and broadcast shopping channels.

Although unrelated to Save the Children's programmes concerning children's education, health, economic security, and physical safety, the licensing social enterprise generates a significant amount of unrestricted revenue ($4.5 [£2.6] million in 2003) and represents millions of dollars in marketing value for the organization.

The social enterprise unrelated to mission is not intended to advance the mission other than by generating income for the organization's social programmes and operating costs. Business activities may have a social bent, add marketing or branding value, operate in an industry related to the not-for-profit parent organization's services or sector, but the profit potential is the motivation for creating a social enterprise unrelated to mission (Box 10.3).

Social Enterprise Models

Social enterprises are designed to accomplish their social and economic value creation objectives. The design process typically begins with a vision for the social enterprise that articulates its purpose in accordance with the not-for-profit's mission. Ideas for how the social enterprise will create value are conceptualized, and then modelled. Often a market study is used to analyze internal and external factors that can inform operational aspects of the model design, these may include: market forces, investment capital, available assets, opportunities and threats, ease of implementation, profit potential, organizational strengths and weaknesses, client needs and capabilities, legal environment, and so on. All social enterprise models fit into the three main archetypal categories noted earlier according to the level of integration between their social programmes and business activities: embedded, integrated, and external.

Embedded Social Enterprise

In the embedded social enterprise business activities and social programmes are synonymous. The enterprise activities are 'embedded' within the organization's operations and social programmes. Practitioners create embedded social enterprises to accomplish their organization's mission. The not-for-profit target population (client) is a recipient of the enterprise, either as the target market, a direct beneficiary, owner, or employee. Social programmes are self-financed through enterprise revenues and thus, the embedded social enterprise can also be a sustainable programme strategy. The relationship between business activities and the social programmes is comprehensive, achieving financial and social benefits simultaneously (Figure 10.2).

Integrated Social Enterprises

In integrated social enterprises social programmes overlap with business activities, often sharing costs, assets, and programme attributes. The enterprise activities are 'integrated' with the organization's operations. Not-for-profits create integrated social enterprises as funding mechanisms to support their operations and social activities; and/or as vehicles to expand or enhance the organization's mission. The latter may be achieved by commercializing social services to new fee-paying markets or by providing new services to existing clients. In integrated social enterprises, the not-for-profit client benefits from investments made in social programmes vis-à-vis earned income, but may or may not be involved in the enterprise's operations. This type of social enterprise often leverages organizational assets, such as expertise, content, relationships, brand, or infrastructure as the foundation for its business. The relationship between the business activities and the social programmes is synergistic, adding value—financial and social—to one another (Figure 10.3).

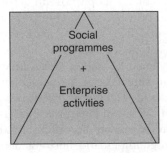

Figure 10.2 Embedded social enterprise.

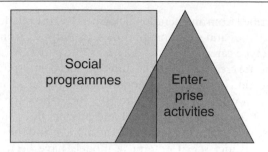

Figure 10.3 Integrated social enterprise

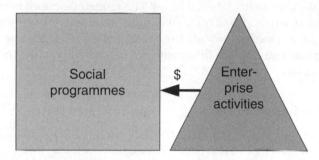

Figure 10.4 External social enterprise

External Social Enterprises

In external social enterprises social programmes are distinct from business activities. The enterprise activities are 'external' from the organization's operations and programmes. Not-for-profit organizations create external social enterprises to fund their social programmes and/or operating costs. Mission relevance and the pursuit of social benefit are not prerequisites of business activities. The not-for-profit client is an indirect beneficiary of revenue and rarely involved in any operational aspect of the external social enterprise. These social enterprises may or may not benefit from leveraging, cost sharing or programme synergies, therefore, to serve their purpose, they must be profitable. The relationship between the business activities and social programmes is supportive, providing unrestricted funding to the not-for-profit parent organization (Figure 10.4).

Operational Models

Seven distinct operational prototypes of social enterprise evidenced and emulated by practitioners around the globe have been identified using a 'practice-to-theory approach'. The characteristics of each social enterprise

213

model are described from an operational perspective: the relationship between its business activities and social programmes, its purpose, its mission orientation, and archetype category. Model diagrams illustrate how social value and economic value are created within the different social enterprise models. Additionally, this section describes how models can be combined and enhanced to achieve maximum value creation. Figure 10.5 shows how the symbols can be used to interpret the diagrams' financial and product flows in relation to the social enterprise, the parent organization, the market, and the clients.

Inasmuch as distinct social enterprise models have been identified, it is equally important to recognize that the field is immature and many innovative examples defy neatly labelled boxes. The models described below are not intended to straitjacket practitioners into a prescribed set of formulas, but rather to guide readers through the social enterprise landscape and help them recognize and embrace the abundance of possibility under the umbrella of a larger vision.

Entrepreneur Support Model

The entrepreneur support model of social enterprise sells business support and financial services to its target population—self-employed individuals or small firms—who then sell their products and services in the open market. The entrepreneur support model is an *embedded* model; the social programme is the business, its mission centres on facilitating the financial security of its clients by supporting their entrepreneurial activities. The social enterprise achieves financial self-sufficiency through the sales of services to its clients and uses this income to cover costs associated with delivering these services as well as operating expenses. In cases where surpluses are generated, the

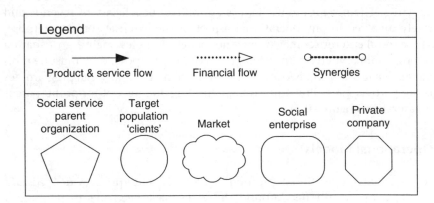

Figure 10.5 Legend for interpreting social enterprise diagrams

Figure 10.6 Entrepreneur support model

entrepreneur support model may use this money to underwrite auxiliary social services for clients such as health education, insurance, etc. (Figure 10.6).

The strengths of the entrepreneurial support model lie in its ability to reach large numbers of clients, and its potential to realize the sustainability inherent in its self-financing model. The mission-centric nature of this social enterprise also serves to guard against losing mission focus. These features have contributed to the success and allure of microfinance, the quintessential social enterprise, which provides financial services to poor entrepreneurs. Though the entrepreneurial support model meets several key objectives, its application is narrow and limited to economic development or programmes that support employment and entrepreneurship. The clients, most often poor or disadvantaged people, are also the paying customers, therefore viability is difficult to achieve without scale.

Economic development organizations, including microfinance institutions, small and medium sized enterprises, and business development programmes, use the entrepreneur support model. Common types of businesses these organizations run are: financial institutions, management consultancies, other professional services, technology, and product firms that support entrepreneurs (Box 10.4).

BOX 10.4 ENTREPRENEUR SUPPORT MODEL EXAMPLE

Pro Mujer, an international women's development organization, was founded in 1990 to empower women to improve their social and economic status. The organization accomplishes its mission by establishing microfinance institutions that provide small working capital loans ($50–$300; £29–£174) to low-income women who invest the capital in productive activities such as retail trading or small-scale production, then sell their products in the open marketplace. Due to the perceived risk and high transaction costs to serve Pro Mujer's target population, these poor women have no access to credit and saving services from formal financial institutions, and are consequently easy targets of money lenders' usury practices. Training in business development and management augments Pro Mujer's financial services by helping women to improve their small businesses and increase their incomes to ensure economic security for themselves and their families. Pro Mujer also provides health education, and connects women and their families to health services.

(Continued)

BOX 10.4   (CONTINUED)

Pro Mujer operates in four countries: Bolivia, Nicaragua, Peru, and Mexico. As of March 2005, the organization provided training and credit to over 100,000 clients, 98 per cent of whom are low-income women, and had a total loan portfolio of $6.5 million (£3.8 million), with less than 1 per cent arrears. The organization's financial model is similar to a bank's, interest is charged on each loan and savings deposits are leveraged for on-lending. The interest spread over significant volume creates a financially sustainable entrepreneur support model (i.e. a microfinance institution): income covers operating and financial costs and loan loss. Factoring in operational and capital costs, regulations, and competitors' prices sets interest rates. Because its clients are so poor, Pro Mujer's goal is to provide financial services as inexpensively as possible without compromising its viability.

The results of an impact evaluation demonstrated that Pro Mujer's clients are able to double their income after two years in the programme. They are also more likely to seek health care for themselves and their children. Moreover, clients tend to increase their community leadership and participation and expand their decision-making abilities. In addition, three of the four of Pro Mujer's microfinance institutions are self-sufficient and have received several awards for the transparency of their financial management.

Market Intermediary Model

The market intermediary model of social enterprise provides product development, market access, and credit services to its target population: small producers (individuals, firms, or cooperatives). The market intermediary model is an *embedded* model: the social programme is the business. Its mission focuses on facilitating clients' financial security by helping them develop and sell their products in high-value markets. The social enterprise purchases the client-made products at fair prices, and then sells the products at a margin. Commissions or mark-up charged on client-made products provides income to the enterprise that is used to pay operating expenses and programme costs (Figure 10. 7).

The advantages of the market intermediary model are similar to the entrepreneur support model concerning its potential for scalability, social impact, mission strengthening, and self-financing. Its application is limited to producers, and difficulties can arise in finding markets for client-made products due

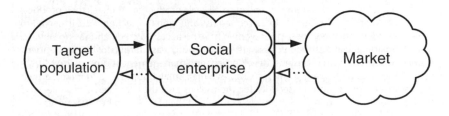

Figure 10.7 Market intermediary model

BOX 10.5 MARKET INTERMEDIARY MODEL EXAMPLE

The Aetas indigenous people of Luzon in the Philippines once lived simply on abundant fish and wildlife and subsistence farming. The plight of these poor mountain people began when a volcano on Mount Pinatubo erupted in the early 1990s and buried their community and its natural resources under volcanic ash and stone. Threatened with starvation, many Aetas migrated to cities to find jobs. Unskilled, poorly educated, and lacking urban savvy, they were exploited for labour and left to live in squalor. Those that stayed stripped the mountain of its few remaining natural resources to survive. Meanwhile, entrepreneurs in Manila discovered the benefits of the acres and acres of stone and rock left behind by the volcano—pumice, which is used in garment factories to produce 'stone washed' denim fashions.

With help from the Asian Institute for Technology, the Aeta people formed a marketing social enterprise to gather, market, and sell the stones to the thousands of garment makers in the Philippines. The marketing cooperative commercializes the informal process of selling pumice to middlemen who pay the Aeta very low prices then realize large profits by selling products to the private sector. As a result of the social enterprise, the Aeta are able to earn a liveable, rather than a marginal income. This alternative livelihood encourages Aetas to say in their community while reducing their reliance on environmentally destructive activities.

---

to market saturation, poor or inconsistent quality, and commodity products. Frequently, quality requirements for marketable products cannot be supported through the market intermediary's decentralized production; thus, the social enterprise may sacrifice scale to serve clients, converting it into an employment model.

Marketing supply cooperatives—such as Fair Trade organizations, agriculture, and handicraft groups—use the market intermediary model of social enterprise. Common types of businesses they operate are marketing or consumer product firms and companies that sell processed foods or agricultural products (Box 10.5).

Employment Model

The employment model of social enterprise provides employment opportunities and job training to its target population: people with high barriers to employment—such as the disabled, homeless, at-risk youth, and ex-offenders—through enterprises that sell products or services in the open market. The employment model is an *embedded* model; the social programme is the business. Its mission centres on developing skills and employment opportunities for its clients. The type of business used in the employment model is predicated on the appropriateness of jobs it creates for clients as well as its commercial viability. Social services, such as soft skills training, physical therapy, mental health counselling, or transitional housing, are built into the enterprise model to provide a supportive working environment for clients. The social enterprise achieves financial self-sufficiency through the sales of its products and services. Income is used to pay

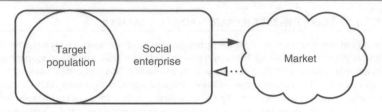

Figure 10.8 Employment model

standard operating expenses associated with the business, including paying liveable wages to clients, and additional social costs incurred by employing the target population (Figure 10.8).

The employment model may operate any business that meets its social and financial goals. Therefore, the organization is not burdened with designing an enterprise from scratch, but may benchmark similar existing businesses and apply industry standards. Modifications to the business model are social in nature such as 'job coaches', shortened working hours, modified workstations to accommodate physical needs, and are thus compatible with the not-for-profit's core competencies. The employment model is mission-centric, and renders direct client impact; however, this model is not scaleable due to the inverse relationship between employing clients and viability. Depending on the type of business, start-up costs and capitalization requirements can be high, barring many would-be practitioners from using this model. Employment enterprises must compete with the private sector while carrying additional social costs associated with employing clients, making marketplace survival a challenge.

The employment model is widely used by disabled-focused and youth organizations, as well as social service not-for-profits serving low-income women, recovering addicts, formerly homeless people, and welfare-to-work recipients. Popular types of employment businesses are: janitorial and landscape companies, cafes, bookstores, thrift shops, assembly work, bakeries, woodworking, and mechanical repair (Box 10.6).

BOX 10.6 EMPLOYMENT MODEL EXAMPLE

Cambodia's long history of war and devastation left a large number of disabled, disenfranchised, and displaced people who face barriers to employment. Many Cambodian women have few economic choices other than to enter the sex trade. The poor become trapped in low-income jobs because their families cannot afford to send them to school. Rural immigrants, who came to urban areas hoping to find a better life, wind up in squatter settlements scratching out a subsistence living picking through rubbish tips. Large numbers of Cambodians physically maimed or disabled in the war are completely marginalized from the workforce, a result of discrimination. The situation has created a huge surplus of labour in Cambodia, yet few institutions provide vocational training to help these people secure relevant jobs.

(Continued)

BOX 10.6 (CONTINUED)

Technology avails an opportunity for poor and marginalized people to start entry level jobs and gain high value workplace experience and marketable skills while earning a liveable wage. Digital Divided Data is a technology-based employment social enterprise that provides vocational training to disadvantaged people in Cambodia. Its clients are landmine victims, abused women, rural immigrants and orphans, and through Digital Divide Data they receive computer literacy and technology training to qualify for entry level and low-skilled jobs in the technology sector.

Digital Divide Data secures contracts for data entry work outsourced by universities and businesses, which provides paid on-the-job training in a supportive environment for its clients and generates income for its operating costs, including fair wages and social costs related to education and training. The combination of paid work experience and computer literacy, coupled with education, prepares clients for higher-paying skilled-work opportunities.

Fee-for-Service Model

The fee-for-service model of social enterprise commercializes its social services and then sells them either directly to the target population: individuals, firms, communities, or to a third party payer. The fee-for-service model is an *embedded* model; the social programme is the business. Its mission centres on rendering social services to clients in the sector in which it works. The social enterprise achieves financial self-sufficiency through fees charged for services. This income is used as a cost-recovery mechanism for the organization to pay service delivery and business expenses, such as marketing and accounting, associated with commercialization. Surpluses (net revenue) may be used to subsidize social programmes that do not have a built-in cost-recovery component (Figure 10.9).

The fee-for-service model's ease of implementation is its blessing and its curse. Charging for social services has long been cast as a not-for-profit cost-recovery vehicle, and does not require the mental leap to 'running a business' that many not-for-profit leaders abhor. As a result, many organizations treat fee-for-service as an income-generating activity rather than as a scaleable business. Even when operated as a business, many fee-for-service activities produce marginal financial benefits, failing to cover costs of the service, let alone subsidize the parent organization. Similarly to the entrepreneur support model, the target population frequently lacks money, and third party payers such as

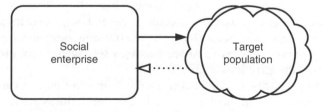

Figure 10.9 Fee-for-service model

BOX 10.7 FEE-FOR-SERVICE MODEL EXAMPLE

Fewer than 5 per cent of books are available for people with 'print disabilities'—the blind or learning disabled—posing a significant barrier to literacy. The only way for most people with print disabilities to enjoy books is to scan them into computers with adaptive technology capable of converting the text into speech or Braille formats. The Benetech Initiative, a Silicon Valley based not-for-profit organization that develops adaptive technology, saw this gap as an opportunity to launch its new social enterprise—Bookshare.org

Bookshare.org is a subscription service that provides an extensive online library of digital books for individuals with print disabilities; many of whom already use the computer-reading machine technology originally developed by Benetech. With a special exemption in US copyright laws, Bookshare.org is allowed to distribute its materials to US residents who have a visual impairment, learning disability, or mobility impairment. Bookshare.org enables thousands of people who scan books to share them, while eliminating duplication of efforts and producing accessible books much faster than other providers at a fraction of the cost. Subscribers download books using Bookshare.org's software in two formats: digital Braille or talking books. In less than three years from its 2002 launch, Bookshare.org already had more than 20,000 books available.

Bookshare.org uses a fee-for-service model. For individuals, a one-off fee of $25 (£14.50) is charged to register and then subscribers pay an annual subscription fee of $50 (£29). In 2004, Bookshare.org launched a group account service, Institutional Access, which enables a school or group to purchase a pre-set number of books to download and deliver directly to qualified students. Income generated from these fees covers the costs to continue expanding the book collection and provides new services to its users. Scale makes viability possible in Bookshare.org's business model. In 2002 membership was 628. This figure grew to over 2,000 in 2004, and Bookshare.org's membership continues to grow rapidly. Breakeven is expected with roughly 10,000 subscribers.

---

insurance companies that can offer viability are largely limited to industrialized countries or specific industries. The fee-for-service mission-centric nature is a plus, yet, when financially successful, this model can test the mission and create internal organizational strife. Then again, the potential application of the fee-for-service model is vast, transcending the not-for-profit sector. Membership organizations and trade associations, educational institutes, parks and recreational facilities, museums, hospitals, and clinics are typical examples of organizations that use this model (Box 10.7).

Service Subsidization Model

The service subsidization model of social enterprise sells products or services to an external market and uses the income it generates to fund its social programmes. The service subsidization is an *integrated* model: business activities and social programmes overlap, sharing costs, assets, operations, income, and often programme attributes (Figure 10.10).

Employed primarily as a financing mechanism—the business mandate is separate from the social mission—nonetheless the business activities are frequently mission-related, serving to enlarge or enhance the organization's

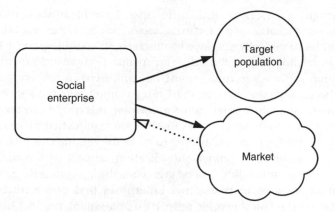

Figure 10.10 Service subsidization model.

mission. Not-for-profits that implement service subsidization social enterprises operate many different types of businesses; though most leverage assets as the basis of their enterprise activities. Commercialization of social services leads to enterprise activities that enhance the mission; whereas leveraging physical assets may result in an enterprise that is very different from the organization's social programmes. The enterprise benefits financially from leveraging and cost sharing and provides a stream of unrestricted revenue to subsidize or wholly fund the parent organization's social services.

BOX 10.8 SERVICE SUBSIDIZATION MODEL EXAMPLE

Associacao Nacional de Cooperacao Agricola (ANCA) works in areas of Brazil where illiteracy rates are as high as 80 per cent of the population. This education not-for-profit provides literacy training and educational services to children, adults, and community activists. While operating its programmes, ANCA recognized a gap in the education market for pertinent leadership and organizing resources for the community activists it serves. In response to this need, ANCA developed training and educational materials for labour movement leaders, and found there was high demand for these products outside their target population. ANCA saw an opportunity to sell its materials and generate supplemental income for its literacy programmes. ANCA created a social enterprise—Editora Expressao Popular (Popular Expression Press)—a publisher and clearinghouse for educational materials for not-for-profit leaders and community activists. Editora Expressao Popular sells periodicals, audiotapes, and publications within Brazil and export markets. The social enterprise enlarges ANCA's mission beyond teaching literacy to facilitating social change. Editora Expressao Popular is integrated into ANCA as a division of the organization. In 2002, the enterprise sold 7,000 books, up from 4,500 the year before. Income is used to cover start-up and operating costs of the press, and to subsidize programmes aimed at ANCA's clients overcoming illiteracy.

Source: Alter, K. (2003). *Social Enterprise: A Typology of the Field Contextualized in Latin America.* Inter-American Development Bank.

The strength of the service subsidization model is its broad application to not-for-profits—organization type, business, sector, or client does not bind it. The model can be strategically employed to increase its social impact by commercializing social programmes. But before an organization can implement a service subsidization social enterprise, it must be competent in rendering its social services, because the organization must run a venture over and above its social programmes. Even when programmes are strong, this model can tax staff and test the mission. Additionally, social subsidization requires that the organization has assets and earns significant income to make the venture worthwhile.

Common examples of service subsidization models that commercialize social service or intangible assets are: consulting, counselling, logistics, employment training, or marketing. Enterprises that utilize infrastructure and capital assets include: leasing, property management, product-based retail businesses, transportation, and copying and printing services (Box 10.8).

Market Linkage Model

The market linkage model of social enterprise facilitates trade relationships between the target population—small producers, local firms, and cooperatives—and an external market. The social enterprise functions as a broker connecting buyers to producers and vice versa, provides market information, and then charges fees for these services (Figure 10.11).

The market linkage model can be either embedded or integrated. If the enterprise's mission revolves around linking clients to markets, and its social programmes support this objective, the market linkage model is *embedded*; the social programme is the business. Income generated from enterprise activities is used to self-finance social programmes. On the other hand, commercializing an organization's social services or leveraging assets, such as trade relationships, also creates market linkage social enterprises and in this case, income is used to subsidize its other client services. In this second example, social programme and business activities overlap following the *integrated* model.

Unlike many social enterprise models, the market linkage customer is the financially attractive private sector, making viability readily attainable. Scalable impact also is achievable, though client scope is limited to producers.

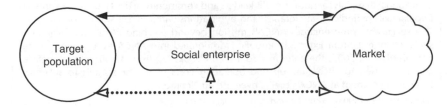

Figure 10.11 Market linkage model

BOX 10.9 MARKET LINKAGE MODEL EXAMPLE

In southern Africa, few economic opportunities exist for the rural poor, many of whom live on annual incomes below $100 (£58). An emphasis has been placed on cash-cropping for employment, though 65 per cent of the region is arid and agricultural cash crops are risky for vulnerable populations, often ecologically inappropriate, and financially unproductive. Employment alternatives residing in the $45 billion (£26.1 billion) global market for natural products have been largely inaccessible for rural African producers. These natural products, made from African plant species, have a multitude of applications: beverages; cosmetic oils; health care products; herbal teas; jams; nutritional supplements; and medicinal products. Because natural products are grown in the wild, rural producers can easily manage their collection and cultivation.

PhytoTrade Africa is a non-profit trade association that promotes sustainable production and Fair Trade, contributing to the economic development of southern Africa. Phyto-Trade's main aim is to develop business partnerships between rural producers and buyers—usually major European natural products companies. In doing so, the social enterprise links rural producers in seven southern African countries directly to source suppliers, buyers, quality control evaluators, and product development specialists. Additionally, it helps its clients secure export contracts and provides a clearinghouse for research and development information on African natural products.

In partnership with another not-for-profit, Southern African Marula Oil Producers Network (SAMOPN), PhytoTrade Africa embarked on a new venture designed to promote a biodiversity-friendly rural production system. Marula oil is derived from an indigenous plant species that is critical to the maintenance of the ecosystem in dryland areas. Commercialization of a range of new Marula products is projected to earn between 8,000 and 10,000 rural producers as much as $8–12 million (£4.6–7 million) per year, giving rural communities—otherwise faced with economic pressure to convert natural woodlands into arable cropland—incentives to invest in sustainable management of dryland ecosystems. SAMOPN helps rural producers with sustainable production and extraction of quality Marula oil, while PhytoTrade Africa facilitates market linkages and product commercialization.

The market linkage model offers easy integration opportunities for trade associations, network organizations, and cooperatives who may add import–export, market research, and buyer–broker services to its other activities. This model works best for organizations in developing countries connecting with Western companies. Trade is a relationship-driven industry, thus barriers to entry exist on the buyer side along with the normal hurdles of cultural misunderstanding between not-for-profit and private companies (Box 10.9).

Organizational Support Model

The organizational support model of social enterprise may incorporate virtually any type of business and sell its products and services to an external market, businesses, the public, or in some cases the not-for-profit client. The organizational support model is an *external* model; its business activities are separate from social programmes. Although the enterprise may have social

223

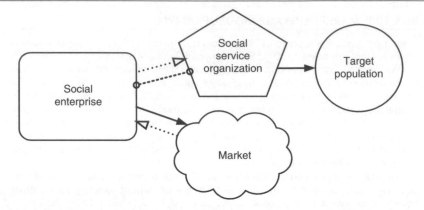

Figure 10.12 Organizational support model

attributes, the organizational support model is created as a funding mechanism to cover programme costs and operating expenses of the parent organization. Therefore, not-for-profits select business activities on their financial merits, and these are not necessarily related to mission (Figure 10.12).

Advantages of the organizational support model are similar to those of the service subsidization model; namely, wide application among not-for-profits and tremendous latitude regarding the type of business organizations operate. The main disadvantage of this model is that it is difficult for not-for-profits to implement. Successful organizational support models fund a significant portion

---

BOX 10.10 ORGANIZATIONAL SUPPORT MODEL EXAMPLE

In many rural areas in Guatemala, residents lack access to basic health services and medicine. Barriers include mountainous topography with few roads, poor distribution systems for health inputs, urban flight of medical professionals, and few sources of stable funding for rural health clinics. Para la Salud, a national health organization, started a chain of village pharmacies to address this problem. The pharmacy social enterprise was designed as a sustainable distribution model for health inputs in rural areas as well as a means to generate funds to subsidize rural clinics. Para la Salud orders medicines and supplies in bulk, which are first shipped to its headquarters in Guatemala City before being sent to rural pharmacies. Through educational campaigns that promote lower cost generic drugs, the organization has worked to counter the effects of brand marketing by large US pharmaceutical companies. Para la Salud's business model uses streamlined systems— centralized purchasing, inventory management, order fulfillment, and delivery—to lower the high costs associated with serving rural areas. The pharmacies have an average profit margin of 20 to 25 per cent, and profits are used to cover the costs of rural community health clinics. To date, Para la Salud's village pharmacy social enterprise enables a community to self-fund its local clinic without external subsidy in four to five years. Currently, Para la Salud operates forty-three village pharmacies serving poor communities in thirteen departments in Guatemala.

of the parent organization's budget, therefore, the enterprise must be highly profitable. Staff and mission challenges similar to the service subsidization model that exist in the organizational support model on a larger scale. This model is best executed by mature and business-savvy organizations (Box 10.10).

Combining Models

Social enterprises combine operational models to capture opportunities in both commercial markets and social sectors. Operational models are like building blocks that can be arranged best to achieve an organization's dual objectives. Models are combined to facilitate enterprise or social programme growth, to increase revenues by entering new markets or businesses, or to augment the breadth or depth of social impact by reaching more people in need or new target populations. Social enterprise model combinations occur within a social enterprise as a 'complex model' or at the level of the parent organization, a 'mixed model'.

Complex Model

A complex model of social enterprise combines any two or more operational models into one social enterprise. Models are combined to achieve the desired impacts and revenue objectives. Operational models that fall into integrated or external social enterprise categories may yield greater financial benefit, whereas embedded social enterprises offer higher social return. Complex models are vehicles to achieve sustainability equilibrium, particularly in cases where financial opportunity does not neatly mesh with social need. Combining models can also serve an organization's growth and diversification objectives, though the added complexity can stretch an organization if growth is not planned and managed carefully. Figure 10.13 illustrates a common example of a complex model: an employment model combined and an organizational support model.

Mixed Model

Many not-for-profit organizations run multi-unit (mixed) operations; each with different social programmes and financial objectives. Units within the mixed model may be related vis-à-vis their target population, social sector, mission, markets, or core competencies. Not-for-profits employing mixed models combine social and business entities to diversify their social services and capitalize on new business and social market opportunities. Like all social enterprises, mixed models come in a variety of forms depending on the organization's age, sector, social and financial objectives and opportunities (Figure 10.14).

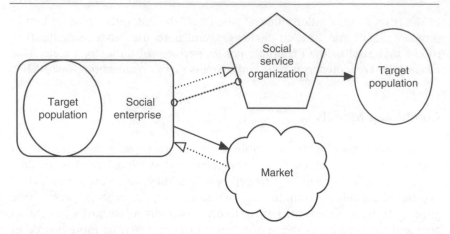

Figure 10.13 Complex model

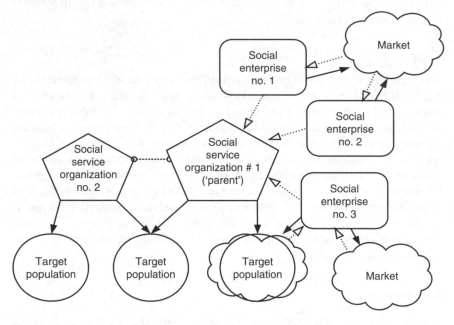

Figure 10.14 Mixed model

Mixed models are common among large multi-sector organizations that establish separate departments or subsidiaries for each technical area—i.e. education, health, economic development, etc.—and mature not-for-profits with established social enterprises. A museum, for example, in addition to educational art exhibits, might have both a for-profit catalogue business and

---

BOX 10.11 MIXED MODEL EXAMPLE

Health Access for All (the name, location, and details of this organization have been changed to preserve anonymity) is a New England based not-for-profit membership organization composed of public health service providers and clinics serving the uninsured and underinsured poor through three linked but separate entities. Health Access for All, the first entity and parent organization focuses on advocacy and lobbying to change legislation to strengthen the health safety net for disenfranchised and at-risk populations. The second entity, Public Health Management Service, is a not-for-profit subsidiary of Health Access for All that provides health care and management consulting services to member public health service providers and clinics. The third structure, Health Access Network, is a for-profit wholly owned subsidiary of Health Access for All. Health Access Network is a group purchasing business that buys bulk pharmaceuticals, office supplies, medical surgical supplies, and laboratory services at discounted, volume-based prices, then sells them to community clinics at a mark-up, but at substantially cheaper prices than retail.

Last year Health Access Network had total sales of $22,370,000 (£12,974,600), and after tax revenues of $1,651,566 (£957,908) for business growth and social investments in its not-for-profit parent. Of this amount, Health Access Network contributed $732,935 (£425,102) to its not-for-profit subsidiary, Public Health Management Service, and its parent organization, Health Access for All, to fund their advocacy and technical assistance activities and overhead. In the same year, purchasing discount medical and pharmaceutical supplies and services through Health Access Network saved community clinics a total of $9,827,307 (£5,699,838), allowing them to render more services to the uninsured and underinsured poor.

---

highly subsidized research and acquisition operation (Dees 1998). The diagram is representative of the complexity, not the conformity, of the social enterprise mixed model (Figure 10.14).

Enhancing Models

Franchise Model

The franchise model enhances social enterprises by addressing not-for-profit challenges of replication and scale. An organization franchises its 'proven social enterprise model', selling it to other not-for-profits to operate as their own business. Franchising helps the organization achieve economies of scale and with it viability or profit. As well, franchising enables mass replication, and thus, increased breadth of scale—geographical coverage—or depth of scale—volume of clients. Hence, the franchise model enhances scalability; social and economic value creation through replication. For example, a café that employs disabled people may be profitable only when it employs twelve or fewer disabled people. However, if franchised, the café social enterprise can create employment for hundreds of disabled people through numerous outlets (Figure 10.15).

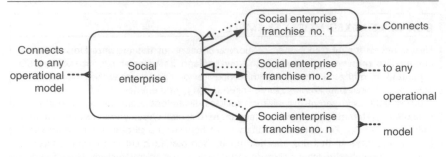

Figure 10.15 Franchise model

Purchasers pay franchise fees to receive the social enterprise model, methodology, and ongoing technical support from the franchiser. Buying a franchise enables a not-for-profit organization to focus on running operations of a proven enterprise, rather than worrying about what type of business to start, which products to sell, or what markets to enter. Becoming a franchiser creates a new social enterprise for the organization that leverages its industry and business expertise and, in turn, creates new social impact opportunities and another source of earned income. The franchise itself can be any successful and replicable social enterprise and may use any model listed (Box 10.12).

BOX 10.12 FRANCHISE MODEL EXAMPLE

In 1999, Accion Centro, a microfinance network organization in Latin America, sought to create a large-scale, sustainable training programme capable of replication. Historically, few training services targeting low-income microentrepreneurs are viable due to the low purchasing power of the target market, high costs to deliver training services, and the inability of these programmes to realize economies of scale. Training is often a lost leader for organizations, used as a marketing strategy to cross-sell other services, because the high development costs can rarely be recuperated from fees. This problem is exacerbated in a market where the paying customer has few financial resources and often opts for 'hands-on' learning in lieu of paid training. Seventy-five per cent of ACCION's market is poor and operate subsistence enterprises. Given the preference, most clients would spend money on a productive asset or credit before paying for training. Yet ACCION realized that the social need for training to help microentrepreneurs increase their business's productivity and income was enormous.

It seemed the impossible was needed: an efficient, low-cost distribution model and a market with money to purchase the training. Accion circumvented these market constraints by targeting institutions rather than individuals and by creating a franchise model to distribute its innovative training programme. The franchise, Diálogo de Gestiones (DdG), was a strategy to achieve objectives of scale and efficient delivery, as well as viable revenue model. DdG licenses ACCION's training programme for three years for a fee of $10,000 (£5,800). In exchange, the institution receives the rights to use the programme, as well as a 'training for trainers' course, a business plan, a system for evaluation, programme curricula updates, ongoing technical assistance, access to a franchisees' online

(Continued)

BOX 10.12 (CONTINUED)

community and virtual support services. Microfinance institutions were DdG's original target market: however, to diversify the risk and to meet unanticipated demand, DdG expanded its market and began selling franchises to NGOs, universities, chambers of commerce, and private businesses.

Results have been impressive. As of May 2003, Diálogo de Gestiones had 41 licensed franchisees selling the training programme in fourteen Latin American countries. DdG had trained more than 500 trainers: 81,430 microentrepreneurs, 69 per cent of whom were women and 20 per cent indigenous people. By October 2002, DdG had achieved 66 per cent operational self-sufficiency before R&D costs, and 52 per cent including R&D and production expenses (as of October 2002). In addition to franchise fees, residual income is earned on sales of course materials, profit margins average 22 per cent and are as high as 50 per cent in some countries.

Source: Alter, K. (2003). *Social Enterprise: A Typology of the Field Contextualized in Latin America.* Inter-American Development Bank.

Private-Not-for-Profit Partnership Model

The private-not-for-profit partnership model of social enterprise is a mutually beneficial business partnership or joint venture between a for-profit company and a not-for-profit organization. Relationships are forged on commercial grounds whereby each partner is contributor and recipient of the venture's success. The partnership enhances the not-for-profit social enterprise by increasing its viability, and its social impact, either directly by reaching more clients through its business model or indirectly by generating funds for its social programmes. The private sector partner benefits by improving goodwill and public image, increasing customer loyalty, lowering costs (labour or R&D), penetrating new markets, attracting more socially conscious consumers and so on, which subsequently translates into higher sales and more profit (Figure 10.16 and Box 10.13).

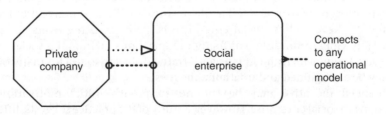

Figure 10.16 Private-not-for-profit partnership model

BOX 10.13 PRIVATE-NOT-FOR-PROFIT PARTNERSHIP MODEL EXAMPLE

Helados Bon is a large progressive ice cream company based in the Dominican Republic, whose interest in diversifying its ice cream led to the introduction of a new flavour—macadamia—and help for the country's ecology. A partnership was forged between Helados Bon and an environmental not-for-profit, Plan Sierra. The business idea leveraged each of the partners' knowledge and assets, marrying Helados Bon's ice cream industry expertise with Plan Sierra's conservation efforts. The social enterprise that emerged helps local farmers grow macadamia trees and reforest farmland through the sale of delicious ice cream. Macadamia trees, which are capable of growing to a height of over 500 metres on infertile land, are ideal for reforestation and conservation of natural resources. In the partnership, Plan Sierra manages and coordinates local farmers growing macadamia nuts that are used to make the new ice cream flavour; Helados operates the production and sale of the macadamia ice cream. The social enterprise earns one peso for each double macadamia ice cream sold to fund macadamia conservation efforts and local farmers gain a steady customer from their macadamia crops. Helados Bon also disseminates information about conservation and the importance of growing macadamia to its customers. Plan Sierra uses the revenue generated by the social enterprise to promote and develop its macadamia programme. The partnership has been a winning proposition for all of those involved: Helados Bon increased its sales; Plan Sierra achieved the reforestation of more than 140,000 hectares with macadamia trees; and farmers benefited with higher paying jobs and marketable crops.

Source: Alter, K. (2003). *Social Enterprise: A Typology of the Field Contextualized in Latin America.* Inter-American Development Bank.

New Paradigms for Social Entrepreneurship

Inasmuch as the early years of social entrepreneurship have been marked by practitioner innovation, they have been equally marred by false promise. This chapter demonstrates that in practice most social enterprise operational models relate to the mission of their not-for-profit parent. Model mechanics show that business activities can serve to strengthen or augment an organization's mission and social activities. Even so, much of social enterprise's potential as a tool for mission accomplishment and social impact is being eclipsed by its lure as a funding vehicle.

Who has not been seduced at one time or another by the promise of 'easy money'? At a time when the funding pie is no longer growing, but competition for a piece is, not-for-profits feel acute pressure to find alternative methods of financing. Nevertheless, social enterprise is, perhaps, being oversold as the new Holy Grail of funding. For many organizations taking on a social enterprise as a funding instrument is a valid strategic objective, still for many others it may be a misguided and unattainable quest.

Financial incentive may be the not-for-profit's initial motivation for engaging in social enterprise. However, a study of the practice suggests different objectives. A 2002 survey (WB&A Market Research 2002) of social enterprises revealed that 78 per cent were mission-centric, and 16 per cent mission-related, whereas only 3 per cent were unrelated to mission.

Moreover, of the five most critical social enterprise impacts cited by practitioners, only one focused on money. The most significant impact was the entrepreneurial culture that a social enterprise brought to its parent organization, followed by self-sufficiency, and third, the ability to attract and retain staff. For the practitioner social programming is already difficult enough, but what not-for-profit leaders do not always realize is that running a business is even harder. The more a social enterprise's economic value creation properties are disaggregated from its social value creation properties, the more difficult implementing a social enterprise can become.

The not-for-profit *raison d'être* is social change. Social impact is the practitioner's motivation for doing their work, obtaining money is only motivating in that it is a necessary means to finance social ends. The issue is less of perpetuating a money myth than it is missing a mission opportunity. One author warns that a social enterprise is worthwhile only if it is an efficient way to serve or support the organization's mission performance (Dees 2004).

Though funding is an essential element of the social enterprise, as a value proposition it does not go far enough. Both literature and practice suggest that social enterprises achieve success when they are executed first to achieve mission and second to earn income. A social enterprise's true promise as well as its future lies in its potential as a methodology for not-for-profit mission accomplishment and organizational strengthening—in its ability to achieve sustainable social impact through its dual value creation properties.

The beauty of social entrepreneurship is that commuting business practices to effect social change offers so much more possibility than just money. New paradigms should stress mission as the cornerstone of the social enterprise, and focus on operational models that maximize social impact. Indeed, social entrepreneurship should kick-the-box-out farther to include cultural transformation and capacity building as additional not-for-profit benefits. These paradigms should encompass concrete strategies and tools to employ social enterprise as a methodology for practitioners to do what they do but better—help them innovate, increase impact and effectiveness, and improve performance. In the advent of these new paradigms old social enterprise models will evolve and new ones will emerge.

Note

1. Many of the social enterprise models in this chapter are drawn from or inspired by a monograph, *Social Enterprise: A Typology of the Field Contextualized in Latin America* (September 2003), commissioned by the Inter-American Development Bank to commemorate twenty-five years of innovation through their Small Projects Fund and

Social Entrepreneurship Programme (SEP). The Inter-American Development Bank must be recognized for the contributions that made this chapter possible.

References

Dees, J. G. (January–February, 1998). 'Enterprising Nonprofits', *Harvard Business Review*, 76(1): 54–67.

——(2004). 'Putting Not-for-profit Business Ventures into Perspective', in S. Oster, C. Massarsky, and S. Beinhacker (2004). *Generating and Sustaining Nonprofit Earned Income*. San Francisco, CA: Jossey-Bass, pp. 3–18.

Reis, T. (1999). *Unleashing New Resources and Entrepreneurship for the Common Good: A Scan, Synthesis, and Scenario for Action*. W.K. Kellogg Foundation.

WB&A Market Research (2002). *Powering Social Change: Lessons for Community Wealth Generation for Not-for-profit Sustainability*. Community Wealth Ventures.

11

The Socially Entrepreneurial City

Charles Leadbeater

Introduction

Rodrigo Muscolevy is tired. For eight hours he has been tramping the streets of Curitiba, a city in central Brazil, pulling his makeshift, light green, handmade cart called *Interprise II* behind him, collecting rubbish to be recycled. On a good day, after two or three outings, Rodrigo can collect enough to earn £5 when he delivers his load to the recycling centre. Today his cart is full with 80 kg of plastic, glass, and metal and he should earn about £2.50. Rodrigo is one of a small army of recycling entrepreneurs created by a remarkable example of mass social innovation orchestrated by Curitiba's city council, one of the most innovative public authorities in the world (see Hawken, Lovins, and Lovins 2001; www.curitiba.pr.gov.br). The way Curitiba council has organized this process of mass social innovation should give us pause to think about how we understand social entrepreneurship (see Leadbeater 1997; Dees 1998; Johnson 2000; Bornstein 2004).

Curitiba has not innovated a stand-alone service or product but an entire system for producing a public good: a cleaner, more environmentally sustainable city. In doing so it has helped to create social value: everyone in the city benefits from what has been done, even though some people like Rodrigo also take away some private value in the form of their earnings. Curitiba council has acted as a 'systemic social entrepreneur', charting the emergence of an entirely new system for dealing with waste which has brought together many different players: waste collectors; households who sort through their rubbish; the recycling centre to which the rubbish goes; and the council refuse service. The council did not develop its own discrete solution that it delivered to the city. Instead it orchestrated a process of bottom-up social change where much of the solution emerged from within the city itself. To achieve this kind of systemwide change, Curitiba has had to adopt a highly networked form of civic organization, working to achieve its goals through a distributed network of players, including microentrepreneurs such as Rodrigo. In this chapter

I will use the example of Curitiba to explore the connections between three ideas: system-level social entrepreneurship; networked forms of organization; bottom-up social change. The argument is simple: innovating at the level of entire systems often entails orchestrating networks of players and, thus, enabling bottom-up social change (for commentary on the relationships between different forms of organization and different types of innovation see, e.g. Nelson and Winter 1977; Gawer and Cusumano 2002; Chesbrough 2003). This is the 'worm's eye view' approach to strategy employed by Grameen Bank and others.

Such an approach helps to highlight some differences between social and business entrepreneurship. Entrepreneurs in the private sector typically succeed by creating superior products and services that attract customers and make higher profits. Social entrepreneurs aim to create social value and bring about social change usually by helping people who often cannot afford market-based solutions to their needs in health, education, and welfare. Social change is not something that can be delivered in the way that a pizza company brings food to your door. Social entrepreneurs seeking systemwide change often need to work through networks that mobilize a mass of microchanges in society.

The Curitiba waste recycling initiative is a prime example of this. Rodrigo does not collect litter from the side of the street but from plastic shopping bags neatly placed on elevated stands outside most houses in the city. People leave out items for recycling—plastic, paper, metal (rubbish that is not rubbish to the people of this city)—twice a week when the city's big green recycling trucks are due to come by. But the council has organized for its large trucks to collect rubbish that is not rubbish late in the afternoon, giving entrepreneurs like Rodrigo a good eight hours to collect the rubbish first. As a result, Curitiba is crawling with thousands of men and boys pulling handmade carts collecting rubbish that is not rubbish. The city gets its rubbish collected at much lower cost to the taxpayer because they need far fewer big green trucks. The population gets a better service. The city's population gets a cleaner environment. Indeed, Curitiba recycles far more rubbish that comparable cities in Europe and the USA as well. Furthermore, about 30 per cent of the city's rubbish is recycled at a centre that mainly employs reformed alcoholics and drug addicts, and young men recently arrived from the countryside looking for work can find a way to make a living as recyclers. As the city grows and generates more rubbish, so does the population of rubbish collectors. Supply rises with demand, far more flexibly than if the council was in charge of planning a centrally organized service. The system as a whole is a prime example of mass social innovation. The system would not exist without the leadership of the council that created the recycling centre, provides incentives for recycling, and promotes the scheme. Yet what makes it all work are the mass of micro-entrepreneurs who collect most of the rubbish and the householders who have collectively changed their behaviour. Between them, they have created a self-organizing solution within a framework provided by the council (see further Johnson 2002).

Structured Self-organization

Curitiba's challenge, like many cities in the developing world, is to encourage order to emerge from the ever-present threat of chaos. Between 1970 and 2004, Curitiba's population grew from 300,000 to more than 2 million. Each year between 20,000 and 30,000 people come to the city from the countryside looking for a better life. Often they have no education, trade, skills, place to live, or sense of what it means to be a citizen of a city. All over town, but particularly along the riverbanks and under power lines, migrants throw up shanty towns that grow quickly as word spreads that a new area of land has been taken over. It takes just a few weeks for a field to become a 'favella' housing thousands of people. Favella are breeding grounds for poor education and bad health, protection rackets, and exploitation. The city council was not prepared to allow that to happen. Pure self-organizing solutions—the shanty-towns—are, in this case, clearly sub-optimal. But top-down, state-delivered solutions also have serious failings.

Curitiba's solution has been structured self-organization. It provides public leadership to encourage people to devise self-organizing solutions: top-down rules, incentives, and tools to allow massive bottom-up innovation. The most striking example of this philosophy in action is Cujaru, a former squatter encampment, on the city's edge which houses 120,000 people on land that was pasture in 1990. As the Cujaru settlement grew, the city got a loan from the Inter American Development Bank to replace the favella's shacks with permanent houses. The Bank stipulated that the council had to contract with a registered builder to build the new homes. Pretty soon builders were throwing up standardized, low-rise, housing units that looked rather like army barracks. The city council called a halt and went back to the Bank with a proposal for a structured, but self-organizing solution. The contractor's houses cost $10,000 (£5,800) per unit. The council argued that if people were allowed to build their own houses, employing their own labour—often family and friends—the cost would be about $3,000 (£1,740). Instead of the area being blanketed by one-size-fits-all, barrack-style housing, Cujaru would have a variety of architectural styles. The council also pointed out that people who built their own homes would look after them and their neighbourhood. If something went wrong with the plumbing, for example, the householders would fix it themselves rather than turning to the council to provide a solution. If the council were the landlord, it would have to employ a large housing maintenance department to carry out the work. Eventually, the council persuaded the Bank that its approach would be far more cost-effective: people would be participants in the process rather than recipients of a top-down service. In the first four months of the revised scheme 10,000 homes were self-built and Cujaru is now a thriving, stable community of more than 120,000 homeowners. Chaotic and unstructured self-organization—the favella—would have created huge problems in terms of health, education, and crime. The traditional top-down solution would have created a landscape of barrack blocks, detested by the residents and maintained at great cost by a reluctant council. Structured self-organization—a well-designed, mass, self-organized solution—trumped both.

Curitiba has practised networked, system-level social entrepreneurship since the mid-1970s. Cassio Taniguchi, who was central to Curitiba's strategy first as the council's chief engineer and then as mayor, reflected on the city's approach, sitting in his mayoral retreat—a log cabin, with a stream running through it, in a forested green park—where he goes several mornings a week with his staff to 'think-and-feel' the city:

No matter how well run we are, we still would not have all the resources we need. We can only get those resources by mobilising more people to participate and take co-responsibility for devising solutions. We cannot organise ourselves in linear ways because people do not live their lives in straight lines.

The council does not have the resources to deliver solutions to all the issues the city faces. That is why it has to design systems that draw in resources and investment from citizens and the private sector. That, in turn, means the council has to operate by orchestrating a network rather than just running an autocratic organization. The results have been impressive. In 1995, Curitiba's income per head was already 40 per cent above the Brazilian average; by 2004, it was twice as high. Thanks to the creation of more than thirty large parks, there are 51.5 sq metres of green space per resident compared with 0.5 sq metres in 1970. The unemployment and infant mortality rates are among the lowest in Brazil and literacy rates are higher than in many cities in the USA and the UK. So, what makes Curitiba work?

Building Blocks of Structured Self-organization

Structured self-organization at a city level requires five key driving elements: leadership, shared platforms, pragmatic philosophy, highly distributed resources, and collaborative civic engagement.

Leadership

The first requirement is leadership, but leadership of a particular, open, and inclusive kind. Curitiba has had a stable core leadership that formed around Jaime Lerner, several times Curitiba's mayor and original architect of the city plan. Many of the specific strategies have been devised by Curitiba's Institute of Public Policy (IPPUC: see further www.ippuc.curitiba.pr.gov.br). About 300 people work at IPPUC in multi-disciplinary teams of architects, engineers, planners, designers, and economists. They are the city's systems designers, responsible for the framework of rules, incentives, interfaces, and tools that make it fit together. But it is not just the institutions and skills of leadership that count but its style and ethos. Since the 1970s, Curitiba's political leaders have mainly been non-politicians. Jaime Lerner trained as an architect and Cassio Taniguchi was one of Brazil's top engineers. Both brought to their office a pragmatic, technocratic, problem-solving style. Their charisma comes primarily from being quiet and thoughtful. That non-egotistical style of leadership is vital for open innovation to draw out contributions from many different people. As Taniguchi put it:

Every time the public sector tries to do something on its own it tends to be a failure. The public sector works best when it encourages contributions from many other people—the private sector and citizens—to solve problems. It is not enough just to respond fast and effectively when people have a problem. Leadership has to go out and actively search for issues to solve before they really become problems.

Jaime Lerner agreed, in a catchphrase that became a slogan for the council: 'We have to take the first step. If we wait for a perfect plan we will be waiting forever.' Curitiba's transformation began in 1972 when Lerner pedestrianized one of the main shopping streets within seventy-two hours of being made mayor.

Self-organization in Curitiba works because it is not a free-for-all. It is structured by clear and simple rules. Major housing developments are allowed only along high-speed bus routes. No one can cut down a tree without council permission and, if permission is granted, two trees have to be planted in its place. Since 1970, about 1.7 million trees have been planted. No buildings are allowed within 200 metres of public parks, to extend the green belt. The historic core of the city, founded by European immigrants in the eighteenth century, has been preserved by strict planning guidelines. Curitiba has grown sixfold in less than three decades and yet it feels ordered, calm, and at ease, in contrast to other fast-developing cities which can seem chaotic, frenetic, and on the verge of break down (see e.g. Joyce 2003; Rose 2003).

Shared Platforms

Second, one of the key roles for public leadership is to create shared platforms, facilities, and infrastructures on which self-organization can then thrive. It was IPPUC engineers who designed the revolutionary roll-on-roll-off system for boarding buses that is at the heart of Curitiba's mass transport system. The city literally flows: Curitiba has the highest rate of car ownership of any city in

Brazil, but even in the rush hour there are no traffic jams. That is because 2,530 buses make 21,000 journeys a day to carry 2 million passengers, along 71 km of bus-only lanes within the city and more than 270 km of feeder routes. More people travel by bus in Curitiba than New York City. The busiest interchanges at the edge of the city handle 35,000 passengers an hour, more than Heathrow airport. Transport policy is closely linked to planning, land use, and economic development. Tall buildings are only allowed along bus expressways. Most of the population live within a short walk of an express bus stop. Curitiba does not have sprawling suburbs in which people have to use cars to get to work. The public transport system, combined with economic development and land use policies, has provided a public platform for Curitiba's development and makes a crucial contribution to economic equality. Poor people can use the buses for free as can pensioners and people making a payment to the council. It is easy for people on the fringe of the city, where the poorer communities lie, to make it to the jobs in the centre.

Pragmatic Philosophy

Third, the city's philosophy is pragmatic rather than perfectionist. As Taniguchi explained, sitting at a long table in the loft of his log cabin: 'We don't make big mistakes because we make lots of small mistakes first.' Open source social innovation thrives on a multiplicity of experiments that allow constant trial and error rather than grand designs (see Raymond 1999; Weber 2004; von Hippel 2005). As resources are scarce in Curitiba, many innovations have to serve more than one purpose. Curitiba is built on a flood plain, criss-crossed by five rivers. Flooding was a major problem when the city began to grow rapidly in the 1970s. The solution has been to build a string of lakes within the thirty parks the city has created. The parks give the city its green feel and act as flood defences. They also discourage favelas: squatters do not invade public parks. Another example of dual-use technologies are the forty-eight 'Lighthouses of Knowledge': small, local, libraries and Internet access points, located next to schools or health centres, which tend to be close to bus interchanges. All are built with a light-house tower that makes them easy to find, but which also serves as a convenient lookout post for the municipal guards who are also based there.

Distributed Resources

Fourth, resources are highly distributed to make it easy for people to use and adapt them to their local needs. Across Curitiba, there are small pockets of resources rather than large, central departments and institutions. In addition to the 48 libraries, there are 106 municipal day care centres, four of which are open 24 hours a day, and hundreds of vocational training centres, which cater for more than 33,000 people a year doing short courses to prepare them for work or to start their own courses. There are 165 health centres, and 1 million Curitibans have an electronic health card that allows them to book an appointment at any centre, regardless of where they live. Most of the 163 schools have Internet connections and many are open beyond school hours for use by the community. Over the past few years all education budgets for capital, maintenance, and teaching have been devolved directly to schools. Elisangel Cabral, the coordinator of the council's business incubator programme, explained how they planned to take their service door-to-door in future, almost like a guerrilla campaign:

Far more people will create jobs and businesses at home in the garage or kitchen than will come to a council incubator. We have to take our service to them rather than expecting them to come to us.

Collaborative Civic Engagement

Fifth, Curitiba adopts a collaborative and conversational form of engagement with citizens to encourage people to take shared responsibility for solving their own problems. City planners have drawn up a detailed social map of the city, highlighting communities blighted by multiple social problems, such as crime, unemployment, and family breakdown. Council staff going door-to-door to collect detailed information on educational attainments, household income, employment, and health compiled the map. They now have a detailed picture of the lifestyles of 10,000 of the poorest families in the city who live in fifty of its poorest neighbourhoods where they have launched collaborative community planning initiatives The city's aim is to provoke a creative conversation within these communities to generate its own momentum for change. Ana Jayme, the project's leader explained:

Getting people engaged in this collaborative model has been really hard and we've had a lot of false starts. We have had to equip people to do it, to give them the support and tools they need. We have to find the real leaders in a community. If we can get them involved, the first twenty people, then it's spread by word of mouth and we get many more people involved. We have to find something positive in the community, whatever it might be, that they can start building upon. Self-esteem is very low in these neighbourhoods. We want to get people to feel involved because unless they do they will not feel like real citizens, people who feel a sense of belonging in the city.

A city like Curitiba needs clear rules to keep order and an infrastructure for transport, education, health, and welfare to provide stability. But a fast-growing city also needs to be able to mutate, adapt, and evolve. Self-organization without leadership all too easily leads to a dead end: the favella. Top-down leadership that stifles self-organization fails to mobilize a wide range of people and resources. The trick is to provide leadership for a process through which people—together—find collaborative solutions.

Networked Social Entrepreneurship

So how does Curitiba's approach shed light on the idea of social entrepreneurship more widely? The idea that a city—rather than an individual or an organization—can be socially entrepreneurial should cause us to reconsider some of the assumptions that have grown up around social entrepreneurship. Curitiba council has acted entrepreneurially in leading the town's development. It has set strategic goals, sought opportunities and then mobilized resources to take those opportunities. In the process it has created tremendous social value: a cleaner environment, better education, and improved levels of health. But the question may be asked: what kind of social entrepreneurship is this?

Definitions of social entrepreneurship vary enormously. But at the core of what many people mean by social entrepreneurship is the social entrepreneur: a person who, rather like the heroes of Silicon Valley, builds an organization from scratch. The venture becomes the embodiment of the social value the entrepreneur creates. Examples of these organizations include: BRAC, in Bangladesh, which has 4.5 million members, provides $425 million (£26.1 million) in microfinance loans a year, and runs schools with 35,000 teachers; and Gente Nueva in Mexico, which runs food programmes, hospitals, loan schemes, and local stores serving millions of people. Both BRAC and Gente Nueva operate at a mass scale, applying many lessons learned from running big businesses —supply chain management, distribution, marketing—to address social issues. The implication of these accounts is that social entrepreneurs make a big impact when they scale up large service organizations, using fairly traditional business methods. These social entrepreneurs are following a model of organizational social entrepreneurship. The implications are fairly clear as well: if we want social entrepreneurs to have more impact we must help them to build larger organizations with finance and management expertise and models of growth—such as franchising and mergers and acquisitions—drawn from the private sector. We know how private sector organizations grow and so generate more impact measured by revenues and sales. We may need to apply the same kind of thinking to scaling up social ventures.

The Curitiba example suggests a very different model of social entrepreneurship and how it can scale: networked social entrepreneurship. In networked social entrepreneurship, the aim is not to grow a single organization but to achieve greater impact through a network of collaborators and partners. An organization—like the council in Curitiba—might be at the core of the network, but most of the impact comes from the reach of the network of partners. That increases the range of resources that can be brought to bear on an issue and multiplies the number of experiments and innovations, allowing solutions to be tailored to particular circumstances. Curitiba council's network mobilize resources beyond the council, resources that lie in households, civil society, and the private sector. The council's aim is not to build an organization that captures and controls resources, but to set off change within civil society. Networked entrepreneurship implies a different model of leadership, governance, and growth. Traditional business tools used to scale organizations will not work if you are trying to scale a network.

Motivations and Impacts

One way to define social entrepreneurship would be through what motivates the actors, i.e. they want to create social value and put a higher value on their social mission than their financial one. This would mean that Rodrigo and the rubbish collectors were not social entrepreneurs. Creating social value accidentally, as an unintended by-product of commercial activities, is not good enough for this definition. The quality of the motivation counts because this is vital in keeping the activity going. Another way to define social entrepreneurship would be through outcomes: anyone who creates lasting social value through entrepreneurial activities is a social entrepreneur. This broader definition would allow Rodrigo and his competitors to be counted as social entrepreneurs. Any organization that acts entrepreneurially to create social value is, therefore, a social entrepreneur. A third approach would be to define social entrepreneurs by the kinds of organizations they run: social entrepreneurs build organizations, usually not-for-profits, which create social value by applying business-like methods to meet social needs. This definition is surely too restrictive because it would count out Curitiba council, which is part of the Brazilian system of government and is, thus, democratically accountable and collectively funded as well as providing a variety of business-like services.

The Curitiba example suggests that we should not define social entrepreneurship by the types of organizations that social entrepreneurs build alone. Organizational solutions will vary enormously depending on the resources and skills available. It would be wrong to associate social entrepreneurship exclusively with a single type of organization or a single sector of society. Instead we should focus on motivations and impact. Many different kinds of organizations—public, private, for-profit, not-for-profit, voluntary, membership-based—can generate significant social value. Social entrepreneurship is a route to social value creation; it can take place in many settings and generate impact through many organizational forms.

The Nature of Leadership in Social Entrepreneurship

A widespread assumption is that social entrepreneurs are charismatic, heroic individuals akin to private sector entrepreneurs who have the courage and ambition to set up and grow businesses: Richard Branson, Bill Gates, Scott

McNealy, and the like. Social entrepreneurship is also often impossible without a dynamic, driving, social entrepreneur. But the 'lone-hero' entrepreneur is only part of the story and in some cases can actually be an obstacle to sustained social entrepreneurship.

Curitiba certainly bears out the argument that dynamic and ambitious leaders are vital to social entrepreneurship. The city's development was led by the very charismatic and visionary mayor Jaime Lerner. But this is a 'quiet' kind of charisma—self-effacing and stressing the contribution of others—leading through persuasion and consensus. Similarly, Taniguchi's leadership style is designed to encourage others to make contributions, out of a recognition that the public sector alone cannot solve social problems. The recognition that complex social problems need partnerships and alliances to solve them has implications for the congruent style of leadership. Alliances and networks need leaders who are politically astute, good at listening and drawing out the contributions of others, and provide an overall sense of direction without dominating. The characteristics of highly ambitious entrepreneurial leaders, who want to leave their mark on the world by building an organization with their name on it, are not well suited to this kind of networked social entrepreneurship.

Curitiba council has sustained its social value creation over more than thirty years by overcoming some of the limitations of a highly individualistic account of social entrepreneurship. Lerner and Taniguchi have made succession easier because they have created ways of thinking and rules of thumb that others can follow and pick up. They created around them a wider team—for example, through IPPUC—which can sustain their innovations. The entrepreneurial leadership of Curitiba city extends beyond the council itself into its partnerships with voluntary organizations and business. Social entrepreneurship in Curitiba has not just been sustained by a flow of remarkable individuals. The real story is that the council has created a culture of social entrepreneurship: a way of thinking and acting, which can evolve and adapt and which supports and sustains social entrepreneurs as they emerge. Curitiba shows that social entrepreneurship can be sustained over several generations by building teams, changing outlooks, and supporting cultures of social entrepreneurship.

Social Entrepreneurship Contexts

Curitiba throws into relief the role of the state and the public sector in social entrepreneurship. Social entrepreneurs often present themselves as distinct from the state, if not in opposition to it. In the developing world, social entrepreneurs often create social welfare, education, and development services in the absence of a state infrastructure or in the face of a state that is widely viewed as corrupt and untrustworthy. In much of the developed world, especially in Europe and parts of Asia, social entrepreneurs operate in a welfare landscape in which the state is a leading player, which thus limits the scope for entrepreneurial entrants. This self-image of the social entrepreneur as a maverick outside the system is sometimes reinforced by academic commentary about the growth of the 'civil sector' that is presented as a social space separate from 'government' and 'business', as if they were camps operating in separate territories in society. Some advocates—Bill Drayton of Ashoka, for example—seem to identify social entrepreneurship exclusively with the rise of the third sector (see, e.g. Salamon, Sokolowski, and List 2003).

The Curitiba story, however, does not fit into a neat academic schema of government, civil society, and business. Nor does it bear out the social entrepreneur's nightmare story of 'state bad/social entrepreneurs good'. In Curitiba, the state has been the leading social entrepreneur, creating an environment in which civil society seems to have thrived and business encouraged through regulations and incentives to act in socially responsible ways. It would be quite wrong to identify social value creation as only being possible in civil society, given the council's essential role in making the systems and infrastructure available. Curitiba should warn us against sweeping generalizations about the relationship between the state and social entrepreneurship. In Curitiba, the relationship between state and civil society has been highly creative. Yet the state takes a wide variety of forms across the world. For example within Europe: more decentralized (Spain) or less (France); low tax (UK) and high tax (Sweden); some have long histories of democracy (UK) others relatively short (Portugal). The state interacts with civil society in quite different ways in different societies: some states work through civil society bodies that they rely upon to deliver social programmes; other states limit the role of voluntary groups. Therefore, macrolevel estimates of the scale of civil society may disguise as much as they reveal about the nature of social entrepreneurship and how social entrepreneurs interact with the public sector: social value creation often emerges from within the public sector. Systemic social entrepreneurship of the kind that Curitiba practises, for example, in creating its waste recycling programme, could not have emerged without the exercise of political power and the mobilization of public resources.

Socially Entrepreneurial Outcomes

The standard account of entrepreneurship in commercial and social settings is that entrepreneurs create new products and services that meet previously unmet needs. The Furniture Resource Centre in Liverpool, for example, brings people into work and give them incomes by serving a market for cheap, recycled furniture. Childline International is using telephone help lines and call centres—familiar in many big businesses—to address the needs of street kids. The Grameen Bank deploys 'barefoot bankers' to get microloans to poor people in Bangladesh who are often beyond the reach of the traditional banking system.

Curitiba has done something slightly different: it has not innovated a product but a whole system. The innovation of a system of recycling—from the householder putting out their recyclables in the morning to the microrecycler dropping them off to the recycling centre in the evening—has allowed an entire city to evolve a new way of dealing with waste. The council has acted as a systems social entrepreneur: designing the way the architecture of the system and the way the components fit together. It has also been a service social entrepreneur: providing a new service in the form of the recycling centre. But the platform it has created has encouraged many other people in the city to act entrepreneurially—in small and large ways—to solve shared problems. The council has allowed the city as a whole to innovate a new solution to shared problems by orchestrating entrepreneurial inputs from a variety of players, of which it is only one. Curitiba has innovated a 'new value domain'—a new way to organize a variety of players in the system collaboratively to come up with a shared solution.[1] That solution is the system itself, not a discrete stand-alone service. Stand-alone organizational social entrepreneurs might be inspiring individuals. Social entrepreneurs who want to change entire systems have to engage with government.

Conclusion

The example of Curitiba shows that to increase the scale of impact a social entrepreneur does not have to increase the scale of their organization. On the contrary, Cassio Taniguchi believes the social system will only have a growing impact by not growing, and so encouraging business, the voluntary sector, and citizens to take more responsibility. The only way to pull off this trick is to work, as Curitiba does, through a range of alliances and networks. Social innovation does not always come from lone, heroic innovators. Social innovation is often the product of joint authorship that combines the inputs of many people. This process cannot be controlled or planned from on high, nor does it emerge spontaneously from below. Social innovation of this kind requires an open, collaborative style of leadership to encourage different players to make complementary commitments and innovations. This kind of leadership is strong on shared values and norms, light on rules and process.

Curitiba's story should caution against an overly prescriptive and narrow definition that identifies social entrepreneurship solely with individual social entrepreneurs who build an organization from scratch to create a growing impact. In this chapter, the traditional, organizational model of social entrepreneurship has been contrasted with a model of networked social entrepreneurship. The latter offers a promising account of much emerging practice, both in government and in the social sector, including NGOs, social movements, and campaigns. Networked social entrepreneurship is a particularly potent way to bring about systemwide social change. The reality is that there is a considerable and, perhaps, growing overlap between these two models of entrepreneurship. The most successful organizational social entrepreneurs work in a highly networked way. The most successful social networks usually have some kind of organization at their core, even if it is only a small one. The interaction between these two models will throw up all kinds of organizational hybrids.

Much of the debate about social entrepreneurship revolves around organizational models, particularly how to finance and support them. That means borrowing lessons from organization building in the private sector, such as venture capital investment, creating equity markets, and business training. Networked social entrepreneurship suggests that we could learn a lot from a much wider range of organizations, including social movements and campaigns, civic councils, and alliances which scale up impact in a different way. These networks are often structured without anyone being in charge, organized without being an organization. Their ultimate goal is to generate social value. Organizational social entrepreneurship and networked social entrepreneurship are different routes to this goal. The most successful social entrepreneurs are not just organization builders; they are network architects and alliance builders as well.

Note

1. Nokia, the Finnish mobile phone company, uses the phrase 'new value domain' to describe its emerging approach to orchestrating global innovation.

References

Bornstein, D. (2004). *How to Change the World: Social Entrepreneurs and the Power of New Ideas*. Oxford: Oxford University Press.

Chesbrough, H. (2003). *Open Innovation*. Harvard, MA: Harvard Business School Press.

Dees, J. G. (1998). *The Meaning of Social Entrepreneurship*, available at http://faculty.fuqua.duke.edu/centers/case/files/dees-SE.pdf

Gawer, A. and Cusumano, M. A. (2002). *Platform Leadership*. Harvard, MA: Harvard Business School Press.

Hawken, P., Lovins, A., and Lovins, L. (2001). *Natural Capitalism*. London: Earthscan.

Johnson, S. (2000). 'Literature Review on Social Entrepreneurship', *Canadian Centre for Social Entrepreneurship Discussion Paper*, available at: http://www.bus.ualberta.ca/ccse/WhatIs/Lit.%20Review%20SE%20November%202000.rtf

Johnson, S. (2002). *Emergence*. London: Penguin.

Joyce, P. (2003). *The Rules of Freedom*. London: Verson.

Leadbeater, C. (1997). *The Rise of the Social Entrepreneur*. London: Demos.

Nelson, R. and Winter, S. (1977). 'In Search of a Useful Theory of Innovation', *Research Policy*, (6): 2–16.

Raymond, E. (1999). *The Cathedral and the Bazaar*. Sebastapol, CA: O'Reilly.

Rose, N. (2003). *The Powers of Freedom*. Cambridge: Cambridge University Press.

Salamon, L., Sokolowski, M., and List, R. (2003). *Global Civil Society: An Overview*. Baltimore, MD: Kumarian Press.

von Hippel, E. (2005). *Democratising Innovation*. Boston, MA: MIT.

Weber, S. (2004). *The Success of Open Source*. Harvard, MA: Harvard University Press.

12

Helping People Is Difficult:
Growth and Performance in Social
Enterprises Working for International
Relief and Development

Alex Jacobs

Introduction

This chapter contributes to debate on the systematic factors that make it difficult for social enterprises to improve their performance. It is argued here that the bureaucratic and organizational arrangements across the sector undermine attempts to improve performance and to strengthen accountability. The chapter considers, particularly, the case of NGOs. These organizations may be defined as independent, NPOs with the stated aim of working for the benefit of poor and vulnerable people in developing countries.[1] This includes NGOs which provide short-term humanitarian assistance and longer-term development support, and which are either international or local in reach. Typically, such organizations work in three areas of social value creation: community level empowerment, welfare service delivery, and humanitarian responses to specific crises. Over recent decades the sector has enjoyed substantial growth (see Edwards and Hulme 1992; Kameri-Mbote 2000, etc.), but evidence shows that their field-level performance remains variable and that yesterday's mistakes may often be repeated today.[2]

NGO Performance

The considered opinion of many respected commentators is that NGO performance in the field is variable. Sometimes they do excellent work, helping people move out of poverty or oppression, contributing to pro-poor changes in local structures, or providing humanitarian aid. At other times, they fall short of these impressive achievements.

The Active Learning Network for Accountability and Practice (ALNAP) is an inter-agency body set up to support the practice of the evaluation of humanitarian action. In 2002, ALNAP reviewed fifty-five evaluation reports and concluded that strong performance in some areas was offset by weaknesses in others:

Food aid interventions generally meet their primary objective of feeding the hungry, although there are serious questions concerning whether targeting is appropriate.... Water and sanitation interventions were also generally successful in meeting physical targets, but sustainability of facilities is a major problem.... Housing is the most problematic sector, and the results of reports on housing support the findings of *Annual Review 2002* concerning the inability of relief interventions to facilitate sound housing reconstruction. (ALNAP 2003: 82)

There is no sectorwide equivalent to ALNAP's annual reviews in relation to development or service provision. But the overall picture presented by commentators is similar: success within limits, doubts about wider impact. As Chambers put it:

The literature on development errors is neither sparse nor all of it recent (see Wood, 1950; Baldwin, 1957; Hirschman, 1967; Chambers, 1973; Cassen et al., 1986; Hill, 1986, Porter, Allen, and Thompson, 1991; Morse and Berger, 1992. (Chambers 1997: 17)

Many others have amplified this theme (see Lewis and Wallis 2000; Smillie 2000). Kaplan (2000: 29) commented:

Development theory has undergone many transformations over the years, and today there is a growing body of thought that is beginning to question not only the various theories by the very validity of the development concept itself.... Questions abound, *but there is little change in development practice*...(original emphasis).

Furthermore, these doubts are not new: '...the impact of NGOs on the lives of poor people is highly localised, and often transitory' (Edwards and Hulme 1992: 104). Some commentators are more positive about NGO performance (particularly NGOs' own published material), others less so (e.g. de Waal 1997). These concerns are mirrored by wider concerns about the efficacy of external aid as a whole (among many examples, see Chambers 1997; Ahmad 2001). The balance of evidence supports the conclusion that NGO performance remains variable.

Variables That Influence NGO Project Success

NGOs themselves, commentators, and academics have reflected on the immediate causes of success (or failure) of NGO interventions. A research project examining these questions in sixteen projects, implemented in four countries, in 1992 concluded:

Successful project interventions were found to be related to a number of different variables.... Three in particular stand out: genuine participation, strong and effective management [at the project level], and skilled and committed staff [at the project level]. (Robinson 1992: 34)

These findings are reinforced by more recent reviews (Fowler 1997: 16; ANLAP 2002: 143). Project failures often centre on inappropriate project design, due to an inadequate understanding of the local context (Smillie 2000) and to pressures from donors (discussed below). Moreover, evidence suggests that NGOs find it difficult to learn from their previous mistakes (Hailey 2000; ALNAP 2002).

These variables can be summarized: successful NGO interventions depend on front-line staff-making high quality judgements (about issues faced and possible responses), having the skills and space to put them into practice, and adapting them as circumstances change.

This chapter argues that systematic factors make it difficult for NGOs to deliver these variables consistently in their fieldwork.

Systematic Factors

NGOs operate in a complex system of financial flows, competing organizational interests, evolving contexts, and changing understandings of humanitarian and developmental practices.

As a result, NGOs are subject to many different pressures, some of which encourage good practice while others do not. Improvements can only be achieved when the factors encouraging positive change outweigh the factors discouraging positive change. For the sake of this argument, the factors discouraging positive change have been organized into four categories:

- Conceptual issues
- Funding pressures (institutional and from the public)
- Internal organizational factors
- External context

Factors in each category are related to aspects of the overall system within which NGOs work, including relationships with their donors, the people they

249

aim to help, regulatory frameworks, and the way they go about their work themselves. The categories are interrelated, but not exclusive.

Conceptual Issues

EMPOWERMENT, SERVICE DELIVERY, OR HUMANITARIAN RESPONSE?

There are no established and widely shared definitions of different categories of NGO activity, such as development empowerment, service delivery, and humanitarian response. What one organization refers to as humanitarian work, another may label service delivery, and a third development. There are areas of overlap between these categories, but also fundamental differences. For example, empowerment requires political engagement, while the delivery of humanitarian aid may require political neutrality.

This can cause confusion at the practical level. NGOs do not always distinguish between these concepts in either their responses or in their organizational or conceptual frameworks. Indeed, due to this, many useful lessons about rehabilitation and development practice can be drawn from evaluations of what is labelled 'humanitarian' work. A great deal of current confusion in debates between politicians, donors, NGO managers, and NGO field staff may stem from misunderstandings at this level.

THE PROBLEM OF PROJECTS

Some services can be delivered through the framework of tightly defined projects with pre-defined activities, inputs, outputs, and outcomes. But empowerment—the approach most widely recognized as contributing to lasting community-level development—cannot (see Chambers 1997; Kaplan 2000; Edwards, Hulme, and Wallace 2000).

The problems associated with overspecified projects are well documented, particularly in what many practitioners see as their most pernicious form: logical framework analysis. This project management technique relies on tight specification of activities, inputs, and outputs.

Ebrahim provided an excellent analysis of the practical impact of logical framework analysis on two established NGOs in India. He points out that '[logical framework analysis] is a technocratic tool: it organises and reduces complex social and political realities into simplified and discrete components of a "project"' (Ebrahim 2003: 86).

This is useful for donors and central managers, who share the responsibility of ensuring that funds are used effectively and so may want to see evidence of well-thought-out plans before committing resources to an intervention. They also have to weigh competing claims for their limited funds, and so need some way of comparing the results of different projects they are considering supporting.

However, Ebrahim (2003: 90) continued,

...by forcing its user to articulate his objectives within a positivist project management framework, [logical framework analysis] actually strips those aims of political, contentious, process-based and ambiguous content. In other words, the logical framework achieves clarity in development planning by de-politicizing development intervention.

This is at odds with Fowler's assertion that 'bottom line of strengthening the poor is clearly political' (Fowler 1997: 6). But, any political activity by an NGO or community is likely to meet with a political response, as established interests are threatened and the balance of power starts to shift. When it comes to project planning, initial assumptions seldom hold.

Tightly specified projects encourage NGO staff to think about complex processes in simplistic terms. As a result, they encourage staff to stop discussing the messy realities of the people they aim to help and instead start trying to force those realities into pre-defined frameworks. Success is determined in terms of whether pre-defined targets are achieved, not whether those targets are relevant. This is inimical to the process of development as discussed earlier, often blocking ongoing reflection on evolving situations and so discouraging dialogue and participation. This creates a serious problem for development agencies: how else can they organize their resources into manageable chunks so as to achieve their goals?

Current debate is noticeably quiet on this point. There is some use of the concept of 'programmes', as a more loosely defined approach to thinking about development. But programmes also have a tendency to attract tight specification, albeit spanning more money or a bigger geographical area.

In the absence of other conceptual units for thinking about how to do development, 'projects' continue to dominate the landscape of NGO action. This is the cause of a great deal of frustration and waste. It inevitably tends to influence how practitioners think about development, overshadowing the ideas of participation and empowerment with the idea of what can be achieved as set out in the project plan.

HOW NGOS THINK ABOUT ACHIEVING THEIR MISSION

NGOs tend to have difficulty explaining how they expect to achieve their missions in practice. Two examples illustrate this.

EveryChild is a mid-sized UK-based NGO, working in eighteen countries around the world. In 2002, it had an annual income of £8 million ($13.8 million). In 2004, its mission statement began: 'EveryChild's mission is to empower families, communities and their governments to provide the best environment for children to thrive and develop...' (EveryChild 2004).

This is a big mission. To achieve it, will require substantial changes at all levels of society. Very substantial economic, political, and cultural institutions, which dwarf any NGO's resources or influence, have a direct impact on whether it can be achieved. EveryChild does not suggest that it can or will achieve this mission on its own. Nor does EveryChild explain how it expects to engage with all those other institutions so as to contribute effectively to 'empowerment'.

However, it is unfair to single out EveryChild. Most NGOs lack an articulated theory of social change. It is a critical omission (Edwards 2004). If NGOs are serious about achieving their important and ambitious missions, then they have to know (or at least have a theory about) what practical steps they can take to contribute to achieving them: particularly as they are normally minnows compared to other institutions. Otherwise, there is the real risk that they respond to symptoms not the systemic causes.

If NGOs cannot explain how their actions contribute to realizing their missions, then they (and their supporters) cannot be sure that they do, in fact, contribute to their missions at all. The next example shows how this can create real confusion about how to help people in practice.

In 2002, the UN and international NGOs launched a major response to what was seen to be the serious risk of acute food shortages in seven countries in southern Africa. Twelve of the largest NGOs spent approximately £260 million ($447.2 million) on this response in a one-year period (Cosgrave et al. 2004).

The Overseas Development Institute (ODI) carried out an extensive study of the international response, with a particular focus on conceptual issues. While external publicity focused on a simple message of drought, hunger, and impending starvation, internally agencies recognized that the situation was more complex. But the study found considerable confusion among agencies as to the nature of the crisis they were facing and how they should respond. As Darcy et al. noted (2003: 17):

The situation in Malawi and Zimbabwe was variously described to the research team as: a humanitarian crisis, an HIV/AIDS crisis, a long-term crisis, a livelihood crisis, a developmental crisis, a governance crisis, a manufactured crisis, and a food security crisis.

Agencies appeared to lack a conceptual model that could link the symptoms of hunger and poverty to long term causal factors, such as lack of investment in rural communities, exploitative market conditions, and political decisions which did not favour the poor. They were not sure how to engage with the major institutions that influenced these factors.

The ODI report concludes that '[there] is reason to think that the models on which much of the prevailing analysis of the Southern Africa crisis is based are inadequate either to explain, or predict' (Darcy et al. 2003: 27). This conceptual confusion had very direct operational implications. Agencies struggled to make decisions about how to assess the situation and what programmes they should launch in response.

Fowler (1997: 45) succinctly summarized the issue: 'Inconsistency between an [NGO's] vision of the world, what it says it wants to be and what it does is a common source of ineffectiveness.'

FUNDING PRESSURES: INSTITUTIONS

A large amount of money that NGOs spend is provided to them by donor institutions for specific activities. Donor institutions include governments and UN agencies, the European Commission, charitable trusts, and other NGOs. Many of these donors are large bureaucracies handling substantial budgets.

Donor institutions have a responsibility to ensure that funds are used effectively and efficiently (defined in broad terms). They have to process and approve many applications, as well as often having to manage relationships with their donors (for instance, member states, in the EC's case). In addition, all funds that come through government or inter-government organizations are liable to political influence.

Donors have a tendency to make these complex problems manageable by setting up bureaucratic processes based on the unit of 'the project'. As discussed earlier, this is often not an appropriate way to 'do development'. Research consistently shows that a donor's requirements for proposals and reports exert a major influence on how NGOs go about their work (Hudock 1995). Ebrahim (2003: 78) commented:

... the information requirements of funders impact NGOs not only by placing demands on their attention but also by promoting positivist and easily quantifiable valuations of success and failure. This is not an intended effect, but a systematic one that emerges from reporting and budgeting protocols that favour 'product' data over 'process' data.

In particular, 'downward accountability' to the people that NGOs aim to help is often squeezed: there is an incentive not to engage with local people if the project plan diverges from their changing realities. In any case, there is only so much accountability that staff can handle and only so many mechanisms that can be set up to provide it.

Ebrahim continued (2003: 92), noting that ' ... the monitoring systems linked to the [logical framework analysis] are not well adapted to [NGO staff's] implementation needs, which require simpler and continuous feedback systems.'

The attempt to force development into project-sized chunks has a number of other implications.

NGOs compete for limited funds, which 'lead to the mushrooming of claims that NGOs make about what they can do with relatively small amounts of money' (Wallace and Chapman 2003: 9). De Waal (1997) saw a parallel with

Gresham's law: bad project proposals drive out good ones. Donors are naturally liable to prefer to fund proposals that claim that they can achieve lasting results quickly rather than uncertain results slowly. Tight timescales add to the pressures. It is clearly crazy for NGOs or donors to consider that lasting social change can be achieved in a few months—but this appears to happen regularly.

There is also evidence that the quality of progress reports that donors receive may, in fact, routinely be rather low (Cosgrave et al. 2004: 125; Wallace and Chapman 2003: 14). One of the factors which encourages low quality accountability is that, according to Ebrahim (2003: 78), 'NGOs resist funder attempts to structure their behaviour'. All in all, the situation adds up to a lack of openness and trust between the funded and the funders at all levels (Wallace and Chapman 2003: 8).

However, as Ebrahim argued, NGOs and donors depend on each other. NGOs have an important role to play in meeting donors' organizational needs. A series of structural issues reinforce donors' power, but NGOs are not powerless. Some can negotiate more than others. If they had a realistic, alternative model to project-based funding then it appears likely that donors would consider it.

Some models are starting to emerge. For example, in the UK the Department for International Development (DfID) funds a number of NGOs through 'Programme Partnership Agreements', which are not tied to tightly specified projects. DfID has agreed to accept progress reports in formats defined by some of the recipient NGOs, for example ActionAid and Save the Children, not using logical framework analysis. This may suggest a way of tackling some entrenched systematic problems (see David and Mancini 2004; Starling, Foresti, and Bānos Smith 2004).

Other donors recognize these limitations. For example, the Good Humanitarian Donorship Initiative (see Harmer, Cotterrell, and Stoddard 2004) has the potential to contribute to progressive change on a major scale. Individual donors like International Development Exchange and Zurich Financial Services Community Trust are also taking steps in the same direction (Hobson 2003; King 2003). However, the donor community is as diverse and as independent as the NGO community and there is little evidence of systematic change of practice across it.

One final and important point in this section is that large international NGOs face the same problems as donors, and tend to come up with the same compromised solutions. They have the same bureaucratic problem of how to parcel up their money and spend it so as to achieve development: whether they are deciding to fund their own projects or other organizations. This reinforces the impression that there are limited alternatives to projects on the table at the moment.

FUNDING PRESSURES: FROM THE PUBLIC

If institutional funding tends to lead to tightly specified projects and the attendant problems of low quality upward accountability, hamstringing local management, and corroding trust between organizations, then funding from individual members of the public brings other pressures.

NGOs receive significant amounts of funding through modest-sized donations directly from individuals. This may be in response to a particular appeal (typically for a humanitarian response) or unrestricted funds that NGOs can use however they choose.

For example, in 2004 Oxfam GB received £76 million ($130.7 million) in direct donations from individuals and £40 million ($68.8 million) in grants from institutions. They spent £19 million ($32.7 million) on fund-raising costs, to generate this income. Over 500,000 individuals (mostly members of the British public) make a regular donation of a few pounds to Oxfam GB every month.[3] Oxfam is the biggest of all the UK NGOs and no other has this many individual supporters. It also demonstrates the size of the prize available from raising funds from individuals: financial security.

NGOs compete on brand for donations from individuals. As Pharoah recently commented (2004), 'big charities have very strong brands in an era when fund-raising depends on branding and direct marketing'. Many NGOs invest in sophisticated marketing operations using many techniques developed in the commercial sector to encourage people to give them money. This is no bad thing. It provides a mechanism for concerned people to give and brings in substantial funds for NGO work. But it also creates a relentless pressure within NGOs to simplify and sometimes sensationalize their media messages, to win more attention and more money.

For example, twelve major UK NGOs combined their fund-raising appeal for the southern Africa response, mentioned earlier. One of their joint press releases, published on 25 July 2002, read: '14.5 million people risk starvation in Southern Africa as the region's food aid crisis deepens. . . . We can stop this crisis if we act now and we have a good opportunity to do so . . . ' (DEC 2002). A picture of an emaciated African child accompanied this emotionally charged presentation of the crisis and 'their' ability to stop it.

More dangerously, brand-driven fund-raising from individuals can create a rod for NGOs' backs: having set up expectations among their donors, they are bound by them; otherwise they risk losing their donors' support. So emotive public messages reinforce the view that millions of Africans are only kept alive by periodic bouts of Western generosity: a far cry from the effective theory of social change that NGOs need to achieve their missions.

NGOs are careful to protect their brand. Typically, a great deal of attention is paid to maintaining their image as effective and efficient development and humanitarian actors. So, for instance, news about projects that do not achieve their stated objectives tend to be buried. This is a powerful incentive against full transparency. The One World Trust recently analysed the accountability of a selection of major NGOs, companies, and international organizations. Its report found:

... international NGOs come close to the bottom in the access to information dimension.... [They] often fail to provide information that is likely to be of significant use to stakeholders, for example, how they are spending their money and how well they have been achieving their aims.... The provision of evaluation material about the projects and programmes of international NGOs is also inconsistent. (Global Accountability Project 2003: iv)

In summary, all efforts to win funds from donors tend to encourage NGOs to present development as something that can be achieved with more certainty, and more quickly, and with the necessary intervention of outsiders, than it actually can. This approach provides a strong incentive to limit the release of any bad news, and so acts to reduce transparency and accountability. Sometimes NGOs resist these pressures; often they do not.

Internal Organizational Factors

NGO Operations Are Complicated and Hard to Manage

It is important to recognize that NGOs face a very difficult management job. A series of factors make managers' lives complicated, including:

- Working with cross-cultural teams (who may speak different languages)
- Distance management (sometimes in places where infrastructure is poor)
- The overwhelming significance of complex local context and external factors (including politics, other development actors, etc.)
- Different activities covering different technical specializations
- Multiple stakeholders operating in a web of relationships and making competing demands on the organization (including client communities, donors, partner organizations, government departments, peer organizations, staff, board members, and others)

Partly as a result of these complexities, NGOs are not tightly managed. Senior field staff work with considerable latitude, using their judgement to work through these issues, often with limited oversight from their direct managers. It could not be different: senior managers cannot possibly have the time to understand all the details and context of each different project.

It is neither a surprise nor a criticism that Ahmad (2001: 185) concluded a review of NGO relationships in this way: 'A major finding of [my] research is that donors and Northern NGOs know very little about the reality in the South and their clients.' It is important that these rich and powerful actors continually recognize that local realities are complicated and how little they know about them.

As Fowler put it (1997: 53), '[a] basic fallacy lies in the idea that [project] documents can ever describe the situation or its dynamics sufficiently to pass judgment without a leap of faith'. Senior managers rely on field staff when deciding how to intervene in any situation. Field staff are the main source of information about any project (and its context). To a great extent, senior managers have to trust their field staff (see Lindenberg and Bryant 2001).

Senior field staff tend to take a similar approach of using their judgement when it comes to implementing NGOs' internal policies. ActionAid's experience of implementing its new Accountability, Learning, and Planning System (ALPS) project provides a good example. The new approach was developed and formally adopted in 2000. But implementation is another matter. Each field unit considered and re-interpreted the approach within the context of their priorities. As a result, it has still not been fully implemented today. David and Mancini (2004: 12) commented that 'the culture of some country programmes was (and, in some cases, remains) quite at odds with ALPS.'

Big NGOs can rarely tell their field staff what to do. Following a study of large NGOs, Lindenberg and Bryant (2001: 56) commented: 'One of the most important barriers to change in NGOs is the strong individualistic and independent style of staff.' This is partly because staff work within loosely managed structures.

Governance Structures

In the UK and many other countries, most NGOs are legally structured as charities. They are governed by boards of voluntary trustees, who, by law, cannot be paid for their service to the organization. The board is responsible for the use of all the NGO's resources to meet its primary objectives. These are often rather general and aspirational mission statements, along the lines of 'the relief of poverty and suffering'. Meeting a few times a year, these boards exercise their responsibility by recruiting a chief executive to run the NGO, setting (or approving) policies and strategy, and overseeing performance. It is a difficult role.

While a variety of election mechanisms are available, the existing board often selects new board members. It is often hard to find good people with the appropriate experience and enough time to be effective. Particularly in large NGOs, board members tend to lack recent field experience. It is even more rare that they are drawn from the communities that NGOs aim to help. The Centre for African Studies (2001: 17) concluded that 'The effectiveness of boards differs from very active ones to those that hardly perform any functions and are mostly used as a rubber stamp for the management.'

This structure has two additional implications: boards tend to be rather distant from field operations; boards can tend to exert a centralizing influence. Trustees rely on their senior managers for information about an NGO's performance. This creates an unavoidable conflict of interest: managers are expected to report both good and bad performance to the people holding them to account. Writing as an NGO chief executive myself, senior staff would not be human if bad news was not sometimes softened. Trustees generally lack the time to understand an NGO's operations in more detail and they may not always have much field experience of their own. A sea of positive publicity, created by NGOs to support fund-raising efforts, may also surround them (Chambers 1997). These factors may encourage them to support managers and to avoid risk.

Unavoidably, boards are a central authority and have central responsibility. This has led them, in some cases, to try to ensure that operations are controlled down through the management chain, which is directly opposed to the conditions necessary for good development practice, as outlined earlier.

For example, Billis and MacKeith (1992: 119) reported on research on large UK NGOs. They found that:

[typically], senior managers perceived themselves to be working within a hierarchy in which authority had been delegated to them by the governing body.... [Subordinate] staff, on the other hand, felt the organisation should be organised in a democratic manner, and that they should be full and equal participants in decisions affecting their work... that agencies should practise what they preached.

Good community-level development practice requires those with power to give it up, and to be led by those without it. Centralized boards do not appear to encourage this. Billis and MacKeith interviewed directors, senior managers, chairs, and other governing body members in ten of Britain's largest development NGOs: and reported that:

Interviewees in seven out of ten agencies mentioned governance as an area in which their organisation needed to re-evaluate and make changes. Overwhelmingly, the issues that seemed most pressing was the question of the skills and expertise of governing body members to fulfil the tasks required of them. (Billis and MacKeith 1992: 120)

Growth

As if things were not hard enough already, many NGOs have been growing at a substantial rate. Not only are they tackling difficult management problems today but also they have frequently found that their systems have been outstripped by the size of the organization tomorrow. NGOs have found themselves running complex operations in many different countries.

Systems are required for all operations (such as defining projects, handling the accounts, recruiting staff). Generally, organizations have struggled to put these systems in place after growth, not before (see Lindenberg and Bryant 2001).

In many cases, this has led to continual processes of organizational change within NGOs. Trustees and senior managers have had their attention taken up on these issues, often concentrating on one system at a time rather than the entire organization. Some systems have been borrowed from the corporate sector (Edwards, Hulme, and Wallace 2000: 12). This has brought much needed discipline in some areas such as financial control. But, without a clearly articulated strategy or sense of methodology, these systems have at times ridden roughshod over the process of development. Some NGOs have tried to standardize complex, diverse, dynamic, and unpredictable circumstances at the cost of being able to respond to realities that are localized.

ActionAid has presented a candid account of the difficulties that these changes created. As Scott-Villiers noted (2002: 6):

Between 1990 and 1998 ActionAid's budget more than doubled, from £20 million ($34.4 million) to £50 million ($86 million), as the organisation expanded to new countries, new activities, and took on more staff. It became increasingly unworkable for Trustees to absorb all the information and make decisions on small matters at local level. In 1995, moves were made towards decentralisation.... In some cases, decentralisation allowed country directors to put their own ambitions before the organisation and in others they moved so far ahead conceptually that they left their staff behind. Meanwhile the reporting and other procedures remained essentially the same, so staff found themselves spending time 'satisfying bureaucratic demands for reports with irrelevant information, while carrying out programme work based on the needs and situations on the ground'. In general there was a tendency for much to be written by fieldworkers that was not used, many decisions to be made by management that were avoided in the field and much energy expended which might have been better spent.

One of the results of this bureaucratic approach was to corrode trust between field staff and central managers and between client communities and field staff. Araújo Freire and Macedo (1998: 78) described the dangers of this:

Any situation in which some individuals prevent others from engaging in the process of inquiry is one of violence. The means used are not important; to alienate human beings from their own decision-making is to change them into objects.

Lack of trust prevents people engaging in the process of inquiry: no trust, no development.

Summary of Internal Organizational Factors

The heart of many of the issues discussed above is that when it comes to field-level development, central organizations exist to support their field staff. The organization is not in itself important; its practitioners are. The organization has a critical role in helping (or sometimes hindering) practitioners. It can also carry out higher-level analysis or action in relation to issues that have to be tackled above the local level.

But many commentators (as well as managers) discuss NGOs as though they function as coherent, managed entities and as though the organization itself is the most important vehicle for action. Too often NGOs fall into the trap of valuing the organization itself and confusing the idea of 'what is good for the NGO' with 'what is good for development'. The issue of brand tends to make this worse.

As the Centre for African Studies' analysis concluded (2001: 26):

Many NGOs have not created enabling environments within which programme staff can perform optimally.... Well-trained professionals can only perform fully when delegated adequate authority to run their programmes and when given an opportunity to fully participate in the decision-making process.

This applies to NGO work around the world. It may be useful, when considering field operations, to recognize the centrality of individual practitioners, and to think of them as a network of individual professionals working under the umbrella of a specific organization.

External Context

The Link Between Performance and Funding

The link between performance and funding is often tenuous. Both institutional and individual donors depend on unverified information from NGOs to make their decisions. This information is often imperfect and liable to distortion. NGOs that can sustain credibility with donors sustain their revenue. This is usually achieved through a combination of factors, such as: brand building, personal relationships, historical reputation, size, and, finally, performance. However, it does not depend on performance alone.

Individual donors have almost no external source of information to check whether an NGO's claims are correct. Institutional donors rarely do much better. Project reports can show short-term success without discussing the wider impact of an intervention. In addition, institutional donors rely on NGOs for implementation so that they in turn can meet their targets and claim success. Funding is often equated to organizational success. In these terms, success can be divorced from the impact of an NGO's work on the ground. There is often no overriding financial incentive for NGOs to improve their field-level performance. For example, the market discipline that governs much of conventional business performance is notably absent.

Regulation

NGOs operate in a lightly regulated environment. Anyone who can raise funds can set up a new organization and start operations. While allowing enormous freedom of action, this also means that there is little independent check on the NGO sector. In the UK most NGOs are registered charities and are regulated by the UK Charity Commission. The Commission provides a basic level of regulation on financial and political matters and can investigate allegations of malpractice. But it does not provide any regulation of the quality of operations. The Charity Commission is not in a position to distinguish between NGO fieldwork that is excellent, indifferent, or even harmful.

NGOs are generally required to register with the state in every country in which they work. But, regulation rarely extends to the quality of their work or the qualifications of their staff. NGOs resist this: as political agents, regulation may be liable to abuse as a way of controlling their activities. This is a real risk. There are some moves towards self-regulation (for instance, through the Sphere (2004) standards or the Philippine Council for NGO Certification). But these are still in the process of being put into action and suffer from a lack of enforcement. It is as yet unclear what level of impact they will have. It is reasonable to conclude, therefore, that at the moment there is very little regulatory incentive for NGOs to improve their field-level performance.

The Link Between Academia and Practice

There is a rich literature of reflection on NGO practices, including: case studies; impact evaluations; academic reviews; journals; conference papers, and many other contributions. Some are widely known and some work has, over a number of years, contributed to fundamental shifts in how NGOs think about and do their work. Others continue to re-invent old truths. Insights from twenty or thirty years ago remain valid, but are sometimes not put into practice.

Maybe this is the case for every field of academic study. But it is striking that the link is weak in NGO work. While some of the most recent, forward-thinking, research suggests that NGOs should reinvent themselves as exemplars of the kind of just society they want to create (e.g. Edwards and Sen 2002), NGO managers continue to make mistakes that have been documented and analysed years ago. This could be seen as analogous to medical doctors not benefiting from the development of new cures for old diseases.

One mechanism that creates this link in other fields is that of professional qualifications. Mandatory qualifications are generally neither required nor enforced for practice in the NGO sector, which is disturbing as their work is so important and can—in extreme humanitarian cases—involve life-saving decisions.

Possible Ways Forward

This chapter noted that NGO performance continues to vary. It has described some of the systemwide factors that make it hard for NGOs to improve their performance. Based on this analysis, it is possible to set out some preliminary thoughts about how to release the energies of NGO staff to achieve greater impact in the field.

As has been discussed above, it is an important point to recognize that there are systematic problems across the sector. Changing one component is no more likely to solve them than changing one tyre on a broken-down car. Furthermore, systemwide change is likely to go against the short-term interests of some actors (either within or between organizations). This is a particular problem due to the highly consensual nature of NGO debate to date.

ActionAid has documented its experience and concludes that the drive, vision, and commitment of a small group of trustees and the organization's most senior managers, including the Chief Executive (who had substantial field experience), were critical in making the ALPS initiative happen. This group set out to discard their old systems, take 'a leap of faith', and create something entirely new. Their trailblazing approach may make it easier for others to go through a similar process. Their leadership role confirms the analysis set out earlier. As the system currently stands, very few external factors can influence NGO performance for the better. Most of the drive for improvement has to come from within. But it can be hard to take on the systemwide issues from this position. Having said that, external factors are not irrelevant, for example, improved practice may depend on the donors' insistence on participation (among other things). Currently, not all donors are so far sighted.

Greater Conceptual Clarity

The confusion between empowerment, service delivery, and humanitarian action muddies the water. It would be useful to distinguish between these different types of intervention much more clearly, at the conceptual level. Inevitably, they overlap in practice. But if the differences were clearly and consistently stated, then there would be a better chance of managing the tensions between them on the ground.

Other areas would also benefit from much greater conceptual clarity. One is the mission that NGOs set themselves and the implied theories of social change that follow from them. Both internal and external actors may reasonably assume that an organization knows how it aims to achieve or to contribute to its mission. By stating missions that are aspirational and often beyond their reach, NGOs risk setting false expectations among all actors about the limits of their impact. This is an important issue. Fowler (1997) has called for

NGOs to recognize the limits of what they can achieve in relation to much more powerful institutions and to rein in their publicity and fund-raising material accordingly. Otherwise inappropriate expectations are fuelled and continue their corrosive effects.

This suggests an area that may be of interest to NGO board members: pushing senior managers on the conceptual clarity of their strategic planning, and on recognizing the limits of what NGOs can achieve in practice.

Alternative Units to 'Projects'

The literature is loud in its condemnation of projects in relation to development, but quiet in proposing alternatives. This is a critical area for further reflection. The sums of money that are handled by NGOs and their donors require bureaucratic systems. If projects choke sensitive implementation, then what other unit can organizations use to organise and fund development?

A more appropriate unit for development may possibly be the community (loosely defined as a group of people with shared interests). NGOs could (and often already do) define interventions in terms of communities. Instead of making a commitment to deliver a project, they could make a commitment to support a community's development for a minimum of three to five years. In practical terms, their intervention would probably include cycles of action and reflection (Araujo Freire and Macedo 1998). This may include projects, but any project would be a sub-unit of the ongoing, community level process of development. It would not be an end in itself.

This could have a number of advantages, including reducing attention on concrete, short-term outputs (and the temptation to define them away from the field) and recognizing the centrality of the development process. It might make it more obvious that it is normally unhelpful to have many uncoordinated development interventions in the same place at the same time. It could also provide a framework for different external actors to contribute to one community's development, so long as they do coordinate their efforts.

Using communities as the conceptual unit for thinking about doing development could potentially help align bureaucratic systems with the reality of good development practice. However, communities are complex systems themselves, normally comprising many different interests and understandings, and subject to external forces. Other units may be more appropriate still. This difficult area needs substantial further research and reflection.

Focus on the Quality of the Process

When it comes to community-level development, the process of empowerment is the only recognized long-term solution to poverty. The process is the cure. So any organization aiming to deliver development could usefully focus on the quality of the process, rather than on its results.

A great deal of effort is currently being put into new impact measurement mechanisms, including approaches to quantify the return on social investment or to set precise targets in advance of implementation and monitor actual impact in comparison to them. But social impact is extremely difficult to pin down and to attribute to specific causal factors. It is also contingent on the circumstances of each particular intervention, often precluding comparison and aggregation across projects.

As described above, it is important for development practitioner on the ground to set and strive for specific results in dialogue with the people they aim to help to reflect on their actions together. These processes should last longer than one project-based intervention, including cycles of action and reflection. However, it is not necessarily important for other managers within an NGO (or donors) to know the details of exactly what specific interventions aim to achieve. It is perhaps more important that they have confidence that respectful dialogue appropriate actions, and reflection are taking place.

It may be useful to understand operational details for the purposes of learning and cross-fertilization. Donors also have a legitimate right to an explanation of what has been achieved with their funds. But detailed demands for project-level results can have a distorting influence. The functions of learning and upward accountability could potentially be separated from the function of monitoring.

ActionAid's model is groundbreaking in this regard. One interesting idea currently being considered is to make finance staff responsible for financial transparency to client communities. This could provide a useful balance to field staff, segregating some of the responsibilities for implementation and transparency. This initiative would have a strong empowering effect, substantially strengthening client communities' knowledge and negotiating position when it comes to discussing programme implementation with field staff (see www.whocounts.org for details). It may be possible to go further and measure the quality of the process. This is already partially being done, but, curiously, normally only in relation to financial probity through internal and external financial audits. It is feasible to imagine that NGOs could audit the quality of their participatory processes and of their learning from cycles of action and reflection. Sensitively done, this need not be overly intrusive. It would provide one of the most crucial quality control mechanisms that NGOs need to provide assurance that interventions really are meeting local people's needs.[4]

This would have the important effect of separating the question 'Are we doing a good job?' from the question 'What are we doing?'. The evidence discussed earlier shows how asking the second question in detail can make it difficult for staff to do a good job in the first place.

One practical implication of focusing on the quality of the process is to define a key question for everyone concerned with the effectiveness of interventions, including donors, board members, and senior managers, namely: what mechanisms does an NGO have in place to foster a strong connection between staff and the people they are trying to help? This connection is the root of much of NGOs' credibility and the foundation of their effectiveness. It may be an important area for trustees to probe.

Releasing the Energies of Practitioners

NGO work depends on committed field staff taking high quality judgements and having the space to put them into practice. Individual field workers' values are the most important factor in creating the conditions for appropriate interventions. When working with client communities, good judgements depend on behaviours including: respectful dialogue, humility, sensitivity to other people's way of seeing the world, genuine transparency about decision-making, self-critical reflection, and a sense of solidarity with the poor and marginalized. If an NGO can strengthen these values in their staff, then their staff may be more likely to make more good decisions about what can be done at the local level.

One implication of this is to reaffirm the critical importance of recruiting the right staff in the first place and ensuring that they have appropriate skills and values. Many sectors handle these problems through professional self-regulating institutes; an approach which may have a great deal to offer the NGO sector (Jacobs 2003).

Another implication of this is to recognize the leadership role of NGO managers: they act as guardians of values and may inspire staff to follow them. This is challenging and very different to other aspects of management. When it comes to people-centred development, decentralization is everything. All other bureaucracy must be fought to limit the distracting systems, forms, and paperwork that prevent field workers from dedicating their energies to the demanding job of working with local people.

Change the Internal Context

At a practical level, it is clearly appropriate to invest in leadership at all levels within NGOs (including the board). This may be the single most important factor that can trigger change across an organization. Thus, it may be useful to provide further opportunities for learning and reflection at the most senior level. Boards may not often invest a great deal in their own development. This may be a critical oversight, which can lead to the organization being held back or confused by board members who do not share managers' understanding. A number of initiatives are currently underway to encourage more discussion and learning among board members, including providing training towards accrediting board members as a way of identifying individuals with the appropriate skills and experience for the role. The analysis in this chapter suggests a number of key questions that board members may find useful to consider, among their other responsibilities:

- Is it clear what an NGO is trying to achieve and how it aims to achieve it in practical terms?

- Do plans, reports, and publicity material recognize the limits of an NGO's potential to contribute to solutions to poverty, in relation to other institutions?

- How are staff encouraged to develop a strong connection with the people they are trying to help?

- What evidence indicates the presence of a strong connection between staff and the people they aim to help?

- Are staff released from as much bureaucracy as possible?

- How are staff encouraged to maintain a strong commitment to the values that embody good development practice?

Change the External Context

An obvious question to explore is what could be done to change the external context to encourage more good practice? Is it unlikely that regulation is the answer here, rather donors may hold the key. It may be possible to encourage more reflection and learning among donors. Everybody involved in NGO work has a shared responsibility in this, including NGOs that submit reports to donors. Furthermore, institutional donors have to recognize their influential position and the responsibilities that come with it. Asking for additional detail is never a minor request in the context of the power relationships between funder and funded. Clearly, donors can exert a powerful positive influence for change.

NGOs have a responsibility to provide institutional donors with realistic descriptions of the issues that they face on the ground, and of the harmful implications of overspecified project planning and reporting. This may be painful and it may be unrealistic to expect NGOs to act in ways that may reduce their funding. But transparency and systemwide improvement demand it.

It would be particularly useful to abandon a particular widely used, and highly inappropriate, efficiency measure: the percentage of funds spent on 'administration' or 'sent to the field'. This provides no indication of the quality of work carried out and simply encourages creativity among NGOs' financial staff. By continuing to reuse this measure, NGOs reinforce an unhelpful understanding of what it means to do development among donors and the public.

Conclusion

This chapter has discussed the key constraints that hold back NGO staff from maximizing their social impact and has proposed some initial ideas for responding to them. It has taken a systemwide view, identifying factors that exist in the relationships between, as well as within, organizations.

It can be concluded that the system of donors and implementing agencies, which has grown up in an unplanned way, now includes structural impediments to good practice. The fundamentals of good practice have been overshadowed by competing bureaucratic concerns, the pressure of raising funds, and a loss of conceptual clarity. With no regulation to rectify the situation, NGO performance continues to vary, swinging between the excellent and indifferent, occasionally reaching the harmful.

However, it is positive to note that NGOs are leading reflection on these critical issues themselves. Further reflection on field practice may help overcome constraints and do more to release the energies of their staff. Finally, the experience of the NGO sector can have wider implications for social enterprise and entrepreneurs more generally in developing innovative organizational structures that actively encourage and reward good practice.

Notes

1. There is an ongoing debate about the precise definition of an NGO. Fowler (1997) provides an overview.
2. For example, see ALNAP's Annual Review (2002): 'Box 1.1 [Housing Provision Following Natural Disasters in Bangladesh] provides an example of how successive evaluations of similar operations in the same country, undertaken over a thirteen-year period by the same bilateral donor, identify similar problems.'
3. Source: Oxfam's Annual Accounts for the year ending 30 April 2004, available from www.oxfam.org.uk, including the section on legitimacy for a note of the number of individual donors. These income figures do not include an additional £66 million ($113.5 million) gross income from Oxfam's trading operations.
4. Some NGOs are already experimenting with this such as ActionAid and Medair, which has implemented Quality Standard ISO 9001, specifically to strengthen its learning.

References

Ahmad (2001). *Understanding the South: How Northern Donor Agencies and NGOs Understand the Needs and Problems of Southern NGO Clients*. Dhaka: Maniruddin Ahmed.

ALNAP (2002). *Annual Review 2002*. London: ALNAP/Overseas Development Institute, Available at: www.alnap.org

—— (2003). *Annual Review 2003*. London: ALNAP/Overseas Development Institute, Available at: www.alnap.org

Araújo Freire, A. and Macedo, D. (1998). *The Paulo Freire Reader*. New York: Continuum.

Billis, D. and MacKeith, J. (1992). 'Growth and Change in NGOs: Concepts and Comparative Experience', in M. Edwards and D. Hulme (eds.), *Making a Difference: NGOs and Development in a Changing World*. London: Save the Children Fund/Earthscan.

Centre for African Studies (2001). *Situation Analysis of NGO Governance and Leadership in Eastern, Southern, Central and Western Africa*. London: Centre for African Studies.

Chambers, R. (1997). *Whose Reality Counts? Putting the First Last*. London: ITDG Publishing.

Cosgrave, J., Jacobs, A., McEwan, M., Ntata, P., and Buchanan-Smith, M. (2004). *Independent Evaluation of the Disasters Emergency Committee's Southern Africa Crisis Appeal July 2002 to June 2003*. London: Valid International, Available at: www.dec.org.uk

Darcy, J., Griekspoor, A., Harmer, A., and Watson, F. (2003). *The Southern Africa Crisis: A Critical Review of Needs Assessment Practice and its Influence on Resource Allocation*. London: Overseas Development Institute, Humanitarian Policy Group, Background Report for Research Paper 15, Available at: www.odi.org.uk/hpg/

David, R. and Mancini, A. (2004). *Going Against the Flow*. London: IDS, Lessons for Change 7.

DEC (2002). *Disasters Emergency Committee Press Release*, 25 July.

Ebrahim, A. (2003). *NGOs and Organizational Change: Discourse, Reporting and Learning*. Cambridge: Cambridge University Press.

Edwards, M. (2004). *Civil Society*. Cambridge: Polity Press.

—— and Hulme, D. (eds.) (1992). *Making a Difference: NGOs and Development in a Changing World*. London: Save the Children Fund/Earthscan.

—— and Sen, G. (2002). *NGOs, Social Change and the Transformation of Human Relationships: A 21st-Century Civic Agenda*.

—— Hulme, D., and Wallace, T. (2000). 'Increasing Leverage for Development: Challenges for NGOs in a Global Future', in D. Lewis and T. Wallace (eds.), *New Roles and Relevance: Development NGOs and the Challenge of Change*. London: Kumarian Press.

EveryChild (2004). Available at: http://www.everychild.org.uk

Fowler, A. (1997). *Striking a Balance: Enhancing the Effectiveness of Non-Governmental Organisations in International Development*. London: Earthscan.

Global Accountability Project (2003). *The Global Accountability Report 1, 2003: Power without accountability*. London: One World Trust, Available at: www.oneworldtrust.org

Hailey, J. (2000). 'Learning for Growth: Organisational Learning in South Asian NGOs', in D. Lewis and T. Wallace (eds.), *New Roles and Relevance: Development NGOs and the Challenge of Change*. London: Kumarian Press.

Harmer, J., Cotterrell, S., and Stoddard, K. (2004). *From Stockholm to Ottawa: A Progress Review of the Good Humanitarian Donorship Initiative*, Humanitarian Policy Group, Research Briefing, 18, ODI, Available at: www.odi.org.uk/hpg

Hobson, S. (2003). 'Grantmaker on the Receiving End', *Alliance Magazine*, 8(4): 42.

Hudock, A. (1995). 'Sustaining Southern NGO Partners in Resource-Dependent Environments', *Journal of International Development*, 7(4): 653–67.

Jacobs, A. (2003). *Concept Paper: An Institute of Humanitarian Managers*. Oxford: Mango, Available at: www.mango.org.uk

Kameri-Mbote, P. (2000). *The Operational Environment and Constraints for NGOs in Kenya: Strategies for Good Policy and Practice*. London: International Environmental Law Research Centre, IELC Working Paper No. 2000–2, Available at: www.ielc.huma.org

Kaplan, A. (2000). 'Understanding Development as a Living Process', in D. Lewis and T. Wallace (eds.), *New Roles and Relevance: Development NGOs and the Challenge of Change*. London: Kumarian Press.

King, A. (2003). 'A Journey into Trust', *Alliance Magazine*, 8(4): 41.

Lewis, D. and Wallace, T. (eds.) (2000). *New Roles and Relevance: Development NGOs and the Challenge of Change*. London: Kumarian Press.

Lindenberg, M. and Bryant, C. (2001). *Going Global: Transforming Relief and Development NGOs*. London: Kumarian Press.

Pharoah, C. (2004). Quoted in *Third Sector*, 3 November.

Robinson, M. (1992). 'NGOs and Rural Poverty Alleviation: Implications for Scaling-up', in M. Edwards and D. Hulme (eds.), *Making a Difference: NGOs and Development in a Changing World*. London: Save the Children Fund/Earthscan.

Scott-Villiers, P. (2002). 'How the ActionAid Accountability, Learning and Planning System Emerged—The Struggle for an Organisational Change', *Oxfam: Development in Practice*, 12: 3–4.

Smillie, I. (2000). 'Relief and Development: Disjuncture and Dissonance', in D. Lewis and T. Wallace (eds.), *New Roles and Relevance: Development NGOs and the Challenge of Change*. London: Kumarian Press.

Sphere (2004). *The Sphere Handbook: Humanitarian Charter and Minimum Standards in Disaster Response*. Oxford: Oxfam/Sphere.

Starling, S., Foresti, M., and Baños Smith, H. (2004). *Global Impact Monitoring: Save the Children UK's Experience of Impact Assessment*. London: Save the Children UK, Available at: www.savethechildren.org.uk

De Waal, A. (1997). *Famine Crimes*. London: James Curry African Issues.

Wallace, T. and Chapman, J. (2003). *Some Realities Behind the Rhetoric of Downward Accountability*. London: INTRAC, Available at: www.intrac.org

13

The Social Entrepreneurship Collaboratory (SE Lab): A University Incubator for a Rising Generation of Social Entrepreneurs

Gordon M. Bloom[1]

Tell me, what is it you plan to do with your one wild and precious life?
'The Summer Day', Mary Oliver

Unleashing a Rising Generation of Social Entrepreneurs: An Emerging University Pedagogy

University education rarely focuses its attention and imagination on teaching students how to turn a vision into reality, how to design and develop social change organizations. This chapter describes aspects of a teaching and transformative learning model developed and launched at Stanford and Harvard Universities to undertake this mission: the Social Entrepreneurship Collaboratory (SE Lab). Its description endeavours to answer several questions: How can universities help create, develop, and sustain a rising generation of social entrepreneurs and their ideas? What new forms of learning environments successfully integrate theory and practice? What conditions best support university students in studying, creating, and developing social change organizations, thinking through their ideas, and connecting with their inspiration? What are the intellectual content and the rationale for a curriculum addressing this at a university?

Consider Uri for example, an Israeli student at Stanford University, whose great-aunt died in a terrorist attack at a Jerusalem bus stop in 2002. He teamed up with Hisham, a Palestinian student at Peter Drucker School of Management, whose cousin was killed by Israeli troops during a demonstration in

270

Nablus (Levy 2003). Rather than fight, these otherwise natural enemies sought to improve conditions in the Middle East by addressing the economic roots of terrorism. Uri enrolled in a new course being co-created by faculty and students at Stanford to teach students about social entrepreneurship and to help them develop their personal passion for social change into concrete plans. He used the course and many other resources to develop Jozoor Microfinance (*Jozoor* means 'roots' in Arabic). Based on the premise that enforced poverty and limited opportunities for Palestinians make terrorism a relatively more attractive option, Jozoor's founders determined that an effective means of improving conditions was to provide microloans to young Palestinian men to start businesses. In 2003, the plan won first place in the Stanford Social Entrepreneurs Challenge business plan competition and now, after many developments and difficulties, there are pilot projects in East Jerusalem and the West Bank.

Bhakti enrolled in Harvard's joint degree programme at the Kennedy School of Government (KSG) and Harvard Business School (HBS) with a desire to contribute to international development in third world countries. She envisioned a programme that would promote development capital for local entrepreneurs, and she had started to form a fast-growing network among graduate students across the USA to help. Many unanswered questions about how best to design and develop an enterprise that would effectively accomplish her goal led her to an innovative social entrepreneurship course at Harvard, which promised insights from academic frameworks and practical examples and feedback and mentorship to help bring the project to fruition. The result for Bhakti and her KSG and HBS team mates Deirdre, Mei, and Mike was the Global Micro Entrepreneurship Awards (GMA), a programme honouring innovative entrepreneurs of small enterprises in developing countries. GMA country teams give awards and identify and provide successful, local entrepreneurs with funding to help them develop their organizations. In addition, GMA winners are honoured at a ceremony where they ring the opening bell of the stock exchange in their respective countries—a public symbol of official recognition of the individual as a major contributor to their country's development. As of 2005, GMA is rolling out in thirty countries thanks to a strategic partnership with the United Nations Development Fund and generous funding from Citibank Foundation which has committed to contributing over $1 million (£580,000) annually to the project.

Like Uri and Bhakti, many university students have a strong desire, drive, and commitment to participate in global social change. Unfortunately, most have little or no opportunity to address and act upon this in their university's formal curriculum, even though improving social welfare through service to the public may be a value cherished by university communities. Many leading universities have a long-standing and now rapidly burgeoning interest in developing and enhancing courses, programmes, and schools that are oriented to practical global problem solving, and that will educate and influence a rising generation of leaders and managers who will face this challenge. Jane Stanford described the mission of the university she and her husband Leland Stanford founded in 1885 as follows:

The university was accordingly designed for the betterment of mankind morally, spiritually, intellectually, physically, and materially. The public at large, and not alone the comparatively few students who can attend the University, are the chief and ultimate beneficiaries of the foundation. While the instruction offered must be such as will qualify students for personal success and direct usefulness in life, they should understand that it is offered in the hope and trust that they will become thereby of greater service to the public (Jane L. Stanford, address to Stanford University Trustees, 3 October 1902; reprinted in Bloom and Scher 2003).

Similarly, the mission of the John F. Kennedy School of Government at Harvard is to 'serve the public interest by preparing leaders for service to society and by scholarship and collaboration that contributes to the solution of public problems' (John F. Kennedy School of Government, Harvard University Facts 2004–5; reprinted in Bloom et al. 2005). The demand for innovation and expansion of programmes in universities for interdisciplinary social problem solving has been catalysed by global circumstances, fuelled by students' and donors' interests, and increasingly embraced in the recent rhetoric of university presidents, including Stanford's John Hennessy and Harvard's Larry Summers (Bernstein 2005; Delgado 2005; Staff Writer *Harvard Gazette* 2005; Gewertz 2006).

So why have universities not made more progress towards developing courses and programmes that satisfy the growing demand for teaching social entrepreneurship? One problem is that tradition has locked university faculties into a tenure system that values and promotes research (inquiry) and scholarship (high theory). Tenure line faculty members thus face little incentive, few precedents, and some risk in designing an innovative curriculum that combines theory and practice—one of the key elements needed for social entrepreneurship to thrive in an academic environment. As noted earlier in this book by Bill Drayton, a crucial aspect of social entrepreneurship involves pragmatic, actionable 'how to's', puzzling out the logistics of the journey, solving problems on the ground, making the pieces fit together.

A second problem is that social entrepreneurship has no clear academic home within most universities. On one side of the university, many humanities, sciences, and public policy faculties suspect social entrepreneurship as a market-oriented, co-optation of social justice and the public good: a wolf in sheep's clothing. On the other side, many business school faculties see social entrepreneurship as an imprecise, compromised semblance of business practices and not at the core of their mission. As a result, the dominant culture amongst both sides of this debate has been sceptical of social entrepreneurship courses.

How then can universities create a new model for a curriculum that does not hopelessly abstract and theorize social entrepreneurship into a dry lecturing, reading, and writing exercise? The SE Lab, a collaboration of committed teams of students, faculty, fellows, and staff first at Stanford University and then Harvard University, has undertaken an alternative approach.[2] It provides students with an opportunity to discover and focus their intelligence, energy, and passion on identifying and confronting social problems of their choice; provides them with a curriculum that integrates theory and practice; introduces them to a broad set of resources supportive of social entrepreneurship within and outside the university; and invites them to co-create a collaborative environment that mentors them in designing and developing solutions and the social change organizations to implement them (see Figure 13.1). By sharing their innovative ideas and approaches to social change, students gain more than the opportunity to develop their individual projects. The understanding, tools, and perspectives they gain through participation in the SE Lab contribute to their success in public, private, or not-for-profit sector careers.

Fusing theory and practice

- Applying theoretical frameworks to the design and development of social entrepreneurship initiatives

Tailored to students

- Seeking to understand what social issues and agenda for change are important, meaningful, and inspiring to each, and orienting the lab to support their needs and passions in the design and development of their projects

Co-created with students

- Co-producing an interactive learning environment within and outside the lab

- Working in teams and partnerships to provide peer support and learning

Supported by extensive resources within and outside the university

- Informal and structured individualized and group mentorship and feedback; access to intellectual and practical advisors

- Collaboration within the lab, within teams, among teams, between the lab and related university resources, and between the lab and resources external to the university

- Broad participation in the lab including not only students and university faculty but also practitioner-faculty, non-enrolled university fellows and staff, invited social entrepreneurs, and social entrepreneurship funders

- Identification of related resources including through participation in business plan competitions and conferences outside the lab

- Multiple role models and examples in person and through readings

---

Figure 13.1 Key characteristics of the SE Lab

The SE Lab is a Silicon-Valley influenced incubator where student teams create and develop innovative pilot projects for US-based and international social sector initiatives. The SE Lab combines academic theory, frameworks, and traditional research with intensive fieldwork, action research, peer support and learning, and the participation of domain experts and social entrepreneurship practitioners. It also provides students with an opportunity to collaborate on teams to develop planning documents (i.e. a business plan, briefing book, funding proposal) for their initiatives and to compete for recognition in the marketplace of ideas. Students in the SE Lab have created innovative organizations serving many different social causes, including fighting AIDS in Africa, promoting literacy in Mexico, combating the conditions for terrorism using microfinance in the Palestinian Territories, and confronting gender inequality using social venture capital to empower women in Afghanistan.

The SE Lab provides a new model in comparison to most graduate and undergraduate curricula. Some professional schools, however, use teaching models with aspects similar to the SE Lab in their application of theory to practical problems. For example, architecture schools use a design studio or 'charette', which teaches architecture by providing a design problem such as building a community centre to help address social needs in a particular location. Projects require not only application of architectural design theories, but also field research regarding the needs of the community. In-class activities include presentations, critiques, and elements of collaboration in the open studio. Similarly, medical schools require significant medical practice under the direction of physician mentors as part of clinical training ('teaching hospital' model), and the aim of bench-to-bedside clinical research includes development and testing new medications, surgical techniques, and therapeutic practices in the delivery of clinical medicine. Engineering schools are also very oriented to the translation of theory in practical applications, and design projects facilitate that aim. Finally, business schools and some public policy schools use case teaching pedagogy to enable students to learn through practical application (in case scenarios) the value of theoretical management frameworks. The SE Lab, however, is unusual in its openness to, and support of, identified interests of students and its utilization of resources throughout and beyond the university to create opportunities for the collaborative development of their organizational designs. In this way, it is a new form of pedagogy, one that moves professional education beyond the case method.

This chapter proceeds as follows. First, I will briefly describe the history of this educational model through its emergence at Stanford and Harvard. Next, I will describe selected aspects of the content of the course and related resources. Finally, I will present some results that demonstrate the potential impact of the model.

The Making of the SE Lab

Some people see things as they are and ask why.
I see things as they never were and ask why not.

—George Bernard Shaw

Despite the close alignment of social entrepreneurship with the universities' missions, as of 2000, neither Stanford nor Harvard offered a course to help students learn to design and develop social change organizations and to become effective social entrepreneurs by applying theoretical frameworks to practical problems. This was true despite the decidedly entrepreneurial nature of universities: 'No better text for a History of Entrepreneurship could be found than the creation of the modern university, and especially the modern American university' (Drucker 1985).

At Stanford, the SE Lab derived from activities, initiatives, and support from the Public Policy Program and Program in Urban Studies in the School of Humanities and Sciences; the Graduate School of Business (GSB) and its Public Management Program (PMP) and Center for Social Innovation (CSI); and the Stanford Institute for International Studies (SIIS). The business school had a long-standing interest in the public good through its creation of the PMP in 1974. In 1999, it further established the CSI, with faculty co-directors Greg Dees, who as a Harvard and Stanford faculty member had created ground-breaking social entrepreneurship courses and authored several pivotal publications in forming the field, and Dave Brady, the business school's senior associate dean for academic affairs and senior faculty in the university's political science department. Though there was significant student interest in social entrepreneurship, there were few courses offered in the business school and the public policy undergraduate curricula to satisfy this demand. I joined the Public Policy Program faculty in Spring 2001 to teach and further develop the courses Social Entrepreneurship: Mobilizing Private Resources for the Common Good, and Business Concepts and Skills for the Social Sector, which were originated by Dees, and quickly understood from the students that further courses were needed. The ensuing Social Entrepreneurship Course Series was sponsored and adopted by the Public Policy and Urban Studies Programs at Stanford, with support from economist Roger Noll as well as Brady (consecutive directors of the Public Policy Program) and the GSB CSI. During the two years beginning in 2001–2, the SE Lab grew to encompass a four course series, including the two original courses, a third course entitled Social Innovation and the Social Entrepreneur: the Creation and Development of US and International Social Sector Organizations, and the year-long, flexible enrolment SE Lab.

The motivation for the expansion of the social entrepreneurship curriculum at Stanford came in large part from students. For instance, in Spring 2001, a group of committed and energetic undergraduate students led by Tariq Ghani and Leela Young created as part of their course project Future Social Innovators Network (FUSION), a special interest group devoted to social entrepreneurship, and undertook the development of a social entrepreneurship lecture series, conference, website (http://fusion.stanford.edu), and many related initiatives. In addition, in 2001–2 a group of graduate students from Management Science and Engineering (MS&E) led by Monica Tran created the Social Entrepreneurs Challenge (Social E-Challenge) business plan competition in the same year. The students wanted more courses and a bigger role in the design of the curriculum; they wanted the course to help them prepare innovative and competitive business plan proposals that they could enter into the Social E-Challenge, and they were eager for faculty mentorship and collaboration. Thus, from its inception, the SE Lab was co-created by the student participants.

A key to the SE Lab's resonance with students in their work at Stanford was an alignment, coherence, and fit with the existing culture and resources of Stanford. From the beginning the SE Lab had a dual mission: (1) to develop a rising generation of social entrepreneurs and their partners, and (2) to create a university incubator for interdisciplinary global problem solving where students develop ideas and social change models into new social entrepreneurship initiatives, collaborating with, and stimulating innovation in the new field. Its design as part lecture course, part case study analysis, part design 'charette', and part start-up incubator was intended to inspire students and provide them with tools, support, feedback, and examples that would help them achieve the SE Lab's mission.

The naming of the SE Lab was serendipitous. In 2001–2, an SIIS-based project on the development of the knowledge economy, called KNEXUS (later the Kozmetsky Global Collaboratory), had a room they called the 'knowledge collaboratory', which was located in the same building as my office and attracted my interest as it was adjacent to the SIIS offices of organization and management scholars Jim March and Woody Powell. A casual conversation about the name with the KNEXUS director Syed Shariq, whose prior work had been with the NASA jet propulsion laboratory, and doctoral fellow Ben Shaw, who had worked at IDEO, the Palo Alto design firm, led to its adoption in the creation of the SE Lab. The term 'collaboratory' captured the essential features of the SE Lab, its collaborative co-creation between students, faculty, practitioners, and other participants; its experimental, inventive laboratory environment; its aim to translate good theory and good ideas into innovative new social change initiatives and models and to develop the leaders and teams that would power them.

Other pivotal milestones for the SE Lab included engaging the participation of the Reuters Foundation Digital Vision Fellows at Stanford, a group of talented practitioner scholars acknowledged for their achievement and interests in international development and technology, with Stuart Gannes as program director. In addition, I recruited Laura Scher, CEO of Working Assets, a social enterprise that donates profits mainly from long distance telephone service revenues to not-for-profit initiatives, to serve as a faculty member in the SE Lab, and Greg Scott, a research fellow and case writer at Stanford GSB with deep experience in international development. Scher, the fellows, and an array of special guests invited to participate in the SE Lab offered a source of inspiration, ideas, and opportunities for students both individually and as a group. They also provided a practical perspective to theoretical discussions and feedback and advice to students about class assignments. The ability to provide individualized and team feedback and advice to students is a critical feature of the learning experience in the SE Lab, particularly because it comes from many sources including peers, faculty, fellows, and practitioners.

There was a similar need for the SE Lab at Harvard. Its academic home since 2004 has been the Hauser Center for Nonprofit Organizations, a university-wide centre (founded in 1997) based at the KSG, with Mark Moore as its faculty director and former Harvard president Derek Bok as its faculty chair. The SE Lab has also benefited from collaboration with the Social Enterprise Initiative (founded in 1994) at HBS and with the Center for Public Leadership at KSG with faculty director David Gergen, and several other centers and schools at Harvard, and the Sociology Department in the Faculty of Arts and Sciences. For the SE Lab pilot in Spring 2005 included Dutch Leonard, senior faculty at the KSG and HBS and faculty co-chair of the Social Enterprise Initiative; Mark Moore, senior faculty at KSG and faculty director of the Hauser Center; Chris Winship, senior faculty in the Sociology Department, Faculty of Arts & Sciences and chair, University Committee on Public Service; and Gordon Bloom, Hauser Center fellow and SE Lab director who joined the KSG faculty in 2005–2006. The course at Harvard was developed during 2004–5 and taught for the first time in Spring 2005 at the KSG as a pilot, and then in Spring 2006 formally became part of the Harvard KSG curriculum, with 50 graduate students and fellows from 20 degree programs at 6 universities enrolled in that inaugural class (Gewertz 2006).

Currently, the SE Lab at Stanford can be structured over one, two, or three academic quarters (ten weeks each), and at Harvard it is currently offered during a semester (sixteen weeks), which in 2005–6 has been expanded to be preceded by a half semester module emphasizing foundational frameworks so that the curriculum now spans the academic year.

Expansion of the KSG's social entrepreneurship curriculum was further catalysed by a recent $10 million (£5.8 million) grant for twenty to twenty-five social entrepreneurship fellowships, given to Harvard by the Reynolds Foundation and announced in May 2005 (Bernstein 2005; Staff Writer *Harvard Gazette* 2005). These evolving models can only provide limited experience and information as we approach the questions this chapter aims to help answer. However, at these universities some determinants of success in the early stages included significant unmet student demand and interest in the SE Lab; gifted and motivated students; abundant intellectual resources for advising, guiding, mentoring students and project teams; an organizational culture in selected schools and programmes which support integrating academic and practical approaches; a supportive academic home for the SE Lab with related senior faculty interest and committed teaching staff; and some initial funding (in both cases for the SE Lab itself less than $10,000 [£5,800]).

A Curriculum Addressing Social Entrepreneurship

The teaching environment of the SE Lab fuses theory and practice, utilizing conceptual frameworks, case studies and examples from the field, and gives students the opportunity to design and develop a social entrepreneurship initiative utilizing the SE Lab as an incubator. While foundational knowledge is important, lectures and readings on theory are not sufficient to prepare students to become social entrepreneurs because much of the skills that are needed to be effective are embedded in applying theoretical frameworks to practical problems.

The course readings introduce students to selected concepts and practices as they are developing in the USA and internationally. The cases and examples from the field are intended to equip students with knowledge of some alternative perspectives and strategies for turning good social ideas into viable and effective ventures. But social entrepreneurship is an emerging field, especially in academia, so many of the animating theories, while useful are still in formative stages.

The background and informational readings provide a framework for in-class discussions and facilitate the collaboration that is necessary for the incubation of team projects, which are the essence of the SE Lab. Later I highlight some of the conceptual frameworks that provide the building blocks for the students' organizational development, and I discuss the ways in which the SE Lab encourages students to apply them in developing their projects.

Introduction to Social Entrepreneurship

The introduction to the course grapples with two central questions: What is social entrepreneurship? And, consequently, who are social entrepreneurs? In preparation for discussion, students read *The Meaning of Social Entrepreneurship* (Dees 1998a) and parts of *The Rise of the Social Entrepreneur* (Leadbeater 1997). In class, using a handout from a Stanford case study on Ashoka, students are presented with over a dozen definitions, varying from *The Economists's* characterization—'a new breed of philanthropists . . . [who] want to solve problems in a specific way'—to the description, 'people who use the techniques of business to achieve positive social change' (Choi and Meehan 2001) (see Appendix 1).

Students are challenged to react critically to Dees' definition (see Figure 13.2). The goals of this exercise are: (*a*) to define and critically examine social

Social entrepreneurs play the role of change agents in the social sector by:
- Adopting a mission to create and sustain social value (not just private value)
- Recognizing and relentlessly pursuing new opportunities to serve that mission
- Engaging in a process of continuous innovation, adaptation, and learning
- Acting boldly without being limited by resources currently in hand and
- Exhibiting heightened accountability to the constituencies served and for the outcomes created

Figure 13.2 Defining social entrepreneurship (Dees 1998*a*)

entrepreneurship and (*b*) to develop a common language to serve as a foundation for the rest of the course.

In a second introductory exercise, students form pairs and discuss with their partners the source of their interest in the course, the social issues that are compelling to them, any personal experiences that have affected their interests, and preliminary ideas for a socially entrepreneurial project. This exercise is one of several designed to help students identify not only the issues about which they feel passionate but also the underlying source of their passion. Some students enter the SE Lab with a very clear idea of what they are most passionate about and how they hope to translate that passion into change. For example, Alyce entered the SE Lab clear about her passionate objections to the sex and slave trade in Thailand and determined to provide the affected women with a way to find alternatives. Through the SE Lab, and collaborating with humanitarian organizations operating in Southeast Asia, Alyce and her team mates Naureen, Evelyn, and Karen designed New Means—a not-for-profit venture to help Thai women leave prostitution and earn a livelihood making beautifully handcrafted cards to sell in the US market. Many students are less clear and simply want to make a difference. In either case, the introductory exercises seek to strengthen students' understanding of themselves, the issues about which they are passionate and why.

We next seek to portray a conceptual overview of the landscape that comprises social entrepreneurship in order for students to begin to envision the place that they and their own work might occupy. As background reading on the nature of not-for-profit and social purpose organizations and as an introductory overview to not-for-profit management, the SE Lab also uses the beginning sections of Oster's *Strategic Management for Nonprofit Organizations* (Oster 1995) and Frumkin's *On Being Nonprofit* (Frumkin 2002). Two additional frameworks stimulate in-class discussion. First, Charles Leadbeater's diagram depicting the sources of social entrepreneurship among the three spheres of economic activity (public, private, and voluntary) highlights the notion that social entrepreneurship occurs at the points of intersection between and among these three sectors, which represent different interests and methods (Leadbeater 1997; see Figure 13.3). Second, Dees' presentation of the Social Enterprise Spectrum provides a view at the level of organization and enables the SE Lab to emphasize that there is a broad continuum of

The Social Entrepreneurship Collaboratory (SE Lab)

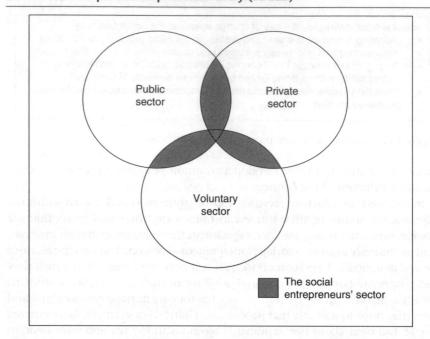

Figure 13.3 Sources of social entrepreneurship (Source: Leadbeater 1997)

		Purely philanthropic ←	→ Purely commercial
Motives, methods, and goals		Appeal to goodwill Mission driven Social value	Mixed motives Mission and market-driven Social and economic value	Appeal to self-interest Market-driven Economic value
Key stakeholders	Beneficiaries	Pay nothing	Subsidized rates, or mix of full payers and those who pay nothing	Market-rate prices
	Capital	Donations and grants	Below-market capital, or mix of donations and market-rate capital	Market-rate capital
	Workforces	Volunteers	Below-market wages, or mix of volunteers and fully paid staff	Market-rate compensation
	Suppliers	Make in-kind donations	Special discounts, or mix of in-kind and full-price donations	Market-rate prices

Figure 13.4 The social enterprise spectrum (Source: Dees 1998b)

available options for organizational design rather than starkly differentiated categories (Dees 1994; Dees 1998b; Dees, Emerson, and Economy 2001; see Figure 13.4). Discussion reveals, for example, that a social enterprise may have commercial features, relying less on philanthropy and operating more like a business in how it acquires resources and delivers its goods and services. Social entrepreneurship initiatives sometimes combine commercial and philanthropic elements in a 'productive balance'. For example, a team of five Harvard SE Lab students, Lance, Minor, Maggy, Amit, and Xochitl developed VIDA Card, a not-for-profit organization to help US immigrants substantially reduce transaction costs and lost value associated with sending $34 billion (£19.7 billion) annually to families overseas. VIDA also redistributes a portion of its earnings in programmes for the development of the home communities. Discussion also facilitates clarification of the motives, methods, and goals of the organization and of the key stakeholders involved including beneficiaries, providers of capital, workforces, and suppliers.

In combination, these frameworks enable students to begin to make distinctions between characteristics of organizations that operate in the different sectors and to clarify what is meant by social entrepreneurship. This also allows students to approach decisions about the structure of the organizations or initiatives they have begun to formulate.

The Process of Social Entrepreneurship: From Inspiration to Reality

As students embark on the creation process, we support them in formulating a value-creating social mission. To this end, one highly effective in-class demonstration involves presenting Kevin Carter's Pulitzer Prize winning photograph from 1994, taken during the Sudan famine (see Figure 13.5).

Seeing the photo shocks students and creates a new level of seriousness around global problem solving. It throws into question the value of the projects under consideration. It provides participants with a new metric against which to measure the seriousness of their purpose and the value and importance of their proposed endeavour. Related discussion encourages consideration of feasibility and potential effectiveness of students' social change models by focusing on the magnitude and intractability of global problems. We highlight obstacles to social change including complicated political structures and human failings, the willingness to create war and conflict, and the preference to turn a blind eye rather than looking at images like this photograph.

We frame the development of specific visions and missions for students' initiatives by presenting distinctions developed and popularized by Collins and Porras in 'Making Impossible Dreams Come True—A Guide to Demystifying Purpose, Mission, and Vision, and Putting Them to Work for You and Built to Last' (see Figure 13.6), which help to clarify boundaries among related concepts (Collins and Porras 1989, 2002). We marry the framework with examples from Ashoka Fellows described in the early chapters of David Bornstein's 2004 book, *How to Change the World: Social Entrepreneurs and the Power of New Ideas*. Using these tools and drawing upon insights based on the introductory exercise about issues of personal importance, we invite students

Pulitzer1994 KevinCarter

The PHOTO in the mail is the 'Pulitzer prize' winning photo taken in 1994 during the Sudan famine. The picture depicts a famine stricken child crawling towards a United Nations food camp, located a kilometre away.

>The vulture is waiting for the child to die so that it can eat it. This picture shocked the whole world. No one knows what happened to the child, including the photographer Kevin Carter who left the place as soon as the photograph was taken.

>Three months later he committed suicide due to depression.

Figure 13.5 Sudan child (Source: Carter 1994)

to draft their own vision and mission statement, and we select examples to critique as a group.

One of the hardest parts for students can be articulating a justification for their ventures. Thus, this process of developing, articulating, and discussing their own and others' visions and missions helps them clarify the rationale for their endeavour. Students' statements evolve over the course of the semester, and we indicate that they should treat their statements as working drafts. For example, Dave, a KSG student focusing on the environment and natural resources, had formerly lived and taught children both in the Boston housing projects and in Cali, Colombia. While in Colombia, several of his students

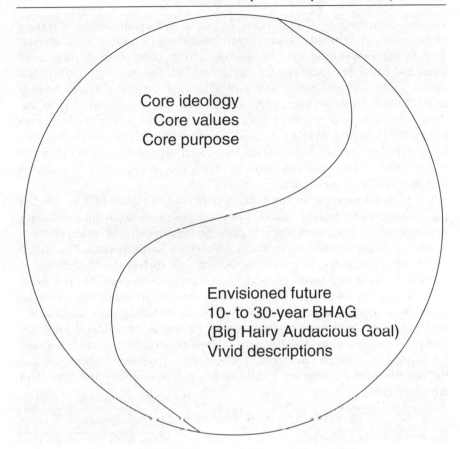

Core ideology
Core values
Core purpose

Envisioned future
10- to 30-year BHAG
(Big Hairy Audacious Goal)
Vivid descriptions

Figure 13.6 The vision framework (Source: Collins and Porras 2002)

were kidnapped and ransomed. Outraged and frustrated by the crime and environmental degradation caused by the country's civil conflict and high unemployment, Dave sought to reduce violence and protect Colombia's natural heritage. With this vision, he and classmate Doug developed FundaCap (Fundacion Capullo or Cocoon Foundation) whose mission was to 'rebuild Colombian communities and sustain our common future' by training ex-combatants alongside ordinary citizens and funding their employment in service to local conservation organizations.

Having covered the critical importance of understanding and adopting a social mission and the key attributes of social entrepreneurship, the curriculum shifts to a process for translating ideas into opportunities and impact: 'All acts of entrepreneurship start with the vision of an attractive opportunity' (Stevenson and Gumpert 1985). The 'Opportunity Creation

Process' developed in 'The Process of Social Entrepreneurship: Creating Opportunities Worthy of Serious Pursuit' provides an introduction and overview of the social-entrepreneurial process and its component parts (Guclu, Dees, and Battle Anderson 2002) (see Figure 13.7). The two main parts of the process involve: (*a*) generating a promising idea and (*b*) attempting to develop that idea into an attractive opportunity. The SE Lab is designed to help students address aspects of this process. By describing the process as an opportunity, the diagram provides a decidedly positive image. The process depicted aims at the level of the individual student/social entrepreneur rather than the organization or economy and helps to clarify the process and commitment required to achieve an impact.

The SE Lab intervenes in the process portrayed in Figure 13.7 at selected junctures. In order to help students develop promising ideas into attractive opportunities, it supports students in drawing upon their personal experiences in order to identify social needs about which they are passionate. The SE Lab facilitates and inspires their assessment of the needs and the importance of addressing them in a broad context for creating public value. It does so by providing examples and perspectives and a positive, collaborative environment for designing and developing solutions, including peer and faculty feedback in the supportive environment of the incubator. Students are often at different stages in the development of their projects (and in their relevant life experiences), but this most frequently enriches the peer collaboration and mentorship opportunities and collective sense of support, learning, and advancement.

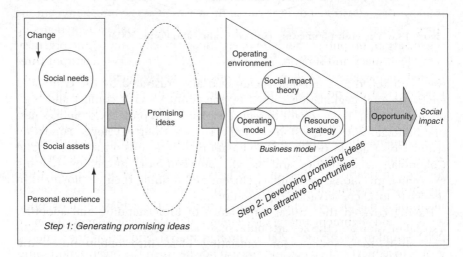

Figure 13.7 The opportunity creation process (Source: Guclu, Dees, and Battle Anderson 2002)

284

Aligning Mission and Strategy in a Social Entrepreneurship Organization

Once a project team has a good working proposition for its mission and a working knowledge of the process of social entrepreneurship, the team can start to develop its plan. A session on creating public value and the Strategic Triangle framework (Moore 1995, 2003) helps students move their ideas into an organizational concept and 'to become more helpful to society in searching out and exploiting opportunities to create public value' (Moore 1995: 21). The lecture and readings provoke a discussion about differences between private sector organizations, in which owners have traditionally sought private gains, and not-for-profit and public sector organizations, which are mandated to seek to create public value. Using student ideas under development, we examine public value and the challenges of the three-sector worldview. For example, in one instance a pair of students intended to develop a for-profit organization, Aquafloor, designed to sell padded pool bottoms to reduce serious pool-related injuries. Their model involved seeking government support for regulatory requirements that would advantage their product. While the organization would clearly benefit individuals who would otherwise be harmed by accidents in swimming pools, faculty and students felt the company's primary aim was to generate individual wealth for its founders and market dominance for the company, and thus was not driven first and foremost by a social mission which fit the SE Lab's working definition of social entrepreneurship. This example raised an inevitable issue, i.e. who is the arbiter of public value?

A useful and flexible framework for helping students design a strategy for creating public value has been the Strategic Triangle: Capacity, Support, Value (Moore 1995, 2003; Leonard 2002; Frumkin 2003: see Figure 13.8). We use the framework to illustrate both the causal links as well as the interaction among three elements necessary for creating a successful social entrepreneurship organization: (*a*) public value, (*b*) operational capacity, and (*c*) the organization's legitimacy and support. The model prompts students to confront three related management challenges: (*a*) mission management, the generative work of creating and re-creating a mission, value proposition, and theory of change to guide the organization; (*b*) operations management, effective mobilization of operational capacity to deliver services; and (*c*) stakeholder management, the building of support and legitimacy within the authorizing environment, i.e. among relevant arbiters of public value including potential funders. In relation to their own projects, we ask students to answer three questions: Is it valuable? Is it feasible? Is it authorizable? The key to successful planning and action is finding the 'sweet spot', i.e. the achievement of coherence, fit, and alignment among the elements of the Strategic Triangle (Leonard 2002; Frumkin 2003; Moore 2003). Through analysis and action, the students' goal is to achieve coherence and consistency between the organization's mission and value creation, the capacity of the proposed organization to carry out

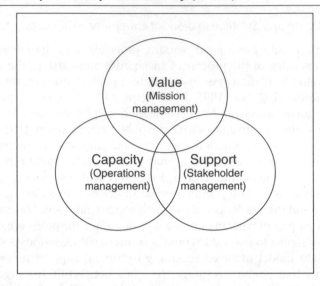

Figure 13.8 Value, Capacity, Support Framework derived from the Strategic Triangle (Adapted from Leonard 2002; Frumkin 2003; Moore 2003)

required operations, and the needs and desires of envisioned stakeholders. Therefore, making decisions and taking actions that will enable an organization to provide public value requires consideration of all three strategic dimensions of organizational management and finding that the proposed course of action simultaneously meets the criteria of all three. The Strategic Triangle framework can be used as both a prescriptive and a diagnostic tool and can be applied together with Kaplan's Balanced Scorecard (Kaplan and Leonard 2005), which similarly provides evaluative feedback on an enterprise's important dimensions.

Oster's six forces chart for not-for-profit industry analysis complements the Strategic Triangle by providing an industry perspective to this discussion and contributes the notion of a competitive environment (Oster 1995; see Figure 13.9). The framework, derived from Porter's Five Forces strategy framework (Porter 1980, 1996), allows SE Lab participants to begin to examine market forces and understand the wide range of stakeholders involved in the creation and market success of their organization. It also allows them to assess the resources that will be necessary to launch and grow their enterprise. Of the need for market analysis, Oster (1995) wrote, 'Nonprofit organizations often begin with a vision. To survive, however, organizations must also understand the economic and political markets in which they operate.'

Most project teams find this framework powerful and helpful, including the Stanford team that participated in founding Camp Kesem (*kesem* means 'magic' in Hebrew), a summer camp whose mission is to help children in

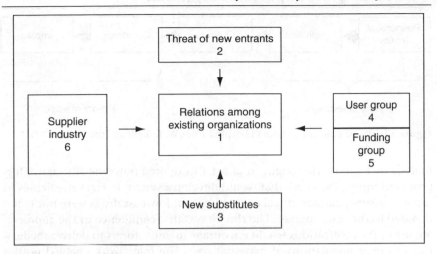

Figure 13.9 Six-forces chart for nonprofit industry analysis (Source: Oster 1995)

families coping with cancer. Inspired by the biblical mission of *tikun olam* (repairing the world) and supported initially by Stanford's Hillel, the group of Jewish and non-Jewish students performed industry analysis to help them convey their merit to the Walter and Elise Haas Fund, a Bay-Area philanthropy, and other key funders and stakeholders. Recognizing that they faced competition from existing and potential organizations providing cancer counselling and support, they sought to differentiate themselves. They did so successfully by identifying and emphasizing that not only would Camp Kesem benefit children whose parents have or had cancer, but it would also benefit Stanford student organizers and camp counsellors by providing profound leadership and care giving opportunities. Their dual-benefit argument succeeded in raising over $300,000 (£174,000) in operating funds. The Camp Kesem project at Stanford hosted its first summer session in June 2001, free of charge to thirty-seven campers. Since then, the project has continued and has grown each year to engage more student volunteers at eight university campuses and to serve more children.

Similarly, the Basic Logic Model framework complements the Strategic Triangle by modelling a value chain and 'theory of change' (W. K. Kellogg Foundation 2001; see Figure 13.10). Many students use this framework to develop and chart their proposed initiative's theory of change, i.e. the chain of causality between resources/inputs, activities, outputs, outcomes, and impact that is assumed by their organizations. The model helps students articulate the process by which their organization proposes to affect a desired change in society. For instance, KSG mid-career student Ron wanted to improve access to medical treatment for urban and rural populations in Africa by encouraging more affordable and reliable delivery of pharmaceuticals to treat, for example,

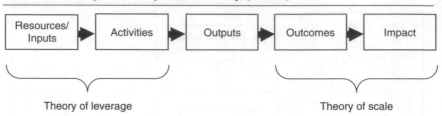

Figure 13.10 The basic logic model (Adapted from W. K. Kellogg Foundation 2001)

malaria in Uganda. He sought to affect this desired outcome through a for-profit enterprise, Pyramed, that would develop a system to track medicines in order to assure pharmaceutical companies that low-cost drugs were not being diverted to the black market. The theory was that confidence in the appropriate use of the medications would encourage manufacturers to deliver medications to poor populations at marginal cost. The framework enabled both a clear articulation of the student's theory of change and valuable discussion about whether this approach was indeed the best way to help people in Africa, or whether the beneficiaries would be primarily the manufacturers and corporate founders. Once their projects become operational, the model may also be used to help social entrepreneurs design and implement effective initiatives, evaluate them, improve them, and adapt to changing conditions.

The SE Lab also uses the Basic Logic Model to help students clarify their organizations' theories of leverage and of scale (Frumkin 2006). The theory of leverage suggests that social change organizations must assess their assets and decide how optimally to combine them into activities based on beliefs about the leverage and strategic advantage of those activities and some understanding of the organization's distinctive capabilities and comparative advantage. For example, high impact social entrepreneur Bobby Sager once commented that his foundation's impact in the developing world is simply leveraged relative to what his dollars could achieve in the USA (Personal meeting with Sager 2002).

Similarly, funders should consider leverage in their social change investment decisions. Frumkin has proposed a hierarchy of leverage for funders, ranging from ideas (most leverage), politics, networks, and organizations to individuals (least leverage), to help funders engage in 'strategic giving' (2006). For example, while funders can invest in social change work by investing in individual leaders in high-touch direct efforts, they may be able to achieve greater leverage by investing in organizations or programmes and allowing flexibility to direct funds where most needed. Investments in network building and guardians (Podolny 2005); politics, public policy and advocacy; or in shaping of fundamental ideas, new models, and creation of new knowledge represent theoretically increasingly leveraged interventions. While the funding community is only one perspective, each social entrepreneurs' theory of change ideally embeds an understanding of how to create public value in a leveraged manner, recognizing the realities of allocating scare resources and the often critical demands of time, especially in projects involving life-threatening situations.

Concerning a theory of scale, the SE Lab considers three models for its achievement, which are not necessarily mutually exclusive: (*a*) grow organic-ally as an organization; (*b*) franchise or license out what the organization does; and (*c*) export the ideas and the model for others to adopt, replicate, imitate, or transform including the public sector. SE Lab discussion conveys the idea that achieving scale is not just about growing your initiative and organization, but it is also about changing the way people see and do things in a way that amplifies the effect (Bradach 1999; Drayton 2000; Wei-Skillern, Battle Anderson, and Dees 2002). We discuss successful examples using each model, enabling students to assess better their own visions for social change. For example, the founder of Pyramed (introduced earlier) sought to develop a tracking system that would benefit as many people as quickly as possible by providing greater access to medications. While the founder preferred a for-profit model, many SE Lab participants felt potential growth would be greater and scale aims would be better achieved through a not-for-profit model that applied an open-source model for the tracking system making it more widely available than a proprietary technology.

The Performance Management Framework builds on the logic models framework (Leonard 2005; see Figure 13.11). It suggests that an organization's theory of change or logic model shapes its management and operations and defines an organizational boundary. Beyond this boundary, different organ-izations' outputs interact with the external environment, and these external outputs affect the organization's outcomes and the resulting impact or social change. An organization's data horizon represents the appropriate boundary of an organization's measurement and evaluation metrics. Feedback from measurement enables social entrepreneurs to manage and adapt their organ-izations in a cycle of learning and continuous improvement (March 1991).

Beyond the data horizon so many external outputs affect organizational outputs that response to an organization's intervention may differ markedly from its intended impact. One moves into the 'realm of cherished theory' as one moves farther away from the organization's boundary. This is where an organization hopes that its outputs have produced outcomes and the desired impact, but where its claims on causation are weak and uncertain. In the realm of cherished theory, and in a complex global landscape, an organization can in fact know little about its true impact on creating social change.

The paper, 'Zeroing in on Impact', and related discussion guides students in moving from aspirations to impact and in making their mission strategic, challenging them to articulate their 'actionable intended impact' and a 'coherent theory of change' (Colby, Stone, and Carttar 2004; see Figure 13.12). Colby and colleagues sought to address the often-weak connection

289

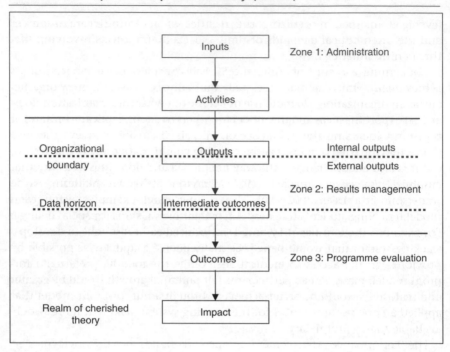

Figure 13.11 The performance management framework (Adapted from Leonard 2005)

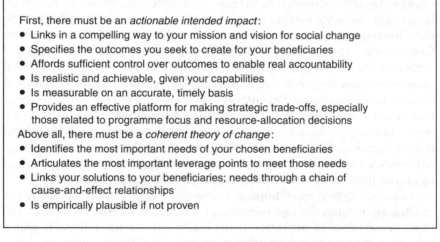

First, there must be an *actionable intended impact*:
- Links in a compelling way to your mission and vision for social change
- Specifies the outcomes you seek to create for your beneficiaries
- Affords sufficient control over outcomes to enable real accountability
- Is realistic and achievable, given your capabilities
- Is measurable on an accurate, timely basis
- Provides an effective platform for making strategic trade-offs, especially those related to programme focus and resource-allocation decisions

Above all, there must be a *coherent theory of change*:
- Identifies the most important needs of your chosen beneficiaries
- Articulates the most important leverage points to meet those needs
- Links your solutions to your beneficiaries; needs through a chain of cause-and-effect relationships
- Is empirically plausible if not proven

Figure 13.12 Intended impact and theory of change (Adapted from Colby, Stone, and Carttar 2004)

between professed mission and actual strategy, resulting in unsatisfactory outcomes. The paper helps students understand and articulate a coherent theory of change beginning with inputs and leading to outcomes and impact. Discussion focuses students on very practical, operations-oriented questions regarding performance (How will you know your work is accomplishing stated goals?), evaluation (What metrics can I track to demonstrate effectiveness to potential funders?), and strategy (How will you know whether your resources are leveraged in the best way?). For example, Harvard KSG mid-career student Giovanna, a native of Vieques Puerto Rico, sought ways to turn her goal of economic development for her homeland (until recently a site of a US military base and bombardment exercises) into a practical initiative. She formulated a strategy for addressing the island's high unemployment and poverty rates through a cooperative venture model. Cooperative participants would develop both an eco-tourism business and a cooperative housing development. To assess its performance, Turismo Vecinal Viequense (Vieques Neighborhood Tourism) identified relevant metrics, including change in the number of participants in the cooperative and clients, per capita income, and a development of alternative, viable financial sources for residents.

Applying Theory to Practical Problems

Of central importance in the SE Lab is applying theory to practical problems. A critical element of the curriculum for teaching students about social entrepreneurship is the design and development of a course project. The project represents an opportunity to collaborate on teams; to conduct field research; to develop planning documents for an initiative designed to address the social problem of their choice; and to compete for recognition in the marketplace of ideas.

Over the course of the semester, student teams create and develop a business plan, briefing book, or funding proposal, and often-innovative pilot projects. One student, April, called her end-term paper an 'Idea Briefing Dossier & Business Plan'. Required elements of the project include: an executive summary; the organization's name; statement of mission and vision; management team and advisors (who students have recruited and enlisted in developing their idea); description of the problem/need the project will address; the theory of change; proposed solution and intended impact; the market served; the strategy/business model, including the operating model and resource strategy; a financial plan; strategic partners; plan for measuring and evaluating project results; pilot project design and implementation (if applicable); references and sources of inspiration.

Assigned readings and in-class exercises and discussion support participants in addressing each of the elements required for the course project, but they represent only a part of the resources provided by the SE Lab (see Figure 13.13). To assist students further in choosing and developing their understanding of

Element of the SE Lab course project	Selected teaching tools	
	Element-specific	Global
Statement of mission and vision	Exercise • In-class introductory exercises • The Summer Day (Oliver 2004) Frameworks and field examples • Mission statement, Stanford University and Harvard KSG (Bloom and Scher 2003; Bloom et al. 2005) • Sudan child (Kevin Carter 1994) • Vision Framework (Collins and Porras 2002) • Vision Contract (Bloom and Nicolson 2003) • Attributes of an Effective Mission (Chio and Meehan 2001) • Johnston's diagnostic tests (Dees, Emerson, and Economy 2001) • Ashoka case studies (Chio and Meehan 2001; Bornstein 2004) Additional references and resources • Collins and Porras 1989 • Chs 2–3, Oster 1995 • Bryson 1995 • Cervantes (*Don Quixote*) 2003 • Carver 1997	Exercises • Abstract and project proposal • Elevator pitch/Social Enterprise Conference Pitch-for-Change • Reflection assignment • Preliminary presentation • Final presentation • Business plan/briefing book • Feedback forms • Social E-Challenge business plan competition Frameworks and field examples Introduction and overview for social entrepreneurship • Defining Social Entrepreneurship (Dees 1998a) • Definitions of Social Entrepreneur; Stanford/Ashoka case (Chio and Meehan 2001) • Sources of Social Entrepreneurship (Leadbeater 1997) • Social Enterprise Spectrum (Dees 1998b) • What Makes Social Entrepreneurs Different? (Dees, Emerson, and Economy 2001)
Theory of change	Frameworks and field examples • Basic Logic Models (adapted from W. K. Kellogg Foundation 2001) • Performance Management Framework (adapted from Leonard 2005) • Intended Impact and Theory of Change (Colby, Stone, and Carttar 2004)	
Developing a strategy and business model	Frameworks and field examples • The Strategic Triangle (Moore 1995, 2003; Leonard 2002; Frumkin 2003) • Six forces chart for nonprofit industry analysis (Oster 1995) • Opportunity Creation Process (Guclu, Dees, and Battle Anderson 2002) • Performance Management Framework (Leonard 2005) • Solomon R. Guggenheim Foundation case (Oster 1995)	

		Business plan development
	Additional references and resources • Kaplan and Leonard 2005 • Colby, Stone, and Carttar 2004 • Dees 1998b • Oberfield and Dees 1991 • Wei-Skillern, Anderson, and Dees 2007	• Ripple Effects business plan (2002) • Harvard Business Plan Competition • Van Slyke, Stevenson, and Roberts 1988
Governance	Frameworks and field examples • Key tasks of nonprofit boards (Oster 1995) • Old work new work (Taylor, Chait and Holland 1996) • Board attributes and best practices (Meehan 2003) Additional references and resources • Oster (1995) • Chait, Ryan, and Taylor (2004) • Fremont-Smith (2004)	• Introduction and overview for social entrepreneurship • Oster (1995) • Frumkin (2002) • Drucker (1985) • Drayton (2000) • Alvord, Brown, and Letts (2004) • Yunus (2003) • Bornstein (2004)
Strategic partnerships	References and resources • Briggs (2003a and 2003b) • Ostrower (2005) • Austin (2004)	Business plan development • Childress (2005) • Brooks (2002) • Rooney in Dees, Emerson, and Economy (2001) • Sahlman (1997)
Financial planning and funding	Frameworks and field examples • Peace games case (Rosegrant and Leonard 2004) References and resources • Chu (2005) • Letts, Ryan, and Grossman (1997) • Sievers (1997) • Dees (1998b)	
Project measurement and evaluation	Frameworks and field examples • Performance management framework (Leonard 2005) • Social return on investment (SROI), Roberts Enterprise Development Fund (Gair 2002) References and resources • Sawhill and Williamson (2001) • Ch. 4 in Dees (1998b) • Kaplan and Leonard (2005) • Kramer (2005)	

* See References for complete citation information.

Figure 13.13 Selected teaching tools of the social entrepreneurship collaboratory*

social entrepreneurship and their course project, the SE Lab introduces students to a broad set of resources within and outside the university supportive of social entrepreneurship and invites them to co-create a collaborative environment that mentors them in designing and developing solutions and the social change organizations to implement them.

Both Stanford and Harvard have excellent, student-organized and student-oriented conferences and a business plan competition that can be helpful to participants in the SE Lab. At Harvard in Spring 2005, the HBS/KSG Social Enterprise Conference and KSG International Development Conference provided perspectives from hundreds of speakers and organizations addressing social entrepreneurship as well as valuable, complementary resources upon which we suggested strongly that students draw. The SE Lab recommends attendance to specific sessions of the conferences. For instance, in 2005 at Harvard's Social Enterprise Conference, students attended a panel with Ashoka founder Bill Drayton and four Ashoka fellows, followed two days later by a special SE Lab session with Drayton. As part of the international development conference, many students also attended a keynote address by C. K. Prahalad on the controversial market-based approach to international development, as articulated in *The Fortune at the Bottom of the Pyramid* (Prahalad and Hart 2004).

In addition, Stanford's Social Entrepreneurship (Social E)-Challenge enjoys impressive university-wide participation and motivates students to develop innovative business plans to address social needs (Levy 2003). Two rounds of competition evaluated first an executive summary and, for finalists, a business plan and presentation. In association with the business plan competition at both Stanford and Harvard, SE Lab participants availed themselves of specialized help sessions on constructing a business plan, performance measurement, and business financing that accompanied these university-based activities.

Harvard SE Lab students were encouraged to participate in a special HBS/KSG Social Enterprise Conference Pitch-for-Change competition in which contestants competed to offer the best funding pitch for their social change organization. The goal was to be able to communicate their idea in a compelling way to a potential funder or strategic partner in a very brief 'elevator pitch'. The written abstract could be no longer than 200 words, the first round pitch 30 seconds, and in the final round, the verbal pitch must be conveyed in no more than 2 minutes with the help of two PowerPoint slides. Criteria for evaluating the pitch included the scale of impact, innovativeness of the idea, likelihood of success, and overall persuasiveness of the presentation. A team of three women from the SE Lab, led by an Afghani-born KSG mid-career student, Masuda, won first prize in the 2005 competition, pitching Impact Capital, a venture capital firm that aims to empower women in Afghanistan. One month later, team members had the opportunity to meet Afghanistan President Karzai and made their pitch, which was well practised and enthusiastically received. Team members have secured some start-up funding and will be in Afganistan conducting fieldwork during Summer 2005 to pilot their plan.

SE Lab class sessions comprise a broad range of formats, including presentations, discussions, and case studies. In addition to the several sessions designed to introduce students to the frameworks discussed earlier, the SE Lab invites participation from domain experts and social entrepreneurship practitioners, both as visiting faculty and as regular participants and mentors in the lab. Practitioner and domain expert participation is a key feature of the lab's impact on students. These individuals bring inspiring examples of successful social entrepreneurship endeavours and help demonstrate how to translate ideas into practice. They also bring extraordinary intellectual capital, connecting students to a local and worldwide network of resources and social entrepreneurs. Special guest lecturers have included faculty and practitioners who add a wealth of knowledge and wisdom that helps students develop as leaders and social entrepreneurs (Figure 13.14).

The style of class sessions varies, but is often Socratic in that discussion leaders act as facilitator rather than lecturer. Discussions challenge both students and guest practitioners to examine critically key issues in social entrepreneurship. Students also engage each other, advising and helping colleagues to develop as leaders and to build their initiatives.

Students complete a series of milestones to facilitate continued progress and timely completion of the course project. Written assignments and in-class presentations afford students an opportunity for feedback on their work from colleagues and faculty and help the SE Lab to develop as a community of learning and mutual support. Assignments include an abstract and preliminary project proposal, an 'elevator pitch', a reflection assignment, executive summary, preliminary and final presentations, and a final business plan or briefing book. Class assignments are linked, where possible, to the social entrepreneurship activities ongoing across the university.

Three weeks into the course, students submit an initial abstract and preliminary project proposal that touch on many of the main elements of the business plan they would eventually submit. The intent of the assignment is to push students to formulate an idea and to provide an opportunity for input. At Stanford, the abstracts meet the criteria for the first stage of the Social E-Challenge.

The elevator pitch requires students to develop a funding pitch for their social change organization. Requirements for the elevator pitch meet the criteria for the HBS/KSG Pitch-for-Change competition.

A mid-course reflection assignment provides a structured exercise to consolidate and make productive events students had experienced through the SE Lab. The assignment asks them to reflect on recent experiences (including SE Lab sessions or events at the social entrepreneurship conference) that impacted their thinking on their project and changed their ideas or perspective, and to

The Social Entrepreneurship Collaboratory (SE Lab)

Speaker	Title or position	SE Lab topic
Bill Drayton	Ashoka founder	Identifying, funding, and supporting
Paul Herman	Ashoka North American Program director	1,400 social entrepreneurs and their international social change organizations
Greg Dees	Co-founder of the Stanford Center for Social Innovation and Duke professor	The nature of social entrepreneurship and social entrepreneurs
Jim Phills	Faculty co-chair, Stanford Center for Social Innovation	Mission and strategy for social innovation organizations
Bill Meehan	Stanford GSB Lecturer, McKinsey director	Aligning mission and strategy
Michael McCullough Ana Rowena Mallari	Quest Scholar co-founders	
Stacy Childress	HBS lecturer	Constructing a social enterprise business plan
Jacqueline Novogratz	Acumen Fund CEO	Sources of social venture funding
Kavita Ramdas	Global Fund for Women CEO	Gender equality and social venture capital models for investing in women in the developing world
Iqbal Paroo	Omidyar Foundation president	Funding social entrepreneurship in
Bruce Sievers	Stanford lecturer, former Haas Family Foundation director	family and community foundations
Peter Hero	Community Foundation Silicon Valley president	
Jed Emerson	Roberts Enterprise Development Fund (REDF) co-founder	Social capital markets and blended value theory for optimal investment of foundation endowments and other resources
Mark Kramer	Foundation Strategy Group co-founder and managing director, Center for Effective Philanthropy co-founder	Evaluating social entrepreneurship organizations
Sarah Alvord	Harvard Hauser KSG Senior Program officer	Societal transformation through social entrepreneurship
David Brown	KSG lecturer	
Eric Dawson	Peace Games founder	Start-ups, growth, and governance
Christine Letts	KSG lecturer and Peace Games board chair	
Laura Scher	Working Assets CEO and Stanford lecturer	Strategy and for-profit social purpose organizations

Figure 13.14 Selected guest lecturers in the SE Lab

discuss the way in which their thinking had changed. It also asks students to describe any ways in which they and their project team felt stuck and what they planned to do about it.

During the second half of the course, students submit a draft executive summary and give preliminary presentations covering all the categories required for their final assignment. This exercise requires students to develop plausible answers to each one of the categories, even if their ideas were not yet well formed. Its intent is to help students understand the strengths and weaknesses of their project and to enable them to seek and receive feedback and suggestions from SE Lab participants.

The final assignment consists of two parts. Student teams first submit a two-page executive summary and make an in-class presentation of their project. The final presentation synthesizes their work and enables students to practise conveying their ideas to potential funders and strategic partners. Students receive additional feedback at this time. Approximately three weeks later, their final completed business plan or briefing book is due. Students aim to create presentations and documents that could be used as their entry in the Social E-Challenge or to share with potential funders. Many indicate that they value the cumulative nature of the learning and final product for the SE Lab, where parts are developed selectively along the way, and then drawn together, augmented, and revised by the end of term.

Signs of Success

> *My life is my message.*
> —Gandhi

The SE Lab aims to create an environment for students to identify a social problem about which they are passionate, to envision a solution to the problem, and move their vision towards reality by designing and developing a social change organization and an agenda for change. According to available measures, the SE Lab has experienced some success in achieving its aim.

First, the SE Lab has performed well on such metrics as course enrolment and student evaluations. One student, Dave, whose email tagline reads, 'If opportunity doesn't knock, build a door. –Milton Berle', reflected on the value of the course:

I have constantly been frustrated at the Kennedy School with my lack of ability to engage deeply in courses, including the ones whose descriptions, syllabi, and readings are of utmost thematic interest to me. I simply muddle through the readings, papers, and problem sets with only one goal—to get done with them so I can move on to more important things. . . . This course, by contrast, is one that I can't stop thinking about. The readings are ones that I mull over and am able to place in context, testing my idea, judging the worth of my enterprise, etc. We ought to have more real-life experiential training at this school. Thank God I was able to take this one before graduating.

For this student at least, the SE Lab delivered on its promise to fuse theory and practice, with powerful results.

Equally importantly, the course has produced concrete outcomes. Students' projects demonstrated their competitiveness in the marketplace for ideas, reaping financial as well as psychic rewards for their efforts. Four of the five winning teams of the Stanford Social E-Challenge in 2003 developed their proposals in the SE Lab. The competition included twenty-nine student teams who competed to create innovative business plans addressing social needs. Venture capitalists judged plans and presentations and awarded the $20,000 (£11,600) prize money (Levy 2003). Similarly, for work developed in Harvard's first SE Lab in 2005, students were awarded the top prize and three of the four additional prizes in the 2005 HBS/KSG Social Enterprise Conference Pitch-for-Change competition. SE Lab students have raised hundreds of thousands of dollars for their initiatives, and in one case known to this author, over a million dollars. In addition, there are SE Lab spin-offs, including courses offered through Stanford's Public Policy Program aimed at health care, environment, and global development, and at other universities.

Students in the SE Lab have created innovative organizations serving many different social causes. For example, Stanford SE Lab student Alex, who lost a close friend to HIV/AIDS, was passionate about helping HIV-infected populations in developing countries. With an initial theory of change that was impractical, the SE Lab supported him in designing and developing a more effective social change model through research, iterative feedback, and by facilitating an extracurricular brainstorming session with AIDS experts and potential partners. He founded a national campaign to raise funds and political support for treatment, which engaged thousands of people, sent thousands of letters to Congress, formed strategic partnerships with one of the leading AIDS activist organizations and the Elizabeth Glaser Pediatric AIDS Foundation, and organized AIDS walks in ten US cities. The initiative recruited dozens of Stanford students and an array of SE Lab members and raised tens of thousands of treatment doses for HIV-infected individuals in seventeen countries.

Jo Microfinance, introduced at the outset of this chapter, was the first place winner in the 2003 Social E-Challenge. Uri led a team of students in developing a business plan to address the economic roots of Israeli–Palestinian terrorism using a microfinancing model inspired by Grameen Bank in Bangladesh. The company gives loans of $200 (£116) to $600 (£348) and basic business training to young Palestinian men who could become targets for recruitment to terrorist groups. Pilot projects are underway in East Jerusalem and the West Bank. In 2005–6, Uri is embarking on a joint-degree programme between Harvard's KSG and Stanford's GSB to pursue dual masters degrees focused on international development and entrepreneurship.

Aid Information Mapping Services (AIMS) for Humanity is a technology-enabled mapping and humanitarian relief project which seeks to improve the speed, accuracy, and quantity of aid to disaster zones, developed at Stanford in collaboration with the Reuters Foundation Digital Vision Fellows Program. The initiative employs novel technology to improve coordination of information that facilitates emergency response to crises such as war, famine, disease, earthquake, and floods that disrupt the lives of millions across the world. Pilot projects in Iraq and Africa have provided crisis workers with maps using imagery collected from unmanned aerial vehicles and satellites that provide a real-time picture of water needs, buildings on fire, locations of mine fields, or a percentage of a population afflicted with illness.

ABCD Español Oaxaca is a literacy project for Mexico, which employs a method for tackling literacy that has been successful in Colombia, Guatemala, and the Dominican Republic. The method involves playing a game that incorporates linguistic principles and is a highly cost-effective way of achieving literacy. Students worked with a local centre for the development and study of indigenous languages to design a pilot project to teach 4,000 people to read and write in their native language in four months.

These projects illustrate the potential impact of combining exercises that tap into people's passion, fieldwork, action research, peer support and learning, and the participation of domain experts and social entrepreneurship practitioners with foundational frameworks. The growth and development of projects in the SE Lab brings to mind an image of my daughter Audrey that I hold dear, and that I shared with the Stanford SE Lab as an introduction to one of the final presentation sessions.

We launched the SE Lab at Stanford when Audrey was 3 years old, the year her brother Jason was born: a time of extraordinary developmental growth for both. That year, Audrey enrolled at Bing Nursery School at Stanford and enjoyed playing on the swings in the large yard in the outdoor portion of her classroom and trying to swing high enough to touch a leaf on the branch of a nearby tree. At the beginning of the year, Audrey was too small and not skilled enough to reach the leaf, but as the year progressed, Audrey grew and was able to swing higher and higher, to stretch forward her feet towards the leaves. The branch also grew towards the swing, and by year end Audrey was able to just touch the lower-most leaf. In the same way, SE Lab students grow and move forward in reaching goals by the end of the semester that they may have been able to envision, but were impossible to achieve at the outset of the SE Lab.

Ultimately, the intellect, energy, passion, and talent of the students themselves provided the core of their success in developing innovative social sector initiatives. While Stanford and Harvard attract superb students and create impressive networks, this model is generalizable to many other universities. The SE Lab created an environment in which the students' ideas and project teams could be unleashed and flourished. Not all projects incubated in the SE Lab are successful nor will all participants in the SE Lab become successful social entrepreneurs. However, the SE Lab supports students to fulfil their longing to be part of a social change movement and gives them the opportunity to create their own path. By helping students to gain confidence and inspiration in their own ability to make a difference through social entrepreneurship, many of them will join the next generation of leaders in any sector.

Notes

1. Acknowledgements: I wish to thank the many gifted students and teaching fellows of the SE Lab at Stanford and Harvard. Stanford student and teaching fellow Alex Bradford and Harvard student Elizabeth McKenna provided important assistance in researching, drafting, and commenting upon an early manuscript for this chapter, based on their experiences in the lab at their universities. SE Lab principals Ashoka founder Bill Drayton and Harvard Hauser Center faculty director Mark Moore gave valued early guidance on the abstract for this chapter at a memorable meeting at Oxford for the first Skoll World Forum on Social Entrepreneurship (29 March 2004), and Oxford Skoll Centre for Social Entrepreneurship Lecturer Alex Nicholls has been a steadfast supporter and patient editor. Most importantly, my Stanford teaching colleague and extraordinary wife Sara Singer who worked tirelessly with me on the final stages of this manuscript, and who together with our two children Audrey and Jason provided love and support without which the SE Lab at Stanford and Harvard would have been inconceivable.

   I am indebted to an extensive group of university colleagues, mentors, and advisors who influenced the SE Lab in its development—some are indicated here. At Stanford's Public Policy Program and Program in Urban Studies, Graduate School of Business and CSI, and Institute for International Studies: Greg Dees, Dave Brady, Roger Noll, Len Ortolano, Jim Phills, Jed Emerson, Laura Scher, Melanie Edwards, Bill Meehan, my wife Sara Singer, and dear friend Mark Nicolson, Cliff Nass, Syed Shariq, Ben Shaw, Joel Podolny, Chip Blacker, Nadine Cruz, Bruce Sievers, Wally Falcon, Alain Enthoven, Mike Spence, Woody Powell, Jim March, David Abernathy, Beth Anderson, Marga Jann, Bill Berhman, and Perla Ni. Harvard's Hauser Center for Nonprofit Organizations at the KSG has been an important home and intellectual incubator for the SE Lab with its seminars and valued conversation partners—Mark Moore, Dutch Leonard, Chris Winship (and our Sociology 136 seminar on nonprofits), Peter Frumkin, Chris Letts, Peter Dobkin Hall, Derek Bok, Dave Brown, Sarah Alvord, Xav Briggs, Tiziana Dearing, Shawn Bohen, Brent Coffin, Liz Keating, Marshall Ganz, Bill Ryan, Marion Freemont Smith, and Paul Hodge. At the Kennedy School's Center for Public Leadership, David Gergen, Ron Heifitz, and Max Martin, and HBS and Social Enterprise Initiative faculty, Jim Austin, Kash Rangan, Jane Wei-Skillern, Allan Grossman, Michael Chu, and Stacey Childress. Their ideas, advice, published and unpublished articles, and example have been helpful and inspiring. And Catherine and Wayne Reynolds, for their magnificent gift to Harvard establishing a pathbreaking fellowship programme in social entrepreneurship and curriculum development fund. All errors in this manuscript are mine.

2. The SE Lab was introduced to the Stanford Public Policy Program curriculum Fall 2002 and into the Harvard Kennedy School Spring 2005.

References

Alvord, S., Brown, D., and Letts, C. (2004). 'Social Entrepreneurship and Societal Transformation: An Exploratory Study', *Journal of Applied Behavioral Science*, 40(3): 260–83.

Austin, J. (2004). 'Institutional Collaboration', in D. Young (ed.), *Effective Economic Decision-Making by Nonprofit Organizations*. National Center on Nonprofit Enterprise and The Foundation Center, pp. 149–66.

Bernstein, E. (2005). 'Giving Back', *The Wall Street Journal*, 13 May: W2.

Bloom, G. and Nicolson, M. (2003) Vision Contract. Stanford University: Social Entrepreneurship Collaboratory (SE Lab).

——and Scher, L. (Spring, 2003). *Public Policy 192—Social Entrepreneurship: Mobilizing Private Resources for the Common Good & Public Policy 193—Social Entrepreneurship Collaboratory (SE Lab) Syllabus*, Stanford University, Public Policy Program and Program on Urban Studies, School of Humanities & Sciences.

——Leonard, H., Moore, M., and Winship, C. (Spring, 2005). *Social Entrepreneurship Collaboratory (SE Lab): Syllabus*, Harvard University, Hauser Center for Nonprofit Organizations, John F. Kennedy School of Government.

Bornstein, D. (2004). *How to Change the World: Social Entrepreneurs and the Power of New Ideas*. New York: Oxford University Press.

Briggs, X. (2003*a*). 'Perfect Fit or Shotgun Marriage?: Understanding the Power and Pitfalls. In Partnerships', *The Art and Science of Community Solving Project at Harvard University*.

Briggs, X. (2003*b*). 'Working the Middle: Roles and Challenges of Intermediaries', *The Art and Science of Community Solving Project at Harvard University*.

Brooks, Z. (2002). *An Introduction to Business Planning for Nonprofits*. The Bridgespan Group, available at: www.bridgespangroup.org

Cerrantes, M. (2003). Don Quixote (a new translation by Edith Grossman), New York: Ecco

Chait, R., Ryan, W., and Taylor, B. (2004). *Governance as Leadership: Reframing the Work of Nonprofit Boards*. New York: John Wiley & Sons.

Chio, J. and Meehan, W. (2001). *Ashoka: Innovators for the Public (North America Program)*. Stanford, CA: Graduate School of Business, Stanford University, Case Number: SM-64.

Childress, S. (2005). *Developing a Social Enterprise Business Plan*. HBS Business Plan Contest Help session, 26 January.

Chu, M. (2005). *Financing a Nonprofit or Social Purpose Organization*. HBS Business Plan Contest Help session, 16 February.

Colby, S., Stone, N., and Carttar, P. (Fall, 2004). 'Zeroing in on Impact: In an Era of Declining Resources, Nonprofits Need to Clarify Their Intended Impact', *Stanford Social Innovation Review*: 24–33.

Collins, J. and Porras, J. (July, 1989). 'Making Impossible Dreams Come True—A Guide to Demystifying Purpose, Mission and Vision and Putting Them to Work for You', *Stanford Business School Magazine*: 12–19.

—— —— (eds.) (2002). *Built to Last*. New York: HarperCollins.

Dees, J. G. (1994). *Social Enterprise: Private Initiatives for Common Good*. Harvard University: Harvard Business School Press.

—— (1998*a*). *The Meaning of Social Entrepreneurship*. Stanford University: Center for Social Innovation, Graduate School of Business, Kauffman Center for Entrepreneurial Leadership, Ewin Marion Kauffman Foundation, available at http://faculty.fuqua.duke.edu/centers/case/files/dees-SE.pdf

—— (January–February, 1998*b*). 'Enterprising Nonprofits', *Harvard Business Review*: 76(1): 55–66.

—— Emerson, J., and Economy, P. (2001). *Enterprising Non-profits: A Toolkit for Social Entrepreneurs*. New York: Wiley Non-Profit Series.

Delgado, R. (2005). 'Through New Initiative, University Amplifies Focus on Global Problem Solving', *Stanford Report*, 4 May.

Drayton, W. (2000). 'The Entrepreneurs Revolution and You', available at: http://ashoka.org/fellows/entrepreneurs_revolution.cfm

Drucker, P. (1985). *Innovation and Entrepreneurship: Practice and Principles*. New York: HarperCollins.

Fremont-Smith, M. (2004). *Governing Nonprofit Organizations: Federal and State Law and Regulation*. Harvard University: Belknap Press of Harvard University Press.

Frumkin, P. (2002). *On Being Nonprofit: A Conceptual and Policy Primer*. Harvard, MA: Harvard University Press.

—— (2003). *Creating New Schools: The Strategic Management of Charter Schools*. Annie E. Casey Foundation, available at: www.aecf.org

—— (2006). *Strategic Giving*. Chicago, IL: University of Chicago Press.

Gair, C. (2002). *Report from the Good Ship SROI*. San Francisco, CA: Roberts Enterprise Development Fund, available at: www.redf.org

Gewertz, K. (2006). *'Caring' Entrepreneurship at KSG: where business and social awareness meet*, Harvard Gazette, 25 May. http://www.news.harvard.edu/gazette/2006/05.25/11-entrepreneur.html

Guclu, A., Dees, J., and Battle Anderson, B. (2002). 'The Process of Social Entrepreneurship: Creating Opportunities Worthy of Serious Pursuit', *CASE Working Paper Series 3*. Duke Fuqua School Duke University: Center for the Advancement of Social Entrepreneurship.

John F. Kennedy School of Government (2005). *Harvard University Facts 2004–2005*.

Kaplan, R. and Leonard, H. (February, 2005). *Aligning Mission, Support, and Capacity in Public Sector Programs*. Harvard University.

Kramer, M. (2005). *Measuring Innovation: Evaluation in the Field of Social Entrepreneurship*. Skoll Foundation, Boston, MA: Foundation Strategy Group.

Leadbeater, C. (1997). *The Rise of the Social Entrepreneur*. London: Demos.

Leonard, H. (May, 2002). *A Short Note on Public Sector Strategy-Building*. Harvard University.

Letts, C., Ryan, W., and Grossman, A. (March–April, 1997). 'Virtuous Capital: What Foundations Can Learn From Venture Capital', *Harvard Business Review*: 36–44.

Levy, D. (2003). 'Social Entrepreneurs Pitch Their Plans: Contest Winners Promotes Peace Through Prosperity Democracy Through Literacy', *Stanford Report*, June 4: 6.

March, J. (1991). 'Exploration and Exploitation in Organizational Learning', *Organization Science*, 2(1): 71–87.

Meehan, W. (Fall, 2003). *Strategic Management of Nonprofits. Course Syllabus.* Stanford Graduate School of Business.

Moore, M. (1995). *On Creating Public Value: Strategic Management in Government.* Harvard: Harvard University Press.

—— (September, 2003). *On Creating Public Value: What Businesses (And Non-Profit Organizations) Might Learn from Government about Strategic Management.* Harvard University: John F. Kennedy School of Government.

Oberfield, A. and Dees, G. (January, 1991). 'A Note on Starting a Nonprofit Venture', *Harvard Business School*: 9-391-096.

Oliver, M. (2004). 'The Summer Day', in *New and Selected Poems.* New York: Beacon Press.

Oster, S. (1995). *Strategic Management for Nonprofit Organizations: Theory and Cases.* Oxford: Oxford University Press.

Ostrower, D. (Spring, 2005). 'The Reality Underneath the Buzz of Partnerships', *Stanford Social Innovation Review*: 34–41.

Podolny, J. (2005). *Social Networks as Ends and Not Means*, presentation to the Skoll World Forum on Social Entrepreneurship, Saïd Business School, Oxford University, 31 March.

Porter, M. (1980). *Competitive Strategy: Techniques for Analyzing Industries and Competitors.* New York: Free Press.

—— (November–December, 1996). 'What Is Strategy?', *Harvard Business Review*: 61–78.

Prahalad, C. and Hart, S. (2004). *The Fortune at the Bottom of the Pyramid: Eradicating Poverty Through Profit.* University of Pennsylvania: Wharton School Publishing.

Rosegrant, S. and Leonard, H. (2004). 'Peace Games: A Nonprofit's Journey From Birth to National Expansion (A) and Epilogue', Kennedy School of Government Case Study.

Sahlman, W. (July–August, 1997). 'How to Write a Great Business Plan', *Harvard Business Review*: 98–108.

Sawhill, J. and Williamson, D. (2001). 'Measuring What Matters in Nonprofits', *McKinsey Quarterly*, 2: 98–107.

Sievers, B. (November–December, 1997). 'If Pigs Had Wings: The Appeals and Limits of Venture Philanthropy', *Foundation News & Commentary*: 44–6.

Staff Writer (2005). 'Reynolds Foundation Creates Unique Fellowship: Program to Focus on Social Entrepreneurship', *Harvard Gazette*, 19 May.

Stevenson, H. and Gumpert, D. (March, 1985). 'The Heart of Entrepreneurship', *Harvard Business Review*: 85–94.

Taylor, B., Chait, R., and Holland, T. (September–October, 1996). 'The New Work of the Nonprofit Board', *Harvard Business Review*, 74(5): 36–44.

W. K. Kellogg Foundation (2001). *Logic Model Development Guide: Using Logic Models to Bring Together Planning, Evaluation & Action*, available at: www.wkkf.org

Yunus, M. (2003). *Halving Poverty by 2015.* London: Commonwealth Institute, 11 March.

Additional Supporting References

Bennis, W. and Thomas, R. (2002). *Geeks & Geezers.* Cambridge, MA: Harvard Business School Press.

Bloom, G. and Nicolson, M. (2003). *Vision Contract.* Stanford University: Social Entrepreneurship Collaboratory (SE Lab).

Bowen, W. (September–October, 1994). 'When a Business Leader Joins a Nonprofit Board', *Harvard Business Review*: 38–43.

Bradach, J. (Spring, 2003). 'Going to Scale', *Stanford Social Innovation Review*: 19–25.

Bradford, A. (ed.) (2003). *Generation Y for the Global Village*. Washington, DC: International Peace Press.

Bryson, J. (1995). 'Clarifying Organizational Mandates and Mission', in S. Oster (ed.), *Strategic Management of Public and Nonprofit Organizations*. San Francisco, CA: Jossey-Bass.

Carver, J. (1997). 'Creating a Mission that Makes a Difference', in *CarverGuides*. San Francisco, CA: Jossey-Bass.

Cervantes, M. (2003). *Don Quixote* (a new translation by Edith Grossman). New York: Ecco.

de Tocqueville, A. (2004). *Democracy in America*. Arthur Goldhammer, trans., New York: Library of America.

Drucker, P. (July–August, 1989). 'What Businesses Can Learn from Nonprofits', *Harvard Business Review*: 88–93.

Emerson, J. (May–June, 2002). 'Horse Manure and Grantmaking', *Foundation News & Commentary*, 43(4): 22–3.

——(May, 2003). *Social Innovation: Blending Profit and Nonprofit Values*. Stanford: Graduate School of Business.

——Tuan, M., Dutton, L., and Kessler, D. (May, 1998). *The Roberts Enterprise Development Fund: Implementing a Social Venture Capital Approach to Philanthropy*. Stanford University: Graduate School of Business.

Gardner, J. (March, 1994). 'The Road to Self-Renewal', *Stanford Alumni Magazine*: 32–5.

Gershenfeld, N. and Mikhak, B. (2005). *Fab Lab: The Center for Bits and Atoms*. Massachusetts Institute of Technology, available at: http://cba.mit.edu/projects/fablab/

Gertner, J. (2002). 'A New World Order: Jed Emerson's Capitalist Utopia. Can Social Value Reward Investors Companies?', *CNN Money Magazine*, 29 October, Available at http://money.cnn.com/2002/10/28/pf/investing/emerson/

Greider, W. (2003). *The Soul of Capitalism: Opening Paths to a Moral Economy*. New York: Simon & Schuster.

Harvard Business Review on Nonprofits (1999). Harvard University: Harvard Business School Press.

Husock, H. (July–August, 2004). 'New Ideas People', *The Philanthropy Roundtable*, available at: www.philanthropyroundtable.org

Kanter, R. (May–June, 1999). 'From Spare Change to Real Change. The Social Sector as Beta Site for Business Innovation', *Harvard Business Review*: 122–32.

Khazei, A. and Fallen, E. (2004). 'Inspiring Future Social Entrepreneurs', *The Boston Globe*, July 5: A11.

Klausner, M. (Spring, 2003). 'When Time Isn't Money: Foundation Payouts and the Time Value of Money', *Stanford Social Innovation Review*: 51–9.

Kuhn, T. (1962). *The Structure of Scientific Revolutions*. University of Chicago: International Encyclopaedia of Unified Science.

Letts, C., Ryan, W., and Grossman, A. (1999). *High Performance Nonprofit Organizations: Managing Upstream for Greater Impact*. New York: John Wiley & Sons.

Martin, M. (2004). *Surveying Social Entrepreneurship*. St. Gallen, Germany: Universitat St. Gallen Center for Public Leadership.

More, T. (1516). *Utopia* (translated and edited by H. V. S. Ogden, Appleton-Century-Crofts, New York 1949).

Peyus, S., Grossman, A., Austin, J., and Hart, M. (November, 1999). *Explore, Inc.* Harvard University: Harvard Business School.

Powell, W. (ed.) (1987). *The Nonprofit Sector: A Research Handbook*. New Haven, CT: Yale University Press.

Putman, R. (January, 1995). 'Bowling Alone: America's Declining Social Capital', *Journal of Democracy*: 65–78.

Timmons, J. (1999). *New Venture Creation: Entrepreneurship for the 21st Century*. Boston, MA: McGraw-Hill.

Van Slyke, J., Stevenson, H., and Roberts, M. (1988). *The Start-Up Process*. Harvard University: Harvard Business School.

Waterman, R. (1979). *Structure Is Not Organization*. McKinsey Staff Paper, McKinsey and Company.

Wei-Skillern, J., Anderson, B., and Dees, J. G. (2002). 'Scaling Social Innovations: A Report from the Front Lines', *Working Paper Social Enterprise Series* No. 25, Harvard Business School, Division of Research.

Winship, C. (forthcoming). 'Policy Analysis as Puzzle-Solving', in *Oxford Handbook of Political Science*. Oxford: Oxford University Press.

The Social Entrepreneurship Collaboratory (SE Lab)

Appendix 1 Social entrepreneur definitions (Stanford Ashoka Case, Meehan 2001)

Source	Definition
Echoing Green Foundation provides money and technical support to early stage social entrepreneurs	Social entrepreneurs are 'catalysts for social change' . . . they are 'risk-takers who have innovative ideas for a new organization or project.'
The Economist (30 May 1998)	'These budding social entrepreneurs, as this new breed of philanthropists like to call themselves, are keen to give away their money themselves (rather than create foundations to do it). They want to solve specific problems in a specific way (rather than just earmark money for some vaguely benevolent purpose). They focus on performance. And they try to make projects self-sustaining (so the recipients do not keep coming back for more).'
Jay Emerson and Fay Twersky, editors of 'New Social Entrepreneurs: The Success, Challenge, and Lessons of Non-Profit Enterprise Creation.' (The Roberts Foundation, San Francisco, 1996)	A social entrepreneur is a 'non-profit manager with a background in social work, community development, or business, who pursues a vision of economic empowerment through the creation of social purpose businesses intended to provide expanded opportunity for those on the margins of our nation's economic mainstream.'
Ewing Marion Kauffman Foundation is an operating and grant-making foundation supporting sustainable programmes and projects that will lead to individual, organizational, and community self-sufficiency	Not-for-profit entrepreneurship is the 'recognition and pursuit of opportunity in fulfilment of a social mission without regard to resources currently under control to create and sustain social value.'
Charles Leadbeater, author of *The Rise of the Social Entrepreneur* (Demos, UK)	'Social entrepreneurs are like business entrepreneurs in the methods they use but they are motivated by social goals rather than material profits . . . [T]heir great skill is that they often make something from nothing, creating innovative forms of active welfare, health care, and housing which are both cheaper and more effective than the traditional services provided by the government.'
The National Center for Social Entrepreneurs provides support to nonprofits by helping them to think and act in an entrepreneurial manner	'Simply stated, ''social entrepreneurs'' are nonprofit executives who pay increasing attention to market forces without losing sight of their underlying missions, and they are driven by a dual purpose:
	-To take programmes that work and make them more available to people (social entrepreneurship is rooted in the core competencies of an organization) and
	-To become less dependent on government and charity.'
New Economics Foundation is a London-based foundation promoting practical and creative approaches for a just and sustainable economy	'Behind many pioneering institutions are often a few individuals who combine the skill for finding new opportunities with a desire for social justice. These are social entrepreneurs. Social entrepreneurs are found in business, in the public sector, working for voluntary organizations, and within communities. They respond to the evident needs around them with innovative ideas and the ability to motivate and empower others and turn their ideas into reality.'
Social Entrepreneurs, Inc. is dedicated to building strong management and operating infrastructures within human service organizations	The goal of social entrepreneurship is to 'measurably enhance the quality of life for individuals and communities by making significant improvements to the capabilities, efficiency, stability, and outcomes of human service organizations.'
The Social Entrepreneurs Network offers practice advice, technical support, and access to expertise for communities wanting to think and act entrepreneurially	'Social entrepreneurs are people who use the techniques of business to achieve positive social change.'
Youth Service America (YSA) is an alliance of organizations committed to community and national service for young Americans	Social entrepreneurs are ' . . . visionary young leaders who have bold, effective, and innovative ideas for national and community service ventures.'

Part IV

New Directions

14

Wayfinding Without a Compass: Philanthropy's Changing Landscape and Its Implications for Social Entrepreneurs

Sally Osberg[1]

Introduction

When asked about the role foundations in general, and the Skoll Foundation in particular, play in advancing the work of social entrepreneurs, Ashoka founder and Chairman Bill Drayton did not hold back. 'What a social entrepreneur needs and what a foundation provides is an almost perfect mismatch' he commented pointedly.[2] Drayton should know. For more than two decades, he has been interacting with foundations and found the experience slow, inefficient, and burdensome, with any resulting grant generally less than appropriate to the scale of his vision and case.

And yet, in the absence of a 'social capital market', institutionalized philanthropy should be the social entrepreneur's best choice, affording the most rational array of financing options: the risk capital needed to get a venture off the ground, the patient capital required to show results, the mezzanine funding that supports expansion, even the 'smart subsidy' to bridge transition from the not-for-profit to market environment. Why, then, is organized philanthropy the source of as much disaffection as it seems to be among social entrepreneurs? And is the perception warranted, or is philanthropy changing in ways that social entrepreneurs will want to understand in order to access its considerable assets—funding, knowledge, and networks—most effectively?

In this chapter, I argue that philanthropy is in the throes of reinventing itself. New philanthropic entrepreneurs and market forces are sparking new innovations in philanthropy that, in turn, are re-drawing the contours of social investing. For social entrepreneurs, navigating this changing terrain offers fresh challenges along with striking opportunities. Understanding how foundations and other philanthropic institutions are changing—and in particular, appreciating trends in the funder–grantee relationship discussed in this chapter—will help social entrepreneurs make better decisions about which foundations to approach at what point in their evolution. In determining those foundations that are best aligned with their own theories of change, whether the kind of interactions a foundation seeks will meet their needs, and how well a foundation's goals and theirs are aligned, social entrepreneurs stand to reap the full range of the new philanthropy's benefits.

This chapter draws primarily on experience and research related to US-based foundations. The particular set of philanthropic institutions discussed represents a small proportion of total financial support for the work of social entrepreneurs on a national scale, although on a global scale private philanthropy, including foundation funds, accounts for 60 per cent of total US international assistance (US Agency for International Development 2002: 146). However, many of the trends noted here might be observed elsewhere, and the implications of funder–grantee relationships apply to social entrepreneurs and funding institutions on a more general scale as well.

The Funder–Social Entrepreneur Mismatch: Sources of Tension and Seeds of Change

According to Aristotle, it is easy to 'give or spend money; but to do this to the right person, to the right extent, at the right time, with the right motive, and in the right way, that is not for every one, nor is it easy'. However, those seeking funds from foundations will have little sympathy with this analysis of the grant maker's conundrum, facing as they do a veritable philanthropic tower of Babel: thousands of entities organized to give away money, each with its own version of determining how much to give to whom for what purpose. In the USA, foundation grant making represents approximately 12 per cent of total contributions, in 2003, some $30 billion (£17.4 billion) of $240 billion (£139.2 billion) (AAFRC Trust for Philanthropy 2004), which accounts for <0.03 per cent of the not-for-profit sector's aggregate income (IRS 2004). Yet, the profile of foundations looms large on the philanthropic landscape, suggesting that the foundation grant is seen more as a hard sought, hard won prize than a more 'rational' source of capital. For the very reasons grant seekers find foundations frustrating, they may also value and seek their support. Enduring application processes and surmounting due diligence hurdles, this line of thought goes, confer credibility in a way that individual contributors' decisions do not. When one factors in the harsh realities of proposal-to-award ratios at the largest foundations—where the odds of getting a grant can be one in 100—it is not hard to appreciate the privileged status of such victories.

Indeed, that sense of privilege seems at the root of most critiques of foundation behaviour. In a recent address, former not-for-profit executive and current foundation president Michael Bailin reprised an all-too-familiar litany associated with the iconic foundation: 'Autocratic, ineffective and wilful', 'elitist', 'cloistered', 'arrogant', and 'pampered' (Bailin 2003). Disappointment, of course, fuels such perceptions, given that grant seekers experience repeated rejection. But even disappointing news can be communicated in a timely and respectful way. Francesca Gardner has described the experience of many who sought an audience with her father, the late John Gardner, during his twenty years with the Carnegie Corporation; even when they left empty-handed, she recalls, they felt valued and important (Gardner 2005). Unfortunately, such experience does not seem yet to be the norm.

Beyond complaints directed towards foundation behaviour is another set of charges aimed at foundation effectiveness. Paul Ylvisaker's observation that foundations' 'dainty dabs of money' (McIlnay 1998: 127) are woefully out of proportion to the scope of challenges foundations should be addressing or Waldemar Nielsen's dismissive comment that 'foundations have been about as consequential as drug stores' in influencing social change is representative of voices raised periodically over decades (Dowie 2001: 12). More recently, critics have pointed to the gap between the lofty goals to which foundations aspire and any logical means of achieving such visions. 'The very nature of philanthropy—working to redress massive social problems or to enhance our civilization—leads ineluctably to goals that are worthy and inspirational, but at the same time ambiguous and unattainable', wrote Mark Kramer (2001).

A subset of this school of criticism is foundations' risk aversion, despite what many feel is their extraordinary ability to back new ideas and absorb the consequences of failure. More than forty years ago, a US Treasury Department Report on Private Foundations described this paradox, noting that while foundations are 'uniquely qualified to initiate thought, experiment with new ventures and dissent from prevailing attitudes', they demonstrate scant appetite for such behaviour (McIlnay: 126). A number of researchers have tracked this aversion to predictable sources: centrist-oriented boards of trustees, professional staff's concerns for their reputations, CEO reluctance to court controversy and deal with the fallout of negative publicity, the constraints of legal compliance. Other areas of more general concern centre on foundation payout, endowment investment, or are political in nature—adherents of either left or right, and their public sector allies, who take issue with any given foundation's perceived bias—and are beyond the scope of this chapter (see, e.g. Klausner 2003).

What we are left with, then, would seem to be two relevant areas of disaffection for social entrepreneurs. The first is their perceived lack of respect from foundations: the timeliness and knowledgeable consideration that would convey the regard most social entrepreneurs feel they have earned. The second, more serious, charge and barrier for social entrepreneurs is foundations' failure to operate strategically along with their corollary aversion to risk.

311

Against the first set of challenges, progress is slowly being made, driven on the one hand by increased media interest in philanthropy and a rash of investigative stories and calls-to-account by attorneys general, and on the other by serious attempts to bring a market orientation to philanthropy. Among the more visible efforts in the latter category are Guidestar, which publishes tax returns and self-reported data online for more than 80,000 US not-for-profit organizations, including foundations, and the Center for Effective Philanthropy's (CEP) Grantee Perception Report, which solicits confidential feedback from grantees for foundations. Rolled out in 2003, the Grantee Perception Report met with initial resistance, but has now been adopted and is in use by sixty-five of the largest American foundations, providing their leaders with confidential, comparative data on grantees' insights about their practices.

Summarizing findings culled from 3,200 not-for-profit grantees of thirty large foundations, CEP confirmed that grantees' impressions of the foundations that fund them are generally positive (Bolduc, Buchanan, and Huang 2004). The three top behaviours grantees value are fairness, clarity, and expertise. Paradoxically, these three can look like yang to the yin of behavioural critiques levelled against foundations. The foundation that is fair in its methods for evaluating applicants will communicate clear guidelines and have well-developed processes for making decisions—processes that are likely, especially over time, to become less responsive or flexible, frustrating the social entrepreneur whose particular needs will rarely slot neatly into the foundation's well-defined cycles and programme areas. Similarly, grantees want foundations to have a vision of change for the field or community in which the not-for-profit works and the networks or expertise to support systemic change. Grantees also value expertise in the programme officers with whom they interact, but those same programme officers more often than not are academically trained within a specific discipline and likely to bring to their analysis of any given proposal the biases of that training and experience, which may leave them less open to more radical, potentially transformative, ideas from social entrepreneurs.

The charge that foundations are ineffective, that they all too often fail to develop robust strategies, to take risks, and to demonstrate entrepreneurial leadership, is a more serious criticism, frequently discussed in the literature. 'Nothing forces a foundation to choose realistic goals or a strategy that will work', wrote Kramer (2001), citing, as have many others, foundations' historical immunity to governmental or market forces. Sustaining innovation in the public and not-for-profit sectors 'will never be easy', added Paul Light (1998), given the public's expectation for quick success and the realities of institutional bureaucracy; it is revealing, however, that in Light's initial five-year study of twenty-six innovating organizations, none was identified in the field of philanthropy.

But as the field of social change has evolved over the past quarter of a century, this profile of organized philanthropy as an academically structured, slow-moving institution locked into the status quo is increasingly at odds with the new reality. Today's institutionalized philanthropy is no longer character-ized predominately by the large private foundations created in the early 1900s, but by the extraordinary influx of new wealth and new ideas flowing into it. In fact, today's philanthropic field is a complex array of models, all of which have at their disposal, or are engaged in creating, a host of strategies, tools, and techniques. Although it is too early to say whether this new wave will achieve the promise of another 'golden age', there is reason to be hopeful. As Dowie (2001: 222) has written, 'Mix enough imagination with enough money over enough time and innovation will lead to change.'

The Context for Change

New wealth created during the 1980s and 1990s, much of it in the technology industry, the long bull stock market of the same period, and a more favourable federal regulatory environment, spurred extraordinary growth in the founda-tion sector, when the number of foundations rose from 23,770 in 1982 to more than 65,000 in 2002 (Commonwealth Fund 2004). When one of the factors in the unprecedented wave of wealth transfer now underway and projected to last over the next five decades, with trillions more dollars expected to flow to charity, the relationship between philanthropy and social entrepreneurship becomes both a relevant and timely issue. In fact, the slope of the trend line for new philanthropic organizations is nearly identical to that representing the growth rate for social sector groups organized and registered in the same period: between 1975 and 2002, the number of US not-for-profit organizations climbed from 400,000 to 1.2 million, with total revenues of $897 billion (£520.3 billion, see Figure 14.1).

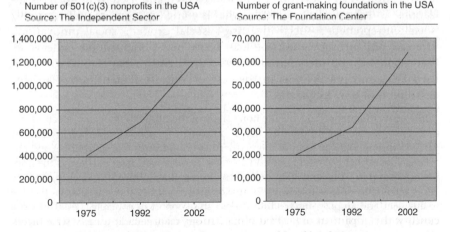

Figure 14.1 The rise in US not-for profits vs. grant making foundations

Of course, most of this phenomenon of new wealth, which has led, in turn, to the dramatic acceleration of foundation formation, arises from the activity of a new generation of entrepreneurs. It is worth reminding ourselves that institutional philanthropy has its origin in the motivations, experiences, and ideas of individual donors. As Nielsen has observed trenchantly,

the first and fundamental fact about foundations is that they do not start with a concept or an organization chart or a strategic plan. A foundation starts with a person, a donor. That human being, by his or her major charitable act, is the fountainhead from which all else—good, bad, or indifferent—flows. (1996: 10)

In many of the best-known cases, significant philanthropic creations—particularly in the modern twentieth century foundation—follow on that human fountainhead's entrepreneurial success. Henry Ford, Andrew Carnegie, and John D. Rockefeller are three of the best-known industrial age pioneers who dedicated themselves to philanthropy in the past century, while Jeff Skoll, Stephan Schmidheiny, Bill Gates, and hundreds of others represent a new generation of entrepreneurs for the new century. Is it any surprise that individuals such as these are bringing to their philanthropy the same innovative ideas, intensity, and drive that they have brought to building successful businesses or that the distinctive characteristics of their experience with, and knowledge of, technology would also inform their philanthropic pursuits?

New Donors, New Models

Typically, the new philanthropy is framed as a quasi-business venture, a paradigm reinforced by a lexicon of phrases invented and used by donors, organizations, and the media to describe what is going on: 'venture philanthropy'; 'social entrepreneur'; 'social investing'; 'social capital'; 'social innovation'; 'strategic philanthropy', and the like. Many new philanthropic endeavours draw upon such business terminology to distinguish what is different about their ideas and practices, as in the case of Venture Philanthropy Partners' description of how it operates:

While many foundations devote the lion's share of their time to the grant selection and award process, we devote the majority of our time to engaging with our investment partners throughout the term of the partnership and in ways that go well beyond our financial investment. A vital part of VPP's value to our investment partners is the non-financial support—the strategic insights, the engaged assistance, the opening of new doors and relationships—that we and our wide network of advisors and contacts provide to augment and amplify our funding. To put this support in concrete terms, we work closely with our partners to help them build strong management teams, create highly effective and engaged boards, gain mission and outcome clarity, define economic models and fund-development strategies to establish financial sustainability, improve product/service models, and develop an information-based management approach that enables a vigilant focus on managing the organization to achieve its desired social outcomes. (Venture Philanthropy Partners 2004)

Obviously shaped by entrepreneurial ways of thinking and engaging and by business approaches to designing and building, this newer philanthropic model is also influenced by its architects' grounding in the fields of science and engineering. Less well explored in the literature, but clearly relevant, is the new philanthropy's resonance with scientific principles: the premise that problems can be solved, the disciplined articulation of a hypothesis, the design of a systematic approach, and the reliance on feedback and evidence.

According to research carried out by Schervish, O'Herlihy, and Havens of the Social Welfare Research Institute of Boston College, the distinctiveness of high-tech donors is not vested in their motivations or their adoption of venture philanthropy as a paradigm. Rather, it is in their insistence on philanthropy that is 'market-conscious' and 'knowledge-based' (Schervish, O'Herlihy, and Havens 2001: 44). In the context of philanthropy, this market-consciousness translates into insistence on feedback from stake-holders—loosely defined as those who stand to benefit from or be influenced by philanthropic investment—a category encompassing other donors and foundations, government, policymakers, social sector leaders, and organizations along with their clients, the media, and the public at large. Elevating the role and significance of stakeholders distinguishes the new philanthropic work from its more traditional antecedents and causes distinctive shifts in the way that work is framed and carried out.

Figure 14.2 integrates three points of orientation for this new generation of market-conscious, knowledge-driven philanthropists: for some, grounding in a value proposition or theory of change or, even more commonly, a strategy, is fundamental, for others, it is the terms of the engagement and relationship with grantees that is most important. Still others begin with the end in mind and focus their work around an ultimate, desired impact, incorporating means for measuring performance against that goal. What is distinctive about this still formative model, however, is the larger dynamic which embraces all three—the value proposition, relationship, and impact—even though the newer foundation is likely to emphasize one dimension as most significant to its identity and work.

Implications of the Model

The dynamic nature of this model reinforces the importance of interdependence with and feedback from stakeholders not just out of a market-consciousness, but because that feedback generates knowledge: about the

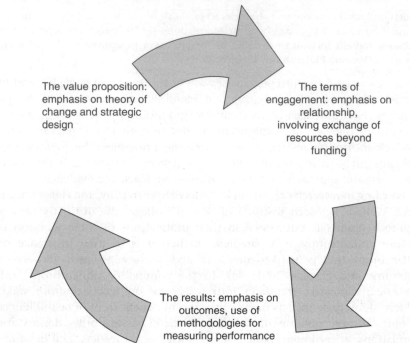

The value proposition: emphasis on theory of change and strategic design

The terms of engagement: emphasis on relationship, involving exchange of resources beyond funding

The results: emphasis on outcomes, use of methodologies for measuring performance towards desired impact

Figure 14.2 Three points of orientation for market-conscious, knowledge-driven philanthropists

dimensions of any problem; the conditions of context; the complexity of change. But regardless of whether a foundation's orientation is to its value proposition, relationships, or impact, its continued learning and progress requires attention to, and learning from, all three dimensions. In practice, the new foundation can be seen to set off from and emphasize a particular orientation, with its work giving rise to new patterns of behaviour, as contrasted in Figure 14.3.

Orientation 1: The Value Proposition

For a foundation that leads from an emphasis on its value proposition or theory of change—which, in turn, shapes the ways it interacts with grantees and assesses its impact—the Edna McConnell Clark Foundation provides an excellent example. During the 1980s, the foundation practised a traditional model of grant making, seeking to effect significant, policy-level change in five core areas: child welfare; middle-school education; criminal justice; neighbourhood redevelopment; and tropical disease research. With the arrival of new CEO Michael Bailin in 1996, the foundation began to examine this model

Traditional patterns of behaviour	Market-based patterns of behaviour
Define the problem	Create value proposition
Invite applications	Seek out partners
Mitigate risk	Tolerate risk
Fund the programme or project	Fund core operations and capacity
Emphasize grant transaction	Emphasize relationship
Vest accountability in grantee	Share accountability
Strive for clarity, consistency	Strive for flexibility, responsiveness

Figure 14.3 Traditional vs. market-based grant giving

in earnest, arriving at the conclusion that the time had come for a change. Bailin described his challenge as strategic in nature, rooted in the foundation's programmatic structure and efforts to 'reform huge, complex, entrenched, multi-billion dollar public systems with a staff of 25 people and around $25 million a year in grants' (£14.5 million, Bailin 2003: 4). As a former grant seeker himself, Bailin acknowledged another flaw in more traditional philanthropic design, which he described as follows:

You come to a foundation with an idea that you hope is worth funding, and you hope to get some money. But first you have to be willing to do what the foundation feels is important to do (and) you try to shoehorn their requests into your other activities, because you are a not-for-profit and you need the money. What you end up doing is taking on an activity that doesn't really belong in your portfolio but fits at the periphery and provides some overhead. That can degrade the quality, focus and effectiveness of a not-for-profit's key programs. (Grossman and Curran 2002: 5)

Influenced by his seventeen years as a grant seeker, Bailin was himself predisposed to think in terms of the foundation's external market, which he concluded was comprised of those organizations on the front lines of social change: 'Foundations succeed when their grantees grow stronger, achieve more, and gain stature for leadership'. This idea became the core of a new strategy for EMCF, one which focused not on vast public systems, but instead on the not-for-profit institutions that were doing the best work within one of those systems. Clark decided to concentrate its work on a single field, youth development, where—perhaps not co-incidentally—it had enjoyed a long-term relationship with social entrepreneur Geoffrey Canada, CEO of the Rheedlen Centers for Children and Families. Over the course of Canada's work with Clark, Canada significantly sharpened his strategy and drove the organization's growth such that the organization under his leadership was re-focused, re-positioned, and even re-named as the Harlem Children's Zone.

The literature describing the foundation's transformation is revealing in pointing out the role Canada appears to have played in reinforcing Bailin's ideas. In remarks that mirror Bailin's own, Canada noted:

Our relationship with the Clark Foundation started in the late eighties. At the time, the Foundation was pursuing a 'homebuilder' child welfare strategy in which all services and support were targeted to keep children in their natural home environment and out of institutions and shelters. We agreed to be a part of their strategy even though it wasn't our main business. We focused more on after-school programs and physical security. But it was at a tough economic time. So we told them it was a great model. It wasn't what we were buying, but it was what they were selling. (Grossman and Curran 2002: 5)

While it may be overstating the case to draw the conclusion that Clark's approach and decision to concentrate in the field of youth development were strongly influenced by the relationship with Canada, it is certainly clear that Canada and his organization were top of his mind as the foundation began implementing its new model, firstly in an experimental way with Canada's organization, the Rheedlen, invited to participate in a series of organizational assessments of five community-based grantees, followed by award of a $250,000 (£145,000) grant to undertake business planning with the Bridgespan group. Canada recalled, 'Mike and Nancy came to me and said that Clark was thinking of making larger, more significant longer-term investments in helping organizations do what they really want to do. We don't know if this is going to work, but we want you to help us test the idea'. Nancy Roob emphasized how critical Canada's role was to this effort: 'My feeling was that this was a real test of Bridgespan's ability to take these private sector tools and actually apply them to a not-for-profit. I felt that Geoffrey Canada was a person whom we trusted to tell us the truth about whether this was a value-added approach to grant making' (Grossman and Curran 2002: 12).

In 2001, as Clark moved forward with full implementation of its new approach, it selected Canada's organization to receive its largest investment: $5.7 million (£3.3 million) over three years. By early 2003, Bailin could already point to early indicators of the success of this investment, and the foundation's new approach:

They have dramatically increased the number of young people they're serving, restructured the board, hired key department heads, and reorganized their management. They now have a new evaluation system and have raised $30 million (£17.4 million, and broken ground) to finance a new building. The result is not just a bigger program, but a better organization. Neither would have meant much without the other. (Bailin 2003: 14).

In fact, Bailin could have made just about the same claims about his own organization. On the other side of its five year transformational process, the foundation had reoriented its board, restructured its management and internal organization, hired key new portfolio managers, and entered into several significant strategic partnerships with youth-serving organizations.

In a profoundly meaningful way, Geoff Canada and his Harlem Children's Zone organization seem to have stimulated, grounded, and ultimately proven the Clark Foundation's shift to a new approach, demonstrating the vitality of social entrepreneurs—on both sides of the aisle—in advancing new paradigms of philanthropy.

Orientation 2: Terms of Engagement

Leading the movement to rethink and construct the terms of engagement between funder and funded are any number of new philanthropic organizations, some of them public charities, some private foundations, all categorized, despite recent efforts to disavow the label, as practitioners of venture philanthropy. Coined first by John D. Rockefeller III in testimony before the US Congress in 1969, venture philanthropy was defined as 'the imaginative pursuit of less conventional charitable purposes than those normally undertaken by established public charitable organizations' and has been a current in the evolution of philanthropy ever since (Ryan 2001: 16).

This style of grant making received a major boost in 1997 with the publication of *Virtuous Capital: What Foundations Can Learn from Venture Capitalists*, which made the case for applying principles of venture investing to philanthropic practice (Letts, Ryan, and Grossman 1997). Authors Christine Letts, Bill Ryan, and Allen Grossman identified six venture capital practices with relevance to foundations; the seminal practice, and the one most commonly identified with venture philanthropy, is characterized as the 'closeness of the relationship', while four of the five remaining practices—establishing performance measures, determining an optimal funding amount, projecting the length of the relationship, and planning for exit—are all contingent upon a far more intimate working relationship, one involving full transparency to all aspects of the endeavour, between both parties. The shift from hands-off or even arm's-length grant making to one in which the grant maker would play a significant role in the organization's affairs—helping to determine strategy, hiring professional staff, or developing a system for tracking performance—is represented by the authors as a shift from 'oversight' to 'partnering'.

In 2002, Mario Morino's Venture Philanthropy Partners documented sixty-nine organizations whose work is predicated on more closely negotiated terms of engagement between the supporter and the supported, with the majority concentrating their work in the USA. Of the 69, 42 are grant makers whose aggregate investment amounted to just over $50 million (£29 million) in 2002, 'not even 0.2% of total foundation grant making...but important nonetheless' (Venture Philanthropy Partners 2002).

Morino's journey and embrace of high-engagement philanthropy is described in his own words as a very personal 'discovery process'. Informed by his experience as a telecommunications industry entrepreneur and grounded in his personal values, Morino reflects many of the characteristics described by Schervish in his study of twenty-six high-tech philanthropists, the most outstanding of which Schervish branded as 'agent-animated' or 'intercessional', the basis for most of the debate about venture philanthropy (Sievers 1997).

Undergirding the bias for high engagement is what Schervish and his associates have identified as the belief 'that human capital is the key to human development'. They go on: 'Not only is human capital seen as the principal tool of philanthropy, it is also its principal output' (Schervish, O'Herlihy, and Havens 2001: 57–8). For a generation of philanthropists who have been involved in the creation of the knowledge economy—where information and understanding are the foundation for wealth creation—this belief is fundamental, representing as it does a seismic shift from the economic paradigm in which wealth is built through the control and exploitation of natural resources such as land, waterways, or oil reserves. Seen in this context, the emphasis on relationships and renegotiated investor–investee terms of engagement is profound in its implications.

Research proving a net positive impact from 'high engagement' grant makers is still nascent, with most of what exists focused on how grantees benefit from their funder partners. In 2000, when Greg Dees published his *Note on Innovations in Philanthropy*, he concluded that 'the venture philanthropy approach, focused primarily on ways to increase the effectiveness of recipient organizations, thus creating greater social impact (with) the basic venture philanthropy model' did not directly address creating value for donors (Jacobson, Anderson, and Dees 2000). More recently, unpublished research carried out by the Hauser Center for Nonprofit Organizations on six such partnerships points again to benefits derived by grantees in the form of larger, longer, more-sustained grant funding and from general management assistance: 'The net result is larger blocks of capital with a relationship that aims to ensure that it is used as a strategic investment in the not-for-profit's organizational capacity' (cited in Ryan 2001: 16–17).

But organizational capacity, in fact, cuts in both directions. As the model has evolved, it has become clear, even if not yet fully embraced in the research, that high engagement funders are deriving significant benefits from their grantee partners. Journalists and others who have begun charting this strand of change in the field have been struck by admissions of learning and testimony to challenges from those migrating from business to philanthropy. 'It's harder in philanthropy to know you did the right thing', observed Patty Stonesifer, President of the Bill and Melinda Gates Foundation, echoing founder Bill Gates's acknowledgement, 'The reason there are big social inequities is because they come from deep, complex, historical pressures. There is no quick fix.... Long-term solutions require thoughtful, committed programs to work' (Byrne 2002: 88). This perspective is echoed by others, such as real estate developer Eli Broad, whose eponymous foundation focuses on education, 'I'm working harder at this than when I was CEO of SunAmerica' (Byrne 2002: 88).

Such testimonials reveal a strong current of humility in this emerging style of philanthropy, another manifestation, I would argue, of the new generation's regard for learning and knowledge. In their interview-based study of high-tech philanthropists, Schervish, O'Herlihy, and Havens underscored the point:

Of course their self-assurance, can-do attitude and relative inexperience can be perceived as arrogant and presumptuous. However, we found only very occasional evidence of such conceit (with respondents') overwhelmingly concerned to educate themselves about the needs they might address, and how best to work with others to meet those needs (Schervish, O'Herlihy, and Havens 2001: 99).

It would seem that even those who enter philanthropy confident in their abilities to add value are chastened by the experience. The high-tech entrepreneur Mario Morino noted, 'The trouble is, a lot of new people came into this cocky. We thought we had all the answers and wanted to do it ourselves ... we should have been more respectful of the people who have done this all their lives' (Byrne 2002: 90). Former venture capitalist and founder of the Entrepreneurs' Foundation Gib Meyers acknowledges the same process of self-discovery, speaking candidly of his early bias towards believing business had the answers and subsequent realization that the effort to demonstrate social benefit required long-term persistence and no small measure of commitment. Emphasis on the terms of engagement, it would seem, is driven not as much by the philanthropic sector's insistence on its need to be in a position of power and influence—the venture capital model—but to position itself for learning and partnership. Indeed, as Greg Dees was early in pointing out, 'Most of the organizations that were being built around these principles were also committed to developing and sharing intellectual capital about the emerging field of venture philanthropy' (Jacobson, Anderson, and Dees 2000: 12).

As if taking his cue from Dees's observation, Morino has dedicated himself to charting the evolution and progress of high-engagement philanthropy since his own entry to the field in 1992, first through personal essays made public on his Morino Institute website, and beginning in 2000, through Venture Philanthropy Partners. Even the titles of these reports are suggestive, with early documents still brandishing the term 'venture philanthropy', while the later ones shift to using 'high-engagement'. More importantly, the contents of the reports themselves evolve from attempts to chart the evolution of the practice in business-like terms, through surveys and documentation, to a far more open-ended report model in 2004—a series of six transcripts of 'dialogues' between high-engagement funders and their grantees, underscoring the process of two-way learning resulting from intentionally close interaction.

321

Of course, interaction and learning between foundations and their grantees has always been a hallmark of healthy and progressive philanthropic practice. When he was a programme officer working in Dakha for the Ford Foundation in the mid-1970s, Bill Fuller recalled getting to know a young professor at Chittagon University who had 'a terrific idea to set up a rural studies programme that would take faculty and students out of the university to do action research at the village level' (World Affairs Council 2004: 51). Ford funded the idea with a small grant. Several months later, Fuller recalls, this same young professor—Dr Muhammad Yunus—returned with another idea, 'that was very different (and . . .) did not appear in the grant letter that was signed by me on behalf of the Ford Foundation'. Of course, Fuller and his colleagues at Ford did agree to fund Dr Yunus' follow-on idea, which was to test the viability of lending to the poor, a concept that ultimately became the Grameen Bank and spawned the $50 billion (£29 billion) microcredit revolution. For Fuller, the lessons for philanthropy were clear: 'First, the obvious lesson that a small grant at the right time with the right person can, in fact, make a difference. But second, in the philanthropy business, never be trapped or blinded by your own goals or objectives, by your letters of agreement, or by the original benchmarks of program success (which) are simply guideposts. Always keep an eye out for the unexpected, which can be a terrific source of creativity and opportunity'. Francesca Gardner recalls that her father John Gardner used to say while he was President of Carnegie Corporation, 'You want the best people with the best ideas to walk through your door' (Gardner 2005). Without John Gardner, would Carnegie have been receptive to Joan Ganz Cooney, with her new idea for the Children's Television Workshop, from which *Sesame Street* was born? Without enlightened and empowered programme officers like Bill Fuller and Adrienne Germaine, would Ford have been willing to renegotiate the terms of engagement with Dr Yunus?

But there is more to the Ford Foundation story, a couple of footnotes that demonstrate the enormous and too often untapped potential of grantee-funder-grantee engagement, and the importance of the 'right' people on both sides of the sector trusting one another enough to renegotiate midstream or supply additional help. Dr Yunus recounts that he benefited particularly from Ford's identification of two American bankers, Shorebank co-founders Ron Grzywinski and Mary Houghton, to serve as his consultants in assessing Grameen's early work. With Ron and Mary as coaches, Yunus was thus prepared to take the next step: to charter Grameen as a bank and to expand it throughout Bangladesh. Ford, in turn, considered how best it could back this move, choosing to exercise an underutilized foundation tool, the programme related investment (Yunus 1999: 113).

As Director of Ford's Program Related Investment Program, Barry Gaberman structured a loan guarantee of $800,000 (£464,000)—in effect, a smart subsidy—which Grameen never needed to draw down but which made its market transition possible. During the first year of this expansion, Grameen's cumulative loan disbursement increased by an additional $10.5 million (£6.1 million)—nearly as much as the total lent during its first five years.

Orientation 3: Results

A third category of emphasis in this emergent grant making model is vested in the results a funder seeks; such funders lead with a desired end in mind. These ends are described in the literature in various ways, as 'measurable outcomes', 'social return on investment', 'impact', 'social value creation', or even more prosaically and simply as 'goals'. Philanthropic ends may be defined crisply, as in Rotary International's determination to eradicate polio by 2005, or in more aspirational terms, as in the Open Society Institute's vision for the global spread of democracy.

For such funders, the development of a theory of change or strategy is derived from a well-defined goal. The Bill and Melinda Gates Foundation, for example, has identified as the goal for its health programme the reduction of global health inequities, which founder Bill Gates characterized as 'a real market failure' (Gates 2001). It is worth recalling that Gates did not arrive at this clarity overnight, but began his philanthropic work closer to home, literally, with technology-focused grants and contributions to not-for-profit institutions working in the Seattle area. In the mid-1990s, Gates, then in his 30s, was still vague about the contours of his philanthropy; focused on expanding Microsoft, he did not envision becoming actively engaged in philanthropy for another fifteen years when he would reach his 50s. As is the pattern for many philanthropists, he began giving in his own community in accordance with his own experience. That changed when he came across the stunning reality of global health—the array of interventions and solutions readily available in the developed world in stark contrast to their absence in developing countries, the human misery exacted by disease, malnutrition, and high mortality rates. 'Bill learned enough about the burden of infectious diseases to believe that his dollars are best used now', noted Patty Stonesifer, President of the Gates Foundation, 'The cost of him being really smart about malaria at 45 versus 65 was extremely worthwhile. The impact of this money over those 20 years could be great' (Byrne 2002: 88).

Once he had arrived at his goal of reducing global health inequities, however, Gates was able to develop a strategy that was both straightforward and bold: to support activities that would help close the gap, including research and testing of new drugs, treatments, and techniques addressing unmet needs in the developing world.

The Gates Foundation organizes its global health work in six programme areas: infectious diseases; HIV/AIDS; tuberculosis; reproductive health; global health strategies; and global health technologies. In pursuing this strategy, Gates looks for leverage not through social entrepreneurs per se, but through large, well-established global networks and partnerships, placing its largest investments in a few large 'bets'—grants ranging upwards to many millions of dollars to organizations that are either staking out a leadership role in the fight against a single disease or problem or are well positioned to lead or accelerate research. Many of the grants are made with an eye to forging alliances with other major donors and aid agencies in order to influence a whole field of funding, which give NGOs the resources to be influential members of these alliances.

The sheer magnitude of the Gates Foundation's grant making highlights an obvious challenge for social entrepreneurship: only rarely is the social entrepreneur's capacity large enough, or its networks well-developed enough, to be able to attract and deploy large scale investments. Social entrepreneur Victoria Hale's Institute for One World Health (IOWH) illustrates how one organization has been able to meet this challenge, and how this has led to new and unforeseen issues.

A pharmaceutical research scientist, Hale created the IOWH out of her own frustration with the limits of market dynamics stunting the development of medicines capable of treating millions of people suffering from infectious— and eminently preventable—diseases in the developing world. Like Gates, Hale has identified the failure of markets to address clearly preventable, as well as more challenging, diseases in the developing world. Furthermore, consistent with her entrepreneur's orientation, she has also cited untapped opportunity, in the form of 'dozens, perhaps hundreds, of potentially life-saving compounds (that) sit on university or drug-company shelves because there isn't a profitable market for them' (Hale 2004). To address this market opportunity, Hale and her physician husband created the world's first not-for-profit pharmaceutical company in 2002:

The idea was simple. With the help of drug companies and their scientists, we would track down compounds that showed promise but weren't being actively pursued. When we found one, the company would grant us development rights through a licensing agreement or a donation of the patent. Then we would develop it, with help from generous donors and the volunteer contributions of time and expertise from pharmaceutical scientists. (Hale 2004)

To ensure success, Hale and her team stressed partnership and collaboration with industry and international research institutions—the kinds of organizations the Gates Foundation had begun to work with as well. Within months of its founding, IOWH had attracted its first grant from the Gates Foundation, $4.6 million (£2.7 million), most of which was focused on testing paromomycin, a therapy with the potential to cure leishmaniasis—a parasitic disease threatening more than 350 million people worldwide and recognized by WHO as a 'neglected' disease, one with special impact on the world's poorest and most vulnerable population that receives little funding or attention. By the end of 2004, IOWH received additional funding from the Gates Foundation, but not alone. It was through an organizational partnership with UC Berkeley and Amyris

Biotechnologies that IOWH was able to attract a significantly larger sum, $42.6 million (£24.7 million), to develop an anti-malarial drug. In funding this effort, Gates was able to address all three of the market gaps he had identified: the failure of visibility; the failure of incentives; and the failure of collaboration. As part of the alliance receiving this support, Hale was now positioned to demonstrate the power of the IOWH model, but not without new ramifications.

While at first glance major investments would seem to be 'the big break' that would launch a social entrepreneur to a significant new level of effectiveness and impact, infusions of such magnitude coupled with the complexity of managing institutional collaborations bring challenges as well. Very large restricted grants can dominate an organization's balance sheet, skew its mission, and overtake efforts to build the diverse financial base and pipeline of activities needed to ensure long-term sustainability. Indeed, in the absence of a broad base of support, US not-for-profits may even face the issue of 'tipping': receiving such a large percentage of their income from a single donor that they fail to meet the 'public support test' that qualifies them as public charities under the Internal Revenue Services tax code.

The Gates Foundation's emphasis on impact also leads it to designate most of its funding for project-specific activities, allocating only a simple percentage for overhead related to administering the grant project. Thus, an organization can become quite large very quickly, without the means to develop the systems to manage that growth or look beyond the immediate future. In addition, other donors may perceive that their support is now superfluous or unnecessary in the face of such large investments—or that their contributions would always be overshadowed by the Gates funding—and, thus, may be reluctant to give just at the time when the organization needs diversified and unrestricted support to build its capacity.

Social entrepreneurs who succeed in attracting order-of-magnitude investments from foundations focused on the achievement of well-defined goals will want to be sure, first of all, that their goals and the funder's are well-aligned. Beyond such an obvious consideration, social entrepreneurs will also want to balance their roster of investors. With a diversified funding base and sufficient consideration for their own institutional development within any negotiated grant, social entrepreneurs can take full advantage of any big break, achieving large-scale and important outcomes while ensuring their capacity to meet future opportunities.

Implications for Social Entrepreneurs and the Path Forward

Together with the organizations and individuals in whom they invest and with whom they partner, collaborate, and learn, a new generation of philanthropists and foundation professionals are reinventing institutionalized giving. The iconic image of a foundation insulated from market forces no longer characterizes the field of philanthropy, a change that social entrepreneurs are helping to bring about. In preparing a recent keynote address for a meeting of the CEP, for example, Surdna Foundation Executive Director Ed Skloot polled not just his colleagues in philanthropy, but an equal number of foundation and front-line not-for-profit leaders, asking them to identify the qualities they most value in their interactions with one another. The answer was honesty, the basis for trust, the very DNA of the sector's effectiveness. 'Giving money well wasn't even mentioned', Skloot noted; instead 'respondents wrote about the need for mutual understanding and a bedrock sense that we're all in this together' (Skloot 2003).

Allow me to become more personal. As CEO of the Skoll Foundation, I have the extraordinary privilege of working with my colleagues on the crest of this wave of innovation, in partnership with a remarkable social entrepreneur, our founder and chairman, Jeff Skoll. For Jeff, this new imperative for philanthropy is rooted in a vision—that the unsustainable world we know today, a dangerously imbalanced world of rich and poor, a world in which suffering and hopelessness breed desperation and violence, does not have to be the world we pass on to our children. This vision, in turn, has shaped the foundation's theory of change. Jeff sees his foundation not as a passive vehicle for redistributing wealth, but as an active means of empowering those with the greatest potential to bring about positive social change. This fundamental idea, that those highest potential agents of change, social entrepreneurs, are vital to tackling the world's greatest problems and creating healthier, more peaceful and prosperous communities, is the foundation's starting place in the schema of the new philanthropy. We are underway in a collaborative process of designing the terms of our engagement with our community of social entrepreneurs, and in determining the impact we want to achieve, mindful that many tough choices lie ahead. And we have also reached out to colleagues and thought-leaders invested in understanding the dynamics of social entrepreneurship within the broader swath of global civil society, believing that we have both the privilege and the responsibility to help build the knowledge that can lead to more effective practice.

For the Skoll Foundation, and so many others, the new philanthropy is a work in progress, the map of its geography still full of uncharted waters. But by understanding that modern philanthropy is changing, and by taking their cues from what is beginning to take shape, social entrepreneurs will be able to navigate this largely unexplored terrain more efficiently, with greater chance of success at the outset and over the life cycle of a relationship. Perhaps most significantly, philanthropy itself has learned that it needs the experience and intelligence of social entrepreneurs to imagine what this brave new world might look like, and how best to venture forward together.

Notes

1. The author wishes to express her appreciation for research assistance, general support, and inspiration from her colleagues at the Skoll Foundation, especially Christy Chin, Ruth Norris, Barbara Kibbe, Avon Swofford, and Terry Nagel.
2. Recorded by consultants at SiegelGale for a stakeholder survey commissioned by the Skoll Foundation over the Summer and Fall, 2002.

References

AAFRC Trust for Philanthropy (2004). *Giving USA 2003*. Washington, DC.

Aristotle, *Nichomachean Ethics*, Book II, Chapter 9, translated by Ross, W. D.

Bailin, M. (2003). *Re-Engineering Philanthropy: Field Notes from the Trenches*, presentation delivered at the Center for the Study of Voluntary Organizations and Service, Georgetown University, Washington, DC, 21 February.

Bolduc, K., Buchanan, P., and Huang, J. (2004). *Listening to Grantees: What Nonprofits Value in their Foundation Funders*. Cambridge: Center for Effective Philanthropy.

Byrne, J. (2002). 'The New Face of Philanthropy'. *Business Week*, 2 December: 88.

Commonwealth Fund (2004). *Annual Report 2004*. Available at: www.cmwf.org/annreprt/2004

Dowie, M. (2001). *American Foundations: An Investigative History*. Cambridge, MA: MIT Press.

Gardner, F. (2005). Author Conversation with Francesca Gardner, January.

Gates, W. (2001). Remarks to the World Economic Forum, 29 January, available at: www.gatesfoundation.org/MediaCenter/Speeches/BillgSpeeches/BGSpeechWEF-010129

Grossman, A. and Curran, D. (2002). *EMCF: A New Approach at an Old Foundation*. Harvard Business School Publishing Case Study No. 9-302-090.

Hale, V. (2004). 'Creating More Paths to Hope', *Newsweek*, 6 December, available at: www.msnbc.msn.com/id/6594602/site/newsweek/

IRS (2004). *Internal Revenue Service: Fall 2004 Statistics of Income Bulletin*. Available at: www.irs.gov

Jacobson, K., Anderson, B., and Dees, J. G. (2000). *Notes on Innovation in Philanthropy*. Stanford University Graduate School of Business Case Study No. SI-05.

Klausner, M. (May, 2003). 'When Time Isn't Money', *Stanford Social Innovation Review*: 51–59

Kramer, M. (May–June, 2001). 'Strategic Confusion', *Foundation News and Commentary*, available at: www.foundationnews.org

Letts, C., Ryan, W., and Grossman, A. (March–April, 1997). 'Virtuous Capital: What Foundations Can Learn from Venture Capitalists', *Harvard Business Review*: 36–44.

Light, P. (1998). *Sustaining Innovation: Creating Nonprofit and Government Organizations that Innovate Naturally*. San Francisco, CA: Jossey-Bass.

McIlnay, D. (1998). *How Foundations Work*. San Francisco, CA: Jossey-Bass.

Nielsen, W. (1996). *Inside American Philanthropy: The Dramas of Donorship*. Norman, OK: University of Oklahoma Press.

Ryan, W. (2001). *Nonprofit Capital: A Review of Problems and Strategies*, prepared for the Fannie Mae Foundation and the Rockefeller Foundation.

Schervish, P., O'Herlihy, M., and Havens, J. (2001). *Agent Animated Wealth and Philanthropy: The Dynamics of Accumulation and Allocation Among High Tech Donors*. Association for Fundraising Professionals, May.

Sievers, B. (1997). 'If Pigs Had Wings', in *Foundation News and Commentary*, November/December. Available at: http://int1.cof.org/fnc/67sievers.html

Skloot, E. (2003). *Philanthropy: What's Love Got to Do with It?*, luncheon keynote speech for the Center for Effective Philanthropy Conference, New York, 10 October, available at www.surdna.org/speeches

US Agency for International Development (2002). *Foreign Aid in the National Interest*, February.

Venture Philanthropy Partners (2002). *Venture Philanthropy 2002: Advancing Nonprofit Performance Through High-Engagement Grantmaking*, report prepared by Community Wealth Ventures for Venture Philanthropy Partners. Available at: www.venture-pp.org/learning/reports/report

—— (2004). Available at: www.venturepp.org/about/approach/index.html

World Affairs Council (2004). Printed transcript of the 2nd Annual Borderless Giving Conference, Global Philanthropy Forum, held 5–6 June 2003.

Yunus, M. (1999). *Banker to the Poor: Micro-Lending and the Battle Against World Poverty*. New York: Public Affairs.

15

Delivering on the Promise of Social Entrepreneurship: Challenges Faced in Launching a Global Social Capital Market

Pamela Hartigan[1]

Introduction

The notion of a global social capital market has been the subject of academic publications in the USA since the mid-1990s.[2] But at the 2002 Annual Meeting of the World Economic Forum in Davos, Switzerland, a panel discussion catapulted the concept to a global stage and captured international attention among social investors, philanthropists, social entrepreneurs, and other thought leaders.[3] During the year that followed, major efforts were undertaken to launch the market—which was baptized as the GEXSI—the Global Exchange for Social Investment.

Over the past twenty years, the growth in the size and global influence of socially oriented activity by the for-profit and not-for-profit sectors has become a factor promising positive transformation of national and international development. The unprecedented emergence of social enterprises all over the world has been a welcome sign of increasing innovation in the service of humanity. In parallel, business entities have been joining in a growing global movement towards CSR. These developments reflect the convergence of the information and communications revolutions and the accumulation of capital on a scale not previously encountered. But they are also responses to market failure and the increasing recognition that governments and the international community simply cannot provide essential public goods and services to all, and that others must support public sector efforts.

As a consequence, a mushrooming universe of diverse actors makes up what is increasingly being called the 'social capital market'.[4] Its salient characteristics are well described elsewhere. One might say that such a market has always existed to provide essential public goods. But it is a strange market.

There is a dearth of credible information concerning the availability and quality of social projects to compare and select. No objective criteria exist. The best opportunities for social impact may go unidentified. In seeking funding for activities, high performing social purpose organizations often find that they are in the same pot with less competent counterparts. Likewise, social investors are accustomed to knowing little about how effectively their money or in-kind contributions have been put to use to make life better for others. How do investors know whether to continue or stop their funding, or whether they should offer something other than funds, such as management advice, financial guidance, or other in-kind support? And other than traditional grants, what other investment instruments are out there for those investors who want or need to make some financial return on their social dollars?

A major consequence of these shortcomings is that conservative investors—who are the majority—continue to fund start-ups with relatively low infusions of capital. As these start-ups progress from early to intermediate and mature stages, the importance of securing significant and diverse types of investments grows larger and, concomitantly, more difficult.

The Schwab Foundation for Social Entrepreneurship became acutely aware of the 'paradox of success' very early on in its own evolution because of its focus on selecting accomplished social entrepreneurs at intermediate and senior stages of development. These social entrepreneurs have moved well beyond their initial concept and communities of implementation, expanding their initiatives to address market and government failures, ultimately benefiting hundreds of thousands of people. Their capacity to continue to scale is often contingent on securing flexible, longer term financing. As a result, the urgency of identifying second-stage financing mechanisms and networking platforms so that social entrepreneurs with replicable models can find the financial and in-kind support they need became a driving force in the creation of the GEXSI.

The Initial Vision and First Steps

The Schwab Foundation for Social Entrepreneurship[5] initiated the GEXSI in February 2001 when it became clear that even outstanding social entrepreneurs selected to the Foundation's network continuously struggled to mobilize resources to expand and strengthen their initiatives. How could it be that the most successful organizations with the biggest impact in their fields could find it so difficult to raise funds?

Additionally, through the Foundation's sister organization, the WEF, it learned that many willing high net worth individuals and corporations lacked credible information on quality initiatives in a range of areas. Thus, the GEXSI was created as a private venture with a public purpose: to render the global social capital market more efficient and transparent and to work on objective performance criteria. The GEXSI was envisioned to be a mechanism that matched high quality initiatives with investors committed to social value creation.[6]

By April 2001, a consortium had been formed comprising Bain & Company, the Soros Foundations, Deutsche Bank, PricewaterhouseCoopers, Foursome (a social venture fund based in the UK), and the Schwab Foundation. As a first step, Bain conducted extensive interviews with high net worth individuals and entities in Europe and the USA to collect information on their companies' or foundations' social investment practices and the degree to which a GEXSI-like platform would be of interest to them. In those interviews, corporate leaders and high net worth individuals identified the same five shortcomings in relation to investing in social initiatives:

1. Information provision with no quality assurance
2. Narrow focus on a specific geographic area or a specific problem
3. Lack of feedback loops or monitoring systems
4. Limited types of investment instruments—mostly grants. What about loans and equity?
5. Tiny number of quality initiatives.

One of the early quandaries faced by the GEXSI consortium was the issue of volume. The number of social purpose organizations around the world was exponentially growing and the life expectancy of these organizations was highly variable. While an all-inclusive GEXSI was intellectually and emotionally exciting, it was hardly feasible from a business perspective as the GEXSI ramped up its operations.

But, as importantly, the number of highly qualified intermediaries providing financial, technical, and other types of support to these organizations was also growing. Each one of these intermediaries was conducting due diligence on potential local partners prior to making any sort of investment, a process taking anywhere between six and eighteen months and often involving site visits to see first hand the work of these social purpose organizations. The GEXSI had not been set up to compete with highly qualified intermediary organizations, the consortium concluded, but to support their efforts and those of the organizations they identified. Thus, from its inception, the GEXSI focused on accrediting intermediary organizations, and the performance principles devised were created for that purpose. This decision significantly influenced the GEXSI's initial direction.

By September 2001, the GEXSI was keen to achieve proof of concept. What better way of doing so than to pilot test the performance principles it had designed, in consultation with community development organizations and other seasoned intermediaries. The WEF's Annual Meeting in 2002, to be held in New York City,[7] was a perfect opportunity to test the GEXSI idea on the high net worth individuals and corporate leaders attending the meeting.

Between October and December 2001, eleven intermediary organizations agreed to participate in this pilot run to test the performance principles that would accredit them to the GEXSI.[8] If they were accredited, they would be rewarded with an opportunity at the WEF's Annual Meeting to showcase initiatives in their social investment portfolios to corporate leaders and high net worth individuals. In this way, potential investors would also get a sense of the range and types of support that typically would be sought through the GEXSI, which could include grants, loans, equity, or equity equivalents as well as in-kind contributions.

Shaping the Performance Principles

It took approximately three months for the GEXSI consortium to finalize the performance principles for accrediting intermediary organizations. Three basic requirements underpinned the development of this framework. Namely, it had to be:

- A comprehensive rating approach applicable to a broad range of organizations, ensuring that all social purpose intermediary organizations met quality standards
- Pragmatic and applicable
- Acceptable among the wide range of intermediary social purpose organizations and investors

Bain spearheaded the groundwork to devise the performance principles by conducting interviews and workshops with over thirty recognized intermediary not-for-profit organizations working around the world as well as a dozen social venture funds and independent experts. It researched publicly available information on the rating of not-for-profit and for-profit social purpose organizations as well as proprietary documents of those collaborating in this effort. In the process of refining the performance principles, it identified cutting edge social purpose organizations that agreed to be part of the pilot effort to test and refine these principles.

The result of this initial work was a draft of eleven Performance Principles grouped into three categories (financial, social portfolio management, and organizational performance), forming the basis for testing the GEXSI accreditation effort (see Figure 15.1).

What follows is a summary of the rationale behind each of the eleven principles. Subsequently, examples will be given of how two of these principles, Management and Monitoring, and Organizational Set-Up, were operationalized in rating a social enterprise.

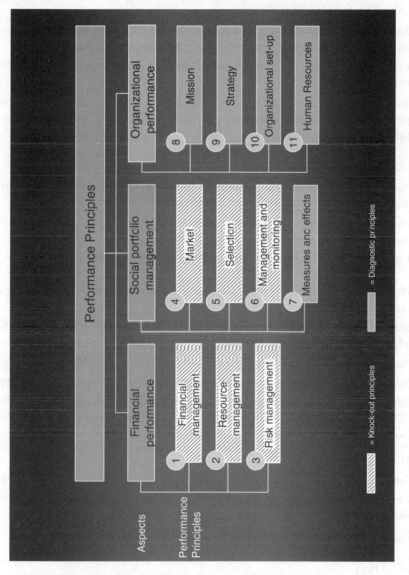

Figure 15.1 Accreditation considers three main aspects

Rationale for Each Principle

Financial Performance

FINANCIAL MANAGEMENT

- Financial accountability and transparency are the bases for trust and cooperation between social investors and social purpose organizations
- Sound financial planning helps focus on important topics and develop sustainable strategies
- Financial Management provides information on whether the organization spends money efficiently and works according to ethical and professional standards

RESOURCE MANAGEMENT

- Diversified financial resources increase the sustainability of the organization and indicates the commitment of a number of investors
- Sound resource management enhances the ability to communicate goals and results
- It provides further confidence that the social impact will be delivered

RISK MANAGEMENT (only for social purpose organizations also providing a financial return):

- Indicates that an organization adheres to policies that reduce risk and safeguard investments and capital
- Policies for portfolio management ensure standardized quality investments
- Policies for assets/liability management are essential to guarantee liquidity
- Current monitoring and recovery plans enhance risk management

Social Portfolio Management

MARKET

- Understanding the organization's market helps focus on core competencies
- Market definition reflects clients' needs, social, economic, and political environment
- Regular updates reflect sensitivity to changes in the market

SELECTION

- Clear criteria consistent with the organization's mission guide initiative choice and demonstrate the core competence of the organization
- The organization's expertise covers the focus of the selected initiative

- The assessment and admission of initiatives is challenging and therefore involves a significant number of experts

MANAGEMENT AND MONITORING

- Monitoring of initiatives delivers ongoing information on current stage and plans
- Active and close 'accompanying' of initiatives assures ongoing quality and fosters sustainability

MEASURES AND EFFECTS

- Social process and impact are defined and clearly stated by the organization
- Methodologies and tools are designed and implemented to gather these measures

Organizational Performance

MISSION

- States the shared vision of all persons working for and with the organization
- A clear, concise, and realistic mission guides the activities of the organization
- Updated mission reflects changes in clients' needs and environment

STRATEGY

- Indicates how the mission is to be fulfilled and the resources allocated by the organization
- Sets inspiring goals and helps measure, document and communicate results
- Coherent planning of long-term and short-term as well as financial and organizational aspects increase likelihood of success

ORGANIZATIONAL SET-UP

- The organization's structure reflects the level of organizational maturity, advances its mission, and increases its impact
- A clear governance structure supports accountability and operational excellence
- Suitable infrastructure ensures effective operations

HUMAN RESOURCES

- Leadership enhances the organization's performance
- Leadership that is actively nurtured enhances staff commitment to mission and strategy

- Competent and professional staff reflect careful recruitment and training policies
- A supportive culture and core values facilitate progress towards fulfilment of the mission

The eleven Performance Principles are divided into two sets: the first six are knockout principles, the remaining five are diagnostic principles. Knockout principles are deemed to constitute the basic elements of an effective social purpose organization. Diagnostic principles provide a deeper understanding of the soundness and consistency of purpose of the entity. The Risk Management principle (Principle 3) is applied only to those social purpose organizations constituted legally as for-profit.

Figures 15.2 and 15.3 provide further detail of two of these Performance Principles. Management and Monitoring (knockout), and Organizational Set-Up (diagnostic). The y-axis of the figures identifies the criteria assessed within the principle. For example, for Management and Monitoring, five criteria are reviewed: ongoing information gathering; ongoing quality assurance; sustainability; exit strategy; and additional evidence. Each of the five is ranked on a scale of 1 to 5 (the x-axis). Those organizations ranking 1 or 2 on any of the six knockout principles would not be accredited to the GEXSI.

The two principles selected (Figures 15.2 and 15.3) illustrate the structure of all the Performance Principles developed and tested. What is readily apparent is the fuzziness between levels 3 and 4 on the x-axis. Additionally, the repeated use in level 5 of the term 'best practice' begs the question of what constitutes such practice. Some have argued that seeking to follow best practice is 'imitation frenzy, as if these fancy labels would make a difference . . . benchmarking and best practice will never get you to the top—merely to the middle' (Ridderstrale and Nordström 2004: 14).

Nevertheless, the principles do broadly discern the difference between more effective organizations and their less effective counterparts. Additionally, the use of exemplary indicators proved to be a useful guide in the assessment and feedback process.

Applying the Performance Principles

Endeavor Global

Endeavor is a not-for-profit entity that was founded on the premise that the key to stability around the world lies in the cultivation of a robust middle class by harnessing the innovative spirit and job-creating capacity of local entrepreneurs. It addresses the problem that in most emerging markets, only a handful of families control the nation's resources and networks. Lacking access and inspiration, entrepreneurs rarely flourish. Endeavor identifies

	1	2	3	4	5
Ongoing info-gathering	• Insufficient and unclear information collected less than once a year from each initiative	• Insufficient or unclear information not covering relevant topics (e.g. finance, current issues)	• Information covers all relevant topics in a meaningful way, updated at least once a year	• Very comprehensive information covering all relevant topics and providing even additional information	• Best practice in ongoing information provision
Ongoing quality assurance	• No possibility to interact with initiative in appropriate manner	• Insufficient interfaces to assure quality of initiatives	• Provision of necessary interfaces to assure quality of initiatives and effective handling of critical issues	• Sustainable and very sound ongoing quality assurance	• Best practice in ongoing quality assurance
Sustainability		• Sustainable development of initiatives is not clearly fostered	• Convincing way of fostering sustainable development of initiatives	• Consistent track record in fostering sustainability	• Best practice in fostering sustainable development
Exit strategy		• No exit strategy exist	• Exit strategy provides practicable way without significant risk	• Very sound exit strategies depending on specific situation	• Best practices in exit strategy and practice
Additional evidence		• No supporting additional evidence	• Further evidence proving fulfilment of criteria	• Further evidence proving very good fulfilment of criteria	• Further evidence proving excellent fulfilment of all criteria

Exemplary indicators

- Written management guides, programme descriptions, and other documents used for management of initiatives
- Reports and monitoring documents
- Processes in place to gather information, assess the quality of initiatives, and to manage initiatives
- Quality of IT systems in place
- Quality of the knowledge available to do the management
- Sustainability of operations, e.g. Number and age of programmes, services offered for initiatives

Figure 15.2 Management and monitoring: The organization manages selected initiatives according to its quality standards and mission

	1	2	3	4	5
Clear governance stucture	• Governance structure is not clearly defined	• The roles of the different entities are not clear (Board, management, department)	• Well-defined governance structure with clear lines of authority and responsibilities	• Very good definition of governance structure; all members act according to the governance structure	• Best practice in clear governance structure
Furthering organizational strengths		• The roles for different entities are not appropriate to the current stage of maturity	• The roles are appropriate to current stage of maturity and regularly revised	• Processes are in place to strengthen the institutional set-up according to current stage	• Best practice in furthering organizational strengths
Accountability		• Lines of accountability are not clearly defined	• Board and management provide full accountability	• Board and managment have proven track record and good credibility	• Best practice in providing accountability
Additional evidence		• No supporting additional evidence	• Further evidence proving fulfilment of criteria	• Further evidence proving very good fulfilment of criteria	• Further evidence proving excellent fulfilment of all criteria

Exemplary indicators

• Organization charts, accountability policies, or other documents for organizational structure and accountability
• Processes in place to define, revise governance structure, and to ensure accountability
• Number of persons involved, their background and knowledge as well as their time allocation

Figure 15.3 Organizational set-up: The organization has a clear governance structure fostering its mission, institutional strengths, and accountability

entrepreneurial leaders, helps them access the training, mentoring, and resources necessary to succeed, and catalyses the local infrastructure to support them. It then promotes its entrepreneurs as role models, delivering a meritocratic message to citizens of the developing world that through hardwork, creativity, and values-driven leadership, individuals living anywhere from any background can turn an entrepreneurial idea into a world-class business venture.

Endeavor's rigorous search and selection process ensures that it identifies individuals with the entrepreneurial capacity to transform their industries, their communities, and potentially even their countries. Founded by Linda Rottenberg and Peter Kellner in 1997, by 2003 Endeavor had selected 174 entrepreneurs from a pool of 9,478. Those selected have generated over 15,000 new jobs and $655 million (£380 million) in revenues. As remarkably, 73 per cent of Endeavor Entrepreneurs are giving back to Endeavor financially or through mentoring. Traditionally, over 90 per cent of new business ventures fail in the first five years, however, 95 per cent of Endeavor entrepreneurs are still operating. Headquartered in New York City, Endeavor operates in Argentina, Brazil, Chile, Uruguay, Mexico, and has expanded to South Africa.

The genius of Endeavor's model lies in its approach to galvanizing commitment to growing a local entrepreneurial culture. Despite all advice from friends, family, and colleagues that there are no entrepreneurs or willing investors in emerging markets, Rottenberg managed to convince some of Latin America's top business leaders not only to donate over $10 million (£5.8 million) to set up Endeavor in their respective countries but also to dedicate their time and passion to the organization and its entrepreneurs. By 2003, Endeavor had created a network of 665 business mentors, engaged 500 angel investors and venture capitalists, and recruited almost 100 top business and academic leaders to its selection panels.

Endeavor agreed to participate in the GEXSI pilot accreditation process in the autumn of 2001. The Bain team spent several days at Endeavor's Headquarters in New York City, reviewing administrative, financial, and strategic documentation and interviewing staff, including top management. That was four years ago, and since then, Endeavor has doubled the number of entrepreneurs in its network (from 100 to 206) and more than trebled the number of jobs they have created through their enterprises (from 6,000 to 20,000). In addition, Endeavor has reconstituted its Board with Edgar Bronfman Jr brought in as Chairman as well as expanded to a new continent. It has secured core funding from the IFC/World Bank and the Inter-American Development Bank, and Citigroup is the most recent core partner to join Endeavor in spreading its efforts. Along the way, Endeavor has been the recipient of numerous national and international awards.

The next section reviews the outcome of the accreditation process as relates to Endeavor. It is important to keep in mind that it is a snapshot of this organization in 2001 not 2005. With respect to Management and Monitoring (Performance Principle 6) Endeavor achieved an overall score of 4/5 (refer to Figure 15.2). Four criteria were assessed within this Performance Principle:

- Ongoing information gathering
- Ongoing quality assurance
- Sustainability
- Exit strategy

What follows are Endeavor's results for this Principle:

CRITERIA: ONGOING INFORMATION GATHERING (Score 4/5)

This criterion is related to the level of ongoing information gathering about Endeavor's selected entrepreneurs as well as the country offices.

Selected Entrepreneurs: Engaged in systematic contact (at least twice a month) with their respective national country office. Several programmes are offered to support the entrepreneurs.

Country Entities: Communicated to each other and to headquarters regularly, at least once a week, often more. The CEO is a member of each national board and represents Endeavor Global. Several meetings a year take place in each country of operations to discuss Endeavor's overall and national strategy.

CRITERIA: ONGOING QUALITY ASSURANCE (Score 4/5)

This criterion is related to continuous monitoring of the quality of the selected entrepreneurs and the country offices.

Entrepreneurs: There are a large number of services available for selected entrepreneurs including:

- *On a global scale*: Silicon Valley Road Show (where they interact with leaders of investment companies): access to MBA students from top-tiered programmes who take internships with Endeavor Entrepreneurs; MIT e-lab
- *At local level*: Mentoring by entrepreneurial business leaders; local road shows; local workshops: educational programme for angel investors

Country Entities: The following indicators demonstrate success on a national level: level of country funding; success of nominated local entrepreneurs in the global selection process; involvement of local entrepreneurs in the national board and network.

CRITERIA: SUSTAINABILITY (Score 4/5)

This criterion is related to the sustainability of the selected entrepreneurs and of the country offices.

- Under the Country Benefactor model, all countries are launched only once funding has been secured for the first four years of operations. The countries then can meet their funding needs through building up country endowments

- Endeavor's national Board and Endeavor Entrepreneurs already have initiated the country endowment in Argentina, on a matching basis. That is, Endeavor Country Benefactors pledged $1 million (£580,000) that was matched by $1 million from Endeavor Argentina's entrepreneurs
- In all Endeavor country offices, the entrepreneurs are selected into the network based on their commitment to donate to the country endowment in the future, in order to sustain the organization
- Endeavor first launched its operations in Chile in 1998. However, unable to raise money from top business leaders, the sine qua non for Endeavor to set up operations in a country (the Chilean government was willing to fund the operation), Endeavor decided to pull out. Realizing the success of Endeavor's operations in Argentina and Uruguay, Chilean business leaders rallied to create the pool of funds needed to sustain Endeavor in Chile
- In the past two years, Endeavor has implemented successfully its strategy for financial sustainability through the Country Benefactor model. The model is fully functional in Chile, Argentina, Uruguay, Brazil, and Mexico

CRITERIA: EXIT STRATEGY (Score 4/5)

- Endeavor will exit a country if private sector funding is non-existent, as such commitment underpins the model and Endeavor's theory of change. The example of Chile (bullet 4 under Sustainability criterion) is an example of how Endeavor's exit strategy leveraged the needed funding to ramp up operations there.
- In terms of when Endeavor exits a country, this occurs at the point where barriers to entrepreneurship have been broken down in that country. At such a time (this has yet to occur in any region), the Endeavor office no longer continues its Search & Selection process for Endeavor Entrepreneurs, or the process will shift focus to more distant regions within the country outside capital cities. Once Search & Selection is no longer needed, country operations will transition to emphasize educational programmes that support entrepreneurship on a broad scale.

With respect to Organizational Set-Up (Performance Principle 10) Endeavor achieved an overall score of 4/5 (refer to Figure 15.3). Four criteria were assessed within this Performance Principle:

- Clear governance structure
- Furthering organizational strengths
- Supportive organizational systems
- Accountability

What follows are Endeavor's results for this Principle:

CRITERIA: CLEAR GOVERNANCE STRUCTURE (Score 4/5)

- Endeavor Global is governed by Endeavor Global's Board of Directors. Each Endeavor country is governed by a local Endeavor Country Board. These governance relationships are enforced through the legal by-laws of each respective legal entity (e.g. Endeavor Global, Endeavor Argentina, Endeavor Brazil, etc.) which outline fiduciary and management responsibilities of the Board of Director members in this oversight capacity. Each Endeavor Board of Directors (global and country-based) also includes at least one Endeavor Entrepreneur to ensure an ongoing feedback loop from the drivers of Endeavor's mission and the direct recipients of its programme's support.

- The Global Policy Committee and Global Advisory Board provide governance for the global organization to ensure control mechanisms that maintain Endeavor's mission, brand, trademark protection, ethical standards, financial policies, and evolution of Endeavor's model and programmes to meet the evolving needs of the organization as it expands globally. (Documentation reviewed: Global Affiliate Agreement as well as Impact Reports.)

  - The Global Policy Committee is comprised of the President of each Endeavor Country Board, the Chair of Endeavor Global, two additional representatives of Endeavor Global Board of Directors and the two co-Chairs of the Global Advisory Board.

  - The Global Advisory Board is comprised of thirty individuals representing a broad constituency base of business, academic, and economic development/emerging market backgrounds. The Global Advisory Board includes the President and one additional member of each Endeavor Country Board of Directors. In addition, the Global Advisory Board includes Endeavor Entrepreneurs, leading members of the academic community in the area of global entrepreneurship, and corporate supporters of global entrepreneurial development.

- The Global Policy Committee has authority to make recommendations to the Endeavor Global Board of Directors regarding new country entry, removal of the right to operate as an Endeavor country (for breach of mission, brand, ethics, etc.)

- Endeavor Global's organizational structure is clearly defined in its organizational chart with programme P&L accountability at the programme manager level, with lines of reporting into the Chief Operating Office (COO)/ Chief Finance Officer (CFO) who reports to the CEO

CRITERIA: FURTHERING ORGANIZATIONAL STRENGTHS (SCORE 3/5)

- Global Affiliate Agreement and global and country by-laws provide for ability to amend these respective legal documents in order to ensure adaptation over time to evolving organizational needs.

- Organizational staffing requirements are analysed and revised annually, based on organizational needs (e.g. for programme and/or new country expansion, etc.). Endeavor Global and Country Boards of Directors evaluate and approve annual budgets and proposed staffing plans, based on organizational needs.

- Roles and responsibilities of global staff members are adapted over time based on evolving organizational requirements to meet needs of Endeavor countries, programme expansion, or expansion to new countries. Job descriptions are created and adapted over time to reflect changing roles and responsibilities based on organizational requirements.

  - Example: Endeavor Global's May 2001 Board meeting discussed the unmanageable number of direct reports into the CEO (fourteen at that time including all US staff and country Managing Directors) in addition to the responsibility for new country expansion and fund-raising. The Board made the recommendation to have the CFO become the COO/CFO to relieve the number of direct reports into CEO. In the resulting current organizational structure, the COO/CFO oversees all US staff members and global operations human resources. The CEO now only has direct reports of Country MDs, COO/CFO, and Fund Development Senior Advisor.

- Self-assessment of organization: Endeavor has had external surveys evaluating feedback from its network of entrepreneurs completed through Avina, a Swiss social investing intermediary organization particularly active in Latin America that also backs Endeavor. The feedback from these surveys has resulted in changes in Endeavor's strategy vis-à-vis its entrepreneurs over time (e.g. involving the entrepreneurs at the national and global levels, programme development, etc.).

CRITERIA: SUPPORTIVE ORGANIZATIONAL SYSTEMS (Score 4/5)

- Endeavor has an extensive IT system and Lotus Notes database through which it runs its international Search & Selection programme that is accessible to all Endeavor countries. This global system enables replication and process focus for its semi-annual Search & Selection process and management of the selection panels.

- Endeavor has a Microsoft Exchange platform for its e-mail, website hosting, intranet, and international contact database. Expense reports are accessible and updated through Endeavor's intranet.

- The global website serves as an information resource and point of knowledge dissemination. The country websites allow online entrepreneur registration for Endeavor's Search & Selection process.

- Endeavor Global is developing an extranet for its Entrepreneurial Services programme; in order more efficiently to store and update data on its global

VentureCorps members and entrepreneurs' needs assessments. This extranet will be available to all Endeavor countries, to facilitate exchange of information on entrepreneur services requirements and updates.

- Annual evaluation during the budgeting process of facilities, equipment, and operational and IT systems ensures adequate support for size of organization and staffing. Current facilities and equipment will be sufficient to support the US organization for the next five years.

- IT systems (hardware and software): Endeavor has an agreement with Microsoft which is renewed annually to donate new software to the global and country organizations in order to meet expanding IT resource requirements (Microsoft donated $150,000 [£87,000] in software in 2000). In 2000, Compaq donated $200,000 (£116,000) in hardware to the global and country organizations to meet hardware equipment and server needs.

- Based on expanding organizational size and IT requirements, Endeavor Global and Endeavor's country offices decided in 2001 to decentralize IT in order more effectively to ensure accountability for IT systems and support. As a consequence, Endeavor's country offices use their own Internet service providers and e-mail domains and hire local IT support for developing and/ or hosting their websites, rather than Endeavor Global developing and hosting all IT, e-mail, and websites centrally. All countries are responsible for updating and maintaining their own contacts.

- Endeavor Global and Endeavor country offices meet quarterly to discuss which IT resources/databases will be shared and used between all countries in order to ensure operational efficiencies.

CRITERIA: ACCOUNTABILITY (Score 4/5)

- Bylaws for Endeavor Global and Endeavor country offices outline fiduciary and governance accountability of the global and country Boards of Directors. Endeavor Global also has one seat on each Endeavor Country Board.

- The Global Affiliate Agreement stipulates annual Endeavor country office reporting to the Global Advisory Board. The Global Policy Committee is accountable for recommending new country entry or removal of the right to operate as an Endeavor country office.

- Endeavor management is accountable to its respective Boards of Directors; meetings are held on a quarterly basis. Management is also accountable to the Global Advisory Board to which presentations are made on an annual basis.

- The Global Advisory Board has been in existence since May 1999 and has enabled Endeavor to adapt to challenges faced as Endeavor has evolved and expanded. Likewise, the global and country boards of directors have assumed full fiduciary accountability for the global and country organizations and have worked with management to ensure that the Endeavor country offices are able to overcome financial challenges and create strategies for sustainability.

Summary

This section on Endeavor's pilot accreditation process to the GEXSI has attempted to capture the depth of the assessment for each performance principle, taking as an example two of those principles. Endeavor's feedback on the process was overwhelmingly positive. To a greater or lesser degree, its feedback reflected that received from the other ten participating intermediary organizations. In general, all expressed that the exercise had been conducted with professionalism and thoroughness and had been well worth the investment of time and effort to prepare for the review. Moreover, such an exercise would have represented significant costs to the organization. Yet it had been provided free.

Evaluating the Process and Managing Intermediary Expectations

Despite the initial positive feedback, the Performance Principles and their respective criteria and scoring had not been derived through an open, participatory process wherein those who would be assessed according to those principles contributed also to their creation. In fact, many social entrepreneurs in the Schwab network had been critical of that very issue. But the time pressure to get a pilot running for the January meeting of the WEF drove the process— the consortium wanted proof of concept and felt that the Annual Meeting was the platform to secure it.

In addition, the intermediaries participating in the pilot process were pragmatic. They were more interested in the possibility of funding for their initiatives than quibbling about the criteria in the eleven Performance Principles and the process of accreditation. Their eyes were on the fact that once accredited through this pilot process, they would have access to a pool of interested investors. A number of them were also highly enthusiastic about the real possibility of creating a global social capital market, and of having participated from the outset in its launch.

Once accredited, the eleven intermediaries worked on getting their initiatives ready to be presented at the WEF's Annual Meeting in New York (2002). This entailed selecting those initiatives among the many in their respective portfolios and boiling down their essence to one page. Figure 15.4 illustrates one of the ten initiatives put forward by Endeavor. All remaining ten intermediaries followed similar formats to that shown in Figure 15.4.

The Initiative: Endeavor Uruguay is pioneering a not-for-profit model to spur growth by offering multi-pronged support to promising business entrepreneurs in emerging markets. Unlike micro-lending institutions, Endeavor Uruguay targets the equally underserved yet slightly up-market sector of high-growth entrepreneurs. Different from private equity groups, Endeavor Uruguay selects entrepreneurs leading companies between $1–$15 million (£580,000–£8.7 million) in sales, but does not make financial investments of its own. Instead, Endeavor offers a comprehensive and locally adaptable model that accelerates the process of new venture and wealth creation

The Challenge: While entrepreneurship is behind the growth of the strongest global economies, entrepreneurs in Uruguay face unique hurdles: lack of entrepreneurial risk taking; few role models; limited access to information: and difficulty attracting capital. Endeavor's six-stage model breaks down these barriers by stimulating the creation of new ventures, developing venture-friendly environments, and communicating local entrepreneurial success stories to achieve a role model effect.

Critical Requirements: A virtual library/interactive website to extend educational programmes will require funding beyond the first four years of operations that will finance the development of additional educational programmes and of infrastructure tools to scale search and selection. These tools will enable expansion into lesser-developed regions of the country and will increase the reach of Endeavor Uruguay's programmes beyond the base of selected Endeavor entrepreneurs.

Impact: In 2000–1, Endeavor Uruguay screened 160 and selected six entrepreneurs, hosted 1,929 attendees at 17 educational conferences; made 96 entrepreneur contacts, and held two peer sessions. Annually, Endeavor Uruguay will screen 200 and select four to six entrepreneurs, host 800 conference attendees, and publish local entrepreneur case studies. With $1.3 million (£754,000) pledged for the first 4 years of operations, Endeavor Uruguay seeks to raise an endowment to fund ongoing operations (entrepreneur equity, grants, donations).

Stage of initiative
Enlargement
(Stages 1–6 of Endeavor Model)

Market information
Uruguay: Econ.Dev/Entrepr.
3,000 Entrepreneurs (3 years)

Kind of investment
Grant or Endowment

Accute ST/LT Needs
$500,000; $500,000/yr. (£290,000)

Total Expenditures
Planned
$1.5 million/3 yr.; $5 million (endowed)
(£870,000/3 yr.; £2.9 million (endowed)

Total Funding to Date
$270,000; $1.3 million 4-yr. pledge
(£157,000; £754,000 4-yr. pledge)

Investment opp this financial year
$500,000

Total Spending this financial year
$231,000

Organizational
Management
Endeavor Global, Inc.
Linda Rottenberg, CEO

Non-financial Support
Management, Marketing, IT

Current investors
IDB; Grupo Velox; Michael
Chu; Banco Comercial;
Francisco de Narvaez; CNI

Figure 15.4 Building a social infrastructure of entrepreneurship and innovation

But while the intermediaries were keen on getting funding for their initiatives, the GEXSI consortium members also wanted to secure additional seed funding to ramp up the GEXSI's activities. Each consortium member had already invested significant amounts of time and funding to get the GEXSI to where it could 'grow legs' and run. GEXSI needed additional funds to do that. To the consortium, the pilot accreditation process had been a means to an end—to illustrate how the GEXSI could work and recruit excited investors. However, for the majority of the intermediaries that had been accredited, the accreditation process was analogous to 'money in the bank' for their initiatives, in many cases regardless of whether the GEXSI itself secured seed investors. In sum, from the outset, the interests of the different stakeholder groups were clearly not aligned because the expectations had not been clear from the start.

PricewaterhouseCoopers, one of the GEXSI consortium members, invested resources in compiling a glossy publication (henceforth known as 'the red book' because of its cover) that contained the intermediaries' investment opportunities. All in all, the red book presented approximately 100 such initiatives, similar to the one presented in Figure 15.4. During the WEF's Annual Meeting, a lunch was organized at Le Cirque, one of New York City's top restaurants. Approximately 100 corporate leaders and ultra high net worth individuals showed up. George Soros and Klaus Schwab made presentations about the importance of the GEXSI platform. Charlie Rose, well-known political analyst and television personality in the USA, moderated the process. A feature article had appeared in the *Financial Times* announcing the GEXSI. Going into the lunch at Le Cirque, the consortium was confident.

By the end of the lunch, each participant had a red book and had skimmed through it. But no deals had been made, no cheques had been written, either for the GEXSI or for the individual initiatives in the book. 'Interesting idea', offered many. 'Too American', quipped others (ironically, only half of the consortium members were US based). No one was ready to commit. Not then. It would take time and a new iteration of the GEXSI.

The GEXSI consortium came together after the New York launch to analyse the next steps. The intermediaries did as well, feeling disappointed. Some felt they had been 'used' by the consortium for its own ends.

There is little doubt that the entire process could have been better managed. In the immediate aftermath, the Performance Principles and the process of accreditation were criticized. The nature of the consortium also was strongly questioned, primarily, the absence of a stronger representation of practitioners and the fact that the Performance Principles had been crafted by strategic business consultants with little experience with social purpose organizations. In addition, should not membership in the GEXSI consortium have precluded participation in the pilot accreditation process? Bain was part of the consortium but was conducting that pilot accreditation process. Two fellow consortium members wanted to be accredited. Did this not introduce the appearance of a bias, benefiting those two intermediaries? Finally, the mix of intermediaries varied widely, from entrepreneurial organizations such as Endeavor and Accion (which are not-for-profits funding for-profits) to more established bureaucratic intermediaries. Should there not have been an effort to separate these 'apples and oranges'? All of these comments have validity.

In addition to shortcomings in the process and in the lack of differentiation among accredited intermediaries, the GEXSI was missing a critical mass of large-scale investors including credible philanthropists and financial leaders willing to make the first move, seeding the GEXSI's initial scale-up as well as supporting a significant number of the offerings put forward by the accredited intermediaries—both evidence of proof of concept and creating a snowball effect.

But for purposes of this chapter, there are two particular questions of interest:

- If the Performance Principles and the process of applying them had been derived through a wider process of global consultation, whereby those assessed owned the product, how significantly would the resulting framework differ from what was initially produced by Bain?

- The process of accreditation to any market, particularly a social capital market, does not guarantee funds will flow to the social purpose organization. What is the optimum way to manage such expectations?

Raising the Phoenix from the Ashes: The Creation of the Keystone–GEXSI Partnership

As the GEXSI momentum appeared to unravel before everyone's eyes, a group of committed observers assessed the situation.[9] They had met in 2002 at the Conference on Finance for Development in Monterrey, Mexico, and formed the Founding Coalition for the Development Market Place (henceforth referred to as the Coalition), the precursor of what has become Keystone, as well as the new iteration of the GEXSI.

One of the major concerns about the GEXSI model among a minority of its consortium members, which persisted throughout its initial phase, related to the fluid relationship between the market component and the accreditation component. This concern became heightened as some consortium members asked to be accredited to the GEXSI during the pilot application of the Performance Principles prior to the WEF's Annual Meeting in 2002. If the GEXSI was to be a credible and transparent marketplace, it became increasingly urgent to create a firewall between the agency that accredited the organizations to the market, and the platform for presenting and finding such investment opportunities.

The initial GEXSI experience helped shape the Coalition's approach. In particular, the Coalition sought to emphasize two components that in its view constituted the underpinnings of any social capital market but, to their mind, had been overlooked by the GEXSI. First, any framework for improving the accountability of social purpose organizations worldwide had to be shaped through a collective process that engaged as many as wanted to contribute.

This would have to include a forum for dialogue and debate relating to accountability issues. Second, a capacity-building component had to be incorporated to improve the accountability of social purpose organizations and help them connect with the resources. These two components have been the cornerstone of the evolution of the Coalition into Keystone and constitute the basis of its core offering.[10]

While there were evident synergies between Keystone and the GEXSI, there was one potential obstacle to making the relationship happen. The two entities had very distinctive 'personalities' that influenced their respective approaches. Investors and strategic business consultants had driven the GEXSI consortium. By nature, it is a group that is highly impatient with form and process. Time is their most precious resource and concrete output drives them. They speak in bullets and power point, indicating a zeal to boil things down to their essence. Need to put together performance principles for accrediting social purpose organizations? In three months these are produced. While experts are consulted, the final product is crafted by a few.

On the other hand, the original Coalition that formed Keystone was much more heterogeneous. Most of its members were used to speaking in documents and stories, not bullets. Process is as important as product, and the way one arrives at the product has everything to do with the acceptance of that product by 'consumers'. Widespread consultation and building consensus are corner-stones of their stakeholder-focused modus operandi. They contend that by engaging in capacity building to achieve organizational transparency and mobilize resources, the social purpose organization's expectations would also be more realistic, averting the backlash the GEXSI had experienced in the aftermath of intermediary disappointments with the lack of investment deals.

Despite these differences, Keystone saw a GEXSI partnership as a way to tap into a wider network of social investors in the USA and Europe. From the GEXSI consortium's perspective, it had learned the hard way that the process for deriving the performance principles was critically important—even if the end product achieved through consensus was similar to the original principles that had been created behind a desk in Munich. Ultimately, Keystone provided the GEXSI with the opportunity to do what it felt most confident at doing—creating new sources of funds and setting up deals.

Much has been written about both GEXSI and Keystone (for information on either see www.gexsi.org or www.accountability.org). The next section will only summarize the distinctive features of both approaches.

The Current GEXSI Approach—The Market Component

While there are a number of substantive advances in the way the GEXSI is now being conceptualized, the major difference between the new GEXSI and its initial approach lies in its inclusiveness. In its first iteration, the GEXSI had sought to accredit only intermediary organizations on the premise that this would increase the volume of quality initiatives in the GEXSI portfolio and also be more cost effective. The current GEXSI seeks to exclude no organization, no matter how small or recently created. It is also cultivating a strong network of venture philanthropists that understand the nature of more engaged social investing.

The GEXSI's organizational structure, too, has evolved from the collective consortium-driven approach in its initial incubation period. GEXSI now has a full time CEO—Dr Maritta Koch Weser—who was part of the original Monterrey Coalition that formed Keystone. The consortium continues to act as a governing board as the GEXSI's product offering matures and grows. Other strong contributors have joined the GEXSI to support its core operations, most importantly, the German Development Agency (GTZ).

The GEXSI has two main products, one focused on for-profit social investment, called the GEXSI Social Investment Partnerships, the other focused on the philanthropic and not-for-profit domain, called the GEXSI Change Initiative.

The GEXSI Social Investment Partnerships are devised to bridge the gap between commercial investors and for-profit grassroots initiatives on a deal or thematic basis. Customer groups in this area include private investors and development agencies, including funds-of-funds and investment guarantors. The focus is on development areas that can attract commercially oriented credit and investment, such as the fields of renewable energy, communication, water and sanitation, housing, sustainable forestry, and enterprise development. For example, GEXSI might bundle a group of high performing initiatives in the area of renewable energies to be presented to one or more interested social investment partners. Operating through the bundled portfolio system is more administratively efficient for the investor than investing in each initiative separately.

The second product, the GEXSI Change initiative, is aimed at those initiatives that are much less likely to go to market, primarily in the areas of education, health, and environmental protection, for example. These require grant finance for longer term and recurrent costs. The Change concept is based on the idea that large scale electronic billing systems, such as those in the utility, communications, online sales, and credit card sectors, offer enormous opportunities worldwide for raising additional funds for social investments at the customer level, on a voluntary, sustainable basis. Transaction costs are minimal. Customers would be given the 'social' choice of rounding up their bill to the next full dollar, euro, rupee, or real. Even with a modest 10 per cent of customers participating, enormous amounts of funding for development would be generated. Such systems could be promoted and developed locally, and for individual participants, contributions would be tiny.

Accountability and transparency for the Change initiative will be assured in association with Keystone. There will be no accumulation of large funds at the level of billing companies. Based on customer preferences, billing systems will channel funds directly to eligible beneficiary institutions.

The GEXSI aims to establish national level franchises with the GEXSI World-wide as the company holding the copyright to the name and brand. The hub size will be minimal, and for technical backstopping, the GEXSI will cooperate with existing centres of expertise. Currently, in the start-up phase, the GEXSI is dependent mostly on grant support. Future funding is envisaged to come from two sources: income earnings from expert services in support of the Social Investment Partnerships and multi-year grants in support of the Change initiative team.

The Keystone Approach—The Ratings Component

Initially focused on civil society organizations in the not-for-profit space, Keystone seeks to promote their effectiveness, trust, and legitimacy by creating the tools for making them accountable to other citizens, businesses, and governments.

Keystone recognizes that any organization or initiative that seeks to advance civil society accountability at a system level—through the creation of generally accepted principles, standards, and guidelines—will generate great suspicion and resistance. Thus, Keystone has replaced the idea of a reporting and accountability model, with a process of coming up with 'generally accepted principles for'. In other words, Keystone runs an inclusive conversation to foster generally accepted principles for civil society reporting and accountability with a view to deriving a framework based on an agreed conception of quality, allowing diverse actors—social investors, activists, citizen organizations—to engage from their distinctive vantage points. By following this direction, Keystone seeks also to enable organizational learning.

Keystone pursues a two-pronged strategy:

1. Keystone Dialogue promotes an open convening space for the discussion and creation of generally accepted principles and guidelines for not-for-profit accountability. As such, it uses the same principles and practices of the 'open source' software movement to write the principles and guidelines of not-for-profit accountability. Thus, Keystone hopes to create a strong incentive for those with an interest in accountability to contribute to the development of their principles. The resulting outputs would belong to all, by use of 'reverse copyright' licences. Differently from other standards initiatives—including those created through wide consultation and consensus such as the Global Reporting Initiative—the outputs would not be the formal responsibility of a specific organization. Rather, quality would be maintained through the self-organizing community of its creators.

2. Keystone 'application hubs' develop and test performance-based ways of reporting, using participatory methods. Working with local partners in different contexts who are direct participants in the open source dialogue, the results of these applications are also fed back into the Dialogue. Current application hubs include the Philippine Council for NGO Certification, the Nelson Mandela Foundation, the Innovation Bazaar, Global Giving, Give Foundation, and the Southern Africa Grant Makers Association.

Keystone has already been able to attract significant funding for its activities.

Coming Together—More or Less?

One of the challenges faced from the outset by the GEXSI–Keystone partnership has been that of timing. The Keystone approach is based on process, testing, and consensus. That takes time. The GEXSI approach requires volume for its social investment partnerships and a mechanism for ensuring the transparency and accountability of recipient organizations for its Change initiative. This is an immediate need.

To allow the GEXSI to move forward whilst ensuring that Keystone remains true to its process and consensus-building orientation, the partners agreed that Keystone would develop a template for use by the social purpose organizations that would serve not only to judge the present and potential future performance of the entity but also help it focus on how it could evolve. The template will be refined as the Keystone application hubs test and improve the framework.

With respect to the verification process for initiatives in the Social Investment Partnership portfolios, Keystone has also provided a template for those organizations and will conduct the monitoring.

While the GEXSI and Keystone have a similar genesis and share, at least at present, some cross-representation in the current governance structure,[11] neither will rely exclusively on the other for pursuing its mission. For example, in the current absence of generally accepted principles for the reporting and accountability of social purpose organizations, the GEXSI has had to find other ways of vouching for the effectiveness and transparency of the organizations that seek to use its market platform.

In so far as Keystone is concerned, there are a host of social market platforms in addition to the GEXSI that are waiting for a product they can use that will be applicable and acceptable as a global framework for assessing the organizations they review and promote.

Conclusion

Rather than being at the end of the trajectory to set up a global social capital market and its accompanying rating frameworks, we are just at the beginning. The faults with the GEXSI's initial effort to design and apply generally accepted performance principles was not with the eleven Performance Principles put forward by Bain. While these could have been improved, in their application these Principles shed much light on the quality and impact of a social purpose organization. The problem with the Principles can be summed up thus: top-down does not work.

But does 'bottom up' measure up? The verdict is still out and will be out for a long time. The core philosophy underpinning Keystone is the importance of engaging in a global participatory process and consensus-building effort in elaborating such principles. But at some point, there has to be a product agreed to and put to use. Meanwhile, the second iteration of the GEXSI has been launched and deals are being made—without generally agreed upon principles for rating social purpose organizations. The same is true of multiple social marketplaces around the world.

So, does having those principles matter in the end for the global social capital market? We think so. One cannot doubt such a need when one witnesses on a daily basis the difficulty high impact social entrepreneurial organizations have in mobilizing the resources needed to ensure the health, growth, and impact of their transformational initiatives.

Clearly, both the GEXSI and Keystone paths are complementary, parallel processes that will converge over time through successive iterations. The transactional world often leads the world of theoretical understanding and refinements, rather than vice versa. Those in social ventures seeking funds and those in social investing entities seeking quality transactions inevitably rub shoulders daily in a world of sub-optimal efforts to transform society for the common good. The challenge to both the GEXSI and Keystone is to harness enough of what is already known to catapult a fragmented, mainly localized, marketplace into a progressively more organized global market with greater social benefit. By degrees, these initiatives are moving jointly in this direction in a concerted, catalytic way, trying to sidestep the many pitfalls along the way.

Until then, we will continue to rely on Thomas Edison's words of wisdom: 'I have not failed. I have found 10,000 ways it won't work'.

Notes

1. The author wishes to express her particular thanks to Linda Rottenberg for agreeing to share the results of the pilot accreditation process with readers who might benefit.

2. Most of the literature on the social capital market has been focused on the USA. However, the characteristics described apply to social purpose organizations and social investors around the world. See any of Jed Emerson's publications including Emerson, J. (1999) 'The US Non-Profit Capital Market: An Introductory Overview of Development Stages, Investors and Funding Instrument', *REDF Box Set* (Roberts Enterprise Development Fund); Emerson, J. (2000). 'The Nature of Returns: A Social Capital Markets Inquiry into Elements of Investment and the Blended Value Proposition', *Social Enterprise Series*, 17 (Harvard Business School).

3. The panel included Jed Emerson, then Executive Director of the Roberts Enterprise Development Fund; Muhammad Yunus, Founder and Managing Director of the Grameen Bank; Bill Drayton, Founder and Chair, Ashoka; Linda Rottenberg, Co-Founder and CEO, Endeavor; and Pamela Hartigan, Managing Director, The Schwab Foundation for Social Entrepreneurship.

4. Most of the literature on the social capital market has been focused on the USA. However, the characteristics described apply to social purpose organizations and social investors around the world.

5. The Schwab Foundation for Social Entrepreneurship was co-founded by Klaus Schwab and his wife, Hilde, in 1998. The Foundation initiated its activities at the end of 2000. Professor Schwab is also the founder and Executive Chairman of the WEF. Both organizations are Swiss-based not-for-profits.

6. GEXSI's business plan will not be discussed in this chapter due to space limitations. However, GEXSI was set up as a not-for-profit organization with a view to becoming self-sustaining in five years of operation.

7. This was the first time in the history of the WEF that its Annual Meeting had taken place outside of Davos, Switzerland. Klaus Schwab moved the venue to express solidarity with New York City in the aftermath of the September 11 terrorist attack.

8. The following organizations were accredited by Bain to the GEXSI using the pilot performance principles: Accion International (USA), Ashoka (USA), Investors in Society Charities Aid Foundation (CAF) (UK), Cascadia Revolving Fund (USA), Citizens Network for Foreign Affairs (CNFA) (USA), Endeavor (USA), Foursome Investments Ltd. (UK), Nonprofit Finance Fund (NFF) (USA), Open Society Institute (USA), The Robin Hood Foundation (USA), and Rockefeller Philanthropy Advisors (USA). For reasons of time pressure given the proximity of the WEF's meeting and the pilot nature of this effort, most of the intermediaries were US based, with two UK exceptions.

9. The institutions and key individuals (acting 'ad personam') include in alphabetical order: AccountAbility (Simon Zadek), the Aga Khan Foundation (David Bonbright), Brugger Consultants/Sustainability Forum (Ernst Brugger), Development Space (Dennis Whittle), Earth3000 (Maritta Koch-Weser), Gesellschaft für Technische Zusammenarbeit-GTZ (Albrecht Graf Hardenberg), The Interamerican Foundation (Carolyn Karr), Medley Consultants (John Goldstein), the Nelson Mandela Foundation (Jon Samuel), and The State of the World Forum (Tom Rautenberg).

10. Access was launched in September 2004 and is a UK-based not-for-profit. Its CEO is David Bonbright, a lawyer and former Director of NGO Enhancement Programmes for the Aga Khan Foundation.

11. Maritta Koch Weser, CEO of GEXSI, was involved heavily in the Coalition which gave birth to Keystone. Pamela Hartigan, Managing Director of the Schwab Foundation

and incubator of the first iteration of the GEXSI, currently represents the Foundation in the GEXSI consortium and is also on the Executive Committee of Keystone.

References

Emerson, J. (1999). 'The US Non-Profit Capital Market: An Introductory Overview of Developmental Stages, Investors and Funding Instrument', in *REDF Box Set*, vol. 2, chapter 10. San Francisco, CA: Roberts Enterprise Development Fund.

Emerson, J. (2000). 'The Nature of Returns: A Social Capital Markets Inquiry into Elements of Investment and the Blended Value Proposition', *Social Enterprise Series*, 17. Harvard, MA: Harvard Business School.

Meehan III, W. F., Kilmer, D., and O'Flanagan, M. (Spring, 2004). 'Investing in Society', *Stanford Social Innovation Review*: 35–41.

Ridderstrale, J. and Nordström, K. (2004). *Karaoke Capitalism: Management for Mankind*. London: Prentice-Hall.

16

Social Entrepreneurship: The Promise and the Perils

Jerr Boschee[1]

Introduction

Social innovators around the world have begun to reach a disquieting conclusion: inspired vision, impassioned leadership, enthusiastic volunteers, government subsidies, and a phalanx of donors are not always enough.

They serve admirably while innovators transform their dreams into fledgling programmes and steer their organizations through early growing pains. But there comes a time, albeit reluctantly, when most founders and their followers begin to understand that living from year to year does not ensure the future—and that is the moment when they begin migrating from innovation to entrepreneurship. It is one thing to design, develop, and carry out a new programme, quite another to sustain it. So they begin turning towards commercial markets, gradually exploring the possibilities of earned income, many for the first time and often with reluctance given their uneasiness about the profit motive.

The moment of realization comes at different stages and for different reasons. Major funders may be experiencing donor fatigue. The initial band of dedicated volunteers and employees might be burning out. Government support for a project could be waning or the cost of delivering services escalating dramatically. It might even be that the organization is on the threshold of significant growth but cannot proceed without new sources of financing.

In the USA, the moment arrived for most not-for-profits in the mid- to late-1990s, although a handful of pioneering social entrepreneurs had been emphasizing earned income since the 1960s and 1970s. Around the world, the moment is dawning today for some of the most successful social innovators, and they are slowly moving away from a dependency model of financing that relies almost entirely on charitable contributions and public sector subsidies. The movement takes two forms:

- Some are working towards sustainability, which can be attained through a *combination* of philanthropy, subsidies, and earned revenue
- Others are seeking self-sufficiency, which can only be achieved through earned revenue alone

However, entering commercial markets poses significant challenges for non-governmental organizations (NGOs), and the purpose of this chapter is to review some of the lessons learned during the past thirty years by not-for-profits in the USA that have turned increasingly towards earned revenue—not-for-profits whose successes and failures serve as both models and cautionary tales for their counterparts in other countries.

This chapter will:

- Summarize six historical forces that led to the emergence of social entrepreneurship in the USA
- Describe five basic principles that have evolved over time
- Present two unexpected outcomes experienced by not-for-profits adopting entrepreneurial strategies
- Identify four types of stakeholder objections
- Analyse the single greatest obstacle encountered by entrepreneurial not-for-profits
- And review fourteen critical success factors emphasized by the pioneers in the field

Historical Context

The pressures on not-for-profits in the USA began to build more than two decades ago. Six of the most damaging have been the following:

- *Depleted reserves*: During the late 1970s, the US economy simultaneously suffered recession and double-digit inflation. The pressures led to sharply escalating costs and tighter budgets for all not-for-profits, the first sign that times were changing. During the next few years, the impact worsened: a national survey in 1977 showed that the average not-for-profit had approximately three months of operating capital in reserve at the end of the year; the same survey ten years later revealed that average capital reserves had fallen to less than four days (Bailey 1990: 4).
- *Diminished support from the public sector*: Driven by the Reagan administration's emphasis on privatization, federal and state spending on social services and the arts began plummeting in the early 1980s, eventually falling by more than 23 per cent (in real numbers) in a single decade (Bailey 1990: 4).

- *Reduced giving by individuals and corporations*: Changes in the US tax code in 1986 also precipitated a substantial drop in giving from wealthy Americans, who by 1990 were donating only 4 per cent of their annual income to charity compared to 7 per cent in 1979 (Williams 1992: 17). A parallel reduction in corporate philanthropy exacerbated the plunge—it failed to keep pace with inflation for six consecutive years after the tax code changed (Kaplan 1995: 77). Overall, the relationship of private contributions to the current operating expenses of not-for-profits in the USA shifted dramatically: in 1960, they covered 59.8 per cent, in 1990 only 31.5 (Hodgkinson et al. 1992: 59). And, by 1997, private giving to human service organizations had fallen to their lowest point in thirty years (Weitzman et al. 2002: 57).

- *More competition for grants and contributions*: The number of 501(c)(3) charitable organizations in the USA has exploded. For every two that existed in 1977, there are more than five today (Weitzman et al. 2002: 5), and they are all appealing to the same potential donors. As one frustrated Foundation executive put it, 'there are just too damn many not-for-profits out there, and they're tripping over each other.'

- *More people in need*: By 1992, one in seven Americans were living below the poverty line (Berg 1993: 2A), including more than one in five children (Berg 1993: 4A) and 18 per cent of families with at least one adult holding a full-time job were still classified as living in poverty (*Star Tribune* 1993). Beyond that, not-for-profits were wrestling with an eruption of new challenges, including HIV/AIDS, homelessness, drug addiction, and an exponential growth in the number of frail elderly persons. According to Catholic Charities USA, four times as many people were seeking help from its member agencies in 1991 than just ten years previously; even more dismaying, only one in four had needed help with basic food and shelter in 1981—ten years later it was two out of three (*Not-For-Profit Times* 1993: 57).

- *A dangerously frayed reputation*: A series of scandals throughout the 1990s also caused many Americans to lose confidence in the sector, including misappropriation of funds by the head of the nation's largest fund-raising body; a pyramid scheme that stole more than $50 million (£29 million) from wealthy philanthropists; and embezzlement in the highest ranks of the Episcopal church. As a result, by 1996, a national poll revealed that only 60 per cent of Americans believed charities were honest and ethical in their use of funds (Toppe and Kirsch 2002: 2).

These and other pressures impinging on not-for-profits in the USA are familiar to NGOs around the world. They pose a daunting challenge, and earned income strategies have become an important part of the response.

Basic Principles[2]

Social entrepreneurs in the USA have identified five basic principles that are fundamental to understanding entrepreneurship for NGOs. In addition to the distinction between 'sustainability' and 'self-sufficiency' described earlier, they include the differences between:

- 'Entrepreneurship' and 'innovation'
- 'Entrepreneurship' and '*social* entrepreneurship'
- 'Earned income strategies' and 'social purpose business ventures'
- 'Innovators', 'entrepreneurs', and 'professional managers'

'Entrepreneurship' versus 'Innovation'

Entrepreneurship is one of the most misunderstood terms in the third sector today. Everybody, it seems, has a different definition of what it means.

Twenty years ago the idea of NGOs acting in an entrepreneurial manner was anathema to most people in the sector: the idea of merging mission and money filled them with distaste. But the phrase social entrepreneur is bandied about freely these days. British Prime Minister Tony Blair praises the emerging tide of social entrepreneurs that is changing the face of England's voluntary and community sector. Senior executives associated with the not-for-profit sector's national lobbying organization in the USA talk about social entrepreneurs who find new and exciting ways to attract contributions and government support for their programmes. Both are right to praise the ingenuity of NGOs—but most of what they are praising has nothing to do with entrepreneurship.

Here is the gist of the problem: unless an NGO is generating *earned* revenue from its activities, it is *not* acting in an entrepreneurial manner. It may be doing good and wonderful things, creating new and vibrant programmes, but it is *innovative*, not *entrepreneurial*.

Why is the distinction so important? Because only earned income will ever allow an NGO to become truly sustainable or fully self-sufficient. Innovation is a precious resource and it served as the primary engine of not-for-profit growth in the USA throughout the 1970s and 1980s. But innovation can take an NGO only so far. It is one thing to create and nurture a new programme—and quite another to sustain it without depending on charitable contributions and public sector subsidies. Smart NGO managers and Board members realize they must increasingly depend on themselves to insure their survival—and that leads them naturally to the world of entrepreneurship.

However, too many NGO executives and trustees continue to use old methodologies and old definitions to improve the impression given by their books and their brochures. It has reached the point where almost everything new in the third sector is called entrepreneurial and the people who create these new approaches (not to mention the people who write about them and underwrite them) walk away satisfied that they have changed the fundamental equation. They have not.

'Entrepreneurship' versus 'Social Entrepreneurship'

According to the dictionary, an entrepreneur is 'a person who organizes and manages a business undertaking, assuming the risk for the sake of profit' (Webster 1982). In a 1998 column for *Inc.* magazine, Norm Brodsky expanded on the definition. 'Starting with nothing more than an idea or a prototype,' he wrote, 'entrepreneurs have the ability to take a business to the point at which it can sustain itself on internally generated cash flow' (Brodsky 1996). Successfully running a business means sustaining it with *earned* income, not grants or subsidies.

Professor J. Gregory Dees of Stanford University formulated the most commonly quoted definition of social entrepreneurship in 1998, but his essay contained a fundamental oversight. He outlines five factors that define social entrepreneurship: adopting a mission to create and sustain social value (not just private value), recognizing and relentlessly pursuing new opportunities to serve that mission, engaging in a process of continuous innovation, adaptation, and learning, acting boldly without being limited by resources currently in hand, and exhibiting a heightened sense of accountability to the constituencies served and for the outcomes created (Dees 1998). He never mentions earned income.

That is not only conceptually flawed, but also psychologically crippling. It lets NGOs off the hook. It allows them to congratulate themselves for being entrepreneurial without ever pursuing genuine sustainability or self-sufficiency. They still return, year after year, to individual donors, foundations, and government agencies.

Without self-generated revenue, NGOs remain forever dependent on the generosity of others, and that is a risk social entrepreneurs are unwilling to take. They are passionately committed to their mission—but they are just as passionately committed to becoming financially sustainable or self-sufficient in order to do more mission! As traditional sources of funding dried up or became less available during the 1980s and 1990s, a growing number of not-for-profits in the USA discovered the importance of paying their own way, and their managers became genuine social entrepreneurs who understood the difference between innovation (doing something new) and entrepreneurship (doing something that makes money).

What, then, is social entrepreneurship? And how does it differ from entrepreneurship per se? A social entrepreneur is any person, in any sector, who uses earned income strategies to pursue a social objective, and a social entrepreneur differs from a traditional entrepreneur in two important ways:

- Traditional entrepreneurs frequently act in a socially responsible manner: they donate money to NGOs; they refuse to engage in certain types of businesses; they use environmentally safe materials and practices; they treat their employees with dignity and respect. All of this is admirable, but their efforts are only indirectly attached to social problems. Social entrepreneurs are different because their earned income strategies are tied directly to their mission: they either start 'affirmative businesses' (known as 'social firms' in the UK) that employ people who are developmentally disabled, chronically mentally ill, physically challenged, poverty-stricken, or otherwise disadvantaged; or they sell products and services that have a direct impact on a specific social problem (e.g. delivering hospice care, working with potential dropouts to keep them in school, manufacturing assistive devices for people who are physically disabled, providing home care services to help elderly people stay out of nursing homes).

- Second, traditional entrepreneurs are ultimately measured by financial results: the success or failure of their companies is determined by their ability to generate profits for their owners. On the other hand, social entrepreneurs are driven by a double bottom line, a virtual blend of financial and social returns. Profitability is still a goal, but it is not the only goal, and profits are re-invested in the mission rather than being distributed to shareholders.

'Earned Income Strategies' versus 'Social Purpose Business Ventures'

Many NGO board members and executives are daunted by the prospect of social entrepreneurship because they think it means starting a business venture, something few know how to do. But creating a business is not the only way to be successful as a social entrepreneur. The most fertile ground for the vast majority of NGOs is something called 'earned income strategies', and they have nothing to do with starting a business venture. The two approaches differ substantially in terms of purpose, expectations, and structure:

- *Earned income strategies*: Every NGO has opportunities for earned income lying fallow within its existing programmes. The opportunities may be tiny, but exploiting them can have a significant cumulative impact. By aggressively turning inward and searching for pockets of existing opportunities, NGOs have been able to register impressive gains, often raising their percentage of total revenue from earned income by as much as 15 per cent within one to three years, a considerable boon to sustainability.

- *Business ventures*: Once an NGO has successfully carried out a variety of earned income strategies, it may want to consider launching a formal business venture—but the goals would be much more ambitious and the strategy completely different. The only reason for an NGO to start a business venture is to exploit a specific opportunity for significant growth and profitability—

361

a substantial difference from earned income strategies, which are designed primarily to cover more of a programme's cost, without any real expectation of making a profit or even reaching a break-even point. The pioneers in the field have also discovered that the chances for success with a business venture increase dramatically if the NGO creates a 'skunk works', a completely separate entity insulated as much as possible from the day-to-day operations of the parent organization. That means having a separate staff, separate compensation policies, and, if necessary, even a separate board of directors in order to achieve as much independence as possible.

'Innovators', 'Entrepreneurs', and 'Professional Managers'

Perhaps the single most important lesson learned by the pioneers in the field has been a deeply personal one that strikes to the very heart of their self-perceptions. So often, NGOs discover (too late) that their entrepreneurial efforts have been doomed simply because they are being led by people with the wrong types of skills. The mistake occurred because they did not truly understand the differences between innovators, entrepreneurs, and professional managers.

Regardless of whether an NGO is attempting to engage in a variety of earned income strategies or trying to launch a third sector business, it is important to understand the differences between the three types of leaders: they are all needed in the evolution of a healthy organization, but at different times, and rarely does an individual possess more than one of the three sets of skills.

Innovators are the *dreamers*: they create the prototypes, work out the kinks—and then get bored, anxious to return to what they do best, which is inventing more prototypes. They are rarely concerned, ultimately, with the long-term financial viability of what they do. Entrepreneurs are the *builders*: they turn prototypes into going concerns—then *they* get bored. For them, financial viability is the single most important aspect of what they do. Professional managers are the *trustees*: they secure the future by installing and overseeing the systems and infrastructure needed to make sure the going concern keeps going.

Unfortunately, often because resources are scarce, NGOs try to shoehorn people into positions where they do not fit, and many of the problems they have when they begin adopting entrepreneurial strategies arise from having an innovator or a professional manager trying to do an entrepreneur's job.

Potential Outcomes

The beauty of making a profit, as we've been able to do during the past 15 years, is that you can do a lot with the money, you can do what you want to do. You can do it how you want to do it for as long as you want to do it and you don't have to make anybody happy except your own Board and staff. You don't have to meet anybody else's expectations. That's a very freeing idea, and once you feel it, you don't want to go back to the confines of any other type of funding.

Kathleen Buescher, president and chief executive officer,
Provident Counseling, Inc., St Louis, MO

When they began entering the commercial markets, social entrepreneurs in the USA were primarily interested in finding new sources of revenue to help them maintain and expand their programmes, but they quickly discovered there was much more to gain than financial returns. In addition to obtaining the freedom described by Kathleen Buescher, two of the most important results have been learning how to sharpen their strategic focus and becoming a more powerful voice for the people they serve.

New Strategic Directions

The concept of 'organized abandonment' began to seep into the USA not-for-profit sector during the late 1980s when management guru Peter Drucker turned his attention to the field and recoiled from what he saw. Too many not-for-profits were becoming increasingly unwieldy, unable to give their clients the attention they deserved because they no longer had the necessary time or resources. And much of the pain was self-inflicted: multi-service organizations were growing frenetically, adding programmes every year, spreading themselves thinner and thinner. Drucker had some blunt advice: If your products or services are not number one or number two in the market, kill them. Rather than trying to be all things to all people, concentrate on doing the best job possible in a few, carefully chosen areas (Sterne 1989: 10–11).

Drucker's advice runs against the grain of the traditional NGO mentality, but most NGO managers eventually do admit they are trying to serve too many masters, and his suggestion gives them a lifeline, a way to simultaneously sharpen their organizational focus and expand their impact. However, the process can be agonizing. It is not easy to kill programmes, especially if they are the pet projects of board members or funders. And there is an important caveat: organized abandonment for NGOs does not mean eliminating a programme just because it fails to generate earned revenue. If the NGO is the best or only provider of a programme that is critically needed, it has an obligation to continue the programme—and a managerial challenge to find other sources of revenue to cover the cost.

In effect, entrepreneurs in the not-for-profit sector in the USA during the 1980s and 1990s discovered a stunning irony: the first rule of entrepreneurship is contraction. And one of the decision-making tools they have been using for the past fifteen years has been 'The Organized Abandonment Grid'® (see Figure 16.1), which enables them to simultaneously analyse the social impact and financial viability of each of their programmes. Once the analysis has been

Social purpose

		Critical	Significant	Some	Minimal	None
		5	4	3	2	1
Financial **Profits** 21% or more	7	Definitely	Definitely	Definitely	Probably	Maybe
11 – 20%	6	Definitely	Definitely	Definitely	Maybe	Maybe
0 – 10%	5	Definitely	Definitely	Probably	Maybe	Probably not
Viability **Losses** 1 – 10%	4	Probably	Probably	Probably	Probably not	Definitely not
11 – 40%	3	Probably	Probably	Maybe	Definitely not	Definitely not
41 – 70%	2	Maybe	Maybe	Probably not	Definitely not	Definitely not
71 – 100%	1	Maybe	Probably not	Definitely not	Definitely not	Definitely not

Notes: 'Profits' and 'losses' are for annual operations and include all direct *and* indirect costs; 'profits' are pre-tax and prior to capital re-investment.

Figure 16.1 The Organized Abandonment Grid®

completed, they can make rational decisions about which programmes to expand, maintain, reduce, divest, or eliminate.

At its heart, organized abandonment requires an NGO to be honest with itself—exceedingly difficult for any organization, NGO or otherwise. But the results have been worth it, and the ultimate winners have been the clients. Social entrepreneurs have discovered that reducing the number of programmes they offer has actually enabled them to serve more people and to serve them better, because they have had the time and resources to expand their most effective and needed programmes, to selectively launch innovative programmes, to create new positioning strategies and marketing plans, and to develop profitable social enterprises.

Speaking Truth to Power

Generating additional revenue, freeing themselves from the expectations of others, re-calibrating their strategic focus and serving more people are not the only benefits social entrepreneurs have derived from adopting earned income strategies or starting business ventures. There is another, subtler, but just as important result.

In his keynote speech at The Fourth National Gathering for Social Entrepreneurs in December 2002, Charles King told his audience about his recent trip to the international AIDS summit in Barcelona. 'It became increasingly obvious during the conference', he said, 'that if we are ever going to seriously address the plague of AIDS, it is not going to be government that leads the way, and it is not going to be corporations. If we are to make any significant progress, NGOs will have to lead the way' (King 2002). But he pointed out that most not-for-profits are dependent on government subsidies and corporate largesse. How then, he asked, can they speak truth to power?

It was a powerful moment for his audience, because social entrepreneurship begins to loosen the chains of dependence. When the individuals and organizations that control the purse strings are also those that must step aside or change their practices, it becomes more difficult for NGOs to speak freely— but, as emphasized by Kathleen Buescher, when the purse strings are severed, the power relationships change.

Stakeholder Objections

The NGOs most prepared for entrepreneurship today are those that have been the most innovative during the past ten or fifteen years. Their challenge is to make the transition from a culture of innovation to a culture of entrepreneurship—but the path is strewn with dangers and the changes do not occur without a considerable shock to the system. Not every not-for-profit is willing to take the necessary steps to complete the transformation: they are beset with nightmares, which typically fall into four categories.

Generic Nightmares

Board members, staff members, clients, customers, and other stakeholders have numerous misconceptions about earned revenue that rise quickly to the surface. They immediately ask questions such as these:

- How can we justify 'making money off the backs of the poor'?
- What happens to quality when we emphasize financial returns?
- Will we have a two-tiered system that ignores people who cannot afford to pay?

They reflexively believe pursuing earned income is 'too risky', predict funders and other stakeholders will object, express concerns about liability exposures, bemoan the absence of models and expertise, and of course retreat behind the 'not invented here' syndrome. In short, they have dozens of reasons not to proceed, including—quite often—a fundamental discomfort with making money.

Logistical Nightmares

The 'resource' question becomes an insurmountable stumbling block for many NGOs. Some of the logistical barriers include:

- Entrenched patterns of behaviour
- Competing priorities
- Inadequate resources (dollars, people, time, and psychic energy)
- Lack of business development, operations, and marketing skills

However, the pioneers in the field have repeatedly demonstrated that when an NGO really wants to do something, it manages somehow to find the resources it needs: being able to do so is almost the sine qua non of entrepreneurship.

The Nightmare of Failure

There are no guarantees, and the possibility of failure is very real. Personal careers can crash and burn. So NGO board members and executives are often concerned about the consequences. If we start down this path and fail, how can we avert a financial disaster? Will it damage our reputation? Can we do it without depleting our energy and resources?

Some of the other questions that plague them are these:

- Will we lose sight of our mission while trying to save it?
- Will we wind up shepherding bloated programmes that never get anywhere (a different type of 'failure')?
- What about opportunity cost? If we fail at this, we have really failed twice.
- What if it causes our best people to burn out or leave?
- How will funders react to future requests for help?
- What about lawsuits?
- Who will get the blame?

The Nightmare of Success

And there is still one more nightmare: success itself. What happens when social entrepreneurs achieve their objectives? Simple: somebody raises the bar. And the entrepreneurs find themselves grappling with questions like these:

- Can we continue to care? Will we lose our hearts when we find our wallets? What about all the people who came to do good and stayed to do well?
- Can we manage rapid growth without overextending our resources?
- What happens if the market changes or the competition toughens or our best people are lured away?
- How will we deal with the inevitable ascending expectations placed upon us by others and ourselves?
- How can we avoid becoming complacent or lazy, resist trying to cover our mistakes with money rather than ingenuity?
- How can we make sure we do not lose control of our mission if we turn to outside investors to fuel our expansion plans?

All these nightmares cause many NGOs to spin their wheels, waiting for the perfect market opportunity, the perfect plan, the perfect time. None of them exist.

The Single Greatest Obstacle

The culture of a traditional NGO, no matter how innovative, is vastly different from the culture of an entrepreneurial NGO. Entrepreneurs have a higher tolerance for risk, a greater appreciation of margins, and an eagerness to compete. Traditional NGOs distrust the capital markets, prefer collaboration to competition, and underestimate the productive capabilities of their disadvantaged employees. They watch other NGOs become increasingly sustainable or self-sufficient, but are unwilling to emulate their practices.

Instead, they criticize. 'My god, the resistance', said Rick Walker, who runs seven small businesses in Marshfield, MA, which employ people with developmental disabilities. 'To a great extent, not-for-profit people are not risk-takers, and their unwillingness to think outside very standard parameters constantly amazes me. Quite frankly, we've had a lot better luck getting people outside the not-for-profit world to understand what we're doing and feel comfortable with it.'

Tony Wagner concurred. He has been astonished by the resistance he has encountered from both the business community and the not-for-profit sector as his not-for-profit in Minneapolis, MN, tried simultaneously to create a business and carry out a social mission by employing people who were economically disadvantaged. 'I've been blown away by the level of misunderstanding and mistrust,' he said. 'For all the writing and talking that's being done about the subject, out there in the world people either don't get it or don't want to get it. They say you have to be one or the other.'

Why does this happen? Why is the embedded culture of an organization so often the single greatest obstacle for trustees and senior executives trying to launch earned income strategies or third sector businesses?

John Maxwell tells a wonderful story in his book *Failing Forward* that illustrates the problem:

Four monkeys were placed in a room that had a tall pole in the center. Suspended from the top of that pole was a bunch of bananas. One of the hungry monkeys started climbing the pole to get something to eat, but just as he reached out to grab a banana, he was doused with a torrent of cold water. Squealing, he scampered down the pole and abandoned his attempt to feed himself. Each monkey made a similar attempt, and each one was drenched with cold water. After making several attempts, they finally gave up.

Then researchers removed one of the monkeys from the room and replaced him with a new monkey. As the newcomer began to climb the pole, the other three grabbed him and pulled him down to the ground. After trying to climb the pole several times and being dragged down by the others, he finally gave up and never attempted to climb the pole again.

The researchers replaced the original monkeys, one by one, and each time a new monkey was brought in, he would be dragged down by the others before he could reach the bananas. In time, the room was filled with monkeys who had never received a cold shower. None of them would climb the pole, but not one of them knew why. (Maxwell 2000: 47–8)

The plight of the monkeys resembles that of many NGOs: people continue doing things but have no idea why. Too many of them suffer from what Joel Arthur Barker called 'paradigm paralysis' (Barker 1989: 26). As Barker pointed out, paradigms can be extraordinarily useful. They help us make sense of the world by organizing incoming data streams and sorting them into categories, helping us decide what to think and do. But paradigms can be a double-edged sword. Blinders are slapped into place and we begin to interpret new information according to our preconceptions. We become frozen. Change becomes our enemy. Individuals and organizations begin to believe the categories they are using are the only ones available, and they slowly become paralysed.

Institutional paralysis can be overcome, with a sufficient dose of courage. But occasionally it takes something dramatic. In the mid-1980s, when the board of directors of a not-for-profit in Louisville, KY, offered Bob Russell the job as CEO, he realized the existing make-up of the board worked against entrepreneurship and agreed to accept the position only if every member of the board resigned. They agreed.

Still another CEO, who ran a sheltered workshop for people who were developmentally disabled, decided to change the basic values of his organization—and in the process invented an entirely new type of business, known today as an 'affirmative business'. On a pleasant summer evening in 1973, John DuRand invited his eleven senior managers to a downtown hotel in St Paul, MN, where he wined and dined them, asked them to sit down and then fired them all. Five minutes later he passed out application forms. 'Starting tomorrow', he said, 'we are no longer a rehab agency, we're a business. Starting tomorrow, we no longer have clients, we have employees. And, starting tomorrow, you are no longer clinicians, you are business managers. If you can get your minds and hearts and souls around that concept, I want you back. If you can't, I'll help you find a job somewhere else.' Nine of the eleven returned to their jobs. Two could not accept the philosophic shift. But, from that day, the culture of the organization changed and the primary goal became the operation of a viable business.

However, regardless of dramatics, cultural change must be systemic. The first step usually has to be taken at the board level. When Charley Graham arrived at his new post in Oregon in the early 1980s, he immediately began promoting the idea of a double bottom line. According to his second-in-command, Roy Soards, 'he told the Board we were never going to be able to employ more people with psychiatric disabilities if we continued operating a sheltered workshop and depending primarily on social service subsidies and charitable giving. He convinced the Board that if we provided quality goods and services, people would buy them and we'd therefore be able to employ even more people with disabilities and help them become self-sufficient.'

Kevin McDonald found that customers appreciated the change. He employs former convicts, prostitutes, and drug addicts, and he built his moving company business in North Carolina primarily through personal selling and word of mouth. 'We didn't have a very big staff', he said, 'just me and two others, and we didn't have much money for advertising. We were just trying to survive as a program. So, I decided to start hitting the pavement and gave a lot of speeches. Went out to the Junior League, the Kiwanis Club, that sort of thing . . . and I found out they were tired of people asking them for a handout. So I told them, "I don't want your money . . . I want your business . . . call us up, let me give you an estimate . . . *use* our services."'

Once they begin paying for actual products or services, customers become increasingly demanding, which puts a further strain on an organization's traditional culture. 'When we started working with Ben & Jerry's', recalled Julius Walls, CEO of Greyston Bakery, which employs former convicts and others with barriers to employment, 'they made it very clear that our product had to always be up to snuff or they wouldn't produce their ice cream with us. They held us accountable as a business and not as their young child. They provided a lot of assistance, but they told us from the beginning that we needed to stand up and be a business, not a sheltered workshop.' When Walls took over the Yonkers, New York, company as CEO, he discovered that the biggest obstacle he faced was helping his employees 'understand what we needed to do to be a sustainable model. We had to understand we were a business with a dual bottom line. Most businesses have one bottom line— economic dividends. (At the time) Greyston also had a single bottom line, but it wasn't the economic one. There was a mentality on the part of the employees that came here that if you're really nice we'll figure something out to keep you and it doesn't matter if you're producing or if the business is doing well. But there came a time when the employees and the business needed to understand that that's not a sustainable model'.

The cultural transformation can turn into a war. 'By the time I got here', remembered Soards, who succeeded Graham as CEO in Oregon, 'there was a demilitarized zone between the production people who ran the factory and the rehab people who provided social services. We had two very strong-willed managers and each of them had their own lieutenants and armies'. The opposing forces fought over resources and, more fundamentally, they fought for the soul of the organization. It took years for the culture wars to subside, and 'it was pretty ugly at times', said Soards. 'The rehab people would sabotage the production people, who often had to rely on the rehab folks for employees. If the production people had a job that had to get done, they were under a lot of pressure, because the rehab people were more concerned about, 'Well, is this the proper training for this individual, they're not ready for work that's too demanding, and why don't you guys find the types of jobs that fit their needs, and no, they can't work after three o'clock because they have to go see their case workers.' We finally had to part ways with the head of the rehab division.'

Hiring people from the for-profit world can be another wake-up call. 'Everything changed', said Dave McDonough, who ran a social enterprise in Los Angeles that employed people who were homeless. 'Right off the top, it was just the way the new people walked and talked and dressed and approached their day. It was a big shock to the rest of us.'

Fundamentally, neither the traditional not-for-profit approach nor the traditional for-profit approach works in a double bottom line environment. See Figure 16.2 (Crossing the Cultural Divide®) for a depiction of the changes

Category	Traditional non-profit mentality	Traditional for-profit (corporate) mentality	Hybrid mentality
Primary benchmark	Social returns	Financial returns	Double bottom line (*'social'* and *'financial'*)
Sine qua non	Year-to-year survival	Ongoing self-sufficiency	Ongoing sustainability
Primary stakeholders	Clients ('the people we serve')	Customers ('the buyers')	Clients *and* customers
Basic approach	Try to do it all	Capitalize on a niche	Focus on selected programs
Attitude towards earned income	Filthy lucre	Staff of life	Means to an end
Attitude towards making a profit	Uncomfortable, 'illegitimate'	*Raison d'etre*	A tool for sustainability
Tolerance for R&D	Short-term (*'cost'*)	Long-term (*'investment'*)	Medium-term (*'investment'*)
Attitude towards taking risks (*'in the commercial marketplace'*)	Generally averse	Necessary evil	Reluctant but willing
Level of commitment when launching a business venture	Conflicted	Committed	Conservative but committed
Strategic planning methodology	Mission-driven	Market-driven	Matrix-driven (*'mission'* and *'market'*)
Market research	All but non-existent	Extensive	Extensive
Segmentation of markets	Minimal	Extensive	Extensive
The 'buyer'	Clients first, then funders	Customers	Customers first, then clients, then funders
Approach to marketing	Tactical	Strategic	Strategic
Determining quality standards	Non-profit usually decides	Customers dictate	Customers and clients dictate
Organizational hierarchy	Fairly rigid	Very rigid	Less rigid
Decision-making process	Consensus	Hierarchical	Empowering
Executive compensation levels	Marginal	Competitive	Increasingly competitive
Employee incentives	Low-risk, low-reward	High risk, high reward	Risk-taking rewarded
Typical attitude towards non-performing employees	Forgiving	Harsh	Tough
Crisis fall-back options (*beyond expense reductions*)	Seek contributions	Acquire debt, sell equity, kill product or service lines	Seek contributions, acquire debt, sell equity, kill programs

Figure 16.2 Crossing the Cultural Divide®
Copyright © The Institute for Social Entrepreneurs

required to create a new, hybrid culture. Many of the elements in the chart are also reflected in the 'critical success factors' discussed in the next section.

Critical Success Factors

In addition to changing their organizational culture, the pioneers in the field have found that a significant number of other factors come into play. Here are fourteen they believe are particularly important.

Candour

Entrepreneurs understandably fall in love with their business ideas—but love can be blind. Starting a new venture, or even an earned income strategy, is difficult enough without being honest about the product or service, market, competition, and resources. The mantra is very simple: 'Beware of yourself!'

Tony Wagner discovered the power of candour when two of his board members took him aside. 'It was probably the darkest day of my career', he recalled, 'I'd gotten into this 'I can't fail' routine. I kept saying, 'Give me one more month and I'll make it work.' And I remember the board meeting very clearly when two guys I respect very highly looked me right in the eye and said, 'Tony, it's over.' It wasn't until that point that I faced reality. As an entrepreneur, sometimes you just can't admit defeat. But I learned a valuable lesson. You need to have people outside you who aren't as passionate or emotionally involved who can ask the hard questions and say the things that need to be said.'

Employees can also be among a social entrepreneur's greatest allies. Rich Gilmartin runs seven businesses in Florida that employ people who are disabled or disadvantaged, and over the years he has learned that some of his best problem solvers are his employees—but only if they know that a problem exists. 'We were doing okay with one of our businesses', he recalled, 'but we weren't generating the type of financial contribution we wanted. We were real close, but we were constantly in the red, so we resigned ourselves that things were as good as they were going to get. But one day the contract administrator who reports to me went to a meeting with our employees and laid it all out. We'd never done that before. The employees had never been told they were in the red—and when they heard about it they basically said, 'We can fix it!' It only took them four to six months to get us into the black.' The experience prompted Gilmartin to open his books to all his employees. 'We now have a very transparent policy', he says. 'If employees want information about what's going on financially or how decisions are being made, we give it to them.'

Candour is especially important as a company begins to expand. 'You have to be careful,' commented Kevin McDonald. 'We started growing so quickly our infrastructure couldn't keep up, so I had to slow things down. We had to be honest with ourselves and be cautious about which jobs to bid on rather than building up a reputation for biting off more than we could chew.'

Clarity of Purpose

What are the driving forces behind a decision to begin adopting or expanding entrepreneurial strategies? The members of an organization's entrepreneurial team must reach a consensus on this issue before they start the planning process because they will be intensely scrutinized once they begin and will need to have a consistent, compelling answer ready for their critics (and there will be critics!). Here are four rationale developed by a not-for-profit in Minnesota:

- *Mission*: We will be able to serve more people
- *Survival*: Our traditional sources of funding are drying up
- *Opportunity*: The market is beckoning, already anxious to buy what we have
- *Freedom*: If we can generate more of our *own* money, we will not be so bound to the priorities and restrictions imposed on us by others

Those four words—mission, survival, opportunity, and freedom—became the rallying cry for the organization's entire planning effort and a major reason for its long-term success.

But there is another aspect of clarity that is equally important, though it forces NGOs onto treacherous soil because circumstances change so rapidly, and that is the answer to the following question: 'What will success look like?' It is important to define some concrete, long-term goals before getting started: they serve as a beacon and a source of energy, and without them social entrepreneurs can lose their way. Rich Gilmartin made sure his employees understood in 2000 that the company intended to grow from $13 million (£7.5 million) to $30 million (£17.4 million) within two years. 'It was a big hairy-assed goal', he laughs, 'but we made it'.

Courage

The typical NGO is plagued by crises. Unless the board and the staff members declare entrepreneurial planning a priority, it will be swept aside by the flood of day-to-day demands. Unfortunately, too many boards are reluctant to commit because they are either risk-averse or searching for a quick fix. Both attitudes are understandable, but they conflict with marketplace realities.

The fact is that some earned income strategies and third sector businesses will fail. Unless the board is willing to accept that fact and take some chances, it should not proceed at all, and the board must also be willing to take a longer view. Too many members still think in terms of 'cost' rather than 'investment', and are therefore reluctant to proceed unless they can see a rapid return. Entrepreneurship does not typically work that way. It takes time. A ten-year study of 814,000 small businesses by the Massachusetts Institute of Technology (MIT) showed that generally significant revenue did not begin to flow until the seventh year (Kirchoff 1997: 461).

Rick Walker knew 'we were heading into uncharted territory, so we formed a New Ventures Committee' eighteen months before he launched his first business. 'We had Board members, staff members, the people we served and their family members. We brought everybody together and talked about doing something that was very, very different from what any of us were used to doing in our job placement program or in our old sheltered workshop model.' Walker believed the committee 'instilled a sense of risk-taking across the organization' and set the tone that made it possible for an entire network of businesses to emerge.

Even now, years later, Walker minimizes his exposure by spreading his risks. 'A lot of people say we're in too many businesses', he said, 'but the issue for me is risk management. Collectively, their impact is large—but each of them is small, so failure wouldn't be critical to the agency as a whole. The point is we need to be prepared to eat our mistakes, and most not-for-profits are not real good at that. For example, each of our little businesses is generating some revenue and creating some jobs, but if the ice cream store continues losing money because we're not able to solve our location problem, I'll kill it. We can't afford those kinds of losses. Or if the bookstore business goes completely kaflooey and starts doing terribly, I'm not going to let it imperil the agency as a whole. Or somebody could build a giant Motel 6 down the street and be better prepared to respond to the market. We don't have pockets deep enough to compete in a situation like that, so it means we'd fold our cards, close our motel and go off in a new direction.'

Of the six businesses operated by Esperanza Unida, which employ Latino members of the community in Milwaukee, WI, two are profitable, three are slightly under water and one is struggling. Over the past ten years, four others have come and gone, but Executive Director Richard Oulahan did not consider that a bad track record. 'You have to take risks', he said. 'Our community and our organization and our Board basically feel we don't have a lot of choice. If we're sitting here losing resources every day and people are being destroyed by our economic system, what do we have to lose if we go out on a limb and try to make something work? You can't be crazy. You've got to be careful. But there's nothing wrong with making mistakes. We've made a lot of them—but we look at them as a natural part of development and growth. Nothing gets done unless you make them! You try one thing and if it doesn't work you try something else. Any time you create something, there are always pieces on the ground around it when it's finished. So we're not afraid of mistakes. We just figure that something's always lost when you create something new.'

'Nothing surprises me any more', said Kevin McDonald. 'I've been doing this sort of thing for 20 years, and I was a street urchin before that. I just know that if you believe in something hard enough and work hard enough, it's gonna happen. You just don't quit no matter how hard it looks. You just keep going.'

Core Values

Critics often ask how it is possible to balance mission and money, to talk about moral imperatives and the profit motive in the same sentence. The answer lies in an organization's core values, a set of four or five basic principles that are clearly articulated, institutionalized, and constantly reinforced. In order for something to qualify as a 'core' value, according to consultant Ronnie Brooks:

- An organization must be willing to accept the consequences
- The value must be freely chosen from genuine alternatives
- It must be acted upon as a regular pattern of action
- It must apply everywhere in the work
- It must last over time
- And the organization must be proud of it

Entering the world of entrepreneurship means NGOs will be confronted by things that have never tempted it before and will need to maintain an internal sense of balance. The rules associated with core values are simple: Identify them before doing anything else, make sure they can be quantified, build them into strategic plans and annual operating plans, monitor them religiously, measure progress periodically, and trumpet results to the world.

Kevin McDonald said that a core value in his company was that 'our employees have to act in a professional manner. When you're dealing with recovering addicts, the first thing you have to do is make sure they're not using drugs. You can't be la-dee-dah about it. The accountability has to be there. You've gotta have discipline, and appearance is really important. Our people are taught to dress, speak, and act professionally. Part of our goal is to change people's perceptions of addicts as street people, and sometimes our people forget that the customer is the person paying the bills. We sort of have to go back to basics. If somebody isn't performing, if they're disrespectful to a customer, we'll have to fire them.'

One of the core values at Gulf Coast Enterprises is emphasizing to employees that they are responsible for *all* the company's resources. Essentially, said Rich Gilmartin, 'we want our people to take ownership of both our tangible and intangible resources, regardless of their specific jobs. We don't want them thinking it's somebody else's responsibility. For example, in most organizations, if you see a visitor who appears to be lost, hopefully a staff member will give that person directions—but, in our system, the expectation is that you'll actually walk them to their destination, no matter what else is going on. That leaves a powerful impression.'

The core values adopted in 1989 by The Affirmative Business Alliance of North America and still in use today are as follows:

- Individuals with mental, physical, economic, or educational disadvantages are capable of holding real jobs, should receive competitive wages, and deserve opportunities for career advancement and profit sharing
- It *is* possible to operate successful businesses while employing substantial numbers of individuals who are disadvantaged
- The first priority of an affirmative business is to operate a viable business, not to employ a specific number of people
- Affirmative businesses treat their employees as employees, not as clients

A Willingness to Plan

According to the US Small Business Administration, 90 per cent of business failures are caused by management mistakes, not by competitors, changes in the market, or other external factors (MEC 2003: 1). Here are three suggestions offered by some of the pioneers in the field to get off on the right foot:

- *Ask for help*: Be sure the planning team includes some 'business mentors', proven entrepreneurs who have successfully built their own small or medium-sized businesses. They will provide a reality check that is invaluable. Also, bring in some 'wild cards', people who may not know much about the organization or even about business per se. Tell them their job is to ask all the 'dumb' questions out loud, to probe the areas others might neglect because they are too close to the table.
- *Put somebody in charge*: The planning team needs to have a leader—a single person. Do not try to lead by committee—and do not require somebody to be the leader in addition to his or her regular job: without a dedicated focus, the process will drift.
- *Create a comfort zone*: Once the entrepreneurial team has been assembled, take some time to make sure everybody involved is comfortable with the organization's strategic framework, and that they know and agree on the answers to the following five questions:
  - What is our vision (how do we want the world to change)?
  - What is our mission (what will we do to bring about that change)?
  - What forces are driving us to adopt or expand earned income strategies?
  - What outcomes do we expect?
  - What core values will guide us?

Most NGOs find it worthwhile to spend one or two meetings at the beginning of the planning process clarifying the answers to these questions and are often surprised at what happens. The 'mentors' and 'wild cards' (and occasionally the insiders) challenge some of the organization's most dearly held assumptions and the answers begin to change.

Building the Right Team

There are at least four critical components to building the right team for a successful third sector business:

- *The leader*: NGOs have historically made three critical mistakes when seeking a qualified leader for their business venture:
  - *Inadequate focus*: 'We started by simply assigning the project as an additional set of responsibilities for one of our senior staff members', said Kathleen Buescher, 'That was a big mistake. It set her and us up for failure. As soon as things started popping, it pulled her away. We should have taken the time early on to find a full-time CEO whose sole interest and total energies could go to developing the company.'
  - *Inadequate compensation*: One of the most severe shocks to the system of an established NGO is discovering how expensive talent can be. The CEO of a third sector business owned by an NGO will frequently earn (or have the opportunity to earn) a much higher salary than the CEO of the parent organization. It takes a courageous parent CEO to let that happen.
  - *Inadequate flexibility*: Few things will de-motivate an entrepreneur more than having to carry out somebody else's business plan. 'Don't be afraid to hire somebody smarter than you—then give them the freedom to operate!' commented Jim Westall, whose business in Port Townsend, WA, takes young men off welfare. 'Use benchmarks to monitor their work— but get out of their way!' In other words, find a CEO first, then let him or her create the business plan.
- *The senior management team*: One of the findings during the ten-year MIT study of 814,000 small businesses during the 1980s and 1990s was this: the survival rate of companies that had at least five people in the brain trust at the beginning was substantially higher than those that had four or fewer. The first thing smart CEOs do is surround themselves with people who have the talents and expertise they lack.
- *Industry expertise*: 'It's relatively easy to enter the temporary help business', noted Roy Soards, who did it successfully in Oregon. 'There aren't many obstacles. But our biggest mistake was not bringing in an expert from the start. We thought this would be a really easy business, and we simply didn't get the expertise we needed. We don't do this anymore. Any time we start a

new business these days we hire expertise first.' Julius Walls of Greyston Bakery could not agree more emphatically. 'It may sound obvious', he says, 'but it needs to be emphasized. We needed to have expertise in bakery science. We understood the art, but we didn't understand the science, how ingredients react with each other and why. We understood how to make our product every day, yes, but if somebody asked us to deviate from what we were doing it wasn't as clear how to change and modify.' And when Bobbie Lenz started searching for somebody to run her bulk mailing business in Duluth, MN, that employs people who are developmentally disabled, she turned to a woman who had significant experience working for the post office. 'It made a very big difference', said Lenz. 'No matter what kind of business you start, you have to be an expert at what you're doing. If you don't do that, you don't have anything to offer. With us, it meant we had to learn the mailing regulations and keep up with constant changes—so our customers wouldn't have to.' Kathleen Buescher pointed out that at least some of the board members for any third sector business should also have experience in the specific industry—not doing so hampered her initial efforts in St Louis. And a thriving direct mail business for women in New York State failed because when times got tough (paper costs, fulfilment costs, and online competition all escalating), there was nobody on the board who understood the nuts and bolts of the business well enough to be helpful.

- *The employees*: Building an effective group of employees—and a viable third sector business— requires NGOs to meet at least three basic challenges:
  - *Recruiting and retaining people with the right attitudes and skills*: NGOs installing an entrepreneurial culture will often have to make some tough choices about staff members. Some of their most loyal, long-term employees will not understand the new culture. Some who do will not accept it. And some of those who embrace it will not have the talents to thrive. Some form of compassionate out-placement is the best solution, for them and for the organization.
  - *Creating a blended workforce*: Most third sector businesses that employ the people they serve develop what is known as a blended workforce. The optimum mix differs depending on the type of business, but 60–75 per cent of the employees are typically drawn from the target population, the rest from the general population.
  - *Firing people who do not perform*: Rick Walker's businesses employ people who are developmentally disabled, but he says 'you've got to be absolutely ruthless about making changes whenever they're needed. We fire people.' Julius Walls is equally adamant. 'We do *not* do make-work', he says. 'We don't have pseudo-welfare jobs or a sheltered workshop. You *must* perform. We have very strict standards.' John DuRand of Minnesota Diversified Industries calls it 'giving people the dignity of allowing them

the opportunity to fail', and Jim Westall says 'there *is* a lot of dignity in knowing what the expectations are and being able to achieve them, being in a workplace where you really feel valued. We benchmark everything, so people know how they contribute to the success of the company. That's tremendously important for them, to know they're part of something significant.'

The Separation Strategy

Paul Firstenberg wrote:

The basic point . . . is that the creation of a successful profit-making component within a not-for-profit environment—the building of a culture-within-a-culture, so to speak—is a difficult business. . . . The chances of successfully doing so will be enhanced if the (profit-making) component is, from the outset, clearly labeled as such, and its different objectives and need for a different operating style are recognized from the start. . . . The greater the separation in terms of form, staffing, oversight, and location, the greater are the chances that the profit-making component will be able to function with the necessary clarity of purpose and operating style appropriate to its objectives.' (Firstenberg 1986: 63–4)

Entrepreneurial business ventures have to move quickly, and they cannot do so if bureaucracy encumbers them. For that reason, any entrepreneurial activity started by an NGO should be kept as separate as possible from the parent organization's other operations. Furthermore, if the goal is to create a profitable third sector business, it is reasonable to incubate the venture internally for a short period of time, but the sooner and more completely it can be separated, the better its chances for success. Part of the separation strategy for a third sector business is a willingness to create an independent board of directors, which should have no more than six or seven members, most of them outsiders:

- Three or four should be proven entrepreneurs, who can provide an invaluable reality check.
- One should be a person in the business of starting businesses (a seed capitalist or an attorney specializing in start-ups).
- One should be the senior executive of the parent NGO (to serve as the conscience of the new company, but not to become involved in operations).
- One should be a champion from the parent board who is specifically charged with protecting the new venture from interference by either the parent board or staff.

Relinquishing control of day-to-day operations in a third sector business is a terribly difficult thing for most NGO board and staff members to do, but, as

Firstenberg points out, it is a fundamentally important strategy, especially when taking a business to scale.

Strategic Marketing

Marketing is *not* a business function—it *is* the business. Marketing begins when the senior management team makes two important strategic decisions: what products or services to offer and what target markets to pursue. Unfortunately, when most social entrepreneurs begin thinking about marketing, they immediately focus on tactics: creating a brochure, writing a news release, offering a discount, etc. Strategic and tactical marketing are certainly related, but strategic marketing is the parent and tactical marketing the child.

The key strategic marketing questions are these:

- Who are our customers?
- What do they want/need/value?
- Can we provide it?
- Should we provide it?
- How should we position ourselves?
- Can we win?

The key tactical marketing weapons are these:

- Packaging (product or service design)
- Pricing
- Distribution channels
- Marketing communications (advertising, publicity, sales promotion, personal selling)

There are two fundamental marketing strategies, both of which are relevant for social entrepreneurs:

- *Market push*: This is the only strategy available when a social entrepreneur is attempting to introduce a product or service that has never before been commercialized (e.g. hospice care in the USA in the 1970s): the entrepreneur must 'push' the new product or service into the market (a process sometimes called 'market development'). It is a long and difficult journey.

- *Market pull*: The situation is different when an NGO is thinking about entering a market already occupied by competitors, which is typically what happens when an established NGO attempts to capitalize on its organizational strengths by starting a business. The temptation is to start with its established products and services, offer them for sale and hope somebody will buy them—but the proper approach is to start with potential customers, discover what they need, then build it. In this way its customers, a vastly preferable situation, will pull the NGO into the market.

Viability First, Not Mission

Perhaps the greatest obstacle Jim Westall sees in running a third sector business is what he calls 'value rubs'. Sometimes, he said, 'you have to make decisions about sustainability that are at least temporarily in conflict with your mission. You just have to do it. You have to depersonalise those conflicts and solve the problem. But in my work with other not-for-profits, I've seen those value rubs absolutely destroy their businesses.'

Implicit in the argument offered by Westall and others is the belief that if the business is not viable, it will not survive—and, if it fails, the entire discussion about social impact becomes irrelevant. Dale Novotny of Applied Industries in Longview, WA, who provides employment opportunities for people who are disabled, made the point succinctly: 'We've always been very focused on being a business first. We're a social service business second'.

Rich Gilmartin ran into a 'value rub' in his Florida janitorial business, which employs people who are developmentally disabled. 'In order to keep our prices competitive', he said, 'we're consistently looking for ways to introduce new technology, and that usually translates into automation or more efficient equipment. For example, we've traditionally had a person manually operating a floor-waxing machine that can do swipes of 24 to 28 inches wide. But now we've identified some labour-saving machinery that's much more expensive on the initial end but will reduce our labour consumption and allow us to hold down costs. That means we'll be employing fewer people in the short run, but in the long run it can make our prices competitive and allow us to secure more contracts and ultimately create even more jobs'.

Focus, Focus, Focus

Over the years, social entrepreneurs have learned some painful lessons about the market. Here are three:

- *Do not wander too far afield*: Too many NGOs are charmed by the promise of an unrelated business, a cash cow that somehow supports its social mission. During the late 1970s and early 1980s, a number of not-for-profits across the USA began to pursue unrelated business income in an attempt to offset the escalating cuts in federal and state funding. However, this meant they were delving into areas unrelated to their social mission, and most of the efforts failed: the not-for-profits were not only trying to start a business (which they did not know how to do), but were also trying to do it in an arena they knew nothing about.

- *Find and define a niche*: The market can be tumultuous and cruel. To succeed, social entrepreneurs must have a sound business concept, regardless of whether they are enhancing an internal programme or contemplating a spin-off business venture. In other words, they need a market niche—a product or service, somebody who wants it, and somebody who is willing and able to pay for it. For NGOs, of course, the last part is frequently the toughest, because the 'client' and the 'customer' are often two different parties. But, as Paul Hawken (1987) noted, the goal of any entrepreneurial effort is to reduce the business idea to its essence—and then continue reducing it until reaching a space that is small enough to defend but large enough to make a profit.

- *Be a player or do not play at all*: This one takes real courage, but it gives NGOs a way to grapple with the classic '80/20' problem that occurs when they devote 80 per cent of their management time to the 20 per cent of their programmes that should actually be eliminated. It is very difficult for NGOs to kill programmes, but finding a home for them in another agency better positioned to provide the service could often mitigate the pain. By doing so, NGOs will simultaneously be freeing themselves to concentrate on the programmes where they are better positioned—and the clients and customers of both NGOs will be better served.

Customer Service

The customer may not always be right, but the customer is always the customer. Once a social enterprise is underway, customer service is the most important factor for ongoing success. For example, one of the biggest surprises for Kathleen Buescher has been discovering that 'when you're working with the corporate sector, everything is negotiable, unlike government contracts where it's 'thou shalt and thou shalt not.' So it's very important to stay in tune with your corporate customers, stay very attentive and sensitive to their needs. We don't want to be just a short-term contractor. We want to be an ongoing resource to supervisors and to management.'

'We will never forget that our customers are the ones who keep us in business', said Kevin McDonald, 'so you have to treat 'em right. They are always right. If we do something wrong, we respond immediately and take care of the problem. That's just so important . . . but people forget that. When customers appreciate what you've done it's the best form of advertising you can get. It's like buying cars: you go back to somebody you're comfortable with.'

Almost by accident, Bobbie Lenz discovered that customer focus gave her company a unique selling proposition. 'Right from the beginning', she said, 'as a not-for-profit, we were always mission driven, always centred on what was best for our clients. But very early in our existence as a business we realized running it successfully meant we had to use the same approach with customers. 'Here we are', we said. 'What do you need? We'll do everything to meet your needs.'' That determination to do what was best for its clients and for its customers emerged from what Lenz called one of her organization's core values: the importance of choice for people who are developmentally disabled.

'That's what our business venture has been all about', she commented. 'These days, customer service is hard to find, but we've bent over backwards to provide extraordinary customer service. We're definitely people-oriented, and that's part of our heritage as a not-for-profit.' She also discovered a practical reason to emphasize customer service. 'Initially', she said, 'here we were, this human service agency with severely disabled people doing mailings, and a lot of people had a problem with that. So we never used the heart on the sleeve, 'Oh, please put these poor people to work', approach. Right from the beginning we said, 'Use us. You need to. It's good business.' That's why referrals and word of mouth have worked so well for us. You need to act like a business, not a human service agency.'

Rich Gilmartin predicted that 'if we're not accessible to the customer, we probably won't be their vendor very long. Customers often tell us that the management for previous vendors stayed at a great distance, never came to talk with them—and if decisions had to be made, the local person was not empowered to make them. So we mount a concerted effort to empower the person on the site to make the greatest scope of decisions possible—and we also have people from our headquarters office travelling to each site on a regular basis, in part to spot problems before the customer sees them and they become big problems.'

One of the obstacles Gilmartin and his staff have managed to overcome has been 'not hearing a message early enough'. As an example, he cited the company's custodial contract on a naval air base. 'They'd been telling us for months we were missing the mark', he remembered. 'They weren't ringing any fire alarms or loud bells, but they were saying improvements were needed here and there. We were listening—we thought—but then we discounted the information and came up with reasons why things were the way they were and why we were doing everything we could be doing. Then they set off the fire alarm. 'We've been telling you for six months that things need to be fixed', they said, 'and we've seen no noticeable attempt to fix them. So now your contract's at risk.' It took us 18 months to eradicate that situation and turn it around. It didn't take that long to fix the problems, but it did take that long for the base to believe our fix would stick.'

Gilmartin also believes his company takes customer service a lot farther than most. 'If you just do what people expect, and that's it', he said, 'they almost don't know you're there—and when it comes time for contract renewal or adding contracts there's no substantial advantage. On the other hand, it makes a difference if you do something a little out of the ordinary—like leave behind your business card with a handwritten note, or leave a Hershey's Kiss on someone's desk, or if you find a $2 bill on the floor and call it to the attention of the ownership instead of shoving it into your pocket and walking away. It can be any number of things.' In many situations, for example, the previous vendor did not wear uniforms. Gulf Coast employees not only wear uniforms, 'but we put our name on them and we let customers pick the colour. It all sets a tone immediately that is different than what the customers expect.'

Quality

'We will make no compromises on quality just because the work has been done by people with disabilities', said Rick Walker. 'If you rent a room at our motel it will be the bloody cleanest hotel you've ever been in. If you go into our ice cream store you'll have a perfect experience. Not, 'Isn't that cute', but 'This is great!' I make life miserable for people around me on that issue.' Walker noted that community scepticism about the ability of his organization successfully to operate its businesses 'can only be overcome in two ways. Number one, don't give them an avenue for an opening by having quality failures. And the other is to outlive the bastards and patiently go about what you've been doing.'

'The customer won't pay for mistakes', said Bobbie Lenz. 'If you screw up, you're costing yourself money, so quality control is essential. You have to do it right the first time.' And Rich Gilmartin believes measuring employee performance is critical. 'Before we started actually doing it', he noted, 'we would sometimes say, 'This is important' and then not measure it, or we'd measure it for a time and stop—and lo and behold performance would deteriorate. So now we do focus groups and have periodic performance meetings with our clients. We track things historically to see if they're on the rise, or flat—or, worse yet, going downward.'

What sets Jim Westall's asbestos abatement company aside from its eight competitors in the state of Washington is its certification as an ISO 14000 provider, an international environmental quality standard. 'You have to be able to document precisely what's happening with the asbestos every step of the way', he said, 'so it can be tracked for at least 20 years. Sometimes we can't remove it, so our job is simply to encase it so it can't be touched.' Being certified gives Skookum an edge on its competitors and also reassures its clients. 'Here we are', laughed Westall, 'telling our customers we'll do asbestos abatement— and that we're going to hire the least capable members of the community to do it! In an area that has a tremendous liability for the customer! And they're going to look at us and say, 'Huh, sure you are!' And we can say we're the only asbestos abatement company in the state of Washington that is ISO certified.'

Aggressive Pricing

When setting pricing strategies, NGOs are gradually learning to think in terms of annual budgets, not just unit costs. For example, successful service companies in the USA typically have a gross profit margin of 40 to 60 per cent on everything they sell—in order to finish the year with an overall net margin (after overhead, payroll, and other internal and external sales costs have been deducted) of 3 to 5 per cent (Timmons 1994: 26). In other words, if it costs $1.00 (£0.58) to deliver a product or service, NGOs need to be charging $1.40 to $1.60 (£0.81 to £0.93).

Of course, abruptly introducing price hikes of that magnitude would come as a shock to most current payers. Nevertheless, any NGO hoping to become increasingly sustainable or self-sufficient will have to consider this approach and, at the very least, begin raising its prices incrementally. Rich Gilmartin's company frequently wins contracts despite having a higher price than its competitors. 'Often', he said, 'the customers have already been there—and realize they may have shot themselves in the foot by going with the lower price. Now they're looking around because they feel like they're not getting what they expected—or maybe they're just asking for a higher level of service.'

Of course, charging a price is one thing; collecting another. Dave McDonough discovered a harsh truth: 'You pay your employees every Friday and you send out invoices once a week, but you don't get paid for 30 or 45 days.' At one point during its history, his Los Angeles social enterprise 'had a bad accounts receivable problem, and we discovered the primary reason was our inability to get our invoices out on time. And then when they did go out they were wrong! So the customer would say, 'Well, this one's wrong, I'll just set it over here.' It was amazing, really. So we hired a woman for our finance department who had a background in collections—and it turned out it wasn't really a collections issue at all as much as it was a follow-up issue. After that we made sure the invoices went out on time, called customers to follow up and in just a few months went from having about 60 per cent of our accounts receivable unpaid after 90 days to having the bulk of them paid within 45 days.'

One of the major pressures on pricing, of course, is competition, which often changes the landscape dramatically. 'There used to be more companies competing with us', commented Kathleen Buescher. 'Now there are fewer, they're a lot bigger, and they've turned employee counselling into a commodity business. And that means pricing has become a very big deal. We used to be able to charge our corporate customers $30 or $35 (£17.4 or £20.3) per year per employee—now it's down to $12 to $18 (£6.96 to £10.44).'

Strategic Partnerships

Few businesses today can survive in the market without forging strategic partnerships. Four of the most powerful types include operational philanthropy,[3] supplier relationships, distributor relationships, and cause-related marketing (or 'licensing'):

- *Operational philanthropy* occurs when a for-profit company creates a business relationship with an NGO instead of giving it a grant—and therefore becomes dependent on the not-for-profit's performance for its own success. For example, Pioneer Human Services in Seattle, WA, employs disadvantaged men and women to manufacture aerospace and sheet metal products for the aircraft, telecommunications, electronic, and other industries (including cargo liners and more than 8,000 other parts for Boeing aircraft). Pioneer businesses also include warehousing, assembly, contract packaging, and food purchasing services, plus a central kitchen facility and a number of retail cafes, and the total annual revenue from all of them is more than $51 million (£29.6 million)—with 99.7 per cent coming from earned income. The company, led by president Mike Burns, recently received national recognition for 'pioneering a new model for social change and setting an agenda for not-for-profit organizations nationwide' (Dahle 2000: 172).

- A *supplier relationship* takes place when either the NGO or the for-profit company supplies personnel, raw materials, and/or finished components to the other. Greyston Bakery is a prime example: it supplies more than 10,000 pounds of 'brownies' and 'blondies' a day—nearly 3 million pounds a year—that are used in five Ben and Jerry's ice cream products in the USA and in its products throughout Europe and the Middle East. Annual sales for Greyston are $4.2 million (£2.4 million), with a 3.7 per cent net profit—and the bakery provides fifty jobs for ex-convicts and others with barriers to employment.

- A *distributor relationship* occurs when either a for-profit company or an NGO channels its products or services to customers through the other organization's network. A common example in the USA takes place when for-profit companies partner with not-for-profits to access federal and state 'set-aside' programmes (in which government contracts are offered first to not-for-profits). Another is the relationship Bobbie Lenz has with the post office. 'They've given us a lot of technical assistance and taught us everything we've learned about the business', she said, 'and, for them, having an organization like us is helpful, because it reduces the number of organizations showing up with bulk mailings that aren't sorted or otherwise ready for mailing. When people like that come to them, the post office sends them to us.'

- *Cause-related marketing* occurs when one organization licenses the use of its name, products, or services to another. The combination can be powerful: it can enhance the reputation and boost the sales of a for-profit company and simultaneously increase the credibility and generate earned income for an NGO. For example, during ninety-day periods in the spring of five consecutive years, each person who used an American Express card in the USA knew 4 per cent of his or her purchase price went directly to Share Our Strength, one of the nation's leading anti-hunger organizations.

The partnership raised $43 million (£24.9 million) and funded more than 1,000 local, state, national, and international organizations. But the goals do not have to be so ambitious: when Clif Bar, Inc., one of the country's leading manufacturers of energy bars, decided to help the Breast Cancer Foundation by creating the LunaBar and donating a percentage of sales to the Foundation, the first year's proceeds were only $5,000 (£2,900)—but they have now grown to more than $300,000 (£174,000) per year, about 10 per cent of the Foundation's annual operating budget.

Conclusion

The rules of the game for NGOs have changed dramatically during the past twenty years. Operating costs have soared, resources available from traditional sources have flattened, the ranks of NGOs competing for grants and subsidies have mushroomed, and the number of people in need has escalated beyond our most troubling nightmares. This chapter has been an attempt to clarify both the promise and the perils attached to social entrepreneurship. And the pioneers in the field have some final warnings:

- *Do not enter the world of entrepreneurship unless you are personally energized by the idea—it is not for the faint of heart*: Do not attempt to do it because you think you 'should' or because others insist. Unless you are ignited by the prospect, unless it drives you out of bed in the morning and sends you charging into the day, it is not for you.

- *Ask yourselves some important threshold questions*. Is this something we really want to do? Is the timing right? Do we understand the risks and are we willing to take them? Are we being realistic about possible results? Do we have enough staying power (money, time, psychic energy)? Have we the right people—and are we willing to give them the freedom, responsibility, and authority necessary for entrepreneurial success? Positive answers to these and other questions will not guarantee success, but they may give you the confidence to proceed.

- *Do not underestimate the resources you will need*: The biggest mistake Jim Westall made when developing his asbestos abatement business was the timeline: 'We thought it wouldn't take nearly the capital or the time. You know, the old 'rosy scenario' planning process. We kept digging into our capital'. And the necessary resources were not limited to money: they also included people, facilities, time, and other scarce commodities. 'In order to get started', said Westall, 'we had to acquire a whole different level of skills. We really had to gear up. We had to train ourselves, and then our employees. It took months and months of pretty intensive work, and we climbed into a large hole before we got out with our first contract. We spent almost half a million dollars buying equipment, travelling, buying people, getting people trained. But we were in it for the long haul.'

- *Watch the numbers, every day*: It became apparent to Tony Wagner early on that his training as a not-for-profit manager did not prepare him for the realities of running a business. 'You've got to have an absolutely brutal discipline about the financial end of the business', he noted, 'I'd been a not-for-profit manager for years, but until we started our business there'd never been a time when I needed daily financial information.'

- *Grow organically*: The most dangerous time for any small business is when it attempts to grow from being a 'big small' business into a 'small big' business. Financial resources are stretched, emotional stress escalates, psychic energy dissipates, and competitors get in the way. 'We made some significant mistakes', admitted Rich Gilmartin. 'We were still operating as though we were a twenty-five to a hundred person operation long after we'd passed that point.' Dave McDonough remembered 'the vacuum effect' when a large customer 'sucked up people from everywhere and became our only focus. It was a shock to the system.' And Richard Oulahan emphasized how important it is for NGOs to sometimes say no, either because it rubs against their mission or because it dangerously extends their resources.

- *Be flexible*: There are no guarantees, no perfect plans. All the other advice offered by the pioneers in the field is simply a way to shape in the field of play: ultimately, success or failure depends on the willingness of social entrepreneurs to do whatever is necessary. As a wise man once said, 'Things turn out best for those who make the best of the way things turn out.'[4]

Making the transition from innovation to entrepreneurship is fraught with dangers. Years ago, Pablo Eisenberg (1992: 22), Founder and Chairman Emeritus of the National Committee for Responsive Philanthropy, wrote that 'far too many charities have...forgotten the distinction between for-profit and non-profit activities, between fulfilling a mission and survival at any cost.... The appeal of non-profit organizations is their commitment to public service...it is not as a shadow private sector.' But, according to Kenneth Mason, the former chairman of Quaker Oats, 'making a profit is no more the purpose of a corporation than getting enough to eat is the purpose of life. Getting enough to eat is a requirement of life. Life's purpose, one would hope, is something broader and more challenging. Likewise with business and profit' (Makower 1994: 31–2).

And not-for-profit executive Robert Harrington may have put it most succinctly, and in terms social entrepreneurs would resoundingly endorse: 'If you want to help the poor people of the world', he said, 'step one is to make sure you're not one of them!'

Notes

1. My thanks go to my research assistant, Josh LaBau, for the preparation of this chapter.
2. Much of the material in this section has been developed jointly with Jim McClurg, vice president of the Social Enterprise Alliance, the leading membership organization for social entrepreneurs in the USA. Mr McClurg previously served for twenty-five years as CEO of Northwest Center Industries in Seattle, WA, one of the most successful social enterprises in the nation: during his tenure, he developed a network of small businesses that generated more than $15 million (£8.7 million) in annual sales, employed 400 adults with disabilities, and reduced grant income to less than 3 per cent of budgeted expenses.
3. Gary Mulhair created the phrase 'operational philanthropy' in 1998 during his tenure as president and CEO of Pioneer Human Services, Seattle, WA.
4. Attributed to former US Vice President Hubert H. Humphrey.

References

Bailey, A. (1990). '1980's Giving Boom Not Matched by Growth for Many Groups,' *The Chronicle of Philanthropy*, 9 January: 11.

Barker, J. (1989). *Discovering the Future Series: The Business of Paradigms*. Burnsville, MN: Charthouse Learning.

Berg, S. (1993). '36,900,000: Americans in Poverty in '92,' *Star Tribune*, 5 October: 6.

Brodsky, N. (1996). 'Who Are the Real Entrepreneurs?,' *Inc. Magazine*, December: 33.

Dahle, C. (2000). 'Social Justice—Pioneer Human Services,' *Fast Company*, April: 9–11.

Dees, J. G. (1998). *The Meaning of Social Entrepreneurship*, Available at: http://faculty.fuqua.duke.edu/centers/case/files/dees-SE.pdf

Eisenberg, P. (1992). 'Corporate Value Could Poison Nonprofits', *The Chronicle of Philanthropy*, 10 March: 20–25.

Firstenberg, P. (1986). *Managing for Profit in the Not-For-Profit World*. New York: The Foundation Center.

Hawken, P. (1987). *Growing a Business*. New York: Simon & Schuster.

Hodgkinson, V., Weitzman, M., Toppe, C., and Noga, S. (1992). *Not-For-Profit Almanac 1992–1993: Dimensions of the Independent Sector*. San Francisco, CA: Jossey-Bass.

Kaplan, A. (ed.) (1995). *Giving USA 1995: The Annual Report on Philanthropy for the Year 1994*. New York: AAFRC Trust for Philanthropy.

King, C. (2002). Remarks by Charles King, Chair, Board of Directors, The National Gathering for Social Entrepreneurs, at the 4th National Gathering for Social Entrepreneurs, Minneapolis, MN, 4–6 December.

Kirchoff, B. (1997). 'Entrepreneurship Economics', *The Portable MBA in Entrepreneurship*, 2nd edn. New York: John Wiley & Sons.

Makower, J. (1994). *Beyond the Bottom Line*. New York: Simon & Schuster.

Maxwell, J. (2000). *Failing Forward: Turning Mistakes into Stepping-Stones for Success*. Nashville, TN: Thomas Nelson Publishers.

MEC (2003). 'Business Success and Failure', *MEC: The Minnesota Entrepreneurs' Club Newsletter*: 1.

Not-for-Profit Times (1993). 'Social Services Gap', February: 7.

Star Tribune (1993). 'Working Poor Grow in Number: 1 in 5 Full-Time Employees Now Counted in Category, Study Says', 7 October: 1.

Sterne, L. (1989). 'Management Guru Calls on Not-For-Profits', *Not-For-Profit Times*, May: 19–21.

Timmons, J. (1994). 'Opportunity Recognition: The Search for Higher-Potential Ventures', *The Portable MBA in Entrepreneurship*. New York: John Wiley & Sons.

Toppe, C. and Kirsch, A. (2002). *Keeping the Trust: Confidence in Charitable Organizations in an Age of Scrutiny*. Washington, DC: Independent Sector.

Webster (1982). *Webster's New World Dictionary*.

Weitzman, M., Jalandoni, N., Lampkin, L., and Pollak, T. (2002). *The New Not-for-Profit Almanac and Desk Reference: The Essential Facts and Figures for Managers, Researchers, and Volunteers*. New York: Jossey-Bass.

Williams, G. (1992). 'Generosity of Wealthy Donors Dropped in 1980's, but Overall Giving Held Steady, Study Finds', *The Chronicle of Philanthropy*, 2 June: 1.

17

Moving Ahead Together: Implications of a Blended Value Framework for the Future of Social Entrepreneurship

Jed Emerson

Introduction

Social entrepreneurship is an emerging field with diverse perspectives, experiences, and visions of our collective future. This diverse community consists of social activists, business people, academics of various stripes, and those involved in government—each with something to offer towards what is simultaneously an evolving exploration and a global coming together of ideas, vision, and new practice.

These differing perspectives hold the promise to shed light on discussions with extremely diverse actors, making use of different languages and terms to describe what are fundamentally similar concepts and challenges. This coming together often leads to a tower of Babel in which terms clearly defined in one application are grossly misused in another, contributing to confusion and wasted efforts. In the context of this closing chapter, the terms social enterprise and social entrepreneurship are simply used to refer to those activities, whether for-profit or not-for-profit, that seek to create and then manage ventures capable of pursuing social, environmental, and economic value: efforts to maximize blended firm value as well as capital performance (see Emerson 2003a, 2003b, 2003c; see Figure 17.1).[1]

While one might easily conclude we are all climbing the same social entrepreneurship mountain, but simply moving up different paths along its sides, if one steps back to take the long view it becomes clear that, in truth, we are each actually pursuing the same path—that of value maximization. This path simply takes us each up the slopes of different mountains along a common, 'value' mountain range. What is striking about all these various conversations and perspectives is the fact that each of these actors—whether

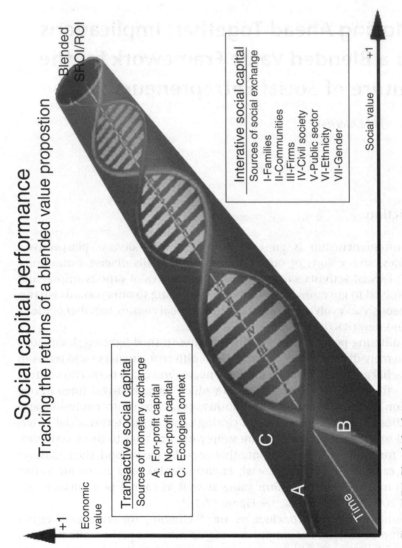

Figure 17.1 Blended value

investor or businessperson, social entrepreneur or philanthropist—is trying to do what is essentially the same thing. They are all circling around the core question of how best to think about value as more than simple economic performance or social impact alone. Whether or not they consciously know it, they are each confronting the reality that value itself is not a single entity, but rather a composite—a blend—of economic, social, and environmental elements.

And it would appear there are many leaders in both the traditional business and social sector arenas that are reaching the same conclusion. Michael Porter, the organizational guru and leading academic on corporate strategy, states in the European Business Forum newsletter, 'In this corporate competitive context, the company's social initiatives—or its philanthropy—can have great impact, not only for the company, but also for the local society... I used to see this area of corporate social performance as the last thing on my agenda ten years ago, but now I agree that social and economic issues are intertwined' (2003).

Porter is not alone as a mainstream business strategist who has concluded that the interests of the firm are inseparable from those of society and planet. Growing numbers of companies are creating not just annual reports on their social responsibility, but actually developing internal management information systems (MIS) to track data and inform managerial decision-making. Indeed, mainstream investment advisors, such as Cambridge Associates, are telling clients that consideration of social and environmental value elements within investing needs to be advanced as a core component of any sound approach to asset management (see Bowers 2003).

Increasingly, it is obvious to many in both the for-profit and not-for-profit sectors that the nature of value is whole. Within this understanding, value is viewed as a blend of discrete elements. To function in ignorance of this reality is to doom oneself to continual underperformance relative to the potential for overall value creation. Having embraced this broader, more catholic understanding of value positions, both organizations and capital can capture the greatest possible amount of full, blended value.

This has a number of very significant implications that fall into the following general categories:

- The nature of the firm
- Capital investment
- Performance tracking
- Development and dissemination of intellectual capital, and
- How we organize both this field and our work within it.

I will touch briefly on each of these elements in turn.

The Nature of the Firm

Perhaps the most important insight we may take from the concept of the blended value proposition is that, from a value creation perspective, there is no difference between a for-profit and a not-for-profit firm. Stated another way, not-for-profits create economic worth and for-profit companies have social and environmental impacts. In today's world one may structure a for-profit with related 501-c-3/charity support organizations and a not-for-profit may have significant interests in a for-profit subsidiary corporation. Corporate structure itself matters only as a strategic means to an end since the venture, whether it is not-for-profit or for-profit, generates value that is whole and blended: consisting of economic, social, and environmental components. Other consideration—such as the type and source of capital sought or the specific type of strategy to be pursued—may have an influence upon which corporate structure is chosen. However, from the perspective of value creation itself, not-for-profits and for-profits both have the potential to create full, blended value.

Given this reality, it is important that we acknowledge that, for the most part, not-for-profit organizations tend to underperform economically, whilst for-profits underperform relative to their social and environmental potential. For example, consider the affordable housing industry. Across the USA there are thousands of community development corporations that have been active over the past two decades, building thousands of units of affordable housing. This is great and largely made possible financially by the sophisticated use of an Affordable Housing Tax Credit. Despite the seeming acumen of leveraging this investment instrument as a means to assist in the financing of new, affordable, units of housing, the sector left significant amounts of economic and environmental value 'on the table' by simply viewing themselves as 'housers'—and producing most of that housing with timber that was clear cut. Had the affordable housing community conceived of themselves as creators of blended value and not simply providers of low-cost housing, they could have approached timber companies with a completely different business opportunity: one based upon the awareness that the affordable housing industry was about to create a massive construction market that could be leveraged to support a new, green demand for timber—which, in turn, would have decreased the market price of such lumber, while making certified sustainable timber available to a substantially broader market.

Or consider that the not-for-profit sector represents fully 7 per cent of the GDP of the USA (see www.blendedvalue.org). Every year billions of dollars flow through the not-for-profit sector. If all that was done was to manage the balance on personal cheque accounts better, we could leverage greater economic value and impact. Yet instead of placing our accounts with ShoreBank or other federally insured community banking institutions, we place our accounts with mainstream financial institutions that function with little regard for the social or environmental interests we profess to advance. There are other examples, but the point remains: while creating great social impact in many other areas, not-for-profits consistently fail to leverage their economic value to then achieve social and environmental value or impacts.

We must strive to realize our traditional notion that somehow for-profits consist of the 'bad guys' and the not-for-profits of 'the good guys' is simply wrong since both organizational forms have the potential to create and maximize all components of value. Our focus needs to be upon form, function, and leveraged relationships—not whether or not the organizational structure is for-profit or not-for-profit.

Capital Investment

In most business school courses on capital finance, students are taught that 'capital will always seek its highest and best use'. This core premise of capital market structure and functioning remains true within a blended value framework, but is augmented by the knowledge that capital markets are themselves lodged within a set of social assumptions regarding the nature of value and how our societies assign worth to any variety of items. Commerce, while operating in the aggregate within 'objective' systems of monetary exchange, is itself grounded within a set of social operating assumptions and values. This reality will remain with us in the future, but what is striking to note is the degree to which increasing numbers of capital market investors are entering these markets with a commitment to managing their investments with reference not only to financial performance and return but also with reference to other, non-monetary considerations of value as well. Two decades ago, the entire arena of socially responsible investing barely existed as a segment of mainstream capital markets. Today, that segment represents over $2 trillion (£1.16 trillion) of investment in the USA alone. Pension funds such as CALPERS (the state pension fund for California with over $180 billion (£104.4 billion) under management), has targeted portions of its portfolio for investing in inner city neighbourhoods in the state and recently announced steps to invest in green and sustainable technologies. This trend will only continue as mainstream investors seek to protect themselves from elements of risk (environmental, social, and otherwise) they fear will negatively affect their financial returns and as progressive shifts in demographics result in an ageing population concerned not simply with financial well-being in retirement, but the long-term well-being of their children and the communities they will leave behind.

As growing numbers of investors enter capital markets with an interest in maximizing both financial returns and social and environmental value creation, new opportunities will also emerge for diverse investors seeking multiple returns to join together and create new funds to provide additional capital to firms seeking to capture their full, blended value potential. These funds will provide needed capital to entrepreneurs engaged in the creation of twenty-first century organizations fulfilling the greatest degree of effectiveness and returns of financial capital, while strategically leveraging that capital to simultaneously generate social and environmental value. As capital networks such as Investors Circle and related emerging angel networks continue to be organized and achieve viable financial returns, combined with these other elements of value, more investors will be drawn into these markets, further expanding the capital options available to entrepreneurs (Emerson, Freundlich, and Berenbach 2004).

While significant changes will continue to take place within mainstream capital investment markets, additional pressures will also grow for philanthropic institutions to develop and pursue investment strategies that maximize the full value of their financial investing practices. In the same way that we might agree poor people cannot spend their way out of poverty and must be engaged in an array of asset development efforts to expand not only their financial assets but personal and other assets as well, foundations must confront the reality that they cannot 'grant their way' out of a troubled world. By focusing upon grants alone, foundations will never begin to approach the true value they have the potential to create.

Yet, today, the majority of foundations view themselves as grant makers, placing primary focus upon how their 5 per cent payout is managed. The reality is that 95 per cent of foundation assets are placed in mainstream investments with little or no consideration of whether those investments are in synch with the institutional goals and mission of the investor organization (Emerson 2003c). As these investors continue to experiment with how best to manage the financial assets of foundations, leading foundations such as Nathan Cummings, Endswell Foundation, and the F. B. Heron Foundation will be joined by other institutions that together will continue to apply pressure on capital markets to respond to and pursue greater opportunities to maximize the full value of both corporations and capital.

In addition to achieving greater asset alignment with their market rate investing, foundations will also need to find ways to continue expanding their overall approach to effective management of their total assets (Emerson 2003c). As more foundations seek to maximize the impact of their work, they will move to engage in strategic philanthropy that seeks to build real, sustainable capacity of investee organizations. As foundations become more intentional in operating as investors in full value, they will also find they need to be more strategically engaged with grantees, transparent in their operating practices, and accountable in a wider variety of ways to those who are stakeholders in their work.

Out of these transformed philanthropic relationships between foundations and social enterprise practitioners, new intellectual capital and knowledge will evolve—intellectual capital that will need to be cultivated and disseminated to its best, most relevant, applications in changing the way practitioners and others approach their work.

While critical to advancing the work of those within a given area of practice, simply improving and building upon the intellectual capital of a single topic area is not enough. Foundation grant making represents less than 3 per cent of the capital flows of the not-for-profit sector and it is clear that their greatest value is not to be found in grant making, but rather in the leverage foundations may achieve through building upon the work they fund. Specifically, foundations interested in maximizing their full value must take the intellectual capital created by their investees and develop more effective platforms for converting that capital into broader educational programmes to help the larger society understand more about the work in which the foundation and its grantees are engaged.

This process of education will also need to include a more sophisticated approach to policy development and advocacy. At the present time, too many foundations shy away from assuming any meaningful role in advancing a policy agenda based upon the work they are supporting. By not taking the logical next step from grant making to learning to policy development, too many foundations are leaving real value unrealized, instead of capturing it to achieve the greatest possible returns in pursuit of their stated institutional missions.

Finally, all foundations—regardless of programme areas—need to realize that everything they do has an effect upon the natural environment. While not every foundation should have a formal environmental grants programme, all foundations must consider the environmental context of the work in which they are engaged and find ways to pursue their core mission while affirming the need for us all to be environmentally aware. Public health programmes should explore how health efforts might include considerations of environmental factors that effect health. Youth and education programmes can seek to integrate some aspect of environmental education into their curriculum. All foundations should examine whether and how their core operating practices may contribute to environmental degradation and how those practices may be modified to minimize negative environmental impacts.

The key and critical challenge for all investors, whether they are managing for market-rate, concessionary, or philanthropic returns, is that they will need to understand how their investing can create and leverage full, blended value in order to achieve the greatest impact possible.

Performance Tracking

Naturally, if we are going to pursue full value and generate multiple returns, we must advance better frameworks for assessing the performance of our investments and the firms in which we invest. While traditional financial return analysis, programme evaluation, double and triple bottom-line reporting, and other approaches are all needed, such tools cannot be allowed to detract from the reality that there is a single, bottom line consisting of multiple value components. Each of the tools we have at hand must be refined and applied within this awareness that what we seek is not simply the ability to track financial, social, or environmental performance, but rather each of these three aspects of value creation is key to achieving and maximizing the total, blended return.

In discussing the challenge of creating more comprehensive and practical performance tracking frameworks, we must first acknowledge that such frameworks will not come about fully formed. Given our familiarity and comfort with numeric and econometric reporting systems, many of us have a tendency to assume such metrics evolved naturally with little effort. In point of fact, the current frameworks used to track and assess economic performance are the outcome of decades of debate and deliberation among business people, economists, financiers, and governmental monitoring and regulatory groups. The Securities Exchange Commission, Financial Accounting Standards Board, Generally Accepted Accounting Practices, and other such common bodies which set the basic ground rules for how to assess rational, financial performance and returns were each the product of a set of actors coming together to decide upon the need for such entities and embracing the frameworks then advanced by such groups. It is naïve to think that the new metrics of the twenty-first century will evolve on their own, as a simple logical outgrowth of our common quest for better measures to capture the full value of our investing and enterprise creation efforts. Such metrics will only evolve over a number of years, if not decades, as diverse actors deliberately work together to propose new ways to assess and track the performance of their capital and firms.

What is required for the field to embrace a common set of performance metrics capable of tracking blended value, is the creation of a network of 'metrics mavericks', each focused upon taking what is known and applying it within their own work—before circling back to the larger 'metrics network' to present and modify their proposed expanded measures on the basis of broad, open-source, feedback. Over time, different actors will embrace various standards of practice and those standards will themselves come to form the foundation of a new, global, framework for understanding not simply economic value creation but social and environmental value as well.

Over past decades, both not-for-profit and for-profit managers have viewed documentation of non-financial reporting as a task imposed from above by funders or regulators. Often, the general feeling of managers has been that this is 'something we must do, but is not something we want to do'. However, what is clear is that as managers begin to understand the critical importance of having effective MIS capable of tracking not only dollar expenditures, but overall firm performance, managers will be able to track critical information more effectively and increase the overall performance of their organizations, whether for-profit or not-for-profit.

This realization will, in turn, result in the continuing migration of MIS from external reporting (in the form of annual reports, programme evaluations, and regulatory documentation) to internal reporting (in the form of 'Social MIS' to track social value performance and creation, as well as the continuing evolution of environmental, health and safety reporting systems within companies). This will all take place as increasing numbers of organizations, whether firms or investor groups, that seek to be 'built to last' come to view the new metrics as central to firm management and the maximization of the value potential of both the firm and strategic partnerships.

Development and Dissemination of Intellectual Capital

Today, we operate with a wide variety of fields of interest and disciplines of focus, each with its own common language and intellectual frameworks. What is clear, however, is that in a world where managers and investors seek to maximize the full, blended value of capital and ventures, future knowledge will emerge less and less from within discrete silos of practice and increasingly evolve from between the silos as growing numbers of actors bridge the gaps that divide our respective works. An easy example is in the arena of social entrepreneurship wherein business acumen, frameworks, and skills are often transferred for application within non-traditional areas, such as managing for-profits for social gain and not-for-profits with market-based business ventures. Neither traditional not-for-profit management nor mainstream business practices suffice to enable today's managers successfully to address the many challenges they confront: that knowledge will emerge from in between the spaces, not from any single business orientation or social sector practice.

This emerging knowledge of how best to manage social enterprise will develop from practice, informed by both reflection and history. Over the years, we have traditionally turned to experts to teach us how to manage a given task or for unique insight into the work in which we are engaged. What is striking about today's discoveries, however, is that they are arising from 'the street', as practitioners and managers grapple with the daily challenges of their work. There is no 'off the shelf' application or standard approach to structuring social enterprise capital, tracking multiple returns, or managing a firm to maximize its full, blended value. Into this vacuum of ideas and practice will rush new concepts and practice.

In this case, the challenge will be to ensure that the work that is evolving out of practice is informed by the work that has gone on before. Too many practitioners confuse their own innovation for innovation in the space as a whole, when in point of fact they simply think their insights are innovations because they are unaware of what others have already achieved. Indeed, a critical role for academia becomes documenting and disseminating the emerging practices within organizations and investor groups in order to support the widest dissemination of that knowledge and broadest application of these tools. Innovation pursued in the absence of knowledge regarding what is already in place is not innovation, but, rather, duplication and useless efforts amounting to little more than multiple reinventions of existing wheels.

Accordingly, there is a crying need for academic institutions to increasingly cultivate intellectual capital driven by a commitment to intellectual curiosity and academic inquiry not donor development. For example, to date, the major initiatives addressing social enterprise, whether at HBS, Stanford Business School, or the Skoll Centre at Oxford, have each come about as a result of donor interest and commitment. For many academics the real challenges of social enterprise, the new metrics, or any number of related areas of interest to those advancing the emerging social entrepreneurship agenda, are viewed as not valid or valued areas for academic work. Until the mainstream faculty of our world's leading academic institutions conclude such areas of focus are valid and consistent with what stands as sound academic work, practitioners will continue to lose the benefit of the scholarship which does reside within the walls of the academy. And yet, as one thinks of the potential value of creating meaningful partnerships between academics and managers, the possibilities for creating not only new approaches, but also entirely new fields of research and practice, seem boundless.

One key opportunity, therefore, is the creation of a new set of relationships linking those in the academy with those within the arena of social entrepreneurship. To date, the majority of relationships tend to be around the writing of cases or creation of curriculum. What is needed is a commitment to moving beyond such low hanging fruit, to the creation of an international network of academic centres of excellence, each of which becomes a regional hub that brings together the most promising social entrepreneurs (whether not-for-profit or for-profit) within a given area. The goal of such an international network will be to assist practitioners in assuring their work and thinking is informed by that of others around the world; and to ensure that the direction and product of academic inquiry is not simply of interest to academics, but is relevant to managers seeking new insights and tools with which to engage in their work. This international network could then work to propose a broad framework for research and inquiry that will then make it possible for efforts in this area to be more effectively coordinated and receive better leveraged impacts.

How We Organize Both this Emerging Field and Our Work Within It

Finally, all of this—our understanding of the venture, investing of all forms of capital, organizational and capital performance tracking, intellectual capital development, and more—affects how we must think about organizing these seemingly disparate areas of activity and innovation. As more and more individuals find each other outside of their traditional areas of focus, we will see growth in the emergence of value networks which will increasingly impact how we organize our work and structure our fields of practice. These networks will be both spontaneous and facilitated, but will, over coming years, be driven by a mutual pursuit of common challenges in structuring capital, advancing new metrics, and leveraging diverse resources to assure maximum impact. These networks will be created as those within any number of silos seek out the answers to the questions before us and begin working across disciplines and limited areas of inquiry to find the broader solutions we require for our success.

Other documents explore this question of value networking at length (see www.blendedvalue.org), however it is worth noting that these value networks will evolve not from the top down—as academics, foundations, and governments struggle to set the agenda—but rather from the bottom, sides, and middle, as practitioners grappling with these issues on a daily basis continue to find each other and create strategic partnerships better to address their respective needs and interests. While such networks may be supported and facilitated, at their best they are member-directed and organic, evolving to meet a felt need or address a particular and shared challenge and then, perhaps, dissolving again back into a set of random—though, now better informed—atoms. Value networks are driven by the felt need personally to overcome a particular issue or potential area of setbacks. They are self-organized and built upon other organizations and networks in existence. By way of example, we have all attended the traditional conference, with speakers on a stage far away and with the real action taking place in the hallways and bars as attendees find each other in an effort to connect and find common ground for future collaboration. In a virtual sense, the process and evolution of value networks follows much the same course as more conventional connecting.

Overview of Blended Value Mapping Process

With these general conceptual understandings in mind, as one looks out over the landscape of those engaged in advancing more than either social impact or financial performance alone, it is clear there are many diverse efforts naturally organizing within a number of discrete areas. If these value networks are to be effective in self-organizing, it becomes critical that actors within these networks be able both to find others and understand the relation between each of their challenges.

To assist actors in these various areas in finding one another, a Blended Value Mapping Process was initiated in 2003. Complete documentation of the process and the Map itself are available at www.blendedvalue.org, so this chapter will provide only a brief overview of the work. The process included a series of meetings with key players in the USA and Europe that occurred in the spring and autumn. These sessions brought together people from five areas of work that were felt to be related:

Capital providers:

- Social investing (institutional)
- Social investing (double bottom line)
- Strategic philanthropy

Capital investees:

- Social enterprise
- Corporate social responsibility

The purpose of these sessions was to explore a very simple, yet complex question: 'Within your area of activity, what would you define as the key leadership examples, resources, and sources of intellectual capital that you would want others to know about?' Based upon these discussions and the ongoing input of a number of key leaders in each space, a map of each of the five areas was created. In constructing the Blended Value Map, a fundamental operating hypothesis of the mapping process was confirmed, namely that each of the five areas of focus was grappling with very similar challenges, yet because practitioners were divided into silos of work, many were not aware of or familiar with resources and efforts underway in related areas of interest. These efforts were divided into cross-cutting themes (see Figure 17.2):

- The capital challenge
- Performance measurement and metrics
- Leadership and organizational capacity development
- Regulatory, policy and tax code

The mapping process confirmed the assumption that a great deal of work within each area was not being leveraged as effectively as it might be, and also lead to the advancement of a theory of change based on the following ideas:

That value networking across each of the five silos of activity—in order to address each of the cross-cutting themes—would help contribute to the creation of a tax and regulatory enabling environment that in turn would lead to the creation of greater efficiencies within capital markets, and, therefore, an increase in the flow of funds into those markets.

And

That the evolution and application of more effective metrics would contribute to social entrepreneurs and firm managers being able to lead more effective organizations, which in turn would lead to increased effectiveness of that capital which was invested in these organizations, whether for-profit or not-for-profit.

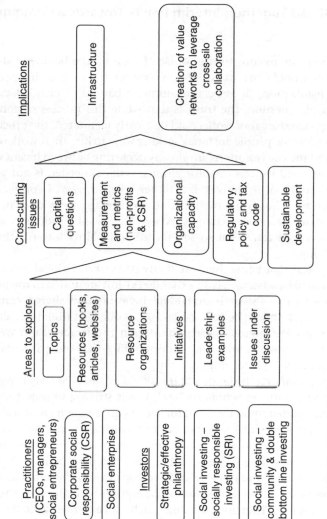

Figure 17.2 The blended value process

Finally, these two shifts would enable actors and organizations within each of the silos of focus to be able to maximize the full, blended value of their efforts and the value created for both shareholder and stakeholder alike.

Moving Ahead Together: Interim Points Towards a Common Future

During various discussions in the course of creating the blended value map, the question would arise as to whether we were trying to initiate a new network, organization, or association under a banner of blended value. An understandable question, the truth is that while this process of connecting and linking related areas of work could be greatly facilitated, the process itself is already underway: people are today seeking ways to link their work with that of others, and the conversations are already occurring between business, social entrepreneurs, and various investor groups. What is needed is not yet more new organizations or initiatives, but rather a better way of connecting the emerging efforts already in motion and to leverage individual insight to achieve sustainable, global change. Where this is all heading is anyone's guess, however we can point to several interim points towards the future that is evolving.

First, it is clear that while there are many parts to this global picture, what may first need to be advanced is an expanded vision grounded in the pursuit of total, blended value for both individual investors and shared community benefit. Our work should be focused less upon our own individual goals and organizational development efforts than upon the larger vision we should each be striving towards with the understanding that our particular efforts are simply a means to achieving that end.

At the event marking the launch of the Skoll Centre for Social Entrepreneurship at the Saïd Business School in 2004, it was striking to note that several speakers commented upon the need for social entrepreneurs to rise above ego in order to embrace a larger vision of our mission and the community we seek to build together. As we look across the landscape of social entrepreneurship it is easy to appreciate the difficulty of the task. Each of us believes in our own specific vision, cause, and purpose and because of this it becomes all too easy for us to confuse the interests of our organization with those of the field of which we are a part. Therefore, we must each strive to re-engage the original passion that brought us forward as leaders. We should seek to maintain a sustained level of objective criticism in order to understand what is best for the larger cause we advance, in addition to our own institutional interests. Having done so, we will then have greater ability to create powerful, strategic partnerships, identify more obvious opportunities for merging organizations to achieve common goals, and significantly enhance our capacity for practising intentional abandonment of underperforming organizations and programmes.

Second, we must seek to understand that our efforts might have greater impact and leverage if we view our respective silos of activity as simply a starting point for our work. Those efforts will have the highest value and impact if they are seen as taking place within a commitment to working together through value networks that build upon connections and leverage total assets. Our goal is not simply to build the field of CSR, social enterprise, or sustainable development, but rather to pursue those efforts with an awareness that what we seek to do is not to build organizations, empires, or silos, but to transform the way mainstream capital markets and organizations function throughout our world.

And, finally, given the nature of knowledge management today and the speed of innovation and change, we should work to create a global web that can function as a dynamic platform of support for the development of the field of social entrepreneurship as a whole. In the words of Douglas Busch of the Intel Corporation, 'Every company has a diagram of the universe in which they are the centre. That's never true. We are all nodes in a mesh.'

Yes, there are certain organizational and personal realities to be acknowledged and operated within, however those realities cannot be allowed to define how we understand our true arena of work or potential impact. We are each part of an emerging, global web of actors seeking to do more than simply make money or create social change. It is not about an either/or but rather a both/and value proposition for most effectively managing capital and organizations. The sooner we recognize that reality, the faster we will be able to advance what will truly be the new organizations we seek to bring into being. These organizations will, in turn, then make use of the new capital structures and finance options we would like to have available in the market. And the performance of capital and organization will both be assessed on the basis of the new, twenty-first century metrics by which we hope to have our efforts judged.

Within an understanding of the value we seek to create as blended value and with an awareness of the fundamental links between each of our efforts, the concepts of 'organization', 'centre', and 'area of focus' all need to be revised out of our twentieth century constructs and brought into new frameworks of understanding and action that we need to advance in order to achieve our goals. The collected chapters of this book are simply a snapshot of a dynamic, global exchange of ideas and emerging managerial practice that promises to open a range of opportunity for us all, developed or developing world, investor, entrepreneur, or citizen. All are welcome, each is needed, and our shared community of a more just, sustainable world will be all the better for our joint efforts. Welcome to our world's common future: step right up!

Note

1. In the context of the many concurrent conversations taking place, a *Blended Value Glossary* may also be of assistance and has been developed as well. Please see, www.blendedvalue.org for a copy of this glossary and support materials.

References

Bowers, R. (2003). *Socially Responsible Investing*. Cambridge Associates European Business Forum, 15, Autumn.

Emerson, J. (2003*a*). 'The Blended Value Proposition: Integrating Social and Financial Returns', *California Management Review*, 45(4): 35–51.

——(2003*b*). *The Blended Value Map*. Available at: www.blendedvalue.org

——(2003*c*). 'Where Money Meets Mission: Breaking Down the Firewall Between Foundation Investments and Programming', *Stanford Social Innovation Review*, Summer: 38–47.

——Freundlich, T., and Berenbach, S. (2004). *The Investor's Toolkit*. Available at: www.blendedvalue.org

European Business Forum (2003). CSR—a Religion With Too Many Priests? Interview with Michael Porter, Copenhagen Business School, September.

Endnote

Alex Nicholls

This book has set out to demonstrate, analyse, and celebrate the dynamic impacts of social entrepreneurial individuals, groups, and networks across the globe. Despite the extraordinary achievements of social entrepreneurship to date, there still remain some serious challenges to its future growth and success. This concluding section will outline four key issues for social entrepreneurs going forward to which further research, embedded in praxis, can significantly contribute.

The first and perhaps the most pressing issue confronting researchers is to contribute towards the development of a market for social 'capital' investments to bring a new level of resources into social entrepreneurship. This is of considerable concern, since whilst earned income strategies may offer a path towards sustainability for a subset of social enterprises within the larger social entrepreneurship spectrum, such approaches will not be appropriate or even feasible for all creative social purpose ventures. Furthermore, for all 'social' start-ups there are major barriers towards accessing finance since they are typically seen as far too risky for conventional capital investment.

According to Emerson (1999*b*, 2003*c*), social entrepreneurs have four main external sources of funding open to them aside from market transactions: social venture funds or venture philanthropy, strategic philanthropy funds within larger institutional funds, foundations and individual donors, and government grants. In the USA this funding amounted to roughly $200 billion in 2001, of which the majority (65 per cent) came from individual donors. However, this investment in social and environmental activities (outside the public sector) that did not attract a direct financial return accounted for only roughly 1 per cent of total investment in the USA.

Generally speaking, social entrepreneurs have little access to mainstream capital markets due to their high-risk profile, lack of established and transparent performance metrics, and long time frames by which success or failure must be assessed (e.g. in health, education, or offender rehabilitation programmes). Consequently, the social capital market has a number of significant problems that inhibit the further development of social entrepreneurship. These are characterized by the striking lack of appropriate financial instruments and the frequent failure to reflect organizational performance in capital allocation. The development of an increasingly rigorous approach to quantifying social return (see, e.g. Emerson 1999a, 2003a, 2003b) offers one part of a larger project that will better assess the relationships between resource allocation, risk, and return in social ventures. Such work would also support the urgent need for more legitimate accountability regimes in the sector (see later).

Similarly, on the supply side the lack of an organized and accessible social capital market often results in potential investors encountering frustration and confusion as they look to fund social projects. Whilst there are a number of such markets under development (see, e.g. Chapter 15), there is no clear evidence on how easy it will be to create a properly functioning marketplace for the social sector. Further research into how to create a fully functioning social capital market is, therefore, of high priority. This should include a survey of available financial instruments (debt, equity, equity-like, guarantees, etc.) to see how they can be applied to the social sector as well as work considering the development of new mechanisms (see, e.g. Emerson and Beceren 2001; Emerson, Freundlich, and Berenbach 2004).

Finally, there needs to be further work done on analysing the capacity constraints at both institutional and organizational levels to absorbing new social finance. Without this piece of the jigsaw, it is unlikely that any progress in driving new resources into social ventures will be truly successful. The example of social enterprises struggling to meet the demands of new public sector contracting in the UK typifies this problem: many do not have the inbuilt capacity to scale quickly nor the access to the resources required to build capacity fast (see, e.g. Hines 2005). Recent work focused on a sample in Manchester, UK (Bull and Crompton 2005), supported this, noting that capacity-building and developing sound management skills still represent major challenges to many social enterprises (see also Collins 2005; DTI 2005).

Three other important areas for future research are all related to the development of a fully functioning social capital market: social venture accountability and governance structures, the use of social impact metrics, and network modelling of strategic social value creation. Each will be briefly considered further in turn.

Today, as noted in Chapter 12, the accountability and governance structures used by social ventures are under increased scrutiny. Traditionally, charities and other not-for-profits have been subject to far less stringent and transparent reporting mechanisms than conventional commercial enterprises, but this is changing. Donors—whether institutional or individual, large or small—are increasingly sceptical of social venture performance and, in concert with other key stakeholders, are often demanding greater accountability from their grantees. Media scare stories about misused funds and a more com-petitive donor landscape are also contributing to this change of emphasis. Future research can contribute to this debate by exploring what underpins a social organization's right to operate and how this can be strategically man-aged. One promising approach is to look at how a social venture generates different levels of legitimacy across its stakeholder groups. Work by Jepson (2005) and Nicholls, Jepson and Jacobs (2006) is already exploring this concept of 'legitimating assets', but more needs to be done.

Over the past five years, scholars, practitioners, and policymakers have established a number of approaches towards managing and measuring social impact, ranging from the highly qualitative, such as the Triple Bottom Line (Elkington 2001), to the more quantitative, such as the Social Return on Investment model (Emerson 1999a; Nicholls 2004). However, there has yet to be any evaluation of the strategic use or social impact of such mechanisms and tools (although see, Aeron-Thomas et al. 2003). Key questions would include:

- Can better social metrics improve resource allocation and generate greater social 'productivity'?
- Do they give access to new resources?
- Is there a relationship between strategic innovation and the use of social metrics?
- Do social metrics make social ventures more accountable?

Finally, whilst many authors note the importance of networks in social venture creation and operation, there has yet to be developed a body of research that explores the implications of such statements. Future research in social entrepreneurial networks should ground its analysis in existing social network theory, ranging from the social capital literature (see, e.g. Putnam 2001; BarNir and Smith 2002; Spence, Habisch, and Schmidpeter 2005) to Actor Network Theory (see, e.g. Callon 1986; Latour 2006), to consider the value of network actions by social entrepreneurs (see, e.g. Nicholls and Alex-ander 2006). One focus of such research should centre on how strategic network building differs in the social sector from the commercial. For example, there is evidence that social entrepreneurs are not constrained by conventional models of competitive markets and, thus, can develop more flexible and altruistic partnerships across their networks, often sharing or even divesting resources and assets to others to advance their larger social mission. Thus, the approach taken by the Fair Trade Foundation in the UK to encourage more competition and new entrants into the Fair Trade market seems to be counter-intuitive in a commercial or mission-driven sense, since it threatens existing social ventures, until such a strategy is reconceived in terms of maximizing social impact across a wider network. From this perspec-tive, it can be seen that growing the market is more important than protecting existing players, even if this means that they go under. It should be noted, however, that this approach, which has recently endorsed the entry of Nestle into the Fair Trade coffee market, is highly controversial.

If these daunting research topics are successfully to be addressed both to help build the academic discipline of social entrepreneurship and to offer real value to practitioners, two things need to be in place. First, as has been noted throughout this book, within social entrepreneurship research there is a need to draw on more established disciplines to build work beyond the purely descriptive. Second, future research should be international in scope if the richness of praxis is to be explored and new theory developed and tested.

The first of these conditions is beginning to be addressed as some more deeply conceptual, theory-based work emerges (see, e.g. Martin 2004; Mair, Robinson, and Hockerts 2006, as well as Nicholls and Cho, Grenier, and Foster in this volume), but there is still far to go and, as was noted in Chapter 7, there are institutional hurdles in place.

In terms of the second criterion, there has also been some progress recently. The International Social Entrepreneurship Research Conference (ISERC), that held its first meeting in Barcelona during 2005, is a clear example of the potential for new international collaborations. Similarly, the ARNOVA network is also committed to adding significantly to the scholarly resource base in social entrepreneurship across countries (see, e.g. Mosher-Williams 2006). Finally, the Skoll Centre for Social Entrepreneurship—with several key partners—is pioneering the development of an online academic network of international researchers working on social entrepreneurship. The network will bring together—for the first time—research and teaching information from around the globe both to encourage new research collaborations and discourage needless repetition of projects. Once completed, the value to practitioners of a single point of access into past and current research in the field via this network should be considerable.

In social entrepreneurship academe, then, we are still witnessing today the birth pangs of the subject as a truly research-based discipline. However, there are, at the very least, encouraging signs of a path towards more mature theory building supported by better empirical data in the future. The increasing institutional interest in the subject across nations and universities can only support this positive progression.

As this volume has demonstrated, social entrepreneurs combine a clear mission focus with boundary blurring innovation and creativity: where others see hurdles, they see opportunities. Social entrepreneurship offers the world the opportunity to address its fundamental problems in new ways that not only ameliorate present need but also ensure future change for the good. This growing band of global social change-makers is relentless and pragmatic, opportunistic and visionary, stubborn and dynamic. If the first discernible wave of social entrepreneurship grew out of established patterns of charity and public sector structures, the next wave—already upon us—is reinventing these structures, tearing down institutional barriers, and generating systemic as well as immediate impact. This second wave of social entrepreneurs and their networks offer the prospect of a new global agenda for positive social change combining the best of progressive charities, the voluntary sector, social movements, and business practice. The potential positive impact of such a potent brew is incalculable both in its direct impact and as a model for larger actions at both policy and grassroots levels. Whilst it would be both impossible and undesirable for the world to be populated exclusively by social entrepreneurs, their role as pathfinders towards a better world is demonstrable. They make clear the potential for change for the better in all societies and empower those who come behind them to carry on the mission. Whether in micro-finance, Fair Trade or renewable energy, social entrepreneurship is leading change on a global scale and these are changes with which we can engage. To paraphrase the words of one old North of England poet, social entrepreneurship demonstrates to everyone that there is nothing they can do that can not be done by all of us too.

References

Aeron-Thomas, D., Nicholls, J., Forster, S., and Westall, A. (2003). *Social Return on Investment: Miracle or Manacle?* London: New Economics Foundation.

BarNir, A. and Smith, K. (2002). 'Interfirm Alliances in the Small Business: The Role of Social Networks', *Journal of Small Business Management*, 40(3): 219–32.

Bull, M. and Crompton, H. (2005). *Business Practices in Social Enterprise*. Manchester, UK: Manchester Metropolitan University Business School.

Callon, M. (1986). 'The Sociology of an Actor-Network', in M. Callon, J. Law, and A. Rip (eds.), *Mapping the Dynamics of Science and Technology*. Basingstoke, UK: Macmillan, pp. 1–16.

Collins, J. (2005). *Good to Great and the Social Sectors: A Monograph to Accompany Good to Great*. HarperCollins.

Davis, G., McAdam, D., Scott, R., and Zald, M. (2005). *Social Movements and Organizational Theory*. Cambridge, UK: Cambridge University Press.

Department for Trade and Industry (DTI) (2005). *A Survey of Social Enterprises Across the UK*. London: Small Business Service, DTI.

Elkington, J. (2001). 'The Triple Bottom Line for 21st Century Business', in R. Strakely, and R. Welford (eds.), *Business and Sustainable Development*. London: Earthscan, pp. 20–43.

Emerson, J. (1999a). 'Social Return on Investment: Exploring Aspects of Value Creation', *REDF box set*, vol. 2, chapter 8. San Francisco, CA: Roberts Enterprise Development Fund.

—— (1999b). 'The US Non-Profit Capital Market', *REDF box set*, vol. 2, chapter 10. San Francisco, CA: Roberts Enterprise Development Fund.

Emerson, J. (2003a). 'The Blended Value Proposition: Integrating Social and Financial Returns', *California Management Review*, 45(4): 35–51.

—— (2003b). *The Blended Value Map*, available at www.blendedvalue.org

—— (2003c). 'Where Money Meets Mission: Breaking Down the Firewall Between Foundation Investments and Programming', *Stanford Social Innovation Review*, Summer, pp. 38–47.

—— and Beceren, M. (2001). *Frontiers in Social Investing and Finance: Understanding and Exploring the Social Value Note*.

—— Freundlich, T., and Berenbach, S. (2004). *The Investor's Toolkit*, Available at www.blendedvalue.org

Hines, F. (2005). 'Viable Social Enterprise—An Evaluation of Business Support to Social Enterprises', *Social Enterprise Journal*, 1(1): 13–28.

Jepson, P. (2005). 'Governance and Accountability of Environmental NGOs', *Environmental Science and Policy*, 8: 515–24.

Latour, B. (2005). *Reassembling the Social: An Introduction to Actor-Network-Theory*. Oxford: Clarendon Lectures on Management Studies.

Mair, J., Robinson, J., and Hockerts, K. (2006). *Social Entrepreneurship*. Basingstoke, UK: Palgrave Macmillan.

Martin, M. (2004). 'Surveying Social Entrepreneurship: Toward an Empirical Analysis of the Performance Revolution in the Social Sector', *Arbeitspapiere Band 2*, University of St Gallen.

Mosher-Williams, R. (2006). *Social Entrepreneurship Issues: Research on an Emerging Field*, ARNOVA Occasional Papers, vol. 3. Colorado, CO: Aspen Institute.

Nicholls, A. and Alexander, A. (2006). 'Rediscovering Consumer-Producer Involvement: A Network Perspective on Fair Trade Marketing in the UK', *European Journal of Marketing*, 40 (forthcoming).

Nicholls, A., Jepson, P., and Jacobs, A. (2006). *Improving the Performance of Social Organizations: Legitimacy as a Tool for Analysis and Strategic Management*, Skoll Centre for Social Entrepreneurship Working Paper.

Nicholls, J. (2004). *Social Return on Investment: Valuing What Matters*. London: New Economics Foundation.

Putnam, R. (2001). *Bowling Alone*. New York: Simon & Schuster.

Spence, L., Habisch, A., and Schmidpeter, R. (2005). *Responsibility and Social Capital*. Basingstoke, UK: Palgrave Macmillan.

Bibliography

AAFRC (2003). *Giving USA 2003*. Bloomington, IN: AAFRC Trust for Philanthropy.

American Behavioral Scientist (ABS) (June, 2002*a*). 'Resources for Scholarship in the Nonprofit Sector: Studies in the Political Economy of Information, Part 1: Data on Nonprofit Industries', *The American Behavioral Scientist*, 45(10).

—— (June, 2002*b*). 'Resources for Scholarship in the Nonprofit Sector: Studies in the Political Economy of Information, Part 2: Resources for Comparative Institutional Research', *The American Behavioral Scientist*, June, 45(11).

Association of Chief Executives of Voluntary Organisations (ACEVO) (2002). *Leading the Organisation: The Relationship Between Chair and Chief Executive*. London: ACEVO.

—— (2003*a*). *Rethinking Governance*. London: ACEVO.

—— (2003*b*). *Replacing the State? The Case for Third Sector Public Service Delivery*. London: ACEVO.

Aeron-Thomas, D., Nicholls, J., Forster, S., and Westall, A. (2003). *Social Return on Investment: Miracle or Manacle?* London: New Economics Foundation.

Alcock, P., Brannelly, T., and Ross, L. (2004). *Formality or Flexibility? Voluntary Sector Contracting*. London: NCVO.

Alter, K. (2000). *Managing the Double Bottom Line: A Business Planning Reference Guide for Social Enterprises*. Washington, DC: PACT Publications.

—— (2002). *Case Studies in Social Entrepreneurship*. Washington, DC: Counterpart International.

—— (2003). *Social Enterprise: A Typology of the Field Contextualized in Latin America*. Washington, DC: Inter American Development Bank.

—— Shoemaker, P., Tuan, M., and Emerson, J. (2001). *When Is It Time to Say Goodbye? Exit Strategies and Venture Philanthropy Funds*. California, CA: Virtue Ventures.

Alvord, S., Brown, L., and Letts, C. (2004). 'Social Entrepreneurship and Societal Transformation: An Exploratory Study', *Journal of Applied Behavioral Science*, 40(3): 260–83.

Amin, A., Cameron, A., and Hudson, R. (2002). *Placing the Social Economy*. London: Routledge.

Anderson, A. and Jack, S. L. (2002). 'The Articulation of Social Capital in Entrepreneurial Networks: A Glue or a Lubricant?' *Entrepreneurship and Regional Development*, 14(3): 193–210.

Aspen (2006), *A Closer Look At Business Education: Social Entrepreneurship/Social Enterprise*, Aspen Institute.

Atkinson, D. (1994). *The Common Sense of Community*. London: Demos.

Austin, J. (2000). *The Collaboration Challenge: How Non-Profits and Businesses Succeed Through Strategic Alliances*. San Francisco, CA: Jossey-Bass.

—— Gutierrez, R., Ogliastri, E, Reficco, R. (eds) (2006), *Effective Management of Social Enterprises*, Harvard: David Rockefeller Center Series on Latin American Studies.

413

Austin, J. Stevenson, H., and Wei-Skillern, J. (2006). 'Social Entrepreneurship and Commercial Entrepreneurship: Same, Different, or Both?' *Entrepreneurship Theory and Practice*, 30(1): 1–22.

—— Leonard, H., Reficco, E., and Wei-Skillern, J. (2005). 'Corporate Social Entrepreneurship: A New Frontier', in M. Epstein and K. Hanson (eds.), *The Accountable Corporation*. Westport, CT: Praeger.

—— Reficco, E., Berger, G., Fischer, R., Gutierrez, R., Koljatic, M., Lozano, G., and Ogliastri, E. (2004). *Social Partnering in Latin America: Lessons Drawn from Collaborations of Businesses and Civil Society Organizations*. Cambridge, MA: Harvard University Press.

Backman, E. and Smith, S. (2000). 'Healthy Organizations, Unhealthy Communities', *Nonprofit Management & Leadership*, 10(4): 355–73.

Badelt, C. (1997). 'Entrepreneurship Theories of the Non-Profit Sector', *Voluntas*: 162–78.

Bakan, J. (2004). *The Corporation: The Pathological Pursuit of Profit and Power*. New York: Constable and Robinson.

Bank of England (2003). *The Financing of Social Enterprises*. London: Bank of England. Available at: http://www.bankofengland.co.uk/financing_social_enterprise_report.pdf

Banks, J. (1972). *The Sociology of Social Movements*. London: Macmillan.

Barendsen, L. and Gardner, H. (Fall 2004). 'Is the Social Entrepreneur a New Type of Leader?', *Leader to Leader*, 34: 43–50.

Barman, E. (2002). 'Asserting Difference: The Strategic Response of Nonprofit Organisations to Competition', *Social Forces*, 80(4): 1191–223.

Baron, D. (2007), 'Corporate Social Responsibility and Social Entrepreneurship', *Journal of Economics & Management Strategy*, 16.3, pp. 683–717.

Bartlett, W. and LeGrand, J. (1993). 'The Theory of Quasi-Markets', in J. LeGrand and W. Bartlett (eds.), *Quasi-Markets and Social Policy*. Basingstoke, UK: Palgrave Macmillan, pp. 13–34.

Baumol, W. (2003). *The Free-Market Innovation Machine: Analyzing the Growth of Miracle Capitalism*. Princeton, NJ: Princeton University Press.

Beck, U. (1992). *The Risk Society*. London: Sage.

—— and Willms, J. (2004). *Conversations with Ulrich Beck*. Cambridge: Polity Press.

Beinhacker, S. and Massarsky, C. (2003). *Enterprising Nonprofits: Revenue Generation in the Nonprofit Sector*. Yale School of Management—The Goldman Sachs Foundation, Partnership on Nonprofit Ventures.

Bernholz, L. (2004). *Creating Philanthropic Capital Markets*. Hoboken, NJ: John Wiley & Sons.

Birmingham Social Economy Consortium (2001). *Social Enterprise: What Implications for the Voluntary Sector?*

Black, L. and Nicholls, J. (2004). *There's No Business Like Social Business*. Liverpool, UK: Cat's Pyjamas.

Blau, P. (1977). *Inequality and Heterogeneity*. New York: Free Press.

BOND (2006), A BOND Approach to Quality in Non-Governmental Organisations: Putting Beneficiaries First, available at: http://www.bond.org.uk/futures/standards/index.htm.

Bornstein, D. (1998). 'Changing the World on a Shoestring', *Atlantic Monthly*, 281(1): 34–9.

—— (2004). *How to Change the World: Social Entrepreneurs and the Power of New Ideas*. Oxford: Oxford University Press.

Borzaga, C. and Defourny, J. (2001). *The Emergence of Social Enterprise*. New York: Routledge.

Boschee, J. (1995). 'Social Entrepreneurship', *Across the Board*, 32(3): 20–5.

—— (1998). *Merging Mission and Money: A Board Member's Guide to Social Entrepreneurship*. Washington, DC: National Center for Nonprofit Boards.

—— (2001a). *The Social Enterprise Sourcebook*. Minneapolis, MN: Northland Institute.

—— (July–August, 2001b). 'Eight Basic Principles for Nonprofit Entrepreneurs', *Nonprofit World*: 15–18.

—— Emerson, J., Sealey, K., and Sealey, W. (2000). *A Reader in Social Enterprise*. Boston, MA: Pearson.

—— and McClurg, D. (2003). *Toward a Better Understanding of Social Entrepreneurship: Some Important Distinctions*. Minnesota, MN: Institute for Social Entrepreneurs.

Bowen, W. (September–October, 1994). 'When a Business Leader Joins a Nonprofit Board', *Harvard Business Review*: 38–43.

Bowers, R. (2003). *Socially Responsible Investing*. Cambridge Associates European Business Forum, 15, Autumn.

Bradach, J. (Spring, 2003). 'Going to Scale', *Stanford Social Innovation Review*: 19–25.

Bradford, A. (ed.) (2003). *Generation Y for the Global Village*. Washington, DC: International Peace Press.

Bradley, B., Jansen, P., and Silverman, L. (May, 2003). 'The Nonprofit Sector's $100 Billion Opportunity', *Harvard Business Review*: 3–11.

Brickell, P. (2000). *People Before Structures*. London: Demos.

Brinckerhoff, P. (2000). *Social Entrepreneurship: The Art of Mission-Based Venture Development*. New York: John Wiley & Sons.

Brock, D. (2006), *Social Entrepreneurship Teaching Resources Handbook*, Berea College.

Brockhaus, R. (1980). 'Risk Taking Propensity of Entrepreneurs', *Academy of Management Journal*, 23(3): 509–20.

Brooks, Z. (2002). *An Introduction to Business Planning for Nonprofits*, The Bridgespan Group. Available at: www.bridgespangroup.org

Brookes, M. (2002). *Funding Our Future II: Understand and Allocate Costs*. London: ACEVO.

Bruyat, C. and Julien, P.-A. (2000). 'Defining the Field of Research in Entrepreneurship', *Journal of Business Venturing*, 16: 165–80.

Bull, M. and Crompton, H. (2005). *Business Practices in Social Enterprise*. Manchester, UK: Manchester Metropolitan University Business School.

Burch, J. (1986). *Entrepreneurship*. New York: John Wiley & Sons.

Burrows, R. (ed.) (1991). *Deciphering the Enterprise Culture: Entrepreneurship, Petty Capitalism, and the Restructuring of Britain*. London and New York: Routledge.

Cabinet Office (2006), *Social Enterprise Action Plan: Scaling New Heights*, London: Office of The Third Sector, available at: http://www.cabinetoffice.gov.uk/third_sector/social_enterprise/action_plan.aspx

Carver, J. (1997). 'Creating a Mission that Makes a Difference', *CarverGuides*. San Francisco, CA: Jossey-Bass.

Callon, M. (1986). 'The Sociology of an Actor-Network', in M. Callon, J. Law, and A. Rip (eds.), *Mapping the Dynamics of Science and Technology*. Basingstoke, UK: MacMillan, pp. 1–16.

—— (1999). 'Actor-Network Theory—The Market Test', in J. Law and J. Hassard (eds.), *Actor Network Theory and After*. Oxford: Blackwell, pp. 35–49.

Casson, M. (1982). *Entrepreneur: An Economic Theory*. London: Edward Elgar.

Casson, M. (ed.) (1990). *Entrepreneurship*. London: Edward Elgar.

—— (1994). *The Economics of Business Culture*. Oxford: Clarendon Press.

—— (2005). 'Entrepreneurship', in D. Henderson (ed.), *The Concise Encyclopedia of Economics*. Liberty Fund: Library of Economics and Liberty. Available at: http://www.econlib.org/library/Enc/Entrepreneurship.html

Catford, J. (1998). 'Social Entrepreneurs Are Vital for Health Promotion—But They Need Supportive Environments Too', *Health Promotion International*, 13(2): 95–7.

Cerny, P. (2000). 'Political Agency in a Globalizing World: Toward a Structurational Approach', *European Journal of International Relations*, 6(4): 435–63.

Chait, R., Ryan, W., and Taylor, B. (2004). *Governance as Leadership: Reframing the Work of Nonprofit Boards*. New York: John Wiley & Sons.

Chamberlain, N. (1977). *Remaking American Values*. New York: Basic Books.

Chell, E. (2000). 'Towards Researching the 'Opportunistic Entrepreneur': A Social Constructionist Approach and Research Agenda', *European Journal of Work and Organizational Psychology*, 9(1): 63–80.

—— (2007), 'Social Enterprise and Entrepreneurship', *International Small Business Journal*, 25.1, pp. 5–26.

China Economic Review (2007), 'Giving Back, Corporate Style', August.

Chio, J. and Meehan, W. (2001). *Ashoka: Innovators for the Public (North America Program)*. Stanford, CA: Graduate School of Business, Stanford University. Case Number: SM-64.

Cho, A. (2006), 'Politics, Values, and Social Entrepreneurship: A Critical Appraisal', in Mair, J., Robinson, J., and Hockerts, K., *Social Enrepreneurship*, Palgrave MacMillan, pp. 34–56.

Clark, J. (ed.) (2003). *Globalising Civic Engagement*. London: Earthscan.

Clark, C. and Gaillard, J. (2003). *RISE Capital Market Report: The Double Bottom Line Private Equity Market in 2002–2003*. New York: Columbia Business School.

—— Rozenzweig, W., Long, D., and Olsen, S. (2004). *Double Bottom Line Project Report: Assessing Social Impact in Double Bottom Line Ventures*. New York: Rockefeller Foundation.

Collins, J. (2005). *Good to Great and the Social Sectors: A Monograph to Accompany Good to Great*. New York: HarperCollins.

—— and Porras, J. (July, 1989). 'Making Impossible Dreams Come True—A Guide to Demystifying Purpose, Mission and Vision and Putting Them to Work for You', *Stanford Business School Magazine*: 12–19.

—— —— (eds.) (2002). *Built to Last*. New York: HarperCollins.

Colby, S., Stone, N., and Carttar, P. (Fall, 2004). 'Zeroing in on Impact: In an Era of Declining Resources, Nonprofits Need to Clarify Their Intended Impact', *Stanford Social Innovation Review*: 24–33.

Commission on Unclaimed Assets (2006), *Social Investment Bank: A Consultation Paper*, available at: *http://www.unclaimedassets.org.uk/CUA_report_16pp.pdf*.

Community Wealth Ventures (2003). *Powering Social Change: Lessons on Community Wealth Generation for Nonprofit Sustainability*. Washington, DC: Community Wealth Ventures Inc.

Cone Communications and Roper Starch Worldwide (2002). *The 2002 Cone Corporate Citizenship Study: The Role of Cause Branding*. Boston, MA: Cone Communications and Roper Starch Worldwide.

Cunningham, K. and Ricks, M. (Summer, 2004). 'Why Measure: Nonprofits Use Metrics to Show That They Are Efficient, But What If Donors Don't Care?' *Stanford Social Innovation Review*: 44–51.

Dabson, B., Plastrik, P., and Turner, R. (2001). *Lessons from the Life and Death of the Virginia Eastern Shore Corporation*. Washington, DC: Corporation for Enterprise Development.

Dacanay, M. (2004). *Creating Space in the Market. Social Enterprise Stories from Asia*. Asian Institute of Management.

Dart, R. (2004). 'The Legitimacy of Social Enterprise', *Nonprofit Management and Leadership*, 14(4): 411–24.

—— (2005). *Unintended Consequences of Social Entrepreneurship: The Complex Structure and Effects of Radical Service Delivery Improvement in a Canadian Human Services Organization*, presented at the International Social Entrepreneurship Conference (ISERC), Barcelona, April.

Davis, G., McAdam, D., Scott, R., and Zald, M. (2005). *Social Movements and Organizational Theory*. Cambridge, UK: Cambridge University Press.

Davis, L., Etchart, N., Jara, M., and Milder, B. (2003). *Risky Business: The Impacts of Merging Mission and Market*. Santiago, Chile: NESsT.

Dees, J. G., and Battle Anderson, B. (2002). 'Blurring Sector Boundaries: Serving Social Purposes Through for-Profit Structures', *CASE Working Paper Series*, 2, Duke Fuqua School.

—— —— —— (2002). *Strategic Tools for Social Entrepreneurs: Enhancing the Performance of Your Enterprising Non-Profit*. New York: Wiley Non-Profit Series.

—— (2003). *Social Entrepreneurship Is About Innovation and Impact, Not Income*, discussion paper on Social Edge. Available at: http://skoll.socialedge.org/?293@218.2JjfaI3NaT-C.0@.1ad86d9e

—— Battle Anderson, B., Wei-Skillern, J. (Spring, 2004). 'Scaling Social Impact', *Stanford Social Innovation Review*: 24–32.

—— —— (2003). 'For-Profit Social Ventures', in M. Kourilsky and W. Walstad (eds.), *International Journal of Entrepreneurship Education: Special Edition: Social Entrepreneurship*. Senate Hall, pp. 1–26.

—— and Battle Anderson, B. (2006), 'Rhetoric, Reality, and Research: Building a Solid Foundation for the Practice of Social Entrepreneurship', in Nicholls, A. (ed), *Social Entrepreneurship: New Models of Sustainable Social Change*, Oxford University Press, pp. 144–68.

—— and Dolby, A. (1991). *Sources of Financing for New Nonprofit Ventures*. Harvard, MA: Harvard Business School, HBS 9-391-097 (revised 1996 by J. Elias).

—— (1994). *Social Enterprise: Private Initiatives for Common Good*. Harvard, MA: Harvard Business School Press.

—— (1996). *The Social Enterprise Spectrum: From Philanthropy to Commerce*. Harvard, MA: Harvard Business School Press.

—— and Elias, J., (1998). 'The Challenges of Combining Social and Commercial Enterprise', an essay on Norman Bowie's University–Business Partnerships: An Assessment, *Business Ethics Quarterly*, 8(1): 1–17.

—— (1998a). *The Meaning of Social Entrepreneurship*. Available at: http://faculty.fuqua.duke.edu/centers/case/files/dees-SE.pdf

—— (January–February, 1998b). 'Enterprising Nonprofits', *Harvard Business Review*: 76(1): 54–67.

Dees, J.G., Emerson, J., and Economy, P. (2001). *Enterprising Non-Profits: A Toolkit for Social Entrepreneurs*. New York: Wiley Non-Profit Series.

Defourny, J., Develtere, P., and Foneneau, B. (eds.) (2001). *Social Economy North and South*. Belgium: Katholieke Universiteit Leuven and Universite de Liege.

de Geus, A. (1997). *The Living Company*. Boston, MA: Harvard Business School Press.

Department for Trade and Industry (DTI), Social Enterprise Unit (2002). *Social Enterprise: A Strategy for Success*. London: DTI.

—— Social Enterprise Unit (2002), *Social Enterprise: A Strategy for Success*, London.

—— (2003). *Public Procurement: A Toolkit for Social Enterprises*. London: DTI.

—— Small Business Service (2004). *Lending to the Social Enterprise Sector*. London: DTI.

—— (2004). *Community Interest Companies: An Introduction to Community Interest Companies*. London: DTI.

—— (2005). *A Survey of Social Enterprises Across the UK*. London: Small Business Service, DTI.

DiMaggio, P. and Anheier, H. (1990). 'The Sociology of Nonprofit Organizations and Sectors', *Annual Review of Sociology*, 16: 137–59.

—— and Powell, W. (1983). 'The Iron Cage Revisited: Institutional Isomorphism and Collective Rationality in Organizational Fields', *American Sociological Review*, 48: 147–60.

Docteur, E. and Oxley, H. (2003). *Health-Care Systems: Lessons from the Reform Experience*. OECD Health Working Papers.

Dorado, S. (2006), 'Social Entrepreneurial Ventures: Different Values So Different Process of Creation, No?', *Journal of Developmental Entrepreneurship*, 11.4, pp. 319–44.

Dowie, M. (2001). *American Foundations: An Investigative History*. Cambridge: MIT Press.

Drayton, W. (2000). *The Entrepreneurs Revolution and You*, Available at: http://ashoka.org/fellows/entrepreneurs_revolution.cfm

—— (2006), 'The Citizens' Sector Transformed', in Nicholls, A. (ed), *Social Entrepreneurship: New Models of Sustainable Social Change*, Oxford University Press, pp. 45–55.

—— (2002). 'The Citizen Sector: Becoming as Entrepreneurial and Competitive as Business', *California Management Review*, 44(3): 120–32.

—— (2005). 'Where the Real Power Lies', *Alliance*, 10(1): 29–30.

Drucker, P. (1985). *Innovation and Entrepreneurship*. London: Harper-Business.

—— (July–August, 1989). 'What Businesses Can Learn from Nonprofits', *Harvard Business Review*: 88–93.

—— (1990). *Managing the Non-Profit Organization*. New York: HarperCollins.

Duccie, G., Stentella, C., and Vulterini, P. (2002). 'The Social Enterprise in Europe', *International Journal of Mental Health*, 13(3): 76–91.

Dunn, A. and Riley, C. (2004). 'Supporting the Not-for-Profit Sector: The Government's Review of Charitable and Social Enterprise', *The Modern Law Review*, 67(4): 632–57.

Ebrahim, A. (2003). *NGOs and Organizational Change: Discourse, Reporting and Learning*. Cambridge: Cambridge University Press.

Economist (2005a), 'Hale and Healthy', April 14th.

—— (2005b), 'Calling an End to Poverty', July 7th.

—— (2005c), 'Good for Me, Good for My Party', November 24th.

—— (2006a), 'The Rise of the Social Entrepreneur', February 23rd.

—— (2006b), 'Special Topic: The Business of Giving', February 23rd.

—— (2006c), 'The New Powers in Giving', June 29th.

—— (2006d), 'The Fight over a Big Idea', July 20th.

—— (2007a), 'Fish versus AIDS', August 30th.

—— (2007b), 'The Clinton Factor', September 25th.

Edwards, M. (2000). *NGO Rights and Responsibilities*. London: NCVO.

—— (2004). *Civil Society*. Cambridge: Polity Press.

—— and Hulme, D. (eds.) (1992). *Making a Difference: NGOs and Development in a Changing World*. London: Save the Children Fund/Earthscan.

—— and Sen, G. (2002). *NGOs, Social Change and the Transformation of Human Relationships: A 21st-Century Civic Agenda*.

Eikenberry, A. and Kluver, J. (2004). 'The Marketization of the Nonprofit Sector: Civil Society at Risk?' *Public Administration Review*, 64(2): 132–40.

Elkington, J. (2001). 'The Triple Bottom Line for 21st Century Business', in R. Strakely and R. Welford (eds.), *Business and Sustainable Development*. London: Earthscan, pp. 20–43.

Emerson, J. (1999a). 'Social Return on Investment: Exploring Aspects of Value Creation', in *REDF Box Set*, vol. 2, chapter 8. San Francisco, CA: Roberts Enterprises Development Fund.

—— (1999b). 'The US Non-Profit Capital Market', in *REDF Box Set*, vol. 2, chapter 10. San Francisco, CA: Roberts Enterprises Development Fund.

—— (1999c). 'Five Challenges in Social Purpose Enterprise Development', in *REDF Box Set*, vol. 2, chapter 11. San Francisco, CA: Roberts Enterprises Development Fund.

—— (2000). 'The Nature of Returns: A Social Capital Markets Inquiry into Elements of Investment and the Blended Value Proposition', *Social Enterprise Series*, 17. Harvard, MA: Harvard Business School.

—— and Beceren, M. (2001). *Frontiers in Social Investing and Finance: Understanding and Exploring the Social Value Note*.

—— (May–June, 2002). 'Horse Manure and Grantmaking', *Foundation News & Commentary*, 43(4): 22–3.

—— (2003a). 'The Blended Value Proposition: Integrating Social and Financial Returns', *California Management Review*, 45(4): 35–51.

—— (2003b). *The Blended Value Map*. Available at: www.blendedvalue.org

—— (Summer, 2003c). 'Where Money Meets Mission: Breaking Down the Firewall Between Foundation Investments and Programming', *Stanford Social Innovation Review*: 38–47.

—— and Bonini, S. (2004). *The Blended Value Map: Tracking the Intersects and Opportunities of Economic, Social and Environmental Value Creation*. Available at: http://www.blendedvalue.org/Papers/97.aspx

—— Freundlich, T., and Fruchterman, J. (2007), *Nothing Ventured*, Skoll Centre for Social Entrepreneurship, available at: http://www.sbs.ox.ac.uk/skoll/research/Short+papers/Short+papers.htm

Bibliography

Emerson, J. and Twersky, F. (1996). *New Social Entrepreneurs: The Success, Challenge and Lessons of Non-Profit Enterprise Creation*. San Francisco, CA: Roberts Enterprises Development Fund.

—— Freundlich, T., and Berenbach, S. (2004). *The Investor's Toolkit*. Available at: www.blendedvalue.org

—— Freundlich, T. (2007), *Nothing Ventured*, Skoll Centre for Social Entrepreneurship, available at: http://www.sbs.ox.ac.uk/skoll/research/Short+papers/Short+papers.htm

—— and Spitzer, J. (2007), *From Fragmentation to Functionality*, Skoll Centre for Social Entrepreneurship, available at: http://www.sbs.ox.ac.uk/skoll/research/Short+papers/Short+papers.htm

Etchart, N., and Davis, L. (2002). *Legal Guide: CSO Self-Financing in Chile*. Santiago, Chile: NESsT.

—— —— (2003). *Unique and Universal: Lessons from the Emerging Field of Social Enterprise in the Emerging Market Countries*. Santiago, Chile: NESsT.

Etzioni, A. (1961). *A Comparative Analysis of Complex Organizations*. New York: Free Press.

—— (1973). 'The Third Sector and Domestic Missions', *Public Administration Review*, 33: 314–23.

Firstenberg, P. (1986). *Managing for Profit in the Not-For-Profit World*. New York: Foundation Center.

Foster, W. and Bradach, J. (February, 2005). 'Should Nonprofits Seek Profits?', *Harvard Business Review*: 92–100.

Fraser, N. (1992). 'Rethinking the Public Sphere: A Contribution to the Critique of Actually Existing Democracy', in C. Calhoun (ed.), *Habermas and the Public Sphere*. Cambridge, MA: MIT Press, pp. 109–42.

Fremont-Smith, M. (2004). *Governing Nonprofit Organizations: Federal and State Law and Regulation*. Harvard University: Belknap Press of Harvard University Press.

Frumkin, P. (2002). *On Being Nonprofit: A Conceptual and Policy Primer*. Harvard University: Harvard University Press.

—— (2003). *Creating New Schools: The Strategic Management of Charter Schools*. Annie E. Casey Foundation. Available at: www.aecf.org

—— (2006). *Strategic Giving*. Chicago, IL: University of Chicago Press.

Fukyama, F. (1995). *Trust: The Social Virtues and the Creation of Prosperity*. London: Penguin.

Gair, C. (2002). *Report from the Good Ship SROI*. San Francisco, CA: Roberts Enterprise Development Fund. Available at: www.redf.org

—— (2005). 'If the Shoes Fits: Nonprofit or For-Profit? The Choice matters', San Francisco: REDF.

Gartner, W. (1988). 'Who is the Entrepreneur? Is the Wrong Question', *American Journal of Small Business*, 12: 11–32.

Gertner, J. (2002). 'A New World Order: Jed Emerson's Capitalist Utopia. Can Social Value Reward Investors Companies?', *CNN Money Magazine*, 29 October. Available at http://money.cnn.com/2002/10/28/pf/investing/emerson/

Giddens, A. (1984). *The Constitution of Society*. Berkeley, CA: University of California Press.

—— (1990). *The Consequences of Modernity*. UK: Polity Press.

—— (1998). *The Third Way*. Cambridge: Polity Press.

—— (2000). *The Third Way and Its Critics*. Cambridge: Polity Press.

Gill, R. (1992). *Moral Communities*. Exeter, UK: University of Exeter Press.

Global Social Venture Competition (2003a). *Social Impact Assessment Guide 2: Defining Social Value and Social Indicators.*

—— (2003b). *Social Impact Assessment Guide 3: Monetizing Social Value / SROI.*

GlobeScan (2002). *The 2003 Corporate Social Responsibility Monitor.* Toronto: GlobeScan.

Grant, W. (1993). *The Politics of Economic Policy.* London: Harvester Wheatsheaf.

—— and Nath, S. (1984). *The Politics of Economic Policy Making.* Oxford: Blackwell.

Granovetter, M. (1985). 'Economic Action and Social Structure: The Problem of Embeddedness', *American Journal of Sociology,* 91: 481–510.

Graves, R. (1952). *The White Goddess.* London: Faber & Faber.

Greider, W. (2003). *The Soul of Capitalism: Opening Paths to a Moral Economy.* New York: Simon & Schuster.

Grossman, A., Letts, C., and Ryan, W. (1999). *High Performance Nonprofit Organisations.* New York: John Wiley & Sons.

Guclu, A., Dees, J., and Battle Anderson, B. (2002). 'The Process of Social Entrepreneurship: Creating Opportunities Worthy of Serious Pursuit', *CASE Working Paper Series,* 3. Duke Fuqua School.

Guthrie, J. (2006), 'Let this social enterprise malarkey bloom', *Financial Times Comment,* May 25th.

Guthrie, D. (2007), 'Social Entrepreneurship and Innovation in China', paper presented at the International Forum on Social Entrepreneurship, Hangzhou, May 27th.

Habermas, J. (1989). *The Structural Transformation of the Public Sphere.* Cambridge, MA: MIT Press.

Habgood, J. (1997). *Faith and Uncertainty.* London: Dalton, Longman and Todd.

Halpern, D. (2005). *Social Capital.* London: Polity Press.

Hammack, D. (ed.) (1998). *Making the Nonprofit Sector in the United States.* Bloomington, IN: Indiana University Press.

Handy, C. (1997). *The Hungry Spirit.* London: Hutchinson.

Hanlon, G. (1998). 'Professionalism as Enterprise', *Sociology,* 32(1): 43–63.

Hannah, L. (1980). 'Questions and Discussion', in A. Sheldon (ed.), *The Prime Mover of Progress.* London: IEA, pp. 127–8.

Hansmann, H. (1996a). 'The Changing Roles of Public, Private, and Nonprofit Enterprise in Education, Health Care, and Other Human Services', in V. Fuchs (ed.), *Individual and Social Responsibility: Child Care, Education, Medical Care, and Long-Term Care in America.* Chicago, IL: University of Chicago Press, pp. 245–71.

—— (1996b). *The Ownership of Enterprise.* Boston, MA: Harvard University Press.

Harding, R. (2004). 'Social Enterprise: The New economic Engine?' *Business Strategy Review,* 15(4): 39–43.

—— and Cowling, M. (2004). *Social Entrepreneurship Monitor: United Kingdom 2004.* London: Global Entrepreneurship Monitor.

—— and —— (2006), *Social Entrepreneurship Monitor: United Kingdom 2006,* London: Global Entrepreneurship Monitor.

Hargrave, T., and Van de Ven, A. (2005), 'A Collective Action Model of Institutional Innovation', *Academy of Management Review,* 31.4, pp. 864–88.

Harold, J., Spitzer, J., and Emerson J. (2007), *Blended Value Investing: Integrating Environmental Risks and Opportunities into Securities Valuation',* Skoll Centre for Social Entrepreneurship, available at: http://www.sbs.ox.ac.uk/skoll/research/Short+papers/Short+papers.htm

421

Bibliography

Harris, J. (1994). *Private Lives, Public Spirit: Britain 1870–1915*. London: Penguin.

Hartigan, P. (2002). *Social Entrepreneurship: What is it?* Available at http://www.schwab-found.org/news.htm?articleid=30&sid=10

Harvard Business Review (1994). *On Nonprofits*. Harvard: Harvard Business School Press.

Hartzell, J. (2007), *Creating An Ethical Stock Exchange*, Skoll Centre for Social Entrepreneurship, available at: http://www.sbs.ox.ac.uk/skoll/research/Short+papers/Short+papers.htm

Haugh, H. (2007), 'New Strategies for a Sustainable Society: The Growing Contribution of Social Entrepreneurship', *Business Ethics Quarterly*, 17.4, pp.743–9.

Hawken, P. (1987). *Growing a Business*. New York: Simon & Schuster.

—— Lovins, A., and Lovins, L. (2001). *Natural Capitalism*. London: Earthscan.

Hayek, F. (1967). *Studies in Philosophy, Politics and Economics*. London and New York: Routledge.

—— (1986). *The Road to Serfdom*. London: Ark (1st pub. 1942).

Hemingway, C. (2005). 'Personal Values as a Catalyst for Corporate Social Entrepreneurship', *Journal of Business Ethics*, 60: 233–49.

Henton, D., Melville, J., and Walesh, K. (1997). 'The Age of the Civic Entrepreneur: Restoring Civil Society and Building Economic Community', *National Civic Review*, 86(2): 149–56.

Hirsch, R. and Peters, M. (1998). *Entrepreneurship*. Boston, MA: Irwin/McGraw-Hill.

Hjorth, D. and Steyaert, C. (2004). *Narrative and Discursive Approaches in Entrepreneurship. A Second Movement in Entrepreneurship Book*. Cheltenham, UK: Edward Elgar.

—— Johannisson, B., and Steyaert, C. (2003). 'Entrepreneurship as Discourse and Life Style', in B. Czarniawska and G. Sevón (eds.), *The Northern Lights*. Copenhagen: Copenhagen Business School Press, pp. 91–110.

Hobbs, D. (1988). *Doing the Business*. Oxford: Oxford University Press.

—— (1991). 'Business as a Master Metaphor: Working Class Entrepreneurship and Business-like Policing', in R. Burrows (ed.), *Deciphering the Enterprise Culture: Entrepreneurship, Petty Capitalism and the Restructuring of Britain*. London and New York: Routledge, pp. 107–25.

Hodgkinson, V., Weitzman, M., Toppe, C., and Noga, S. (1992). *Not-For-Profit Almanac 1992–1993: Dimensions of the Independent Sector*. San Francisco, CA: Jossey-Bass.

Home Office (2004a). *Citizenship Survey: People, Families and Communities*. London: Home Office.

—— (2004b). *Patient Capital*. London: Civic Renewal Unit.

Husock, H. (July–August, 2004). 'New Ideas People', *The Philanthropy Roundtable*. Available at www.philanthropyroundtable.org

Hutton, W. (1996). *The State We're In*. London: Vintage.

—— Giddens, A. (eds.) (2001). *On the Edge: Living with Global Capitalism*. London: Vintage.

Institute for Social Entrepreneurs (2005). *Social Entrepreneurship: A Glossary of Useful Terms*. Available at: http://www.socialent.org/pdfs/GLOSSARY.pdf

Jack, A. (2007), 'Beyond charity? A new generation enters the business of doing good', *Financial Times*, April 5th.

Jackson, E., Draimin, T., and Rosene, C. (1999). 'A Window on the Future of Partnerships', *Civil Society*, 2: 56–74.

Jacobs, A. (2006), 'Helping People is Difficult: Growth and Performance in Social Enterprises Working for International Relief and Development', in Nicholls, A. (ed), *Social Entrepreneurship: New Models of Sustainable Social Change*, Oxford University Press, pp. 247–69.

Jain, P. and Moore, M. (2003). 'What Makes Microcredit Programmes Effective? Fashionable Fallacies and Workable Realities', in *IDS Working Paper*, 177. University of Sussex: Institute of Development Studies.

James, E. (1989). *The Nonprofit Sector in International Perspective*. Yale, CT: Yale Studies on Nonprofit Organizations.

—— and Rose-Ackerman, S. (1986). *The Non-Profit Enterprise in Market Economics*. London: Routledge.

—— (2003). 'Commercialism and the Mission of Nonprofits', *Social Science and Modern Society*, 40(4): 29–35.

Jepson, P. (2005). 'Governance and Accountability of Environmental NGOs', *Environmental Science and Policy*, 8: 515–24.

John, R. (2006), *Venture Philanthropy: The Evolution of High Engagement Philanthropy in Europe*, Skoll Centre for Social Entrepreneurship, available at: http://www.sbs.ox.ac.uk/skoll/research/Short+papers/Short+papers.htm

—— (2007), *Beyond The Cheque: How Venture Philanthropists Add Value*, Skoll Centre for Social Entrepreneurship, available at: http://www.sbs.ox.ac.uk/skoll/research/Short+papers/Short+papers.htm

Johnson, S. (2000). 'Literature Review on Social Entrepreneurship', *Canadian Centre for Social Entrepreneurship Discussion Paper*. Available at: http://www.bus.ualberta.ca/ccse/WhatIs/Lit.%20Review%20SE%20November%202000.rtf

Jones, T. (May, 1994). 'A Customer by Any Other Name: Rethinking the Donor Relationship', *Advancing Philanthropy*: 12–18.

Joyce, P. (2003). *The Rule of Freedom*. London: Verso.

Hines, F. (2005). 'Viable Social Enterprise—An Evaluation of Business Support to Social Enterprises', *Social Enterprise Journal*, 1(1): 13–28.

Kaldor, M. (2003). *Global Civil Society: An Answer to War*. London: Polity Press.

—— Anheier, H., and Glasius, M. (eds.) (2003). *Global Civil Society Yearbook 2003*. Oxford: Oxford University Press.

Kanter, R. (May–June,1999). 'From Spare Change to Real Change. The Social Sector as Beta Site for Business Innovation', *Harvard Business Review*: 122–32.

Kaplan, A. (ed.) (1995). *Giving USA 1995: The Annual Report on Philanthropy for the Year 1994*. New York: AAFRC Trust for Philanthropy.

Kaplan, R., and Norton, D. (1996). *The Balanced Scorecard*. Boston, MA: Harvard Business School Press.

—— (2002). 'The Balanced Scorecard and Nonprofit Organizations', *Balanced Scorecard Report*: 2–6.

Keane, J. (2003). *Global Civil Society?* Cambridge, MA: Cambridge University Press.

Kelly, G., Mulgan, G., and Muers, S. (2002). *Creating Public Value: An Analytical Framework for Public Service Reform*. London: Prime Minister's Strategy Unit.

Kennedy, C. (2001). *Business Pioneers: Sainsbury, John Lewis, Cadbury*. London: Random House.

Kent, C., Sexton, D., and Vesper, K. (1982). *Encyclopaedia of Entrepreneurship*. New Jersey, NJ: Prentice-Hall.

Kim, M., and Davis, S. (2007), *Social Entrepreneurship Faculty Directory*, Ashoka Global Academy.

Kirby, D. (2003). *Entrepreneurship*. London: McGraw-Hill Education.

Kirchoff, B. (1997). 'Entrepreneurship Economics', in *The Portable MBA in Entrepreneurship*, 2nd edn. New York: John Wiley & Sons.

Klausner, M. (Spring, 2003). 'When Time Isn't Money: Foundation Payouts and the Time Value of Money', *Stanford Social Innovation Review*: 51–9.

Klein, N. (2007), *The Shock Doctrine*, Penguin.

Kramer, M. (2005). *Measuring Innovation: Evaluation in the Field of Social Entrepreneurship*. Skoll Foundation, Boston: Foundation Strategy Group.

Kriesi, H. (1995). *New Social Movements in Western Europe: A Comparative Analysis*. London: University College Press.

Kuhn, T. (1962). *The Structure of Scientific Revolutions*. University of Chicago: International Encyclopaedia of Unified Science.

Kotler, P. and Andreasen, A. (1995). *Strategic Marketing for Non-Profit Organisations,* 5th edn. New York: Prentice-Hall.

LaPiere, R. (1965). *Social Change*. London: McGraw-Hill.

Lasprogata, G. and Cotton, M. (2003). 'Contemplating 'Enterprise': The Business and Legal Challenges of Social Entrepreneurship', *American Business Law Journal*, 41(1): 67–114.

Latour, B. (2005). *Reassembling the Social: An Introduction to Actor-Network-Theory*. Oxford: Clarendon Lectures in Management Studies.

Leadbeater, C. (1997). *The Rise of the Social Entrepreneur*. London: Demos.

—— and Goss, S. (1998). *Civic Entrepreneurs*. London: Demos.

Leat, D. (1993). *Managing Across Sectors: Similarities and Differences Between For-Profit and Voluntary Non-Profit Organizations*. London: Centre for Voluntary Sector and Not-for-Profit Management, City University.

—— (2003). *Replicating Successful Voluntary Sector Projects*. London: Association of Charitable Foundations.

LeGrand, J., and Bartlett, W. (eds.) (1993). *Quasi-Markets and Social Policy*. Basingstoke, UK: Palgrave Macmillan.

—— (2003). *Motivation, Agency, and Public Policy: Of Knights and Knaves, Pawns and Queens*. Oxford: Oxford University Press.

—— (2007), *The Other Invisible Hand*, Princeton University Press.

Letts, C., Ryan, W., and Grossman, A. (March–April, 1997). 'Virtuous Capital: What Foundations Can Learn From Venture Capital', *Harvard Business Review*. 36–44.

—— —— —— (1999). *High Performance Nonprofit Organizations: Managing Upstream for Greater Impact*. New York: John Wiley & Sons.

Lewis, D. and Wallace, T. (eds.) (2003). *New Roles and Relevance: Development NGOs and the Challenge of Change*. London: Kumarian Press.

Light, P. (1998). *Sustaining Innovation: Creating Nonprofit and Government Organizations that Innovate Naturally*. San Francisco, CA: Jossey-Bass.

—— (2002). *Pathways to Nonprofit Excellence*. Washington, DC: Brookings Institution Press.

Lindle, J., Lingane, A., and Walters, L. (2000). *Social Return on Investment: A Practitioners Perspective*. Berkeley, CA: Haas Business School. Available at: http://www.haas.berkeley.edu/groups/socialventure

Lister, S. (2003). 'NGO Legitimacy—Technical Issue or Social Construct?' *Critique of Anthropology*, 23: 175–92.

Mair, J., and Marti, I., and Schoen, O. (2005). *Social Entrepreneurial Business Models: An Exploratory Study*, IESE Working Paper Series 610.

—— Seelos, C. (May–June, 2005). 'Social Entrepreneurship: Creating New Business Models to Serve the Poor', *Business Horizons*, 48(3): 241–6.

—— Marti, I. (2006). 'Social Entrepreneurship Research: a Source of Explanation, Prediction, and Delight', *Journal of World Business*, 41: 36–44.

—— —— Borwankar, A. (2004). 'Social Entrepreneurial Initiatives Within the Sustainable Development Landscape', *International Journal of Entrepreneurship Education*, 2(4): 1–14.

—— Robinson, J., and Hockerts, K. (2006). *Social Entrepreneurship*. Basingstoke, UK: Palgrave MacMillan.

—— and Seelos, C. (forthcoming), 'Profitable Business Models and Market Creation in the Context of Deep Poverty: A Strategic View', *Academy of Management Perspectives*.

Makower, J. (1994). *Beyond the Bottom Line*. New York: Simon & Schuster.

Mancino, A. and Thomas, A. (2005). 'An Italian Pattern of Social Enterprise: The Social Cooperative', *Nonprofit Management and Leadership*, 15(3): 357–69.

March, J. (1991). 'Exploration and Exploitation in Organizational Learning', *Organization Science*, 2(1): 71–87.

Martin, M. (2002). 'Between Entrepreneurship and Surveillance: an Interpretive Political Economy Perspective on the Globalizing Organization', *Entwicklungsethnologie*, 11(1): 83–110.

—— (2004). 'Surveying Social Entrepreneurship: Toward an Empirical Analysis of the Performance Revolution in the Social Sector', *Arbeitspapiere Band 2*, University of St Gallen.

Martin, R. (March, 2002). 'The Virtue Matrix: Calculating the Return on Corporate Responsibility', *Harvard Business Review*: 3–9.

Maslow, A. (1973). *The Farther Reaches of Human Nature*. Harmondsworth, UK: Penguin.

Maxwell, J. (2002). *Failing Forward: Turning Mistakes into Stepping-Stones for Success*. Nashville, TN: Thomas Nelson Publishers.

McCarthy, H., Miller, P., and Skidmore, P. (2004). *Network Logic*. London: Demos.

McClelland, D. (1961). *The Achieving Society*. Princeton, NJ: Van Nostrand.

McIlnay, D. (1998). *How Foundations Work*. San Francisco, CA: Jossey-Bass.

McKinsey & Company (2001). *Effective Capacity Building in Nonprofit Organizations*. Washington, DC: Venture Philanthropy Partners.

McLaughlin, T. (1998). 'Social Enterprise: Everyone Can and Should Learn From It', *Nonprofit Times*, 13: 18.

Meehan III, W., Kilmer, D., and O'Flanagan, M. (Spring, 2004). 'Investing in Society', *Stanford Social Innovation Review*: 35–41.

Meyer, J. (2000). 'The 'Actors' of Modern Society: The Cultural Construction of Social Agency', *Sociological Theory*, 18(1): 110–20.

—— and Scott, R. (1992). *Organizational Environments: Ritual and Rationality*, Newbury Park, CA: Sage.

—— and Zucker, L. (1989). *Permanently Failing Organizations*. Newbury Park, CA: Sage.

Moore, G. (2004). 'The Fair Trade Movement: Parameters, Issues and Future Research', *Journal of Business Ethics*, 53: 73–86.

Moore, M. (1995). *On Creating Public Value: Strategic Management in Government.* Harvard University: Harvard University Press.

Morrin, M., Simmonds, D., and Sommerville, W. (2004). 'Social Enterprise: Mainstreamed from the Margins?' *Local Economy,* 19(1): 69–84.

Mosher-Williams, R. (2006). *Social Entrepreneurship Issues: Research on an Emerging Field,* ARNOVA Occasional Papers, vol. 3. Colorado: Aspen Institute.

Mosher-Williams, R. (2007), *Research on Social Entrepreneurship: Understanding and Contributing to an Emerging Field,* ARNOVA.

—— (2007), *Research on Social Entrepreneurship: Understanding and Contributing to an Emerging Field,* ARNOVA

Mulgan, G. (2005). *Value Maps.* London: Commission on Architecture and the Built Environment.

National Council for Voluntary Organisations (NCVO) and Landry, C. (1996). *The Other Invisible Hand.* London: Demos.

—— (2007), *UK Voluntary Sector Almanac 2007.*

—— (2007), *Social Innovation,* Skoll Centre for Social Entrepreneurship, available at http://www.sbs.ox.ac.uk/skoll/research/Short+papers/Short+papers.htm

Nelson, S. (1999). 'What Can Managers Learn From Nonprofits?' *Harvard Management Update,* No. U9912B. Harvard, MA: Harvard Business School.

Nicholls, A. (2004). 'Social Entrepreneurship: The Emerging Landscape', in S. Crainer and D. Dearlove (eds.), *Financial Times Handbook of Management,* 3rd edn. Harlow, UK: FT Prentice-Hall, pp. 636–43.

—— and Cho, A. (2006) 'Social Entrepreneurship: The Structuration of a Field', in Nicholls, A. (ed), *Social Entrepreneurship: New Models of Sustainable Social Change,* Oxford University Press, pp. 99–118.

—— and Opal, C. (2005). *Fair Trade: Market-Driven Ethical Consumption.* London: Sage.

—— Jepson, P., and Jacobs, A. (2006). *Improving the Performance of Social Organizations: Legitimacy as a Tool for Analysis and Strategic Management,* Skoll Centre for Social Entrepreneurship Working Paper.

—— (2006). 'Social Entrepreneurship', in D. Jones-Evans and S. Carter (eds.), *Enterprise and Small Business: Principles, Practice and Policy,* 2nd edn. (forthcoming). Harlow, UK: FT Prentice-Hall.

—— Nicholls, J. (2007), 'Social Impact Measurement and Planning for Innovation', paper presented at the 3rd International Social Entrepreneurship Conference, Copenhagen, June 18th.

—— (2008), 'Capturing the Performance of the Socially Entrepreneurial Organisation (SEO): An Organisational Legitimacy Approach', in Robinson, J., Mair, J., and Hockerts, K. (eds), *International Perspectives on Social Entrepreneurship Research,* Palgrave MacMillan (forthcoming).

—— Moore, M. (forthcoming), 'The Competitive Advantage of Organizational Legitimacy: Lessons for Business from Social Entrepreneurship', Skoll Centre for Social Entrepreneurship.

Nicholls, J. (2004). *Social Return on Investment: Valuing What Matters.* London: New Economics Foundation.

—— (2006), 'Playing the Field: A New Approach to the Meaning of Social Entrepreneurship', *Social Enterprise Journal,* 2.1, pp. 1–5.

—— and Pharoah, C. (2007), *The Landscape of Social Finance*, Skoll Centre for Social Entrepreneurship, available at: http://www.sbs.ox.ac.uk/skoll/research/Short+papers/Short+papers.htm

—— (2007), *What is the Future of Social Enterprise in Ethical Markets?*, London, Office of The Third Sector, available at: http://www.cabinetoffice.gov.uk/third_sector/Research _and_statistics/social_enterprise_research/think_pieces.aspx

Nielsen, W. (1996). *Inside American Philanthropy: The Dramas of Donorship*. Norman, OK: University of Oklahoma Press.

Nyssens, M. (ed) (2007), *Social Enterprise*, Routledge.

Oberfield, A. and Dees, G. (January, 1991). 'A Note on Starting a Nonprofit Venture', *Harvard Business School 9–391–096*. Harvard, MA: Harvard Business School.

Offer, A. (2006), *The Challenge of Affluence*, Oxford University Press.

Osborne, S. (1998). *Voluntary Organizations and Innovation in Public Services*. London: Routledge.

Osbourne, D. and Gaebler, T. (1992). *Reinventing Government*. Reading, MA: Addison-Wesley.

Oster, S. (1995). *Strategic Management for Nonprofit Organisations: Theory and Cases*. Oxford: Oxford University Press.

—— Massarsky, C., and Beinhacker, S. (2004). *Generating and Sustaining Nonprofit Earned Income*. San Francisco, CA: Jossey-Bass.

Ostrower, D. (Spring, 2005). 'The Reality Underneath the Buzz of Partnerships', *Stanford Social Innovation Review*, 34–41.

Parsons, S. (1988). 'Economic Principles in the Public and Private Sectors', *Policy and Politics*, 16(1): 29–39.

Paton, R. (2003). *Managing and Measuring Social Enterprises*. London: Sage.

Paul C. Light, P. (2006), 'Reshaping Social Entrepreneurship', *Stanford Social Innovation Review*, Fall, pp. 47–52.

Pearce, J. and Kay, A. (2003). *Social Enterprise in Anytown*. London: Calouste Gulbenkian Foundation.

Peredo, A., Chrisman, J. (2006), 'Towards a Theory of Community-Based Enterprise', *Academy of Management Review*, 31.2, pp. 309–38.

—— and McLean, M. (2006), 'Social enterpreneurship: A critical review of the concept', *Journal of World Business*, 41, pp. 56–65.

Perkin, H. (1992). 'The enterprise culture in historical perspective: birth, life, death—and resurrection?' in P. Heelas, and P. Morris, (eds.), *The Values of Enterprise Culture: A Moral Debate*. London and New York: Routledge, pp. 36–60.

Perrini, F. (ed) (2007), *The New Social Entrepreneurship*, Edward Elgar.

Pfeffer, J. and Salanick, G. (1978). *The External Control of Organizations: A Resource Dependence Perspective*. New York: Harper & Row.

Pharoah, C., Scott, D., and Fisher, A. (2004). *Social Enterprise in the Balance: Challenges for the Voluntary Sector*. West Malling, UK: Charities Aid Foundation.

Pointer, D. and Orlikoff, J. (2002). *The High-Performance Board*. San Francisco, CA: Jossey-Bass.

Porter, M. and Kramer, M. (December, 2002). 'The Competitive Advantage of Corporate Philanthropy', *Harvard Business Review*: 3–14.

Powell, W. (1987). *The Nonprofit Sector: A Research Handbook*. Yale, CT: Yale University Press.

Bibliography

Prahalad, C. and Hart, S. (2004). *The Fortune at the Bottom of the Pyramid: Eradicating Poverty Through Profit*. University of Pennsylvania: Wharton School Publishing.

Putnam, R. (1994). *Making Democracy Work: Civic Traditions in Modern Italy*. Princeton, NJ: Princeton University Press.

—— (2001). *Bowling Alone*. New York: Simon & Schuster.

—— (ed.) (2004). *Democracies in Flux: The Evolution of Social Capital in Contemporary Society*. New York: Oxford University Press.

Raynolds, L., Murray, D., and Wilkinson, J. (2007), *Fair Trade. The Challenges of Transforming Globalization*, Routledge.

—— —— —— (eds) (2007), *Fair Trade. The Challenges of Transforming Globalization*, Routledge

Reis, T. and Clohesy, S. (1999). *Unleashing New Resources and Entrepreneurship for the Common Good: A Scan, Synthesis, and Scenario for Action*. New York: Kellogg Foundation.

Renard, M.-C. (2002). 'Fair Trade Quality, Market and Conventions', *Journal of Rural Studies*, 19: 87–96.

Ridderstrale, J. and Nordström, K. (2004). *Karaoke Capitalism: Management for Mankind*. London: Prentice-Hall.

Ridley-Duff, R. (2007), 'Communitarian Perspectives on Social Enterprise', *Corporate Governance*, 15.2, pp. 382–93.

Roberts Enterprise Development Fund (REDF) (1999). *Social Purpose Enterprises and Venture Philanthropy in the New Millennium—Practitioner Perspectives*. San Francisco, CA: Roberts Enterprises Development Fund.

—— (2002). *An Information OASIS: The Design and Implementation of Comprehensive and Customized Client Information and Tracking Systems*. San Francisco, CA: REDF.

Robinson, J., Mair, J., and Hockerts, K. (eds), *International Perspectives on Social Entrepreneurship Research*, Palgrave MacMillan.

Rockefeller Foundation (2003). *Social Impact Assessment: A Discussion Among Grantmakers*. New York: Rockefeller Foundation.

Rose, N. (2003). *The Powers of Freedom*. Cambridge: Cambridge University Press.

Ryan, W. (January–February, 1999). 'The New Landscape for Non-Profits', *Harvard Business Review*: 127–36.

Sacks, J. (2002). *The Money Trail. Measuring Your Impact on the Local Economy Using LM3*. London: New Economics Foundation.

Sagawa, S. (2000). *Common Interest, Common Good: Creating Value Through Business and Social Sector Partnerships*. Boston, MA: Harvard Business School Press.

Salamon, L. (1994). 'The Rise of the Nonprofit Sector', *Foreign Affairs*, 73(4): 109–22.

—— (1997). *Holding the Center: America's Nonprofit Sector at the Crossroads*. Cummings Foundation.

—— (2000). *The Tools of Government*. Oxford: Oxford University Press.

—— (2003). *The Resilient Sector: The State of Nonprofit America*. Washington, DC: Brookings Institution Press.

—— and Anheier, H. (1999). *The Emerging Sector Revisited*. Baltimore, MD: Johns Hopkins University.

Salamon, L., and Anheier, H. (1997), *Defining the Nonprofit Sector: A Cross-National Analysis*, Manchester University Press.

—— Sokolowski, M., and List, R. (2003). *Global Civil Society: An Overview*. Baltimore, MD: Kumarian Press.

—— Anheier, H., List, R., Toepler, S., and Sokolowski, W. (eds.) (2003). *Global Civil Society: Dimensions of the Non-Profit Sector*. Baltimore, MD: Johns Hopkins University.

Sanfillipo, L., and Lawlor (2007), 'Measuring Real Value: A DIY Guide to Social Return on Investment', New Economics Foundation, available at: http://www.neweconomics.org/gen/z_sys_PublicationDetail.aspx?pid=241

Sawhill, J. (2001). 'Mission Impossible? Measuring Success in Nonprofit Organizations', *Nonprofit Management and Leadership*: 36–44.

—— and Williamson, D. (2001). 'Measuring What Matters in Nonprofits', *McKinsey Quarterly*, 2: 98–107.

Say, J.-B. (2001). M. Quddus and S. Rashid (eds.). *A Treatise on Political Economy*, London: Transaction Publishing.

Schumpeter, J. (1950). *Capitalism, Socialism, and Democracy*, 3rd edn. New York: Harper & Row.

—— (1980). *Theory of Economic Development*. London: Transaction Publishing.

Scott, W. (2001). *Institutions and Organizations*, 2nd edn. London: Sage.

Schoening, M. (2003). *Global Trends in Financing the Social Sector*. Geneva: Schwab Foundation.

Shane, S. and Venkataraman, S. (2000). 'The Promise of Entrepreneurship as a Field of Research', *Academy of Management Review*, 25(1): 217–26.

Shaw, E. (2004). 'Marketing in the Social Enterprise Context: Is It Entrepreneurial?' *Qualitative Market Research: An International Journal*, 7(3): 194–205.

—— Carter, S. (2007), 'Social entrepreneurship; Theoretical antecedents and empirical analysis of entrepreneurial processes and outcomes', *Journal of Small Business and Enterprise Development*, 14.3, pp. 418–29.

Sheldon, A. (ed.). *The Prime Mover of Progress*. London: IEA.

Shore, B. (1995). *Revolution of the Heart: A New Strategy for Creating Wealth and Meaningful Change*. New York: Riverhead Books.

Silvia Dorado, S. (2006), 'Social Entrepreneurial Ventures: Different Values So Different Process of Creation, No?', *Journal of Developmental Entrepreneurship*, 11.4, pp. 319–44.

Skocpol, T. (2003). *Diminished Democracy: From Membership to Management in American Civic Life*. Oklahoma, OK: University of Oklahoma Press.

Smallbone, D., Evans, M., Ekanem, I., and Butters, S. (2001). *Researching Social Enterprise: Final Report to the Small Business Service*. Middlesex University: Centre for Enterprise and Economic Development Research.

Social Enterprise Coalition (2003). *There's More to Business Than You Think. A Guide to Social Enterprise*. London: SEC.

—— (2004). *Unlocking the Potential: A Guide to Finance for Social Enterprises*. London: SEC.

Social Enterprise London (SEL) (2000). *Enterprise for Communities—Creating Sustainable Social Enterprises*. London: SEL.

Social Enterprise Zones Task Force (2007), *Social Enterprise Zones*, Conservative Party, available at: http://www.conservatives.com/pdf/socialenterprise.pdf

Spear, R. and Bidet, E. (2003). *The Role of Social Enterprise in European Labour Markets*, EMES Working Papers Series 3/10.

—— (2005). 'Social Enterprise for Work Integration in 12 European Countries: A Descriptive Analysis', *Annals of Public and Cooperative Economics*, 76(2): 195–231.

Spence, L., Habisch, A., and Schmidpeter, R. (2005). *Responsibility and Social Capital*. Basingstoke, UK: Palgrave Macmillan.

Spengler, J. and Ford, T. (2002). *From the Environmentally Challenged City to the Ecological City.* Available at: http://www.earthscape.org/p3/ger01/ger02.pdf

Spinosa, C., Flores, F., and Dreyfus, H. (1997). *Disclosing New Worlds: Entrepreneurship, Democratic Action, and the Cultivation of Solidarity.* Cambridge, MA: MIT Press.

Spitzer, J., Emerson J., and Harold, J. (2007), *Blended Value Investing: Innovations in Real Estate,* Skoll Centre for Social Entrepreneurship, available at: http://www.sbs.ox.ac.uk/skoll/research/Short+papers/Short+papers.htm

Sprinkel, G. (1997). *Beyond Fund Raising: New Strategies for Nonprofit Innovation and Investment.* New York: John Wiley & Sons.

Stevenson, H. and Gumpert, D. (March, 1985). 'The Heart of Entrepreneurship', *Harvard Business Review*: 85–94.

Sullivan Mort, G., Weerawardena, J., and Carnegie, K. (2003). 'Social entrepreneurship: Towards conceptualisation', *International Journal of Nonprofit and Voluntary Sector Marketing*, 8(1): 76–88.

Sullivan, D. (2007), 'Stimulating Social Entrepreneurship: Can Support From Cities Make a Difference?', *The Academy of Management Perspectives*, 21.1, pp. 77–8.

Szelenzi, I. (1988). *Socialist Entrepreneurs.* Cambridge: Polity Press.

Tarrow, S. (2001). 'Transnational Politics: Contention and Institutions in International Politics', *Annual Review of Political Science,* 4: 1–20.

Taylor, B., Chait, R., and Holland, T. (September–October, 1996). 'The New Work of the Nonprofit Board', *Harvard Business Review,* 74(May): 36–44.

Taylor-Gooby, P. (1999). 'Markets and Motives: Trust and Egoism in Welfare Markets', *Journal of Social Policy,* 28(1): 97–114.

The Economist (2004). 'Philanthropy: Doing Well and Doing Good', 29 July.

—— (2005). 'The Good Company: A Survey of Corporate Social Responsibility', 22 January.

Thekaekara. S., and Thekaekara, M. (2007), *Social Justice and Social Entrepreneurship,* Skoll Centre for Social Entrepreneurship, available at: http://www.sbs.ox.ac.uk/skoll/research/Short+papers/Short+papers.htm

Thompson, J. (2002). 'The World of the Social Entrepreneur', *International Journal of Public Sector Management,* 15(5): 412–31.

—— Alvy, G., and Lees, A. (2000). 'Social Entrepreneurship—A New Look at the People and the Potential', *Management Decision,* 38(5): 328–38.

Tilly, C. (2004). *Social Movements: 1768–2004.* London: Paradigm.

Timmons, J. (1999). *New Venture Creation: Entrepreneurship for the 21st Century.* Boston, MA: McGraw-Hill.

de Tocqueville, A. (2004). *Democracy in America,* Arthur Goldhammer, trans. New York: Library of America.

Toppe, C. and Kirsch, A. (2002). *Keeping the Trust: Confidence in Charitable Organizations in an Age of Scrutiny.* Washington, DC: Independent Sector.

Tracey, P., and Jarvis, O. (2007), 'Toward a Theory of Social Venture Franchising', *Entrepreneurship Theory and Practice,* 31.5, pp. 667–85.

Treasury (2003). *The Green Book. Appraisal and Evaluation in Central Government.* London: HM Treasury.

Venkataraman, S. (1997). 'The Distinctive Domain of Entrepreneurship Research. An Editor's Perspective', in J. Katz and R. Brockhaus (eds.), *Advances in Entrepreneurship, Firm Emergence, and Growth*, vol. 3. Greenwich, CT: JAI Press, pp. 119–38.

von Hippel, E. (2005). *Democratising Innovation*. Boston, MA: MIT.

Voss, Z., Voss, G., and Moorman, C. (2004). 'An Empirical Examination of the Complex Relationships Between Entrepreneurial Orientation and Stakeholder Support', *CASE Working Paper Series*, 6, Duke Fuqua School. Available at http://www.fuqua.duke.edu/centers/case/documents/workingpaper6.pdf

W. K. Kellogg Foundation (2001). *Logic Model Development Guide: Using Logic Models to Bring Together Planning, Evaluation & Action*. Available at: www.wkkf.org

Waddock, S. and Post, J. (1991). 'Social Entrepreneurs and Catalytic Change', *Public Administration Review*, 51(5): 393–402.

Walker, P., Lewis, J., Lingayah, S., and Sommer, F. (2006), *Prove it! Measuring the Effect of Neighbourhood Renewal on Local People*, available at: http://www.neweconomics.org/gen/newways_socialaudit.aspx

Warren, M. (2003). 'The Political Role of Nonprofits in a Democracy', *Social Science and Modern Society*, 40(4): 46–51.

Weerawardena, J., and Sullivan Mort, G. (2006), 'Investigating social entrepreneurship: A multidimensional model', *Journal of World Business*, 41, pp. 21–35.

Weisbrod, B. (1998). *To Profit or Not To Profit: The Commercial Transformation of the Nonprofit Sector*. Cambridge: Cambridge University Press.

—— (Winter 2004). 'Pitfalls of Profit', *Stanford Social Innovation Review*: 40–7.

—— and Lindrooth, R. (2004). 'Do Nonprofit and For-profit Organizations Respond Differently to Incentives? Behavior in the Mixed Hospice Industry', *Working Paper* 05–13, Institute for Policy Research, Northwestern University.

Wei Skillern, J., Anderson, B., and Dees, J. G. (2002). 'Scaling Social Innovations: A Report from the Front Lines', *Working Paper Social Enterprise Series*, 25, Harvard Business School, Division of Research.

—— Austin, J., Leonard, H., and Stevenson, H. (eds) (2007). *Entrepreneurship in the Social Sector*, Sage.

Weitzman, M. (2002). *The New Nonprofit Almanac & Desk Reference: The Essential Facts and Figures for Managers, Researchers, and Volunteers*. San Francisco, CA: Jossey Bass.

Westall, A. (2002). *Value Led, Market Driven*. London: IPPR.

Wilkinson, J. (1997). 'A New Paradigm for Economic Analysis? Recent Convergences in French Social Science and an Exploration of the Convention Theory Approach with a Consideration of its Application to the Analysis of the Agro-Food Sector', *Economy and Society*, 26(3): 305–39.

Young, D. (ed.) (2004). *Effective Economic Decision-Making by Nonprofit Organizations*. The Foundation Center.

Young, W. and Welford, R. (2002). *Ethical Shopping*. London: Fusion Press.

Yunus, M. (1999). *Banker to the Poor: Micro-Lending and the Battle Against World Poverty*. New York: Public Affairs.

—— (2003). *Halving Poverty by 2015*. London: Commonwealth Institute.

Zadek, S. (1998). 'Balancing Performance, Ethics, and Accountability', *Journal of Business Ethics*, 17(13): 1421–41.
Zietlow, J. (2001). 'Social Entrepreneurship: Managerial, Finance and Marketing Aspects', *Journal of Nonprofit and Public Sector Marketing*, 9(1–2): 19–43.

Selected Websites

Acumen Fund—www.acumenfund.org
Alliance Magazine—www.allavida.org/alliance/alliancehome.html
ARNOVA (Association for Research in Nonprofits Organisations and Voluntary Action)—www.arnova.org
Ashoka—www.ashoka.org
BRAC—www.brac.net
Bridges Community Ventures—www.bridgesventures.com
Bridgespan—www.bridgespangroup.org
Centre for the Advancement of Social Entrepreneurship at Duke University—www.fuqua.duke.edu/centers/case/
Centre for Social Innovation at Stanford University—www.gsb.stanford.edu/csi
Charities Aid Foundation—www.cafonline.org
Charity Bank—www.charitybank.org
Charities Evaluation Service—www.ces-vol.org.uk
Community Action Network—www.can-online.org.uk
Community Development Finance Association—www.cdfa.org.uk
EMES—www.emes.net/en/index.html
European Venture Philanthropy Association (EVPA)—www.evpa.eu.com
Futurebuilders—www.futurebuilders-england.org.uk
Guidestar (USA)—www.guidestar.org; (UK)—www.guidestar.org.uk
GEXSI—www.gexsi.org
Grameen Bank—www.grameen-info.org
Institute for Social Entrepreneurs—www.socialent.org
Keystone—www.keystonereporting.org
NESsT—www.nesst.org
Net Impact—www.netimpact.org
New Economics Foundation—www.neweconomics.org
New Philanthropy Capital—www.philanthropycapital.org
New Profit Inc—www.newprofit.com
REDF (Roberts Enterprise Development Fund)—www.redf.org
RISE (Research Initiative in Social Entrepreneurship)—www.riseproject.org
School for Social Entrepreneurs—www.sse.org.uk
Schwab Foundation for Social Entrepreneurship—www.schwabfound.org
Skoll Centre for Social Entrepreneurship at the University of Oxford—www.sbs.ox.ac.uk/skoll
Skoll Foundation for Social Entrepreneurship—www.skollfoundation.org
Social Audit Network—www.socialauditnetwork.org.uk
Social Edge—www.socialedge.org

Social Enterprise Alliance—www.se-alliance.org

Social Enterprise Coalition—www.socialenterprise.org.uk

SEKN (Social Enterprise Knowledge Network)—www.sekn.org

Social Enterprise London—www.sel.org.uk/home.aspx

Social Enterprise Magazine—www.socialenterprisemagazine.org

Social Enterprise Unit (Department of Trade and Industry: Small Business Service, UK)—www.sbs.gov.uk/sbsgov/action/sitemap?r.11=7000000412&topicId=7000000412

Social Entrepreneurship Initiative at Harvard Business School—www.hbs.edu/socialenterprise

Sustainability—www.sustainability.com

UnLtd—www.unltd.org.uk

Venturesome—www.cafonline.org/venturesome

Young Foundation—www.youngfoundation.org.uk

Index